BRITISH POLITICS
AND THE
GREAT WAR
Coalition and Conflict 1915–1918

BRITISH POLITICS
AND THE
GREAT WAR

Coalition and Conflict 1915 – 1918

JOHN TURNER

YALE UNIVERSITY PRESS
NEW HAVEN AND LONDON · 1992

Design based on an original by Gillian Malpass

Set in Monotype Bembo at the University of London Computer Centre
and printed and bound at The Bath Press, Avon, Great Britain.

Library of Congress Cataloging-in-Publication Data

Turner, John, 1949 May 18–
  British Politics and the Great War : coalition and conflict, 1915–1918 / John
Turner.
    p. cm.
  Includes bibliographical references and index.
  ISBN 0-300-05046-1
  1. Great Britain – Politics and government – 1910–1936. 2. World War,
1914–1918 – Great Britain. I. Title.
  DA577.T86 1992
  941.083–dc20   90–50994
                                               CIP

CONTENTS

ACKNOWLEDGEMENTS

I beg to acknowledge the gracious permission of Her Majesty the Queen to reproduce extracts from Lord Stamfordham's papers in the Royal Archives at Windsor. For permission to publish quotations from privately owned collections and other copyright material I am also obliged to Mr Julian Amery, Viscount Addison, the Trustees of the Beaverbrook Foundation, Mrs Mary Bennett, Baron Bonham-Carter, Sir Simeon Bull, the University of Birmingham Library, the Syndics of Cambridge University Library, the Master, Fellows and Scholars of Churchill College in the University of Cambridge, Dr P.M. Cowburn, Lord Craigmyle, the Earl of Crawford and Balcarres, The Earl of Derby, Mr Robin Dower, the Secretary of the Confederation of British Industry, the Hon. Mrs Crispin Gascoigne, Earl Haig, Vice-Admiral Sir Ian Hogg, the Librarian of the National Library of Ireland, the Marquess of Lothian, the Warden and Fellows of New College, Oxford, The Warden and Fellows of Nuffield College, Oxford, Lord Robertson, Sir Henry Rumbold, the Keeper of the Records of Scotland, Mrs Simon, the Librarian of Sheffield University Library, the Earl of Selborne, Mrs R.M. Stafford, and the Librarian (Manuscripts and Archives) of Yale University Library. I have quoted from the Ramsay MacDonald Diaries with the permission of the Keeper of the Public Records, taking note that the contents of the diaries were, in MacDonald's words, 'meant as notes to guide and revive memory as regards happenings and must on no account be published as they are'.

I have also quoted extensively from collections held by libraries and other institutions, namely the University of Birmingham Library, the British Library, the Bodleian Library, Cambridge University Library, the House of Lords Record Office, the Liddell Hart Centre for Military Archives (King's College, London), Liverpool City Library, Newcastle University Library, Nuffield College, Oxford, the Public Record Office, the Harry Ranson Humanities Research Center, the Modern Records Centre at the University of Warwick Library, and the Wiltshire County Record Office. Like all historians I owe a debt of gratitude to the keepers, librarians or curators of these institutions and their staffs, not only for formal patient and enthusiastic help over many years of research. Because of the nature of my subject I have made special demands on the House of Lords Record Office and the Department of Western Manuscripts of the Bodleian Library, which therefore merit special acknowledgement.

This book has taken a long time to write, and my intellectual debts are beyond numbering. Many are implied in the footnotes and bibliography, but I must particularly acknowledge Cameron Hazlehurst and Martin Gilbert, under whose supervision I first approached the study of the First World War two decades ago, and Maurice Cowling, whose unique blend of scepticism and support was applied to this project when it first began to take shape. I have learned a great deal from my colleagues and friends in the University of London, in particular Kathleen Burk, Peter Dewey, David French and John Ramsden. The work of two of my former research students, Kevin Jefferys and Robert Fitzgerald, has also made me think noticeably harder about some of the issues discussed in the book. A particular debt of gratitude is owed to John McCarthy, once of the History Department at Yale and now a computer scientist at Berkeley, who taught me to be suspicious of numbers, and William Miller who generously made available the machine-readable file of election statistics on which my study of the Coupon Election is based. But none of these scholars should feel any responsibility for my interpretation of politics in the Great War: the perversity is all my own. I have also tried the patience of John Nicoll and Rosemary Amos at Yale University Press.

Historians place special burdens on their families. My children have never known me when I was not writing this book, and in the circumstances have been very decent about it. My wife Sara has supported and cajoled me throughout the project: without her this book would never have been finished, and it is dedicated to her. But it also honours the memory of my father, Edward John Turner, who was born in the First World War into a staunch Liberal family and died as this book was going through the press.

London, February 1991

TABLES AND FIGURES

ABBREVIATIONS

A.B.C.C.	Association of British Chambers of Commerce
A.S.E	Amalgamated Society of Engineers
B.C.U.	British Commonwealth Union
B.E.A.	British Engineers' Association
B.E.A.M.A.	British Electrical and Allied Manufacturers' Association
B.E.P.O.	British Empire Producers' Association
B.M.A.	British Manufacturers' Association
B.T.C.	British Trade Corporation
C.I.G.S.	Chief of the Imperial General Staff
C.M.L.S.C.	Central Munitions Labour Supply Committee
C.M.S.	Central Materials Supply Committee
C.W.C.	Clyde Workers' Committe
D.o.R.A.	Defence of the Realm Act
E.A.C.	Employers' Advisory Council
E.E.F.	Engineering Employers' Federation
E.O.C.	Economic Offensive Committee
E.P.A.	Employers' Parliamentary Association
F.B.I.	Federation of British Industry
I.L.	Industrial League
I.L.P.	Independent Labour Party
I.S.T.C.	Iron and Steel Trades Committee
J.I.C.	Joint Industrial Committee
L.R.C.	Labour Representation Committee
N.A.C.	National Advisory Council (Ministry of Munitions)
N.A.E.E.	National Alliance of Employers and Employed
N.C.E.O.	National Confederation of Employers' Organisations
N.E.C.	National Executive Committee (of the Labour Party)
N.E.F.	National Employers' Federation

N.D.P.	National Democratic Party
N.I.C.	National Industrial Conference
N.L.C.A.	National Light Castings Association
N.U.A.	National Unionist Association (see N.U.C.U.A.)
N.U.C.U.A.	National Union of Conservative and Unionist Associations
S.E.F.	Shipbuilding Employers' Federation
T.U.C.	Trades Union Congress
U.B.C.	Unionist Business Committee
U.D.C.	Union of Democratic Control
W.E.A.	Workers' Educational Association

1

THE WAR AND BRITISH POLITICS

This book is a study of British politics under the shadow of defeat. Its purpose is to identify, describe and explain the transformation of British party politics in the later years of the First World War. Its focus is upon the Lloyd George Coalition which held office from December 1916 to December 1918, because it was during that government's term of office that most of the upheavals which shaped the inter-war political system took place. But no account would be complete which did not recognise the importance of the Asquith Coalition which preceded it — a much-abused and much-misunderstood episode in British politics — or the response of the electorate to the political opportunities of the 'Coupon' election which immediately followed the war.

The book is about policy as well as politics, because the First World War saw a crisis of the state as well as a discontinuity in party relationships. Politicians recognised the possibility of military collapse, and feared that revolution would follow it, or even precede it as it had done in Russia. To prevent defeat they tightened the state's hold on British society, and so increased the risk of revolution. Their solution to this dilemma was to destroy the pre-war party system in the hope that a new alignment of parties would keep them in power, inhibit social upheaval, and make it possible to win the war. The most powerful weapon in this great work of destruction and renewal was the threat of a general election, which was deployed effectively by the Lloyd George Coalition after the spring of 1917.

Political parties naturally tended to split along lines of weakness, and the issues which divided them during the war were not all new. There were obvious continuities between the political developments of war and the predicaments faced by the four major parties — Liberal, Conservative (otherwise called Unionist), Labour and Irish — in the decade or so before the war. Many contemporaries were convinced the war had swept away the certainties of the Victorian and Edwardian system, and many wanted nothing more than to have them back. But what Trevor Wilson has memorably called the 'rampant omnibus' of war quite obviously did not bear down on a stable and untroubled political community. Religion, class, nationality and gender divided the British in 1914, and continued to divide them after the war. Parliamentary leaders before the war had little time to relax between episodes of bitter conflict within as well as between their parties; during and after the war they easily retained their adversarial habits, and only a few of them had made new friends or new enemies. Many of the important party-political changes of the first three decades of the century, of which the most important is undoubtedly the rise of the Labour Party at the expense of the Liberals, were manifestly happening before the war and continued after it.

It is therefore a risk to isolate a short period such as this, and make it bear a great weight of explanation. The justifications for doing so in this book are that the war as a catalyst accelerated the pace of some changes, that decisions taken in the heat of war significantly altered the direction of change, and that in some important respects the war had a conservative or even reactionary effect which nullified changes which might otherwise have occurred. This last consideration is perhaps the most important reason for examining wartime politics in such fine grain. A great weight of scholarship, more or less openly accepting the tenets of Whig history, bears down on the First World War. Whether by encouraging change benignly, or by the stimulus of revolutionary threat, the war is held to have shaped the progress of twentieth-century Britain. But closer inspection reveals both revolution and counter-revolution going off at half cock in the heat of war. This suggests an urgent need to reinterpret both the war and, at a remove, the history of the twentieth century as well.

Another reason for taking a fairly narrow period is that the political history of the war is too important to be left to political historians and biographers. The tradition of writing history as 'one damned thing after another' has very properly withered. The sophisticated thematic studies which have superseded it, whether they cover political ideas, institutions, voting behaviour or any other topic, have many advantages but one signal drawback: they cannot easily recreate a world in which everything seemed to be happening at once. British politics in the climax of war was just such a world, and the changes which emerged from it were the fruit of chaos. To explain them without grappling directly with that chaos would be misleading and unsatisfactory.

I have tried to reduce chaos to some sort of order by taking a broadly chronological approach to the history of party and personal conflict, and by looking at, and outward from, the world of a small group of influential politicians, in government and opposition. These men — no women had any significant political role at this level — were in the epicentre of political change. They could not control events, but some of them controlled government departments, and those who were forced into opposition were in touch with many of the forces in the wider society which were contending about 'who gets what, when, how'.[1] In this way I have tried to go beyond the limits of the 'high politics' approach to historical explanation, but I readily acknowledge the influence of 'high politics' in everything that follows.

The need to explain policy and politics simultaneously determines the structure of most of the chapters in this book, which set discussions of grand strategy, manpower policy, industrial relations or the state of Ireland beside accounts of the political strategy and tactics of the politicians who were trying to manage the war and at the same time foresee the post-war world which it would bring. Politicians under pressure worked with very limited and usually distorted views of the larger society. Even their knowledge of political organisations outside Westminster was partial. Their own views, rather than an objective reality, determined their actions. There has not been space in this book to try to correct all their misapprehensions; but some of their more important superstitions are contrasted with what can be discovered about political changes out of doors.

The final chapters have a different perspective and a different form. The 'Coupon' election of December 1918 was the culmination of wartime political machinations, and it was the first time for nearly eight years that the political élite had confronted the mass electorate. Moreover the 1918 Representation of the People Act had created a new electorate, 40 per cent of whom were women and just under 20 per cent of whom were men who would probably not have been enfranchised under the pre-war statutes. For the politicians, it was a new world. Although the decision to call the election is studied at the top, the results are examined at the bottom, regionally and quantitatively. In studying the election, it is possible to address some questions about the long and short term social change which helped to create the post-war political world. A chapter on capital and labour examines part of the new political landscape brought into being by the war. Politicians' relationships with organised businessmen, with trade unionists and with the rank-and-file movement reflected profound changes in the distribution of power. To complement this the quantitative study of the election results illustrates the new political geography of the post-war world.

This introductory chapter sets out a schematic political history of the war in which the rest of the chapters will fit, and summarises the historiography

---

[1] This was Harold Lasswell's attempted definition of the essence of politics as an activity in the title of *Politics: who gets what, when, how* (New York: McGraw-Hill, 1936).

of the war. It also examines the political baggage which Britain's leaders were carrying in 1914. Neither the recent history of political change nor the themes of political argument in the Edwardian period proved easy to forget even in the heat of war. Just as many of the generals would rather have fought the old battles than face the intractable horrors of the Western Front, so the majority of practising politicians were not ready to give up the battleground of Tariff Reform, imperial expansion, land values, unemployment insurance, the Welsh Church and Irish Home Rule. Their dismay was palpable when in 1917 and 1918 the political world seemed to move beneath their feet.

The First World War: the Politicians' View

Twenty years of patient diplomacy had ensured that when a major European war broke out in 1914 it would be fought between the Entente Powers — France, Russia and Great Britain — and the Central Powers — Germany and Austria-Hungary. The Liberal government under H.H. Asquith, and the British public, entered the conflict in 1914 expecting a short struggle, brought to an end by the success of British sea-power and the armies of the Entente. Party conflict was briefly suspended by agreement, but Westminster politicians realised rather sooner than the general public that this happy state could not last for long. Turkey joined the war on the side of the Central Powers and Italy, the third power in Germany's Triple Alliance before the war, could not at first be wooed to the Entente cause even though the Italian government declined to recognise any commitment to the Central Powers. In November 1914 the battle in France came to a halt, with fixed trench lines stretching from the Channel to the Alps. In Britain the withering of optimism corroded the political truce. In May 1915, buffeted by a newspaper 'scandal' over the supply of shells to the armies in France and by the resignation of the First Sea Lord, Admiral Lord Fisher, in protest against the Dardanelles campaign, Asquith reconstructed his Cabinet as a coalition. This headed off demands for a general election, which neither Asquith nor the Unionist leader Andrew Bonar Law wished to see. It did not produce military success or political harmony. The new coalition Cabinet argued about conscription, which Unionists (except for Arthur Balfour, a former prime minister) wanted and Liberals (except for David Lloyd George, the Chancellor of the Exchequer, and Winston Churchill, who had once been First Lord of the Admiralty) did not; and about the wisdom of continuing the Dardanelles campaign, which did not divide them so clearly on party lines. Cabinet ministers rearranged their private lists of friends and enemies. Back-bench M.P.s looked on, suspicious of their leaders' intentions. For those outside the governing circles 1915 was a year of frustration and bewilderment.

Nineteen-sixteen, by contrast, was a year of unprecedented disaster abroad and alarm at home. The 1916 offensive on the Western Front — the Somme campaign — was even bloodier and no more effective than the campaigns of 1915. In the Middle East, where the year had begun with a humiliating withdrawal from the Dardanelles, British forces in Mesopotamia were forced to surrender to the Turks at Kut-el-Amara. In Eastern Europe the German army knocked Romania out of the war and brought the Russian army to a halt. In Ireland a small rising on Easter Monday was turned into an historic rebellion by the brutality and incompetence of the military authorities. At home the spring brought engineering strikes. Military conscription, introduced in stages in January and June, was supposed to rationalise the use of manpower, sending enough men of the right quality to fight and keeping back those needed to maintain the industrial war effort. Instead it showed how fragile was the balance between military and industrial needs. The harvest was poor, and fears of food shortage were aggravated by the threat of a submarine campaign against the British merchant fleet. Britain's financial strength was drained by the purchase of munitions in the United States: by the end of the year the authorities were in constant fear of a run on sterling which would have brought the war effort to a full stop.

Accordingly, the first suggestion from within the Cabinet that Britain should give up the struggle and seek the best possible terms from Germany was made on 13 November 1916, in private, by Lord Lansdowne, a former Foreign Secretary in the Conservative government of 1902–5 and now a senior minister in the Coalition. No one who mattered could be found to agree with him, but there was nothing fanciful about the account he gave of Britain's predicament. From the autumn of 1916 to the late summer of 1918 no serious politician could avoid thinking about the prospect of defeat. In the circumstances political instability was to be expected. Surprisingly, perhaps, the revolution in British politics at the end of 1916 was confined to the highest levels. Asquith was levered out of office on 6 December by Lloyd George and a group of Conservative politicians. A new coalition government was presented to the House of Commons, which had taken no part in its conception except to express disgruntlement, and the regime continued in being.

The credit for this smooth transition belongs to the much-despised Asquith Coalition, which had done important work by containing discontent on the Right and on the Left alike. But by the autumn of 1916 it had reached the limits of its strength. Hitherto it had been able to command a parliamentary majority so long as it could retain its cohesion at

Cabinet level. This had been proved in June, when the Military Service Act, extending conscription to married men and extending the age limits, had been passed despite the distaste it aroused on the Liberal back benches. But with the Liberals divided by conscription, and the Irish Nationalists distanced from the government by the Easter Rising and its aftermath, this majority now depended on the Unionist back bench. In the autumn of 1916 a substantial minority of Unionist M.P.s had lost patience with the government, though the malcontents were not united on a single issue. In the famous Nigeria debate on 8 November 1916 almost half the Conservatives voting opposed the government. The Conservative opposition was led by Edward Carson, the Irish Unionist leader, who had resigned from the coalition ministry in October 1915 to urge greater vigour in the prosecution of the war. Within the Cabinet, Lloyd George led a critical minority which demanded a reconstruction of the government's machinery for taking decisions and enforcing them on soldiers and civilians alike. Using the parliamentary crisis, Lloyd George enlarged his following among ministers and in the last days of November and the first week of December brought about Asquith's resignation. Most of the Liberal ministers followed Asquith out of office. Lloyd George constructed a ministry with some Liberal and Labour support, which was nevertheless dominated by Unionists, including Carson. It was a revolution at the top, engineered by party leaders, ratified by a bewildered House of Commons, and accepted with apparent equanimity by 'public opinion'.

The new prime minister and his colleagues wanted to take a grip on war policy, improve the machinery of government, and re-assert civilian control over strategy. The first aim was to be achieved by ditching Asquith and his Liberal allies. The second was attempted through a small War Cabinet with supreme powers of decision, supported by a number of new ministries to control vital economic functions — food supply, shipping, manpower allocation and eventually post-war reconstruction. The control of strategy was also to be achieved by the exertions of the War Cabinet. In the event the expected improvements did not come to pass for many months, and civilian control of strategy was never fully achieved. Nineteen-seventeen managed to be worse than 1916 on most counts, except that the United States joined the war on the Entente side in April in a move which just counterbalanced the collapse of Russia.

The economic storm which had been building up in earlier years finally broke in the spring and early summer, which were marked by extensive industrial disorder. By the end of the year another manpower crisis had appeared, made far worse by the War Cabinet's failure to stop the generals' mounting another Western offensive — on this occasion the Third Battle of Ypres, better known as Passchendaele. The German submarine campaign brought food stocks almost to nothing in the weeks before the 1917 harvest, and the harvest itself was threatened by the shortage of skilled manpower. The War Cabinet, caught between the Scylla of military defeat and the Charybdis of economic collapse, cast desperately about them for ways to keep the war going. From the Liberal opposition, and from sections of the Labour movement, the pressure for a negotiated peace became steadily more insistent.

The climax came in March 1918. A German offensive, the first since 1916, nearly broke the British Army. In the first frantic days, the government searched everywhere for men to throw into the breach. Age limits and fitness limits were extended, and a delicately constructed Irish policy was ruined by applying conscription to Ireland and offering Home Rule in the same breath. The outcome of the battle was in the balance until June, when the energy of the German attack was exhausted. For much of the summer it was assumed that the war was once more in stalemate, and the government's new machinery was deployed in scraping up the men and resources for the 1919 battles. The machinery itself was better than it had been in 1917, but the economic position was much worse. The situation was saved by the effective intervention of the American army, which was at last deployed in strength in France, and by the inexorable collapse of the social and economic structure of Germany. By October the early defeat of the Central Powers was expected, and the Armistice was concluded on 11 November. The First World War had been lost rather more than it had been won.

A few days before the Armistice, Lloyd George asked the King to grant an early dissolution to allow the Coalition to fight an election as soon as possible after the war. Election planning had begun in 1917, when the Coalition's political managers had decided to consolidate the new government's support by going to the polls during the war. The move had been postponed because the provisions of a new franchise bill could not be implemented until 1918, and by then the polarisation of politics had become clear. Liberals and Conservatives in the Coalition were prepared to stand together against a common enemy comprised of the anti-Coalition Liberals and the anti-war minority of the Labour Party. Peace broke out before the Coalition's plans had matured, and the pro-war section of the Labour Party declined to join the common front. As a result, the 1918 election ranged Conservatives and Coalition Liberals, backed by a joint letter of support from Lloyd George and Bonar Law which has passed into history as the 'Coupon', against Labour and the Asquithian Liberal rump.

The Coalition's resounding victory, by 473 seats to 234 (of whom 73 were Sinn Feiners who declined to take their seats), posed more questions than it answered. The simplest, and the most important in the medium term, was the question of who had really won the election: Conservative managers claimed the credit for their party, while Lloyd George's friends claimed a personal victory. During the peacetime coalition government, Conservatives' confidence in their own unaided strength grew steadily, until a revolt of the back benches helped to overthrow Lloyd George in 1922. An equally potent, and closely connected question, was whether the Labour Party had performed well. With sixty members, it had improved on its pre-war representation, but only by putting forward many more candidates than at any previous election. It was critically important for all politicians to know whether this had been the party's best possible performance, in favourable conditions, or a minimum result obtained when the tide was running unusually heavily against it. On the answers to these two questions depended a third. Had the war done permanent damage to the prospects for Liberal reunion, and thus for Liberal survival? Answers to two of these three critical questions had emerged within three years: Labour had under-performed in 1918, and the Liberals were no longer capable of reunion. The other question no longer seemed critical, and the Conservative Party duly found Lloyd George expendable in 1922. The way was clear for the three-party politics of the inter-war years, in which the Conservative Party held most of the good cards, and only another war could reshuffle the deck.

The First World War: the Political Historians' view

No one writing about the First World War can pretend to be treading on ground 'hitherto neglected by historians', and this book is heavily influenced by what has been written before. British historians have traditionally favoured narrative for party-political history. As explained above, this seems to have many virtues in studying an intense and complex period of change, but it has drawbacks. The transition from polemical memoir to the party history of the First World War was made, but only just, by Lord Beaverbrook, in *Men and Power* and *Politicians and the War*. Although Beaverbrook knew the principal actors and in his later work had the advantage of exclusive access to the papers of leading figures including Lloyd George, he was interested in powerful men rather than in the uses of power. A large body of scholarship, reaching into the minutest detail, has grown up to refute his accounts of political interaction at the top.[2] The result is that historians now know in greater detail than ever before who ate whom for breakfast, but few historians of Cabinet-level politics have succeeded in breaking away from Beaverbrook's pattern of thought,

[2] Peter Fraser, 'Lord Beaverbrook's Fabrications in *Politicians and the War 1914–1916*', *Historical Journal*, xxv (1982), 147–166; John O. Stubbs, 'Beaverbrook as Historian: *Politicians and the War, 1914–1916* reconsidered', *Albion*, xiv (1982), 235–253.

which was to see the rise and fall of ministries as the ultimate *explanandum*. I have tried to take a wider view of the motivations of politicians. At the other pole in conventional party history stand the histories of voting behaviour, which try to explain the rise and fall of parties in terms of the changing preferences and changing social structure of the electorate. Following the questions posed by Matthew, McKibbin and Kay, who argued that the new franchise in 1918, rather than the political experience of war, occasioned the rise of the Labour Party,[3] the final chapters of this book try to confront this problem directly. There is already a thriving tradition of non-quantitative work which has challenged Matthew *et al.*'s assumptions, and it is unlikely that this subject will stand still. Underlying it is an ambiguity, or uncertainty in the definition of class which bedevils all work on voting allegiance. During the war, when the language of class identity was thrown into turmoil by the example of the Russian revolutions, yet more difficulties of interpretation appear.

A third important category in the historiography of party in the First World War is 'high politics'. The term is taken to mean an attitude to evidence and a set of beliefs about the mental world of politicians and the relationship between thought and political action. It was invented by Maurice Cowling,[4] who argues that political rhetoric, dealing as it seems to do in ideas and principles, was in fact a tool used by politicians to achieve particular effects, usually national cohesion and acceptance of the it status quo, and that the private intentions of politicians as revealed in their private correspondence were directed to getting and keeping power.[5]

The high politics tradition encompasses some variation in the focus of interest. The only exponent to take an interest in the First World War, Michael Bentley, cast his net widely, to include any Liberal back-bencher whose opinions about passing events could be discovered.[6] Nevertheless Bentley clearly shares Cowling's view that 'issues of substance' — policy questions — were of strictly limited significance; they are both interested almost exclusively in explaining the language which politicians used to discuss their problems. This has odd effects when applied to the First World War. Although both historians attach great symbolic importance to particular policy decisions and election results they care little about how these decisions and results came about: their concern is the intellectual,

---

[3] H.C.G. Matthew, R.I. McKibbin and J.A. Kay, 'The Franchise Factor in the Rise of the Labour Party', *English Historical Review*, xci (1976), 723–752.

[4] Maurice Cowling, *1867: Disraeli, Gladstone and Revolution* (Cambridge: Cambridge University Press, 1967); *The Impact of Labour* (Cambridge: Cambridge University Press, 1971); *The Impact of Hitler* (Cambridge: Cambridge University Press, 1975).

[5] The whole corpus, clothed in the decent obscurity of a learned language, is discussed by Michael Bentley, 'Party, Doctrine and Thought', in Michael Bentley and John Stevenson, eds, *High and Low Politics in Modern Britain* (Oxford: Clarendon Press, 1983), pp. 123–153.

[6] Bentley, *The Liberal Mind* (Cambridge: Cambridge University Press, 1977).

or 'doctrinal' constraints which prevented Liberals from doing anything to change them and allowed the Conservatives use them in consolidating their strength. This rather contemptuous attitude to 'psephology' has created tension between the high politics school and historians of voting behaviour. But there is no good reason not to combine the two perspectives, which are trying to explain different manifestations of the same thing.

Party history is also intimately related to the political history of class. Most historians will agree that voting preferences depend in part on the voter's conception of his place in society, though there is plenty of room for argument about how and how much it so depends. The latest contribution to the discussion of class and status during the First World War, by Bernard Waites, makes a clear attempt to link sociological theory with historical change.[7] Modern studies of industrial relations, especially by Ian McLean, J.M. Hinton and Alastair Reid, qualify and extend the assumption that political attitudes were determined by socio-economic experience;[8] and in the history of the war, political outcomes seem to become intelligible only if the determining effect of long-term social change is interpreted in the light of short-term political and economic expedients. This is the approach preferred in this book.

The First World War also offers an excellent opportunity to synthesise government and party-political history, which has been seized by historians whose view of the state is essentially Marxist. Keith Burgess is the most explicit, arguing that by making the working-class movement into an insurrectionary force, the war obliged the state, as an instrument of the bourgeoisie, to respond with counter-revolutionary policy.[9] The same point has been made for the immediate post-war period by Mark Swenarton in his discussion of the 'Homes fit for Heroes' housing programme.[10] This is the strong version of Trotsky's dictum that 'War is the locomotive of history', as applied to Britain. The weak version is found in Arthur Marwick's study of *The Deluge*, which casts a wan and faintly Whiggish light over the ruins of pre-war society with its observation that

> Doubtless a new age in Britain would have been ushered in more slowly and more agreeably if there had been no war, if social and political forces, spared its distorting

---

[7] Bernard Waites, *A Class Society at War: England, 1914–1918* (Leamington Spa: Berg, 1987).

[8] J.M. Hinton, *The First Shop Stewards' Movement* (London: Allen & Unwin, 1973); Ian McLean, *The Legend of Red Clydeside* (Edinburgh: John Macdonald, 1983); Alastair Reid, 'Dilution, Trade Unionism and the State in Britain during the First World War', in S. Tolliday and J. Zeitlin, *Shop Floor Bargaining and the State* (Cambridge: Cambridge University Press, 1985), pp. 46–74.

[9] Keith Burgess, *The Challenge of Labour: shaping British society 1850–1930* (London: Croom Helm, 1980), pp. 153–194.

[10] Mark Swenarton, *Homes Fit for Heroes* (London: Heinemann Educational Books, 1981).

effects, had been left to march more closely in unison. But the war is a historical fact.... 11

How far the working class was insurrectionary between 1914 and 1918, and how far the war itself had been responsible for making it so, are questions often approached through the history of industrial relations, though their implications are political in any but the narrowest sense. The large literature on the evolution of employment relations in the late nineteenth and early twentieth centuries is therefore immediately relevant to the political history of the war. The response of the state, by contrast, is all too often taken for granted as a counter-revolutionary reflex, hardly discussed in any historiographical context at all. This is an unnecessary self-denial: the history of counter-revolution can be approached through a conventional political narrative, through 'high politics', and through administrative history. All these methods are acknowledged at different points in the course of this book, though the emphasis lies on the response of the governors rather than the initiatives of the governed.

The historian of the First World War must also recognise an apparent sea change in political ideas. Two major books describe the evolution of the intellectual centre-left during the war: J.M. Winter's *Socialism and the Challenge of War* and Peter Clarke's *Liberals and Social Democrats*.12 Both are concerned with thought as it developed outside governing circles, in opposition or at best on the periphery of power. Both make it clear that the fragmentation of pre-war progressive values under the stress of war was a real problem for the intelligentsia, but leave it to others to decide whether this had wider political implications. Clarke in particular contrasts 'moral' reformers like J.A. Hobson and L.T. Hobhouse, who were demoralised and confused by the war, with 'mechanical' reformers like the Webbs who emphasised its opportunities. But the Right in wartime Britain also thought, even though it had less cause for doubt or reflection: and the output of right-wing publicists suggests that some tendencies of right-wing thought were strengthened by the war and that a principled resistance to democracy was alive and well, and hardly furtive in its operation.13

Another area of political thought which historians of the war have tended to avoid is the development of new non-socialist prescriptions for economic organisation: between Guild Socialism and the atavism of the Gold Standard there was a range of *étatiste*, corporatist and downright

---

11 Arthur Marwick, *The Deluge: British society and the First World War* (London: Macmillan, 1965), p. 314.

12 P.F.Clarke, *Liberals and Social Democrats* (Cambridge: Cambridge University Press, 1978); J.M. Winter, *Socialism and the Challenge of War* (Cambridge: Cambridge University Press, 1974).

13 Lord Selborne, whose opinions are laid out in George Boyce, ed., *Crisis of British Unionism* (London: Historians' Press, 1987) represented the voice of cautious moderation; more extreme views can be found in e.g. F.S. Oliver, *The Anvil of War* (London: Macmillan, 1916).

muddled proposals for national regeneration, which often depended on tariff protection for their success and were to re-emerge into respectability after the disastrous economic episode of 1929–31. These developments in ideas had an influence in governing circles at least comparable to that of the surviving progressives. They leave their mark in the language used by many of the most influential actors in their comments on the quality and purpose of the Lloyd George coalition. Their practical outcome, in the reconstruction proposals of the Coalition before and during the general election, therefore receives some attention below. The most prominent right-wing critics of the status quo were associated with the demand for the modernisation of the British economy through some sort of collaboration between labour and capital at the expense of the existing party system. The proposition that the war was the climax of a 'modernisation crisis' in early twentieth-century Britain is part of a rich, if often misleading seam of ideas.[14]

Finally, an important and controversial interpretation has been suggested by 'corporatist' writers, applying the terminology of an influential school of German historiography to the rather different personalities and conditions of wartime Britain. The bare bones of their case, best expressed by Keith Middlemas, is that the apparatus of the state suffered an overload during the war, and that to prevent the breakdown of order both politicians and the representatives of organised economic interests collaborated to 'extend the boundaries of the state' to include such bodies as the Trades Union Congress and the National Confederation of Employers' Organisations.[15] This view differs from that of the 'modernisation crisis' largely in the emphasis it puts on formal institutions, and on the concentration on tripartite relationships in which the state played a part rather than bilateral bargaining between employers and labour. Many historians have found it hard to credit that the T.U.C. and the N.C.E.O. had the organisational competence, let alone the political will, to assume any part of the burdens of governing after the war. But the practical convenience of dealing with economic interests through representative associations, rather than in detail, did lead ministers and other politicians to look to organised business and organised labour during the war and afterwards. An analysis of wartime politics must assess how this process affected 'who got what' and 'how'.

Each of the approaches outlined above has something essential to contribute to an understanding of political change during the war, but combining them is not easy. The conventional narrative of the first part of

---

[14] R.J. Scally, *The Origins of the Lloyd George Coalition* (Princeton: Princeton University Press, 1975); R.P.T. Davenport-Hines, 'Trade Associations and the Modernization Crisis of British Industry, 1910–35', in Hiroaki Yamazaki and Matao Miyamoto, eds, *Trade Associations in Business History* (Tokyo: University of Tokyo Press, 1988), pp. 205–226.

[15] Keith Middlemas, *Politics in Industrial Society* (London: André Deutsch, 1979).

the book therefore gives way in the concluding sections to a more formal analysis of themes. It has been difficult to avoid rough edges and crude seams, but I hope that only the unavoidable ones are left.

Parties and Society before 1914

PARTIES IN CRISIS

In the sixty years before 1916 the political parties collectively enjoyed more influence and prestige than ever before or since. As the main instrument of power in British society, they were of absorbing interest to educated men. Yet even before the war, the threat to their position was obvious. As the functions of the state expanded, people found other ways to influence it. Pressure groups, whose flowering in the nineteenth century had helped to make the Liberal Party, weakened their ties with all political parties. Some, like the suffragettes, were forced into extra-parliamentary methods by the hostility of party organisers. Employers' groups and trade unions began to deal directly with government departments, as the complexity of legislation and the extent of state intervention in the labour market increased. Meanwhile, as popular expectations of the state grew steadily, the party system was blamed for the state's failures: failure to improve the lives of the poor, failure to win the Boer War quickly and cleanly, failure to keep up with foreign economic competition. The fashionable political language of the Edwardian decade, which emphasised 'national efficiency', implicitly denigrated party; and many who used that language openly looked forward to the eclipse of the party struggle. The political history of the war is in part an account of the parties' competition with other power-hungry institutions.

Historians have identified the years which led up to the First World War as years of 'crisis' for both the major parties in Britain, and for parliamentary government as an institution. The Conservatives were first to be hit. In 1900 a Conservative government under the Marquess of Salisbury fought and won a 'khaki election' in the first flush of enthusiasm for the Boer War. Two years later, when Salisbury handed over the reins to his nephew Arthur Balfour, the government's position had already been weakened by the sorry performance of British armies in South Africa. Although a military victory was achieved in 1902, the government's reputation never recovered. At home the passage of the 1902 Education Act stirred up old antagonisms between the Conservative Party and the Nonconformist churches. In the following year Joseph Chamberlain, himself a lapsed Nonconformist from a business background, with little sympathy for the

landed Anglicans who controlled the Conservative Party, left the Cabinet
to launch a campaign for Tariff Reform.

This reversal of sixty years of economic policy split the Unionists between extreme Tariff Reformers, committed Free Traders, and an undecided centre group led by Balfour, whose indecision on the subject was
the beginning of his own downfall. In 1906 these divisions over Tariff
Reform helped the Liberals towards a massive electoral victory. Within
the Unionist Party Tariff Reform went from strength to strength and became the main plank in the platform for the two elections of January and
December 1910. Nevertheless committed Tariff Reformers, rather than
fellow-travellers, were not in a majority in the parliamentary party, and
the strength of the movement lay in the extra-parliamentary Tariff Reform
League. A double defeat in 1910 led first to the fall of Balfour, replaced
in 1911 by Andrew Bonar Law, and then to the abandonment of Tariff
Reform as an electoral commitment in 1913. Bonar Law, a compromise
candidate whose election prevented a damaging struggle between Austen
Chamberlain, Joseph's son, and Walter Long, was a determined but insecure leader. During his first years in office the defence of the Union
with Ireland, which had defined the party since 1886, once more became
its first priority: but rather than healing the wounds of Tariff Reform, it
exposed the party to a new threat. By the beginning of 1914 the Conservative leadership was committed to supporting armed insurrection in
Ulster, if the Unionists in Ulster thought that that was the only way to
escape from a Home Rule parliament.

The measure of the crisis in Conservatism was that the leadership had
escaped from its difficulties over Tariff Reform only to find itself at the
mercy of political decisions taken either by Unionists in Ireland or by
the Liberal Party at Westminster. This led to serious factional divisions,
stimulated by the leadership ambitions of Walter Long and his identification with the Unionists of Southern Ireland.[16] The Conservative and
Unionist Party was the result of merger between the older Conservative
Party and the Liberal Unionists who had broken away from Gladstone in
1886: the contemporary practice of calling it simply 'the Unionist Party'
signified that Unionism was a convenient and necessary lowest common
denominator of Conservative opinions.[17]

The crisis for Liberalism was less immediate, and many would say that it
was only invented in 1935 by George Dangerfield, whose classic account
of the *Strange Death of Liberal England*[18] is a starting point for many inter-

---

[16] Richard Murphy, 'Faction in the Conservative Party and the Home Rule Crisis, 1912–14',
History, lxxi (1986), 222–234.

[17] Alan Sykes, *Tariff Reform in British Politics 1903–1913* (Oxford: Clarendon Press, 1979), esp.
chs 10–13.

[18] George Dangerfield, *The Strange Death of Liberal England* (London: Constable, 1935).

pretations. Like the Conservatives, the Liberals had been embarrassed by the Boer War. Their difficulty was that the party split down the middle, with one section supporting Conservative policy and the other opposing it root and branch. Internecine bickering was turned into Liberal electoral success largely by the Conservatives, who obligingly made their own quarrels very public after 1903. In that year, looking ahead to the election, the Chief Whip Herbert Gladstone made a secret arrangement with Ramsay MacDonald, secretary of the Labour Representation Committee, to allow a free run to a number of Labour candidates in return for Labour withdrawals in other seats where the anti-Conservative vote might have been split. Thirty Labour M.P.s were returned to parliament in 1906, of whom twenty-four were unopposed by Liberals because of the pact. Thirteen of these were from Lancashire or Cheshire. In the event, the deal was not justified by the circumstances, since the Liberal majority in that election was so large; but it was a tangible sign of Liberal anxieties about the intentions of a largely working-class electorate.[19] The Liberals also had internal problems. Henry Campbell-Bannerman, their leader, was a traditional radical who had opposed the Boer War. Up to a third of his party, including three of his closest lieutenants, were Liberal Imperialists who had supported the Conservative policy.[20] In the event Campbell-Bannerman was able to take H.H. Asquith, Sir Edward Grey, and R.B. Haldane into his Cabinet without conditions or concessions. He also included a Welsh radical, David Lloyd George. The new government had few specific electoral commitments, and its first years were unexciting save for the early signs of a constitutional clash with the House of Lords. Anticipating later appeals to the 'watchdog of the Constitution', Balfour encouraged Unionist peers to block some Liberal measures which the impotent Unionist minority in the Commons particularly disliked, such as licensing reform and the repeal of crucial clauses in the 1902 Education Act.

Serious proposals for social and economic reform were only seen when Campbell-Bannerman retired in 1908, making way for Asquith to become prime minister. Cabinet reorganisation brought Lloyd George to the Exchequer and Winston Churchill, a former Conservative and a refugee from Tariff Reform, to the Board of Trade. Lloyd George and Churchill were the instruments, and to a great degree the makers, of a social policy which extended the state's range of action in society. Churchill had no prior commitment to or experience of social or economic problems. Lloyd George, though his experience of urban England was limited, had already made a mark at the Board of Trade by trying to tackle some of

[19] Frank Bealey, 'The Electoral Arrangement between the Labour Representation Committee and the Liberal Party', *Journal of Modern History*, xxviii (1956), 353–373.

[20] T. Boyle, 'The Liberal Imperialists', *Bulletin of the Institute of Historical Research*, lii (May 1979), 48–82.

the problems of British manufacturers, and he had also intervened prominently in an industrial dispute on the railways. The two men between them generated enormous controversy and some legislation between 1908 and 1911. The greatest controversy followed Lloyd George's 1909 Budget, which taxed more people in more ways than anyone had attempted before. Conservative resistance took the form of a popular campaign and a direct challenge through the veto power of the House of Lords: this in turn led to an election fought by the Liberals as a contest of 'Peers vs. People', which resulted in a narrow Liberal victory in January 1910.[21]

Hardly deterred, the Conservatives hung on in their resistance both to the fiscal intentions of the budget and to the proposal that the powers of the Lords be cut down. The issue was sharpened by the influence of the Irish party, whose votes were now needed to pass the Budget in the absence of an absolute Liberal majority in the Commons. Their price for support was the abolition of the Lords' veto, which stood between them and the attainment of Home Rule. An agreement between the Cabinet and the Irish in late April would have led to a showdown, but for the death of Edward VII on 7 May. To avoid entangling the new king in a serious constitutional crisis, the Cabinet agreed to negotiations with the Conservative leadership, which only broke down in November. Ostensibly the subject was constitutional reform, but, not for the first or last time, the precipitating cause had been Irish Home Rule, and the determination and bitterness of Unionist opposition had the effect of suspending all other Liberal legislation for the year. A passionate desire to be rid of the problem caused Lloyd George to propose a coalition in these circumstances, but this was not attractive to party organisers on either side. The final collapse of negotiations in November led to another election, in which the Liberals suffered a net loss of three seats and finally became a minority government.[22]

The second 1910 election allowed the Liberals to pass a Parliament Act which severely weakened the Lords' veto. In short order they also passed the National Insurance Act, which extended limited unemployment and sickness insurance to some of the working population. Aside from this their policy options were limited. Their parliamentary majority depended on the support of the Irish and the Labour Party: if the Irish supported the Conservatives on any issue, the Labour vote, 42 at full strength, would not be enough to carry the day. This curtailed activity

---

[21] Bruce K. Murray, *The People's Budget* (Oxford: Clarendon Press, 1980); Neal Blewett, *The Peers, the Parties and the People. The general elections of 1910* (London: Macmillan, 1972).

[22] John D. Fair, *British Interparty Conferences: a study of the procedure of conciliation in British politics, 1867–1921* (Oxford: Clarendon Press, 1980), pp. 77–83, recognises the coalition proposal as a tactic to escape deadlock; Scally, *Origins of the Lloyd George Coalition*, pp. 172–210 treats it as the first phase of the wartime political crisis.

on any subject about which the Irish were indifferent or hostile, such as education or temperance, and did little to help other overdue legislation such as franchise reform or the disestablishment of the Welsh Church. In effect, the election of December 1910 enforced a return to Home Rule as the main objective of Liberal policy. A bill was introduced in April 1912 which, almost by accident, took no account of the separate identity of the Protestants in Ulster: Ulster's reaction, supported by the Conservatives in England, precipitated a crisis which lasted until the outbreak of war.[23]

Ulster was not the only cross which the Liberal Cabinet and Party had to bear. The campaign for women's suffrage split the party: it had widespread back-bench support but little following in the Cabinet and no sympathy at all from Asquith. Quite apart from the philosophical problem of deciding what was the best settlement for the franchise, the government bungled the day-to-day handling of the suffragettes' campaign.[24] The government's policy of active intervention in major industrial disputes, which had begun when Lloyd George was President of the Board of Trade and was continued under Churchill and later by Reginald McKenna, led it into difficulties during an upsurge of strike activity brought about mostly by developments outside the government's control. Improved trade union organisation and coherence, and the fluctuation of real wages in major industries, encouraged sympathetic strikes and syndicalist movements in many trades; the most alarming example, from the government's viewpoint, was the threatened strike by the Triple Alliance of railwaymen, miners and dockers in 1914.[25] Besides the embarrassments of government, the Liberal Party was also weakened by divisions within its own back bench over social reform, and by periodic Cabinet crises over naval expenditure. On his translation from the Home Office to the Admiralty in October 1910 Churchill switched sides in the debate between social and defence expenditure, ensuring that the Naval Estimates were thoroughly controversial. The Liberal government's predicament in 1914 was plainly stated by Lloyd George at the Mansion House in July 1914: the combination of a rail strike and disturbance in Ulster would produce 'the gravest [situation] with which any Government in this country has had to

[23] The clearest account is in Patricia Jalland, *The Liberals and Ireland: The Ulster Question in British politics to 1914* (Brighton: Harvester Press, 1980). See also Ronan Fanning, 'The Irish Policy of Asquith's Government and the Cabinet Crisis of 1910', in A. Cosgrave and D. McCartney, eds, *Studies in Irish History presented to R. Dudley Edwards* (Dublin: University College, 1979), pp. 279–303.

[24] Brian Harrison, *Separate Spheres: The opposition to women's suffrage in Britain* (London: Croom Helm, 1978); Harrison, 'Women's Suffrage at Westminster 1866–1928', in Michael Bentley and John Stevenson, eds, *High and Low Politics in Modern Britain* (Oxford: Clarendon Press, 1983), pp. 80–122.

[25] For a measured account of the causes of strike activity in pre-war Britain, see James E. Cronin, *Industrial Conflict in Modern Britain* (London: Croom Helm, 1979), pp. 74–109. On developments 1911–13 see Standish Meacham, ' "The Sense of an Impending Clash": English working class unrest before the First World War', *American Historical Review*, lxxvii (1972), 1343–64; G.A. Phillips, 'The Triple Industrial Alliance in 1914', *Economic History Review*, 2nd series, xxiv (1971), 55–67.

deal for centuries.'[26] Such was the atmosphere of government: an atmosphere which almost inevitably lent a false perspective to the outbreak of war over an assassination on the other side of Europe.

THE GRASSROOTS: RELIGION AND NATIONALITY

In moving thus from crisis to crisis at Westminster, politicians were merely reflecting, in a distorting mirror, the political preoccupations of the whole United Kingdom. The political culture of party activists and ordinary voters was slow to change, and lent a continuity to political debate which sometimes frustrated Westminster politicians: hence Lloyd George's impatient lunge at coalition in 1910.

Religion, nationality and class were the major political variables. Religion defined some of the social differences between Conservative and Liberal M.P.s[27] and voters, and gave politicians the language of bigotry to exploit. Other things being equal (though they rarely were) the Liberal Party relied on the Nonconformists, while the Conservatives looked to Anglicans, both practising and nominal. It was in some cases difficult to separate the political effects of religion from those of nationality. In Wales and Scotland, especially in rural and mining areas, the dominance of the Liberal Party was even greater than religious allegiance would predict, while the great religious revival in Wales in 1904–5 was reflected in buoyant support for Liberalism.[28] The Nonconformist revival in numbers was not confined to Wales, however, and between 1902 and 1905, when the Free Churches were most active politically, the number of their adherents throughout the United Kingdom was rising by rather more than 2 per cent per year. Even so, communicant members of the Free Churches did not amount to more than 5 per cent of the population: their influence outweighed their numbers because· of the efforts put into political organisation.[29]

Religious bigotry, which could just as well be called ethnic or nationalist rivalry, varied in its political significance from place to place. In Liverpool, Conservative politicians relied on anti-Irish and anti-Catholic sentiment to sustain popular Toryism. The Liberal Party, as the custodian of Home Rule, had to compete with Labour competition for Irish working-class votes. On Clydeside, another stronghold of immigrant Irish communities, the strength of the United Irish League favoured the Lib-

[26] Cameron Hazlehurst, *Politicians at War* (London: Jonathan Cape, 1970), p. 28.

[27] In 1900 40% of Liberal M.P.s and 7% of Conservative M.P.s elected were identified as Free Churchmen; in December 1910, 39% of Liberals and 2.5% of Conservatives. Stephen Koss, *Nonconformity in Modern British Politics* (London: Batsford, 1975), pp. 227–236.

[28] K.O. Morgan, *Wales in British Politics, 1868–1922* (Cardiff: University of Wales Press, 1970), pp. 217–18.

[29] Koss, p. 44, citing the 1906 *Free Church Year Book*.

erals except on rare occasions (such as the 1906 Bridgeton election); in
Manchester there was considerable local co-operation between Irish and
Labour politicians.[30]   In East London, where Jewish refugees from the
Russian pogroms of the 1890s were heavily concentrated, anti-semitism
was exploited by Conservative and Liberal politicians alike, except when
they were putting up Jewish candidates in Jewish wards.   Correspondingly, London Jews were politically active in both the Liberal and the
Conservative interest, and were over-represented in proportion to their
numbers at both local and national level.[31] The effects of religion showed
little sign of flagging before the war. The redress of grievances, especially
in education, and the strengthening of class antagonism persuaded many
middle-class English Nonconformists to switch to the Conservatives in the
1890s. But this drift was temporarily halted by the Conservatives' 1902
Education Act, which seemed to reverse the liberalising tendency of previous legislation.[32] Celtic liberalism was unshaken before the war, and the
divisive local effects of anti-Irish and anti-semitic feeling in English cities
were maintained up to and beyond 1914.[33]

Religion and nationality as popular issues helped to settle the agenda
for politicians at Westminster. From 1870 to 1902 religious argument
in parliament took the form of regular tinkering with the provisions of
Gladstone's 1870 Education Act, which had set up elected school boards
with rating powers in areas where voluntary denominational education
was deemed inadequate. The 1902 Act, introduced by the Conservatives
to create a unified structure in which education throughout the country
would be the responsibility of the usual authorities of local government,
was framed with Anglican interests in mind.[34] It horrified the Nonconformist churches, who saw it as an attempt to put 'religion on the rates',
and guaranteed that repeal would have a high priority for any Liberal
government. The Liberals brought in a bill in 1906, very soon after

[30] See Alan O'Day, *The English Face of Irish Nationalism* (Dublin: Gill Macmillan, 1977); R. Davies,
'The Liverpool Labour Party and the Liverpool Working Class', *North West Labour History Bulletin*,
vi (1979–80), 2–14; O'Day, 'The Irish Influence on Parliamentary Elections', in Roger Swift and
Sheridan Gilley, eds, *The Irish and the Victorian City* (London: Croom Helm, 1986); Steve Fielding,
'Irish Politics in Manchester 1880–1914', *International Review of Social History*, xxxviii (1988), 261–284.

[31] G. Alderman, *London Jewry and London Politics, 1899–1988* (London: Routledge, 1989), pp.
29–30; Henry Pelling, *Social Geography of British Elections 1885–1910* (London: Macmillan, 1967), pp.
42–48.

[32] D.W. Bebbington, 'Nonconformity and Electoral Sociology, 1867–1918', *Historical Journal*, xxvii
(1984), 633–656.

[33] K. Lunn, 'Political Anti-semitism before 1914: fascism's heritage', in K. Lunn and R.C. Thur-
low, *British Fascism* (London: Croom Helm, 1979), pp. 20–40; A. Shallice, 'Orange and Green and
Militancy: sectarianism and working-class politics in Liverpool, 1900–1914', *North West Labour History
Bulletin*, vi (1979–80), 15–32.

[34] Benjamin Sacks, *The Religious Issue in the State Schools of England and Wales, 1902–1914* (Albuquerque, N.M.: University of New Mexico Press, 1961); Morgan, *Wales in British Politics*, pp.
181–198.

their return to power, but this was thrown out by the House of Lords in 1907. The Liberals then faced sustained pressure from the Nonconformist churches to enforce a new religious settlement in education. Two other bills failed; the Liberals entered the January 1910 election pledged to make non-denominational (i.e. non-Anglican) education available to all; and education was discussed in that election very largely as a religious issue. In 1911 the Board of Education began to draft yet another bill. While some educational reformers saw this as an opportunity to reform the curriculum and improve the system in other ways, most members of the Cabinet and most Liberal M.P.s saw it as a resolution of the denominational question, in favour of their own supporters.[35] The proposals were still under discussion in July 1914, and emerged in a new form as part of the Lloyd George Coalition's social reform proposals in 1918.

Another issue forced on to the political agenda by Nonconformist sensibility was temperance. This, after education, was the most popular 'fad' of the late Gladstonian Liberal Party. Various schemes for promoting temperance, from outright prohibition to the municipalisation of liquor retailing, had been favoured by politically active Nonconformists, who had tried to impose their views on the Liberal establishment. The United Kingdom Alliance, one of their vehicles, was the most effective instrument for agitational campaigning since the National Education League of the 1870s. Conservatives had consistently opposed temperance policies since Gladstone's 1872 Licensing Act, and the brewery interests were solidly Conservative.[36] When the Conservative government introduced its own Licensing bill in 1904 it had little credit left in the Nonconformist communities, and the measure confirmed the incompatibility between the party and organised Nonconformity. In 1906 the new Liberal government came under heavy pressure to repeal the clauses which gave landlords a vested pecuniary interest in their licences, and duly succumbed. Their predictable humiliation in the Lords inflamed temperance leaders to further abuse of the pusillanimity of Liberal Cabinet ministers and the wickedness of the Conservatives. This was another issue which remained alive during the war, an opportunity for ingenious politicians and a trap for the unwary.

These were issues which concerned all of England and Wales, and the temperance movement was also strong among Free Churchmen in Scotland. A third denominational issue was no less contentious for being confined to Wales. The disestablishment of the Anglican Church in Wales had long been an objective for Welsh Nonconformists. A series of campaigns, over the payment of tithes, the refusal of permission for Nonconformist

[35] Geoffrey Sherington, *English Education, Social Change and War, 1911–20* (Manchester: Manchester University Press, 1981), pp. 9, 21–39.

[36] A.E. Dingle, *The Campaign for Prohibition in Victorian England* (London: Croom Helm, 1980).

burials in Anglican churchyards, and the education issue, had left a tradition of agitation which was strengthened by the religious revival. Under the 1906–14 Liberal governments the pressure for Welsh disestablishment was unremitting. Politically active Nonconformists ranked it above Irish Home Rule in importance, and the movement had a figurehead and sometimes a leader in Lloyd George, who retained the associations he had made in the 1890s with the leaders of political Nonconformity.

The opposition to Welsh disestablishment naturally sprang from the Conservative Party, but not equally from every section of it. Political Anglicanism was focused on the Cecil family: the three sons of the third Marquess of Salisbury, his nephew Arthur Balfour, and his son-in-law, Lord Selborne. The fourth Marquess, 'Jem' Salisbury, and his younger and cleverer brothers Lord Robert and Lord Hugh ('Linky') Cecil took every opportunity to raise the political temperature and rally opposition to disestablishment proposals, especially in the Lords. Their enthusiasm and rigidity enabled Lloyd George to portray the arrogance and selfishness of contemporary Anglicanism, to the delight of his Nonconformist allies. Self-conscious Protestantism was also able to make political capital over the dispute within the Church of England over the adoption of allegedly Catholic ritual forms.[37] The disestablishment of the Welsh Church was an item of contentious business which the wartime political truce never quite suppressed; and Robert Cecil, after going through a war with a prime minister he hated, acquiescing in the Coalition's attack on the independence of the generals he so much admired, and tolerating the casual denigration of the landowning classes to which he belonged, finally resigned from the ministry at the very last minute over the unsatisfactory reference to the Church in Wales in the Coalition's election manifesto.

Although the Conservative Party could be relied upon to oppose all the political aspirations of the Nonconformist churches, political Nonconformity was not an unalloyed blessing for the Liberals. Nor was it as effective as sheer numbers might suggest. Avowed Free Churchmen accounted for 157 Liberal M.P.s after the 1906 election[38] which made them a substantially larger pressure group on the government side than the Irish (with 83 members).[39] This was not enough to endear them to the Liberal leadership. For one thing, the leaders and activists in the Free Churches could easily bully Liberal candidates into subscribing with both hands to temperance, Welsh disestablishment and non-denominational education, but they could not guarantee that their middle-class co-religionists would ac-

---

[37] See G.I.T. Machin, *Politics and the Churches in Britain 1869–1921* (Oxford: Clarendon Press, 1987), pp. 274–310.

[38] Thirty-nine per cent of the parliamentary party, compared with 6 Nonconformists (3%) among the Conservatives.

[39] Koss, *Nonconformity*, p. 228.

tually vote Liberal. Some Free Church leaders and M.P.s were awkwardly hostile to Irish Nationalist aspirations, because the Nationalists, besides being Roman Catholic, were markedly unhelpful about temperance and education. This left bemused Liberal Cabinets with the problem of satisfying two quarrelsome and incompatible factions; and after 1910, when the Nonconformists lost 53 M.P.s, proportionately as many as the Liberal Party in general, while the Nationalists managed to gain a seat, the Irish had the more effective claim to attention. Nevertheless the link between Nonconformity and Liberal politics, established under Gladstone, was resilient enough to survive into the war, and to colour the rhetoric and the calculations of politicians who had grown up with it. Nonconformist issues, and Nonconformist political reflexes, were called into play for the general election at the end of the war, and religious affiliation has even been identified among the determinants of voting choice after the war.[40]

Religious politics could not easily be separated from nationalist politics, either at Westminster or in the country. Although Welsh and Scottish national identities were associated with distinctive political behaviour, the most significant nationalism was in Ireland.[41] The three essential hatreds of Victorian Ireland — between Catholic peasant and Anglican landlord in the South, between Catholic and Protestant industrial workers in the northern towns, and between the Presbyterians of the six north-east counties of Ulster and the whole of Southern Irish society — were muted in the Edwardian years. Wyndham's Land Act of 1903, which fostered the spread of owner-occupation and the consolidation of farms into economic units, helped to pacify the rural south. Moderate prosperity and the absence of any real threat of change kept Ulster quiet. The growth of linguistic separatism in the rural south, based on the Gaelic Athletic Association and the Hibernian League, was counterbalanced by the rise of a Nationalist but Anglophone culture in Dublin, associated particularly with the Abbey Theatre. Although the Nationalist Party retained its dominance throughout the southern counties, there was no real threat of disorder to back up the constitutional struggle at Westminster. This period of equilibrium was

[40] William Miller and Gillian Raab, 'The Religious Alignment at English Elections between 1918 and 1970', *Political Studies*, xxv (1977), 227–251.

[41] A reminder: before 1922 *Great Britain* meant the large island divided between England, Wales and Scotland; the *United Kingdom* included Great Britain and Ireland; *British* meant 'appertaining to the United Kingdom' to Irish Unionists, but 'appertaining to Great Britain' to Irish Nationalists. *Ireland* consisted of four 'historic' provinces, Munster, Connaught, Leinster and Ulster. Ulster included nine counties, of which four — Londonderry, Antrim, Down and Armagh — had Protestant majorities. Tyrone and Fermanagh were evenly divided between Protestant and Catholic, while Cavan, Monaghan and Donegal were predominantly Catholic. *England and Wales* was a single administrative unit with a single legal code. *Scotland* had its own legal system and civil administration, as did *Ireland*: Ireland was governed by a Chief Secretary, usually in the Cabinet, and a Viceroy representing the monarch, through departments corresponding to the departments of English government, except that all foreign relations and defence were the responsibility of the relevant ministries in London.

ended when the Liberal government pushed aside the House of Lords veto which had blocked Irish Home Rule since 1893. The new Home Rule bill introduced in April 1912 provoked Ulster Protestants and southern Nationalists in turn to create and arm 'volunteer' organisations, and gave further impetus to the development of separatist ideologies in the south. At the outbreak of war Ireland was in uproar, with the greatest threat of disturbance coming from the north. Irish tensions also had consequences in Great Britain: in 1905 it was estimated that 98 seats in England and Wales, and 26 in Scotland, had a significant Irish vote. Almost all of them (92 and 22 respectively) were held by the Liberals in 1906.[42]

The Home Rule bill also provoked a new discussion of regional devolution in Great Britain. Except in the Irish-influenced seats, the British electorate cared little about Irish Home Rule. This indifference was exploited by Conservative politicians, whose commitment to the Union, like that of the Liberals to Home Rule, exceeded that of most of their supporters in Great Britain. Conservative arguments against Home Rule were tailored to each audience. In Liverpool and Glasgow, and in Liberal areas like Cornwall where Wesleyan Methodism offered fertile ground, hostility to 'Rome rule' from Dublin was played up. Conservatives in suburban England harped on the integrity of the Empire, while in the Lancashire cotton districts they warned of the threat of Irish customs barriers. But one of the most promising lines of resistance lay in the proposal that all of the United Kingdom should be given some measure of 'Home Rule'. This was a good gambit because it threatened to divide the Liberal Party. One reason for wanting devolution to regional parliaments, popular with some Liberals, was that the congestion of business in the Westminster parliament was a drag on social reform.[43] But devolution also appealed to disgruntled Welsh Liberals and some English Conservatives, in both cases because it would free the Westminster parliament from the others' parochial prejudices; while a body of imperialist thought held that it was a precondition of closer imperial unity.[44] This made a tactical opportunity for Conservatives who wanted to guarantee Ulster a devolved status separate from Southern Ireland, or who merely wanted to wreck the bill. The Liberal Cabinet, from their viewpoint wisely, ignored it as a solution to the Irish problem. 'Federalism' nevertheless became part of pre-war

[42] Memo by Herbert Gladstone, n.d. (1905), BL Add. MSS 46109, ff. 28–35. See also pp. 18–19 above and I.S. Wood, 'Irish Nationalism and Radical Politics in Scotland, 1880–1906', *Journal of the Scottish Labour History Society*, ix (1975), 21–38.

[43] See for example the editorial stance of the *Political Quarterly*, an academic journal of political science supported by Liberals in Oxford.

[44] J.E. Kendle, 'The Round Table Movement and "Home Rule All Round"', *Historical Journal*, xi (1968), 332–353; Patricia Jalland, 'United Kingdom Devolution, 1910–14: political panacea or tactical diversion?', *English Historical Review*, xciv (1979), 757–785.

political language, with a recognised body of support.[45] The nationality question was still open in 1914.

While the British agonised over the problems of nationality and religion, they were also acutely aware of class differences. On the one hand, it was widely agreed that by 1914 the electorate was dominated by the working class, in the sense that working-class men enjoying the householder franchise under the 1884 Reform Act outnumbered middle-class electors even when the various plural votes were taken into account.[46] On the other hand the same working-class men continued to vote for parties dominated by the middle classes, choosing between them on grounds which included religious and nationalist prejudice and straightforward deference to local employers. The only party which openly claimed to represent a particular class, the Labour Party, acquired a substantial existence only in 1900 and was weak, both in parliament and in the country, until the outbreak of war.

From these well established points historians have diverged, some claiming that the survival of the Liberal Party proves that class politics was irrelevant, some asserting that the mere existence of the Labour Party condemned the Liberal Party to death sooner or later. Most are agreed that the Conservative Party retained a large proportion of working-class votes, even beyond Merseyside and the areas dominated by armament industries or defence establishments. Careful studies of Lancashire have shown that while deference in industrial areas lost its power to determine working-class electoral choices in the first decade of the twentieth century, the beneficiary was the Liberal Party, not the Labour Party, and that the Liberals had become the party of the working class by 1910, leaving Labour on the sidelines.[47] Equally careful studies of London have shown a rapid erosion of Liberal support among working-class voters, whose preference for the Labour Party was well established by the outbreak of war.[48] In the West Riding of Yorkshire, according to another account, Labour was gaining strength in an atmosphere of working-class political consciousness, but this strength was manifested in local authority elections,

---

[45] George Boyce, 'Federalism and the Irish Question', in Andrea Bosco and John Pinder, eds., *The Federal Idea* (forthcoming).

[46] But there are differences over how much: see Duncan Tanner, 'The Parliamentary Electoral System, the "Fourth Reform Act", and the Rise of Labour in England and Wales', *Bulletin of the Institute of Historical Research*, lvi, 134 (1983), 205–219 and Neal Blewett, *The Peers, the Parties, and the People: the general elections of 1910* (London: Macmillan, 1972), and his earlier article 'The Franchise in the United Kingdom, 1885–1918', *Past and Present*, xxxii (Dec 1965), 27–56.

[47] P.F. Clarke, *Lancashire and the New Liberalism* (Cambridge: Cambridge University Press, 1971); Patrick Joyce, *Work, Society and Politics* (Brighton: Harvester Press, 1980).

[48] Paul Thompson, *Socialists, Liberals and Labour: the struggle for London 1885–1914* (London: Routledge & Kegan Paul, 1967).

not in parliamentary contests.[49] One recently published synthesis suggests that neither Liberal social reforms nor the electoral 'Progressive Alliance' between Liberal and Labour were enough to save Liberalism from the consequences of being a middle-class party; another, rather foggily, that in the circumstances the Liberals were doing rather well.[50] It is hardly surprising that the most recent major study of the rise of Labour should describe the process of political and electoral change as 'fragmented'.[51]

Over-generalisation is obviously out of place here: class evidently had different political significance in different places and historians should be more careful than they have usually been in generalising from local studies to integrated theories of class politics. But this does not mean that class was a random factor in British politics on the eve of war. Two processes of change were at work: changes in social structure and class identification, brought about mostly by economic change; and changes in the relationship between class and political choice, brought about by largely by political organisation and the daily work of politicians. Working together, these two processes created the socio-economic environment of party politics on the eve of war; amplified by the war, they contributed to the outcome of the Coupon election. Neither process worked in the same way in every part of the country, and neither is an entirely satisfactory explanation on its own. An extra difficulty arises in defining 'class'. The definition used by historians in trying to explain political allegiance often focuses on men's role in the labour process; the definition of class used by historians studying electoral behaviour is necessarily concerned with what can be measured in the census, which is usually confined to the industries in which men worked; the definition used by modern political scientists emphasises patterns of consumption and position in the labour market.

Socio-economic change in the years before the war, as it applied to politics, was mostly the result of structural change in the economy, exacerbated in its effects by foreign competitive pressure. The 'Great Depression' of 1873–1896 squeezed manufacturing profits and cut export prices; while the 'recovery' at the turn of the century was muted by foreign competition in staple products such as textiles, coal, steel, ships and engineering goods. To reduce wage costs, employers introduced new working practices and payment methods which changed social relationships in the workplace and created antagonism between them and their employees.

[49] Keith Laybourn and Jack Reynolds, *Liberalism and the Rise of Labour, 1890–1918* (London: Croom Helm, 1984); see also Martin D. Pugh, 'Yorkshire and the New Liberalism', *Journal of Modern History*, 1 (1978), 1139–1155.

[50] George L. Bernstein, *Liberalism and Liberal Politics in Edwardian England* (Boston: Allen & Unwin, 1986); Michael Bentley, *The Climax of Liberal Politics: British Liberalism in theory and practice 1868–1918* (London: Edward Arnold, 1987) esp. pp. 138–152.

[51] Duncan Tanner, *Political Change and the Labour Party* (Cambridge: Cambridge University Press, 1990).

One method, much favoured in the textile and coal-mining industries, was to bring about agreements in which wage levels would be based on the market price of the product; another, fairly common in engineering, was to introduce machinery which would allow less skilled, and therefore less expensive workers to produce goods. Especially when costly machinery was involved, employers turned to piecework and bonus systems which would encourage faster work and greater productivity. These innovations were introduced to different degrees in different industries and regions, but wherever they appeared they had the effect of stimulating the trade union movement. Sliding-scale agreements and other forms of arbitration depended on the existence of an organised body of workers with which to negotiate. The introduction of self-acting machinery threatened the high earnings and autonomy of skilled workers, and encouraged existing trade unions to defend 'craft privileges'; but since it was usually accompanied by piecework and bonus systems which affected all production workers, the common interest of all workers could overcome 'craft' exclusiveness and stimulate broader co-operation between groups of workers. Wage differentials were compressed and the work autonomy and bargaining position of skilled workers was weakened. In the short term this caused resentment between skilled and semi-skilled workers: in the medium term it created a more homogeneous working class. Moreover, employers who had invested heavily in machinery, and even some who had not, found that they needed to maintain continuity of production in order to service their debts. Semi-skilled workers could therefore benefit from the extra leverage of trade union organisation, as witnessed by the growth of the 'New Unions' from the 1880s.[52]

Employers in the 1890s met resistance to their efforts to maintain profits, but their response to industrial unrest was robust and effective. At company level a combination of industrial welfare and the deliberate use of 'premium bonus' payment systems discouraged union membership and eroded workers' solidarity; employers' associations were able to combine in lockouts and strike-breaking efforts; and political and legal action, undertaken by umbrella organisations such as the Liberty and Property Defence League and by the larger employers' federations, whittled away at trade

---

[52] There is a large literature on this, partly reviewed in John Turner 'Man and Braverman: British industrial relations', *History*, lxx (1985), 236–242, and in John Turner, 'Industrial Relations and Business History', in Charles Harvey and John Turner, eds., *Labour and Business in Modern Britain* (London: Frank Cass, 1989), pp. 1–5. See especially Mike Holbrook-Jones, *Supremacy and Subordination of Labour* (London: Heinemann Educational Books, 1982); Craig R. Littler, *The Development of the Labour Process in Capitalist Societies* (London: Heinemann Educational Books, 1982); Jonathan Zeitlin, 'The Labour Strategies of British Engineering Employers, 1890–1922', in Howard F. Gospel and Craig R. Littler, *Managerial Strategies and Industrial Relations* (London: Heinemann Educational Books, 1983), pp. 25–54; Alan McKinlay and Jonathan Zeitlin, 'The Meanings of Managerial Prerogative: industrial relations and the organisation of work in British engineering, 1880–1939', in Harvey and Turner, *Labour and Business*, pp. 32–47.

union strength, particularly in the area of legal immunities during strike action.[53] The 'employers' backlash' of the 1890s linked the socio-economic changes which began in the 1880s to the political movements of the new century.

The net effect of the whole of the employers' backlash on the working class as electors is much more problematic. Undoubtedly the process which began in the 1890s brought certain heavily unionised industries round to Labour. The miners, whose union's allegiance to Labour was slow to mature, were among the party's most reliable supporters by 1918; even so there was no parliamentary election contest before 1914 in which more than half of the miners voting supported a Labour candidate.[54] But in industries where workers' allegiance to their unions was not so strong or so simple, the effects were mixed. Industrial relations in the engineering industry gave the employers the upper hand until the outbreak of war. Employers' tactics tended to divide one union from another, leaving the Amalgamated Society of Engineers (A.S.E.) as an embattled defender of the economic privileges of skilled men. Even when A.S.E. leaders, including G.N. Barnes, took an active part in Labour politics it could not be assumed that A.S.E. members would support him, let alone that the semi-skilled men still excluded from the A.S.E.'s protection would follow the lead of the industry's most privileged union. Craft loyalties under pressure turned some men into radicals, but it was a radicalism only in defence of their craft, not a firm basis for co-operation with other trade unionists.[55] The intra-class tensions which had reinforced Liberal voting in the 1890s were perpetuated, and as a result the engineering centres were less profitable for Labour than the mining communities before the war.

The electorate's response to industrial developments was further complicated by the wide variation in management styles during a period of rapid managerial change. During the nineteenth century 'employer paternalism' based on a personal relationship between master and men in family firms, however large the firm, had been important in maintaining political allegiances, especially in smaller industrial communities. Hence Blackburn (a two-member seat) returned a Conservative until 1910 because the town's industry was dominated by the Hornby family; other communities

[53] Robert Fitzgerald, *British Labour Management and Industrial Welfare, 1846–1939* (London: Croom Helm, 1988); Joseph Melling, 'British Employers and the Development of Industrial Welfare, c. 1880–1920', University of Glasgow Ph.D. thesis, 1980; Geoffrey Alderman, 'The National Free Labour Association: a case study of organised strike-breaking in the late 19th and the early 20th Century', *International Review of Social History*, xxi (1976), 309–336; Arthur J. McIver, 'Employers' Organisations and Strike-breaking in Britain, 1880–1914', *International Review of Social History*, xxix (1984), 1–33.

[54] Roy Gregory, *The Miners and British Politics, 1906–1914* (Oxford: Oxford University Press, 1968), p. 189.

[55] See especially Reid, 'Dilution, Trade Unionism and the State...' in Tolliday and Zeitlin, *Shop Floor Bargaining and the State*.

had seen a change in political allegiance when family management was superseded by professional management from the new limited companies, often themselves created by mergers. Employer paternalism could work to the advantage of either of the older parties, depending on the inclinations of the employer, and was probably responsible for a great deal of the supposedly 'popular' Toryism of the late nineteenth century as well as for the willingness of much of the working class to stay with the Liberals until the First World War.

The impact of changing management styles can be illustrated by three areas in which shipbuilding and the associated engineering work was the principal economic activity: Jarrow, Barrow-in-Furness, and the Clyde. The technology and skills employed in these areas were similar, and developed in similar ways between 1890 and 1914. All three areas built both merchant and naval vessels, though the balance in Barrow was weighted towards the navy and in Jarrow towards merchant shipping, with the result that technology was probably more advanced, and skills more at a premium, in Barrow. What is known of living standards suggests a well-stratified working-class society, in which a 'labour aristocracy' of the most skilled craftsmen was prominent. It has been estimated that 37 per cent of the Barrow labour force worked for Vickers, of whom a high proportion were skilled and reasonably affluent workers.[56] The important differences between these areas lie in the ownership and management of their principal industries. Jarrow was dominated by Palmer's Shipbuilding and Iron Company. This had been founded by Sir Charles Mark Palmer, a coal-owner, in the 1860s. The Palmer company was a classic North-Eastern vertically integrated concern, taking in every stage in the production of ships from the mining of coal through the making of iron and steel to the manufacture and outfitting of ships' hulls: its Jarrow plant included rolling mills and an engine works, and was the economic heart of the town. Charles Mark Palmer first won the North Durham constituency, where Jarrow lay, in 1874, and remained M.P. for the division and later the Jarrow division until his death in 1907. At the by-election Pete Curran of the I.L.P. narrowly took the seat from Palmer's son, Godfrey Mark Palmer, but Palmer took the seat back in 1910 and retained it until 1922 when at last it fell to Labour in common with almost all of the Durham constituencies.[57]

[56] Elizabeth Roberts, 'Working-Class Standards of Living in Barrow and Lancaster, 1890–1914' *Economic History Review* 2nd series, xxx (1977), 306–319; Elizabeth Roberts, 'Working-Class Standards of Living in Three Lancashire Towns, 1890–1914', *International Review of Social History*, xxvii (1982), 43–65.

[57] A.W. Purdue, 'The Liberal and Labour Parties in North-Eastern Politics 1900–14: the struggle for supremacy', *International Review of Social History*, xxvi (1981), 1–24.

The enduring power of Liberalism was also notable on the Clyde, even though there were no 'company towns' like Jarrow. Despite the rise of aggressively expanding companies such as John Brown's and the Weir group, Glasgow employers were local employers, very often committed Free Traders who were Liberal for that reason. They took a harsh line against the A.S.E., with the result that Barnes was able to take the Blackfriars constituency in 1906 and hold it until his retirement, but this did not lose them the sympathy of all the working-class electorate, and the threat from Labour was therefore contained at that level.[58]

Contrast these experiences with that of Barrow-in-Furness, where the Elswick works was owned by Vickers Ltd. Vickers's installations covered the same range of skills and thus the same labour force as Palmer's in Jarrow or John Brown's on the Clyde, but they were managed as part of a national firm without a strong local personal identity. Industrial relations were more abrasive than in Jarrow. In 1885 and 1886 a director of the Barrow steelworks won in the Conservative interest, and the Conservative held the seat until 1906. The Barrow seat was first won for Labour by Charles Duncan in 1906 (with no Liberal opposition): in the 1920s, with somewhat different boundaries, it was exchanged between Labour and Conservative, and it spent the 1930s in Conservative hands. Barrow returned its last Liberal M.P. in 1885; Liberalism had never since then been a serious challenger to the Conservatives, who were supported by Vickers and the steelworks. Liberal withdrawal under the 1903 pact was a proper reflection of the balance of power between Liberal and Labour in the constituency. The difference between Barrow-in-Furness on the one hand and Glasgow and Jarrow on the other might be explained as the result of 'regional differences' in the strength of Liberalism; but underlying those differences were differences in the typical relationship between employer and worker, and the role of employers in local politics, which affected the rate at which Labour was likely to grow.

Employer paternalism did not guarantee the suppression of Labour, nor was Labour necessarily its only opponent. The St Helen's constituency, economically subordinate to the Pilkington glass-making interests, fell to Labour in 1906, was lost to the Conservatives in December 1910, won back in 1918 with an unusually large Labour poll, and kept with only a short interruption (1931–1935) for the next seventy years. Labour's early political strength in St Helens owed something to the large number of miners in the constituency, and much to the anti-union fervour of the Pilkington family, whose members found themselves defeated by Labour candidates in local elections before the turn of the century. Nearby North-

---

[58] This, of course, is only a partial explanation of working-class Liberalism in the west of Scotland, which also owes much to the Irish issue and to the influence of the Nonconformist Churches: see above, pp. 18–19, 23.

wich, held for the Liberals by Sir John Brunner of the Brunner-Mond company, succumbed on the withdrawal of the Brunner-Mond interest not to Labour but to Conservative, and has been in Conservative hands since 1918. In this case it may be doubted if Labour had any latent strength at all. Crewe, another company town in which the Chief Engineers of the railway works adopted the social role of local employers, saw the struggle between Conservative and Liberal, rather than Labour, survive well past the First World War.[59]

Managerial diversity and change is relevant to the politics of the First World War because the pressures of pre-war economic competition were amplified and distorted by the war itself. Munitions business strained local economies; labour shortages tilted the industrial balance in favour of the unions, then state action, such as compulsory dilution of labour by women, shifted it back again; the impact of conscription, felt to be both arbitrary and highly selective in its impact on different sections of the working class, set men against one another, against their employers, and against the state. The unpredictable political communities of industrial Britain set limits on what politicians could do in pursuit of victory. Their responses to the tightening of the state's hold on the economy made themselves felt in the post-war election and thereby helped change the party system for ever.

Before 1890 working-class involvement in party politics reflected the interest taken by the Liberal and Conservative parties in the expanded electorate of 1867 and 1884. Unorganised workers, by far the majority, were absorbed by the 'parties of social integration' which the old parties had become: team-spirit, smoking concerts, and deference to the political views of powerful employers accounted for voting choices.[60] The Conservative Party was the most ambitious integrating party, with the Primrose League offering plenty of opportunity for working men and their wives to become part of a political community.[61] Organised workers were influenced by their trade unions, almost always in a Liberal direction even when this tended to ally them with their employers. A widespread commitment to Free Trade, fostered by the available sources of popular education, and a firm reliance within the trade union movement on free bargaining in an open market, bolstered their loyalty to the Gladstonian party.[62] Some antagonism between employer and worker could be resolved within Lib-

[59] Patrick Joyce, *Work, Society and Politics* (London: reprinted, Methuen, 1982); P.F. Clarke, 'British Politics and Blackburn Politics, 1900–1910', *Historical Journal*, xii (1969); T.C. Barker, *The Glass-makers: the rise of an international company, 1826–1976* (London: Weidenfeld, 1977); Diane Drummond, 'Crewe: the society and culture of a railway town, 1842–1914,' London University Ph. D. thesis, 1986.

[60] J.A. Garrard, 'Parties, Members and Voters after 1867: a local study', *Historical Journal*, xx (1977), 145–163.

[61] Martin Pugh, *The Tories and the People, 1880–1935* (Oxford: Blackwell, 1985), pp. 25–42.

[62] Robert Currie, *Industrial Politics* (Oxford: Clarendon Press, 1979), pp. 26–56.

eralism: the coal-miners' unions, in particular, could dominate the local organisations of the Liberal Party in South Wales and parts of the northern English coalfields, but were generally content to leave parliamentary seats to the coal-owners or to share the representation.

Rising industrial unrest had a direct impact in the early 1890s. The establishment of local Trades Councils created a focus for joint action by trade unionists. Besides offering a measure of mutual support during strikes, the Trades Councils became active in local politics, supporting candidates for municipal elections, and began to confront the resistance of local Liberal Associations to the adoption of working-class parliamentary candidates. Where strong Trades Councils met strong resistance, especially where deferential feelings towards employers were diffused in large cities or attenuated by the absence of a resident employer, the Independent Labour Party, founded in Bradford in 1893, was able to gain support.[63]

The very limited success of the I.L.P. reflects the difficulties inherent in an independent working-class bid for political influence at this time. Its direct appeal was to active trade unionists, the very group which nourished the longest tradition of attachment to Gladstonian Liberalism. It is not surprising that the party returned no M.P.s in the 1895 election and only two in 1900. Although the I.L.P. was unequivocally a class party, few members of its natural constituency were willing as yet to vote on class lines. Even where the I.L.P. gained temporary success, the established parties soon used established means to re-assert themselves; a case in point was the Jarrow by-election mentioned above.

The establishment of the Labour Representation Committee (L.R.C.) in February 1900 did not signify a great shift in working-class political preferences. It was a tactical opportunity seized by some I.L.P. activists, including Keir Hardie and Ramsay MacDonald, to secure the practical and financial support of the trade unions for independent working-class candidates. Hardie and MacDonald were active socialists, as were a number of the more successful trade union organisers (such as Curran and Will Thorne, a Gasworkers' leader like Curran who became a Labour M.P.), but there is little evidence of enthusiasm for socialism among the rank and file of trade unionists, even those whose leaders were socialists themselves. Even the trade union leaders who took an active part in the L.R.C. were most concerned to secure legislative action in favour of trade unions, to overturn the results of the Taff Vale judgment and the other legal judgments which had preceded it. As a result the L.R.C., known as the Labour Party after the 1906 election, was neither a socialist party nor very obviously the party of the majority of the working class. It could

[63] J. Reynolds and K. Laybourn, 'The Emergence of the Independent Labour Party in Bradford', *International Review of Social History*, xx (1975), 313–346; Deian Hopkin, 'The Membership of the Independent Labour Party, 1904–10: a spatial and occupational analysis', *ibid.*, 175–195.

best be described as the political organ of some, but not all, trade unions. It is significant that scarcely more than half the votes cast at the 1899 Trades Union Congress, representing 546 thousand out of 980 thousand affiliated members, supported the idea of the L.R.C. Even as more trade unions affiliated to the party, notably the miners who in 1908 brought with them 14 former Liberal working-class M.P.s, the party before the war could only claim to represent certain sections of the working class in certain parts of the country.

But for those sections of the workforce whose experience at work had produced a lasting hostility to their employers, the Labour Party was clearly important, and grew in importance during the Edwardian decade. The Amalgamated Society of Engineers, troubled by the downgrading of skilled labour and fairly consistently defeated in its encounters with the Engineering Employers' Federation, provided a number of prominent M.P.s; so did the Amalgamated Society of Railway Servants, which had had to fight for any recognition by the railway companies. The miners, whose homogeneous and isolated communities and peculiarly horrible working conditions strengthened their political cohesion, had worked out a common set of demands before the turn of the century, which included public ownership of the coal mines. The point of this was to strengthen their hand in wage bargaining, and not until 1908 (or in some places even much later) was it widely felt to be inconsistent with stolid Liberalism.[64]

Support for the Labour Party before the war, then, was based on the decisions of groups of workers who had particular reason to move away from the established parties, and took advantage of the erosion of the habit of deference to local employers. It was not the consequence of a generally perceived awareness of class. To anticipate the argument of later chapters, the consequence of war was to encourage more groups of workers to take this step. But what of those members of the working class who did not vote Labour? The working-class electors described above, who had the opportunity to vote Labour, but chose not to, are the most intriguing to historians and political activists who find their action deviant and incomprehensible. But many had no opportunity: the largest number of parliamentary candidates put up by Labour was 78, in the January 1910 election, and even in municipal elections the party could only muster at most 501 candidates (in 1912, when British Socialist Party or Social Democratic Federation candidates, who had disaffiliated from the party, added another 95). Fewer than 150 out of the Great Britain's 560 territorial constituencies had a Labour organisation before the war, far

[64] Gregory, *The Miners and British Politics*; G.A. Alderman, 'The Railway Companies and the Growth of Trades Unionism in the late Nineteenth and early Twentieth Century', *Historical Journal*, xiv (1971), 129–152; J.B. Jefferys, *The Story of the Engineers* (London: Amalgamated Engineering Union, 1946).

fewer than were exposed to the influence of the Primrose League.[65] Many more who are claimed as potential Labour voters did not have the vote, though this remains one of the most controversial issues in the literature.

Outside the workplace the factors influencing working-class votes are elusive. Both of the major political parties had a stereotype of the working-class voter. Liberalism was reckoned to be the preserve of the more educated working man, and since educated working men were in short supply both parties guessed that the least educated were Tories. The Conservative Party took this as the result of uninstructed common sense, the Liberals as the worst consequences of jingoism and drink. The result was much the same. Although the Conservative Party was better at jingoism and xenophobia it did not have a monopoly before the First World War: during the Boer War voters could choose between Conservative jingoes who scorned the Boers and Radical anti-semites who condemned the financiers in whose interest, allegedly, the war was being fought. During the Edwardian decade the Conservative Party, especially in the West Midlands, exploited imperialism and anti-German sentiment to manufacture a populist imperial conservatism which would outflank trade unionism as well as the Liberal Party, and bind together businessmen, clerks and skilled and unskilled manual workers.[66] Earlier the Primrose League had also taken its share of support from the 'respectable' working class, though the political balance within that ill-defined group has not been carefully estimated.[67]

In this context Chamberlain's 1903 appeal for Tariff Reform was born, the first serious attempt at a political programme which linked the material prosperity of the poor directly to imperial expansion. This 'squalid argument' horrified leading Liberals, some of whom wished they had thought of it first. It also confirmed the beliefs of those in both parties who thought that crude and materialist appeals were the best way to deal with the incipient problem of working-class solidarity. In 1918, when debating the future appeal of the Lloyd George Coalition, Liberals and Conservatives looked back for lessons from the working-class politics of 1900–14. Throughout the war, indeed, they had striven to understand the rapid changes of stance in the workforce in terms of what they knew about pre-war issues and preferences, drawing on their stock of preconceptions about 'the working man' to complement what they knew about Irish and Nonconformist voters. Some of their folk wisdom, but not all, improved their navigation through the fogs of post-war politics.

---

[65] Calculations exclude Ireland and the University seats. On Labour organisation see Ross McKibbin, *The Evolution of the Labour Party, 1910–1924* (Oxford: Clarendon Press, 1973), pp. 20–47, and Tanner, *Political Change and the Labour Party, passim*.

[66] R.P.T. Davenport-Hines, *Dudley Docker* (Cambridge: Cambridge University Press, 1984), esp. pp. 55–84.

[67] Pugh, *Tories and the People*, pp. 158–161.

'Class politics' was not just the politics of the working class. Pre-war parties added to their armoury two sorts of appeal to the middle classes, depending on which enemy seemed most threatening, and how the middle classes themselves were perceived. One approach adopted by Conservatives in the 1890s was to identify a certain strand of Liberalism with various forms of social intervention, and to construct an alliance of property owners and employers against it. The Liberty and Property Defence League was the first and best known manifestation, but just as much work was done by the opponents of municipal trading and of the many schemes of land reform canvassed by the Liberals when in opposition.[68] The rapid growth of central government expenditure, and hence of taxation, which took place after 1900 gave this movement all the justification it needed. Because the Liberals were the more expensive party, and also because they were in power at the end of the period when the cumulative cost was greater, they were the victims of the middle-class backlash, and the solidarity of this 'middle class' increased as time, and legislation, passed. The opposition to municipal trading was in fact at its most intense in the first three years of the century. The Industrial Freedom League, founded in 1902 to stamp out public ownership of utility supplies, was led by Lord Avebury, a former Liberal M.P., and attracted a great deal of support from the Cobdenite section of the party. Although it had some big business connections, its membership was largely drawn from the rank and file of the chambers of commerce in the major cities. It did not stem the tide of collectivism, but nor did the passage of time reconcile its supporters. The 1909 Budget made further demands on middle-class incomes, earned and unearned, which the Conservatives exploited through the Budget Protest League; and the passage of the National Insurance Act in 1911 convinced many employers that the Liberal Party in its present guise had nothing to offer them.[69] Steadily these developments helped the Conservative Party to consolidate a hold over small businessmen and salary earners, as well as the wealthier middle classes, which they had first established in the 1890s.

The Liberal answer to this challenge required a rather different definition of the middle class. Instead of the purely economic definition favoured by the Conservatives, who lumped all property owners and all the moderately affluent together, the Liberals emphasised national and sectional loyalties. This allowed them to appeal to the Welsh and Nonconformist middle class

[68] Richard Roberts, 'Businessmen, Politics, and Municipal Socialism', in John Turner, ed., *Businessmen and Politics. Studies of Business Activity in British Politics, 1900–1945* (London: Heinemann Educational Books, 1984), pp. 20–32; Avner Offer, *Property and Politics*, (Cambridge: Cambridge University Press, 1983) pp. 161–220, 377–400.

[69] J.R. Hay, 'Employers' Attitudes to Social Policy and the Concept of Social Control, 1900–1920', in P.M. Thane, ed., *The Origins of British Social Policy* (London: Croom Helm, 1978); Hay, 'Employers and Social Policy in Britain: the evolution of welfare legislation, 1905–14', *Social History*, (1977), 435–456; Charles Macara, *Recollections* (London: 1922), pp. 217–225.

in the hope that the pain of religious grievances would blot out the pain of extra taxation. Their other ploy was to separate the *rentier* from the gainfully employed: a technique particularly attractive to Lloyd George, who made an attack on aristocrats and landlords the centrepiece of his defence of the 1909 Budget. The Budget of 1914 made further progress towards redistribution within the middle classes, in its open attack on the finances of landed estates.[70]

The best that can be said of these Liberal efforts is that they were very optimistic, and reflected the difficulty which all politicians found in getting behind what they read in the newspapers and heard from lobbyists and from each other. Although the middle class was no more a homogeneous mass than the working class, there is strong evidence that religious and occupational divisions became less important predictors of political differences as the nineteenth century retreated into memory. The great gulf between Liberal business and Tory agriculture had been bridged in the 1860s, at first by bankers who readily adopted the manners and the politics of the aristocracy, and increasingly by manufacturers influenced by anti-collectivism or the desire for tariff protection. Although the process was far from complete by 1914, the tendency of social change among the élite was to produce a single, intermarrying and predominantly Conservative upper class distinguished by the amount of its wealth, not by its source.[71] The same process was at work among the less wealthy middle classes, though it was less advanced. What was left of vertical occupational divisions among the middle classes was mostly expressed in regional differentiation, with a fairly robust Liberal tradition in Northern English and Welsh industrial towns (encroached upon by Conservatism in the commercial districts) and in the Central and South-Western agricultural areas, which was counter-balanced by Conservative hegemony in the South-East, the West Midlands, and West Lancashire.[72] There were also potential differences of view and interest between white-collar workers living on small and insecure salaries and the more prosperous professional and commercial middle class whose manners they imitated, but historians have been unable to discover anything intelligible about them. Clerks and shopkeepers were recruited into the mass organisations of both political parties, finding in them a welcome opportunity to acquire status. But social aspiration, like deference, could cut either way, and it has not been established whether the

[70] José Harris, 'The Transition to High Politics in English Social Policy, 1880–1914', in Michael Bentley and John Stevenson, *High and Low Politics in Modern Britain* (Oxford: Clarendon Press, 1983), pp. 77–78.

[71] W.D. Rubinstein, 'Wealth, Elites and the Class Structure of Modern Britain', *Past and Present*, lxxvi (1977).

[72] For definitions of the Central, South-Western, South-Eastern and West Midlands areas see the Appendix and Pelling, *Social Geography*, both of which draw on areas defined by C.B. Fawcett in *Provinces of England* (London: Williams & Norgate, 1919).

lower middle classes were more or less inclined than their immediate social superiors to move from Liberal to Conservative in the Edwardian years.[73]

Politics as a profession was largely a preserve of the upper and middle classes, except that the Labour Party relied almost entirely on trade union officials of working-class origin and the small number of 'Lib-Lab' M.P.s, mostly miners, were deliberately chosen for their working-class origins. While the Conservatives were gaining ground among middle-class voters, and the Liberals seeking working-class support, Liberal M.P.s and the local leaders of Liberalism were drawn almost exclusively from the middle class. After the 1910 elections the occupational differences between Liberal and Conservative M.P.s were much more pronounced than the known differences between Liberal and Conservative middle-class voters. Although both parties were led by career politicians, whose ideological inclinations and political experiences were more important than their fathers' occupations, back-bench M.P.s had important occupational links with the real world outside the chamber. Landowners, bankers and former soldiers and public servants were strongly represented among the Conservatives, but scarcely present at all on the Liberal benches. Businessmen, especially manufacturers, were heavily outnumbered among Conservatives, while they retained an important place among Liberal M.P.s. This partly justified the claim that the Liberals were the party of business, or in a more modern terminology the party of wealth creation, while the Conservatives were society's parasites. In fact the Tariff Reform movement had begun to shift the balance by 1914, by hounding Conservative Free Traders out of their seats. Local Conservative associations, particularly in the West Midlands, were falling under business influence and the next general election, if held in 1915 as planned, would have seen many more businessmen among Conservative candidates. One effect of this was that the Liberal Party was able to develop the charge that business participation in Conservative politics was tinged with corruption.[74]

By 1914, then, British politics had not been completely assimilated to a class-based political structure, but it had gone a great deal of the way. Economic imperatives and the evolution of the labour process had come to determine the political perceptions of many, if not most voters. The major parties had begun to identify their potential supporters according to their socio-economic experience, and the Labour Party had made this

---

[73] Gregory Anderson, *Victorian Clerks* (Manchester: Manchester University Press, 1976); Pugh, *The Tories and the People*, pp. 137–153.

[74] Sykes, *Tariff Reform in British Politics*; Davenport-Hines, *Dudley Docker*; A.J. Marrison, 'Businessmen, Industries and Tariff Reform in Great Britain 1903–1930', *Business History*, xxv (1983); Frantz Coetzee, 'Pressure Groups, Tory Businessmen, and the Aura of Political Corruption before the First World War', *Historical Journal* (1986), 833–852; on the class background of Liberal M.P.s see Bernstein, *Liberal Politics*, pp. 13–17; for Unionist M.P.s see McEwen, 'Unionist and Conservative Members of Parliament', p. 83.

identification its *raison d'être*. The Liberals were losing their grip on the middle classes, though without provenly gaining the allegiance of the industrial working class, while the Conservatives were consolidating their appeal to all property owners and salary earners. Yet the old identifications remained to confuse both historians and the working politicians whose livelihood depended on making sense of a changing reality.

Political Argument

While adapting to the dynamics of social change, all the parties, except perhaps for the Irish Nationalists, were suffering from an ideological bewilderment in 1914. Most of the trouble could again be traced to Britain's changing place in the world. The end of the Victorian boom in the 1870s and the rapid advance of competing industrial economies forced both parties to reconsider the value of economic *laissez-faire*. Competition for formal empire in Africa, like competition for informal empire in Latin America, forced politicians to take a practical interest in foreign policy, especially when it produced a war in 1899. Finally the condition of urban society, revealed by the great social surveys of the late nineteenth century but also thrust on the attention of central government by the breakdown of funding in the existing welfare system, presented the parties with policy decisions which the electorate expected them to resolve. Both of the established parties developed new doctrines, quite different from the classic doctrines of their nineteenth-century century forebears. The Liberals, indeed, were readier to develop new ideologies than to recognise that their political audience had changed. The Labour Party, by contrast, adopted many of the Liberals' ideas but addressed them to a different audience.

The major polarities in British political argument were between collectivist and individualist approaches to social problems; between free trading and protectionist approaches to the problem of economic retardation; between imperialists and critics of empire; and between supporters of Britain's great power role and miscellaneous critics of British foreign policy. Sometimes a whole range of attitudes was contained within a single party, and sometimes each pole was readily identified with a party, but these were special cases: for the most part the old allegiances were simply at a tangent to what was being discussed by politicians, polemicists and journalists. During the war these doctrinal stances were further refined and distorted — it became commonplace to appeal to the traditional arguments while abandoning traditional practices — but the direction and passion of wartime politics can hardly be understood without a sympathetic knowledge of pre-war political debate.

The most extreme polarisation was over social reform. At one pole were the socialists and liberals whom Peter Clarke has jointly labelled 'social democrats'. The axiom which bound them together was that certain social problems could only be solved by state action, and that the state was morally justified in infringing the liberty and taxing the property of some citizens to correct the worst examples of poverty. In party terms most of those who held this view were Liberals, describing themselves as New Liberals as distinct from loyal adherents of *laissez-faire*.[75] But the most extreme of their opponents could be found in either of the established parties, and a powerful minority in the Labour movement would also reject their enthusiasm for the state. It is conventional to argue that the New Liberals were principally concerned to provide an attractive alternative to socialism. This was largely true of the two most prominent politicians who took up New Liberal ideas, Winston Churchill and David Lloyd George, and possibly also of Herbert Samuel and Charles Masterman, two of the more notable New Liberal writers who combined philosophising with practical politics. But many of the New Liberal authors, including J.A. Hobson and L.T. Hobhouse, expressed views which were indistinguishable from those of contemporary self-styled socialists.[76] Hobson in particular was influenced by Saint-Simon and Ruskin, from whom he derived in part his 'underconsumptionist' explanation of economic sluggishness. Hobson's critique of imperialism, published in 1903 and based on his reactions to the Boer War, was written on parallel lines to Rudolf Hilferding's work on the same subject. The general theme, that imperial expansion was a consequence of underconsumption in a capitalist economic system, was later used to great effect by Lenin. While Hobson thought of imperialism as an aberration of capitalist democracy, Hilferding and Lenin took it as a defining feature of the system,[77] and therein lay a characteristic difference between the New Liberals and contemporary Marxists. The New Liberals, almost to a man, believed that the system was capable of salvation without fundamental alteration of its economic structure, and that was why they believed the state had so large a role to play.

Differences of view between New Liberal and socialist writers faded into the metaphysical haze when they confronted the real world within Britain. Both were convinced of the wickedness of the 'individualist fallacy', so they both recommended collective action to remedy agreed evils. This produced a 'progressive' agenda, which included the redistribution

[75] H.V. Emy, *Liberals, Radicals and Social Politics 1892-1914* (Cambridge: Cambridge University Press, 1973) is still a valuable source for a party history of the 'New' Liberalism, though Bernstein's *Liberal Politics* sets the phenomenon in a broader context.

[76] See Michael Freeden, *The New Liberalism: an ideology of social reform* (Oxford: Clarendon Press, 1978); Stefan Collini, *Liberalism and Sociology* (Cambridge: Cambridge University Press, 1979).

[77] P.F. Clarke, *Liberals and Social Democrats* (Cambridge: Cambridge University Press, 1978), pp. 47–51, 90–99.

of wealth by taxation and welfare payments, the direct provision of some social services, such as education, and the abandonment of expansionist foreign policy. In foreign affairs and in the matter of Free Trade the progressives were at one with traditional Radicalism. In other questions they found themselves opposed to old-fashioned Radicalism, whose priorities they did not share, to traditional Gladstonian attitudes, which limited the role of the state, and to the new aspirations of the Liberal Imperialists which conflicted with their internationalist ideals. If intellectuals could slip into this symbiotic blend of socialism and non-socialism without ideological trauma, so too could practical politicians. Without worrying much about the precise ideological significance of their policies, the Liberal Cabinets of 1906–11 carried out a good deal of the progressive agenda. School meals, the school medical service, old age pensions, wages boards, and above all the beginning of sickness and unemployment insurance in the National Insurance Act of 1911, were the defining elements of practical progressivism, underpinned by the working parliamentary alliance between the Liberal government and Labour M.P.s and the Irish party. Conservative sympathy for this point of view was extremely limited. A Unionist Social Reform Committee, composed largely of very junior or otherwise insignificant M.P.s, discussed the same issues and two of its members, Waldorf Astor and Henry Cavendish-Bentinck, crossed the floor to vote for the National Insurance Act.[78]

The progressive element in the Liberal social legislation of the period was not undiluted. Obvious examples of Radical but non-progressive legislative activity are the Education bill of 1906 and the Licensing bill: measures which the Conservative House of Lords was, interestingly, much readier to block than social measures which had a smaller emotional charge. After the difficult passage of the National Insurance Act, the Cabinet, when it could see past Ireland, cast around for new social policies and came up with two: extension and consolidation of the National Insurance Act, and the Land Campaign. Both these moves were inspired by Lloyd George at the Exchequer. The insurance proposals were 'progressive' and prosaic; the Land Campaign was to be the basis of the next general election campaign, and its content of progressive aspirations for redistribution through revaluation was heavily adulterated by appeals to Henry George and the 'single tax' movement of the 1890s.[79] This, together with the festering ed-

[78] Most of its back-bench members were ardent Tariff Reformers. The most prominent sympathiser was F.E. Smith. See Jane Ridley, 'The Unionist Social Reform Committee 1911–14: Wets before the Deluge', *Historical Journal*, xxx (1987), 391–413.

[79] H.V. Emy, 'Lloyd George as Social Reformer: the Land Campaign', in A.J.P. Taylor, ed., *Lloyd George: twelve essays* (London: Hamish Hamilton, 1971); Roy Douglas, 'God gave the Land to the People', in A.J.A. Morris, ed., *Edwardian Radicalism, 1900–1914* (London: Routledge & Kegan Paul, 1974); B.B. Gilbert, 'David Lloyd George, the Reform of British Landholding and the Budget of 1914', *Historical Journal*, xxi (1978), 117–141.

ucation issue and the problem of Welsh disestablishment, kept traditional Radicals emotionally occupied.

The polarity between Free Trade and protection saw the Tariff Reform League and the political inheritance of Joseph Chamberlain taking the lead on the protectionist side. The disputation between Tariff Reformers and Free Traders was carried on at many levels. In purely economic argument the Tariff Reformers owed a debt to German theory and German practice. The leading British academic exponent of a protective tariff, W.J. Ashley, cited Friedrich List's *Der nationale System der politische Ökonomie* as a principal theoretical authority, while the relative economic success of the German economy within the *Zollverein* was taken as a test of the theory. Ashley and his ally W.A.S. Hewins, who was for a time Director of the London School of Economics before becoming a Conservative M.P., were by inclination and training economic historians rather than abstract theorists. The novelty of their argument was that it was empirically based, resting on the collection of bulky statistics both by government and private industry to prove the need for tariffs. Its weakness was the crude logic with which it handled the evidence, its almost wilful defiance of the body of economic theory then being developed by Alfred Marshall and his followers, and its excessive reliance on uneven and suspect data provided by sectional interests through the business-financed Tariff Commission.[80] Economists of the older British tradition weighed in against it with enthusiasm. Marshall, who had reoriented the discipline in 1890 with his *Principles of Economics* was reticent, but Arthur Pigou, his successor in the chair of economics at Cambridge, laid about the Tariff Reformers in a series of polemics.[81] Pigou's argument, that protection would shelter inefficiency, raise costs, reduce Britain's international competitiveness, and if adopted worldwide gravely reduce the volume of world trade, was almost universally accepted on the Liberal side. Most of the theoretical case for and against Tariff Reform had been expounded before the end of 1903 when Joseph Chamberlain first launched it as a political movement. The same arguments reappeared, often from the same hands, whenever protection was contemplated, as it was during the war.

This academic discourse had a limited effect on other levels of Tariff Reform debate. Except for Arthur Balfour, who produced his *Economic Notes on Insular Free Trade* in 1903, the politicians and businessmen who were interested in Tariff Reform rarely bothered with its intellectual ba-

---

[80] Marrison, 'Businessmen, Industries and Tariff Reform...'; Bernard Semmel, *Imperialism and Social Reform: English social-imperial thought 1895–1914* (New York: Anchor, 1968).

[81] A.C. Pigou, *The Riddle of the Tariff* (London: Brimley & Johnson, 1903); *Protective and Preferential Duties* (London: privately printed, 1906); *The Great Inquest* (London: The Pilot, 1903). See A.W. Coats, 'Political Economy and the Tariff Reform Campaign', *Journal of Law and Economics*, xi (1968), 181–229.

sis.[82] Business demands for tariff protection had a long history; despite the dogmatic rhetoric of Free Trade, some manufacturers had never subscribed to the full rigour of *laissez-faire*, preferring the government at the very least to elbow foreigners out of the way in overseas markets and make life difficult for exporters to Britain.[83] The full range of business sentiment in the last quarter of the century had been laid out in evidence to the Royal Commission on Depression in Trade.[84] In broad outline the cotton textile, shipbuilding and coalmining industries were opposed to tariffs, as was the City of London, while protectionism was more popular in the engineering trades, woollen textiles, and some sections of the iron and steel industry; but exceptions were legion. Protectionist demands faded from view when Salisbury's government declined to take them up after 1886.

By the time political interest in Tariff Reform revived in 1903, business sentiment had changed. A very strong protectionist lobby had developed in the electromechanical industry: the manufacturers of generators, large electric motors, electric railways and the like, who faced fierce competition for large contracts from American and German firms with greater technical expertise and larger domestic markets.[85] The City of London had also shifted its ground slightly, with an important minority of bankers developing an interest in some form of protection.[86] Meanwhile the producers of primary iron and steel goods hardened their views, fearful of dumping especially by German, French and Belgian suppliers.

When Joseph Chamberlain launched the Tariff Reform movement in 1903, and set up the Tariff Commission in 1904 to produce 'objective' and 'impartial' evidence of the economic consequences of Free Trade, there was therefore no shortage of businessmen to put time and money into the venture. Although some of those who did so shared Chamberlain's larger vision of imperial unity through imperial preference, a majority were simple protectionists, who disliked dumping whether it

[82] A.J. Balfour, *Economic Notes on Insular Free Trade* (London: Longman, 1903). That Balfour was reckoned an opponent of political Tariff Reform lends irony to his defence of its principles; but the economics of Tariff Reform is full of irony, for Marshall, who wrote powerfully against it in academic journals, was strongly sympathetic to the same German authors who had inspired Ashley and other Social Darwinists. Donald Winch, *Economics and Policy* (London: Hodder & Stoughton, 1969), pp. 37, 67, 69–70; H.W. Macready, 'Alfred Marshall and Tariff Reform, 1903', *Journal of Political Economy*, lxiii (1955), 259–267.

[83] B.H. Brown, *The Tariff Reform Movement in Great Britain 1881–98* (New York: Columbia University Press, 1943).

[84] *Depression of Trade and Industry: reports and minutes of evidence*, P.P. 1886, xxi C. 4715; xxii, C. 4715–I; xxiii, C. 4794.

[85] Hugo Hirst, 'Two Autobiographical Fragments', ed. R.P.T. Davenport-Hines, *Business History*, xxviii (1986), pp. 124 ff.

[86] See e.g. John Turner, 'Sir Vincent Caillard', in David Jeremy, ed., *Dictionary of Business Biography. Volume I* (London: Butterworth, 1986), pp. 564–567.

came from Germany or Canada. Tariff Commission and Tariff Reform League activity brought many businessmen into politics on the Conservative side. In some areas protectionist businessmen dominated the local activities of the party.[87] Anti-protectionist sentiment also brought businessmen into politics, though many Free Traders in the business community seem to have derived their economic doctrines from their party allegiance rather than vice versa. Some anti-protectionist manufacturers took the standard Cobdenite view that protection, because it implied food taxes, would put unacceptable pressure on wage costs by raising the cost of living. Others were more concerned that because it would raise the price of semi-manufactured goods, like steel billets, it would make fully manufactured goods more expensive and in that way reduce international competitiveness. Protectionist manufacturers were often more concerned with semi-manufactured goods anyway, and argued simply that protection would preserve vulnerable industries in Britain from extinction. Protectionists argued, with more or less conviction, that a strong home market would provide a basis for exports, just as it did in Germany. Neither side was much inclined to look beyond its own particular line of business. Like the theoretical economic arguments, these debating points were well rehearsed by the outbreak of war.[88]

The tariff controversy would not have been launched by economists, and businessmen could not have taken it far without support from practising politicians. The Tariff Reform movement addressed many political problems, not the least of which was Joseph Chamberlain's ambition to lead the Conservative Party. When he launched it in Birmingham in 1903 it attracted longstanding protectionists, but politicians liked it for other reasons.[89] Chamberlain's presentation of the case for a reform of the tariff structure was notable for its ambiguity of motive and meaning. On the one hand he emphasised the importance of protecting the home market and thus guaranteeing employment to British workers. On the other hand he hoped that import duties would raise revenue for social reform and thus avoid increases in direct taxation. Either of these benefits might have come about, but, as contemporaries quickly pointed out, probably not at the same time. Moreover Chamberlain and his supporters emphasised the benefits to imperial unity of a tariff wall around the Empire, which would allow preferences to be given to exporters from the Dominions in return for freer British entry to their markets. This, if

---

[87] Marrison, 'Businessmen, Industries and Tariff Reform...'; Davenport-Hines, *Dudley Docker*, pp. 55–79

[88] Reviewed in P.J. Cain, 'Political Economy in Edwardian England: the Tariff Reform controversy', in Alan O'Day, ed., *The Edwardian Age: conflict and stability 1900–1914* (London: Macmillan, 1979), pp. 35–59.

[89] On the party politics of Tariff Reform see Alan Sykes, *Tariff Reform in British Politics* (Oxford: Clarendon Press, 1979).

fully effective, could nullify both the other advantages. There were also major doubts about the impact on working-class incomes. Political Tariff Reformers maintained that the benefits of steady employment at higher wages would outweigh the costs of higher food prices, though the businessmen involved were less enthusiastic about the higher wages. Liberals, who noted that the higher food prices were inevitable while the steady employment and higher wages were not, made great and effective play with the reduced size of the 'Tory loaf' in the 1906 election campaign.[90] Essentially the leading Tariff Reformers appear to have been misled by their own rhetoric into believing that Tariff Reform would be popular with the working-class electorate. Their 'squalid' appeal to materialism apparently fell flat because working-class voters did not believe that the mess of pottage was big enough to make it worthwhile trading in their Free Trade birthright. Long after 1913, when the Conservative leadership had backed away from Tariff Reform, keen Tariff Reformers were still insisting that Tariff Reform was the only really 'democratic' appeal open to the Conservative Party.[91]

While one strand of Conservative opinion saw Tariff Reform as an answer to the Liberals' appeal among working-class voters, another saw it as a solution to the problem of public finance. The success of the 'progressive' appeal was evident, and most Conservatives, excluding the few who complained about the 'petted' working classes, realised that some state welfare expenditure was essential if only to maintain economic efficiency. But who was to pay for it? Rosebery's Liberal government had taken the first step by imposing death duties: a technique which ironically had been devised by the Board of Inland Revenue under Alfred Milner, later to become a major figure in the Tariff Reform movement. This tended to soak the rich, which was precisely what Sir William Harcourt had intended in 1894.[92] By 1903 anticipated expenditure, both on welfare and naval armaments, had grown so much that there were now not enough of the rich to soak. Governments in the twentieth century had to find ways to make the working classes pay at least some of the cost of their own welfare benefits and the cost of defence, even when the only benefit most would receive was the old age pension. The choice lay between the extension of indirect taxation on consumption, which would have most impact on those who saved little and consumed most of what they earned, and an extension of direct taxation by imposing income tax on low and

---

[90] A.K. Russell, *Liberal Landslide* (Newton Abbot: David & Charles, 1973), pp. 172–182.

[91] See e.g. Sir Joseph Lawrence to Bonar Law, 16 July 1918, House of Lords Record Office, Bonar Law Papers (B.L.P.) 83/5/15.

[92] On the trouble he caused within the party, see David Brooks, *The Destruction of Lord Rosebery: from the diary of Sir Edward Hamilton, 1894–1895* (London: Historians' Press, 1987), pp. 13–42, 127–144.

middling incomes. The Liberals, as outlined above, chose the latter, with a modestly progressive scale of income tax and a 'surtax' on higher incomes, and the further expedient of contributory insurance to fund much of the welfare bill. The Conservatives, who took the plunge first, chose to argue for indirect taxation. Tariff Reform was the Edwardian focus for discussion about the redistribution of wealth.

Tariff Reform also intersected with another of the great Edwardian polarities, the discussion of empire. Tariff Reform was a clear party issue, which split the Conservative parliamentary party into three parts and left the Liberals intact. The empire debate was not so clear cut. The most explicit positions on empire were held by the small number of Cobdenite Liberals who would have been glad to see the back of it, and by the equally small group of imperialists surrounding Chamberlain and Milner who were keen on the 'closer union' and ultimately the 'organic union' of those parts of the Empire inhabited by white men.[93] But there were Little Englanders within the Conservative Party, and realists who recognised that the white Dominions did not want closer union; while the Liberals included the self-styled Liberal Imperialists as well as the pro-Boers. Discussion of empire had an economic and a strategic component. The economic argument in favour of empire was that British territories overseas provided easy markets, outlets for investment and settlement, and reliable and cheap sources of raw materials. Crude economic imperialism of this sort was absorbed into protectionist Tariff Reform by such groups as the Business Leagues in the West Midlands, who regularly put forward somewhat shady businessmen with property or mining interests abroad as Conservative parliamentary candidates. The counter-argument was that markets, investment opportunities and raw materials could all be had more cheaply and securely in the world outside the Empire. Europe and the United States were Britain's main markets and main recipients of exported capital, while South America had the market behaviour of an imperial dependency without the cost and trouble of administering it. Imperialists would counter this by citing India, the only dependency with an entirely satisfactory trade balance with the mother country, which also paid the whole cost of its own administration and defence; they would then shift the ground of argument towards the strategic.

The strategic argument for empire was partly dependent on the economic argument. Given that Britain had an empire, it was important that it should be viable. Viability meant defensive security against a possible aggressor, and in the 1880s and 1890s this required the Empire to expand in Africa, so that Britain should not be left behind in the 'Scramble', or

[93] Walter Nimocks, *Milner's Young Men: the 'kindergarten' in Edwardian imperial affairs* (London: Hodder & Stoughton, 1970); J.E. Kendle, *The Round Table Movement and Imperial Union* (Toronto: University of Toronto Press, 1975).

outflanked. Expansion in its turn increased the cost of defence. Whether trade followed the flag or vice versa, a large bill for troops and battle-ships always tagged along at the rear of the column. Colonial defence was recognised as a problem of finance and administration in its own right in 1895, with the establishment of a Colonial Defence Committee by the Salisbury government. Behind the calls for closer union of the white em-pire lay the hope that Canada, Australia and New Zealand would pay for some of the ships which patrolled their waters, and the fear that unless they did so the 'empire on which the sun never set' would bankrupt its proprietors.

The necessity for an integrated colonial defence was a point of agree-ment between most Conservatives and the Liberal Imperialist section of the Liberal Party, which included not only Rosebery — an outsider even before he left the party in 1902 — but three articulate leaders in Asquith, Haldane and Grey and a membership which on some definitions included up to one third of the parliamentary party in 1905.[94] The Liberal Imperi-alists had first emerged as a distinct tendency within the party in opposition to Gladstonian foreign policy. Rosebery himself, as Foreign Secretary in 1892–4, had offended old Gladstonians and some younger Radicals by outspokenly continuing the foreign and colonial policy of his Conser-vative predecessor, largely that of scrambling for Africa.[95] Many Liberal M.P.s supported Chamberlain's policy at the Colonial Office after 1895, and were brought into sharp conflict with fellow Liberals during the Boer War. Until 1903 Liberal parliamentary candidates would not infrequently describe themselves as supporters of Chamberlain's ideas, and the electorate knew this to be a vision of the Empire as 'white man's country' and, to a less prominent degree, a rejection of the importance of Irish Home Rule.[96]

1906 thus provided further opportunities for continuity in policy when Grey went to the Foreign Office, Haldane to the War Office, and Asquith to the Exchequer. The Liberal Cabinet, which was in any case inclined to leave defence and overseas matters to departmental ministers, did noth-ing to reverse the trend of Conservative policy, which in the years since the Boer War had strengthened the central administration of imperial de-fence by setting up the Committee of Imperial Defence, reformed the structure of the army, and begun to provide for the 'reconstruction' of South Africa as part of the Empire.[97] This made for arguments over tim-

---

[94] See the discussion in Bernstein, *Liberal Politics*, pp. 27–46; H.C.G. Matthew, *The Liberal Impe-rialists: the ideas and politics of a post-Gladstonian elite* (Oxford: Clarendon Press, 1973).

[95] Robert Rhodes James, *Rosebery* (London: Weidenfeld, 1963).

[96] See e.g. Cecil Harmsworth, *Pleasure and Problem in South Africa* (London: Harmsworth, 1908). Harmsworth, younger brother of Lord Northcliffe, was Lloyd George's private secretary from May 1917 to December 1918.

[97] Nicholas D'Ombrain, *War Machinery and High Policy: defence administration in peacetime Britain 1902–1914* (Oxford: Clarendon Press, 1973); John Gooch, *The Plans of War: the General Staff and*

ing with the Conservatives, but arguments of principle with some of their own back-benchers.[98] The Liberal government also made a large symbolic commitment to the Empire by holding an Imperial Conference in 1911 and sponsoring George V in his elaborately stage-managed visit to India in 1911.[99]

Debates about defence and foreign policy, going beyond the question of empire, also produced a consensus between the 1906 government and its Conservative opponents and splits between the government and its back-bench supporters. Although at the time this took foreign affairs almost completely out of Westminster politics it stored up trouble which helped to split the Liberal Party during the war. In taking over the Foreign Office Grey took over the pro-French and ultimately anti-German policy set in motion by his Conservative predecessor, the Marquess of Lansdowne. Grey's manner of work is now well documented: an aloof and almost secretive attitude even to the Cabinet enabled him to take crucial decisions without much scrutiny, and thus bring about the Triple Entente, a working military relationship with France and Russia whose diplomatic implications were never fully discussed until after the outbreak of war in 1914. The cost of naval defence, inflated by technological change and by the dynamics of an arms race with Germany, exposed the Cabinet to criticism from Liberals who preferred to spend the money on welfare. More corrosive than this objection, which could partly be met by economic growth and the expansion of taxation, was the Radical objection to being locked in continental alliances. In November 1911 a Foreign Affairs Group appeared in the House of Commons. Its leaders included Noel Buxton and Arthur Ponsonby, later to emerge as radical critics of the Lloyd George regime. Although it had dissolved in confusion by the middle of 1915, it was on the opinions of this anti-alliance group in the first months of war that Grey's subsequent reputation, and some of the fate of the Liberal Party, depended.[100]

British military strategy c. 1900–1916 (London: Routledge & Kegan Paul, 1974); David French, *British Economic and Strategic Planning 1905–1915* (London: Allen & Unwin, 1982); L.M. Thompson, *The Unification of South Africa, 1902–1910* (Oxford: Clarendon Press, 1960); George Boyce, ed., *The Crisis of British Power* (London: Historians' Press, 1990).

[98] Howard S. Weinroth, 'The British Radicals and the Balance of Power, 1902–1914', *Historical Journal*, xiii (1970), 653–682; A.J.A. Morris, *Radicalism against War, 1906–1914* (London: Routledge & Kegan Paul, 1972); and generally F.H. Hinsley, ed., *British Foreign Policy under Sir Edward Grey* (Cambridge: Cambridge University Press, 1977).

[99] John Kendle, *The Colonial and Imperial Conferences 1887–1911* (London: Longman, 1970).

[100] Hinsley, *British Foreign Policy*; see Clarke, *Liberals and Social Democrats*, pp. 164-5 and Keith Robbins, *The Abolition of War: the peace movement in Britain, 1914-1919* (Cardiff: University of Wales Press, 1976), pp. 20–22 for the pre-war activity of the group and the Denman Papers, in the Bodleian Library, for its experience during the war. The group revived, with a Labour membership including Ramsay MacDonald, some time in 1916, and is mentioned in the Public Record Office, PRO 30/69/1753, Ramsay MacDonald Papers, Diary, *passim*.

The views of what A.J.P. Taylor has called the 'troublemakers' were eclectic in origin, their main point of agreement being a dislike of Grey's style and of the practical result of his policy.[101] One strand was a Progressive disdain for Russia, a vital link in the strategic scheme of the Triple Entente. That Russia was anti-German was evident, but to the Radicals nothing favourable was known about the country. Its constitution was archaic, its foreign policy outside Europe was brutal, and it had recently been humiliated in its war with Japan. It was notorious for state-sanctioned atrocities against the Jews.[102] In the Balkans, a spiritual home for some prominent Radicals, Russia's profession of disinterested concern for Slavic aspirations was widely disbelieved. Russia was tainted, and it was indecent to make such an alliance for no better reason than to encircle Germany. Other Radicals were more pro-German than anti-Russian, seeing definite value in economic relations with Germany and sharing the view of Haldane (not himself a pro-German in any political sense) that German culture and education were of an enviable standard, particularly when compared with that of France[103] Here the anti-Grey Radicals found themselves in uncomfortable agreement with some elements of the imperialist Right, who warmed to the idea of a pan-Teutonic world alliance including Germany and the Anglo-Saxon races of Britain, the Empire and the United States.[104]

Pacifists, Little Englanders and true internationalists were outnumbered on the Liberal side, when compared with the often belligerent enthusiasts for small nations, but their voice was still heard. The Peace Society, founded in 1816, was peripheral to Liberal politics. The more engaged anti-war critics were either convinced, like Norman Angell, that war was very unlikely because it was economically irrational, or resigned, like Hobson and H.N. Brailsford, to the possibility that capitalist competition would produce war in any case.[105] Among members of the socialist societies, who like pacifists in the Liberal Party were prominent in the Labour movement more for their energy than for their numbers, the internationalist implications of socialism were well understood. A common dislike of Grey's

[101] A.J.P. Taylor, *The Troublemakers: dissent over foreign policy, 1792–1939* (London: Hamish Hamilton, 1957); Morris, *Radicalism against War*.

[102] D. McLean, 'English Radicals, Russia and the Fate of Persia, 1907–1913', *English Historical Review*, xciii (1978), 338–352.

[103] A notable example was David Mason, M.P., a prominent advocate of peace by negotiation during the war.

[104] E.g. Cecil Rhodes: see Semmel, *Imperialism and Social Reform*.

[105] Writers on British pacifism almost invariably focus their accounts on the period after the outbreak of war in 1914: Martin Ceadel, *Pacifism in Britain, 1914-1945: the defining of a faith* (Oxford: Clarendon Press, 1980); Marvin Swartz, *The Union of Democratic Control in British Politics during the First World War* (Oxford: Clarendon Press, 1971). But see Howard Weinroth, 'Norman Angell and *The Great Illusion*: an episode in pre-1914 pacifism', *Historical Journal*, xvii (1974), 551–574; and the essays by F.M. Leventhal, Swartz and Weinroth in Morris, ed., *Edwardian Radicalism*.

foreign policy had thus prepared a political alliance between parts of the
Labour movement and parts of the Liberal back bench even before war
broke out and 'proved' that the policy was wrong. This moved even a
few erstwhile Liberal Imperialists, like Charles Trevelyan, towards a breach
with the party leadership.

Underlying these sharply polarising discussions of empire, foreign policy,
defence, and even the reform of the tariff structure, was a pervasive anxiety
about British power in the world. None but the blindest politician could
fail to realise that relative economic backwardness threatened the country's
future prosperity and its diplomatic position alike. When the Boer War
showed that Britain's military reach was also finite, this insight became a
collective paranoia. By a strange inversion, in a society where the state
stood largely aloof from economic activity, it was the state rather than
the economic system which was held to blame. The general idea that
something was badly wrong united a wide range of people with very
diverse political and social values. It also produced a convergence of
political language, so that almost every Edwardian politician was loudly
in favour of something called 'National Efficiency': efficiency being a
difficult thing to criticise.[106]

Most of those who used the term saw the nation as a military unit
whose success depended on its economic and military performance, but
the differences between them were as great as the similarities. One school
of thought was most interested in institutional reform of the defence machinery.[107] Another was concerned with the military potential of the
civilian population. This was prominent in the report of the Commission
on Physical Deterioration — anxious to know why so many volunteers
were medically unfit for military service — but it was close to the surface
in some of the evidence to the Royal Commission on the Poor Law.[108]
The most extreme statement of this point of view came from the National Service League, a pressure group which was founded in 1902 to
promote compulsory service, but which moderated its demand to compulsory military training and grew in strength after 1905 when Field Marshal Lord Roberts became its head. Many Conservatives, especially Tariff
Reformers, justified social reform to sceptical audiences as a contribution
to military efficiency, but the National Service League appealed to some
Liberals too. J.E.B. Seely, later Secretary of State for War in the Liberal
Cabinet, was a founder member of the League in 1902.[109] An outspoken

---

[106] G.R. Searle, *The Quest for National Efficiency: a study in British politics and political thought, 1899–
1914* (Oxford: Blackwell, 1971).

[107] *Report of the War Office Reconstitution Committee, P. P.* 1904, Cd 1932; D'Ombrain, *War Machinery and High Policy*; Gooch, *The Plans of War*.

[108] *Report of the Inter-Departmental Commission on Physical Deterioration, P.P.* 1904, Cd 2175; *Report
of the Royal Commission on the Poor Law and the Relief of Distress, P.P.* 1909, Cd. 4499, xxxvii, 1.

[109] He was at that time still a Conservative M.P.

concern for the economic potential of the same unhappy members of the urban working class, often to be heard from Liberals and Fabian socialists, was slightly more pacific, but it, too, seemed to value economic activity as the foundation of military strength. This line of argument, in any of its guises, was usually associated with an organic metaphor of the state. If the community was to prosper, all its parts must be healthy. This saved the necessity of thinking too hard about the ultimate purpose of reform.

So pervasive was 'efficiency' that every serious political group appropriated it to some extent. Even temperance reformers could point to the greater physical 'efficiency' that would result from universal abstinence. This occasionally led to a blurring of distinctions between political opponents, which could be used mischievously by others. Lord Hugh Cecil enjoyed pointing out the common features between the 'programme of State interference in foreign and colonial trade which we know as "Tariff Reform"' and socialist intervention in the economy: he concluded that 'anything like high protection in this country would smooth the way for Socialism'.[110] But the relations between high protectionists and socialists were in fact no smoother than those between Conservatives and Liberal Imperialists. Substantial differences over the practical implementation of 'efficient' policies prevented the appearance of a 'National Efficiency' coalition at any time before the war. On the other hand the language of National Efficiency provided a convenient fig-leaf for coalition proposals in 1910, when at the height of the constitutional crisis Lloyd George proposed a coalition to the Conservatives on a programme including what he later described as 'national training for defence, the remedying of our social evils and a fair and judicial enquiry into the workings of our fiscal system' as well as action on the liquor trade, the railways, and the housing problem.[111]

Lloyd George's plans have become notorious. One historian has made them the centrepiece of his account of the origins of the 1916–18 Coalition, claiming that Lloyd George's willingness to make a deal with the proponents of Tariff Reform and compulsory military service, to reform local government, and to make deals about Ireland behind the backs of the Irish Nationalist party, indicated a conversion to the cause of National Efficiency which finally came to fruition with the appointment of Carson, Milner and Austen Chamberlain to the ministry in December 1916.[112] This is based on a heavy gloss on the circumstances and the document

---

[110] Lord Hugh Cecil, *Conservatism* (London: Williams & Norgate [Home University Library], 1912), p. 194.

[111] D. Lloyd George, *War Memoirs* (Popular edn., London: Odhams, 1938), I, 21–22; 'Memorandum on Formation of a Coalition' 17 Aug. 1910, House of Lords Record Office, Lloyd George Papers (L.G.P.) G/46/3/81, reprinted in K.O. Morgan, *The Age of Lloyd George* (London: Allen & Unwin, 1971), pp. 150–155.

[112] Scally, *Origins of the Lloyd George Coalition*.

itself. Lloyd George's August memorandum mentioned the problems of poor education and technical training, reorganisation of inland transport and commercial regulation, control of liquor, and imperial defence, but his actual proposals were even less specific than his own later gloss: he certainly started with no reference to an enquiry, 'fair and judicial' or otherwise, about tariffs. His argument was rather that party rivalries should be eliminated first; only then could 'the various problems connected with State assistance to Trade and Commerce' be investigated impartially. After discussion with the Unionists, a text of a working agreement was produced in October which included 'A full and impartial Enquiry . . . into the working and results of our Fiscal System' with no changes to be made until that enquiry had been completed.[113]

The 1910 scheme was in fact an attempted political fix to get the Liberals out of a tight corner. To work at all, it had to offer benefits to both parties, and it was convenient to dress it up in the currently fashionable political language. To suggest important ideological similarities between Lloyd George and the Conservative leaders, amounting to practical agreement on any of these points, is to rewrite the past.

Crisis or no crisis, the interval between the Boer War and the First World War was a period of conflict more than of consensus. Nonetheless, the political argument of wartime was conducted in the same language, and reflected many of the themes which preoccupied politicians before the war. It allowed old opponents to come together within a common vocabulary which they could use to persuade or delude the new electorate. Perhaps the most deluded, and afterwards the angriest, part of the electorate consisted of those who had been working since before the war for state action in support of the industrial economy. The 'modernisers' in British industry, usually associated with the electrical engineering and chemicals sectors which had most to gain from technological innovation and most to lose from German competition, had long been working not only towards tariff protection but also a reform of the patents legislation and (in some cases) improvements in welfare provisions. A few of these men, notably Dudley Docker of the Metropolitan Carriage, Wagon and Finance Company, Hugo Hirst of the General Electric Company, and Saxton Noble of Nobel's Explosives, cherished the hope that a reform of the party political system would contribute to the structural modernisation of British society that they wanted. They had been disappointed by the Conservative Party's withdrawal from Tariff Reform, and they were to be disappointed again when the war signally failed to give them the changes they sought.

---

[113] Memo. in L.G.P. C/6/5/1, also quoted in Scally, pp. 375–386. Nor does the text support the exposition in Don M. Cregier, *Bounder from Wales* (London: University of Missouri Press, 1976), p. 151.

Winners and Losers

Caught up in this flux of argument, and struggling to make sense of the changing social foundations of politics, British politicians in August 1914 were contemplating a future which was complicated, unpredictable, and almost certainly disagreeable. Under the terms of the Parliament Act an election would take place in 1915. Neither side was confident of victory, and for both major parties a defeat would have meant recrimination and, probably, attacks on the leadership with incalculable consequences for party unity and coherence. The 'rampant omnibus of war' — mounting the pavement in Trevor Wilson's trenchant metaphor and scattering pedestrians — bowled over not just the ailing Liberal patient, but also an adolescent Labour Party and a dyspeptic and distracted Conservatism. After it had passed, only two of the victims staggered convincingly to their feet. The purpose of this book is to explain their good fortune.

In the history of party politics, the war is inevitably identified with the decline of Liberalism. The party lost its hard-won dominance of parliament, the Liberal Cabinet broke up into warring factions, the ideological coherence of the Liberal movement was undermined, the network of class and interest group allegiances which had bound the party to its voters was destroyed. Two Liberal prime ministers successively led the country, and divided the party between them after the war. To the historian trying to explain the transformation of politics between 1914 and 1918, the fate of Liberalism inevitably dominates the picture, and it is very tempting to recount the story of the war as a drama of party suicide on a grand scale.

Such temptation must be resisted. It was the internal problems of other parties, especially the Conservatives, which brought heat into the politics of war. Bonar Law's leadership of the Conservative Party, never very secure, was further weakened. Back-bench groupings were established to criticise the leadership. Old controversies such as Tariff Reform retained their power to divide the party, while new issues such as franchise reform and agricultural wage control divided front bench from back when the party leaders urged compromise with the Liberals. Because party organisers and most activists believed that the Conservatives had won the 1918 election single-handed, the leadership's willingness to continue co-operation with Lloyd George was misunderstood and resented; but suspicion of the Coalition, and fear that the exigencies of war would force the party to make unwelcome concessions to other parties and social groups, pre-dated the election. Conservatives who believed that the government might at any moment grant Home Rule to Ireland, or disestablish the Welsh Church, or make huge concessions to trade union demands, could rarely rest easy in their beds.

The experience of the Labour Party during the war is more difficult to sum up because explanations are needed at three levels: parliament, the labour movement out of doors, and the electorate. In parliament the Labour Party split at the beginning of the war. The anti-war minority was led by Ramsay MacDonald, who was forced to resign as chairman of the party. It included most of the I.L.P. members and it was a source of leadership for the pacifist[114] Union of Democratic Control. The majority, dominated by trade union sponsored M.P.s, followed Arthur Henderson into coalition with Asquith in 1915 and Lloyd George in 1916. On both occasions Henderson was appointed for his party's parliamentary votes rather than his *beaux yeux* or his expected contribution to policy but his followers did not seem to mind. Lloyd George promised special attention to Labour's views when constructing his coalition in December 1916. Although Henderson resigned from the War Cabinet in August 1917, the Labour majority stayed with Lloyd George until November 1918. After resigning, Henderson undertook a major reorganisation of the party, giving it a new constitution which contrived both to strengthen the trade union element and increase the party's ostensible commitment to socialism. There was only very little sign of a convergence of views within the parliamentary party over the crucial issue of the war. At the end of the war, however, the majority pulled out of the coalition, made friends with the minority, and set up shop again as an opposition party. The transition was uncannily smooth, with only a few ruffled feathers and bruised careers.

The movement of opinion within the trade unions, and its relationship to the behaviour of the Labour Party, is no simpler to follow. Union hierarchies gained some influence in government. The Ministry of Munitions, established under Lloyd George's leadership during the first days of the Asquith Coalition, made a practice of involving trade union representatives on committees which dealt with wages, hours, and the sensitive question of 'dilution' of skilled labour with unapprenticed male and female workers. By bringing union leaders closer to government it separated them from their members. Rank-and-file movements flourished as pressure on wages, prices and working conditions increased during 1915 and 1916. Shop stewards' committees articulated grievances which union officials seemed to ignore. Strikes came in waves, one of the worst being in the spring of 1917.

The occasion of the 1917 strikes was the withdrawal of concessions to skilled engineering unions which allowed them to determine which of their members were called up into the army, but the strikers were also influenced by the erosion of real wages and the example of workers'

---

[114] More accurately *pacificist* in the terminology used by Martin Ceadel in *Pacifism in Britain*, pp. 3–6, 60–61. The U.D.C. did not take an absolute stand against any war at all. See also Robbins, *Abolition of War*.

control which they dimly perceived in Russia. It was the beginning of a steady movement of working-class opinion away from support for the war, which alarmed government and trade union leaders alike. While the once 'patriotic' trade unions gained greater influence in the reorganised Labour Party, the weight of opinion within the unions moved against the war and the Coalition, and the distance between the leadership and the rank and file markedly diminished.[115] Over the winter of 1917–18 food shortages further strained working-class loyalty to the war. The government even revised its published war aims to appease the doubts of trade unionists, among others, and began to prepare an election programme specifically to limit working-class disaffection. The extent, the timing, and the cause of movements in working-class opinion need careful attention, for the sake of their influence on war policy in the short term and on the social basis of political allegiance in the longer term.

Although such fundamental changes in Conservative and Labour politics must be emphasised simply because they have been understated before, there is no case for treating Liberal politics during the war simply as a residual category of explanation. The Liberal Party was no passive victim of events: Liberals did plenty to destroy their own party, for what seemed to be good reasons at the time. The chronology of Liberal self-destruction is well known. The Cabinet carried an overwhelming majority of its own number and a comfortable majority of the parliamentary party into the war. These majorities could not withstand the disappointments of the early months of war, and the 1915 Coalition was necessary to create a firm parliamentary basis for government. Pre-war malcontents, from all sides of the party, were easily disillusioned by the new administration and its policies, and a Liberal opposition emerged in the Commons. This opposition outlived the Asquith Coalition, and slowly transferred its allegiance to Asquith, its old enemy, during the course of 1917. Meanwhile a good number of the ministerial Liberals of 1914–16 had crystallised their opposition to Lloyd George. The 1915 Coalition broke up because its ministerial members differed in their prognosis of military victory, defeat or stalemate, but the language they used to justify themselves was deliberately cast in the form of a debate on Liberal principles and party loyalty. It is this artificial debate on philosophic themes which has survived into historical writing as the main explanation of Liberal decline during the war. Yet the real problem for Liberalism was not to reconcile 'Liberal principles' with

---

[115] This change over time partly resolves the passionate dispute over 'rank-and-fileism' between Jonathan Zeitlin on the one hand and Richard Price and James Cronin on the other, conducted as '"Rank and filism" in British Labour History: a critique', *International Review of Social History*, xxxiv (1989), 42–102. Price and Cronin are clearly right to discern tension between shop stewards and elected officials; Zeitlin is also right to observe that for most purposes shop stewards and elected officials were on the same side, and opposing the government.

the need to fight a total war, but rather to reconcile Liberal organisation and rhetoric with the need to defeat the threat of class-based political insurgency when the total war had been fought. During the Lloyd George Coalition the Liberal Party was sacrificed to the need to defeat the Labour movement in a general election.

In explaining these changes I have not attempted to write a history of politics in wartime from the declaration of war to the Armistice, because I wish to stress the importance of the strategic and economic crisis of the war. This coincided almost exactly with the Lloyd George Coalition. The political changes of 1916 to 1918 owed much to the Asquith Coalition and the wartime experience of the Liberal government which preceded it. These links are recognised and elaborated below. But if there are continuities to note between 1915–16 and 1917–18, there is also a strong case for arguing that the first Lloyd George government saw the consummation and resolution of Edwardian political traumas. The Conservative Party finally exorcised the demon of Tariff Reform; in future it might lose elections for them but it would not threaten the integrity of the party. The Liberals finally divided along lines which at least partly reflected pre-war divisions; the Labour Party at last made a working arrangement out of its contradictory commitments to socialism and trade unionism. The Irish problem *at Westminster* was made to disappear as early as May 1917. The nation's response to the strategic and economic predicament of 1917–18 was not just a background but a catalyst to these changes. The result was neither revolution nor counter-revolution. Lack of faith in the efficacy of the party-political system, which had been obvious before the war, was aggravated by a growing disillusionment with the power of the state to bring about constructive change. But if the old system could not be made to work, it had shown that it was able to smother any serious competition. The history of the Lloyd George Coalition is the essential bridge between the 'strange death of Liberal England' which George Dangerfield arbitrarily assigned to the years immediately before 1914, and the 'impact of Labour' which Maurice Cowling has no less arbitrarily postponed until 1920.

2

THE ASQUITH COALITION
April 1915 to April 1916

Steps are in contemplation which involve the reconstruction of the government on a broader, personal and political basis.

Asquith in the House of Commons, 19 May 1915

It is a queer unpalatable prospect for those of us who remain in this mixed company. At the worst it cannot last long.

Walter Runciman to Herbert Samuel, 26 May 1915

I really believe that none of us now have any political principles but that everything is a question of expediency.

Bonar Law to Lord Buxton, 17 June 1915

...although we had won no victories our credit was splendid.

Reginald McKenna, 21 March 1916

I am glad you are reading the Book of Job: I think I must refresh my memory of it.
Asquith to Hilda Harrisson, 10 December 1916[1]

At a critical moment in May 1918, with German forces menacing the British line in France and the Lloyd George Coalition about to lose a vote of confidence, disaffected Conservative M.P.s were brought to heel by a very junior member of the government who 'got up and tried to bring them back very firmly to the principal point, that this was a manoeuvre to get in Asquith...'.[2] Without the nineteen months of the Asquith Coalition from May 1915 to December 1916 to remind critics of what was past and what might come again, the twenty-four month survival

---

[1] *Parliamentary Debates: House of Commons* Fifth Series (hereafter *H.C. Debs*, 5s), lxxi, 19 May 1915, col. 2392; Runciman to Samuel, House of Lords Record Office, Samuel Papers A/48/6; Bonar Law to Buxton, 17 June 1915, Bonar Law Papers; War Committee Minutes, 21 Mar. 1916, P.R.O. CAB 42/11; Desmond MacCarthy, ed., *H.H.A.: letters of the Earl of Oxford and Asquith to a friend* first series, 1915–22 (London: Geoffrey Bles, 1933), p. 13.

[2] L.S. Amery's diary, 8 May 1918, in John Barnes and David Nicholson, eds, *The Leo Amery Diaries. Volume I: 1896-1929* (London: Hutchinson, 1980), p. 220.

of the Lloyd George coalition after December 1916 is nearly impossible to explain. The experience divided the Liberal leaders, embroiled the already divided leadership of the Conservative Party in responsibility for failure in the war, and convinced most of the Conservative Party that there was something worse than Lloyd George, namely Asquith. Without these preconditions it is hard to see how Lloyd George's premiership could have survived more than a few months. But for all its reputation as a calamitous and humiliating interlude, the Asquith Coalition was a serious attempt to grapple with the implications of an industrial war. The government identified the major needs for state intervention in the economy, and took the decisions of principle which would allow them to be met. In some areas it also set up administrative machinery to do the job. It kept going through two disastrous summer campaigns in the West, and two humiliating defeats in the Middle East, despite deep-rooted conflicts of personality and major disagreements of principle over strategy and the military-industrial balance. It was ousted, like its predecessor, in a palace revolution when the Conservative leaders could no longer contain their own quarrels: and the House of Commons knew even less of what was wrong in December 1916 than they had in May 1915. This is not a triumphant record, but nor is it a story of unmitigated failure.

The Origins of Coalition

The move to a coalition was not expected until a few weeks before Asquith called for the resignation of the last Liberal Cabinet on 17 May 1915.[3] On the outbreak of war in August 1914 the prime minister had used the threat of coalition, successfully, to persuade some of his reluctant colleagues not to resign. Until the beginning of 1915 the Liberals had retained the upper hand in politics, by luck and sleight of hand in equal measure. A safe parliamentary majority had been attained by putting the Home Rule bill on the statute book, to pacify the Irish members, with a Suspending Act postponing its operation until the end of the war which allowed Carson and other diehard Ulster leaders to reassure Unionists that Home Rule would never come into effect. Censorship and journalistic optimism together had secured the public's confidence in the conduct of military operations, though the Western Front was static and the government's Eastern strategy was incoherent. The Liberal back bench, though shaken by entry into the war, had reached an equilibrium, with a badly disaffected minority and a majority which either supported the war or simply trusted

---

[3] Cameron Hazlehurst, *Politicians at War* (London: Jonathan Cape, 1971), *passim*.

its leaders.[4] Asquith, whose public calmness had not yet reached the point of inanition, was still an asset. Lord Kitchener, hero of the Sudan and South African campaigns, who had been plucked from Egypt and hastily appointed as a non-political Secretary of State for War in August 1914, had not yet revealed his clay feet except to his Cabinet colleagues.[5] Signs of trouble for the ministry were limited to a storm of spy mania which broke on the head of the unfortunate Home Secretary, Reginald McKenna;[6] a row pending between the government and the press over the limitation of direct reporting from the front; and murmurs of discontent among munitions suppliers and their workers about the unpredictable effects of the government's purchasing policies.[7] Until January 1915 only the spy scare was translated directly into a parliamentary attack on the ministry's competence, and that was limited to the Home Office.

The fall of the Liberal Cabinet came about, directly and indirectly, because of its loss of grip on the direction of the war. At the end of December 1914 Lloyd George at the Exchequer, Churchill at the Admiralty and Maurice Hankey, the secretary of the War Council, each produced a paper recommending an alternative to the strategy of concentration on the Western Front.[8] Their alternatives were not precisely the same, but they represented a trend which encouraged the Cabinet to approve a naval attack on the Bosphorus to strike at communications between Germany and Turkey and thus put Turkey out of the war. The detailed story of how this grew into the combined naval and military operation in the Dardanelles is beyond the scope of this book:[9] but grow it did, and by April 1915 it had created uncontrollable tension between Churchill as First Lord of the Admiralty and Admiral Lord Fisher, the First Sea Lord, about the safety of the proposed naval operations and the wisdom of diverting ships from other duties to the Near East. The Dardanelles campaign was only one consequence, albeit an important one, of a Cabinet argument about war aims

---

[4] Michael Hart, 'The Liberal Party in Parliament and the Constituencies, 1914–1922', Oxford University D.Phil. thesis, 1982.

[5] T. Royle, *The Kitchener Enigma* (London: Michael Joseph, 1985). Kitchener was the British Agent and Consul-General in Egypt, and thus the effective ruler of the country. At the outbreak of war the War Office was vacant because of the resignation of J.E.B. Seely over the Curragh affair, in which Unionist officers serving in Ireland had at first been allowed to decline to take action against the Ulster Volunteers in the event of armed opposition to Home Rule. Asquith was combining the job with his other responsibilities.

[6] David French, 'Spy Fever in Britain, 1900–15', *Historical Journal*, xxi (1978), 355–370.

[7] Guildhall Library, Minutes of the Associated British Chambers of Commerce, December 1914.

[8] Hankey's paper is printed in Lord Hankey, *The Supreme Command 1914–1918* (2 Vols, London: Allen & Unwin, 1961), I, 244–250; Lloyd George's in his *War Memoirs*, I, 639; Churchill's in *World Crisis*, 1915, p. 44.

[9] David French, 'The Origins of the Dardanelles Campaign Reconsidered', *History*, lxvii (1983), 210–224.

which set Lloyd George and Churchill against Grey, whom they attacked for diplomatic inactivity in the Balkans, and against the War Office.

Meanwhile the Cabinet was brought face to face with Kitchener's incompetence in procuring munitions for the huge armies he proposed to send to France. This confrontation had its own irony, since Kitchener was one of very few ministers who realised the immense scale of social and economic change which the war demanded; unfortunately he was quite unable to imagine the political and administrative steps which would be necessary to bring it about. At this stage the War Office restricted its purchasing to approved suppliers, who then tried to corner the market in raw materials and skilled manpower to enable them to fill orders which were vastly greater than their capacity. As a direct result of this policy the orders were not fulfilled and the rest of the engineering sector, along with many other sectors of industry, was badly disrupted. The rush to recruit all able-bodied men to the forces also unbalanced the labour force.[10] Unwilling or unable to co-ordinate its recruiting sergeants with its purchasing officers, the War Office managed to disrupt the economic stability on which victory depended.

These difficulties reacted on the political world in two ways. Individual 'scandals' were brought to light by interested parties. The engineering employers complained to their M.P.s, many of whom were Birmingham Conservatives, about inefficiencies in munitions production. Senior officers in France blamed the government for keeping them short of shells, and made sure that the press and visiting Conservative M.P.s were thoroughly briefed. Admiral Fisher, though deeply uncommunicative when it suited him, finally contrived his resignation on 15 May in the most public manner, and also made sure that Bonar Law knew about it immediately. Information of this sort was readily available to the press. When printed alongside 'spy scandal' material, but without a reasoned account of the military progress of the war, it sent a clear message that any vague doubts about what was going on should be focused on the performance of the government, and not, for example, on the armed forces.

At the same time senior politicians on both sides of the House were aware of disquiet about the machinery for making policy at the highest level, and had their own anxieties about the content, or even the existence, of the government's overall strategic plan. Senior Conservatives knew about the progress of the war because Bonar Law and Lansdowne (the Conservative leader in the Lords) were officially given copies of War Office and Foreign Office telegrams, whose contents they relayed to their most senior colleagues. Austen Chamberlain, as a former Chancellor of

---

[10] But even at this early stage the Admiralty was able to intervene to keep skilled men at work in the shipyards: see Ian Beckett, 'The British Army 1914–1918: the illusion of change', in John Turner, ed., *Britain and the First World War* (London: Unwin Hyman, 1988), p. 104.

the Exchequer, had been consulted early in the war about the management of public finance during the emergency. Arthur Balfour was a member of the War Council, largely through the accident that the War Council was formally a sub-committee of the dormant Committee of Imperial Defence, of which Balfour was a member. In 1914 these channels merely carried information which complemented what Conservative leaders heard directly from their friends in the army and navy. In January 1915 the War Council took on a new role, under pressure from Lloyd George and Churchill. It began to consider strategy in the East and in the West, and how resources should be found for fighting the war, though the two problems were not explicitly joined in discussion.[11] This implied a much greater degree of responsibility, which caused Balfour to worry that his position on the War Council would prejudice his party,[12] and opened up an unsettling discussion of priorities. Lloyd George in particular urged his colleagues on with a powerful memorandum on 22 February.[13] On 10 March Lansdowne and Bonar Law attended the War Council's meeting about policy towards Constantinople: Asquith and Churchill (who had suggested the invitation) thought they were unhelpful and the two Conservatives declined to come again in case it jeopardised their hold on their own back bench. For all that, Asquith ordered that they should from then onwards receive the Council's papers, and their inner knowledge of government was increased just as its problems began to mount.

The Cabinet dispute about the mobilisation of the economy was conducted at two levels. Within Cabinet Lloyd George, with support from Churchill, argued for a high level of state intervention, directed to expanding industry's capacity to produce munitions. Kitchener wanted to achieve the same end by a rather different route, concentrating labour and materials on existing War Office suppliers, while a faction in the Cabinet led by Walter Runciman (President of the Board of Trade) and Reginald McKenna (Home Secretary) wanted to expand production without controls, simply by using the price mechanism. Lloyd George steadily overtook the other protagonists, winning permission to introduce a Defence of the Realm (Amendment) bill, which reached the Statute Book on 15 March and gave the government power to control the engineering industry. On 19 March he brought about the 'Treasury Agreements' with

---

[11] See David French, 'Business as Usual', in Kathleen Burk, ed., *War and the State* (London: Allen & Unwin, 1982), p. 26, arguing that 'Naval and military policy was decided apart from economic policy.' This depends on a somewhat artificial distinction between the War Council and the Cabinet (see Turner, 'The Higher Direction of War' in the same volume), but accurately reflects the compartments in which strategic thought was confined by most ministers.

[12] Balfour to Lansdowne, 9 Jan. 1915, quoted in Hazlehurst, *Politicians at War*, pp. 160–161; see also Turner, 'The Higher Direction of War', pp. 58–59.

[13] D. Lloyd George, 'Some Further Considerations on the Conduct of the War', 22 Feb. 1915, P.R.O. CAB 37/124/40.

some leading trade unionists in the munitions industries, which provided for the abandonment of the strike weapon and of some restrictive practices, in return for a guarantee that restrictive practices could be reimposed after the war and that munitions profits would be held down.[14] On 23 March he even persuaded Asquith to set him up as chairman of a Munitions of War Committee, though the War Office still retained the power to veto its work. This was substantial progress towards central control of munitions production, which disconcerted the partisans of 'business as usual'.[15]

Any further movement faced public as well as Cabinet resistance, and Lloyd George dealt with this at a different level. On 28 February he told an enthusiastic Welsh Nonconformist audience that 'Drink is doing us more damage in the War than all the German submarines put together', and proceeded over the next month to collect evidence for this remarkable assertion from various employers including the chairman of Swan Hunter, who was a leading figure in the pre-war temperance movement. The factual basis of this exercise, as Lloyd George soon admitted, was 'mostly fudge'.[16] Its purpose was to soften up traditional Liberal supporters for the extension of state control by creating a sense of emergency, and in this it was a success.[17]

But Lloyd George's obsession with drink, irritating though it was to his colleagues, was not enough to create a political crisis in May 1915. There was, indeed, a good deal of public complacency, especially on the Liberal side. A.G. Gardiner, editor of the *Daily News*, published a remarkable encomium in the very month of the government's downfall, observing that 'Mr Asquith's administration seems as firmly seated as at any moment in its history' and that the country's central faith in its rulers was 'absolute, unquestioning, and wholly unprecedented, and it is as marked on the Conservative side of politics as on the Liberal.' He continued:

> ...the efficiency of the Government remains a matter of universal agreement. The boldness of its measures, the promptness with which they were put into operation, the far-seeing scope of its preparations, and the sense of unity and momentum behind its action have impressed the nation profoundly and given it a feeling of security which events have done nothing to weaken. The extent to which England has provided, not only the material and financial resources of the Allies, but their

[14] See Chris Wrigley, 'The Ministry of Munitions: an innovatory department', in Burk, *War and the State*.

[15] H.W. Massingham to Runciman, March 1915, Newcastle University Library, Runciman Papers, WR 166, cited Hazlehurst, p. 208.

[16] Reported by Christopher Addison, *Four and a Half Years* (2 Vols, London: Hutchinson, 1934), I, 73. The exaggeration was not as great as it might seem. In January 1915 there were only 21 German U-Boats in service, eight of them obsolete, and their assault on British trade routes was badly planned. See Avner Offer, *The First World War: an agrarian interpretation* (Oxford: Clarendon Press, 1989), p. 355, citing German naval records.

[17] John Turner, 'State Purchase of the Liquor Trade in the First World War', *Historical Journal*, xxiii (1980), 589–615.

intellectual energy and initiative is well understood, and there is in no quarter any disposition to refuse to the Government the main credit for the satisfactory course of the campaign.[18]

The downfall of the Liberal Cabinet was engineered in a hurry, because Asquith and Bonar Law, who each faced future difficulties in dealing with their own parties, seized a chance to escape into coalition. The catalyst was Admiral Lord Fisher's resignation on 15 May, which Asquith guessed would further erode public confidence in his government. Bonar Law, tipped off by Fisher himself, saw Lloyd George at the Treasury and warned that a major parliamentary row was unavoidable. In response Lloyd George 'inveigh[ed] against much in the conduct of war. In particular he said that Kitchener had "put lies into his mouth" as to the supply of munitions and that the situation was altogether intolerable.'[19] Later that day Asquith summoned Bonar Law to 10 Downing Street by telephone and in a 15-minute discussion agreed on a plan of coalition with an interim division of offices. Historians have devoted much effort to reconstructing the mental events which brought about this quick agreement. The most plausible view is that both wished to avoid a direct confrontation which might lead to a general election: Bonar Law because he would probably lose control of his party, which was already chafing at the leash, and Asquith because he feared that both his party and his Cabinet would dissolve into fragments.[20]

The Balance of Power

The coalition which emerged after a week of vigorous negotiation did avert a general election, but it could not prevent a parliamentary row. Asquith's distribution of offices was skilfully contrived to maintain the Liberals' hold on the substance of power. The greatest disappointment for Asquith was that Kitchener proved immovable. Lloyd George moved to a newly created Ministry of Munitions from the Exchequer, where he was replaced by McKenna. Balfour went to the Admiralty in place of Churchill, whom the Conservative back bench detested and who was demoted to the Duchy of Lancaster. Haldane was ejected, also in deference to Tory backwoodsmen who thought he was 'pro-German', and replaced as Lord Chancellor by Buckmaster, a Liberal, supported by Sir Edward

[18] A.G. Gardiner, *The War Lords* (London: J.M. Dent, 1915), p. 63.

[19] Memorandum by Austen Chamberlain, reporting Bonar Law's oral report to Lansdowne and himself, 17 May 1915, Birmingham University Library, Austen Chamberlain Papers 2/2/25.

[20] Martin Pugh, 'Asquith, Bonar Law and the First Coalition', *Historical Journal*, xvii (1974), 813–836.

Carson, the leader of the Ulster Unionists, as Attorney-General. Austen Chamberlain went to the India Office (in place of Lord Crewe), Walter Long to the Local Government Board (in place of Herbert Samuel). Bonar Law himself went to the Colonial Office, a post vacated by Lewis (Loulou) Harcourt, who for the previous six months had been suffering from heart disease and had delegated much of the work to a private secretary.[21] This extraordinary appointment is evidence of Bonar Law's capacity for self-abnegation, but also of Asquith's low estimate of his administrative ability and determination to exclude him from real influence over the conduct of the war. Whatever fire-eating Tory back-benchers might have thought, the Liberal leaders did not expect their new Conservative colleagues, except for Balfour, to contribute anything useful towards victory. They were there for the parliamentary votes they could command.

This distribution of offices predictably inflamed the Conservative right wing, one of whom described it as 'the old vat ... half-emptied of its former contents and filled up with new wine; but it was the same vat, and the predominating flavour remained the same ... '.[22] Liberal back-benchers were equally distressed, though except in a few cases they were more bewildered than angry. Radical critics of the old Cabinet now declared that they were 'released completely for the first time from party allegiance', and Charles Hobhouse, whose fevered gossip from inside the Cabinet persuaded many politicians and even some historians that Lloyd George and Churchill had plotted the whole thing, announced 'the end of the Liberal Party as we have known it'.[23] The distribution of offices made little impression on them: it was the very fact of coalition, which seemed to give Conservative ministers the power of life and death over the ministry, which rankled. Moreover they believed, with good reason, that 'we shall live under conscription and martial law'.[24] The conscription issue was to shape the history of the new government for more than a year.

But before conscription came the Dardanelles. It is perhaps surprising that a straightforward question of military dispositions should create such a stir in a ministry whose most fundamental divisions were about conscription and voluntary service or Free Trade and Tariff Reform, and whose members could readily remind themselves of pre-war quarrels over Ireland or land taxes.[25] But when the Conservative ministers came into office

[21] Lewis Harcourt was the son of Sir William Harcourt, who had been Chancellor of the Exchequer in the Rosebery government and protagonist of death duties. Loulou was renowned for his loyalty to his father's career, but for little else. The private secretary in question was J.C.C. Davidson, who later became chairman of the Conservative Party.

[22] F.S. Oliver, *Ordeal by Battle* (London: Macmillan, 1916) p. i.

[23] Ponsonby to Trevelyan, 22 May 1915, University of Newcastle Library, Trevelyan Papers CPT 4; Hobhouse to Runciman, 28 May 1915, *ibid*. Runciman Papers WR 162.

[24] Trevelyan to Mary Trevelyan, 21 May 1915, Trevelyan Papers, cited Hazlehurst, p. 287.

[25] See e.g. Long to Bonar Law, 4 Apr. 1915, B.L.P. 37/1/8.

they were full of bitterness against any scheme associated with Churchill, and were well primed by their military friends, led by Sir John French and Sir Henry Wilson, to distrust any diversion of men from the Western Front. The immediate result was the establishment of the Dardanelles Committee, a committee of Cabinet whose remit was to report on the advisability of winding the operation down. The committee consisted of Asquith, Grey, Crewe, Lloyd George and Churchill for the Liberals; Kitchener; and Bonar Law, Balfour, Lansdowne, Curzon and Selborne for the Conservatives.[26]

This was the first of a number of finely balanced committees with which Asquith tried in subsequent months to hold his new coalition together. It was a deft manoeuvre. Conservative distrust of the Liberal Cabinet's 'colossal blundering' in the Near East was a potent force for disruption. Faced with naval and military advice that withdrawal would be costly in men and equipment, and the diplomatic argument that Britain's need for allies in the Balkans required a show of resolution, Selborne changed his mind and prevailed on his colleagues. To Bonar Law he explained in addition that 'We could not face the consequences in India . . . . It would mean rebellion now. In these respects the consequence of withdrawal would not differ from the consequence of defeat.'[27]

The committee never reported formally; but by deciding on 7 June to sanction the despatch of more troops it committed the government in practice to continuing the operation. In the short and unhappy life of the Dardanelles campaign this three-week gap between the local commander's request for troops and the decision to send them was probably a fatal delay. In the rather longer life of the Coalition it was a precipitate decision which secured Conservative complicity in the most public blunder of the war. The Conservatives seem to have regretted their acquiescence soon enough: in July they vetoed a visit to the Dardanelles by Churchill because of doubts 'as to the reception that public opinion might give to such an act, for which the Govt would be held collectively responsible . . . '. Perhaps this would be another Antwerp.[28] But by consenting to the general pattern of military

[26] This body is not to be confused with the Dardanelles Commission, a parliamentary body set up in 1916 to enquire into the mishandling of the operation. Lord Curzon (George Nathaniel Curzon, Marquess Curzon of Kedleston) was a former Viceroy of India who had had a bitter feud with Kitchener; he had been associated with the Diehard element in the Conservative Party until he had made enemies by advising submission to the Parliament Act. Lord Selborne, the second Earl, began his career as a Liberal Unionist M.P.; he was High Commissioner in South Africa from 1905 to 1910, then a leading Tory peer. His correspondence is published in D. George Boyce, ed., *The Crisis of British Unionism* and *The Crisis of British Power*.

[27] Selborne to Bonar Law, 7 July 1915, B.L.P. 51/1/10.

[28] Curzon to Churchill, 20 July 1915, Churchill Papers 21/37, cited in Martin Gilbert, *Winston S. Churchill, Volume III: 1914-1916* (London: Heinemann, 1971), p. 513. In October 1914, when visiting the front as an observer, Churchill had organised a rearguard defence of the city, even offering to exchange the Admiralty for the military command of forces in Antwerp. His actions were heavily

operations which had been established under their despised predecessors, the Conservatives signalled that they would be staying in coalition for a few months at least.

Conscription and Confusion

At once the balance of power which Asquith had created was tested by the conscription issue. Conscription had a significance which political history tends to distort. In parliamentary terms the question of whether men should be compelled by law to join the armed forces divided an identifiable group of Liberal and Labour back-benchers from other members of their own parties, and from the whole of the Conservative Party. Outside parliament the conscription question was dominated by the opinions and treatment of conscientious objectors. Conscientious objection to military service was tolerated, to a surprising degree, by the legislation which was eventually passed in 1916: it required a finely tuned conscience to adopt a position which would actually lead to punitive action by the state, and those who had such a conscience were ready to expound it at length. Moreover, inequities in the treatment of conscientious objectors were seized upon by anti-war groups as a convenient stick with which to beat the government, more popular and generally palatable than a campaign for a negotiated peace with Germany which was what most of the anti-war groups really wanted but dared not seek. As a result, conscription was treated by those whose opinions have become historical sources as predominantly an ethical question. This was true also on the Conservative side, where determined conscriptionists treated the rational arguments against conscription as obstacles to be outflanked rather than serious intellectual problems to be tackled. Compared with the elevated language which politicians used about the right of the state to compel its citizens to take enemy lives and risk their own, the manoeuvres which occupied the Asquith Coalition from July 1915 to June 1916 may seem sordid and demeaning. Asquith's later critics were happy to treat them as such. But the problem faced by the ministry, and well concealed behind the moral debate, was about the use of finite resources and about the nature of decision-making and responsibility in a parliamentary government at war. Those two problems, just as profound in their implications for the future as the divided conscience of the 'Liberal mind', were the Asquith Coalition's poisoned legacy to its successor.

Asquith's first move in response to direct Conservative demands for conscription was to shunt the question, like the Dardanelles, into the sid-

criticised in the Conservative press and by Walter Long; they are defended in Gilbert, pp. 103–134.

ing of a Cabinet Committee. This produced the National Registration bill, which reached the Statute Book on 15 July and provided for a national census of manpower use which was to be taken on 15 August. As a compromise, this convinced neither side. Liberal M.P.s recognised it as a first step to conscription, and Conservatives dismissed it as procrastination. A further Cabinet Committee under Crewe, known as the War Policy Committee, then examined the need for manpower and the best way of meeting it. Asquith tried, half-heartedly, to finesse this committee by leaving out Bonar Law, who was an ardent conscriptionist, and appointing Curzon who was much less ardent, but this had little effect. The other members were Churchill, Selborne, Austen Chamberlain, and Arthur Henderson, the token Labour member of the government who was nominally President of the Board of Education. The committee set out to quantify the army's needs, which could then be compared with the numbers of available men revealed by the national registration. It examined a number of ministers and officials, but the argument of substance was between Kitchener, who insisted that the men could be raised entirely by voluntary means, and Lloyd George who argued for compulsion. Crewe reported that the committee could not agree because the evidence was contradictory: in fact all but Henderson and Crewe himself had decided that conscription was essential, and this dissenting majority submitted its own report.[29] No less important was the committee's conclusion about how many men were needed. Taking the advice of the War Office, which in essence meant asking Kitchener, the committee suggested planning for an army of seventy divisions. This figure was to play as great a part in the Cabinet's impending struggles as the voluntary principle itself.

By the middle of October 1915 it was clear that conscription delimited one section of the Cabinet from the other. Lloyd George and Churchill were the only Liberal proponents of conscription; Balfour the only Conservative defender of the voluntary principle. This was anything but a secret struggle. The National Service League, established before the war under the inspiration of the legendary Lord Roberts to press for peacetime conscription on the continental model and now led by Lord Milner, was in full cry with the scarcely covert support of Long and Carson in the Cabinet.[30] Lloyd George had been flying kites for universal conscription, both for the army and for industrial work, in public speeches since June. In Manchester on 3 June he proclaimed:

---

[29] Supplementary Memorandum to the Report of the War Policy Committee, 3 Sept. 1915. P.R.O. CAB 37/134/3.

[30] F.S. Oliver's *Ordeal by Battle*, which at pp. 309–400 contains a sustained denunciation of voluntarism and a eulogy on Lord Roberts (who died in November 1914), was reprinted seven times between June and October 1915.

I say to those who wish us to dismiss conscription for the time being as a means of levying armies for fighting abroad: 'You ought not thereby to assume that it is unnecessary in enabling us to mobilize the industrial strength of the country.'[31]

The Conservative press, which had taken the Coalition in its stride and continued to abuse the Liberals at every opportunity, took him up, with Northcliffe's *Times* and *Daily Mail* in the lead. The response from the Liberal newspapers was predictable, but it was generally assumed that their attacks on compulsion, Northcliffe and Lloyd George were directly inspired by Liberal Cabinet ministers, among whom McKenna was the main suspect.[32] From their interpretation of Cabinet disputes grew the presumption that Lloyd George was plotting to overthrow Asquith, an assumption which was shared by Liberal back-benchers.[33]

The Labour Party's response to conscription was determined by the vagueness of the proposals: although individual Labour M.P.s and probably many of their supporters would have accepted military conscription as a means of enforcing equality of sacrifice, the conscriptionists changed the ground of argument by seeming to include industrial conscription. When workers already suspected that the Defence of the Realm Acts and the Munitions of War Act were being used by employers to alter agreed patterns of work and payment, thus increasing profits on non-munitions work and permanently injuring the trade union movement, it was no time to be suggesting more stringent direction of civilian labour. This was an issue which would unite the normally right-wing and 'patriotic' trade union members of the parliamentary party with left-wingers of pacifist or 'peace by negotiation' sympathies. Strong emotion could be guaranteed, inside or outside parliament, from all sides.

The intensity of this emotion tended, then and later, to simplify what was a complicated wrangle within the Cabinet over a number of related issues of war policy. Most ministers saw conscription as the fundamental problem. At the same time important decisions were being made about the war economy in the Budget, but since these divided the Cabinet into the same factions as the conscription issue their real significance was not apparent until the following year.[34] The immediate issue, however, was

---

[31] *The Times* 4 June 1915.

[32] See Stephen Koss, *The Rise and Fall of the Political Press in Britain. Volume 2: the twentieth century* (London: Hamish Hamilton, 1984), pp. 282–285; A.J.P. Taylor, ed., *Lloyd George: a diary by Frances Stevenson* (New York: Harper & Row, 1971), p. 60, diary entry for 17 Sept. 1915.

[33] Pringle to Runciman, ? August, 1915, Runciman Papers; Richard Holt Diary, 15 Sept. 1915, Holt MSS, cited Bentley, *The Liberal Mind*, p. 31.

[34] McKenna's autumn Budget was the first attempt to come to grips with the problem of paying for the war without permanently crippling the British economy. Together with very large increases in income tax and an Excess Profits Duty, both intended among other things to reduce inflationary pressure on the economy and to ensure that expenditure was met in some part from taxation as well as from borrowing, McKenna imposed import duties on certain luxury goods.

Kitchener's failing grip on the direction of military policy. In the August campaign in the Dardanelles — the landing at Suvla Bay and the attack on Sari Bair and Chunuk Bair — the incompetence of local commanders and the response of the Turkish defenders under Mustafa Kemal[35] had inflicted heavy casualties on the British and Anzac divisions, and halted them in vulnerable positions. During the recriminations at home, it was revealed that Kitchener had arranged with the French military authorities to mount a further offensive on the Western Front, reversing the decision reached by an Anglo-French ministerial conference in July. This commitment, apparently undertaken because French troops in France needed an offensive to improve their morale, was defended by Kitchener on the memorable but unsatisfactory grounds that 'we had to make war as we must, and not as we should like to'.[36]

This seemed to make it impossible to reinforce the Dardanelles, but in early September the Western Front attack was cancelled and the French offered four divisions for the Dardanelles campaign. On 8 September the Western Front attack was reinstated, and Kitchener could not tell his colleagues whether or not the four divisions were still available for the Dardanelles. Nor could he explain whether the British forces in France had sufficient gun ammunition for an offensive, and an enquiry by Lloyd George and Long on 10 September revealed that Sir John French, who wanted to mount the attack, thought that he had shells enough for six days attack under normal conditions, but no more. As Lloyd George was quick to point out, this promised a repeat performance of the battle of Neuve Chapelle, which had brought down the last Liberal government.[37] This muddle, as much as conscription, set the Conservative ministers against Kitchener. On 14 September, as reported by Lloyd George's mistress Frances Stevenson, Curzon dined with Churchill and Lloyd George to launch a conspiracy. The likely basis of co-operation was no longer in doubt, and Cabinet-level links were now being established which would make plausible the conspiracy charges against Lloyd George which became part of Liberal legend. Curzon assured his Liberal colleagues that

> ...the Tories are going to approach the P.M. & say that they cannot proceed any longer under the present state of things. They will demand conscription and the removal of K. from the W.O., as being incompetent and having failed to grasp the military situation. D. [Lloyd George] & Churchill will throw in their lot with

---

[35] Kemal was later to re-enter history as Kemal Ataturk. The attack was bungled by Sir Frederick Stopford, who failed to press on until Turkish reinforcements had taken up positions on high ground overlooking the British positions. See Gilbert, *Winston Churchill Volume III*, pp. 518–521 and Lord Hankey, *The Supreme Command*, I, 390–402 for clear accounts of the work of 'this wretched inert corps' at Suvla.

[36] Dardanelles Committee, 20 Aug. 1915, P.R.O. CAB 42/3/16.

[37] *Stevenson Diary*, p. 58.

Curzon & his followers, for D. says he cannot possibly be a party any longer to the shameful mismanagement and slackness.[38]

Kitchener's relations with his colleagues deteriorated further when the Germans entered Belgrade on 9 October. Kitchener did not know what the War Office had known for 20 hours, that the invaders had crossed the Danube, and when it was revealed Carson scribbled in a note to Lloyd George that 'K does not read the telegrams — & we don't see them — it's intolerable'.[39]

Cabinet in Crisis — October 1915

If this had brought about a simple contest, Kitchener versus the rest, the Cabinet crisis of October 1915 would have been shorter and more far-reaching in its effects. But Kitchener had friends, of a kind. The prime minister's wife had been pestering him since August to support 'Grey, Crewe, Arthur Balfour, McKenna and Runciman' against 'Curzon, F.E. Smith, Winston and Ll. George' over conscription. Asquith had the same feelings in October.[40] Though Kitchener's 'friends' were agreed on their opposition to conscription, all of them had opposed the renewed offensive on the Western Front. His opponents, on the other hand, agreed only that he was an incompetent, and their own views on military policy were wildly divergent. Carson resigned on 12 October, giving as his reason that the Dardanelles Committee had just refused to recommend an expedition to support Serbia. Selborne, another passionate exponent of action in the Near East, later described this as 'a somewhat slender occasion' for leaving a government whose methods he despised.[41] Lloyd George had intervened at the Cabinet meeting to oppose a paper by Kitchener which recommended the despatch of 150,000 men to Gallipoli after the French offensive in the West was over.[42] Churchill, another malcontent, was at the same time on uncertain terms with Lloyd George because the latter did not trust his personal ambitions, while the two men combined to persuade C.P. Scott, editor of the *Manchester Guardian*, to

---

[38] *Ibid.*, p. 59.

[39] Carson to Lloyd George, n.d. (Oct. 1915), L.G.P. F/97.

[40] Margot Asquith to Kitchener, 18 Aug. 1915, Public Record Office, Kitchener Papers P.R.O. 30/57/106. F.E. Smith, later Lord Birkenhead, was Solicitor-General. Though a violent controversialist who had stood out for his condemnation of Liberals during the Ulster crisis, he was a close personal friend of Winston Churchill. His inclusion in the ministry furnished 'a certain element of comic relief' to Gardiner and those who thought like him, because of Smith's willingness to break the law over Ulster. Gardiner, *War Lords*, p. 82.

[41] Memorandum by Selborne, n.d. [after June] 1916, Bodleian Library, Selborne Papers 80/285.

[42] *Stevenson Diary*, 12 Oct. 1915, p. 66.

throw his paper's weight behind a policy of concentration on the Eastern theatre. Churchill, supported in this instance by Curzon and Selborne, wanted a further push in the Dardanelles; Lloyd George wanted a campaign to reinforce Serbia.[43]

On the day of Carson's resignation Kitchener brought forward a quota system for recruitment, under which districts would be expected to produce by voluntary means the number of men indicated as available by the National Register, and any shortfall would be made up by a ballot of the remaining eligible men. In this ingenious scheme, reminiscent though it was of colonial methods of raising troops among subject peoples, Kitchener was supported in Cabinet by Churchill, Curzon, Lloyd George and at least five other Conservatives, and opposed by Asquith, Runciman, McKenna and Simon, thus reversing the pattern of allegiances to which he was accustomed.

At this point, on the evening of 12 October, Churchill and Lloyd George pressed Asquith to send a telegram to Romania and Greece offering military support if those two countries would come into the war on the side of the Entente, now that Germany and Austria had invaded Serbia and Bulgaria had joined the Central Powers to take part in the attack. The Conservative press was in full cry against Grey and the Foreign Office for diplomatic inactivity in the Balkans. The state of play in the Cabinet crisis at this point was summarised by Grey in conversation with Robert Cecil, reported to Selborne:

> E.G. told me more [about the conscription dispute]. It seems more a question of numbers and finance with [him] than anything else. He is also greatly enraged at the methods by which the controversy has been carried on. He regards the recent attacks in the Press upon himself as an attempt to utilise our Diplomatic misfortunes in order to get rid of a dangerous opponent of the Compulsionist plans and he regards the whole campaign as unscrupulous and rather sordid. To some extent I agree with him. But I only mention all this to show the kind of temper he is in. He is disposed to look round for some sufficiently strong reason to justify him in fighting out the quarrel to the bitter end. He talks very bitterly of the threats of resignation — threats which he thinks would never have been seriously made but for our military misfortunes. He talks of advising the Prime Minister to resign, if such resignation should come to pass and leave L.G. to form a Government. And I imagine that is what is intended. It is clearly inevitable if any considerable number of resignations take place.[44]

There is a clear implication here that the members of the Cabinet were at each others' throats but had almost forgotten why. By the following evening Lloyd George, Churchill, and '6 of the Tories' had decided to

[43] Trevor Wilson, ed., *The Political Diaries of C.P. Scott* (London: Collins, 1970), pp. 139–144.

[44] Cecil to Selborne, 12 Oct. 1915, Selborne Papers 80/55. Robert Cecil, second son of the 3rd Marquess of Salisbury, was Under-Secretary of State at the Foreign Office.

resign.[45] Their motives, as relayed by Walter Runciman to Charles Hob-house, were about as mixed as those of the last-ditchers on the other side, whose own position was also in some doubt:

> Lansdowne, Curzon, Law, A. Chamberlain were for leaving the Cabinet if con-scription were not proposed. Law chiefly because the Gallipoli peninsula was not abandoned and Chamberlain because of his position as reversionary leader. Curzon qualified his desire to resign by a declaration that in that event his criticism would be confined to any subject of actual disagreement. Balfour and Long would remain in whatever happened, to carry on the Govt. A.J.B. being against and Long for compulsory service. With them [evidently the resigners] would go Churchill who was pining to get abroad to the Dardanelles, and Ll.G who saw no opening to a leadership, and was much afraid that he had muddled the Ministry of Munitions, for which he would be called to account, and thought he had better get out of harness while there was yet time to throw the blame on someone else. The P.M. was still a convinced voluntaryist, but equally determined on keeping the Govt. together, and was trying to find a hypothetical formula of a Bill falling due 3 months hence! McKenna who was the P.M.s only confidant was determined to resign as was W.R. and these two thought Loulou would also go, if conscription was carried in Cabinet. K. had been won over, and had told the Cabinet he wanted 35,000 men a week, whereas his departmental people had only asked for 30,000. Simon characteristically could only express his determination to stand by the P.M. Henderson had a violent altercation with Ll.G. and told him and the Cabinet squarely that Labour would resist conscription by every means, in and out of Parliament.[46]

On the 13th Asquith himself was offering to resign and, according to Frances Stevenson's report,[47] some of the Conservatives (it is not clear which ones) were urging Lloyd George to take the premiership. Margot Asquith was convinced that he wanted to accept,[48] but he made no moves to do so on 14 October. At the War Committee meeting of 15 October Asquith unveiled the 'Derby scheme'. This elaborate compromise, which was apparently invented by Asquith and was never submitted formally to the Cabinet,[49] had a little in common with Kitchener's scheme of the previous week. Men between 18 and 41 on the National Register were to be canvassed by local recruiting committees, who would ask them to pledge to join the forces when summoned. Single men were then to be taken first, and Asquith was to tell the Commons on 2 November that he had 'no abstract or a priori objection of any sort to compulsion in time of war' and that he 'would certainly say that the obligation of the married man to serve ought not to be enforced, or to be held binding on him unless and until, I hope by voluntary effort, but if it be needed, in the last

[45] *Stevenson Diary*, 19 Oct. 1915, p. 69.
[46] Hobhouse diary, 14 Oct. 1915, *Inside Asquith's Cabinet*, p. 255.
[47] *Stevenson Diary*, 19 Oct. 1915, p. 69.
[48] M. Asquith to Elibank, 15 Oct. 1915, National Library of Scotland, Elibank Papers, 8803.
[49] Curzon, Austen Chamberlain and Selborne to Asquith, 3 Nov. 1915, Selborne Papers 80/75.

resort by other means, as I have explained, the unmarried men are dealt with.'[50] The Earl of Derby, Kitchener's Parliamentary Secretary, a Tory magnate and a prominent conscriptionist, was drafted in to administer the scheme, but played no part in its devising. This brought the Cabinet crisis to an end, but only just. Asquith wrote to Kitchener on the 17th to warn him that

> what is now going on is being engineered by men (Curzon, and Lloyd George and some others) whose real object is to oust you. They know well that I give no countenance to their projects, and consequently they have conceived the idea of using you against me... So long as you and I stand together, we carry the whole country with us... Cannot you say that, while you aim at, and would like to obtain 70 divisions, the thing should be done gradually and with general consent... [51]

The prime minister fell ill on 18 October and was out of action for the rest of the month. Kitchener observed: 'he is a great man; I thought he had exhausted all possible sources of delay; I never thought of the diarrhoea'.[52] While he was laid up Carson made his resignation public, with a call for conscription which had not been part of his original complaint. Selborne, not apparently realising that Asquith was seriously ill, remarked that the prime minister 'must have been mad' to allow him to read his letter of resignation in the Commons, since it contained 'some most unjustifiable mad and mischievous statements'. It also held up the government to ridicule 'which it deserves but it is not seemly from him'.[53] Walter Long, to whom complaint came naturally, chose 19 October to deliver a generalised homily on the ineffectiveness of the government.[54] On 21 October the Cabinet, in Asquith's absence, decided that the Dardanelles Committee, recently renamed the War Committee, was too big to transact business effectively, and ought to be reduced to a small number of ministers without departmental responsibilities.[55] This ultimatum Asquith was obliged to accept, though he postponed its implementation until after the parliamentary announcement of the Derby scheme. On 1 November he returned to work, bringing his proposed Commons statement to his Cabinet colleagues. Chamberlain, Curzon, Selborne[56] and probably Lloyd George[57] threatened to resign when they heard his text, and in deference

[50] *H.C. Debs*, 5s, lxxv, 2 Nov. 1915, 521, 524.

[51] Asquith to Kitchener, 17 Oct. 1915, Kitchener Papers P.R.O. PRO 30/57/76.

[52] Selborne to Robert Palmer, 20 Oct. 1915, Selborne Papers 109/93.

[53] Selborne to Robert Palmer, 2 Nov. 1915. Selborne Papers 109/104.

[54] Long to Asquith, 19 Oct. 1915, Bodleian Library, Asquith Papers 15. During the crisis Long had in fact been working to preserve the Coalition: Long to Bonar Law, 17 Oct. 1915, B.L.P. 51/4/18.

[55] Crewe to Asquith, 21 Oct. 1915, Asquith Papers 8.

[56] Selborne to Palmer, 2 Nov. 1915, Selborne Papers 109/104.

[57] Lloyd George to Margaret Lloyd George, 1 Nov. 1915, in K.O. Morgan, *Lloyd George: family letters 1885–1936* (London and Cardiff: Oxford University Press and University of Wales Press, 1973)

to their views the promise to conscript single men before taking married men was inserted.

In reasonable confidence that no one was about to leave him, and that the Derby scheme would keep the conscriptionists quiet if not happy, Asquith now set about reconstructing his small War Committee. Even this was not as simple as he might have hoped. Carson used the Commons debate of 2 November to launch an intemperate attack on his former colleagues and their methods, recommending that instead of setting up a new War Committee Asquith should merely reduce the size of his Cabinet to five or six members. Asquith had anticipated him:

> Mr Pitt, when he carried on the great war against France, had . . . a Cabinet of seven or nine, but the exiguity in size of that Cabinet did not prevent him from committing great blunders, or from suffering from many strokes of ill-fortune. For myself, I do not think there is any numerical specific against either want of foresight or want of good luck . . . [58]

This did not convince Carson, who by now had a substantial back-bench following, nor did it much impress Asquith's critics who remained in Cabinet. A new War Committee, consisting only of Asquith, Balfour and Kitchener, met first on 3 November, but Bonar Law, with Lloyd George's support, threatened to resign if Kitchener was not removed from it. Asquith met this demand by sending Kitchener on a mission to the Middle East, from which the whole Cabinet hoped, vainly, that he would never return. He left on 4 November. The next attempt at a committee consisted of Asquith, Lloyd George, Balfour and Lansdowne, but McKenna insisted on being a member, and Lansdowne declined.[59] The committee was announced on 11 November, with Bonar Law in Lansdowne's place and McKenna's name on the list. This new body stood some chance of improving the quality of policy decisions. It sat frequently, it was at first not too large for conversation, and it began to call for specific information from the service departments. Its weaknesses, eventually to prove fatal, were that McKenna and Lloyd George were barely on speaking terms, that Kitchener was in due course to come back and could not be kept out of its meetings, that it still had to win the support of a divided Cabinet, and that other ministers soon began to attend its meetings regularly, so that by the turn of the year it was often a group of nine or more. It is unlikely, though, that the 'numerical specific' had as much to do either with its early success or its ultimate failure as the lack of a shared strategic vision.[60]

p. 180.

[58] *H.C. Debs*, 5s, lxxv, 2 Nov. 1915.

[59] *Stevenson Diary*, p. 72.

[60] See Turner, 'The Higher Direction of War' for further discussion of the mechanisms of Cabinet

The First Conscription Crisis, December 1915 — January 1916

Debarred by the existence of the Derby scheme from discussing conscription until the time limit had expired, the War Committee liquidated one of its outstanding political problems by resolving to evacuate the Dardanelles. Even this decision could not be carried out until it was approved by the Cabinet, which unlike the committee did not have a natural majority for evacuation. By then the pledge implicit in the Derby scheme had fallen due, after the closing date had been extended from 30 November to 15 December. Of the 2.2 million single men not enlisted before the scheme was announced, about 840,000 attested and about 300,000 were medically rejected, leaving just over a million outside the scheme. About 1.35 million married men had attested, secure in Asquith's pledge that they would not be taken before the single men. Derby had proved one part of the the compulsionists' case, that the available manpower would not come forward under the voluntary system. The resulting upheaval in the Cabinet was shorter and more decisive than the tribulations of September to October, and its immediate effects on politics outside Downing Street were more extreme. The Cabinet expected to discuss the question on 28 December. Asquith was implicitly threatened by resignation from McKenna, Runciman, Simon and Grey if conscription went ahead, and from Lloyd George and the Conservatives if it did not.

The argument between conscriptionists and their opponents in Cabinet had now reached a fine dialectical point. The anti-conscriptionists had arrived at some insight into the problem by October, at which time their opponents were inclined to duck it. Robert Cecil put the conscriptionist view of the anti-conscriptionist case to Selborne:

> I am told that every member of the Cabinet would accept compulsion if it were clearly shown that the number of men necessary to win the war cannot be otherwise obtained. But those who are opposed to compulsion say (1) the number of men asked for is not really necessary or desirable and (2) the number really necessary can be obtained by voluntary recruiting.
>
> As to (1) the question is partly military and partly financial. So far as it is military it can surely be settled beyond legitimate doubt by getting separate and reasoned opinions from two or three leading soldiers say K, Murray[61] and W. Robertson.[62] The financial question is more difficult — if it be true that the difference between 50 and 70 divisions would mean a reduction of our subsidies to Russia it might mean a positive loss of men to the Allied forces if we added 20 divisions to our own contingent. On the other hand I am satisfied that public opinion would reject the financial argument in the face of strong military pronouncements. And indeed financial prophecies are too uncertain to be relied on....

government during the war.

[61] Sir Archibald Murray, then the Chief of the Imperial General Staff (C.I.G.S.).

[62] Then Chief of Staff in France: he became C.I.G.S. in December.

As for (2) the matter seems to me perfectly simple. Once you know your requirement you have merely to see what result the present system is bringing in and if it is insufficient the case is complete... [63]

In fact there was more to the case, both for and against, than Cecil imagined. Lloyd George, in his evidence to the early War Policy Committee, had argued that 'every man and woman was bound to render the services that the State required of them, and which in the opinion of the state they could best render'. When he was questioned more closely, by Crewe, on whether this meant direction of civilian labour he declared that: 'I think if you had compulsory military service you could work the rest all right.'[64] This was a cogent analysis: military conscription, though politically difficult, was easier to get than complete direction of labour, and could be used to the same effect. He put this case to a wide public by releasing an edition of his wartime speeches, putting out the preface (in advance of publication) on 13 September as he was laying his plans with Churchill and Curzon to force Asquith's hand.[65]

This line was not received well by anti-conscriptionists. The T.U.C., then holding its annual congress, was full of delegates who held that 'the governing class is using the opportunity of the war to alter the institutions of the country so that any kind of resistance against industrial oppression can be put down'.[66] Another kind of objection came from Liberal ministers. McKenna knew that Scott of the *Manchester Guardian* was a regular visitor to Lloyd George and might have guessed that he would take the view that 'I regard compulsory military service as in itself a great evil, but I would unhesitatingly accept it, as I believe would most of its opponents if it could be shown to be necessary for the purpose of winning the war':[67] McKenna was therefore quick to respond by briefing L.T. Hobhouse, the deputy editor, about his contrary views on 24 September.

McKenna's objection is not so much that it would divide the country, as that we are unable to stand it industrially. He argues 'We have to provide 1,590 millions viz about 2/3 of the national income for the war. All the Allies make calls on us... The Allies have plenty of men, but not equipment. There is a limit to what you can get from the U.S.A. You must in any case pay for what you get... Therefore you must keep our own industry going...' I said 'Would you then actually stop recruiting?' He said, No, but I would go slowly. We can get on as long as only 5 or 10,000 a week are being drawn away, but if it goes much faster exports fall, the exchange

[63] Cecil to Selborne, 12 Oct. 1915, Selborne Papers 80/55.

[64] War Policy Committee, 18 Aug. 1915, CAB.

[65] *Stevenson Diary*, 15 Sept. 1915, p. 59. The edition, *From Terror to Triumph* was published by Hodder & Stoughton.

[66] Reported to Graham Wallas by Beatrice Webb, who was there. Clarke, *Liberals and Social Democrats*, p. 176.

[67] Scott to Lansdowne, 17 Sept. 1915, Balfour Papers, British Library, Add. MSS 49864, 112–115. Scott had visited Lloyd George on 3 and 5 Sept: Wilson, *Political Diaries of C.P. Scott*, pp. 131–136.

goes against us etc . . . . He wholly scouts defeat. Where are we touched? We can go on ten years if they will only leave industry alone . . . . There are 100 ways of winning the war and only one of losing — conscription.

This was a sophisticated defence of the anti-conscriptionist position, and it accords with modern research on the manpower capacity of the country in 1915.[68] The exchange rate against the dollar had been worsening since the early summer, with a crisis in August.[69] Scott observed that Lloyd George had misrepresented it to him as timidity, 'making a bogey of the adverse American exchange'.

George himself was for enlisting all the able-bodied men not needed for his munitions work and financing the war by our investments — i.e. our four thousand millions invested abroad and the French two thousand millions. I should think McKenna has a much saner judgement than he on a question of that kind and I am glad to know what is his real position — particularly as to our ability to stand a long war.[70]

It was this case which McKenna and Runciman pressed in Cabinet before and after December 1915. Roy Jenkins has shrewdly observed that McKenna did so 'in too intelligent a way' when he gave evidence to Cabinet committees. 'When he patiently explained that it was not so much money as the physical allocation of resources, or the "depletion of industry" as it was then called, which was the trouble [Kitchener and Austen Chamberlain] became mystified and unconvinced.'[71] Clearly Cecil, in some ways a representative conscriptionist, also credited Kitchener and Robertson with a military foresight which he thought impossible in financial matters. In the event it took only twelve months of Lloyd George's medicine to produce the financial and economic crisis which McKenna had foreseen. By December 1916 the sterling–dollar exchange was on the point of collapse and Britain faced the possibility of a sudden and ignominious forced withdrawal from the war: but by then Lloyd George was in 10 Downing Street and McKenna was out of office.

Because the anti-conscriptionist case did not depend on an unqualified principle, it was not an insuperable political obstacle to Lloyd George and his Cabinet allies. On 27 December Lloyd George returned to London from a rowdy meeting with trade unionists in Glasgow to find the

[68] Keith Grieves, *The Politics of Manpower* (Manchester: Manchester University Press, 1988), at p. 22 observes that 'the demand for 35,000 recruits per week was a grossly inflated target which any system in an industrial society after sixteen months of war was unable to meet.'

[69] Kathleen Burk, *Britain, America and the Sinews of War 1914–1918* (London: Allen & Unwin, 1985), pp. 62–67.

[70] Hobhouse to C.P. Scott, 24 Sept. 1915; Scott to Hobhouse, 26 Sept. 1915, Wilson, *Political Diaries of C.P. Scott*, pp. 137–138.

[71] Roy Jenkins, *Asquith* (London: Collins, 1964), p. 436.

Cabinet in furious disagreement about whether the time had come to redeem Asquith's pledge to the married volunteers under the Derby scheme. Reckoning that Asquith's own decision, if he could be induced to make one, would determine the result, he sent a message through Lord Reading that if Asquith decided for conscription he would support him even to the point of a general election; if not, he would resign but would not take office in a Conservative-led government. This evidently swayed Asquith, whose desire to trust Lloyd George's good intentions was remarkably long-lived. His conclusion in the Cabinet meeting which finally took place on 29 December was that Derby's figures, showing a minimum of 300,000 single unattested men who might be fit for service, required him to fulfil his pledge to married volunteers. Lloyd George's challenge, based firmly on political calculation, had removed all semblance of rational argument from the discussion. Runciman and McKenna had based their threats of resignation on the case that raising an army of 67 divisions would break the British economy. Asquith offered no rebuttals — when pressed to think he had in the past agreed with them — and responded with a purely political analysis:

> . . . some of Squiffy's friends in the Cabinet would have liked to contend that 300,000 was a negligible quantity, but old Squiffy wouldn't have that at any price. Of course anyone else, especially anyone with the leadership of men in him, would have seized this moment to pass universal service for the war. But not he; the one thing he cares about is the parliamentary situation of the moment. By saying to Liberals and Labour 'You never objected to my pledge, how can you object to its fulfilment? I am going to fulfil it but not one hairsbreadth beyond it', he evades the question of principle and reduces his parliamentary difficulties for the moment to a minimum.[72]

He also reduced his Cabinet difficulties. Sir John Simon, the Home Secretary, resigned, quoting the principle of voluntary service. McKenna and Runciman, who did not have a principle to quote, stayed; so did Grey, who was persuaded that he was indispensable. So did Lloyd George.

Although the Commons posed no serious threat to the government when the measure was introduced, the extent of disturbance among Liberals was a portent of future difficulties. Twenty-seven Liberal and nine Labour M.P.s voted consistently against the Military Service Act.[73] The

---

[72] Selborne to Robert Palmer, 2 Jan. 1916, Selborne Papers 109/133.

[73] That is, voted five or more times against the government in the nine divisions on the bill. A total of 145 members found something to dislike in the bill, but 54 of these were Irish members who lost interest after voting against the first reading, once it became obvious that Ireland was to be excluded. The Labour hard core comprised W.C. Anderson, J.R. Clynes, Frank Goldstone, Ramsay MacDonald, Thomas Richardson, Philip Snowden, J.H. Thomas and George Wardle. Wardle and Clynes later joined the Lloyd George Coalition government and some Labour men notably sympathetic to the Coalition, including James Parker, G.N. Barnes, C.W. Bowerman, John Hodge and Barnet Kenyon, were among the open but less pertinacious opponents of the bill.

Liberals among them were immediately threatened with a witch-hunt by a newly formed Liberal War Committee led by Handel Booth, Sir Arthur Markham and Sir Henry Dalziel. On the other hand Simon joined an anti-conscription committee consisting of Richard Holt, Leif Jones, J.H. Whitehouse, and J.H. Thomas (for Labour). Students of the 'Liberal mind' have taken this to be a turning point in its history, at which a division between 'Asquithians' and 'Lloyd-Georgites' became a reality.[74] Bentley observes that 'If at the beginning of 1916 there did not exist two "camps", the positions which the factions would adopt eleven months later were already apparent.' This statement should however be treated with considerable caution.

At the very least, the Liberal Party should be seen in three parts (not including extra-parliamentary activists and voters, who were not being consulted at this point): the front bench, the back bench, and the extra-parliamentary intelligentsia. These groups talked to one another, sometimes in a common language, but the words and thoughts of one should not be put in the mouths of another. The intelligentsia was divided, but as Clarke's analysis makes clear it was muddled rather than polarised.[75] The back bench was disturbed, but it would be difficult to show that more of the back bench were disturbed in January 1916 than had been disturbed in August 1914 on the outbreak of war, May 1915 on the announcement of the Coalition, or August 1915 when the National Registration Act was passed. There was more noise in January 1916, but it came from the same people as before, each perhaps protesting a little more shrilly, but unable to increase their numbers. Their warlike opponents were also much the same, with Handel Booth taking the lead in promoting a witch-hunt with the same enthusiasm as when proposing a coalition in early May 1915, before Asquith had thought of it. Only a small minority of the back bench, whose views and separate identity had been clear since the middle of 1915, were profoundly upset by the Military Service Act. In no sense did the anti-conscriptionist back-benchers represent Asquith's views, or those of Runciman who in 'declin[ing] to be swindled with my eyes open' was protesting not at the affront to Liberal principle but at the irrationality of the conscription decision and Asquith's submission to political blackmail in Cabinet by Lloyd George.[76]

The front bench was split on different lines from the back bench, and was moved by different enmities and different concerns, but it too had been divided long before December 1915. The personal tension between McKenna and Runciman on the one hand and Lloyd George on the

---

[74] Bentley, *Liberal Mind*, p. 37; Clarke, *Liberals and Social Democrats*, p. 177.

[75] Clarke, *Liberals and Social Democrats*, esp. pp. 164–181.

[76] Runciman to McKenna, 23 Jan. 1916, Churchill College, Cambridge, McKenna Papers 5/9. Cf. Bentley's interpretation of this, *Liberal Mind*, p. 36.

other could be traced back to the National Insurance Act.[77] Moreover, front-bench divisions, being based partly on personal chemistry and partly on arguments about means rather than ends, could be overcome. In the middle of January, when emotion over the conscription crisis had hardly subsided, McKenna was involved in an effort to persuade Lloyd George to take the War Office, and in the course of discussion offered to 'bury the hatchet'. According to Lloyd George 'they parted very good friends'.[78] It was not to last, but it should not be dismissed as an example of how Liberals in Cabinet could sometimes behave.

Labour, Conscription and the Coalition

In the short term the Labour Party suffered more than the Liberal Party from the first conscription crisis, just as it had suffered more from the outbreak of war. Labour's presence in the Coalition, in the persons of Arthur Henderson, William Brace and George Roberts,[79] was controversial from the first. When Henderson was invited, the National Executive Committee agreed that he should accept but the parliamentary party disagreed by nine votes to eight. A joint meeting of the parliamentary party and the National Executive then decided to send him anyway, but the parliamentary party was still opposed by a small majority. When conscription was first contemplated the T.U.C., the Labour National Executive and the parliamentary party decided to oppose it, and their response to the Derby scheme was to found the Labour Recruiting Committee to prove that the men could be found by voluntary means alone. When the failure of the scheme was widely known a conference was summoned to discuss the movement's next step, but by the time it met, on 6 January 1916, the bill had been introduced; but it had Henderson's support, so that the collective leadership was bound to be thrown into turmoil.

Nearly 800 delegates gathered, and by a majority rejected the organisers' suggestion that Labour M.P.s be permitted a free vote. Instead a card-vote majority of 1,998,000 to 783,000 'recommend[ed] the Labour Party in Parliament to oppose the measure in all its stages'. Henderson and MacDonald presented the opposing views. Henderson insisted that he could not leave the government without destroying the Coalition, and

[77] Hazlehurst, *Politicians at War*, pp. 106–107.

[78] *Stevenson Diary*, 31 Jan. 1916, p. 91.

[79] Henderson was Secretary of the Party and *de facto* leader of the pro-war majority; he became President of the Board of Education. Brace was a miners' M.P. from South Wales; he became Parliamentary Under-Secretary at the Home Office. Roberts, a printer from Norwich, had been Labour's Chief Whip, and became a Coalition whip. He was later Minister of Labour and the only one of the three to support the post-war Lloyd George Coalition.

that if he was instructed by the conference to oppose the bill he would resign his seat and fight a by-election on the issue.[80] For this he was generally abused, with Philip Snowden prominent among his attackers.[81] MacDonald's speech embraced every possible objection to conscription. By arguing that 'the principle of compulsion cannot be restricted to this measure' he appealed to the self-interest of the major unions; by proclaiming that 'You can win the War, and in winning it pay such a price that the nation will have lost' he was (probably) conjuring up the spirit of Liberal principles. By declaring that '[t]he function of our movement . . . is to co-ordinate the demand of the military expert with other national demands . . . . National life is not maintained by soldiers only even in time of war' he was both stealing McKenna's clothes and coining the most remarkable definition of the functions of the Labour Party that many of the delegates would ever have heard or ever hear again.[82] But they cheered him to the echo and passed the resolution he supported. The National Executive, meeting immediately afterwards, voted 16 to 11 to withdraw from the Coalition.

This momentous decision was reversed after Asquith had promised the N.E.C. on 12 January, inter alia, that there was no question of industrial compulsion and that married men would not be conscripted. A few days later the annual conference, the first to be held since the outbreak of war, contrived to pass the first part of a resolution which declared its opposition to the bill, but reject the second part which proposed to agitate against it. It then confirmed, by a very large majority, the N.E.C.'s decision to stay in the Coalition, and passed by 1,500,000 to 602,000 a motion which 'pledge[d] the Conference to assist the Government as far as possible in the successful prosecution of the War'.[83] MacDonald, understandably, 'beg[an] to doubt as to the future of the party'.[84] It was threatened as much by muddle as by the rancour of its internal divisions.

The reality of those divisions, though, is in no doubt, and the January conference opened a rift which did not begin to heal until the autumn of 1917. Snowden noted that the large card-vote majority for 'assist[ing] the Government as far as possible in the successful prosecution of the war' was achieved by the block votes of four unions, against 69 other trade unions, 39 trades councils, 41 local Labour parties and all the socialist societies.

[80] Philip Snowden, in An Autobiography (2 Vols, London: Ivor Nicolson & Watson, 1934), I, 393, observes that when his appeal was rejected '[h]e did not go down to Barnard Castle to seek the opinion of his constituency, but contented himself by writing a letter to his agent'.

[81] Snowden, like Ramsay MacDonald, was an I.L.P. member without trade union affiliations. He had been M.P. for Blackburn since 1906, and was later to be a notoriously conservative Chancellor of the Exchequer in 1924 and 1929–31.

[82] Labour Leader, 8 Jan. 1916, for a full conference report.

[83] Snowden, Autobiography, pp. 394–395.

[84] PRO 30/69/1753, MacDonald Diary, 29 Jan. 1916.

The anti-conscriptionists in the parliamentary party immediately began to work with the Liberal anti-conscriptionists, ignoring their own party's organisation and leadership. The choice of speakers in the debate on the Military Service bill was concerted between Liberal and Labour members. According to Snowden's estimate the anti-conscriptionist group at this point numbered 39, with 'three or four' pro-war Labour M.P.s prepared to join them in a vote against conscription: this is close to the figure suggested by the divisions on the bill. The disgruntled pro-war Labour men, who were probably Charles Bowerman, J.R. Clynes, Barnet Kenyon and Will Thorne,[85] represented proportionately a much larger shift of opinion in the Labour Party than could be discerned at this point among the Liberals, and correspondingly a greater threat to the integrity of the party. That the conflict was very largely, though not entirely, between sponsored trade union M.P.s on the one hand taking a pro-war position, and on the other hand members with stronger roots in the I.L.P. and the other socialist societies resisting conscription and the Coalition, made the potential damage greater.

Labour politics in the country, as witnessed by industrial activity and the recent by-election in Merthyr Tydfil, were equally confused. In some areas strike movements suggested that conscription was as unpopular as dilution: but in Merthyr, only recently the epicentre of the South Wales miners' strike, the strikers' leader C.B. Stanton, standing as an independent pro-war Labour candidate, had in November at the height of speculation about conscription defeated the official Labour nominee and entered parliament as a conscriptionist.[86]

With both Labour and Liberal critics in disarray, the divided government had a fairly easy passage in the debates on 5 and 6 January. The Irish party voted solidly against the measure, but withdrew their opposition when Ireland was exempted from the bill. The anti-conscriptionists from Great Britain, whose numbers in the lobbies peaked at 45, were put under heavy pressure. The Liberal whips reportedly threatened that Asquith would dissolve the House if the hostile vote reached 150, and that the Tories would win the subsequent election. Some Liberals were clearly influenced by this pressure: Charles Hobhouse, ostensibly a leader of the anti-conscriptionist committee, 'presided at 2 o'clock at one of its meetings and 2 hours later spoke for the Bill', as did J.M. Robertson, and their

[85] This was a mixed bag. Bowerman was Secretary of the T.U.C., and member for Deptford since 1906; Clynes, of the General and Municipal Workers, had been member for N.E. Manchester since 1906 and had been vice-chairman of the P.L.P.; Kenyon, though elected as a Lib-Lab member for Chesterfield, had since February 1914 only accepted the Liberal whip; Thorne, a convinced socialist who had founded the Gas-workers' Union and the General and Municipal Workers, was member for West Ham.

[86] Anthony Mor-O'Brien, 'Keir Hardie, C.B. Stanton and the First World War', *Llafur*, iv (1986), 31–42.

colleagues only got half the number of supporters they had expected.[87] Some, including some of the reluctant members of the Cabinet, had evidently been influenced by the argument that the principle of compulsion had been accepted, but deferred, in October: this was merely the passive enactment of that decision, now that the Derby scheme had failed. For whatever reason, and there were as many reasons as tea-room discussions, the resistance misfired and the Coalition survived.

New Year – Old Problems

Parliamentary success or no, January 1916 was anything but a new beginning for the Asquith Coalition. Of the great problems of 1915 only the Dardanelles expedition had gone away, and that was to return soon enough: the Cabinet decided on 19 January to resist parliamentary demands for a 'Suvla inquiry', but in the end they had to give in and the Dardanelles Commission was set up. Kitchener, the greatest problem of all in the eyes of some of his colleagues, was still in place. Above all, the decision to conscript single men had not implied a decision of principle on more fundamental problems. At the Cabinet meeting of 31 December, after the conscription decision had been taken, ministers fell to arguing about the size of the army. McKenna forced the issue by insisting that financial constraints made it impossible to maintain an army of 70 divisions in the field; Runciman stated for the Board of Trade that industry could only stand losses of 20,000 men a week, while the General Staff were proposing to recruit 32,000. Lloyd George, Curzon, Bonar Law, Chamberlain and Selborne set upon them with the revealing argument that although no one had ever authorised the War Office to recruit a 70-division army, the authorities had been openly working to that figure since the summer. McKenna, who had only the previous day agreed with Robertson, the C.I.G.S., to work towards an army of 54 divisions in France with a few reserve divisions at home,[88] repeated his point. Even with the army at its present size the war was costing £5 million a day and the country's deficit would mount to £600 million by March 1916 and £2,000 million a year later. This was the argument the Cabinet had ducked when it should have settled it in September: now it was referred to a Cabinet committee, consisting of Asquith, McKenna and Chamberlain.

---

[87] *Scott Diary*, 10–11 Jan. 1916, p. 169. Neither Hobhouse nor Robertson voted against the bill, nor against the fuller Military Service bill passed on 9 May.

[88] Lord Hankey, *The Supreme Command* (2 Vols, London: Allen & Unwin, 1961), II, 472, confirmed by Hankey's diary for 30 Dec. 1915, Churchill College Cambridge, Hankey Papers.

If the crisis in December over conscripting single men had shown Cabinet government at its most unreflective, the 'Military Finance Committee' cruelly exposed the limits of rational thought under which any wartime Cabinet laboured. One Chancellor of the Exchequer and two former Chancellors were confronted with a mountain of evidence from the Treasury about reserves, overseas debt, and the exchange rate, from the Board of Trade about labour supply and production, and from the War Office about the need for troops in the next campaigning season. Except for the Treasury's evidence, much of which related to easily countable things like Treasury Bills and bank deposits, these figures were fragile estimates with little foundation in fact. The Board of Trade had some idea of the movement of labour into the forces,[89] but no model of the economy with which to assess labour demand; the War Office was estimating for a campaign the like of which had never been seen, using arbitrary casualty rates and guessing about the weather. To bring the two sides together involved no more than a vigorous cooking of the books, in which Asquith and Hankey were engaged for a full month. Then the committee's report, drafted by Chamberlain to guarantee its acceptance by the conscriptionist faction in the Cabinet, was produced 'to the intense relief of all concerned'.[90]

The Cabinet politics of the Asquith Coalition in the early spring of 1916 were partly hidden from parliament and the newspaper-reading public. Some issues of major importance to ministers were veiled. Colonel House's peace proposals, discussed below, were kept very quiet.[91] Although the proposals were rejected, the rejection was not a mere reflex, and it implied a decision of principle on a much greater matter which was never discussed explicitly. The compromise by the Military Finance Committee and the decision taken at the end of December to mount a major offensive in the West, both involved a gamble on victory in 1916 in preference to conserving resources for a long war. That this had to be a decision at all was difficult even for some ministers to grasp, and not all seem to have realised fully that it had been made; and it was far beyond the intellectual reach of those back-benchers who busily formed Liberal and Unionist 'War Committees' to agitate for 'a more vigorous prosecution of the war'. The debate of 5 and 6 January showed that, as before, while many Liberals treated conscription as a matter of moral principle, most Conservatives and conscriptionist Liberals treated it equally narrowly as a technical question of how to extract soldiers from the civilian population.

---

[89] Peter Dewey, 'Military Recruiting and the British Labour Force during the First World War', *Historical Journal*, xxvii (1984), 199–224, discusses the validity of its sample surveys.

[90] CAB 37/142/11. The process is described by Roskill *Hankey: man of secrets* (London: Collins, 1970) pp. 241–245; Jenkins, *Asquith*, pp. 436–438; Hankey, II, 471–473.

[91] See J. Milton Cooper, 'The British Response to the House-Grey Memorandum: new evidence and new questions', *Journal of American History*, lix (1973), 958–971.

The question of how long the war would or could last was ignored on the back benches.[92]

On some issues ministers leaked like sieves. The possibility of reinstating Lord Fisher at the Admiralty was thrashed out in the newspapers, and McKenna and Runciman tirelessly expounded their economic reasons for limiting the size of the army and the rate of recruitment to any editor intelligent enough to understand them. Lloyd George's dissatisfaction with the administrative efficiency of the Cabinet and War Committee was well known to the *Morning Post* as well as to the *Manchester Guardian*, because Lloyd George took care to see both editors.[93] On the Conservative side Curzon was keen to make an issue of air defence, with the assistance of Northcliffe's papers, though Northcliffe wanted to be Minister for Air himself. Lord Selborne had a plan for increased agricultural production to which neither Cabinet nor War Committee would listen,[94] and this too was widely known by the press and thus by the back benches. These became the stuff of parliamentary excitements.

The Politics of Economic Warfare

In these excitements the Unionist War Committee took a leading part. Its appearance in January 1916 owed much to Carson, who became a figurehead while the work of the committee was organised by Sir Frederick Banbury and Ronald McNeill.[95] The Unionist War Committee claimed by March 1916 to include most of the back-bench Conservatives not on active service in the forces, perhaps 150 members, and it soon began to behave as a Conservative party in exile, focusing the discontent felt by the back bench at the conduct of the Asquith Coalition. Overlapping with it was the Unionist Business Committee, drawing its inspiration from Walter Long and organised by Long's trusted ally Sir William Bull, and W.A.S. Hewins, former Director of the London School of Economics and former secretary of the Tariff Commission. The U.B.C. was a year older than the Unionist War Committee; its membership had at first been confined

---

[92] John Burns considered it incessantly in his diary, but never in public places. British Library, Add. MSS 46338, Burns Diary, *passim*.

[93] E.g. the meeting between Lloyd George, Hughes of Australia, Donald of the *Chronicle* and Gwynne of the *Morning Post* on 10 March, J.M. McEwen, ed., *The Riddell Diaries* (London: Athlone Press, 1986), p. 148.

[94] Selborne's paper is in Selborne Papers 127/167.

[95] McNeill (who spelt his name variously until 1927 when he was created Baron Cushendun) was an Ulster Unionist, barrister and author. He held minor offices in Baldwin's governments in the 1920s. Banbury, a stockbroker, was at some time chairman of the Great Northern Railway and of the R.S.P.C.A. He was opposed to all forms of change, from socialism to Summer Time, and never held office though he was made Privy Councillor in 1916.

to businessmen or Tariff Reform activists, and its early activities had been confined to matters of direct interest to businessmen, such as munitions production, raw material supplies, and the excess profits duties. Though it excluded ministers and office-holders, it had the formal sanction of Bonar Law, who had ostensibly appointed Walter Long to be its first chairman. In the hands of Bull and Hewins it mutated during 1915, and by the beginning of 1916 it was acting on the one hand as a power-base for Long as a 'candid friend' of Bonar Law's leadership of the party, and on the other hand as a pressure group for a large extension of protectionist measures during and after the war. Its contacts outside the House included a number of leading trade and manufacturers' associations, but far from becoming a tool of external business interests it was able to use those interests to further its own views. When the Unionist Business Committee and the Unionist War Committee were not raising the parliamentary temperature over the passing incidents of the day, they were engaged in a persistent lobby about economic warfare and post-war economic policy.

From the viewpoint of a busy Cabinet and a bemused Liberal back bench the first four months of 1916 were dominated by conscription, but in the longer term the upheaval in economic policy was quite as important. In September 1915 McKenna's first war Budget had been produced during an earlier conscription row. Its proposals to raise a small part of the additional cost of the war by taxation, though much bolder than Lloyd George's earlier efforts, were less prominent than its introduction of import duties on motor cars and luxury goods. This abrupt abandonment of Free Trade was variously explained as an attempt to reduce demands for tonnage and as a revenue-raising measure. McKenna's contemporary private explanation, which seems almost as inadequate as the official account, is that it was an attempt to discredit protectionism as a policy and thus undermine the Conservative attack on McKenna's war economics.[96] Whatever its origin, Tariff Reformers thought they saw a small victory, and the more suspicious Liberals recognised a sell-out. Thomas Lough described it bluntly as 'the price we are paying for a Coalition Government', an interpretation which McKenna and his Financial Secretary, Edwin Montagu, were at pains to refute.[97] During that round of discussion McKenna presented the new duties as a consistent part of his strategy of limiting imports, limiting civilian consumption, and protecting the country's financial resources for making war. During the next two months a new note entered official presentation of policy. Runciman, on 23 December, took the very un-Cobdenite line that '...I think, so far as commerce is concerned, Germany is a beaten nation, and our object is to see that she

---

[96] Thus Mond to McKenna, 14 Oct. 1915, Churchill College Archive Centre, McKenna Papers MCK 5/10.

[97] *H.C. Debs*, 5s, lxxvi, 12 Oct. 1915, cols 1218–1276; 13 Oct. 1915, cols 1378–1436.

does not get her head up and carry on the same activities when the war is over.'[98]

This was at the time an attempt to recast existing policy in a language which would deflect the Conservative back-benchers of the U.B.C., but over the next four months it was a language which seemed to take command of policy. With no obvious reluctance, the Liberal ministers adopted post-war protectionism as a reasonable measure. At first they were merely under pressure, mostly from U.B.C. members but also from the *Morning Post* and *Daily Mail*, to strengthen the blockade against Germany: a press campaign against the government's White Paper of 4 January took wing as soon as the conscription crisis was over, in the form of fierce attacks particularly on Grey and Runciman. Runciman also met Hewins's demand for post-war economic co-operation with the Dominions by giving an extra hostage to fortune, remarking that 'Our second consideration [after the Dominions] will be the extent to which we can help those who have been fighting with us and for whom we have fought.'[99] Hardly more than a month later Edwin Montagu confided to an audience in his constituency that

> it is not a part of Liberalism not to recognise altered conditions.... We in the past conducted trade as a peaceful pursuit. We in the past treated all nations as nearly as we could equally. But look back at the history of this war, and see the use Germany made of her trade, and just ask ourselves the question whether we can ever afford or dare to let that happen again.[100]

McKenna himself began to promise state help to traders after the war.[101]

This new openness to the demands of strident Conservative back-benchers was part of McKenna's attempt to build a convincing war policy which depended on economic pressure rather than what he saw as a policy of denuding industry to fill an over-sized army. It was not his fault that his opponents wanted both the economic war and the comb-out; but he should have realised that they would do so, and his propensity during this period for walking open-eyed into trouble almost justifies Asquith's complaint that he had 'proved himself unstable mentally and morally'.[102] Meanwhile the Board of Trade recruited businessmen to a number of advisory committees on post-war industries.[103] Some of these committees were already at work when the French government appealed for

---

[98] *H.C. Debs*, 5s, lxxvii, 23 Dec. 1915.

[99] *H.C. Debs* 1915–1916, 5s, lxxvii 10 Jan. 1916, cols 1299–1394, esp. cols 1357–1358.

[100] Quoted in *Liberal Magazine*, xxiv, 270 (Mar. 1916), 68.

[101] Addressing the Association of British Chambers of commerce, quoted *ibid.*, 72.

[102] Jenkins, *Asquith*, p. 438.

[103] In a longer perspective, discussed in Chapter 10, this exposed the limits of businessmen's influence on politics and policy during the war. But at the time some found it sinister.

a joint conference on post-war economic policy. The announcement, on 7 March, alerted Liberal suspicions and a fierce campaign was waged throughout March and April. But for the renewal of the conscription dispute, this would no doubt have continued, but since the same people were involved in both arguments post-war trade fell into a political backwater. Unnoticed save by a few, the government was able to accept the elaborate agreements of the conference, including trade discrimination against Germany after the war, and set up the Balfour of Burleigh Committee to advise on their implementation. The impact on some sections of Liberalism was enormous; J.A. Hobson not only condemned it as 'a complicated form of folly', but took it as an excuse for resigning from the party and published a broadside against *The New Protectionism* which rightly identified the prime movers as the new business element in the Conservative Party. Parliamentary Liberals were more relaxed about it in public, and only Simon took a strong stand in the House. In private, it helped to convince the critics of Asquith, McKenna and Runciman that it was unsound to compromise with Conservative principles, and thus further isolated the Asquithians in their own party.

The Second Conscription Crisis

When the crisis came in April nothing could distract the Commons from the conscription issue. Although neither the Conservative ministers nor Lloyd George had ever believed that the necessary troops could be raised without universal conscription, the impulse for a change in policy on this occasion came from outside the government. Carson and the Unionist War Committee launched an agitation on 29 March, concentrating on the grievances of attested married men, and by mid-April this was so obviously popular that Asquith was forced to promise a statement on recruiting. The Military Finance Committee was reconvened, as had been intended when it gave its first report in February. With evidence that the February targets were not being met, but also that shipbuilding and dock work were beginning to suffer because of over-enlistment, the committee concluded that further compulsion would not solve the immediate problem and recommended three minor measures instead: taking powers to send overseas the Territorials enlisted 'for home service only', arranging to recruit 18-year-olds directly they reached that age, and extending the service of time-expired regular soldiers. Lloyd George now found the opportunity to 'forc[e] an issue' which would improve the management of the war. He insisted on immediate general conscription, expecting support from the Conservatives, and insisted that the report be referred to the Army Council for an opinion. The Army Council obliged with a demand for conscription, and took the chance to renege on the February compromise by insisting on recruiting to a target of 70 divisions or more. The Conservatives, on the other hand 'ratted almost to a man'.[104] Bonar Law circulated a letter to his colleagues on 13 April, arguing that if they left the Cabinet there would inevitably be an election; even if the Conservatives won, opposition to conscription from outside parliament would necessitate martial law; and that their case for leaving now would be much weaker than it would have been in January, or than it would be in April if the Military Finance Committee had actually said that compulsion was necessary. He concluded indecisively, remarking that 'I think that if all the Unionist members decided to remain in the Government we should secure for the present the support of the majority of our Party; but I am convinced that the discontent which exists now would become increasingly evident, and that before long our position might be impossible.'[105]

The Army Council report braced most of the Conservatives, but Lloyd George found Bonar Law in 'a state of abject funk' on 16 April, and it was only on the 18th that Bonar Law committed himself to resigning if Lloyd George resigned.[106] The result was another committee, on the size of the army, which met for a single session on 18 April to reconcile the Army Council with the Military Finance Committee. On the day of its meeting Asquith went to the Commons to postpone his promised statement. The next day the Cabinet was presented with a report, largely inspired by Lloyd George, which recommended setting a fairly high weekly recruiting target with the promise that general conscription would be introduced if it were not met. On this they could not agree, and Asquith went once more to the Commons, which was now in a state of uproar, to announce that the Cabinet was divided but might have made up its mind by the following week. But by 20 April the Cabinet had indeed reached an agreement very close to Lloyd George's initial suggestion, and the result was explained to the back benches in a Secret Session on the 25th.[107]

The Cabinet crisis over extending conscription had thus been brought to an end by a decision to postpone any extension for the moment. The political logic of this outcome exemplifies the almost random quality of Coalition decisions in 1916. Both Frances Stevenson and C.P. Scott agreed in their diary accounts that Lloyd George had intended to use conscription as an excuse for resigning from a Cabinet in which he had lost confidence. Instead of resigning, he brought the Cabinet round to a

[104] *Stevenson Diary*, 17 Apr. 1916, p. 105.
[105] Memorandum by Bonar Law, 13 Apr. 1916, B.L.P.
[106] *Stevenson Diary*, 17 Apr., p. 106, 19 Apr., p.107.
[107] See R.J.Q. Adams and Philip Poirier, *The Conscription Controversy in Britain 1900–18* (London: Macmillan, 1987), pp. 154–170.

compromise which neither achieved conscription nor broke the government, and Miss Stevenson had it on 18 April that 'D. is working so hard to avoid a smash.'[108] Finally he told both Stevenson and Scott that it was 'either too soon or too late'[109] to resign and that his time would come in five or six weeks, when it would have been shown that the men could not be raised by the methods then being discussed. This leaves a major problem of explanation, uncharacteristically ducked by Lloyd George's most recent biographer,[110] but settled by Wilson (in a sense hostile to Lloyd George) in the observation that 'Lloyd George's interest was in office, not opposition. He would only quit the government if by so doing he ensured its collapse and his own prompt reinstatement.'[111] This is supported by Scott's own contention that

> Previously he had said that his real motive was dissatisfaction with the whole conduct of the war and a desire to avoid further responsibility for this and to recover his independence and right of public criticism — that the question of conscription was in fact only the occasion and not the cause of his intended resignation.... By consenting to compromise George had reversed this order of importance and had made compulsion the dominant issue and the conduct of the war subordinate. The fact is that, though he has again and again talked of resignation and threatened it, he has always shrunk at the last minute.[112]

The flaw in Scott's reasoning, and ultimately in Wilson's, is that Lloyd George's use of conscription was not merely instrumental: he wanted conscription for its own sake, as he had explained in September 1915, to help maintain some control over the use of labour across the whole economy.[113] This was not the reason usually given by Conservative conscriptionists, most of whom were preoccupied with the number of 'shirkers' in the population.[114] Since Conservatives were concerned above all about the number of men in the army they were swayed by the argument that compulsion, after the political costs had been paid, would make no difference in the short term: Lloyd George was looking further into the future. The Conservative ministers were therefore lagging behind Lloyd George's enthusiasm until 17 April, when the Army Council's opinion was available as a substitute for thought. By 18 April Bonar Law was prepared to resign with Lloyd George, but Lloyd George had won his

---

[108] *Stevenson Diary*, p. 107.

[109] *Scott Diary*, 13–20 Apr. 1916, p. 199.

[110] John Grigg, *Lloyd George: from peace to war 1912–1916* (London: Methuen, 1985), pp. 335–337.

[111] Editorial matter to *Scott Diary*, p. 196.

[112] *Scott Diary*, 13–20 Apr., p. 200.

[113] See above, p. 74.

[114] But cf. Selborne to Robert Palmer, 2 Jan. 1916, Selborne Papers 109/133: '... universal military [service]... is already overdue, as the only way to give the army every man that can be spared without unduly depleting essential industries...'.

case within a day, when Henderson abandoned his objections after a talk with Sir William Robertson. There were therefore no resignations, Lloyd George told the newspapers that he was satisfied with the outcome, told Frances Stevenson that he would wait another few weeks before resigning, and prepared to go to a public meeting to take credit for holding the Cabinet together.[115] Liberal Cabinet members felt bruised, and leaked accordingly to the *Chronicle* and the *Daily News*, but the damage to relations within Cabinet was less than had been felt in December and January. Asquith, who had blamed Lloyd George for raising the issue prematurely, and pronounced himself 'mortified' by the row, recovered rapidly. Lloyd George insisted that Asquith was the only prime minister who could carry conscription through parliament. Conservative ministers were patently relieved to have held the Coalition together.

Predictably, the Conservative back benches did not want the cracks in the ministry to be papered over so thoroughly. The Secret Session was a failure, and when Long introduced the Cabinet's bill on 27 April it was fiercely attacked. Two days later the Cabinet decided to introduce general conscription after a very brief discussion which opened no further controversies: although conscription might split the ministry, anything else would destroy its power in the Commons.[116] The measure was introduced on 2 May and finally enacted on the 25th. It provided for compulsory enlistment of all males between 18 and 41, subject to the exemptions for reserved occupations, medical unfitness, and conscientious objection which had applied to single men conscripted under the January Act.

Resistance from the Labour party and the anti-conscriptionist Liberals was markedly weaker than in January. The Labour parliamentary party passed a resolution against general conscription on 15 April, and just before the Secret Session a joint meeting of the parliamentary party and the National Executive, addressed by Asquith, Kitchener and Bonar Law, decided to summon a national conference.[117] Their resistance did not survive the Secret Session. The conference was called off when the parliamentary committee of the T.U.C. decided to support the government's proposals. Although the T.U.C. had accepted the Cabinet's first proposals for minor extensions, rather than the general conscription which emerged from the Commons session of 27 April, the general flavour of Labour's parliamentary attitude to military service can be judged from Asquith's observation on 12 May that

The speeches made last Thursday, particularly from the Labour benches, encouraged the belief that there was a general desire to settle the whole matter, with all the

[115] *Stevenson Diary*, pp. 106–109.
[116] Asquith to the King, 29 Apr. 1916, Asquith Papers 8.
[117] N.E.C. Minutes, 26 Apr. 1916, Labour Party Archives, NEC 8A.

controversy and heated feeling it has produced, once and for all, and to get it finally out of the way at the earliest moment.[118].

In the major divisions on the bill, only ten Labour M.P.s voted against the government: Will Thorne, George Wardle and William Adamson, who had opposed January's bill, consented to the new measure.[119] Labour opposition to the war was in retreat. Liberal opposition was also steadied at 28 members in the major divisions, against the 27 who had consistently opposed the introduction of the earlier bill.[120] Although Lloyd George later called the opposition 'trivial',[121] the House divided frequently during the passage of the bill, and in all 42 Liberal members voted against the government four or more times, a figure comparable to the 38 who had voted more than once against the January measure. That Liberals could be found to object to details in the measure without objecting to its substance is significant: although Bentley is right to remark that the events of 1916 'sharpened and deepened' the rifts in the parliamentary Liberal party, they scarcely increased the size of the dissentient minority. Already the greatest division in the Liberal Party was at the top, not in the ranks of M.P.s.

Lloyd George's Cabinet critics were generous with the press, especially Robert Donald of the *Daily Chronicle*, and the antipathy felt towards him by Liberal editors persuaded Lloyd George to take his case to a well-reported public meeting at Conway on 6 May, and deny in public that he was attempting to take Asquith's place as prime minister. He later claimed that this political infighting had deflected him from launching another 'National Efficiency' campaign. Moreover, Riddell had warned him that working-class opinion was against him, and he was busy answering press attacks on him which he imputed to Bonar Law.[122] His performance at Conway convinced his followers, and further persuaded the irreconcilables that Lloyd George was not to be trusted: but since many of the irreconcilables were fiercely critical of Asquith, the balance of sympathy within the party was hardly affected.

---

[118] *H.C. Debs*, 5s, lxxxii, 12 May 1916.

[119] Adamson was secretary of the Fife Miners' Association and had been M.P. for Fife since 1910; he was later chairman of the Party, and led it in parliament against the Lloyd George Coalition from 1918 to 1921. The main body of anti-conscriptionist Labour members can thus be identified as William Abraham (a Welsh miners' M.P.), W.C. Anderson, J.R. Clynes, Frank Goldstone, Walter Hudson (a railwayman and member for Newcastle), Fred Jowett (I.L.P. from Bradford), Ramsay MacDonald, Thomas Richards (a miner from South Wales), Thomas Richardson, Philip Snowden, and J.H. Thomas. All were to be more or less staunch opponents of the Lloyd George Coalition.

[120] There were some defectors, such as Percy Alden, W. Clough, Richard Denman, W.A. Gelder, E.C. Rees and Penry Williams. Some members, such as E.H. Lamb, who had not voted on the introduction of the January bill but opposed in committee, did oppose the introduction of the May bill.

[121] *War Memoirs*, p. 39.

[122] Addison, *Four and a Half Years*, I, 202; J. McEwen, ed., *The Riddell Diaries*, pp. 154–155.

Rebellion in Ireland

As a threat to the integrity of the Coalition, conscription was rapidly overtaken by the Irish rebellion which broke out on 24 April. Asquith and every other member of the Cabinet was more concerned at that moment with the Secret Session, and Selborne observed that 'The real attitude here is that no-one takes the thing as other than the usual Irish tragic comic opera but that everyone thinks that [Augustine] Birrell [the Chief Secretary] is a scandal.' Since the military suppression of the rising seemed to be quick and effective, the main concern of British politicians in the first few days was to get a new civilian administration, with Birrell quickly removed from his post. Selborne noted that

> Since this Cabinet was formed last May Birrell has never once mentioned the subject of Ireland and we have had no knowledge whatever of the state of affairs there. As everything seemed calm we assumed that it was calm. Now it appears that Birrell and [Sir Matthew Nathan] have had any number of warnings which they neglected on principle.[123]

Birrell's resignation was accepted on 1 May, and Nathan's on the 3rd.

For the moment, that was the limit of political action; and the future course of Irish politics was determined by the peculiar mixture of muddle and ferocity with which the Commander-in-Chief, General Maxwell, dealt with the situation. On 6 May the Cabinet considered its policy towards the punishment of captured rebels, but by then the military authorities had already executed twelve prisoners, including Padraic Pearse, who had proclaimed the independence of the Irish nation from the steps of the General Post Office. The Cabinet sent Maxwell a weak telegram, hoping that executions would now cease unless the cases were unusually grave, but James Connolly and two others were shot after it arrived. It was soon known that Connolly had been carried to his death on a stretcher and shot while sitting in a chair, because his wounds were too grave for him to stand; and that Sheehy Skeffington, a journalist innocent of any connection with the rising, had been summarily shot by a deranged British officer. Though Asquith, who took temporary charge of the Irish administration and visited Dublin from 11 to 18 May, concluded that this was 'fewer bad blunders than one might have expected with the soldiery for a whole week in exclusive charge',[124] it was enough to turn opinion in Ireland more firmly against the British connection, and it also gave Irish groups in the United States ample material with which to maintain

---

[123] Selborne to Lady Selborne, 26 Apr. 1916, Selborne Papers 102/195.
[124] J. A. Spender and C. Asquith, *The Life of H.H. Asquith* (London: Hutchinson, 1932), pp. 215–216.

a steady flow of funds and support for the separatist Sinn Fein movement which now began to grow.

British efforts to resolve the problem were focused upon the Dublin Castle administration and on Westminster politicians and took little account of the determinants of political sympathy within Ireland. These efforts did not succeed even in their own terms: had they succeeded they would probably not have quelled the separatist movement in southern Ireland.[125] Birrell, giving evidence to the Commission of Inquiry on 19 May, observed that Irish separatism had been shrinking away for twenty years, but had been revived by the war, doubts about the government's sincerity about Home Rule in the light of the Suspending Act, the resort to illegal methods by the Ulster movement, and the appointment of Carson to the Coalition Cabinet in May 1915. The analysis was difficult to fault, but he was at that moment the last person that any Conservative politician was likely to believe.

Asquith's decision to deal with the Irish crisis by a direct political fix, involving only the Westminster leaders of the two Irish parties, was typical of his belief in the resilience of pre-war party ties. Like most British prime ministers, even Lloyd George after him, he assumed in defiance of the evidence that Irish leaders could control their followers. He therefore set Lloyd George to bring about an agreement between Carson and Redmond. Between 23 May and 8 June Lloyd George undertook what has more recently been known as 'shuttle diplomacy': without bringing the two parties together in one room, he produced a draft settlement which both sides could agree to recommend to their followers. The Home Rule Act would be introduced immediately, with an Amending Act to exclude the six counties, and the Irish members, from North and South, would remain at Westminster. After the war an Imperial Conference would meet to settle the future of Ireland, and the permanent exclusion of the six counties would be considered then. By 18 June this had been accepted by both Nationalist and Ulster Unionist activists in Ireland, and published as a White Paper. The problem was now to get it ratified by Conservatives at Westminster. This proved impossible, partly because back-bench Unionist peers led by Lord Midleton and Lord Salisbury mounted a campaign against it, but mostly because of the efforts of Long, Lansdowne and Selborne within the Cabinet.

Selborne's subsequent account of Cabinet discussions and the Unionist perception of them is illuminating as an example of the trials of politicians in a coalition divided by a common language of euphemism and allusion:

---

[125] See D. Fitzpatrick, *Politics and Irish Life* (Dublin: Gill Macmillan, 1979) on the penetration of separatism into Irish political culture during the war.

I do not believe that it crossed the mind of one single Unionist member of the Cabinet that the bringing into existence during the war of Home Rule in any shape or form could possibly form part of such a settlement. I understood, and I believe that my Unionist colleagues understood, that an effort was to be made to get the Ulster Unionists and the Nationalists of Ireland to agree to the exclusion of Ulster or of a part of Ulster from the operation of the Government of Ireland Act, and in addition to see whether there were any safeguards which would induce the Unionists of the South, Centre, and West of Ireland to accept a government and parliament in Dublin for the rest of Ireland. If an agreement on these points could be reached an Act amending the Government of Ireland Act would be passed during the war, but it never entered our heads that anyone contemplated bringing in the Government of Ireland Act, amended or unamended, modified, into operation during the war. I say this as confidently in respect of Lord Lansdowne, Lord Curzon, Lord Robert Cecil, Mr Austen Chamberlain and Mr Walter Long, as of myself. I believe it to be true also of Sir F.E. Smith, Mr Bonar Law, and Mr Arthur Balfour, but, as they subsequently adopted a somewhat unexpected attitude, I do not state it of them with the same confidence as of the others.... Under these circumstances we all concurred in approving the Prime Minister's Commission to Mr Lloyd George. This was where we went wrong. Knowing Mr Asquith and Mr Lloyd George we ought to have insisted on joining some Unionist like Lord Robert Cecil or Mr Austen Chamberlain to Mr Lloyd George in the negotiations.[126]

Selborne's misplaced serenity had been based on a memorandum written by Asquith immediately on his return from Dublin,[127] in which the prime minister remarked that the Home Rule Act could not come into operation until the end of the war. A watching committee was appointed, consisting of Long and Lansdowne as well as Lloyd George and Asquith, but it met only once, on 1 June, to hear Lloyd George's report that the Nationalists were prepared to accept exclusion, but wanted the immediate application of Home Rule as a *quid pro quo*. Long and Lansdowne were later reported to have been unhappy, but did not tell their colleagues outside the committee at the time. Meanwhile, whether before or after the meeting of 1 June, Lloyd George appears to have persuaded Asquith that it would be essential to introduce Home Rule during the war, and then have taken the proposals to Carson and Redmond as though they were the agreed policy of the Cabinet.

Long and Lansdowne repudiated the proposed settlement as soon as they saw it in the newspapers, and Selborne, on hearing Long's account on 16 June, immediately proffered his resignation. These moves provoked a fierce row within the Conservative leadership, with Bonar Law, Balfour and F.E. Smith defending the scheme against an attack from their Cabinet colleagues, led by Long.[128] The Conservative back bench was also

---

[126] 'Memorandum on the Crisis in Irish Affairs which caused my Resignation from the Cabinet June, 1916' by the Earl of Selborne, 30 June 1916, Selborne Papers 80/226.

[127] H.H.A., 'Ireland: the actual situation', 19 May 1916, CAB 37/148/13.

[128] W.H.L. 'The Proposed Irish Settlement', 21 June 1916, CAB 37/150/11; A.J.B., 'Ulster and the Irish Crisis', 24 June 1916, CAB 37/150/17.

roused, partly by Long's loyal assistant Bull,[129] and the result was a major challenge to Bonar Law's leadership in which for once both his principal rivals, Long and Chamberlain, were united. Within the Cabinet Asquith postponed a breach by setting up a committee to draft extra clauses which would protect imperial supremacy in Ireland during the war. This deflected Lansdowne and Long from resigning, and on 5 July the Cabinet agreed to the clauses and put them to Redmond, who also accepted them. This would have secured an agreement if Lansdowne had not glossed the arrangements heavily in a speech in the Lords on 11 July.[130] After this all enthusiasm for a settlement on the Nationalist side evaporated, and Lloyd George's proposals were a dead letter. On 27 July the Cabinet abandoned them and reverted to the rule of Dublin Castle, with Lord Wimborne once more to be Viceroy and H.E. Duke, a Conservative lawyer, to be Chief Secretary.[131]

Questions of War and Peace

The strategic riddle faced by the Asquith ministry in the middle of 1916 included the problem of allocating resources between industry and the army which had been at the centre of the two conscription crises, but was much wider in its significance. Britain was fighting the war as part of the Entente, with only a limited influence over the military or economic policies of her partners. Her role in the war was to provide troops and a naval blockade in support of the Entente's military activity, to supply munitions, essential raw materials, and shipping to her allies as well as her own forces, and increasingly to raise loans and lines of credit in the United States to pay for her own purchases and those of the Allies. These diverse objects conflicted with one another, as McKenna at the Treasury repeatedly pointed out, and it was essential from Britain's point of view to strike a balance between military and economic activity which would fend off bankruptcy until the war could be won. What was worse, there was no 'best course' for Britain which did not take account of the behaviour of the other Allies. As Grey remarked to the War Committee in February 1916, not for the first or last time, 'Germany has taken care to make it known to our Allies that each one of them individually, or at any rate France and Russia, could have peace tomorrow on comparatively favourable terms,

---

[129] Richard P. Murphy, 'Walter Long and the Conservative Party 1905–1921', University of Bristol Ph.D. thesis, 1984, ch. 4.

[130] *H.L. Debs* 5s, xxii, 645–652, 11 July 1916.

[131] Asquith to the King, 27 July 1916, Asquith Papers 8. Wimborne was cousin to Winston Churchill and elder brother of Frederick Guest, who became Lloyd George's Chief Whip. His family were comfortably, and corruptly, established as Liberals in control of Dorset.

if they would separate themselves from us'.[132] Strategic discussion within the British Cabinet had been dominated by this problem since the middle of 1915. A belief in the unreliability of the Allies was one of the strongest arguments for spending resources of men and money quickly, in order to bring the war to a swift conclusion: this was the strategic gamble of 1916.

The Cabinet divided on this issue into two clearly defined camps, with Lloyd George and the Conservatives (except for Balfour) on one side and the Liberals on the other. Their divisions on the other major issue, of whether to make the main effort on the Western Front, were much less clear-cut. In the later months of 1915 most of the Cabinet was unhappy about the policy of committing most of Britain's effort to the war in France and Flanders, but ministers were divided about whether Gallipoli or Salonica was the better theatre for an Eastern initiative, and the advice given by Kitchener and the General Staff was inadequate and confused. The failure of the battle of Loos (launched on 25 September) brought on an open revolt both against Kitchener's methods and against the high command of the British army in France. Sir John French was sacked at the end of November, to be replaced as Commander-in-Chief by Sir Douglas Haig. A few days later Sir Archibald Murray, who had himself only two months previously replaced Sir James Wolfe Murray ('Sheep' Murray to Winston Churchill) as C.I.G.S., was replaced by Sir William Robertson, formerly the Chief of Staff in France. With the support of Asquith and the War Committee, Robertson dictated his terms to Kitchener. As C.I.G.S., he was to be the sole source of military advice to the War Committee, and the sole channel through which the War Committee's orders were to be transmitted to the army. The Secretary of State was to be reduced to the traditional role of providing troops for the campaigns, a more humiliating limitation because the other traditional job of supplying equipment had been given to the Ministry of Munitions. The 'Kitchener–Robertson agreement' was operated very harmoniously, largely because the two men agreed that the only route to victory was 'attrition': forcing the enemy to expend his resources of men and munitions until they were exhausted, in the hope that the Entente could last longer. The greatest change brought about by the change of personnel was therefore not a change of policy, but the mere fact that Robertson, and the staff officers he brought with him from France, were convinced and articulate exponents of the need for concentration on the Western Front, and they had automatic access to the War Committee.[133]

An Allied military conference at Chantilly in December 1915 decided that in the 1916 campaigning season a series of wearing-out operations

[132] 'The Position of Great Britain with regard to her Allies', 18 Feb. 1916, P.R.O. CAB 42/9/3.
[133] French, *British Strategy and War Aims*, pp. 161–163.

should be mounted, in the expectation that Germany's manpower would thereby be exhausted by August 1916. At the end of the month Robertson persuaded the War Committee to accept these plans, which would require the British army to do most of the fighting in the West at least until the summer, when France's 1915 losses would have been made good. These intentions were soon diverted in the Military Finance Committee, where Lloyd George argued that there would not be enough munitions to begin an offensive until June.[134] This argument was a means to a political rather than a military end: Lloyd George wanted conscription, and was trying to bring about a compromise between conscriptionists and anti-conscriptionists in the Cabinet. Nevertheless his intervention had important strategic consequences. In February the Germans attacked in force at Verdun, rather than saving their strength for an attack on Russia which the General Staff had expected. After first welcoming this as an opportunity to exhaust the German armies, the General Staff were alarmed to discover that the French line was unexpectedly weak and that the French army might be unable to take any part in wearing-out operations in the spring or early summer. This led to disagreement between Haig and Joffre, the French Commander-in-Chief, which was finally resolved by an agreement that the main attack would begin in July on the Somme, where Joffre had wanted it, but that Haig would not be obliged to mount major operations in the spring. By this time the British Cabinet had begun to redivide, with Lloyd George speaking firmly against any resumption of the offensive in the West, and Asquith, Grey and Bonar Law strongly supporting Robertson's demand that the generals should be allowed to decide the timing and purpose of the attack. A firm decision, supporting Robertson, was finally reached on 7 April. The next strategic move was to be the battle of the Somme.

Only very occasionally did politicians entangled in strategic discussion remember that the war was not an end in itself. In 1915 only a handful of M.P.s had permitted themselves to question the wisdom or justice of Britain's participation in the war. The I.L.P. members had broken away from the majority of the Labour parliamentary party, and the 'Radical Group' of Liberal members[135] had held meetings until February 1915, but there was no energetic public movement in favour of bringing the war to an end by negotiation rather than force of arms. Even the Union of Democratic Control, which acted after September 1914 as an umbrella for Labour and Liberal critics of the war, was insistent that its policy was

---

[134] Proceedings of the Committee on the Co-ordination of Military and Financial Effort, 13 Jan. 1916, P.R.O. CAB 27/4.

[135] See above, pp. 46–47.

not to 'Stop the War'.[136] In October 1915 there was still a debate within the U.D.C. about whether the time was ripe to admit that some people thought that negotiation was an idea worth exploring.[137] A campaign led by E.D. Morel changed the mind of his U.D.C. colleagues. In November 1915 C.P. Trevelyan raised the possibility of negotiation in the Commons, after the German Chancellor had made an apparently conciliatory speech.[138] By February 1916 Trevelyan and Snowden were ready to start a discussion on war aims in the Commons.

Snowden opened the debate, on an amendment to the Consolidated Fund bill, taking the position that a decisive military victory could only be achieved at the cost of ruining the country, and that

> What has kept the Allies united in this trouble is the menace of a powerful and unconquered Germany, but when Germany has been crushed and ruined then that cohesion will fall apart. Germany will cherish designs for the restoration of her national position, and she will find new Allies and another Great War will only be a matter of time.[139]

This observation, which seems less remarkable in retrospect than it did at the time, was accompanied by a telling quotation in which the *Deutsche Tageszeitung*, discussing the 'Runciman programme' for post-war economic policy towards Germany, welcomed Runciman's speeches 'because they give the official confirmation as to what the British Government thinks of the state of things after the War'. This drew an extended but dismissive answer from Asquith. He denied that Germany's leaders had shown any disposition to negotiate, and reiterated a passage from an earlier speech which promised that Britain would 'never sheathe the sword which we have not lightly drawn' until Belgium and Serbia were restored, France's borders secured, and 'the military domination of Prussia is wholly and finally destroyed'.[140]

In the hiatus between two conscription crises, this drew a pointed enquiry from the *Morning Post*: 'Has it never occurred to Mr Asquith that so far he has not succeeded in unsheathing the sword? It is partly drawn but Mr Asquith thinks it better not to throw away the scabbard until next week, or perhaps the week after.'[141] Asquith's position was not so crudely

---

[136] See Clarke, *Liberals and Social Democrats*, pp. 174–180 for the gyrations of Liberal Radicals in support of the war.

[137] MacDonald to C.R. Buxton, Oct. 1915, cited Swartz, p. 77.

[138] Morel, a journalist, was best known to the public for his exposure of Belgian atrocities in the Congo before the War. Trevelyan, who was related to the other well-known Trevelyans, had been a Liberal member since 1899; he had resigned from the Parliamentary Secretaryship at the Board of Education in protest at the decision to go to war.

[139] *H.C. Debs*, 5s, lxxx, 720, 724, 23 Feb. 1916.

[140] *Ibid.*, 736–737. He was referring to a speech of 9 November 1914.

[141] *Morning Post*, 25 Mar. 1916.

inconsistent as his right-wing enemies implied, though McKenna, Runciman and Grey among his Liberal colleagues were certainly prepared to consider negotiations for the same reasons that led them to resist conscription. In fact the government's attitude, or rather attitudes, to a negotiated peace were far from simple. The day before Trevelyan's motion was debated, Grey had signed an agreement with Colonel House, special emissary of President Woodrow Wilson of the United States. This took the form of a memorandum of a conversation between the two men based on previous conversations between House and a number of French and British politicians, including Asquith, Grey, Balfour, Reading and Lloyd George. The thrust of House's proposal was that if the Entente Powers stated their war aims, President Wilson would propose a conference of all the belligerents, and if Germany refused or made unreasonable demands, the United States would enter the war on the side of the Entente. In mid-February the British Cabinet wanted to see this proposal carried further. No irreconcilable positions had yet been adopted. On 22 January McKenna had told Hankey that 'we should probably get a better peace now than later when Germany is wholly on the defensive . . .'.[142] On 23 February, before the Commons debate, Grey and Runciman lunched with Lloyd George, who later told Frances Stevenson that Grey was 'frankly pessimistic' and agreed with McKenna in wanting American mediation. Lloyd George at this point was opposed to it, because public opinion would not stand it, but he had ostensibly supported the idea only the previous week once it was understood that no conference would take place without a preliminary statement of peace terms.[143]

It took some weeks for Wilson's reply to be prepared, and it was only on 21 March that the War Committee had the chance to discuss its response to Wilson's fatefully adverbial telegram, which promised that if Germany's demands were pitched too high the United States would 'probably' join the war on the side of the Entente. An American historian has noted in this meeting 'the squabbling ineptitude [which] ruled out the kind of bold, difficult choice that was required',[144] but this is to underestimate the degree to which the participants were by now rehearsing prepared roles. Asquith had already decided that the approach was 'humbug, and a mere manoeuvre of American politics'.[145] Grey introduced the question by asking whether the naval and military advisers thought that the Allies would strengthen their position over the next six months. If they did, he thought that 'we could get better terms then with or without the intervention of the United States'. If not, the offer should be pursued.

---

[142] Hankey Diary, 22 Jan. 1916, Hankey Papers. Hankey agreed with him.
[143] *War Memoirs*, p. 411.
[144] Cooper, 'The British Response', p. 965.
[145] Hankey Diary, 16 Mar. 1916, Hankey Papers.

Robertson, who had been forewarned by Hankey, opposed negotiations. Bonar Law urged that public opinion would not stand a peace based on the status quo ante, an argument which suggests that he had been talking to Lloyd George. In response to McKenna's remark that the country could carry on so long as the army did not withdraw labour too rapidly from the civilian economy, he observed that 'credit depended on success, and this could only be achieved by withdrawing the manhood of the country in sufficient volume to ensure success this year...'. McKenna disputed this and responded that 'although we had won no victories our credit was splendid'. Perhaps realising that his colleagues were by now incapable of having new ideas about the war, Asquith pushed the discussion towards a close; Balfour declared that 'at present the proposal was not worth five minutes' thought'; and after some mutterings from Kitchener and Lloyd George about the weakness of the Russian army, the meeting expired. House was sent a discouraging reply.[146]

Except that Lloyd George seemed to have no decisive opinions, the contents of this discussion could have been predicted for months past. Asquith's lack of interest in a negotiated peace, and his apparent willingness to accept Kitchener's hopes for a successful Western offensive, reveal him as one of those whose fundamental instinct was to gamble on an early victory, an instinct which he shared with his Conservative colleagues. Those who felt otherwise — McKenna with his fear of collapsing credit, Lloyd George with his conviction that the war could last until 1918[147] — had no common ground from which to oppose him. In the Commons the idea of a negotiated peace was so unpopular that the government was never under serious pressure to contemplate it. The Labour Party in parliament was even less determined to resist the war than it was to resist conscription. On the Liberal side, when C.P.Trevelyan protested in March about the unnecessary restrictions of the Defence of the Realm Act, he felt obliged to make the remarkable point that 'I am not in favour of stopping the War at this point. I am in the same position with regard to the continuance of the War as my Right Hon. and learned friend [F.E. Smith]; I do not want to stop it at present at any price.'[148] In April, when Chancellor Bethman-Hollweg told the Reichstag that Germany would evacuate Belgium and end the war if her vital interests could be safeguarded, Asquith responded by telling a French parliamentary delegation that the evacuation of Belgium was insufficient without adequate guarantees and reparations. He also squashed

[146] Cooper, 'The British Response' discusses this meeting at length. The full minute is in P.R.O. CAB 42/11, War Committee Minutes, 21 Mar. 1916.

[147] See *Stevenson Diary*, p. 103, entry for 12 Mar. 1916. Although Lloyd George was speaking for effect on this occasion, his insistence that 'the war cannot be brought to a successful conclusion for us until then' is consistent with his other attitudes in 1916.

[148] *H.C. Debs*, 5s, lxxxi, 23 Mar. 1916, 444–445.

an attempt by David Mason, a Liberal M.P. who had resigned the party whip in protest against the war, to open the subject out in the Commons.

Even in May, when the body of anti-government opinion in the House was readily identifiable and well used to action in the conscription debates, Arthur Ponsonby[149] and Ramsay MacDonald could scarcely hold members' attention for a motion criticising the Cabinet and Foreign Office for failing even to ask the German government about the terms on which peace negotiations could begin. On that occasion it was Grey who came down to the House to utter a flat refusal to contemplate negotiations; and the Cabinet's critics, led by Joseph King and William Pringle,[150] quickly passed on to further consideration of conscription. This coyness on the part of the opposition was all the more remarkable since on 24 May the War Committee had once more discussed the House–Grey memorandum, and according to McKenna

> They had not reached a decision, but that he, the P.M., Grey and Balfour had been in favour of accepting President Wilson's good offices, owing to the black financial outlook, while Bonar Law and Ll. George were averse.[151]

If the proponents of a negotiated peace had pressed hard, or appeared to win any sympathy in the House, the Cabinet's integrity might have been threatened. Instead the almost unsupported voice of David Mason raised weary questions throughout July and August about the nature of Britain's war aims and the steps being taken by the Foreign Office to discover Germany's policy. Asquith responded to all questions about peace terms, even friendly ones, with a refusal to discuss them on the floor of the House, and capped it all by telling Ponsonby that he would not undertake to recall parliament if there were any sign of negotiations during the recess.[152] Even so the possibility of American mediation was a real one, because Wilson was fighting an election campaign and had domestic political reasons for a diplomatic intervention. Possible British responses were discussed in the War Committee on 10 August, and in the course of reflecting upon them the Cabinet was drawn into the ministry's last, fatal political crisis. Once again, the lack of a clear, shared view on the nature of the war which was being fought left Coalition leaders vulnerable to paralysing distractions.

---

[149] Ponsonby was the son of one of Queen Victoria's private secretaries. He had been a diplomat and private secretary to Campbell-Bannerman before entering the Commons at a by-election in 1908. He was a founder of the Union of Democratic Control.

[150] King, a barrister and author, had been a Liberal member for N. Somerset since 1910. Like many other anti-war Liberals, including Trevelyan and Ponsonby, he joined the Labour Party after the war. Pringle, another barrister, sat as a Liberal for N.W. Lanarkshire. Though once thought a potential ally, he was later a thorn in the side of the Lloyd George Coalitions.

[151] Hankey Diary, 24 May 1916, quoted Roskill, *Hankey: man of secrets*, I, 274.

[152] *H.C. Debs.*, 5s, lxxxiv, 11 July 1916, 176–177; 24 July 1916, 1412; lxxxv, 8 Aug. 1916, 864; 21 Aug. 1916, 2267–2268; 22 Aug. 1916, 2479.

The Politics of Muddle

With the Cabinet's acceptance of a strategic gamble and the collapse of the Irish settlement, all the necessary conditions for the fall of the Asquith coalition were in place. For more than a year the Coalition had survived because even its most discontented supporters calculated that only the coalition could carry through the policies they wanted to see. The Conservative leaders, especially Bonar Law and Balfour, were convinced that the dissolution of the coalition would bring about a general election which would be fatal in wartime: only Asquith could restrain the partisanship of the Liberal back bench. Lloyd George wanted conscription, but believed that only Asquith could carry it through the Commons: a number of Conservatives shared his view. On the other side McKenna and Runciman saw the Coalition as the only alternative to a Conservative government, and were therefore profoundly unwilling to resign. The unity of the Conservative party was never secure. Bonar Law faced Carson as a focus of back-bench opposition; he looked over his shoulder to Walter Long, an old rival whose own contacts with the back benches were good. The true believers in Tariff Reform looked to Chamberlain or Carson as much as to Bonar Law himself, and the numerous survivors of the Tory landowning caste could identify their fortunes with Selborne,[153] who had already resigned, or with Lansdowne who might resign at any moment. But at least there was no single pretender to Bonar Law's uncomfortable crown.

Almost from the beginning the ministry had been so badly divided that its survival was in doubt. Asquith regularly confided to his female friends — and once, failing a convenient female, to Lord Kitchener — his despair at his colleagues' mutual hatreds. He held them together partly because for each individual the survival of the Coalition seemed preferable to the alternative, partly because no two issues divided the Cabinet in precisely the same way. McKenna and Lloyd George were almost invariably on opposite sides: but even they could agree about Kitchener. The Dardanelles 'evacuationists' did not correspond to the 'anti-conscriptionists', nor to the supporters of the Irish settlement. The generals' best friends over conscription were their worst enemies over military strategy on the Western Front. A *putsch* was always round the corner, but it would only come if enough ministers could be persuaded to agree about something for long enough to join it.

This, though, was no real security for a government at war which had continuing problems to solve. The most general complaint against the Asquith Coalition was that it suffered from a form of pernicious anaemia:

---

[153] Selborne was not an hereditary landowner, but he usually behaved like one, and was in any case married to the Marquess of Salisbury's sister.

because its members were forever wrangling about some great or small issue they rarely had time to make sensible decisions in good time about mundane subjects. Some of the worst offenders were those associated with the loudest calls for a 'more vigorous prosecution of the war'. Carson was a bad and indecisive administrator whose performance in the Lloyd George Coalition at the Admiralty eventually had to be brought to an end by promotion to the War Cabinet. In March 1916 Lloyd George observed that 'Bonar Law is limp and lifeless; Balfour can never make up his mind about anything'; and Hankey, who had every opportunity to see ministers at work, noted at the end of the year that 'Bonar Law is by common consent the poorest figure on the present War Ctee.'[154] Lloyd George and McKenna, the Cabinet's most capable members, disliked each other too intensely to co-operate for long, and consumed a great deal of energy arguing over matters of great strategic importance which might otherwise have been applied to 'getting on with the war'.

Inevitably there accumulated a list of damaging muddles whose public revelation discredited the ministry as the year's campaigning drew to its fruitless close. For example, a row between the Admiralty and the War Office over the control of military aviation was allowed to rage uncontrolled from January 1916 to the fall of the ministry.[155] Far worse was the failure of the Admiralty to take any effective steps against submarine warfare, which left Britain's food supplies at risk during the worst harvest of the war.[156] Public and parliamentary anger was roused by the battle of Jutland on 31 May: through poor training, poor communications, indifferent leadership and technical insufficiency, but mostly through ill-luck, the Grand Fleet suffered proportionately worse losses than the German High Seas Fleet and failed to win the great naval victory which all had expected in the first and last set-piece naval encounter in the war. The Coalition was blamed. Governmental failures were blamed, with even less justice, for the failure of the Mesopotamia campaign and the surrender at Kut-el-Amara on 29 April. Lloyd George later described this as 'a perfect example of what military administration is capable of if entirely freed from civilian "interference"' and an example of 'mismanagement, stupidity, criminal neglect and amazing incompetence'.[157]

Nearer home, as but one example of the internal damage to the Coalition caused by secondary matters, the supply of food was always in doubt. When Selborne took over the Board of Agriculture he was anxious about

---

[154] *Stevenson Diary*, 11 Mar. 1916, p. 102; Hankey Diary, 3 Dec. 1916, Hankey Papers.

[155] Brief description in Roskill, *Hankey*, I, 251–252. Lloyd George's chapter, in *War Memoirs* pp. 582–584, is amusing.

[156] A.J. Marder, *From the Dreadnought to Scapa Flow*, Vol. 5 (London: Oxford University Press, 1961).

[157] Lloyd George, *War Memoirs*, I, 480, 483.

the country's dependence on imported food. He appointed a commission under Lord Milner,[158] which in July 1915 recommended the expansion of domestic wheat production through the device of a guaranteed minimum price for wheat, with an enquiry into agricultural wages. Asquith responded simply that 'In my opinion there is not the least fear that any probable or conceivable development of German submarine activity can be a serious menace to our food supply',[159] and the Cabinet took no action. In the latter part of 1915 some progress was made in establishing a wheat reserve and the Wheat Commission took in hand all overseas purchases of grain, and arranged also to handle the purchases of the European allies. This exercise revealed that competition for shipping between the allies and between different purchasing agencies could also threaten supplies. The general problem of shipping induced the Cabinet to set up a shipping control committee in January 1916. Selborne returned to the subject of increasing home supplies, but could not get the War Committee or the Cabinet to discuss it,[160] and the matter was still open when he resigned over Ireland. He was replaced by the Earl of Crawford and Balcarres, who had the same difficulty: Lloyd George records, as a regular event in Cabinet, Crawford's 'despairing cry for a few minutes' consideration before lunch of his anxieties about the food of the nation', and Crawford's diaries confirm his frustration, which was shared by other junior ministers.[161] Meanwhile the 1916 harvest was exceptionally bad, and the submarine campaign did reduce, appreciably, the stocks of wheat available in the country. [162] When Lloyd George's Coalition took over, very little had been done to increase the supply of home-grown food, but there was a ready-made policy and a ready-made controversy to go with it, which came to fruition in the 1917 Corn Production Act. Other examples of muddle which became particularly pressing in the final months of the ministry are discussed in the following chapter.

---

[158] Alfred Milner, Selborne's predecessor as High Commissioner in South Africa from 1897 to 1905, was associated after his return to Great Britain with an ideologically extreme imperialism, with Tariff Reform, and with Diehard resistance to Liberal policies, in particular the Parliament Act.

[159] Asquith to Selborne, 16 July 1915, Selborne Papers 80/23.

[160] See Selborne to Hankey, 15 May 1916, Selborne Papers 80/167 and Hankey's reply of 16 May that Asquith had told him not to put it on the War Committee agenda 'at present', *ibid.*, 80/168.

[161] *War Memoirs*, I, 584; Crawford's diaries are published as John Vincent, ed., *The Crawford Papers*, (Manchester: Manchester University Press, 1984). Crawford was the 27th Earl, but his family fortune was based not on land but on the ownership of most of the coal under Wigan. He was a Unionist M.P. and Chief Whip from 1911 until he succeeded to the title in 1913. He served in the early months of the war as a medical orderly in France.

[162] Peter Dewey, *British Agriculture in the First World War* (London: Croom Helm, 1988); L. Margaret Barnett, *British Food Policy during the First World War* (London: Allen & Unwin, 1985); Avner Offer, *The First World War: an agrarian interpretation* raises many interesting questions about the significance of the food supply without answering them.

Political Consequences: Liberal Decline and Labour Progress

The political consequences of the Asquith Coalition are fiercely disputed. For the Liberal Party Michael Bentley has insisted that the form of the Liberal split was determined by the events of January 1916 and Asquith's manoeuvrings afterwards, which left his followers disillusioned. Michael Hart prefers to argue that the Liberal back bench was loyal in its votes and only bitter in its private correspondence. Hart is wrong to deprecate the importance of private grief, but right to emphasise the small number of the truly disaffected. Bentley is right to contrast private anger with public displays of reluctant loyalty, but wrong to underrate the importance of backbenchers who did not keep diaries. Most diarists were troubled by the Coalition, but they were few:[163] among the backbenchers whose only contribution to posterity is their recorded votes, Liberal solidarity was not much affected by the Asquith Coalition. Moreover, the other two British parties were equally damaged, though they showed it in different ways. The Conservatives developed not one but two back-bench pressure groups in the Unionist Business Committee and the Unionist War Committee, whose support for the 'vigorous prosecution of the war' was much more consistent than their support for the Party's leader. The Labour Party divided on the same lines as the Liberals, except that the two sides were more evenly balanced; and the peculiar constitution of the party, in which many decisions were taken by a National Executive Committee in which the majority were not M.P.s, led to ludicrous and damaging changes of mind such as the decision, ultimately, to support conscription in May 1916. Within the effective 'leadership of the Labour Party' — a rather indefinite institution which included the N.E.C., the parliamentary party meeting as a caucus, and the Parliamentary Committee of the T.U.C., with considerable overlapping membership between the three groups — the Coalition always had the support of a majority, but never a very large one.

A more elusive problem is the political impact of the Asquith months in the country. Without a source of direct information about public attitudes to compare with the records of Mass Observation in the Second World War, historians are forced back on the patchy and unreliable information with which politicians went about their business. For the most part, contemporaries used the familiar broad categories of pre-war politics to organise their knowledge of the people's thinking. 'The Free

---

[163] Holt, MacCallum Scott, and Burns are the main diarists, of whom MacCallum Scott was the only one who retained any sympathy with the Coalition. The correspondence collections normally cited are weighted heavily towards Cabinet members (McKenna, Runciman, Asquith, Harcourt) or back-benchers who voted against the government in the conscription divisions, and their correspondents (Burns, Holt, Ponsonby, Simon, Dickinson, Gilbert Murray and Lord Courtney), and are *ipso facto* untypical of the body of the Party.

Churches' constituted one such category whose importance, as noted in Chapter 1, lay in their organisation as much as their raw numbers. 'Labour' was another category which contemporaries rightly distinguished from the political Labour movement. 'Working men' or 'the wage-earners' constituted an unknown quantity to most active politicians, which was to be approached either by newspapers, through its employers, through mass meetings or, sometimes, through its trade union leaders. So long as no general election was in contemplation, the opinion of the mass of civilians who were not in the forces or in the war industries was of little consequence; on the rare occasions when politicians did refer to it explicitly, they took their view of it from the popular newspapers, principally the *Daily Mail*.

Among these categories the fate of the Free Churches is of interest because of its intimate relationship with the Liberal Party. The outward and visible sign of Nonconformist political activity was the public utterance of a small number of prominent ministers and a smaller number of recognised laymen, together with the editors of the leading Free Church journals of whom Sir William Robertson Nicoll of the *British Weekly* was the best known and certainly the most influential. This little élite, never very harmonious even in peacetime, was irrevocably split by the war. In the first days of war a very large proportion of Free Church leaders turned almost overnight from principled pacifists convinced of the need for world disarmament to equally principled supporters of the war. Robertson Nicoll wrote an anti-war leader which delighted Ramsay MacDonald in the *British Weekly* of 31 July, and a pro-war leader which equally delighted Lloyd George on 7 August.[164] After the excitement had died down, leaving most of the Nonconformist press and preachers heavily committed to a British victory, the issues most relevant to Nonconformist politics were Drink and conscription. The drink question in March and April 1915 had the predicted and intended effect of rallying the Free Churches to Lloyd George's support; when the government's tactic switched from abstinence or prohibition to state purchase, there was an immediate flight of sympathy, though the Conservatives in the new Cabinet were held responsible. On other issues the *British Weekly* and some leading churchmen followed Lloyd George, as the most prominent Nonconformist in the Cabinet. Robertson Nicoll did not conceal his impatience with Asquith and his desire to see Lloyd George in his place, and the Rev. J.H. Shakespeare, whose son subsequently became Lloyd George's secretary, took it upon himself to pray openly for the destruction of Germany, just like any Anglican vicar. Others, more 'moderate', adopted policies from somewhere in the centre of the Liberal Party, resisting conscription for reasons

[164] Koss, *Nonconformity*, pp. 127–128.

of principle: 'Admit Conscription, and the Kaiser is not far behind'.[165] Whichever line was taken, the political Free Churches were dissatisfied with the Asquith government: but at the same time the Churches' active rejection of pacifism and the manifest irrelevance to wartime concerns of the education issue, Welsh Disestablishment, and passive resistance merely reduced the importance of Nonconformity as a political category.

'Labour' — as a category rather than as a party — was contrastingly raised up. Whatever the long term effect of the war on 'class politics', the short term effect was clear enough, and some aspects of it can be dated precisely to the period of the Asquith Coalition, just as others were the product of developments in 1917 and 1918. After the Treasury Agreements of March 1915, and even more so after the passage of the Munitions of War Act in June, which supplemented DoRA as a means of managing the munitions industries, the government's chosen instrument for dealing with the industrial workforce was the trade union hierarchy. This was not wholly adequate to the conditions in the engineering industry, where workers saw their unions as allies in the effort to keep control of the labour process. When the government, with support from union leaders, began to propose changes in working practices, shop-floor resistance began to threaten the authority of the leaders of the Amalgamated Society of Engineers. 'What is the use in coming to terms with the leaders when the men behind them also insist on being consulted?' lamented Lloyd George in the middle of 1915.[166] This challenge became more serious during 1915 because of a sharp, though temporary, decline in real wages, which affected most industrial workers, and considerable local disruption in the West of Scotland caused by the movement of labour to the shipyards and engineering factories of the Clyde. The Munitions of War Act was largely directed to the control of labour; the promises to control employers' profits, inherent in the Treasury Agreements, were insufficiently carried out; and the formidable legal powers taken in the Act to control strikes were soon challenged. The first important case was the South Wales miners' strike of July and August 1915. The miners were determined to gain some benefit from the large increase in coal-owners profits; and the government, after first considering using the legal powers available to them, finally brought about a settlement by conceding most of what the miners wanted and imposing this on the owners. Lloyd George scored a personal success, at the expense of Runciman who had wanted to limit concessions and imprison a few strikers. On this occasion Lloyd George was particularly anxious not to force the miners to concede, because the miners' union was particularly well disciplined: he told the Welsh union organisers

[165] *Ibid.*, p. 133.
[166] Lloyd George to Henderson, 15 June 1915, L.G.P. D/17/4/1.

approvingly that 'Your men always follow your leaders'.[167] The contrast between this and his response to the A.S.E. is revealing. It reflected a long-held view of the best way to deal with organised interests, and it was a misjudgement of the temper of industrial workers during the war which persisted dangerously into his premiership.[168]

The difference between persuading trade union leaders and persuading their members was graphically illustrated on the Clyde. The Ministry of Munitions was determined to introduce flexible working practices and, soon afterwards, to introduce semi-skilled and female labour in the engineering shops. The first strike over a demarcation dispute broke out in late July 1915; another more serious outbreak in August led eventually to the imprisonment of three strikers in October, by which time the whole of the Clyde district was aroused. This coincided — the causal and personal links are much disputed — with a rent strike in Glasgow which involved the local Labour movement and took the form of marches, defiance of the police, and some small riots.[169] Although the agitation in the shipyards and engineering works had strong syndicalist roots, the rent strike had deeper origins in the community politics of the city. It posed the question, though at this stage it was no more than a question, of whether the war might not bring out a latent challenge to the entire social system. For the moment, though, the government's response was to treat the immediate symptoms with a Rent Restriction Act and an Amending Bill to the Munitions of War Act which offered concessions over the enforcement powers of the original measure.

The winter of 1915–16 saw a rapid development in the influence of the Clyde Workers Committee, the shop stewards' organisation in the West of Scotland. This alarmed Lloyd George, who talked of 'guerrilla war' in the workshops, and embarrassed the official trade union leaders. It also surprised the shop stewards, who found themselves in December 1915 involved in what their historian has called 'a unique breakthrough from the wilderness of sectarian politics; suddenly they found themselves in the leadership of a genuine mass movement.'[170] The Ministry of Munitions began to impose a policy of 'dilution', dividing tasks previously performed by skilled workers and introducing women and non-union workers into the engineering shops. The C.W.C. resisted, circulating pamphlets which clearly contravened the Defence of the Realm Act, and Lloyd George tried to rally the workforce against the shop stewards' leadership by a

[167] Wrigley, *Lloyd George and the British Labour Movement*, p. 123.

[168] For a fuller exposition, see John Turner, '"Experts" and Interests: David Lloyd George and the dilemmas of the expanding state, 1906-1919', in Roy Macleod, ed., *Government and Expertise in Britain 1815-1919* (Cambridge: Cambridge University Press, 1988).

[169] David Englander, *Landlord and Tenant* (Oxford: Oxford University Press, 1983), chs 10–12.

[170] James Hinton, 'Rank and File Militancy in the British Engineering Industry, 1914-1918', London University Ph.D., 1969, p. 164.

personal visit to Tyneside and the Clyde over Christmas 1915, whence
he returned to enter the Cabinet crisis over conscription. The visit culminated in a disastrous meeting on Christmas morning: although Lloyd
George probably won the sympathy of most of his audience, the minority
was extremely hostile and its attitude was reported in the local socialist
newspaper, *Forward*, which Lloyd George immediately ordered to be suppressed. The government moved promptly to impose dilution and break
the C.W.C. The technique adopted was to choose grounds on which the
shop stewards would not attract automatic support. On 2 February the
Worker was suppressed, and on 7 February three shop stewards were arrested. Although 2,000 men struck in response, the strike collapsed when
the arrested men were released on bail. Unrest flared up again in March
when David Kirkwood, the shop stewards' convenor, was forbidden to
move freely in Beardmore's works: on this occasion a number of factories
were hit by strikes, but the government arrested and deported a number of
shop stewards on 24 March. Within 5 days the main body of strikers had
returned to work and ordinary working was resumed a few days later.[171]

The defeat of the Clyde engineers' strike was an important temporary
victory for the government. Dilution was introduced rapidly, and munitions production increased so that in the 1916 offensive the army in
France was adequately supplied with ammunition for the first time. Success had been achieved by narrowing the issues in dispute, and the larger
problems raised by the rent strike were held in uneasy abeyance. While
national trade union leaders and the Labour Party at parliamentary level
accommodated themselves to the government, the Trades Councils at local level exploited the potential link between conscription, state control
of industry, and local welfare grievances to consolidate Labour's appeal to
the working class as a whole. Pensioners and soldiers' wives, as well as
the industrial workers from whom Labour's strength traditionally sprang,
were drawn into the movement's natural constituency. The co-ordination
of this effort by the Workers Emergency National Committee, though
somewhat haphazard, helped to make Labour a class party, rather than the
largely industrial party which it had been before the war.[172] Under the
Asquith Coalition, the government's response to Labour was limited to
the tactical handling of industrial disputes. With the advent of the Lloyd
George Coalition, new problems and new attitudes broadened its attack,
so that what had been a tactic of containment became a strategy, albeit
half-hearted, of counter-revolution.

[171] See Wrigley, *David Lloyd George and the British Labour Movement*, pp. 149–163.

[172] Royden Harrison, 'The War Emergency Workers' National Committee', in Asa Briggs and
John Saville, eds, *Essays in Labour History 1886–1923* (London: Macmillan, 1971); Noel Whiteside,
'Industrial Welfare and Labour Regulation in Britain at the Time of the First World War', *International
Review of Social History*, xxv (1980), 307–331.

The Asquith Coalition in Retrospect

Historical assessments of the Asquith Coalition are almost uniformly hostile. It was, certainly, a badly divided ministry and its major policy decisions were questionable. Its diplomacy was unimaginative, it took no direct control of strategy, it wasted time over economic controls, and it stumbled over manpower policy. It lost the sympathy of parliamentary supporters from both the main parties. But the most extreme contemporary critics were themselves part of the problem, and lack of foresight was not confined to Asquith, Runciman, McKenna and Grey. The fundamental differences within the Cabinet were over real problems to which no available solution was obviously right. Conscription and the Eastern strategy are the most striking examples. Lloyd George's later experience showed that it was impossible to maintain an effective Eastern strategy in defiance of the military hierarchy, and that it was prudent not to try. The decision to gamble on victory in 1916, to which all conscriptionist and anti-negotiation thinking pointed, and which Bonar Law, Curzon and others pressed in Cabinet, was shown to be wrong, largely for the reasons urged at the time by McKenna, Runciman and Grey. The fact that McKenna and Runciman were wrong about other things, in particular in underestimating the possibility of squeezing more out of the economy by more direct controls, does not invalidate their other points. Indeed, their case for postponing the imposition of comprehensive economic controls rested in part on the same set of arguments: they wished, in effect, to prosecute the war with *less* vigour, in the hope of surviving to the end. On the main issue they were defeated. For better or worse, the Asquith government did impose universal conscription as its critics wanted. It would have made no practical difference to the conduct of the war if it had done so earlier, since the constraints of munitions and training were paramount, and conscription neither encouraged the generals to use the troops more effectively nor greatly improved the exploitation of labour at home. The decision to sacrifice the civilian economy to war purposes by heavy borrowing abroad and withdrawing labour rapidly for the army seemed necessary at the time to the likes of Bonar Law and Lloyd George. In retrospect it also helps to explain some of the permanent weaknesses of the British economy after the war, which the anti-conscriptionists predicted. Moreover the military authorities so mis-handled the troops they were given, with aid and advice from many of the conscriptionists, that by the autumn of 1917 the war was in fact unsustainable without American assistance. 1917, if it proved anything, showed that all sides in the controversies of 1916 were wrong in some important particular.

Asquith's own liability for the ministry's defects must be seen in this

light. He entered the Coalition as a last resort. He had no desire to
share power on equal terms with Conservative ministers whose abilities
he despised, and whose behaviour in office tended to confirm his opinion
of them. On the main issues tackled during his premiership, conscription, Ireland, and the negotiated peace, he had clear views. He opposed
conscription because of its effect on the country's economic strength, and
he opposed negotiation because he was confident of the country's power
to win. He was committed to getting an Irish settlement but indifferent
to details, as he had been before the war, so long as the warring parties
could agree. For nineteen months he faced colleagues who continually
threatened resignation but, as he began to learn, never really wanted to
go. Only second-rank ministers like Simon and Selborne valued an honest freedom higher than the opportunities of office. His rational response
was to trim, holding his Cabinet together to save the nation from a Conservative government or a general election, both of which he reasonably
thought were less desirable than the *status quo*. Often enough the only way
to avert a break was to postpone decisions, and during the two conscription crises some days or even weeks were lost in preserving the integrity
of the Cabinet.

    But it should not be assumed that all delays and blunders of the war
were the responsibility of Asquith and his style of Cabinet leadership.
The incompetent obstinacy of the British military and naval authorities
was a force to be reckoned with, and the civilian administration was
uneven in quality. The greatest error of Asquith's administration was to
sanction the renewal of the offensive on the Western Front in the summer
of 1916. This decision was taken on the advice of Kitchener, whom
most of his colleagues by now despised, and of Sir William Robertson,
the C.I.G.S., who had been appointed in December 1915 with carefully
defined powers which made him the only channel of military advice to the
government. When ministers insisted on circumventing the Secretary of
State for War by strengthening the role of the senior military adviser, and
then resorted frequently to the *ex cathedra* statements of the General Staff
to justify the call for conscription, they diminished their own influence on
strategy. Lloyd George and the Conservative ministers were particularly at
fault in this respect, though Asquith himself preferred to leave warfare to
the generals and the Conservative back bench and the Conservative press
were permeated by military influences.[173] The egregious errors in civilian
administration were often errors of co-ordination, but these were made
much worse when a powerful ministry with a strong leader refused to

[173] Unofficial contacts between Conservative ministers and the military hierarchy are noted, for
example, in the diaries of Sir Henry Wilson, in the Imperial War Museum. Press contacts were
maintained by Lt. Col Repington, the military correspondent of *The Times*, and even through family
connections: Maxse, the editor of the *National Review*, was the brother of General Sir Ivor Maxse.

co-ordinate its actions with another. The Ministry of Munitions poached labour from the Admiralty's shipyards; the War Office enlisted the Ministry of Munitions's skilled fitters. In due course the responsible ministers settled their differences at high level. When the War Office recruited a high proportion of skilled ploughmen, the President of the Board of Agriculture could only bleat. These were serious problems, some of which were still unsolved at the end of the war, two years after Asquith's fall.

The consequences of the Asquith Coalition were thus very largely determined before the final crisis which led to its downfall. It could not be an immortal ministry; and when it fell it would inevitably leave its successor with major problems, in a political landscape hugely changed by the war. The Labour movement, though not the parliamentary Labour Party, was aroused. Ireland was a mess. The economy was overheating. The generals were out of control. Liberal ministers were at each others throats; their Conservative colleagues were no more, but no less, rancorously divided than ever. Parliament was operating under a political truce whose meaning was increasingly unclear to M.P.s., and old-fashioned party warfare was transferred to the press, with the result that more people knew about it than would have done if it had been confined to parliament. And into this far from cloudless sky drifted the Battle of the Somme.

3

THE 'DECEMBER CRISIS'
April to December 1916

...he complained bitterly that he had not been heard in his own defence;...that he was still a Liberal and had never done anything divergent from Liberal policy which his colleagues had not also done; and that he had rendered some services to Liberalism which entitled him to consideration.

Samuel's note of a conversation with Lloyd George, 7 Dec. 1916.

The Asquithian excuse for their downfall which attributed it all to a Press plot will not hold water. The power of the Press is greatly exaggerated — but apart from that L.G. needed no plot — All he had to do was to hold a pistol at Asquith's head whenever he chose, because he was the strongest man....however unpopular or mistrusted he was in the House, he carried much more weight in the country than Asquith, who was almost everywhere looked on as a lazy & dilatory man.

William Bridgeman's 'Diary', Dec. 1916.

Balfour, Law, Cecil, Curzon and others have allowed or used LG to destroy Liberal Govt. then Coalition and now the Gentlemen of England serve under the greatest cad in Europe.

John Burns's diary, 8 Dec. 1916.[1]

The reconstruction of the government in December 1916 was in a sense a palace revolution: but unlike the fall of the last Liberal government it was not a surprise to M.P.s. To describe it as a crisis, confined to the first few days of December, is a courtesy to convention, but it is easier to understand as the denouement of a long historical drama which began with the formation of the Asquith Coalition. The real crises of the piece came in April and July 1916, when the Asquith government's proposals respectively for military service and the Irish settlement were rejected by the Conservative Party in the House of Commons. So long as Conservative support for the Coalition was intact, Cabinet disagreements could be

---

[1] Samuel's note, 7 Dec. 1916, House of Lords Record Office, Samuel Papers, A/56/3; Bridgeman 'Diary' for Autumn 1916, reprinted in Philip Williamson, ed., *The Modernisation of Conservative Politics: the diaries and letters of William Bridgeman, 1904–1935* (London: Historians' Press, 1988), p. 112; Burns Diary, 8 Dec. 1916, B.L. Add. MSS 46338.

weathered; without it, the ministry was doomed. This chapter therefore describes the long process of decline as a single episode, without separating the last febrile strugglings of the Asquith regime from the developments which preceded and explained it.

The April conscription crisis revealed two things about the relationship between the Asquith ministry and its parliamentary supporters. On the one hand Lloyd George got his way by playing a strong hand. He knew that if he chose to resign over conscription he would have the support of a majority of the Conservative back bench, but that in doing so he would confirm his unpopularity in the Liberal Party. His popularity with right-wing 'ginger groups' and his tribulations at the hands of Liberal anti-conscriptionists have been amply documented and discussed. On the other hand, the Conservative leaders who 'funked' resignation were rapidly losing the sympathy of their followers. Austen Chamberlain, who thought of himself as a robust conscriptionist, remarked in April that 'I think my own party in the House quite unreasonable, & I find it difficult to submit to their... critical attitude.'[2] The difficulty for dissatisfied Conservatives was that all the plausible alternative leaders except for Carson were still in the Cabinet and apparently determined to stay there. While Carson's War Committee kept up pressure on the back benches, some of his associates began to attempt arrangements with Lloyd George. Geoffrey Robinson,[3] and Waldorf Astor M.P.[4] approached Christopher Addison to suggest that Lloyd George should immediately resign and seek a reconstruction of the government with Lord Milner as prime minister and Lloyd George as second in command. Addison described this as 'utterly absurd', and concluded that 'evidently the Conservative Party is hard put to it to find a leader other than Carson and they now feel the serious handicap of Carson's past performances'. He told Astor that Lloyd George '...was second in command already and it was an impossible position; but I would infinitely rather that he was second to a first rate man, if a lazy and undecided one like Asquith, than to a second-rate wind-bag like Milner'.[5] Nevertheless he was interested in the back-bench reaction to 'the muddle which has recently been made', and invited Astor to meet Lloyd George, together with David Davies, M.P., a member of the Liberal War Committee. At this meeting Lloyd George declined to resign, and instead prepared for a public agitation for 'Win the War' committees, in which

[2] Chamberlain to Samuel, 9 Apr. 1916, Samuel Papers A/155/IV/48/150.

[3] Editor of *The Times*. Robinson, later Dawson, was a former member of the Milner Kindergarten in South Africa.

[4] 1879–1952. Son of William Waldorf Astor, an American millionaire who later accepted a peerage. Astor was one of only two Unionist M.P.s to vote for the National Insurance Act in 1911. He was the proprietor of the *Observer* and a financial supporter of the 'patriotic labour' groups favoured by Lord Milner.

[5] Addison Diary, 1 May 1916, Bodleian Library, Addison Papers 97.

he wanted the support of the Liberal War Committee and Astor's political friends. The foundations of an important political alliance were laid.

The evidence for Lloyd George's political intentions at this juncture is mixed. The proposed 'National Efficiency' campaign would certainly have raised political tension and brought the Cabinet under fire from the Conservative Party. Lord Riddell, after observing a short conversation between Lloyd George and Davies on 28 April, recorded that ' . . . evidently he contemplates a new party — a dangerous experiment at such a time . . . . I did not tell him how unpopular he is with the working classes, who think he is endeavouring to shackle them.'[6] Yet Addison a week later described him as 'utterly disinclined to force the pace for any selfish purpose'[7] in his conversation with Astor. He had met Milner in the autumn of 1915, and in March had talked to Milner's 'Ginger Group', a motley group including Milner, Carson, Astor, F.S. Oliver, Henry Wilson and occasionally L.S. Amery.[8] During this period Milner and Oliver were openly trying to undermine the government by inducing leading members to resign, but Lloyd George's reluctance to contemplate resignation suggests that rather than be used by the Milnerites, he hoped to use them to keep up pressure on his Cabinet colleagues. The difficulty of getting Conservative leaders to resign would in any case have discouraged Lloyd George from doing so, had that ever been his intention.

Two processes now began to threaten the delicate political equilibrium of the Asquith Coalition. Lloyd George was transferred from the Ministry of Munitions, first to deal with the Irish settlement and then to take over the War Office after Kitchener's death. His new positions gave him more substantial reasons for resigning than he had had before, which will be discussed below. Among his potential supporters on the Conservative back benches, impatience with the ministry began to overwhelm loyalty to their leaders. In March Amery had found the Unionist War Committee 'all in an awful stew at the idea of passing a resolution about universal compulsory service lest it should in any way make things awkward for Bonar Law'.[9] This timidity began to evaporate after the conscription

---

[6] *Riddell Diaries*, p. 154.

[7] Addison Diary, 2 May 1916, Addison Papers 97.

[8] John Marlowe, *Apostle of Empire* (London: Hamish Hamilton, 1976), p. 249. F.S. Oliver was a director of Debenham and Freebody, but also a polemicist for federal solutions of sundry political problems and author of a biography of Alexander Hamilton. Before the war he had been closely identified with the National Service League, and in 1916 was an active proponent of universal conscription. Leopold Amery was a *Times* journalist from 1899 to 1909 but also a firm admirer of Milner. He was M.P. for Birmingham South from May 1911 and an enthusiastic Tariff Reformer. General Sir Henry Wilson was a regular officer, at this point commanding IV Army Corps. He had been closely concerned with Ulster's resistance to Home Rule, and was in regular contact with Conservative politicians including Bonar Law as well as Carson.

[9] John Barnes and David Nicholson, eds.,*The Leo Amery Diaries: Volume I, 1896–1929* (London: Hutchinson, 1980), 21 Mar. 1916, p. 128.

crisis. While the loyalists remained loyal, different sections of malcontents found fuel for their grievances.

The first target was the apparent lack of action about the Paris Resolutions: Beaverbrook reported at length to Bonar Law in June that Tariff Reformers in parliament and in the country were angry at the apparent complaisance of the leadership,[10] and when colonial matters came up in the Supply debate on 3 August the Unionist Business Committee whipped its members to brace the government's stand against Free Trade opposition.[11] This was circumspectly encouraged by Walter Long, who helped to found a new political grouping. A number of businessmen were brought together in October, with the assistance of Colonel Grant Morden, a shady Canadian entrepreneur.[12] Bull's record reveals both tone and content:

> In the cloakroom was Hugo Hirst the Chairman of the General Electric: — he sidled up to me & whispered
> I say this is a bleeding dinner isn't it?
> I beg your pardon?
> Well you know what I mean — I have come to be bled.
> How?
> Well what I want to know is how much shall I put down?
> I said I do not know.
> It turned out afterwards it was correct — 18 more or less millionaires turned up — Sir William Beardmore, Saxton Noble, Kindersley of the Bank of England & Lazard Bros, Sir Vincent Caillard, Sir Henry Samuel, Lee Wood of Brown Shipley & many others.
> Walter Long made a speech & the London Imperialists was formed: nearly every man put themselves down for £1000 & I was made Hon. Secretary — with a paper on which was written down £10,400.
> This to [illegible] London in Imperial interests like Liverpool... 13

Meanwhile Liverpool's interests had also been active, and were in some part responsible for the challenge to the government which was mounted

[10] Beaverbrook? to Bonar Law, 6 June 1916, House of Lords Record Office, Beaverbrook Papers, C/203.

[11] Bull's copy in Churchill College Archive Centre, Bull Papers, 4/14.

[12] Morden, who had parliamentary ambitions, attempted to ingratiate himself with Conservative leaders by giving them Stock Exchange tips. He was frequently bankrupt after the war and committed suicide in 1932. See John Turner, 'The British Commonwealth Union and the General Election of 1918', *English Historical Review*, ccclxviii (1978), 528–559.

[13] 'Diary Notes', 20 Oct. 1916, Bull Papers 4/14. Grant Morden later became involved in the 'Cellulose Scandal' in which large quantities of government money were squandered on a plant to manufacture aircraft 'dope', enriching Morden and a few of his friends without producing significant quantities of cellulose. Donald Coleman, 'War Demand and Industrial Supply; the "dope scandal", 1915–1919', in J.M. Winter, ed., *War and Economic Development* (Cambridge: Cambridge University Press, 1975), pp. 205–227. Of the others mentioned, Beardmore, Saxton Noble and Caillard were armaments manufacturers, the rest bankers. The 'Liverpool interests' were almost certainly the British Empire Producers' Organisation.

on 8 November 1916 in the 'Nigeria Debate'. The House divided on the Colonial Office's proposal to sell captured German palm-oil enterprises in West Africa to the highest non-German bidder. The Unionist War Committee was active on behalf of Liverpool merchants who wished, against the desire of the Colonial Office, to preserve their new-found monopoly behind a tariff barrier.[14] The trade warriors of the Conservative Right were on the march.

The Irish proposals also stimulated back-bench groups, one including Walter Guinness and such senior party figures as Sir George Younger and John Gretton, and another clustered around a young Diehard, Lord Willoughby de Broke, who raged that 'we ought to smash the Coalition ... it is simply an entrenchment for every pernicious & "democratic" fallacy.'[15] Although on this issue feeling in the parliamentary party almost certainly did not represent feeling in the country,[16] it was so hostile that Bridgeman, a junior whip, guessed that in a vote 'B. Law would have had 60 percent in his favour, though reluctantly so'.[17] On this occasion Carson was on the same side as Bonar Law, but this merely shows that the Unionist War Committee followed him because they liked his views, not because they trusted his judgement unquestioningly.

With Ireland and the Paris Resolutions setting a tone of suspicion and discontent on the Unionist side, developments over the summer sealed the fate of the Asquith Coalition. Disputes over the franchise, leading to a demand for extensive reform, reinforced the antagonism between Liberal and Conservative back-benchers and reminded them that there would be no automatic political truce after the war. The failure of the Somme campaign concentrated minds on the need for a change in war government, while discontent in the factories raised the prospect that it was beyond the power of any government to strike a balance between military and civilian demands on the economy. In this climate the political crisis broke, ostensibly over the machinery for controlling war policy. At the end of November the government was in grave difficulty. Seven days later it had given way to a new Coalition, promising dynamic action to reverse the drift to failure.

---

[14] The substance is expounded in J.O. Stubbs, 'The Impact of the Great War on the Conservative Party', in Gillian Peele and Chris Cook, eds, *The Politics of Reappraisal 1918-1939* (London: Macmillan, 1975), pp. 28–29.

[15] Willoughby de Broke to Lord Boutwood, July 1916, House of Lords Record Office, Willoughby de Broke Papers WB/11/64.

[16] 'Summary of Views of Provincial Papers', n.d. [June 1916] B.L.P. 63/6/65.

[17] Bridgeman Diary, 7 July 1916, Bridgeman Papers.

The Franchise Factor

The high summer of 1916, just before the parliamentary recess, was marked by a directionless irritability among the government's critics. Apart from an attempt by Churchill to intervene again in politics after a period of self-imposed exile in the trenches, no specific objection to war policy was mounted. In any case the government's principal enemies were unlikely to be convinced by Churchill's thesis that the offensive was futile. Instead the Liberal and Unionist War Committees combined to embarrass the government over the enfranchisement of servicemen. This effort illustrates the remarkable effect of war upon the political meaning of difficult issues. The reform of the franchise had of course been a highly contentious issue before the war: not only had women's suffrage divided the parties, but the Liberals hoped to alter the plural voting provisions of the 1884 legislation, which they thought gave their opponents an advantage. Here was a straightforward partisan issue, of the type which might have been expected to fade away during the war.

Nevertheless, the franchise issue grumbled along after the outbreak of war, since some means had to be found of enabling electors who had joined the forces to cast their vote if there were a general election. The sudden invention of the Asquith Coalition prevented an immediate election without ruling out the possibility indefinitely, and the Coalition Cabinet was forced to go on considering the problem of an ageing and manifestly imperfect register. They first passed an Elections and Registration Act in July 1915, which kept the 1914 register in force until December 1916. Then they put forward another Parliament and Registration bill in December 1915 which, as well as extending the life of parliament and further postponing any work on the register, provided a means for passing the Plural Voting bill which had been introduced in March 1914 and would have lapsed under the Parliament Act but for an elaborate technicality in the new measure.[18] This caused a row in the Commons, where Bonar Law was blamed by his followers for giving in to Liberal pressure; but the conscription crisis was in full swing by the time the bill left the Lords, and the life of parliament was duly extended, though only for eight months so that an election would be due in August 1916. M.P.s who wanted, or feared, the possibility of an election, were increasingly anxious that they would have to fight on an outdated register with many electors either disqualified on residence grounds by their war service, disqualified by having been forced to seek poor relief during the economic dislocation of the early months of war, or simply prevented from voting by being in the trenches.

---

[18] The 1916 session was to be treated as though it immediately followed the 1914 session.

All sides converged during the summer of 1916 on the conclusion that something would have to be done about the register. Some thought that a simple *ad hoc* wartime register would be adequate, with a shortened residence qualification (to allow for geographically mobile munitions workers) and a temporary wartime register for servicemen; others thought a full-scale revision of the franchise was necessary or desirable. As one historian has put it, 'the Cabinet was in the position of fearing to ask for a further extension of Parliament's life without preparing for a new register, and yet appreciating that any registration proposal would . . . risk dissolving the Commons into pre-war parties, thus bringing about the election they were trying to avoid.'[19] Within the Cabinet pre-war party allegiance had little to do with it. Lloyd George wanted a soldiers' register and told Addison that 'the Tories in the Cabinet are supporting the . . . idea'; but Walter Long, at the Local Government Board, resisted it as unworkable, while a number of Conservatives in and out of the Cabinet were already toying with a more general extension of the suffrage. Meanwhile Henderson, expressing the collective view of the Labour Party, wanted universal male suffrage on a simple residential qualification, and a limited female suffrage; while among the parliamentary opposition both Simon and Carson from opposite sides loudly demanded enfranchisement, on the grounds of war service, for both the troops and the munitions workers. In mid-July, hoping to put the issue off for a few months, the Cabinet proposed a Select Committee to discover whether it was practicable to draw up a new register. In the Commons it was received rather as a previous awkward compromise, the piecemeal extension of military service proposed in late April, had been received. The ministry could find few friends, and the proposal was withdrawn amid noise, with a commitment to do something more substantial.

When the Cabinet did offer concrete reform, they were rewarded with the abuse which they had feared. After prolonging the life of parliament again with an Elections bill introduced on 14 August, they proposed a new register which would include all male householders qualified by 12 months' residence (the pre-war qualification), together with all those whose names appeared on the 1915 register (which had been determined on the basis of information largely gathered before the outbreak of war) who would have been disqualified by war service, whether in the forces or in the munitions factories. Led by Carson and Simon, the back benches harried this measure for its inadequacy and injustice. They demanded variously the full enfranchisement of fighting soldiers, even 18-year-olds, which was demanded by back-bench Unionist peers led by Salisbury, and women's suffrage as demanded by the Women's Social and Political Union and the

---

[19] Martin Pugh, *Electoral Reform in War and Peace* (London: Routledge & Kegan Paul, 1978), p. 63.

Labour Party. To fend off another defeat, Asquith offered a constitutional conference, which in due course turned into the Speaker's Conference on electoral reform. Nothing had been decided by the beginning of the recess, and the franchise issue in parliament seemed to be yet another demonstration that the Coalition Cabinet was sadly out of touch with its nominal supporters.

Clearly, though, there was more to the situation than a dispute between the front benches and the back. Protagonists of the soldiers' vote had more in mind than justice. Conservative Central Office believed that many Conservative M.P.s were afraid of the result of a wartime election in which soldiers would be excluded and 'shirkers and Conscientious Objectors' would be well represented on the register,[20] and observers in France believed that if the troops had the vote they would cast it against Asquith.[21] Some hoped that war service would have a permanently beneficial effect on the working classes' attitude to Conservatism. Lloyd George, for his part, had agents canvassing opinion in the army in France, who told him that 'without exception Ll.G. is their man',[22] and Addison was kept busy in May looking up political precedents from the American Civil War.[23] Lloyd George exhorted his admirers in May to agitate for soldiers' votes as 'the next effective step to be taken'.[24] Among this group the ultimate purpose was to replace Asquith as prime minister, though Lloyd George's own ambitions were probably more modest than those of his supporters.

Some Conservative protagonists of reform had a longer view. A leading Manchester Tory reckoned in June that '... there are nowadays large numbers of Liberals and even some Labour men whose political views are really now the same as ours and we want to make it as easy as possible for them to come over to us'.[25] Conservative Party managers began talks with the 'Patriotic Labour' movement sponsored by Lord Milner. On 23 June the junior whip William Bridgeman accompanied Steel-Maitland, the party chairman, with George Younger M.P. and the Sheffield M.P. James Hope, to meet Victor Fisher, the leader of the 'New British Labour Party' and Labour sympathisers including John Hodge M.P., C.B. Stanton M.P., and James Seddon:[26]

[20] *Ibid.*, p. 61, citing Steel-Maitland to Bonar Law, 13 June 1916, Bonar Law Papers 64/G/8.

[21] Henry Wilson to Page Croft, 30 Aug. 1916, Churchill College Archive Centre, Page Croft Papers 1/20.

[22] Not that these opinions should be relied on as an account of the views of the common soldier: David Davies, a keen but erratic Lloyd Georgian, discussed politics with 'a few officers of various grades' to elicit their views. Davies to Addison, 17 May 1916, Addison Papers 4.

[23] Addison to Davies, 23 May 1916, *ibid.*

[24] Addison Diary, 8 May 1916, Addison Papers 97.

[25] Woodhouse (Vice-chairman, Manchester Conservative and Unionist Association) to Derby, 13 June 1916, Derby Papers Lancashire 2/8.

[26] Steel-Maitland, M.P. for Birmingham East, was head of Conservative Central Office from 1911 to 1916. His political roots lay in West Midlands protectionism, and he had been Austen Chamberlain's

Their programme is to fight the I.L.P., & the Pacifists & Syndicalists & they advocate protection provided the high standard of wages is part of the protective policy, national service, an imperial policy, & the restriction of output (sic). They are ready to see Agriculture protected, & would oppose any attack on Church property. They suggest a working arrangement with the Unionist Party for 5 years after the war on these lines — and for my part I think we ought to agree as it is the only way to fight syndicalism & ultra-socialism which are bound to be very dangerous after the war.[27]

The problem was to attach voters to such a programme, and here franchise reform had its uses. Selborne, by now independent after breaking with the government over Ireland, expounded the possibilities to a sceptical Salisbury:

Personally I think it would be most unjust to women and dangerous to the State to enfranchise the adult fighting man and no women. Dangerous to the State because I firmly believe in the steadying influence of the women voters in essentials and in the long run. Unjust to women because I believe that the interests of labour women, and of the woman's view of certain social matters, would be ruthlessly sacrificed...

When I said I was prepared for a bold course I referred to the post-war or permanent franchise.

On theory I would always enlarge the franchise by stages. But I think that the history of the war has settled the question for us. In my judgement the way that the men of our race have behaved in this war has made adult manhood suffrage inevitable; we shall have to do in one stage what I should have preferred to do in several...

I do not believe that 23 million voters will act any differently to 15 or 12. I think that a labour government is not likely to do worse now with a huge electorate than a radical government was able to do and was likely to do with the present electorate. On the whole I should prefer the labour government now. Before the war I should have been more afraid of their attitude on imperial questions. I am not afraid of that now. Of course things will be done which I vehemently dislike, but those things were already being done before the war; and the war has confirmed the intense belief which I have had now for a good many years in the instincts and intentions of my fellow countrymen and women.[28]

private secretary before he entered parliament. Younger, a Scottish brewer, was a formidable figure in the National Union who succeeded Steel-Maitland as chairman from 1917. Hope was an assistant Whip. Of the Labour men, Hodge was leader of the major steel trade union, Stanton a fiercely pro-war miners' M.P. who had recently won a by-election against an official Labour candidate in South Wales. Seddon, who had sat as Labour member for Lancashire Newton from 1906 to 1910, had been President of the T.U.C. in 1914. Victor Fisher, whose main occupation was as a journalist, had left the Labour Party in 1914.

[27] Bridgeman notes, 23 June 1916, *Modernisation of Conservative Politics*, pp. 103–104. Charles Duncan (Barrow-in-Furness; General Secretary of the Workers Union), Will Crooks (Woolwich), James O'Grady (E. Leeds; President of the T.U.C. in 1898) and Alexander Wilkie (Dundee; founder and General Secretary of the Shipwrights' Association) were named as definite sympathisers among Labour M.P.s; Stephen Walsh (Lancashire Ince; active in the Miners' Federation), John Sutton (Manchester East; a miners' M.P. like Walsh, but also a Rechabite) and J.R. Clynes (Manchester North East; a cotton spinner by trade, later President of the General and Municipal Workers, the only prominent anti-conscriptionist in the group) were noted as possible supporters.

[28] Selborne to Salisbury, 25 Aug. 1916, Bodleian Library, Selborne Papers 6.

Pressed further by Salisbury, he urged that 'the existing franchise gives organised labour a larger share of power than it is entitled to considering its proportion to the whole population, and I think that an enlargement of the franchise, and especially the introduction of women voters, will tend to correct the error.'[29] Franchise reform, in short, was not a nine-day wonder among idle M.P.s in the silly season: it was an issue on which to break the Asquith Coalition in the short term, and in the long term to break the Liberal Party.

The Strategic Dilemma

Asquith's parliamentary skills were just enough to keep a divided opposition at bay during the summer and early autumn. The final downfall of the ministry was brought about by forces working from within, which took advantage of the political tension outside, and to some extent encouraged it. Until the final weeks of the Somme offensive on the Western Front, the Cabinet had always been able to hope, against the evidence, that it would be possible to reach a consensus about which war to fight and how to fight it. In November, almost exactly two years after the trench lines had been established, that hope finally collapsed. Lloyd George and his associates then broke the Coalition to get a new war policy, using as a battering ram a House of Commons which barely understood the issues involved.

The generals had been given their heads on April 7 by a War Committee decision which sanctioned the renewal of the offensive on the Western Front. The course of the strategic 'debate' over the next three months showed how difficult it was for the Asquith Coalition to run a war while arguing about matters of fundamental political conviction like the Irish settlement. Largely preoccupied with the rebellion and its political consequences, the Cabinet in May had also to live through the aftermath of their bungling over the Military Service Act. Then on 5 June Kitchener was drowned on his way to Russia, leaving a vacancy at the War Office which was at first filled by Asquith himself. Asquith, understandably, did not enquire further into a strategic decision which had already been taken. He was ready to be impressed by the improvement in men and methods since his last temporary tenure of the War Office after the Curragh incident,[30] and final preparations for the summer offensive went on largely in France. Lloyd George, rather reluctantly, agreed on 17 June to take

[29] Selborne to Salisbury, 12 Sept. 1916, *ibid.*

[30] Asquith to Lloyd George, 6 July 1916, quoted John Grigg, *Lloyd George: from peace to war* (London: Methuen, 1985), pp. 361–362.

over the War Office, but postponed his entry into the office until 6 July, by which time there was no further work to do in Ireland. He made no change in the Kitchener–Robertson agreement, and even accepted as his parliamentary under-secretary Lord Derby, described by Lloyd George's biographer as 'the soldiers' pet'.[31] The course of war in May and June diverted attention from criticism of the generals' strategy on the Western Front. The Austrians first attacked on the Italian front on 15 May, with enough effect to persuade the British government to send a small quantity of guns and equipment to help the retreating Italians.[32] Then, early in June, the Russian attack under Brusilov caused casualties amounting to between one third and one half of the Austro-Hungarian army.[33] Together with the entry of Romania into the war on 17 August, this activity marked what a recent historian has called 'the high point of Allied success' in the early years of the war.[34] The Anglo-French attack on the Western Front should have been the final blow which brought the Central Powers to sue for peace, and thereby brought strategic debate in Britain to an end.

But of course it did not. The attack on the Somme, a greater and more futile catastrophe for the British army than any which its own or anyone else's generals had ever inflicted upon it, began with a week of bombardment. On 1 July 57,000 men became casualties in the first attack, which won an area of about three square miles.[35] Although by the end of the month the rate of loss had slowed down to about 18,000 a week, it was clear within days that Haig's plan had failed. It is also clear now that Haig had within a few days changed his plan, or rather changed it back to what it had been before the detailed planning of the offensive in March and April. Kitchener, Robertson and the War Committee had sanctioned the offensive on the assumption that it would not be a bid to break through the German lines. Haig had elaborated this into a plan to get 'a combined force of French and British across the Somme and fighting the enemy in the open'.[36] When this manifestly failed to happen, he reverted to the previous conception of what he was doing, killing as many Germans as possible with no great regard for territorial gains. This enabled him to claim success, and although it did nothing to please

---

[31] Grigg, *Lloyd George: from peace to war*, p. 360.

[32] David French, *British Strategy and War Aims, 1914–1916* (London: Allen & Unwin, 1986), p. 203.

[33] Norman Stone, *The Eastern Front, 1914-1917* (London: Hodder & Stoughton, 1975), pp. 232–263.

[34] French, *British Strategy*, p. 210.

[35] See Martin Middlebrook, *The First Day on the Somme* (London: Allen Lane, 1971), *passim*, and cogent new material in Trevor Wilson, *The Myriad Faces of War* (Oxford: Polity Press, 1988), pp. 323–337.

[36] National Library of Scotland, Haig Papers, Diary, 5 Apr. 1916, cited in French, *British Strategy*, p. 202.

ministers who thought the casualties were disproportionate to the alleged gains,[37] it made it difficult for them to resist his demands for more troops.

Such was the predicament inherited by Lloyd George when he took over the War Office. Lloyd George's personal dilemmas in this office reflect the difficulty shared by the whole Cabinet. Once the offensive was started it was dangerous to decry its success, because its purpose was to convince the Germans that Entente resources were great enough to wear down the Central Powers and that the Entente governments were willing to carry on to the end. The new Secretary of State seems to have realised very rapidly that Haig's tactics were wrong, but he supported the strategy of a combined Allied offensive and could not bring political pressure to change the army's tactics in the way he had used his contacts with the press and the back bench to stoke up the fires for conscription. The entry of Romania into the war, which was settled by the Treaty of Bucharest on 17 August, seemed to justify the combined strategy, and even the Anglo-French force in Salonika seemed on the point of doing something useful in a diversionary attack on the Bulgarians. The Cabinet as a whole, conscriptionist and anti-conscriptionist, Conservative and Liberal, was under pressure from the Dardanelles and Mesopotamia commissions. All the political pressures were towards solidarity with colleagues, and Churchill's returning to the Commons at Carson's inspiration to attack the conduct of the Somme offensive found little sympathy from within the Cabinet.

The political atmosphere was markedly changed by the rapid collapse of the Romanian army and by the sudden deterioration of Lloyd George's relations with the military hierarchy. On 11 September, during an extended visit to France, he questioned Marshal Foch[38] about British tactics on the Somme, observing that 'he gave Haig all the guns and ammunition and men he could use, and nothing happened'. This implied criticism was reported to Haig, to Joffre, to Robertson and, through Haig's staff, to the *Morning Post*, which attacked Lloyd George on 28 September.[39] This incident marked the beginning of a fierce campaign of press leaks which led Lloyd George to instruct the Army Council to prevent communication between officers, officials and the press, and led Robertson to appeal directly to the King for support.[40] Lloyd George was humiliated by the shackles of the Kitchener–Robertson agreement, which enabled

---

[37] Runciman to Samuel, 8 July 1916, Samuel Papers A/46.

[38] Ferdinand Foch commanded the French forces in the north in the battle of the Somme, but was then *dégommé*. He was to return, at Lloyd George's instance, as Allied *generalissimo* in April 1918: see below, p. 287.

[39] See Grigg, *Lloyd George*, pp. 380–384 for an account of this visit; Sassoon to Northcliffe, 14 Sept. 1916, British Library, B.L. Northcliffe Dep. 8.

[40] D.R. Woodward, *Lloyd George and the Generals* (London: Associated University Presses, 1983), pp. 107–113.

his subordinate to ignore him. He was even more frustrated by the real strategical impasse brought about by the standstill on the Somme. Now that both the 'breakthrough' and the 'wearing out campaign' had come to an indeterminate conclusion, he wanted to support Romania by reinforcing the Balkans. He openly attacked Robertson's position on 9 October in the War Committee,[41] only to be met by a threat of resignation and a particularly blatant leak to Northcliffe.[42] This protracted feud had a profound effect on Lloyd George's political position. For the first time since the previous autumn he found himself opposed by the majority of the Conservative press. Ireland and his tenure of the War Office had separated him from many of his erstwhile allies in the Cabinet, without improving his relations with McKenna and Runciman. This made it more difficult than ever to get his own way within the Cabinet, and presaged the final downfall of the Asquith ministry.

The Crisis Breaks

The final act of the drama was surprisingly disconnected from the episodes which had seemed to make it possible. On 3 November, at the War Committee, Lloyd George set out a comprehensive indictment of Britain's strategic policy and its execution. It was a performance comparable in range to his memorandum of 22 February 1915, which had done so much to establish the conditions for a Coalition. His main contention was that the policy of attrition had failed, because Entente losses had exceeded enemy losses in the 1916 campaigns; but he also took the opportunity to condemn the government's lackadaisical attitude to economic controls, warning that the endurance of the civilian population would be tested unless further steps were taken to guarantee the availability of transport and food. Taking a stand on the need to maintain popular morale, he demanded that strategy should be framed to produce real victories, by which he meant a shift of emphasis to the East. The Cabinet agreed to arrange an inter-Allied conference to take political decisions about the strategy for 1917, which was intended to pre-empt the conference of generals to be held at Chantilly on 15 November. On the face of it Lloyd George, who was by now talking of the Somme offensive as 'a bloody and disastrous failure',[43] had achieved a considerable *coup*, undoubtedly helped by Robertson's absence from the meeting. He had taken a position which gave him

[41] War Committee, 9 Oct. 1916, P.R.O. CAB 42/21/3.

[42] On which see *Stevenson Diary* for 12 Oct. 1916, p. 115; Northcliffe to Sassoon, 18 Oct. 1916, B.L. Northcliffe Dep. 8.

[43] Churchill College Archive Centre, Hankey Papers, Diary, 1 Nov. 1916.

common ground with a majority of his colleagues, and could hope to use the inter-Allied conference as a lever against Robertson and Haig.

In the event the conference went wrong, for reasons which even now are not entirely clear. Robertson contrived to have the two conferences held simultaneously, so that the politicians would have to consider the generals' plan rather than vice versa. Then Asquith refused to read out the whole of a 'most gloomy document' which Lloyd George had prepared for the conference, on the grounds that it would 'outrage Robertson and do no good'.[44] Instead a 'bowdlerised and attenuated form' of it was read to an informal meeting with French ministers.[45] The generals agreed to repeat the combined offensive of the previous campaigning season, including an effort in the Balkans in which the Salonika army, reinforced to 23 divisions, would attack in concert with the Russian and Romanian armies in the north. These proposals were approved by the politicians, even though Robertson and Joffre had declined to send substantial reinforcements to Russia or Salonica. The politicians also resolved to keep control of strategy in their own hands, though it is difficult to see in this anything more than a form of words.[46]

The significance of this meeting for the fall of the Asquith government is a puzzle. Strategy was not the only, or necessarily even the most important issue between Lloyd George and his colleagues. Lloyd George told Hankey on 17 November, and repeated in his memoirs, that the Paris meeting convinced him that it was essential to bring about a change in the direction of the war.[47] However, on 18 November he told Frances Stevenson that the conference was 'very satisfactory in the decisions which they came to',[48] and his subsequent actions were consistent with a longer-hatched plan, concerned as much with the civilian economy and even with the survival of the political system as it was with strategy. Before his return he wired to request a meeting with Bonar Law, which would have taken place if Bonar Law had not already arranged to dine with Sir Henry Wilson to discuss the military situation.[49]

Since early November, in fact, Lloyd George had been involved with Carson in a complex attempt to put pressure on the Cabinet to get what Beaverbrook called 'a War Council with autocratic powers'.[50] Beaverbrook's preoccupation with the demand for change in the machinery of

[44] Hankey Diary, 9 & 11 Nov. 1916.
[45] Hankey, *The Supreme Command*, II, 560.
[46] War Committee, 21 Nov. 1916, P.R.O. CAB 22/72.
[47] Hankey, *Supreme Command*, II, 562–563.
[48] *Stevenson Diary*, p. 124.
[49] Beaverbrook, *Politicians and the War*, p. 337.
[50] *Ibid.*, p. 314.

government, shared by most subsequent writers,[51] is misleading because Lloyd George (if not Carson) was anxious about specific policies on the home front. Warning of the prospect of 'a terrible upheaval in the country' if the civilian economy were allowed to drift any further, he was pressing the Cabinet to appoint a food controller and a shipping controller.[52] He was also determined to push on with the direction of industrial labour, which he had rejected as unnecessary in 1915, but which now found support from the Manpower Distribution Board and from Edwin Montagu, his successor at the Ministry of Munitions. It is noteworthy that in November 1916 he helped to break the Asquith Coalition in the cause of industrial compulsion of a degree that his own administration was never to attempt. In the last days of November Lloyd George was not apparently trying to overthrow the government: but he found fault with almost every facet of the government's policy, and he was prepared to use the well-tried methods of intrigue, resignation threats and outside leverage to get those policies changed.

It is more obvious in a longer perspective than it was at the time that the political crisis of November and December 1916 was the product of the Somme. It was not that the administration was held responsible for the scale and futility of the losses — indeed early in the parliamentary session it was held that 'success' on the Somme was strengthening the ministry[53] — but that failure to win a significant victory, however 'victory' was defined, had momentous consequences for the conduct of the war. The 1916 offensive had been intended to bring about an early victory, before the Entente was forced by economic and financial constraints to accept an unfavourable peace or the mediation of a forbiddingly unbiased American President. To get that result, the government had knowingly weakened the civilian economy and hugely increased Britain's overseas debt. For victory it would have been worthwhile, but instead of victory there was stalemate, with the economic consequences predicted by the anti-conscriptionists. The army began to worry at the end of July that losses could not be replaced without further calls on industrial labour: this led to the establishment of the Manpower Distribution Board to adjudicate between government departments.[54] At the end of August Britain had to take over a huge tranche of France's external debt, while telling France, Russia and Italy that it was no longer possible to meet Allied demands for

---

[51] E.g. J.M. McEwen, 'The Struggle for Mastery in Britain: Lloyd George versus Asquith, December 1916', *Journal of British Studies*, xviii (1978), 131–156.

[52] War Committee Minutes, 13 Nov. 1916. P.R.O. CAB 42/24/5.

[53] Bridgeman's 'Diary' for Autumn 1916, in *Modernisation of Conservative Politics*, p. 110.

[54] On the machinery of manpower control, see Keith Grieves, *The Politics of Manpower 1914–1918* (Manchester: Manchester University Press, 1988), esp., for this period, pp. 40–62.

shipping and supplies at anything like the rate at which they were made.[55] At this point the Allied combined offensive hung in the balance. Even before it began to falter ministers and senior officials began to reassess military-financial strategy for 1917. This had stark, if predictable consequences. McKenna decided that in financial terms the Entente would be completely dependent on the United States by June 1917.[56] Robertson, on the other hand, concluded that Germany would be able to go on fighting until 1918, and that Britain would have to prepare to do the same, though he did not suggest how his manpower demands would enable industry to do so.[57] This marked the final breakdown of the consensus which had been engineered in April to enable the Cabinet to pass the second Military Service Act.

The impending collapse of the frail strategic consensus goes a long way to explain the otherwise surprising episode of the 'knockout blow' interview which Lloyd George gave to an American reporter on 26 September.[58] The Cabinet's policy of the moment was to discourage American mediation for a negotiated peace, and diplomats were making the point explicitly in Washington.[59] In that sense Lloyd George's public statement was hardly more than a repetition of the same point in inimitably crass language, which he judged would appeal both to the American public and to readers of the *Daily Mail* when Northcliffe, who had set the interview up, decided to publish it. Asked to give 'the British attitude toward the recent peace talk', he said that 'The fight must be to a finish — to a knockout blow' and insisted that 'The whole world — including neutrals of the highest purposes and humanitarians with the best of motives — must know that there can be no interference at this stage.' The only thing wrong with this was the tone, and Spring-Rice in Washington reported that even this was effective in the United States. Grey was somewhat less tolerant, complaining immediately that it was wrong to warn Wilson off in public and that mediation might now be ruled out for ever, but even he confessed 'admiration and assent' for most of the interview.[60]

The more substantial, but less noticed point was that Lloyd George now spoke in terms of a very long war, observing even that 'Time is the least vital factor' in Britain's ultimate victory. This was Robertson's view, but Balfour and Grey opposed it in Cabinet, and evidence from both the Treasury and the recruitment figures tended to contradict it. During October there was more and more evidence that Germany's economic resources,

[55] French, *British Strategy and War Aims*, p. 225; Kathleen Burk, *The Sinews of War*, pp. 78–80.
[56] Burk, *Sinews of War*, pp. 80–83.
[57] War Committee Minutes, 3 Nov. 1916, P.R.O. CAB 42/23/4.
[58] A full text is in Grigg, *Lloyd George*, pp. 424–428.
[59] French, *British Strategy and War Aims*, p. 228.
[60] Grigg, p. 429. Lloyd George, *War Memoirs*, p. 511.

as exploited by the German government, were enough for her to prevail in a longer struggle.[61] Behind the public and parliamentary excitements of Lloyd George's battle with the generals, the Asquith Coalition was re-fighting, with a more desperate intensity, the battles of December 1915 and April/May 1916. The fall of the Coalition should therefore be seen not just in the context of the Nigeria debate and the link between Lloyd George and Carson, but in the contemplation of failure and the political challenge from an industrial labour force which in late 1916 seemed un-willing to make any further concessions to the needs of the state. One side, represented by Lloyd George, wanted to make further demands, on labour as well as the rest of industry; the other side, represented by a soli-tary Lansdowne in the Cabinet, wanted to stop fighting; the undecided middle did not want to follow either course to its logical conclusion.

The manpower situation was critical because it had become apparent that outright resistance to further dilution and conscription might suddenly cripple industrial output, and recruiting, even before it was strangled by an absolute shortage of labour. After its successes on the Clyde earlier in the year the Ministry of Munitions had increased its pressure on the munitions labour force. Dilution was pressed ahead. Works holidays were postponed, at Whitsun and in July.[62] Colonial, Irish and in some cases military labour was employed, against objections from the unions and many individual English workmen. One of the most controversial expedients to improve labour productivity was to press for the extension of dilution to non-government work. This enraged the trade unions and the Labour Party, because employers were invited to use the coercive powers of the state to increase profits on private work: but it was entirely consistent with the policy of maintaining the country's trading strength as the basis for a protracted war.[63] Meanwhile the ministry's attempts to save money by keeping wages down continually provoked small strikes over pay and conditions, which were usually settled by small wage increases. During 1916 even munitions wages were rising much more slowly than the cost of living, and discontent was accordingly widespread.[64]

General discontent over dilution and pay created the conditions for a major confrontation between the skilled engineering unions and the gov-ernment over recruitment, which came to a head in November. The War Office's practice of recruiting skilled men from protected occupa-

[61] For recent discussions of comparative economic strength, see T. Balderston, 'War Finance and Inflation in Britain and Germany, 1914–1918', *Economic History Review*, 2s, xlii (1989), 222–244, and Offer, *Agrarian Interpretation*.

[62] Addison, rightly, thought this a risk to Lloyd George's standing with the unions. Addison Diary, 22–29 May, Addison Papers 97.

[63] Wrigley, *David Lloyd George and the British Labour Movement*, p. 169.

[64] C.J. Wrigley, 'The First World War and State Intervention in Industrial Relations 1914–1918', in C.J. Wrigley, ed., *A History of British Industrial Relations: Volume II* (Brighton: Harvester, 1987).

tions was economically nonsensical: the political dangers were seen in Sheffield and Glasgow during the summer, and on 16 November fitters in Sheffield went on strike over the case of Leonard Hargreaves, an A.S.E. member who had been conscripted. The initiative had been taken by the local shop stewards' committee, and on the day before the strike a union official told the ministry that 'the officials of the union cannot prevent an eruption taking place'.[65] To protect the standing of the unions, the government agreed within two days to the 'Trade Card Scheme', which gave local A.S.E. officials almost complete control over the recruitment of their members and brought the strike to an end. Shortly afterwards the scheme was extended to other skilled unions, by a conference chaired by Lloyd George. Although this was a tactical victory for the government, it could not be denied that the Ministry of Munitions was caught in a pincer movement between the shop stewards and the union hierarchies. To avoid making concessions to the shop stewards, it had to make slightly different concessions to the unions. Thus were revealed the political, rather than economic, limits of the policy of 'thorough' now being advocated by Lloyd George and the army. On 10 November Lloyd George lunched with Albert Thomas, the French Minister of Munitions, and Ramsay MacDonald. MacDonald found the Secretary of State for War 'a little depressed, as well he may be', but the main thrust of a 'very friendly talk' was that 'L.G. foreshadowed some more repression of liberties.'[66]

Another sort of political limit was illustrated by Lansdowne's intervention after the 'knockout blow' speech, which came in the form of a Cabinet paper on 13 November. It is possible to make too much of Lord Lansdowne, partly because of his much more important public intervention in late 1917, and partly because Lloyd George made too much of him in his war memoirs.[67] He was not at this stage known in public as a protagonist of negotiations. Nevertheless his memorandum was a good summary of the anti-conscriptionist case of earlier days. He argued that manpower and industrial resources were running out, and that neither the British army nor the Allies were likely to bring off the 'breakthrough' on which the strategy of 1916 had been predicated. Any offer of peace or mediation should therefore be taken seriously.[68] Lansdowne's worries

---

[65] Proceedings of a conference at the Ministry of Munitions, 15 Nov. 1916, P.R.O. MUN 5/57/320/15; Bill Moore, 'Sheffield Shop Stewards in the First World War', in L. Munby, ed., *The Luddites and Other Essays* (London: Michael Katanka Books, 1971), pp. 245–261.

[66] MacDonald Diary, 18 Nov. 1916. PRO 30/69/1753.

[67] Lloyd George, *War Memoirs*, pp. 514–520. Lloyd George's suggestion (p. 514) that Lansdowne's remarks 'startled the Cabinet' is absurd. For the 'Lansdowne letter' of November 1917, see below, pp. 248–252.

[68] 'Terms on which a Peace might be considered', 13 Nov. 1916, CAB 37/159/32.

added to the Cabinet's difficulties in the middle of November, while Lloyd George was urging his colleagues to defy all economic and political doubt.

Most of the story of how this internal Cabinet struggle about policy became an external parliamentary struggle about power has been told, at length, by Beaverbrook, and corrected by later historians.[69] Lloyd George was already in touch with Carson before the Nigeria episode, and dined with him on the evening of the debate.[70] Back-bench M.P.s were expecting trouble, but unsure of its nature: Burns wrote of the House as 'dreary, uninteresting, almost moribund' on 26 October, of a 'disconcerting' rumour of a separate peace between Germany and Russia on 31 October, coupled with a rumour that 'G[rey] AJB[alfour] and L[ansdowne] had definitely decided against LG', and that 'AJB, BL and others are increasingly leaving the troublous questions to P.M. and Liberal Ministers' on 2 November.[71] No matter that this was a bad guess at the internal discussions of the Cabinet: what mattered was that outsiders could sense that the Cabinet was about to break up. The Conservative Party was clearly at odds with itself over Ireland, and the two back-bench committees were dissatisfied with Bonar Law's leadership. In early November Bonar Law was gaining ground over Carson, and the celebrated Nigeria debate has been described as 'a minor triumph' for his leadership, since his majority among Conservatives was higher than in the previous division.[72] But he could not count on further gains, and by 12 November he had made it clear to his confidant Max Aitken, and through him to Lloyd George, that he was contemplating resignation.[73]

Lloyd George, Carson and Aitken met on 13 November, and according to Frances Stevenson it was suggested then that Lloyd George should form a ministry, which he refused to do.[74] Then followed Lloyd George's efforts in Paris. On his return he met Bonar Law and Carson on 20 November; and after he had reassured Bonar Law that he had not helped Carson to concert the opposition in the Nigeria debate, the three men hatched the plan for a new War Committee of three people. At this point they imagined themselves in the parts.[75] The details of machinery were not significant: what Lloyd George wanted was 'someone to support him and less opposition to face' in Cabinet, and he thought that Carson and Bonar

---

[69] See pp. 8–9 above.

[70] n.d. Memorandum by Stamfordham, RA GV 1048A/6.

[71] Burns Diary, B.L. Add. MSS 46338.

[72] Stubbs, 'Impact of the Great War on the Conservatives', p. 29. In a division on 26 October 68 Conservatives had voted against the government, 19 in favour: over Nigeria the government had a majority of 72 to 65 among Conservatives.

[73] Beaverbrook, *Politicians and the War*, p. 305.

[74] *Stevenson Diary*, 14 Nov. 1916, p. 123.

[75] This is Beaverbrook's account in *Politicians and the War*, pp. 342–343, accepted by Lloyd George in *War Memoirs*, p. 586 and, as to this part, not challenged by subsequent writers.

Law could be relied upon.[76] His complaint about the existing Cabinet was not its intellectual weakness or its methods, but the presence of too many 'able men with strong opinions'. By contrast, 'Bonar Law ought to be kept in cold storage and brought out when you want him to make a speech. He makes good speeches, but in Council he is not so good.'[77]

With a 'wave of anxiety'[78] spreading through the Cabinet, and secondary figures like Walter Long believing that 'things are as bad as they can be and I really don't believe the Gov. can usefully and creditably go on much longer',[79] the future of the ministry was at the mercy of a conflict of personalities. Specific demands about policy and machinery began to take second place, and now appear in the story as a means to the end of reconstructing the government. On Friday 25 November, after a number of meetings with Carson and Lloyd George, Bonar Law wrote to Asquith proposing a small War Committee with Lloyd George as chairman. After considering it over the weekend, Asquith refused, arguing that it would undermine his own authority because it would appear to have been 'engineered' to enable Lloyd George to succeed him as prime minister 'not perhaps at the moment, but as soon as a fitting pretext could be found'.[80] This appears to have put Carson, Bonar Law and Lloyd George in a position of some confusion. The most likely reading of Beaverbrook's opaque account of the next two days is that Bonar Law lost his nerve and started to work for a compromise between Lloyd George and Asquith, while Carson became more determined to break the government.

The crisis had become public knowledge on Thursday 23 November through H.A. Gwynne,[81] the editor of the *Morning Post*, who had written a strong leader at Carson's inspiration praising Lloyd George as a potential 'saviour'. This provoked Gardiner[82] in the *Daily News* of Friday 25th to warn Lloyd George to 'refuse the proffered crown of the *Morning Post*', and the cat was out of the bag and running. After Asquith's rejection of the Lloyd George–Bonar Law–Carson plan, the Liberal press took up the issue, and on Wednesday 29 November both the *Daily Chronicle* and the *Westminster Gazette* carried leader comment which was openly critical of 'delay and indecision' in the Cabinet. Up to this point only the *Morning*

[76] *Stevenson Diary*, 22 Nov. 1916, pp. 126–127.

[77] *Lord Riddell's War Diary*, 26 Nov. 1916, p. 223.

[78] *Crawford Papers*, 18 Nov. 1916, p. 365.

[79] Long to Derby, 14 Nov. 1916, Derby Papers, Public Life Papers.

[80] Jenkins, *Asquith*, p. 180. Asquith's reply was partly drafted on 26 Nov. 1916 at the Wharf, and the text exists in the Bonar Law Papers.

[81] H.A. Gwynne had edited the *Standard* from 1904 to 1911 and the *Morning Post* since 1911. He was a man of tumultuous hatreds, always willing to see treacherous conspiracies among Liberal politicians.

[82] A.G. Gardiner was one of the most prolific as well as the most respected of Liberal journalists. He remained loyal to Asquith throughout the war.

Post, which in Gwynne's hands was a political mouthpiece for Carson, and *The Times* which was run by its editor Geoffrey Robinson as an extension of the anti-Asquithian ginger group around Carson and Milner, were deliberately concerting their public statements with the private discussions of politicians. The rest were working on, and perhaps working up, a political atmosphere. On Friday 1 December Lloyd George took direct steps to broaden the newspaper campaign against the present structure of the government by seeing Burnham, the proprietor of the *Daily Telegraph*, and Northcliffe who owned the *Daily Mail* as well as *The Times*; Aitken promised the explicit support of the *Daily Express*, and Lloyd George appears also to have leaked his preferences to Sir Henry Dalziel of the Liberal War Committee, who owned the Sunday *Reynold's News*.[83] These proprietors fulfilled their promises over the weekend, but they had been pre-empted by Friday's *Evening Standard*, which had apparently been inspired by J.W. Pratt, M.P., secretary of the Liberal War Committee,[84] to appeal to Lloyd George to 'do your part without counting the cost'. In this way, press comment came to reflect the nuances of private discussion rather well: as the terms of discussion shifted from policy to structure and thence to personalities, so the content of newspaper criticism changed.[85]

On 30 November — long after the crisis had become a public issue — the Conservative members of the Cabinet met to hear from Bonar Law about the progress and purpose of his negotiations with Lloyd George and Carson. This appears to have been the first time that most of them learned about direct contacts between the three men, and their reaction was generally hostile though their reasons for disliking the proposals varied significantly. Robert Cecil, who had the previous day tried to deflect the proposal for a new small War Committee by proposing a 'Committee of National Organisation' for the home front under Lloyd George's chairmanship, objected to an arrangement with Lloyd George, as did Chamberlain and probably Curzon, on the grounds that Lloyd George was not to be trusted and that Asquith was therefore to be preferred.[86] Long disliked Lloyd George while openly preferring him to Asquith as a war leader,[87] while Lansdowne, according to Beaverbrook, wanted to keep

---

[83] Dalziel, M.P. for Kirkcaldy, was a generous contributor to Liberal funds. He is not to be confused with Davison Alexander Dalziel, the Conservative M.P. for Brixton, who was also a newspaper proprietor.

[84] M.P. for Linlithgow; he was later a Lloyd George Liberal Whip, and later still a member of Mosley's New Party.

[85] On the role of the press in the crisis see Stephen Koss, *The Rise and Fall of the Political Press in Britain: Volume II the twentieth century* (London: Hamish Hamilton, 1984), pp. 298–306; J.M. McEwen, 'The Press and the Fall of Asquith', *Historical Journal*, xxi (1978).

[86] Memorandum by Cecil, 27 Nov. 1916, P.R.O. CAB 37/160/21; *Crawford Papers*, pp. 368–370. Asquith prudently accepted this proposal in the War Committee on 29 November.

[87] Long to Bull, 2 Dec. 1916, Bull Papers 4/14; Long to Bonar Law, 2 Dec. 1916, Wilts. Record Office, Long Papers 947/563, and reprinted in Beaverbrook, *Politicians and the War*, pp. 368–369.

Asquith because he recognised Lloyd George as the greatest obstacle to a negotiated peace.[88] The majority at the meeting, Lansdowne dissenting, therefore demanded that Bonar Law press for two committees, one for civil and one for military affairs, rather than for the Lloyd George–Carson plan. Beaverbrook has correctly observed that in taking on his Cabinet colleagues Lloyd George had at this point one doubtful Liberal ally, Montagu, and Bonar Law had no Conservative allies at all. But this is not the whole truth, since Long had certainly made up his mind that the present regime would have to fall and thought he had the backing of Conservative M.P.s,[89] while most of his other colleagues were convinced of the need for some major change, if not the change which Bonar Law envisaged.

The proposal for a civil committee, which had first been suggested by Robert Cecil, carried its own political baggage. Cecil's original idea had been for a committee under Lloyd George to force through a measure of industrial compulsion. In his 27 November note he suggested a three-man committee under Lloyd George to work in close collaboration with the War Committee — which Cecil probably expected to be claimed by Asquith. The point of the civil committee was to replace the ineffective Manpower Distribution Board, which had by now completely succumbed to the hostility of the Ministry of Munitions, and had, for example, been kept on the sidelines in the Trade Card dispute. Asquith, in accepting the proposal, took care to put Samuel and Runciman on the committee to counterbalance the compulsionist instincts of Cecil and Chamberlain. The War Office had proposed compulsory national service to the War Committee on 20 November, and supported this with a fierce memorandum from the military members of the Army Council on the 28th,[90] and on 30 November the War Committee accepted it.[91] Runciman immediately wrote in protest to Hankey, alleging that the Board of Trade and representatives of organised labour had not been consulted. In view of this his appointment to the committee was understandably taken by the compulsionists as an attempt by Asquith to hamstring any strong move towards extending conscription or compulsory industrial service.

With only unsteady support from Conservative Cabinet opinion, Lloyd George now made a direct demand for a three-man War Committee from which the prime minister would be excluded, and which would have powers to give orders to the departments. The only limit to its authority was to be the prime minister's residual power to refer a question

[88] Beaverbrook, *Politicians and the War*, pp. 373–374.

[89] Long to Lansdowne, 1 Dec. 1916, Lansdowne Papers, cited by R.P. Murphy, 'Walter Long, the Unionist Ministers, and the Formation of Lloyd George's Government in December 1916', *Historical Journal*, xxix (1986), 737.

[90] 'Supply of Men for the Army', 28 Nov. 1916, P.R.O. WO 162/28.

[91] Hankey Diary, 30 Nov. 1916, Hankey Papers.

to the full Cabinet for decision. Meeting Lloyd George on 1 December, Asquith insisted that the prime minister should be the active chairman of the committee, but otherwise accepted the substance of the proposals apart from 'the delicate and difficult question of personnel'.[92] Lloyd George discussed Asquith's response with Bonar Law on the Friday evening, and on Saturday 2 December sent the prime minister's written reply across to Bonar Law with the stirring reminder that 'The life of the country depends on resolute action by you now.'[93] Resolute action had to wait until the next day, when the Conservative ministers (except for Lansdowne) met three times at Bonar Law's house, Pembroke Lodge. At the first meeting, to which according to Beaverbrook (who was in the house but not at the meeting) the ministers 'arrived with copies of "Reynold's" newspaper', a letter was drafted calling on Asquith to resign to permit a reconstruction of the ministry. Beaverbrook, but nobody else, has suggested that this was a manoeuvre in support of Asquith; Crawford, Curzon and Chamberlain all let it be known that they intended some drastic reconstruction of the ministry in which Lloyd George's abilities would be recognised by real influence.[94] Bonar Law's colleagues were annoyed that Lloyd George's position had been made public, but there is only speculation to support the suggestion that they collectively threatened resignation because 'they feared ... that a new arrangement might be made between Lloyd George and Asquith, with Bonar Law weakly acquiescing, while they themselves remained little more than bystanders.'[95] The course of events was too rapid and too obscure to permit such a clear-cut or unanimous calculation.

Bonar Law took the resolution to Asquith, and relayed its content without showing him the text: but since the text was drafted collectively in terms of deliberate ambiguity, this is unlikely to have made much difference. Asquith, after discussion with Bonar Law, assumed that the resolution threatened his position, and was not a gesture of support. This perception is important: Bonar Law was not a dissimulator, and Asquith was never anything but extremely shrewd about the political meaning of the poses struck by his colleagues. That Asquith believed the situation to be dangerous for him is better evidence for the state of the crisis than the recollections of individual Conservatives, let alone Beaverbrook's later glosses. His response was to summon Lloyd George and make a quick and fairly amicable deal which conceded the appointment of a War Commit-

[92] Both men produced documents, which are reprinted in full in Beaverbrook, *Politicians and the War*, pp. 387–389.

[93] Beaverbrook, *Ibid.*, p. 406.

[94] *Ibid.*, p. 417; Austen Chamberlain to Lord Chelmsford, 8 Dec. 1916, Birmingham University Library, Austen Chamberlain Papers AC 15/3/8, part-reproduced in Austen Chamberlain, *Down the Years*, pp. 115–128; Curzon to Lansdowne, 3 Dec. 1916, Lord Newton, *Lord Lansdowne*, pp. 452–453; *Crawford Papers*, pp. 371–372.

[95] McEwen, 'Struggle for Mastery in Britain', p. 143.

tee under Lloyd George and postponed the discussion of personnel until Monday. This was conveyed to Bonar Law who, like Lloyd George and Asquith, thought that the crisis was thereby brought to an end.

Bonar Law's colleagues, meeting for the third time in the evening, were surprised to learn that he had not read Asquith the text, but most of them appeared to accept the outcome of the meeting.[96] Chamberlain, Curzon and Cecil apparently did not accept it, but there is considerable doubt about whether they went so far as to go to Asquith that evening or even the next day to express their support for him against Lloyd George, as Beaverbrook alleged.[97] Even if they did, most reports of what they said are consistent with the view that they wanted a reconstruction under Asquith which would give effective control to Lloyd George, not a breach which would exclude Lloyd George from the government. Asquith now commissioned Crewe to prepare a scheme for a new War Committee, and retired to bed, though not before writing to Pamela McKenna that 'the "Crisis" shows every sign of following its many predecessors to an early and unhonoured grave'.

He was proved wrong by the appearance in Monday's *Times*, *Morning Post*, and *Manchester Guardian* of accounts which depicted the settlement as a personal defeat for him at the hands of Lloyd George. It is now known that the responsibility for this lay with Carson, in so far as it was not the obvious conclusion for any alert editor to draw and an obvious point for an established critic of Asquith to make. Since all three editors were known partisans of Lloyd George, their responses might easily have been predicted. Asquith reacted with anger, whether real or feigned, and wrote to Lloyd George, protesting that 'unless the impression is at once corrected that I am being relegated to the position of an irresponsible spectator of the War, I cannot possibly go on.'[98] As Lloyd George's most recent biographer observes, this was 'far from being an outright repudiation of the previous evening's arrangements', and Lloyd George hoped to avoid a breach by writing a conciliatory reply.[99] There is no satisfactory evidence besides Beaverbrook's assertions that Asquith had any other important discussion with Cabinet colleagues from either party before seeing the King at 12.30 to ask permission to reconstruct his government. He returned to the House of Commons where, according to Beaverbrook's account, he saw Bonar Law and told him that his enthusiasm for the new arrangement had cooled because his Liberal and Conservative colleagues were opposed

[96] *Crawford Papers*, pp. 371–373.

[97] McEwen 'Struggle for Mastery in Britain', 149; Murphy, 'Walter Long', 738–739; Fraser, 'Lord Beaverbrook's Fabrications'; the major source is Chamberlain's account cited above, which is contradictory both in detail and in the general thrust of its interpretation.

[98] The correspondence is reproduced in Lloyd George, *War Memoirs*, pp. 590–591; in Jenkins, *Asquith*, pp. 504–509; and in many other accounts.

[99] Grigg, *Lloyd George*, p. 460.

to the new War Committee. Bonar Law then pursued him to Downing Street after Question Time where

> ...he found Grey, Harcourt, and Runciman, waiting outside the Cabinet Room with the Premier inside. He got hold of Bonham-Carter and asked him to take in a message to the effect that he wished to see the Premier urgently and in advance of the waiting Liberal colleagues. He was duly admitted, but found Mckenna closeted with Asquith. He then urged on the Prime Minister very strongly the necessity of standing by Sunday's agreement on the appointment of a War Council.
>
> ...Failing to receive any satisfactory reply, Bonar Law made it clear beyond all possibility of doubt that if the War Council scheme was not adopted he would break with Asquith.[100]

If this happened — and there is no independent corroborative evidence that it did — it suggests that the fall of Asquith's government was determined by a decision taken by Asquith alone, or perhaps with McKenna's advice. Roy Jenkins, Asquith's biographer, states that Asquith then wrote his second letter of the day to Lloyd George, recording his conclusion that 'it is not possible that such a Committee could be made workable and effective without the Prime Minister as its Chairman' and declining to move Balfour from the Admiralty or include Carson in the War Committee; Asquith is then supposed to have dined with Edwin Montagu and 'refused to discuss the situation at all'.[101]

The most immediate surviving contemporary account of discussions within the Liberal section of the Cabinet, a narrative by Herbert Samuel, is at odds with these printed accounts.

> On the evening of Monday Dec 4 the Prime Minister asked me to come to Downing St where were also Grey, McKenna, Harcourt and Runciman. Henderson came in later. The P.M. explained Lloyd George's proposals, which were in effect that the War Committee of the Cabinet should consist of Ll.G, Bonar Law, Carson and Henderson, that the P.M. should see its agenda before its meetings, have a veto on its decisions, and, while not usually attending its sittings, have the right to be present when he wished. He asked me when I came in whether I thought his acceptance would be an abdication of his position and be inconsistent with his responsibilities as P.M. I said I thought it would. The others were all of the same opinion. I expressed the view that the country desired both the P.M. and Ll.G. to be in the Govt., and that if the latter went, the Govt. would be greatly weakened in the eyes of the country and of the Allies. At the same time Ll.G.'s proposals were quite unacceptable. All the Liberal Ministers advised the P.M. that the right course would be for him to resign and throw upon Ll.G. the duty of forming an administration, the present position being intolerable, and quite sure to recur at short intervals. Several thought that Ll.G. would not be able to form a Govt. and that if he were it would not last. I said I thought he could and would, but that the House of Commons would probably not support it, and before long it would be for the King to choose whether he would

[100] Beaverbrook, *Politicians and the War*, p. 451.
[101] Jenkins, *Asquith*, pp. 507–510.

grant a dissolution or not. Henderson also thought that Ll.G. could form a Govt., and that several of the Unionists would join it. The P.M. expressed no final view, but said he feared that if an Ll.G.–Carson Government was formed Labour would break away and the pacifist movement would become formidable. But he was not prepared to agree to terms which would lead to a demand for fresh surrender. Grey and Runciman were strongly for immediate resignation, and the rest concurred. We were told that the Unionist members of the Cabinet had tendered their resignations the day before, but in no unfriendly spirit and in the belief that to put the possibility of an Ll.G. government to the test was the only way to place matters on a sound footing.[102]

It appears from Samuel's account that it was only after this meeting that Asquith sent his second letter of the day, withdrawing from the compromise. Unless this account is deliberately misleading, it suggests that the first collective discussion of the crisis by senior Liberal ministers happened in the evening of 4 December, not the morning as Beaverbrook has stated. It is unlikely that Asquith would have explained the proposals if he had already been through them before. Asquith's account of the attitude of the Conservative ministers is vague, at least in Samuel's report of it, and decidedly optimistic. Crawford records that Lansdowne saw Asquith at 5 p.m., but no reliable contemporary source has any other Conservative minister calling on Asquith on the Monday.[103] If Lansdowne was the source of Asquith's information, his own firm prejudices against Lloyd George might well have led him to paint a favourable picture of his colleagues' intentions.

Samuel's story allows Beaverbrook's tortuous explanation of Asquith's withdrawal from the compromise of 3 December to be simplified. Beaverbrook alleged that Asquith was forced to withdraw from his compromise with Lloyd George because of Liberal pressure, but decided instead to compel Lloyd George to resign, using the *Times* leader as an excuse, and if necessary fight an election. Bonar Law's intervention in the afternoon of 4 December thwarted that plan, whereupon Asquith turned to his third plan, to resign and 'prove that the rebels could not form an alternative ministry'.[104] To support this elaborate plot, Beaverbrook almost certainly invented a meeting of Liberal ministers in the morning of 4 December. His account of the meeting between Bonar Law and Asquith is uncorroborated, but since it came from Bonar Law himself it is probably reliable. Beaverbrook then describes a critical evening meeting, but cites in evidence a record made by Montagu, who according to Samuel was not present, which mentions ministers not present and includes statements which Samuel attributes to a meeting at 5 p.m. the following day, Tuesday

---

[102] Memorandum by Samuel, 5 Dec. 1916, Samuel Papers A/56/1.
[103] *Crawford Papers*, p. 372.
[104] Beaverbrook, *Politicians and the War*, p. 428.

5 December. On the whole Beaverbrook's account, based on Montagu's note of events, has the ring of fiction about it.

The more likely course of events is that described above, though many doubts and obscurities remain. Lloyd George went into the crisis wanting a reconstruction which would remove his Cabinet opponents. This did not necessarily mean that he needed to be prime minister. Bonar Law and Carson wanted to support him, if necessary to the point that he would replace Asquith. Other leading Liberals were the Cabinet opponents Lloyd George wanted to remove, and defended themselves accordingly; other leading Conservatives, although they shared Asquith's preference for supporting the generals against civilian interference, were so unhappy about every other aspect of his leadership that they were quite content to see the Cabinet dissolved. The assertion that they were rallying in support of Asquith will not hold water except for Lansdowne and Robert Cecil: the leaders who counted — Long, Curzon, Austen Chamberlain, Derby and Balfour — wanted changes far more drastic than Asquith contemplated. Clearly there were misunderstandings, and Asquith assumed a far greater friendliness on the part of Conservative ministers than he should have done. Samuel's note suggests that Bonar Law's intervention on Monday afternoon had not affected his view of them. There is nothing but surmise to support Beaverbrook's contention that Asquith at any point hoped that Lloyd George would resign in isolation.

The Death of the Asquith Coalition

Sunday had ended with an apparent resolution of the crisis in a brief statement issued from Downing Street that the prime minister 'has decided to advise His Majesty the King to consent to a reconstruction of the Government'. Monday ended with a letter from Asquith to Lloyd George which would necessarily provoke Lloyd George's resignation. Outside the Cabinet and the inner circles of party this development had been expected with more certainty, and in many places more enthusiasm, than in Downing Street. Milner, who confessed that 'I cannot see what Ll.G. is waiting for'[105] was *parti pris*; Ramsay MacDonald merely remarked sourly on 'the Brutus which is to kill Caesar';[106] Christopher Addison, who had been a distant observer of the crisis during the previous week, decided 'on [his] own account' to canvass Liberal M.P.s about their willingness to support a Lloyd George Cabinet;[107] and Josiah Wedgwood wrote in asking for a

---

[105] Milner to Lady E.Cecil, 5 Dec. 1916, Milner Papers 353/136.
[106] MacDonald Diary, 3 Dec. 1916, PRO 30/69/1753.
[107] Addison, *Four and a Half Years*, p. 274.

job, coupling his request with the bizarre advice that 'if you are in need of Liberals you can probably bribe Harcourt to join you by offering him the Colonies'.[108] Before hearing of Asquith's final withdrawal from the compromise Lloyd George had been investigating Labour and Conservative opinion for himself, interviewing the chairman of the Conservative Party, Arthur Steel-Maitland, early on 5 December, and making approaches to J.H. Thomas, the Labour M.P. for Derby. Thomas had been suggested by Lloyd George's crony, David Davies, as an alternative Labour member of the new War Committee, perhaps because Henderson had made a public statement of support for Asquith on the previous Saturday.[109] Although the final breach was far from certain, no one could ignore the possibility that it would come, and come soon.

During the course of the day on Tuesday 5 December it became clear that Asquith's gamble had failed. Lloyd George's letter of resignation reached Asquith around noon. At 1 p.m., according to Montagu, the Liberal Cabinet ministers met again-and decided that Asquith's only course was to resign himself, calling Lloyd George's bluff. They were consciously committing their fate to the mercy of the Conservative ministers, ostensibly believing, as they had heard the previous evening, that they had offered to resign 'in no unfriendly spirit'.[110] They were sadly disappointed. Curzon, Cecil, Chamberlain and Long had met at 11 a.m on Tuesday. Whatever their views had been on Sunday, they had concluded on Monday, in full knowledge of the newspapers' interpretation of events, that the decision to offer resignation had been the right one; and by Tuesday their main concern appears to have been to look to the future rather than to preserve an Asquith Cabinet from which Lloyd George had resigned.[111] When Curzon, Cecil and Chamberlain were summoned to Downing Street at 3 p.m. they therefore refused to continue without Lloyd George, and equally firmly refused to promise that they would not serve under Lloyd George. They then betook themselves to a meeting at the Colonial Office with Bonar Law. The outcome of this meeting was a collective decision by all the Conservative ministers that their resignation must stand, and a letter to this effect was carried back across the road by Curzon.

The Liberal ministers, with Henderson, had met again at 5 p.m. to hear Asquith's report of his conversation with Curzon, Cecil and Chamberlain, and also to hear the contents of two letters written by Balfour from his sickbed. Balfour had made it clear that he would not co-operate in any

---

[108] Wedgwood to Lloyd George, 4 Dec. 1916, L.G.P. F/94/1/1.

[109] R.K. Middlemas, ed., *Thomas Jones: Whitehall Diary: Volume I 1916–1925* (London: Oxford University Press, 1969), p. 6 (Jones to E.T. Jones, 6 Dec. 1916).

[110] Jenkins, *Asquith*, p. 512.

[111] Crawford Diary for 4 Dec. 1916, *Crawford Papers*, p. 372; Chamberlain to Chelmsford, 8 Dec. 1916, Austen Chamberlain Papers AC 15/3/8. Murphy, 'Walter Long', and Fraser, 'Lord Beaverbrook's Fabrications', effectively destroy Beaverbrook's account of these transactions.

attempt to obstruct Lloyd George's plans for a new War Committee. Rather than see Lloyd George resign from the ministry, he would resign himself.[112] At 6 p.m., before any decisions had been taken, Curzon turned up with the Conservative ultimatum. This precipitated matters, and the Liberal ministers confirmed their earlier decision to resign *en bloc*, with Asquith at their head. Asquith himself does not appear to have led his colleagues towards this decision with any enthusiasm.

> The P.M. said that he could not accept Ll.G.'s proposals for a War Committee, partly because the position suggested for himself was inconsistent with his tenure of the office of P.M., partly because the suggested personnel of the committee would render it a most inefficient body, unless it was to be no more than a cloak for one man control. He foresaw grave evils from a change of administration, partly because it would mean a divided nation at home, partly because himself and Grey being so definitely identified with the war from the outset, the effect upon the Allies would be bad. (Grey did not concur in this, as Ll.G. equally personified the policy of carrying the war on to victory). He also foresaw that a general election might be the outcome, and this would be a great disaster. He evidently did not like the surrender to a revolting minister involved in resignation. However, we were all strongly of opinion, from which he did not dissent, that there was no alternative. We could not in any case carry on without Ll.G. and without the Unionists and ought not to give the appearance of wishing to do so.[113]

The waiting Curzon was informed of the decision, and Asquith set off to Buckingham Palace to tell the King.

Samuel's account tells strongly against the view that Asquith's resignation was a tactical gamble, made in the expectation that Lloyd George would be unable to form a Cabinet. The picture is that of a proud man resigning with great reluctance and under some pressure from his colleagues, because the Conservative defection had made his position untenable. Asquith's belief in his own indispensability, deftly punctured by Grey, did not quite extend to a belief in political invulnerability. But there had been a very major gamble on the previous day, undertaken on the basis of information about the intentions of the Conservative ministers which was palpably unreliable, even if not actually false at the instant when it was called into account. There is no doubt that some Conservative ministers, among whom Chamberlain and Cecil stand out, had a far higher personal regard for Asquith than for Lloyd George, but it was a grave mistake to infer from this that they would not accept Lloyd George as an alternative prime minister. Cecil's efforts, which might have included a visit to Asquith on Sunday or Monday,[114] and certainly included a written suggestion on Tuesday 5 December that Asquith should con-

[112] These letters are reprinted in Beaverbrook, *Politicians and the War*, pp. 475–477.

[113] Samuel, 'Resignation of Asquith Government', 5 Dec. 1916, Samuel Papers A/56/1.

[114] Cf. Fraser, 'Lord Beaverbrook's Fabrications'.

sider serving under Lloyd George,[115] were perhaps critical, in that they stiffened Asquith when his power to resist Lloyd George was inadequate, and then undermined him when the full results of his folly were becoming apparent. Above all, Asquith's irreducible conviction of his own right to be prime minister was a determining factor. He presented the problem to his Liberal colleagues on Monday 4 December as a problem of personal relationships and of his dignity as prime minister, and did not deviate from that interpretation of what was happening. His repeated assurances that he had 'no personal feeling of *amour propre* in the matter' ring hollow.[116] With the exception of Grey, his most trusted colleagues played up to him and thus ensured their own eclipse.

The Making of a Ministry

It was not immediately apparent that Lloyd George would succeed to the premiership. The King called on Bonar Law to form a ministry. Without explicitly refusing to do so, Bonar Law explained that 'he had come to the conclusion that he must decide between following Mr Asquith and Mr Lloyd George and, as he believed the latter would win the war before the former could do so, he had decided to follow Mr Lloyd George', and went off to consult his friends. He first consulted Asquith, who refused to serve, and in the morning before returning to the palace went with Lloyd George to see Balfour to ask him to persuade Asquith to change his mind. The upshot was a meeting at Buckingham Palace at 3 p.m. on Wednesday 6 December between Balfour, Bonar Law, Asquith, Henderson and Lloyd George. On this occasion Balfour asked Asquith to serve under Bonar Law; and Henderson, who 'did not believe he could get his Party to support any Government of which Mr Asquith was not a member', urged him to agree. Asquith made to decline, but agreed to take the proposition to his friends.[117] The state of play was immediately known in Whitehall. At 4.30 Arthur Murray discussed the situation at the Foreign Office with Eric Drummond, Grey's private secretary.

It appears that Bonar Law said almost at once that he could not form a government, and the King, therefore, sent for Lloyd George. The proposition has been put forward that Asquith should join the Government. Lloyd George and Bonar Law have offered him any position he likes... He has not yet made up his mind whether

---

[115] Chamberlain to Chelmsford, 8 Dec. 1916, Chamberlain Papers AC 15/3/8; Cecil to Asquith, 5 Dec. 1916, reprinted Grigg, *Lloyd George*, pp. 465–466.

[116] E.g. Asquith to Bonar Law, 6 Dec. 1916, B.L.P. 81/1/1, when he declined to serve under Bonar Law.

[117] Memorandum by Stamfordham, Dec. 1916, RA GV K1048A/1.

he will join. The Chief Whip, John Gulland, is very averse to this course, saying that the Liberal Party would not stand it, and that it would be humiliating.

While I was in Eric D's room McKenna came in to see Grey. It appears that McKenna is afraid that Asquith is going to agree to the forementioned proposition, and wishes Grey to dissuade Asquith from it. Grey was to see Asquith at 5.15. Grey himself was in two moods about it, but on the whole against Asquith joining the new Government.[118]

It is not clear what evidence, if any, McKenna had for his fears. By 6 p.m. the whole group of Liberal ministers (Asquith, Grey, McKenna, Buckmaster, Runciman, Harcourt, McKinnon Wood, Tennant, Montagu, Crewe and Samuel), together with Henderson, had resolved that Asquith should not join the ministry, and Bonar Law was told.[119] He returned to the King. Lloyd George was summoned, and undertook to form a government.

Lloyd George's task was not straightforward, though the path to the premiership was rather clearer than he thought when he returned to Frances Stevenson after seeing the King. He was 'at the W.O. till after midnight, . . . conferring with B. Law Carson, & others', and decided that Bonar Law would try to bring round 'the hostile section of the Unionist party' while Lloyd George would 'see what he could do' with Labour.[120] On the Conservative front bench there was less hostility than might have been supposed. Curzon and Cecil, though dismissed as hostile by Frances Stevenson, had decided to back Lloyd George at the Colonial Office meeting of Conservative ministers in the afternoon of Tuesday 5 December, 'as a public duty, if required'.[121] Long had almost certainly decided to accept a Lloyd George premiership on the Tuesday, and told a group of Unionist Business Committee M.P.s on the Wednesday that he would support one if it came about.[122] The major source of resistance was Austen Chamberlain, who told Arthur Steel-Maitland on Tuesday that he certainly would not join a Lloyd George government. This conversation, which Chamberlain described as 'so humid that it may have left you under a misapprehension' about what Steel-Maitland should do, seems to have consisted of the two Birmingham M.P.s each urging the other to join a new government while declining to join himself.[123] Chamberlain's reluctance grew from his extreme personal dislike of Lloyd George

---

[118] Arthur Murray's diary, 6 Dec. 1916. Elibank Papers 8815.

[119] Crewe's memo in Spender and Asquith, *Asquith*. Asquith to Bonar Law, 6 Dec. 1916, B.L.P., 81/1/1.

[120] *Stevenson Diary*, 6 Dec. 1916, p. 133.

[121] *Crawford Papers*, p. 375.

[122] See the discussion of Long's intentions in Murphy, 'Walter Long', p. 740.

[123] Chamberlain to Steel-Maitland, 5 Dec. 1916, Scottish Record Office, Steel-Maitland Papers 390; Steel-Maitland to Chamberlain, 7 Dec. 1916, Chamberlain Papers AC 15/3/19.

...whom I profoundly distrust — no doubt a man of great energy, but quite untrustworthy; who does not run crooked because he wants to, but because he does not know how to run straight; who has tired out the patience of every man who has worked with him and most of those who have worked for him; who let his nearest colleagues down over conscription at the critical moment and then took the question up again when he thought the audience more favourable and the limelight more concentrated on himself...124

Chamberlain had also objected stridently to the composition of the War Committee proposed by Lloyd George on 1 December, remarking later that

I certainly would not have served under such a Committee nor would Curzon and Cecil. We have little confidence in Bonar Law's judgement and none in his strength of character. Carson was a great disappointment in the three months during which he sat in Asquith's Cabinet. He is an Irish sentimentalist as Lloyd George is a Welsh one. He and Bonar Law would merely have emphasized Lloyd George's failings whilst echoing his views, and these are known to have been at variance... with those of the General Staff... [Henderson] is a very good fellow, but on all the larger issues of policy he would have been a cipher.125

Both these outpourings were written after Chamberlain had accepted the India Office in Lloyd George's government. His change of heart was rational and hardly even surprising. At the beginning of the crisis he shared the general belief that the Asquith ministry could not continue. His objection to Lloyd George's plan of reform was to the personnel of the committee, not the idea of structural change. His attitude to the possibility of Lloyd George becoming prime minister resembled Balfour's. It was not necessary for him to be part of such a government, and he would not wish to be part of it, but as he wrote to Steel-Maitland, he had 'no desire to dissuade *anyone* from joining the reconstructed Gov't.' He changed his mind because Curzon, pressed to join the War Cabinet, accepted a place in the ministry on patriotic grounds during the course of Thursday 7 December, following an inclination which he had previously made clear. With Cecil (*contra* Beaverbrook's account) taking the same view, Chamberlain was isolated: he would have felt even more isolated if he had known that Walter Long had already accepted the Colonial Office but sworn Lloyd George and Bonar Law not to tell Chamberlain that he had been approached first.126

Chamberlain was finally squared at a meeting in the evening of 7 December, attended by Long, Curzon, Cecil, Chamberlain, Lloyd George

---

124 Chamberlain to Hilda Chamberlain, 14 Dec. 1916, Austen Chamberlain Papers AC 15/3/10.
125 Chamberlain to Chelmsford, 8 Dec. 1916, Chamberlain Papers AC 15/3/8.
126 Long to Chamberlain, 7 Dec. 1923, Austen Chamberlain Papers AC 15/3/20; Bull Papers, Diary 8 Dec. 1916, 4/14. See the interesting discussion of this point in Murphy, 'Walter Long', pp. 741–742.

and Bonar Law. This meeting, reduced to writing by Curzon, covered a number of controversial points arising from Lloyd George's discussions with the Labour Party, and the composition of the ministry.[127] The issue on which Chamberlain fixed in explaining his change of mind was the composition of the new War Cabinet. This point he made in letters to Chelmsford on 8 December and to his half-brother Neville on 11 December,[128] telling the latter that 'we have got the three things I thought most necessary for the public service — the inclusion of Curzon & Milner in the War Committee & the formal constitution of the War Committee as the Cabinet.' His attitude to Curzon was critical:

> I told Curzon on Saturday the 1st when I first learned of Lloyd George's terms & their rejection that tho' after the 'Die-Hard' business, when I felt his desertion bitterly, I had said that I would not go tiger-shooting with him again, yet values changed & opinions had to be reconsidered. I had seen him at work & learned to appreciate his 'qualities'. I would serve *under* the proposed Cmtee if he were added to it but not otherwise.

Whether or not this fully explains his motives it is a good story. With the adherence of Chamberlain and Curzon, as well as Carson and Lord Derby who were committed already, the Conservative component of the new administration could command widespread support on the back benches. Lloyd George and Bonar Law believed that the back benches would follow their leaders, and were not disappointed. With their adherence assumed, Lloyd George could tell the King that he could form a ministry.

The Liberal Party presented greater problems. By the time he undertook to form the ministry Lloyd George could have been in no doubt that most of his former Liberal colleagues would refuse to join him. He therefore wasted no time on asking them, but in the evening of 7 December, after seeing the Unionist ministers and after kissing hands, he asked Herbert Samuel to see him and offered him the Home Office, explaining that

> ...he had felt he could not approach his Liberal Colleagues in the Cabinet until it became clear that he would be able to form a Government, because they might feel honour bound to stand by Asquith and not help to get the new administration started. But now that it was certain that it would be successfully formed he felt at liberty to do so. There were, however, only two whom he would wish to approach, and only two places that he had kept open.[129]

---

[127] Reprinted in Beaverbrook, *Politicians and the War*, pp. 520–527; original in Austen Chamberlain Papers AC 15/3/6, and elsewhere.

[128] Chamberlain to Chelmsford, 8 Dec. 1916, AC 15/3/8; Chamberlain to Neville Chamberlain, 11 Dec. 1916 *ibid*. 15/3/7. The 'Diehard' reference is to Curzon's recommendation to the Conservative peers to concede the passage of the Parliament Act in 1911.

[129] Memorandum by Samuel, 7 Dec. 1916, Samuel Papers A/56/3.

These two were Samuel and Montagu. Samuel declined on the grounds that he had no confidence in the new ministry's capacity to survive, and that he thought it a patriotic duty to maintain 'an opposition of men of experience in administration who could form an alternative government if things went wrong'. Lloyd George 'wished he could tell me what Asquith had said about that when he made the same suggestion as to his own attitude', and defended his own actions when Samuel added that he 'greatly disliked the way the change had come about'. The two men parted, according to Samuel, on 'friendly terms', but Samuel's refusal was decisive. Montagu, who earlier in the week had tried to mediate between the two sides, was somewhat less decisive. Although he declined offers made to him on 7 December, he left it open to Bonar Law to offer him a junior post at the Treasury a week later; but this he also declined, leaving it until July 1917 to enter the Lloyd George Coalition as Secretary of State for India. For the moment, Asquith's closest colleagues, to a man, chose opposition. This left Lloyd George to find some other way of balancing his Cabinet and ensuring the support of the Liberal back bench.

Part of the work had been done in advance. The Liberal War Committee, led by Frederick Handel Booth,[130] Sir Henry Dalziel and David Davies, could offer between 30 and 40 reliable votes, and these were the majority of the 49 'out and out' supporters revealed by Addison's canvass of 4 December. A number of lists were compiled by Addison and Kellaway[131] during 4, 5 and 6 December, the last of which claimed support from 126 members, in addition to the 49 out-and-outers. From the surviving documents this number can only be reached by double-counting. Some of the claimed supporters, such as John Hinds and James Hogge, were anti-conscriptionists who could only have been included by an optimist.[132] Some of the 'doubtful' supporters made clear by their votes before and after the change of government that they were quite hostile to Lloyd George. Altogether, Addison's canvass leaves much to be desired as evidence, and the strongest interpretation that it will bear is that a large number of Liberals were quite perplexed about the respective merits of Asquith and Lloyd George as war leaders.[133] Their attachment to a new ministry might be secured by successful policy and reassuring appointments, but nothing could be guaranteed in advance.

[130] A Liberal coal-owner. He was M.P. for Pontefract, 1910–1918.

[131] Frederick Kellaway, a journalist, was elected for Bedford in December 1910. He held junior office throughout the Lloyd George Coalitions.

[132] Hogge was a persistent critic of all wartime governments. Hinds was a Welsh Baptist whose political base was in Carmarthen. He was much friendlier to the Coalition than many anti-conscriptionists, and took the Coupon in 1918.

[133] J.M. McEwen, 'Lloyd George's Liberal Supporters in December 1916: a note', *Bulletin of the Institute of Historical Research*, liii (1980), 265–272.

Reassuring appointments were difficult to make. Addison, formerly Lloyd George's deputy at Munitions and a close collaborator in the later stages of the Cabinet crisis, was appointed to the Ministry of Munitions. Lord Rhondda, a coal-owner, who as D.A. Thomas, M.P. had been a leading Welsh Liberal of the faction opposed to Lloyd George, was given the Local Government Board. Sir Alfred Mond went to the Office of Works, against the wishes of the King.[134] Gordon Hewart became Solicitor-General.[135] Sir Robert Munro eventually became Secretary of State for Scotland.[136] This was not much of a team to put up against the best and brightest of pre-war Liberalism, who were now to be found on the opposition front benches. To strengthen the Liberal element in the Coalition, Lloyd George contemplated inviting Lord Rosebery to be Lord Privy Seal, but this was 'unfavourably received' by his Conservative colleagues on 7 December.[137] Winston Churchill was blackballed by the same meeting. Further Liberal talent had to be sought outside, in the form of Herbert Fisher, then Vice-Chancellor of Sheffield University, who accepted the presidency of the Board of Education.[138] Fisher was at least a confirmed Liberal, but he had no parliamentary experience at all. Though Fisher, Addison and Rhondda were later to prove themselves in demanding administrative and political jobs, the lack of well-known Liberals was embarrassing, and the next few days were consumed in matching Liberal back-benchers to vacant or newly created under-secretaryships.

The other two parties to be considered were the Irish Nationalists and the Labour Party. Direct participation in government by the Irish party was inconceivable in late 1916 because of the Easter Rising and the bungled settlement which followed it. Lloyd George had to promise the Conservatives that they were not joining a Home Rule government, and Redmond could not join anything else without losing control of his party. The Labour Party, on the other hand, might be turned. Besides its parliamentary forces, which might be critical to the ministry's survival if there was any doubt about Liberal reliability, Labour M.P.s might somehow control the Labour movement outside the House. Though it seems absurd

[134] Mond, son of the founder of Brunner-Mond chemical company, spoke with a German accent. He was later chairman of Imperial Chemical Industries. He sat successively for his company's pocket boroughs, Chester and Swansea, but in 1926 fell out with Lloyd George and became a Conservative.

[135] Hewart, a K.C., had been a Leicester M.P. since 1913, sharing the seat with Ramsay MacDonald. He remained a Coalition Liberal, as Attorney-General in the post-war Coalition, but left politics in 1922 to become Lord Chief Justice. In *The New Despotism* (London: Ernest Benn, 1929) he made an almost hysterical attack on the growth of state power since the war.

[136] Munro was a Scottish lawyer, M.P. for Wick since 1910 and Lord Advocate since 1913. He held his new job until 1922 and became a judge on the fall of the Lloyd George Coalition.

[137] Yet he persisted until 8 December: Bonar Law to Lloyd George, 8 Dec. 1918, L.G.P. F/30/2/2.

[138] Fisher had already made his greatest mark on education as a fellow of New College, Oxford, where he had helped to educate a good deal of Milner's kindergarten and many others. His best books had been written. He was reckoned in 1916 to be an Asquithian.

in retrospect, Lloyd George and his Conservative collaborators behaved as though they believed that this was possible, and they were encouraged in their belief by the peculiar structure of the Labour leadership, in which the parliamentary party and the T.U.C. were interlocked. Because of Henderson's clear support for Asquith over the weekend, Lloyd George had already made his approaches to J.H. Thomas of the National Union of Railwaymen, with whom he breakfasted on the morning of 7 December;[139] but Henderson had decided by 6 December to back the Lloyd George ministry.[140] He then sought to persuade his colleagues during the Thursday morning. After meeting at the Central Hall, Westminster ('appropriately, a Wesleyan Methodist place & the home of the most self-seeking & worldly spiritualism' recorded MacDonald), Labour M.P.s and the National Executive Committee called on Lloyd George at noon. All the Labour recollections of this meeting are from witnesses hostile to Lloyd George.

> The Ll.G. performance was remarkable. It consisted of blarney & promises of the vaguest kind & he spoke for three quarters of an hour. As soon as we were assembled Sir Edward Carson walked through the room like a sick vulture. Henderson had reported to us at the first meeting the Ll.G. promises & he made them much more generous than Ll.G. himself did. A colleague when it was all over said to me 'George has been on a fishing expedition and he has caught his trout'. It was humiliating to see the subserviency of most of our men, their anxiety to please Ll.G & protect him from a close examination. They swallowed everything & were glad to do so.[141]

Some of the promises were in fact quite clear: Henderson was to be put in the new War Cabinet, and Ministries of Labour and of Pensions were to be created and given to Labour M.P.s. On other matters Lloyd George kept his choices more open. Faced with a demand to extend state control of coal mines and the merchant shipping fleet, he agreed to take over more coalfields but did not promise the same treatment for shipping. On industrial conscription the Labour members asked for, and got, what they believed to be a pledge not to introduce it; but Lloyd George later told the Conservative ministers that he had merely promised a 'Derby scheme' for civilian manpower.[142] The Labour leaders went away and decided to support the ministry by 19 votes to 12.[143] Except for Thomas's support for the ministry, the Executive divided into the same minority and majority groups as it had done over conscription.

[139] *Whitehall Diary*, Jones to E.T. Jones, 7 Dec., p. 8.
[140] MacDonald Diary, 6 Dec. 1916, MacDonald Papers PRO 30/69/1753.
[141] MacDonald Diary, 7 Dec. 1916, PRO 30/69/1753.
[142] Transcript of 7 Dec. 1916 in L.G.P. G/245.
[143] Labour Party Archive, N.E.C. Minutes, Vol. 10, 7 Dec. 1916.

The formation of the new ministry was all over bar the shouting in the mid-afternoon of 7 December, and Lloyd George's meeting with Conservative ministers in the evening merely ratified the adherence of all the important Conservative leaders. Lloyd George was 'in high spirits' by the Thursday afternoon, and Thomas Jones found him on the morning of Friday 8 December 'in fine fettle — said he had put a month's work into yesterday and that the King was "amazed" at his making a Cabinet so swiftly'.[144] There was much left to be done: Bonar Law's postbag was full of applications and supplications, while Thomas Jones records a constant ebb and flow of minor and not so minor appointments occupying the new prime minister's time until the weekend.[145] But victory had been won when Lloyd George kissed hands on the evening of 7 December.

A New Beginning?

Lloyd George's natural exuberance at a challenge met and a contest won makes it difficult to assess what he thought he had achieved and what he had intended to achieve by his actions since the beginning of December, or indeed by the general thrust of his policy since the middle of the year. Equally, the very 'high-political' and private nature of the crisis in December makes it difficult to link the actions of the politicians involved either with the problems of policy which had preoccupied them up to 30 November, or the political structure in which they had been working, and which their feverish Cabinet-making had, though they hardly knew it, altered beyond hope of restoration. But these connections must be made if the crisis is not to be trivialised.

The crisis in December 1916 was short and intense because it was driven in large part by personal animosities and impatience. McKenna and Lloyd George, in particular, were at loggerheads and Lloyd George openly blamed McKenna for causing the rift between himself and Asquith, and for keeping it open against the better inclinations of the two principals after the weekend's agreements. It is unlikely that the ministry could in the event have long survived the Unionists' threat of resignation on Sunday, whatever its inner meaning, but Arthur Murray's evidence certainly suggests that McKenna was working right to the end to ensure that no reconciliation between the two men was possible. In the other party, Chamberlain and Long and most of the other senior Unionists privately despised their leader Bonar Law, while Lansdowne had become an

---

[144] *Stevenson Diary*, p. 134; *Whitehall Diary*, p. 10.

[145] B.L.P. 81/1/16–24 and 84/6/1–12 will serve as examples. Lloyd George's activity is chronicled in *Whitehall Diary*, pp. 10–15.

opponent of his war policy. Senior Conservatives therefore worked independently of their leader and of one another, giving confusing signals
to Lloyd George as well as to Asquith about what support was to be relied upon in what circumstances. This played up particularly dangerously
to the paranoia in the Asquithian camp. The role of Carson as a King
Charles's head to both the Liberal and most of the Conservative members of the Cabinet must not be underestimated either: if Carson's name
had not been associated with Lloyd George's schemes, resistance to them
would have been much slighter. But it is not enough merely to represent
the leaders of the Asquith Coalition as a pack of squabbling children, or
as men obsessed by the struggle for office. Their personal rivalries had
roots in differences of policy, and their relative power was determined as
much by their support outside the Cabinet as by their internal alliances,
important though those were in the final days.

The conventional account, which is Beaverbrook's account, concentrates on the steady withdrawal of Conservative support for the Coalition,
which seemed to put Bonar Law in a weak position *vis à vis* Carson and
forced him into alliance with Lloyd George. This was clearly not the
whole truth, and it distracts attention from the unsteady nature of Liberal
support for the Coalition. There were so many groupings in the House of
Commons that it is meaningless to single out Carson's supporters on the
Unionist War Committee as the pivotal group. Only about two-thirds of
the Unionist War Committee members who voted, 65 out of 95, supported Carson in the Nigeria debate. According to William Bridgeman

> Carson had a bad case, but Unionists were in a bad temper & very nearly half voted
> against the Govt., but the division was good for Asquith as the rest of the House
> was solid. L.G. was significantly absent. On the other hand it was bad for Bonar
> Law who had announced some time before that if the majority of the Unionist party
> voted against him, he should resign the leadership. He was only saved by about half a
> dozen votes. However the victory gave Asquith & his friends the most overweening
> confidence & they went on in their usual desultory way.[146]

The effects of misbehaviour on the Unionist back bench could be
equalled, to take one example, by the combined voting forces, in a normal
turnout, of the Irish party and the anti-conscriptionist Liberals. More than
forty Liberals had shown themselves prepared to vote against the government during the Military Service divisions in March, and an exceptional
turnout might find any of these men in the opposition lobby. Whatever
the 'Asquithian' ministers thought they were defending in Cabinet, plenty
of their nominal supporters had written them off as captives to militarism.
The Liberal War Committee, for its own reasons, had meanwhile ceased

---

[146] *Modernisation of Conservative Politics*, p. 111. This account was of course written in February
1917, and the interpretation may itself be a gloss.

to feel confidence in Asquith, McKenna, Runciman and Grey, though not in Lloyd George. But even when added together, these two groups did not amount to a majority of the Liberal M.P.s regularly present in the House in 1916. The attitude of the anonymous mass of Liberal middle opinion also contributed to the fate of the Asquith Coalition, for it was the faltering allegiance of these men which made it impossible for Asquith's friends to contemplate going on without Conservative support. Most Liberal M.P.s cared, but few knew, what was the best policy for victory. The subtleties, and for that matter even the great simplifications of Eastern vs. Western strategy and long vs. short war, were beyond them. Dr Hart has remarked that most of them supported the government — any government — throughout the war, on the principle that it was their function or even their constitutional duty to do so. In the last days of the Asquith Coalition this was not a good enough reason to prefer Asquith to Lloyd George. Nor did personal loyalty to an old and trusted leader count for very much by the time the new leader was in place, patently enjoying the almost united support of the Conservative Party. A profound intellectual inertia among a body of men who could not find Asquith's leadership inspiring helped to carry Lloyd George to victory. The angry men in the party either hated Asquith or hated Lloyd George, but those who most hated Lloyd George despised Asquith, with Grey, Runciman and McKenna, for abetting his rake's progress to Prussianism. Among the bewildered majority the party crisis over conscription, far from splitting the party, had merely prepared the way for Liberals to support Lloyd George.

On the Conservative side the same controversies over war policy had had equally corrosive effects. The extreme opinions in favour of a 'vigorous prosecution of the war', which were popular with the back bench were those associated with Carson, whose abilities in government were despised by his colleagues. Among M.P.s the Conservatives were least affected by the doctrine that patriotic and constitutional principle should lead them to support the government of the day: their loyalties were to their party and their class. Feelings of loyalty to the party's leadership, which inhibited many back-benchers from supporting Carson, were associated not with Bonar Law but with one or other of the party's independent chieftains. Derby had the Lancashire party in his pocket. Austen Chamberlain had considerable influence in Birmingham to complement the ideological inheritance of Tariff Reform. Walter Long, despite his *persona* as a Tory squire, had little local support but a strong national position based on his championship of Irish Unionism. Balfour still mattered to the surviving Unionist Free Traders and to landed Conservatives, including Derby. Bonar Law only held the reins of party leadership with the consent of these men and this consent depended as much on policy as on personal rivalry. In short, Chamberlain and Derby were committed to supporting the General Staff against any criticism; Long was opposed to any Irish settlement which did not protect the Southern Unionists; Chamberlain, Long and Curzon wanted industrial conscription. For all these reasons they were glad to see the back of the Asquith regime, but would not consent to a Bonar Law government. Mutual rivalry prevented them from choosing one of their own number to lead the party. The great irony was that their lukewarm support for Bonar Law made it all the more certain that Lloyd George, who opposed every one of these positions except industrial compulsion (which was eventually dropped), would attain the premiership.

The Labour Party, too, played an important role in these transactions without getting very much of what it wanted except the abandonment of industrial compulsion. The behaviour of the parliamentary Labour party was remarkably similar to that of the Liberals. The minority, led by MacDonald, was displeased with the Asquith government and displeased with the Labour leadership. The majority supported the government of the day because they thought it a constitutional duty. On certain issues, such as conscription and industrial compulsion, they regretted the Asquith government's attitude, but had no reason after the Executive Committee's interview with Lloyd George to believe that a Lloyd George administration would be any worse. On the issues which distinguished Labour from Liberal M.P.s, principally the welfare of working-class civilians, more was to be expected from a new government committed to food control than from the procrastinations of the Asquith regime. The Ministry of Labour was a direct bribe. In this way the change of government made little immediate difference to Labour politics, except to offer a small but indefinite hope of improvement.

It is a mistake to see the December crisis as an encapsulated palace revolution; equally a mistake to represent it as a climacteric in the development of British politics, in which the structure of party and government was remade by great forces of change. Many adjustments in British politics, such as the changing personnel and attitudes of M.P.s in the two major parties, antedated the formation of the Lloyd George Coalition. The machinery of government was changed, but not revolutionised by the new regime; the new War Cabinet differed in style from its immediate predecessors but its aims when it was set up were remarkably similar. The participants in the crisis were not primarily concerned to preserve or replace a regime, to introduce or deflect 'war socialism', or to take long views of the development of the British state. Nor, on the other hand, were they obsessed by minor personal rivalries. Their main concern was to regain control, if they could, of a situation in the war and in British politics which was becoming dangerously out of hand.

4

THE CONSOLIDATION OF THE MINISTRY
December 1916 to May 1917

It is true L.G. was very unpopular with his own side & with Labour, but one thing Asquith & Co had not calculated was the strength of a new Premier who has a lot of appointments at his disposal, & many more Liberals remained with L.G. than was expected, simply in the hope of getting something. Labour was also won over by the opportunity of office quite out of proportion to their numbers.

Bridgeman 'Diary' for Autumn 1916, written February 1917.

There was, indeed, no hint of active opposition.... The ex-Premier's noble and magnanimous, if somewhat pathetic, speech made a profound impression on his audience...

Arthur Murray's account of the Reform Club meeting of 8 December 1916.

In a few months time, the new Govt. will be as unpopular as the old, and my belief is that we and every other country will fall into the hands of the socialists before we are very much older. Asquith and his crowd will join with the Irish and Labour people and constitute a solid opposition which will gradually become a stop the war opposition. It is a great mistake to suppose that because a few Labour M.P.s have been given billets, the Labour party itself has been squared...

Lord Newton to Sir Horace Rumbold, 12 December 1916

As I told you I think you will be driven into real opposition ultimately by your supporters...

Bonar Law to McKenna, 15 December 1916[1]

---

[1] Bridgeman 'Diary' for Autumn of 1916, Bridgeman Papers; Murray's note in Elibank Papers 8815; Newton to Rumbold, 12 Dec. 1916, Bodleian Library, Rumbold Papers 18/183; Bonar Law to McKenna, 15 Dec. 1916, B.L.P. 84/6/15.

The new prime minister and his government faced a double challenge. The new political settlement depended on the old parliament, whose intentions were unknown; and the problems of winning the war, which had toppled the Asquith administration, were brought no nearer a solution by its fall. The timing and pretext of the change had drawn attention to the machinery of high policy. Lloyd George abandoned the full Cabinet altogether, and replaced the War Committee by a small War Cabinet of five, meeting almost daily under his own chairmanship. It included Bonar Law, who as Chancellor of the Exchequer was the only full member to have departmental responsibilities, Curzon, Henderson and Milner, who was taken in as a surrogate for Carson. Balfour, the new Foreign Secretary, was a regular attender. This unusual, and obtrusively Unionist, body had supreme responsibility for all aspects of war government, while departmental ministers got on with their business and in theory brought only essential decisions to the War Cabinet. This was as near as any wartime government got to the 'numerical specific' which Asquith had sarcastically dismissed in 1915. In practice the War Cabinet held larger and larger meetings and after the spring of 1917 began to delegate its work to subcommittees and even to individual members. As a result it never attained the supposed ideal of a compact supreme executive body. It was, as the excluded Walter Long pointed out resentfully, a 'dictatorship in commission', and its real function was to confine decisions to a small body of men who would obstruct the prime minister as little as possible because they agreed with him on important questions.

Although Lloyd George and his War Cabinet could expect a period of grace, their political survival ultimately depended on success. To add to their difficulties, there was little agreement upon what success meant. Lloyd George himself and his War Cabinet colleagues all wanted a drastic overhaul of military policy: to them success meant, among other things, a major revision of the Chantilly agreement. Unfortunately a strong faction on the Conservative back bench would not contemplate any interference with military prerogatives, and the General Staff was in no mood for concession. Another object of the *putsch* against Asquith and his Liberal colleagues had been to press forward the plans for industrial compulsion which Montagu had been devising in November; but this had ostensibly been abandoned as a condition for Labour's support of the new government. At the same time new problems rapidly arose to which the expressed aims of the new War Cabinet provided no answers. On 12 December the Central Powers proposed peace negotiations in a note to the United States government. No terms were stated, but some appropriate response was clearly necessary from Britain and the other Allied powers.[2]

---

[2] Text of the note in Lloyd George, *War Memoirs*, II, 653–654.

The British government had also to consider the sterling crisis, foretold by McKenna and the anti-conscriptionists earlier in the year, and now realised in the decision by the Federal Reserve Board of the United States on 30 November to advise American banks not to extend further loans to the belligerents.[3] Strategy and manpower questions weighed most heavily on the War Cabinet's mind, determining what Lloyd George and his colleagues had to do. What they could do was constrained politically by the mood of the back benches. This was influenced by the revival of two old issues, the latent antagonism between the major parties over agriculture, and the resurrection of the Irish Question. By May 1917 the growth of the Liberal oppositions in Parliament, and a sharp reminder of the power of labour in the workplace, challenged the ministry and forced the War Cabinet to reconsider its future.

Strategy and Politics

Faced in the last hours of the crisis, on 7 December, by Curzon, Cecil, Chamberlain and Long all insisting that he should retain Haig as Commander-in-Chief of the British armies in France, Lloyd George was forced to accede simply to keep the new Coalition together.[4] His military policy for the rest of the war was hamstrung by this initial compromise: if at any point he wished to dismiss or over-rule Haig as Commander-in-Chief, or Robertson as C.I.G.S., he had to face opposition from Unionist ministers outside the War Cabinet. But Lloyd George's policy was not dictated by simple political cowardice, nor, to put it another way, was he restrained from treacherous attacks on the generals only by the staunch patriotism of his Unionist colleagues. Many of the twists in military policy in 1917 and 1918 can, of course, be traced to an essentially political problem: Lloyd George and the War Cabinet were reluctant to concentrate on the Western Front at the expense of all other theatres of war, but never dared to order the army to follow another policy. But there was more to the strategic debate than a struggle between 'Lloyd George and the Generals' or between 'Easterners and Westerners'. During these most difficult years of the war the protagonists — Lloyd George, the War Cabinet, the General Staff, and the high command in France — were responding to all aspects of the problem at once, not just to the crude categories of news-

---

[3] Kathleen Burk, *Britain, America and the Sinews of War*, pp. 83–86.

[4] 'Memorandum of Conversation between Mr Lloyd George and certain Unionist ex-Ministers, December 7 1916', India Office Library, Curzon Papers, MSS Eur. F 112/130, cited Beaverbrook, *Politicians and the War*, p. 526.

paper correspondents like Repington.[5] On the other hand, the politicians and editors who furnished the chorus were starved of information and expertise and were manipulated shamelessly by the principals. If the military reality of war was made in the trenches and on the factory floor, the political reality was made by the attitudes of editors and journalists, and the response of politicians and the public to what they were told in the press.

The first phase of military policy-making after the Chantilly conference[6] occupied the first five months of 1917, and thus corresponded fairly closely to the new government's period of consolidation. The change of government in Britain was soon followed by a smaller cabinet upheaval in France. The new French government replaced Joffre by General Nivelle.[7] The two new administrations, with the Italian government, resolved to modify the Chantilly plan in two ways: some further resources were committed to the Salonika front, and Joffre's plan for the spring offensive on the Western Front was replaced by Nivelle's scheme, which was to begin with a diversionary attack by the British armies at Arras to draw off German reserves, and follow through with a fierce attack by the French armies on the Aisne. The French and British governments made an agreement at Calais in February, which in effect subordinated the British army to the French commander. In early March Haig and Robertson rebelled against this arrangement, and although the War Cabinet seriously considered sacking Haig, the result was a new agreement which protected Haig's freedom of action. Nivelle's plan, which depended on new and supposedly less costly offensive tactics, was begun on the assumption that it would be halted if quick results were not achieved. In the event the British diversionary attack succeeded (with the capture of Vimy Ridge), but Nivelle's own attack did not. Mutinies broke out in the French army in April and Haig, after first insisting that the attack be continued despite its failure to produce decisive early results, began to press in May for permission to resurrect his Flanders plan. Permission was granted by an anguished War Policy Committee, specially constituted by the War Cabinet on 8 June to re-examine the military situation. This marked the end of the Coalition's first attempt to gain control of military policy. The cost of this defeat at the hands of the generals was a new offensive — the third battle of Ypres, better known as Passchendaele — which began on 31 July and was allowed to continue until 10 November despite its failure to win ground and its disastrous cost in casualties.

[5] Charles à Court Repington had been a regular soldier who was forced to leave the army in 1904 by Henry Wilson because of adultery with a fellow-officer's wife. He became military correspondent of *The Times* in 1904, and retained close links with the General Staff both in London and in France.

[6] See above, pp. 124–125.

[7] Robert Nivelle had distinguished himself at the defence of Verdun in 1916. He had a British mother and spoke fluent English.

The strategic debate in the early months of the Lloyd George Coalition was of course a continuation of previous arguments. The political decline of the Asquith Coalition and the slow intellectual bankruptcy of strategic discussion had proceeded side by side. In September 1916, for two reasons, it had begun to seem possible that some change would be possible in the New Year. The first reason was Romania's belated entry into the war against the Central Powers, which raised once more the possibility of creating a pro-Entente bloc in the Balkans, a chance which had already been bungled twice in 1915 with the expeditions to Gallipoli and Salonika. It was as true in 1916 as it had been in 1915 that the loyalty of the Balkan powers depended on adequate military and political support from Britain and France. Without this the Romanian army stood little chance against Bulgarian, Austrian and German forces, and furthermore the allegiance of Greece, divided politically between the pro-Entente Venizelos[8] and the pro-German King Constantine, would go to the side which seemed most likely to win the Balkan war. In September Lloyd George, with patchy support from his civilian colleagues on the War Committee, had pressed the General Staff to reinforce the Salonika expedition and urged that Robertson be sent to Russia to concert the Entente's military support for the Romanian army. Lloyd George had just led an attempt to persuade the Staff to send an expedition to Red Sea port of Rabegh, to bolster up Sherif Hussein's revolt against the Turks.[9] This broad push towards Eastern ventures was more defensive than offensive — in each case, the purpose was to avoid a humiliating defeat for Entente policy rather than to start something new — but it had set a tone for Lloyd George's interaction with the Staff.

September's other contribution to the government's difficulties had been the encounter between Lloyd George and the command in France during and after his visit to the Western Front in the middle of the month.[10] The episode of the Foch interview was significant because it set the line of argument between Lloyd George and the General Staff: for the next four months he emphasised the superiority of French tactical methods on the Western Front.

By early November 1916 these arguments had been brought to a head, and the War Committee had decided both to proceed with an inter-Allied political conference in Paris to examine whether in 1917 'a decision might not be reached on another front', and to set up a military conference in Russia, attended by the 'principal generals' from the West: Robertson,

---

[8] Eleutherios Venizelos, a radical politician of Cretan origin.
[9] War Cabinet Minutes, W.C. 2, 11 Dec. 1916; W.C. 11, 19 Dec. 1916, CAB 23/1.
[10] See pp. 123–124.

Joffre and Cadorna.[11]   The proposal to get Robertson out of the way for a few weeks was typical of Lloyd George's incorrigible ingenuity, and enraged the C.I.G.S. But its significance soon passed, as Lloyd George himself cooled towards the idea, and its only legacy was an increment in the mutual distrust of Robertson and Lloyd George. The conference with the French duly took place in Paris on 15 November as described in the previous chapter, with Lloyd George's draft statement put to the Allied ministers in a form emasculated by Asquith, and duly agreed. It was not thought inconsistent, except by a downcast Lloyd George and an eminently satisfied Haig, that this harmony should be accompanied by an uncritical acceptance of a military plan invented by Joffre and Haig which was quite discordant with it.

While the failure of the Paris meeting was clearly a catalyst for action, the reversal of its decisions was not the only purpose in Lloyd George's mind and, as we have seen, not the only factor in the collapse of the Asquith Coalition. The tension between Lloyd George on the one hand and Robertson and Haig on the other had actually diminished during November and December. Robertson willingly supported Lloyd George's attack on Lansdowne's suggestions for a negotiated peace, and by early December was prepared to express support for Lloyd George's efforts to strengthen the civilian administration of war and, by implication, overturn Asquith. This probably reflected his confidence that whatever the constitutional arrangements in Great Britain the General Staff could maintain its hold on the direction of Allied strategy.

Robertson's confidence was justified by the attitudes of Unionist ministers in the new Coalition, if not by the composition of the new War Cabinet. Of the four Unionist leaders who had insisted that Lloyd George retain Haig as commander-in-chief in France, one (Curzon) was a member of the War Cabinet and all the others held office. In public, the reason for the change of government, so far as it was discussed at all, was not connected to changes in strategy, and the press campaign against 'interference' earlier in the autumn had been won by the War Office. Moreover Derby, the soldiers' friend, was promoted from Parliamentary Secretary to Secretary of State for War.

Consequently Robertson's first interventions at the new War Cabinet were confident, and directed to mopping up any doubts about the result of the Paris conference. On 9 December he took the opportunity to urge rapid disengagement from the Salonika front, on the grounds that 'None of the objects for which we went to and remain in the Balkans can now be attained... We ought therefore to withdraw altogether from the country, but as this proposal is probably not practical at the moment,

---

[11] Luigi Cadorna was Commander-in-Chief of the Italian army.

for political reasons, we should, at the most, definitely adopt the policy
of holding Salonika defensively.'[12] He was less combative, but still firm,
about the Rabegh expedition, merely remarking that he had always advised
against it. Salonika was the principal strategic issue discussed in December,
because of the political instability of Greece. The pro-Entente Venizelists
with their alternative government at Salonika were constantly trying to
overthrow the Royalist government in Athens. The situation had been
aggravated by a clash between Royalist troops and British and French
marines in Athens in early December. The Allied governments imposed
a blockade and demanded that Constantine's troops be withdrawn from
Thessaly, where they might constitute a threat to the Salonika forces.
The diplomatic overtones were complex: the French positively wanted
to advance the Venizelists, the Italians positively feared Venizelos because
they preferred Greece to be weak. As a result the War Cabinet was forced
to elaborate its own policy before meeting the new French government
on 26/27 December, and Robertson had plenty of opportunity to urge
his views and concert them with the Admiralty. By 27 December he
had settled on the argument that the Salonika expedition could not be
supplied with sufficient men or munitions unless it was maintained on
the defensive and its line reduced. Every change in the Balkan situation
which was mentioned by the politicians gave him further ammunition: if
either a German invasion of Macedonia or an anti-Entente rising by the
Greek government was feared, all the more reason for digging in close to
Salonika and preserving the security of the force. The inconsistencies in
French military advice about Salonika were exploited to the full.

The tone of early strategic discussions at the War Cabinet shows why
Robertson could usually succeed, quite apart from his greater access to
expertise and relevant detailed information. The Chantilly programme
had many weaknesses, especially that it was over-optimistic about the
capacity of the Entente forces in the West to draw off German strength
from Eastern theatres, but it was at least coherent in its intentions. A
review presented to the new prime minister on 8 December by Hankey
supported a 'gigantic offensive in the West next year', simply because it
offered some chance of winning the war.[13] The Eastern alternatives which
had been proposed conflicted not only with the Western alternative, but
also with one another. Thus Hankey could observe on 26 December
that

> The new War Cabinet are really up against it, as they don't believe in Robertson's
> 'Western Front' policy, but they will never find a soldier to carry out their 'Salonika'
> policy. Moreover the complete breakdown of shipping renders the later policy

[12] War Cabinet Minutes, W.C. 1, 9 Dec. 1916, CAB 23/1.
[13] CAB 42/19/2.

impracticable, and they won't recognise it. I am inclined to think they will come a cropper before long.[14]

Apparently indifferent to this risk the War Cabinet tried to use foreign governments as a lever against Robertson. A scheme to reinforce the Italian front was developed just before Christmas, and thrust upon the French, who frankly preferred their own Salonika scheme. The proposal was then carried to Rome, where it was the subject of some spectacular chicanery which is now very well documented: before Lloyd George and Hankey could reach Cadorna, the Italian Commander-in-Chief, to persuade him of the merits of the scheme, Robertson had persuaded him of its failings, and the conference merely remitted the question to soothing hands of the general staffs, where it was to remain until the disaster at Caporetto.[15]

Lloyd George's frustration at this defeat does much to explain his sympathy for General Nivelle's modifications to the Chantilly plan, put forward in mid-January. Where Joffre's Chantilly document had suggested simultaneous but otherwise uncoordinated attacks by the Entente armies on a wide front, Nivelle proposed a co-ordinated attack on two short fronts, in which the British attack would be a diversionary move before a decisive French attack in the south, on the Aisne. Lloyd George accepted this scheme when shown it on 15 January, apparently because Nivelle undertook to use the artillery tactics — short but heavy bombardments exploiting surprise on a relatively narrow front — which the prime minister had favoured since his discussions with Foch and other French generals the previous September, and also because Nivelle suggested that his attack could easily be broken off before casualties became intolerably heavy.[16]

What was later to be known as the Nivelle Offensive was at this point just as acceptable to Haig as the Chantilly plan, and Haig thought that Nivelle was a better general than Joffre. Nivelle wanted to change the French army's tactical plan from the slow-moving attack proposed by Joffre, not to change Haig's methods, and he had a more aggressive tone, which Haig favoured. An exchange of letters between Haig and Nivelle on 6 and 11 January had settled the guiding principles of their co-operation. To the three phases of diversionary attack (British), main attack (French), and exploitation of breakthrough (both armies), Haig insisted on adding a fourth: that if the Channel ports were not being relieved as a side-effect of the larger plan, Nivelle would at some time in the summer relieve British divisions in the south which could then be transferred north for an attack

---

[14] Hankey Diary, 26 Dec. 1916, Churchill College, Hankey Papers 1/1, quoted in Roskill, *Hankey: man of secrets*, p. 348.

[15] The conference is described concisely by Woodward, *Lloyd George and the Generals*, pp. 139–141.

[16] *Stevenson Diary*, 15 Jan. 1917, p. 139; Conference Proceedings in CAB 28/2.

into Flanders.[17] This Nivelle accepted, and the plans were therefore put to the British War Cabinet as an agreed proposal.

Although Haig regretted that the War Cabinet forced him to take over more of the French line than he would have liked, and regretted the early date of the attack, these were relatively minor questions at this stage. It was only as the details of the expected offensive had to be settled with Nivelle, and as he realised that the division of responsibilities made it likely that 'We shall have heavy losses with the possibility of no showy successes',[18] that Haig's reservations began to overtake his enthusiasm. Soon after the meeting of 15 January he began, through Robertson, to prepare his ground for a breach with Nivelle. Nivelle, aware of coolness and suspicious, despite the agreements made, that Haig would try to thwart the French attack in order to forward his own Flanders plan, responded with specific requests for co-operation and messages to Lloyd George that Haig was 'inelastic and unaccommodating'.[19] This merely confirmed what Lloyd George already thought, and precipitated another confrontation between Lloyd George and the generals. By early February he had apparently resolved to formalise Haig's subordination to Nivelle.[20]

The argument between the two commanders was about the adequacy of railway transport behind Haig's army: Haig argued that he could not take part in the attack without a huge improvement in the performance of the French railway network. This had long been a handicap to offensive action in France, and this is perhaps why the War Cabinet suspected that Haig, who had dismissed the problem during the Somme campaign, was now using it as an excuse for his unwillingness to co-operate with Nivelle. This was somewhat unfair, since Haig had taken Sir Eric Geddes on to his staff and into his confidence in the autumn, and supported his efforts to improve both the main network and the light railways which brought supplies to the front.[21] When Haig asked for an Anglo-French conference about railways in mid-February[22] the War Cabinet took their opportunity, deciding that 'as between Haig and Nivelle, Ll.G. should support the latter'.[23] Their motives for expanding the discussion to include the system of command were explained for the King's benefit by Curzon, who emphasised that French generals, in particular Nivelle, were very much cleverer than British generals, in particular Haig, but referred also to the political advan-

[17] Haig Diary, 6 Jan. 1917, quoted Blake, *The Private Papers of Douglas Haig*, pp. 190–191; Haig to Robertson, 11 Jan. 1917, King's College London, Robertson Papers I/23/2/4.

[18] Haig Diary, 7 Feb. 1917, Haig Papers 110.

[19] Hankey Diary, 17 Jan. 1917, Hankey Papers.

[20] E. Spears, *Prelude to Victory* (London: Jonathan Cape, 1939), Appendix IX, p. 546.

[21] See Keith Grieves, *Sir Eric Geddes: business and government in war and peace* (Manchester: Manchester University Press, 1989), pp. 27–39.

[22] Haig Diary, 13 Feb. 1917, Haig Papers 110.

[23] Hankey Diary, 24 Feb. 1917; War Cabinet Minutes, 24 Feb. 1917, CAB 23/1.

tages of thrusting the whole responsibility for the 1917 campaign on to the French.[24] The conference took place in Calais on 26–27 February. The result was a compromise, achieved only after tense discussion, in which Haig was subordinated to Nivelle, but only for the period of the offensive.

Even this limited 'Unity of Command' was resented by both Haig and Robertson, and the immediate aftermath of Calais was an acrimonious correspondence between Nivelle and Haig which Haig thought Nivelle was conducting 'in very *commanding* tones'.[25] Much of his suspicion arose because Nivelle wanted Sir Henry Wilson, whom Haig neither liked nor trusted but who spoke better French than any other senior officer, to be liaison officer between the two headquarters. Haig also took care to warn the King that 'no great difficulty should occur in carrying on just as I have been doing, *provided* there is not something behind it,' and harped upon the theme that unity of command threatened to mean that British divisions would be incorporated in French army corps.[26] The King's entourage spoke of Lloyd George's 'ultimate intention of breaking up the Monarchy and introducing a republic with himself at the head'.[27] Meanwhile the higher ranks of the army got to work on Unionist politicians: Sir Hubert Gough entertained Walter Long at the headquarters of the Fifth Army and 'rubbed into him the madness of making any change in the control of the Army now', while Leo Maxse of the *National Review*, almost certainly at the instance of his brother, General Sir Ivor Maxse, urged Austen Chamberlain not to allow Lloyd George to interfere with the army.[28]

Robertson also supported Haig's efforts, writing for the War Cabinet a fierce critique of the Calais agreement, which Haig sent on to Nivelle.[29] Haig's move, understandably, prompted Nivelle to suspect that he intended to go back on the agreement. From this followed a formal message from the French to the British government, insisting that Haig should stick to his word, and an informal request from Nivelle to Lloyd George that either Haig should be replaced by Sir Hubert Gough, or the British army should be divided into two groups, each to be commanded by a British general 'acting in conformity with my plans and keeping in close touch with the War Committee'.[30]

[24] Stamfordham, 'Memorandum on a Conversation between Lord Curzon and Lord Stamfordham on Sunday 4 March 1917', RA GV Q1079/6.

[25] Haig Diary, 28 Feb. 1917.

[26] Haig's correspondence with the King is reprinted in Blake, *Private Papers*, pp. 203–206.

[27] Clive Wigram, quoted in Sir Henry Rawlinson's diary, 12 Mar. 1917, Churchill College, Rawlinson Papers 1/7.

[28] Rawlinson Diary, 13 Mar. 1917; Maxse to Chamberlain, 12 Mar. 1917, Chamberlain Papers 13/3/68.

[29] G.T. 93, 2 Mar. 1917, CAB 24/6; Woodward, *Lloyd George and the Generals*, pp. 151–152.

[30] Eric Drummond to Lloyd George, 7 Mar. 1917, covering the French note, LGP F/3/2/14; TS note, n.s., 7 Mar. 1917, LGP F/162/1.

Meanwhile the German army had made a brilliant strategic retreat (not, for once, a euphemism) from an uncomfortable salient to the Hindenburg line, which ran almost straight from Arras to Soissons and which had been heavily fortified during the winter. Haig's written warning that the German withdrawal prejudiced the whole basis of the offensive, together with Nivelle's complaint against Haig, prompted Lloyd George to seek a showdown. On 7 March the prime minister asked Hankey to prepare a memorandum on the merits of sacking Haig or keeping him. Since January Hankey had been complaining that Lloyd George was always wanting him to say that Haig should be dismissed, and that he always refused. This renewed request put him to further embarrassment: but the result, a huge handwritten memorandum reiterating his strategic analysis, is one of the most valuable documents for historians of strategy during the war.[31] Its significance lies not only in Hankey's own background as a Royal Marine officer with strong sympathies for amphibious operations and a close identity with the 'navalist' strategic tradition, but also in its continuity with previous expositions of the case against the Western Front. The retention of Haig, the government's abrogation of the initiative in strategic debate, and the attack in Flanders which finally led to the bloody tragedy of Passchendaele, was in March 1917 a logical consequence of the premises which underpinned the 'Eastern' strategy; and this paradox largely explains the War Cabinet's otherwise inexplicable decision to support Haig's plan in June.

Hankey had identified himself as an opponent of set-piece land battles since his service as a junior officer in the secretariat of the Committee of Imperial Defence before the war.[32] After December 1914 his strategic arguments had crystallised into those of an 'Easterner', arguing for an indirect approach even to the tactical problems of the Western Front. He was a strong opponent of conscription on the grounds that a large army would distort the war economy which was Britain's particular strength; and through consistency he had now reached the same opinion which Lloyd George had reached via a wide detour in early 1916: that the only hope for the Entente lay in careful husbandry of resources. He had therefore synthesised the 'navalist' and the 'Western' arguments, and supported Haig's desire to follow through the Somme campaign with an attack to liberate the Channel ports, which would reinforce Britain's naval advantage. This point was reiterated in his appreciation of military policy prepared for Lloyd George on 8 December, two days after the new government was formed: 'the maintenance of seapower is the first consideration' but

---

[31] Holograph note by Hankey, 8 Mar. 1917 (1.30 a.m.), CAB 63/19.

[32] For a full but idiosyncratic discussion of his influence on strategic policy, see Avner Offer, *The First World War: an agrarian interpretation*, esp. pp. 235–239. A more conventional view is in Stephen Roskill, *Hankey: man of secrets*.

therefore 'I think that an offensive is absolutely unavoidable, although I have still the gravest doubts whether we can smash the German army by means of it.'[33]

Professor Woodward, who has written most recently and in greatest detail on this subject, observes that Lloyd George's response to this strain in Hankey's thought was simply to ignore it, and press on with his own plans for an offensive in Italy. 'In reality,' Woodward writes, 'the one-front approach he harped upon amounted to any front but the western front.'[34] This was certainly what Haig and Robertson thought at the time; but it is not what Lloyd George actually suggested, either to the London conference with the French on 26–27 December, or to the Rome conference for which a careful paper was prepared at the end of December.[35] His proposals, which were worked out with Hankey's assistance and conformed closely to the strategic analysis of the 8 December appreciation, were for an attack in Italy in the early spring, followed by a Western offensive later. In short, although what he wanted was to postpone the Western campaign *sine die*, what he asked for was a Western campaign with two Eastern moves, Italy and Salonika. In Rome he discovered that the French wanted the Salonika campaign but not the Italian, the Italians were lukewarm about both, and the British military advisers only wanted the Western offensive, which the French government also supported. Although Lloyd George had found himself in a political embarrassment because his reliance on foreign governments to support him against his own soldiers had backfired, the soldiers were also embarrassed because their political victory was achieved at the cost of supporting their second best Western offensive, at the expense of the Flanders campaign.

In the light of these transactions, Hankey's conclusions, on being asked in March whether Haig should be replaced, acquire a new significance. His first contribution was to make the clear political point that among the War Cabinet, whose members he had polled, only Bonar Law would support Lloyd George in sacking Haig. Taken with what was readily known about the attitude of politicians outside the War Cabinet, this was conclusive in itself, because the government could not survive the episode. But his military advice was in some ways more subversive of Lloyd George's position, for he recommended that Haig should be allowed to make his Flanders attack instead of falling in with Nivelle's more southerly plans.

On the whole this seems to me good sense. Instead of attacking over ground that has been fought over until it is so pitted and pock-marked that even tanks can hardly get about; instead of advancing over a barren region devoid of any strategi-

[33] CAB 42/19/2.

[34] Woodward, *Lloyd George and the Generals*, p. 135.

[35] Hankey's paper, with supporting material is in CAB 63/19.

cal objective, where communications are difficult — instead of this we strike into relatively new country, where the enemy must either fight or surrender important objectives...Moreover the expulsion of the enemy from the Belgian coast is not only a primary British interest, but the War Cabinet have repeatedly insisted that from the point of view of the allies as a whole, viz. that of combatting submarine warfare, it is of almost vital importance...

I consider...that there are very strong *prima facie* grounds for a re-opening of the whole question of the plan with the French Government. We should begin by simply asking whether they agree in the General Staff's view as to withdrawal to the Hindenburg line. If they do...we should press strongly for a change of plan, and that our special interests on the Belgian coast should be considered.

The events of 7–8 March were a turning point in the strategic direction of the war. Lloyd George was evidently convinced that it was politically impossible to sack Haig. It followed that he was forced to support Haig and Robertson in their demands for a revision of the Calais agreement. The critical change of temper can be seen in Robertson's reports to Haig of the War Cabinet meetings of 6 and 8 March. Whereas on 6 March 'the Prime Minister seemed to think that you had at the back of your mind the upsetting of the Calais agreement', on 8 March 'there was much excitement yesterday and the usual amount of suspicion, but by today the atmosphere had cleared a good deal and I think that good may come out of evil perhaps after all'.[36] Clive Wigram, the King's equerry, reported that 'H.M. thinks the War Cabinet is afraid' of Haig, and this seems more than likely.[37] Moreover, although even Haig recognised the impossibility of changing plans at that point, the War Cabinet on 14 March formally approved Haig's wish to prepare for a Flanders attack in the event of failure of the Nivelle scheme.[38] In itself this decision so limited the War Cabinet's options after Nivelle's failure that the decision in favour of the Third Ypres campaign was irresistible, and the deliberations of the War Policy Committee in June were almost superfluous. The restoration of the political advantage held by Haig and Robertson did not have to wait for Nivelle's failure and disgrace.

In any case, failure was not far behind. On 19 March Briand's government, which had nourished Nivelle and his plan, was overthrown and replaced by a new ministry under Ribot. Painlévé, the new War Minister, was an exponent of an Italian strategy, but even he found it too late to stop the Nivelle offensive in its tracks. The British attack towards Arras began on 9 April. The French attack, delayed for six days by bad weather, was launched along a 25-mile front along the Aisne on 16 April, and by 18 April it was obvious to Henry Wilson and the French officers on

[36] Robertson to Haig, 6 Mar., 8 Mar. 1917, Robertson Papers I/23/11, 12.
[37] Haig Diary, 9 Mar. 1917, Haig Papers 111.
[38] *Ibid.*, 14 Mar. 1917.

Haig's staff that this major thrust had failed.[39] This encouraged the French government to set about replacing Nivelle by Pétain. For the next ten days the French government took pains to assure Haig that the offensive would be continued, but neither Haig nor Lloyd George believed them. When Pétain was appointed Chief of Staff on 29 April, Haig immediately wrote to Robertson that 'I think the time has nearly come for me to take up the "alternative plan" in earnest... But pressure on the German army must not be relaxed in the meantime.'[40] Thus ended the new Coalition government's first attempt to control the haemorrhage of manpower on the Western Front.

Manpower, December 1916 — May 1917

While Lloyd George and his civilian colleagues struggled to impose a strategy on the High Command which would limit casualties, they were engaged in a struggle of equal intensity to increase the supply of manpower for industry and the army. More ministers, more ministries, and more of the organised elements in politics were caught up in the effort to increase manpower and so, for the time being, manpower supply was more contentious in public than the control of strategy.

The new government's first move has been heavily and justly criticised. Instead of setting up a department to deal with manpower, to work alongside the new Ministries of Food and Shipping, the War Cabinet set up two, the Ministry of Labour and the Department of National Service. Neither was given the job of finding or controlling manpower. The Ministry of Labour incorporated the labour departments of the Board of Trade: the Employment Department (which ran the Labour Exchanges), the Chief Industrial Commissioners Department (which in peacetime had been the government's main instrument in industrial conciliation), the Trade Boards Department, and the Labour Statistics Department. It had been formed as a ministry which could be given to the Labour Party in part-payment for services rendered in setting up the Coalition, and its first minister was John Hodge, a 'rampaging and most patriotic working man' or 'a buffoon' according to the contemporary source preferred, the leader of the Iron and Steel Trades Confederation and acting chairman of the Labour Party. The ministry's principal asset was the Labour Exchange network, which offered a ready-made national organisation for controlling labour

---

[39] Rawlinson Diary, 18 Apr. 1917, reporting Wilson's views, Rawlinson Papers 1/7.
[40] Haig to Robertson, 29 Apr. 1917, Robertson Papers I/23/25.

supply.[41] But the task of forming a policy for the better use of civilian labour was given instead to the department of National Service.

It is tempting to sneer at the Department of National Service. It gave Lloyd George, writing his memoirs in the 1930s, a chance to snipe at Neville Chamberlain, the first director.[42] But mere personal incompetence cannot explain the chaos of manpower policy in the first months of the new government. As conceived, the new department was to have been responsible both for military recruiting under the Military Service Acts, and for the administration of a compulsory civilian national service scheme which had been foreshadowed in the last fatal deliberations of the Asquith Cabinet. The compulsory civilian scheme devised by Montagu before the fall of the Asquith government was rejected out of hand by the Labour Party: this is hardly surprising in view of Lloyd George's undertaking on 7 December to give them a civilian 'Derby scheme' first.[43] On 19 December the War Cabinet approved in principle a voluntary National Service scheme for civilian labour; in January the Manpower Distribution Board was incorporated into the Department of National Service to provide the machinery for allocating labour between industries.[44] Neville Chamberlain, Austen's half-brother, was appointed in a hurry at his brother's suggestion when Montagu refused to join the new administration. Besides the responsibility for attracting and allocating civilian workers, he was given authority over the enlistment machinery and the tribunals established under the Military Service Acts and previously administered by the Local Government Board. Chamberlain was asked for a plan which would use this huge improvised bureaucracy to get both civil and military recruits. Colleagues were soon alarmed, Lloyd George observing that 'this is one of the few cases in which I have taken a pig in a poke, and I am not very sure of the pig'.[45] When Chamberlain finally presented his scheme on 19 January he was roughly handled by the War Cabinet. His proposal to withdraw all but a tiny handful of exemptions from the 18–22 age group was rejected in favour of a schedule of the numbers which could be withdrawn from the essential industries. Instead of allowing him to take over the Employment Exchanges, the War Cabinet merely ordered the Ministry of Labour to lend the Exchanges. Lloyd George and Milner, the War Cabinet member who was to take most responsibility for manpower

[41] Rodney Lowe, 'The Ministry of Labour, 1916-19: a "still, small voice"?', in Kathleen Burk, ed., *War and the State* (London: Allen & Unwin, 1982), pp. 108–134; see also Keith Grieves, *Politics of Manpower* and Rodney Lowe, *Adjusting to Democracy* (Oxford: Clarendon Press, 1986), chs. 2 and 4. On Hodge see A. Griffith Boscawen, *Memories* (London: John Murray, 1925), p. 207 or W. Runciman to Asquith, 29 Jan. 1917, Runciman Papers WR 161(1).

[42] *War Memoirs*, pp. 804–812; cf. Lowe, *Adjusting to Democracy*, pp. 113–114.

[43] Labour Party Archives, N.E.C. Minutes, 7 Dec. 1916.

[44] War Cabinet Minutes, W.C. 11, 19 Dec. 1916, CAB 23/1.

[45] Riddell's diary, 14 Jan. 1917, *Riddell Diaries*, p. 183.

questions, now agreed that Chamberlain was inadequate.[46] Nevertheless he remained in office until August 1917: a living warning of the difficulty faced by the Coalition in finding capable men to fill important jobs.

Chamberlain's misfortune in having the wrong-shaped head and failing to impress the War Cabinet has rather overshadowed the difficulty of his position. It was not merely that his chief weapon in organising civilian labour, industrial conscription, had been denied him, as Lloyd George grudgingly conceded.[47] The War Cabinet also kept to itself the power to allocate labour between military and civilian uses. They could hardly have done otherwise, for the issue could have split the Coalition. Prothero, for the Board of Agriculture, immediately challenged the instruction to release 30,000 men for military service by the end of the month. Lloyd George, supporting him, ran into the opposition of the Tory landowning bloc, represented by Derby at the War Office and even more prominently by Walter Long.[48] Derby and Long, both highly influential among Tory back-benchers, were unbending conscriptionists. They were also large landowners who opposed the policy of ploughing grassland, on which the Board of Agriculture's food production plans were based. When Long presided over a conference of Prothero, Derby, and Lord French, the Commander-in-Chief, Home Forces, there was little doubt that the War Office would have its way.[49] But it was ominous that two senior Unionists could pre-empt policy, forcing men from civilian employment into the army with the implied threat of parliamentary action by the government's nominal supporters. Equally ominous was the aggressive posture of Addison, who argued that only his officials at the Ministry of Munitions could decide which were key employees.[50]

This guerrilla warfare between departments, though increasingly awkward as the year wore on, was as nothing compared to the trade unions' response to increasing pressure on industrial employees. The ink was scarcely dry on the Trade Card agreement in November when Addison and Sir Stephenson Kent at the Ministry of Munitions began to make private plans to replace it with legislation to regain control from the unions.[51] During December and January the ministry's main concern was to increase the rate of dilution of skilled by semi-skilled labour, but during February

---

[46] War Cabinet Minutes, W.C. 39, 19 Jan. 1917, CAB 23/1; Thornton Diary, 18 Jan. 1917, Bodleian Library, Milner Dep. 23/1.

[47] *War Memoirs*, p. 809.

[48] Lloyd George to Derby, 22 Jan. 1917, L.G.P. F/14/4/6.

[49] The result was reported to W.C. 42, 23 Jan. 1917, CAB 23/1.

[50] W.C. 41, 21 Jan. 1917, CAB 23/1. Grieves, *Politics of Manpower*, pp. 95–98, expands fully on Addison's objections.

[51] Addison, *Four and a Half Years*, p. 256; this was written on 17 October, before the scheme was even in operation. Memo. by Kent, 21 Nov. 1916, P.R.O. MUN 5/57/320/16, cited Wrigley, *David Lloyd George*, p. 186.

the War Office began to press for amendments to the scheme. Officials of the unions involved, of whom the A.S.E. was the most prominent, were summoned to a set-piece meeting on 2 April at which they were addressed by Robertson and Jellicoe on the severity of the military situation. Henderson then told them that the Trade Card scheme would have to be replaced by a more selective method of protecting essential workers.[52] The next three weeks were consumed in consultations between the union officials and their members, and between officials and the ministers involved, principally Addison and Henderson. On 27 April the War Cabinet decided to introduce the new Schedule of Protected Occupations on 7 May. Henderson had warned that there was 'undoubtedly grave unrest' in the country: Addison 'believed that the men would yield if the Government took a firm line'.[53]

Henderson was right, but the reasons for discontent were more varied than the withdrawal of the Trade Card scheme. The first of the 'May Strikes' began in Manchester on 30 April, ostensibly over dilution and the Trade Card scheme; but subsequent walkouts in Coventry, Barrow and Sheffield, organised by the Rank-and-File movement in defiance of union executives, were based on a variety of grievances among which dilution, wages and especially food prices were prominent. To exorcise the spectre of Rank-and-File, which threatened the very foundations of government's industrial relations policy, Addison and Henderson rushed to negotiate with the A.S.E. executive about the new Schedule of Protected Occupations, which they believed to be the root of the trouble. In a series of meetings they agreed not to call up skilled men before all dilutees in each area had been enlisted and not to call up any man over 32. This was a misjudgement. Despite these major concessions the union executives were unable to get their members back to work, and the strike continued, with arrests and deportations, until it was settled by Addison's efforts on 21 May.

The political consequences of the strike for the Coalition and its relations with the Labour movement were immense. The consequences for military recruiting and the War Cabinet's attitude to manpower use were no less significant. Lloyd George and his colleagues behaved as though the rumpus over the Schedule had caused the strikes, even though the strikes went on after the Schedule had been agreed. Quite possibly this was the only way to convey to Robertson and Haig that an industrial society could not be drained of too much skilled manpower without collapse. Nevertheless there is a disingenuous element in Lloyd George's suggestion to Robertson on 26 May that the army could now expect 'only scraps', and his insistence in the War Policy Committee in July that:

---

[52] Proceedings of conferences on 2 and 3 Apr. 1917, MUN 5/62/322.
[53] War Cabinet Minutes, W.C. 127, 27 Apr. 1917, CAB 23/2.

> The C.I.G.S. in a speech the other day said the nation was prepared to do anything as long as it was clearly told what was expected of it. Unfortunately that is only partially true. The nation was told that we wanted the young men out of the munition yards. Our efforts provoked a strike which lost us hundreds of guns and aeroplanes and did not in the end give us the men.

The efforts had not provoked the strikes on their own. Even in the summer of 1917 there was plenty of evidence that the introduction of the schedule was only of incidental relevance to the industrial unrest. Most disputes were about wages and conditions.[54]

On the other hand, the strikes were a powerful dialectical weapon for a War Cabinet which had now been reduced to conducting its manpower arguments with the military authorities by bluff. The War Cabinet's attitude to the use of manpower was stated, with some subtlety, by Hankey in April:

> Man-Power is now the most difficult of the problems which the War Cabinet has to face under the economic head. Their policy has never been very explicitly defined and may in time lead to a difficult parliamentary situation. On the one hand the War Office are clamouring for more men, and contend that, with the terrific offensive of 1917 just begun the army is below strength and is only receiving about half the recruits for which it has budgeted. On the other hand the demands for shipbuilding and agriculture are ever more insistent and in the uncertain condition of our economic future, and with the probability of a prolongation of the War, the Government feel it to be more and more dangerous to mortgage the future by reducing our manpower by any drastic steps. Although some relief may be obtained from the National Service scheme now being overhauled by Lord Milner and Mr Henderson, it is certain that the army will be very low for drafts by the end of the summer campaign... Although it has never been formulated in the War Cabinet Minutes it is understood that the policy of the Government is first, by keeping the War Office short to compel the soldiers to adopt tactics that will reduce the waste of manpower...[55]

If Hankey was right, the inner logic of the War Cabinet's position was that it did not wish to allot more manpower to the Western Front, preferring instead to maintain Britain's economic position for the war and the post-war period; the external reasoning, as presented to the soldiers in the War Policy Committee, was that, whatever its wishes, the War Cabinet *could* not send more men to France because of the likely political consequences. Certainly Lloyd George made little effort to defend his manpower policy to the soldiers except in political terms. In the confrontation over manpower which was to come in July 1917, each side used an elaborate bluff, relying on the other to be frightened by difficul-

[54] A. Reid, 'Dilution, Trade Unionism and the State in Britain during the First World War', in S. Tolliday and J. Zeitlin, eds., *Shop Floor Bargaining and the State*, pp. 46–74.

[55] Memo. by Hankey, CAB 63/19.

ties which it was not expected to understand. The politicians conjured up political bogies; the soldiers military ones. In the event the politicians were more afraid of military failure than the soldiers were concerned about political unease: and the soldiers were to win this critical war of nerves.

Although military demands were very large, and conceived without any apparent reference to the balancing needs of industry and agriculture, the War Cabinet's position in early 1917 was always vulnerable because of the inadequacy of the Department of National Service. Chamberlain, on appointment, had been given a very confusing brief. Lloyd George's promise to the Labour Party had effectively excluded the compulsory direction of civilian labour. This, in turn, made it impossible for Chamberlain to take a strategic view of the balance between civilian and military manpower needs. Instead he began a major publicity campaign, calling in January for an 'Industrial Army', and launching in February the National Service scheme, which fulfilled Lloyd George's promise of a 'Derby Scheme for labour'. Its essence was that men would enrol voluntarily, and undertake to be relocated if they were needed on essential war work. The inherent silliness of the scheme was that most of those who enrolled were, predictably, either unsuitable or already engaged on war work — the roll eventually included two admirals and a director of the Bank of England — and therefore added very little to the pool of available labour.[56] Meanwhile the determination of priorities was jealously guarded by the Ministry of Munitions. An inevitable result was that the department was the object of sustained ridicule in the press, both for its failure to impose compulsion and for muddles in its attempts to match men to jobs. This was the sort of public debate which the Lloyd George government could ill afford.

Food, Politics and the War Effort

The supply of food, both to the civilian population and to the army, was another major economic problem faced by all wartime governments, which troubled the Lloyd George Coalition from the beginning. Like the munitions supply, the supply of food depended on existing economic structures which were forced to change by the war; like the munitions makers, farmers and landowners were deeply entrenched in the political system. Governments who tried to control the food supply were entering a political minefield. Economic dogma could not keep government

[56] Grieves, *Politics of Manpower*, pp. 90–148. The Parliamentary Select Committee on National Expenditure produced a damning indictment of the department in its *First Report* (*P.P.* 1917–18, iii).

departments out of the market for food, but vested interests and administrative ignorance could, and in the event did, hamper efforts to bring about great and effective change.[57]

The most intense political manifestation of food problems was of course the fear of unrest caused by starvation. The Asquith Coalition had established Royal Commissions on the Wheat Supply and the Sugar Supply, to intervene in the market and thus protect the population against shortage and excessive price rises. Lloyd George's government, more enthusiastic about visible action, established a Food Controller, who after a long time produced a rationing policy, hoping that control could eliminate the risk of food queues and thus of revolution. Potential food riots were a permanent source of anxiety to the War Cabinet. Actual food riots, though rare, were met with vigorous policing: John Burns noted in July 1917 after an episode of anti-German violence directed partly against food shops, 'Out in the streets large numbers of police patrols on horseback and many P.C. and S. Constables in readiness for explosion of shop-breaking and disorder similar to what occurred yesterday.'[58] The grievance most commonly expressed by trade unionists was not over shortages and high prices as such but over profiteering, in which food profiteering was only a part. On the other hand, the Coalition was regularly in trouble with landowners and farmers, mostly loyal supporters of the Conservative Party, who were affected by food production policy.

Neither the political problem nor its economic background were created by the war. Economically, Britain's agricultural system had entered a new phase in the 1880s, as the powerfully depressing effects of cheap North American and Australian wheat began to take hold. Farmers in England turned away from grain farming towards a mixed husbandry laying much stronger emphasis on stock raising. Wales and Scotland continued to supply store cattle for fattening on English farms, and in some areas even animal feed was imported as grain instead of being grown on the holding. As a result, in the words of Walter Long at the height of the political agitation over the food production programme, 'This grass land is our capital.'[59] The process of accommodation to new economic realities had not been easy, and had taken its toll both on tenant farmers and their landlords. Although the traditional pattern of landholding in England — large estates let to substantial tenant farmers who in turn employed wage labour — was not to change dramatically until after the war, the immediate

[57] See L. Margaret Barnett, *British Food Policy in the First World War*; and Peter Dewey, *British Agriculture in the First World War* (London: Croom Helm, 1988), which concentrates on the economic history of agriculture and the effects of policy.

[58] Burns Diary, 10 July 1917, B.L. Add. MSS 46339. See also Panikos Panayi, 'Anti-German Riots in London during the First World War', *German History*, vii (1989), 184–203.

[59] Long to Bonar Law, 22 Sept. 1917, B.L.P. 82/4/20.

impact of the 1880s depression had been to reduce rent-rolls and cause landlords to sell some of their holdings, in some cases to tenant farmers who became freeholders. Either landlords or tenants or farmers owning their own holdings had had to find the capital to lay down pasture, an expensive and lengthy business. However it had come about, the effect had been to create a firm vested interest in pastoral farming. The situation even had its Irish twist. One result of the success of Wyndham's Land Act in 1903 had been to release Irish land for sale on an open market, and further the process of consolidation of holdings not for increased arable and dairy productivity — as the policy-makers of the Department of Agriculture and Technical Instruction had intended — but for stock raising. As in England, this diminished employment and depressed wages for agricultural labourers and created a class of prosperous grass farmers.

In England the politics of agriculture was well understood in the early twentieth century. With some well-documented exceptions[60] the deferential structure of rural society led farmers to follow their landlords into the Tory Party. Liberal strength in the English counties, when it came after 1885, was based on labourers' votes. The antagonism between farmers and landlords on the one side and the Liberals on the other was exacerbated by the popularity among Liberals of Henry George's single tax scheme for land reform, and by the demonstrable political success of Lloyd George's Land Campaign in 1912. By the beginning of the war the work of land valuers from the Inland Revenue, putting into effect the provisions of the 1909 Budget, was a constant source of complaint, much worked upon by Conservative politicians such as Long.[61] Agricultural Wages Boards, also established by the reforming pre-war government, caused similar annoyance. As a result the farming community was ready to dislike any government which had Liberal involvement or was connected with Lloyd George. State intervention of any kind was likely to be resisted, not only because of the farmers' cultural dislike of governments and interference, but because this particular government had a poor record.

Home-grown wheat was important to the war effort because of the submarine threat to the imported supply, but pre-war discussions of the wheat problem had assumed the superiority of the British navy over the German; plans were made to blockade Germany, but not to protect British food supplies by import substitution.[62] Agricultural policy during the war was slow to develop, but when it did appear it tended to follow a pattern which farmers had come to expect from Liberal governments. Under the

---

[60] Janet Howarth, 'The Liberal Revival in Northamptonshire, 1880–1895', *Historical Journal*, xii (1969).

[61] Long to Bonar Law, 4 Apr. 1915, B.L.P. 37/1/7.

[62] See Offer, *Agrarian Interpretation*, pp. 285–317.

Asquith Coalition Lord Selborne's committee on food production[63] recommended a guaranteed minimum price for wheat of 45s. a quarter, to
be operated so that no farmer could take advantage of it unless it could be
shown that he had increased his wheat output (or that he had one fifth of
his total land under wheat). The committee assumed that the effect of this
would be to increase agricultural wages, but that if by chance it did not,
steps should be taken by the government to increase them. Consequently
they recommended an inquiry into agricultural wages and earnings. This
was to become the pattern for policy recommendations during the war.
On this occasion it was allowed to drop, largely because Asquith did not
believe that the German submarine campaign should be taken seriously;
and a minority of the committee, Verney and Lord Inchcape, respectively
a landowner and a shipowner, insisted that existing patterns of commerce
and cultivation were better than anything the main report proposed, especially for post-war developments.[64] Selborne warned that without some
such policy, and perhaps even with it, compulsory tillage might become
necessary to increase the supply of home-grown food; and he developed
his thinking to include post-war agricultural policy, recommending that a
sub-committee of the Reconstruction Committee should consider extending the price guarantee indefinitely.[65] Although nothing at all happened
under the Asquith government, all the elements of a policy which would
bring the farming community into conflict with the government were
present in Selborne's report.

The situation became far more urgent when the 1916 harvest failed,
and even more so when the German submarine campaign intensified in
late 1916 and was finally declared 'unrestricted' in February 1917. When
Lloyd George's government took office, a combination of personalities
highly favourable to action in agricultural matters soon led to controversial moves. Milner entered the War Cabinet, and Prothero went to
the Board of Agriculture, prepared to tell the War Cabinet within days
of his appointment that an extensive tillage campaign, based on the recommendations of the departmental committee, was a political necessity.[66]
The institution of a Food Production Department within the Board was
intended to demonstrate a commitment to home food production, and
the Board also prepared a Corn Production bill, which was presented to
the Commons in the spring of 1917, embodying the proposals first made
in the departmental committee's report. But for the 1917 harvest the

[63] Including Milner, R.E. Prothero, Lord Inchcape, A.D. Hall, Sir Harry Verney M.P., Charles
Fielding, E.G. Strutt, and J.A. Seddon M.P.
[64] See above, pp. 102–103 and Stephanie Jones, *Trade and Shipping* (Manchester: Manchester
University Press, 1989), pp. 115–117.
[65] G. Boyce, *The Crisis of British Unionism*, pp. 134–141.
[66] W.C. 5, 13 Dec. 1916, CAB 23/1.

principal instrument of policy was the general power given to the President of the Board of Agriculture under the Defence of the Realm Act (D.o.R.A.). The Board made orders under D.o.R.A. requiring farmers to cultivate derelict land and in some instances to plough up pasture for grain crops. Compulsory tillage orders were applied by local inspectors acting under the authority of the board and on the advice of County War Agricultural Executive Committees made up of farmers and landowners.[67] They were often resisted, both by landlords and their tenants, and thus set neighbour against neighbour as well as against the government. This made for entertaining politics, as the still-powerful agricultural lobby within the Conservative Party battled with the government and its own conscience.

A greater piquancy was lent to the situation by divisions among ministers. As former chairman of the departmental committee, Milner naturally took an interest in agriculture, and on a number of occasions was appointed by the War Cabinet to be an 'overlord' for agricultural matters. Against him Walter Long and Lord Derby, the largest landowners in the Cabinet, took up positions against the tillage campaign, and made Prothero's life particularly difficult. Since Derby as Secretary of State for War was responsible for the conscription of ploughmen into the army, and Long as chairman of the Petroleum Committee had to find petrol for tractors, there was plenty of room for obstruction and disagreement. Added to this was tension between Prothero and the Food Controllers, first Devonport and then Rhondda, who in their attempts to control food prices declared maximum prices for staple foodstuffs such as potatoes, without direct consultation with farmers, and in order to limit meat consumption made regulations about slaughtering which disrupted the livestock market. Prothero and Rhondda made widely reported speeches condemning one another's departments by implication.[68] Devonport suffered the added embarrassment of Charles Bathurst, his Parliamentary Secretary and supposedly his mouthpiece in the Commons, who told everyone who would listen that he heard very little about his department's policies and disliked most of what he heard.

The policy of the new government was laid down by the War Cabinet in January. Prices for the 1917 crop were to be fixed under D.o.R.A. regulations, the War Office and the Board of Agriculture were to cooperate about agricultural labour, and the Food Controller was to regulate consumption.[69] The policy was immediately blown off course when the War Office declared that it would be necessary to take 30,000 men from agriculture by the end of January. Questioned by the Duke of Rutland at a

[67] For an account of the work of the committees, see Dewey, *British Agriculture*.

[68] This was at its worst in the winter of 1918, when food queues were especially tiresome: see e.g. Prothero to Lloyd George, 28 Feb. 1918, L.G.P. F/15/8/30.

[69] W.C. 33, 12 Jan. 1917, CAB 23/1.

meeting of the National Union of Conservative and Unionist Associations on 18 January, Prothero disclaimed responsibility, saying that the War Office had made the figure public without waiting for his reaction. This prompted Pike Pease (the Postmaster-General) to complain to Bonar Law and Albert Illingworth to Lloyd George. Illingworth observed that the War Office's action was 'likely to create a great reactionary feeling and active demonstrations against the Government' among the urban working class, while Pike Pease insisted that 'the result of the war may depend on agricultural production'.[70] On the other side Walter Long, believing that 'the pinch for men must come in April and May — even before', decided that he could not 'attach so much importance to crops which will not be available until the real struggle is over' and offered Prothero little support.[71] Lloyd George was responsive to complaints, and pressed Derby to slow down recruitment from agriculture. The War Cabinet set up a committee under Long to resolve differences between the War Office and the Board, as a result of which the War Office agreed to provide 15,000 Home Army reservists to work on the land; but the combined arguments of the War Office and the Department of National Service under Neville Chamberlain led to the conclusion that men were needed more in France than on the land.[72]

Prothero was more successful in gaining War Cabinet support for his long-term proposals. He elaborated his policy to Lloyd George in January, insisting that agriculture was 'politically . . . the most assailable point of the Government's position', and brought it to the War Cabinet on 14 February.[73] His scheme, based closely on the Milner committee's recommendations, was accepted intact, but opponents of the minimum wage provision were alerted by the War Cabinet minute and reopened the question on the 17th, achieving the suspension of that aspect of the scheme. Long remained acutely discontented, writing to Bonar Law the next day:

The effect on Agricultural labour must be bad as the inferior labourer, the old, the feeble, the dull, the crippled will all be dismissed.

The proper industry for G.B. is cattle-raising; also for Ireland, this plan is going to hit these industries very hard. Of course you must include Ireland.

The Setting up of Land Courts, for this is what Board of Agriculture control means, and Wage boards by *us* will ruin our Party.

The corn grower, a minority and the faddists, have beaten the stock farmers, the majority and the backbone of the country. But it is settled; in normal times I would resign at once, but I recognise the position and therefore don't even talk of it. I think the policy of fixing an artificial price is radically wrong and unsound, but I

[70] Pease to Bonar Law, 19 Jan. 1917, B.L.P. 81/2/18; Illingworth to Lloyd George, 19 Jan. 1917, L.G.P. F/28/4/1.
[71] Long to Prothero, 20 Jan. 1917, Long Papers 947/585.
[72] W.C. 42, 23 Jan. 1917; W.C. 45, 25 Jan. 1917; both in CAB 23/1.
[73] Prothero to Lloyd George, 11 Jan. 1917, L.G.P. F/15/8/3; W.C. 66, 14 Feb. 1917, CAB 23/1.

agree if you adopt it you must control rents and wages. I don't think you will have any serious trouble in the House but if you have and want me to speak I shall of course be ready.[74]

The parliamentary situation was not then critical. F.D. Acland, who had been advising Prothero without being taken entirely into his confidence, wrote at length to Asquith predicting accurately what subjects would be raised in Lloyd George's speech on food questions, which was down for a secret session on 23 February.[75] Runciman, who answered the prime minister's speech for the opposition was 'critical but not hostile', and the government's chief difficulty, according to the Radically minded Ilbert, who observed from the clerk's box, was the guaranteed minimum price which 'cannot affect this years' supply, & may have mischievous effects in the future'.[76] In fact the government's policy as then presented seemed to favour the farmer, and it was not until the Corn Production bill had been drafted and was ready for submission, in May, that grumblings of opposition became serious. In the mean time, critical attention was focused on the Food Controller, Lord Devonport. Bathurst trembled for most of March and April on the brink of resignation on the ground that Devonport's lack of policy was 'nothing less than a crime against the nation'.[77] Discontent about sugar prices and shortages, fears of shortages of imported wheat, a muddle about potato prices, and a feeling in Lloyd George's immediate circle that Devonport had no coherent rationing policy, led to angry clashes between the Food Controller and the prime minister. Internal disharmony was to become public embarrassment when the Corn Production bill was finally introduced in May.

The Irish Question

The government's stability in early 1917 depended on its ability to deflect political problems which were not directly about the war, and of these the most malignant, traditionally, was the Irish question. The Chief Secretary was H.E. Duke, a Unionist, who had succeeded Birrell in July 1916 and retained his post in the new government.[78] On 9 December Lloyd George summoned Redmond to discuss the new government's attitude

[74] Long to Bonar Law, 18 Feb. 1917, Long Papers 947/563

[75] Acland to Asquith, 18 Feb. 1917, Asquith Papers 18.

[76] House of Lords Record Office, Ilbert Diary, 23 Feb. 1917.

[77] Bathurst to Bonar Law, 30 Mar. 1917, B.L.P. 81/4/39; Bathurst to Milner, 19 Apr. 1917, Milner Papers 45.

[78] Eunan O'Halpin, 'H.E. Duke and the Irish Administration, 1916–1918', Irish Historical Studies, xxii (1981), 362–376.

to Ireland. He told the Nationalist leader that he had 'no intention at present of making any move for settlement of the Irish question'; but promised to resist any proposal to conscript Irishmen unless Home Rule were passed at the same time, and in the short term promised to suspend martial law and release untried prisoners held since the Easter Rising.[79] This studied neutrality about Home Rule, justified by constant reference to discussions with Carson and Bonar Law, was ominous for Redmond and his party. Although the Lloyd George government was, for lack of choice, more active in Irish politics than its two wartime predecessors, its action was always determined in the end by a paralysis of will in face of Unionist opposition. It need not have been so limited if the pressures of war on Great Britain had been less acute. During the war it was the Irish party which fell victim; after the war, as a direct consequence of the extinction of the Nationalists, the Union itself broke down. In the spring of 1917 it was still possible to hope that the new government could find a more benign solution, and the effective abandonment of that hope was an important sign that the Lloyd George Coalition was presiding over a metamorphosis in British politics.

Optimistic Nationalists, especially those who were not at Westminster, could believe in December 1916 that they were

> ... going to have a very great opportunity more especially if Sir E. Carson enters the Cabinet ... with the Liberal Party in fairly solid opposition, L. George's government appears to me to be very much at the mercy of the Irish Party. The Labour Party ask for a settlement of the Irish controversy from the Government they have joined; and a government containing Sir E. Carson can more easily than any other propose Home Rule of the right brand for all Ireland.[80]

But this would hold good only if the government could be persuaded to move quickly, since Sinn Fein was fast eroding the Nationalist vote.

Squeezed between Sinn Fein and the government, Nationalist leaders pleaded for Home Rule, but still reserved the right to attack the ministry on whose goodwill their political survival depended. Unionist ministers were not conciliatory. Long complained of Duke's 'deplorable' decision to release the Easter Rising prisoners, while Carson and Crawford believed that

> The Nationalist Party is now fencing to strengthen its electoral position, and is in some ways stronger than during the Autumn. There are however many good judges who think that a general election would sweep half of them from their seats. This

[79] Holograph notes by Redmond, 9 Dec. 1916, Bodleian Library (microfilm) Redmond Papers 15,189.

[80] Bishop O'Donnell (of Raphoe; a Nationalist) to Redmond, 10 Dec. 1916, Redmond Papers 15,217.

view is shared by Redmond and his friends [and] will tend to keep them on their good behaviour . . . [81]

Lloyd George, though sympathetic to Home Rule in private conversation with Nationalists, maintained in public that he was not free to settle without Ulster's consent and was pledged not to coerce Ulster into a Home Rule scheme.[82] In this climate Redmond and his colleagues took up a scheme put forward by Duke in mid-December. This would have set up a statutory commission of five Irishmen to put the Home Rule Act into operation for the whole of Ireland 'at earliest possible moment with necessary amendments', with a committee of Dominion politicians to act as referee when, as was expected, the Commissioners disagreed among themselves.[83] Much depended on the willingness of the Dominion prime ministers, expected in London in March for the Imperial War Conference, to act as brokers between the government and the Irish parties. Billy Hughes, the Labour prime minister of Australia, was an outspoken Home Rule sympathiser who depended on Irish-Australian votes: he urged Lloyd George in January to introduce Home Rule immediately, and T.P. O'Connor[84] thought him 'the best man for us' at the conference.[85]

But the Nationalists could not afford to wait quietly for the Imperial Conference. In late January Derby renewed the War Office case for Irish conscription: 'When we are putting all this pressure on English labour to find men for the Army, you are sure to get a cry as to why should England provide it and Ireland not contribute its proper share.'[86] This move, supported by Robertson in advice to the War Cabinet, put further pressure on the Irish party's negotiating position, since they were pledged to prevent conscription by all means in their power. On this occasion Duke advised that 'with a national settlement in Ireland conscription could be applied without grave risks and that without such a settlement it could be done but at the cost of much disturbance and some bloodshed now and intensified animosities later.'[87] The War Cabinet accordingly made its manpower plans without including Ireland; but the knowledge that the proposal was being discussed raised anxieties within the Nationalist Party. At the beginning of the parliamentary session in February Redmond

---

[81] Long to Bonar Law, 16 Jan. 1917, B.L.P. 81/2/16; Crawford Diary, 6 Jan. 1917.

[82] Lloyd George to Hughes (prime minister of Australia) 18 Jan. 1917, L.G.P. F/32/4/2; 'Confidential Memorandum', unsigned, 27 Jan. 1917, Redmond Papers 15,189.

[83] Redmond, 'Interview with Duke' 13 Dec. 1916, Redmond Papers 15,186.

[84] T.P. O'Connor was an author and journalist and Irish Nationalist M.P. for the Scotland Division of Liverpool; the only Nationalist to sit for a British constituency and the second longest to survive in politics, after Joseph Devlin, who held a Northern Ireland seat.

[85] Hughes to Lloyd George, 13 Jan. 1917, Lloyd George Papers F/89/1/1; O'Connor to Redmond, 22 Jan. 1917, Redmond Papers 15,215.

[86] Derby to Lloyd George, 25 Jan. 1917, L.G.P. F/14/4/18.

[87] Duke to Lloyd George, 30 Jan. 1917, L.G.P. F/30/2/8.

put down a motion calling for Ireland to be given 'the free institutions long promised her'. This was calculated to embarrass the government in dealings with the United States, and provoked the War Cabinet to a 'preliminary' discussion of Ireland on 10 February.

Lloyd George himself was delegated to find a way out which both Ulster and the Nationalists would accept. He dealt principally with Carson for the Unionists and with O'Connor for the Nationalists, since Redmond was ill. O'Connor at first believed that his motion would succeed in shifting the government towards a statutory commission of the sort proposed by Duke. He did not expect to get Lloyd George's support 'to bully Carson into the acceptance at once of a Unitarian Parliament — by which I mean a Parliament for all Ireland,'[88] and his strategy was to let the government wriggle on the horns of the Ulster dilemma:

> I am fairly in touch with Lloyd George, but I see him as little as possible and tell him as little as possible. He is dreadfully indiscreet and I am perfectly sure that the only way we can carry the solution which appears to me the only possible one, is by holding our tongue about it and having it sprung on Carson and the rest of them without any previous notice. Any talk about it would immediately bring into existence as before the diehard factors, which are as malignant as ever and whose power to destroy any settlement still partially remains.[89]

Lloyd George had therefore to deal first with his Unionist colleagues. With the aid of his 'Garden Suburb' of private advisers, he worked out a plan to turn the problem over to a convention of representative Irishmen.[90] Balfour and Bonar Law pondered variants of an amendment to O'Connor's motion which would postpone discussion to the end of the war unless Irishmen could agree among themselves.[91] The Garden Suburb, in concert with Carson, then produced a draft speech for Lloyd George stressing the importance of 'a united Ireland, in a United Kingdom, in a united Empire'.[92] Lloyd George took this to O'Connor, who warned him of 'disaster' if it was delivered:

> you will first have a violent speech, probably by Dillon, and then probably some dramatic course by us in order to arouse public attention, such as getting up and leaving our seats and declining to take any part in the division. This of course to be followed by an appeal to the opinion of the world from the House of Commons, and especially by an appeal to the American people.

---

[88] O'Connor to Joseph Devlin, 15 Feb. 1917, Redmond Papers 15,215.

[89] Ibid.

[90] Turner, *Lloyd George's Secretariat*, pp. 87–89.

[91] Balfour to Bonar Law and v.v., 24 Feb. 1917, L.G.P. F/30/2/14. Carson to Lloyd George, 3 Mar. 1917, L.G.P. F/6/2/18.

[92] Kerr to Lloyd George, 3 Mar. 1917, L.G.P. F/89/1/3.

Faced with this prospect Lloyd George undertook to let the debate, now set for 7 March, be adjourned to allow a staged debate in favour of an agreed settlement. After this interview O'Connor remained optimistic, reporting to Redmond that Lloyd George favoured a statutory commission and was prevented only by Carson, who in turn was prevented from agreeing to a settlement only by fear of losing his hold over the Ulster Unionists: this encouraged O'Connor to think that Lloyd George could, if he wished, force Carson's hand.[93]

O'Connor was wrong, and his negotiating strategy misfired. Asquith agreed only to 'think over' a request for help. Lloyd George was advised that although the Irish members were 'increasingly critical and obstructive', the House was sympathetic to the government.[94] On 7 March the War Cabinet bowed to Carson's reservations.[95] In the House that afternoon 'the Treasury bench was not well staged for placating Home Rulers. L.G. sat between Bonar Law on his left and…Carson on his right.' The prime minister's speech merely called for an agreed settlement, and was vigorously heckled by the Irish members. Redmond, returned to health, made a brief, bitter speech and led his party from the chamber.[96] The Irish members then convened a private protest meeting; issued, as they had previously warned Lloyd George they would do, an appeal for the support of world public opinion; and made a direct approach to the American President through Norman Hapgood, a counsellor at the United States embassy.[97]

If this was failure for O'Connor, it was also a failure for the government, now anxious to bring the United States into the war on the Entente side. Lloyd George's Garden Suburb renewed its attempts to win some concession from the Ulster Unionists in time to bring a feasible plan before the Dominion prime ministers. Finally, on 20 March, Carson advised Lloyd George that 'I do not believe Ulster would agree to come in [to a Home Rule scheme] on any conditions; but I think the conditions which could be offered to her should be ascertained and should be included in any amending Bill, so as to leave it open to Ulster at some later period to accept these terms,' He suggested a 'consultative assembly' of Ulster members of the Westminster parliament and delegates from a Dublin parliament, which would meet to deal with matters of interest to the whole of Ireland.[98] On 22 March the War Cabinet rehearsed all its reasons for grasping the

[93] O'Connor to Redmond, 5 Mar. 1917, Redmond Papers 15,215; O'Connor to Lloyd George, 6 Mar. 1917, L.G.P. F/42/6/13.

[94] W. Astor to Lloyd George, 5 Mar. 1917, L.G.P. F/83/1/2.

[95] War Cabinet Minutes, W.C. 90, 7 Mar. 1917, CAB 23/1.

[96] Courtney Ilbert Diary, 7 Mar. 1917; 91 *H.C. Debs*, 5s, 7 Mar. 1917, 425–500.

[97] Hapgood to House, 9 Mar. 1917, House Papers 466/I/69/4114; *The Times*, 9 Mar. 1917. For the warning see Astor to Lloyd George, 7 Mar. 1917, L.G.P. F/83/1/3.

[98] Memo. by Carson, 20 Mar. 1917, Scottish Record Office, Lothian Papers 566.

Irish nettle: 'the increasingly serious nature of the Sinn Fein movement, . . . the political situation, the general trend of public opinion, as recently evidenced in the London and Provincial Press of various shades of political thought, and to the great desire of all parties — and conspicuously the Labour party, — to find a solution' and decided to refer the question to a commission even after the Dominion prime ministers, in the absence of Hughes, had refused to become involved.[99] Lloyd George took the proposal to Devlin[100] and O'Connor. The latter reported to Redmond:

> Joe and I then saw Lloyd George; we did not consult him, so practically it is a deadlock. L.G. says that the Orangemen still insist on the 6 counties and was hopeless of getting them to move from that position. We told him he ought to defy them; he says he could not.
>
> He then made a second and almost as ridiculous a proposition . . . that if a vote were taken there should be two-thirds of a majority to secure inclusion, at the same time characteristically refusing to apply the same rule for exclusion. Joe and I told him quite plainly that any such proposition could not be accepted by the Nationalists. L.G. followed up with great triumph the concessions he supposes himself to have got from the Orangemen . . . [101]

This exchange marked a low point in relations between the government and the Irish party, but the irrepressible O'Connor still saw some hope because Lloyd George had opened the question of 'county option': a method of avoiding irrevocable partition by letting each Ulster county decide in a plebiscite whether it wished to be included in a Home Rule plan. Given the right terms Nationalists could reasonably hope that two of the six 'Ulster' counties, Tyrone and Fermanagh, would vote to be governed by a Dublin parliament, leaving only Londonderry, Antrim, Down and Armagh to cling to the Union. O'Connor at first hoped that Lloyd George and the Liberal back-bencher, Sir Henry Dalziel were 'playing a deep game for the purpose of compelling the Orangemen into county option',[102] but soon concluded that the prime minister was 'hopeless' on the point, as were the Ulster Unionists. The only hope seemed to lie in the House of Commons.[103] The Nationalists' urgent need for a plausible settlement was now intensified by the South Longford by-election, a 'deplorable tangle' in which three contenders for the Nationalist nomination wrangled with each other and with the local Catholic hierarchy as Sinn

[99] War Cabinet Minutes, 22 Mar. 1917, CAB 23/1; Long to Lloyd George, 22 Mar. 1917, L.G.P. F/32/4/54; Public Archives of Canada, Borden Diary, 22 Mar. 1917.

[100] Joseph Devlin, M.P. for West Belfast, represented Northern Catholics in the leadership of the Nationalist Party. He was first elected for N. Kilkenny in 1902, and was M.P. for Fermanagh and Tyrone when he died in 1934.

[101] O'Connor to Redmond, 29 Mar. 1917, Redmond Papers 15,215.

[102] Ibid.

[103] O'Connor to Redmond, 2 Apr. 1917, ibid.

Fein moved in strongly to capture votes.[104] Meanwhile negotiations with the government were hampered by temperamental differences within the Nationalist leadership. Dillon was irritated by O'Connor's optimism and willingness to keep on meeting Lloyd George, while Dillon's combative style in debate alarmed some of his colleagues.[105]

The War Cabinet, believing wrongly that the Irish party would apply pressure by obstructing the Parliament bill, which had to be passed in April if a general election was not to be held at a very inconvenient moment, wrestled with the incompatible demands of Ulster and the Nationalists.[106] On 17 April it discussed and rejected both of the expedients then being canvassed: temporary exclusion until the end of the war, when constitutional arrangements would be reviewed, and the alternative of a commission of Dominion prime ministers. Instead of evolving a compromise scheme which could be presented to both sides, it was decided to prepare a bill based on county option which could then be submitted to an Irish conference during the committee stage of its passage through parliament.[107] A drafting committee was set up, consisting of Curzon, Addison and Duke, but it was soon deflected by the news that the Nationalists would not accept the provision that 55 per cent of a county's voters would be required to support inclusion in the Home Rule area. Since Carson had registered his dissent from the county option plan, on the opposite ground that Ulster Unionists would think it was too easy for a county to be incorporated in the Home Rule area, county option was abruptly dropped and the drafting committee reverted to the idea of a 'clean cut' excluding the six counties until three years after the end of the war.

O'Connor and Devlin saw Lloyd George on 29 April and reported his attitude as 'extremely unsatisfactory'.[108] On 3 May they learned from C.P. Scott, who had discussed Ireland at breakfast with Lloyd George, that the prime minister was determined on exclusion because Bonar Law would lead the Unionists out of the government if Carson resigned over the issue.[109] Scott did not reveal to his Irish friends that the government intended to turn the question over to a committee of Irishmen during the

---

[104] Dillon to Redmond, 12, 13, and 14 Apr. 1917, Redmond Papers 15,182.

[105] J.J. Clancy to Redmond, 29 Apr. 1917, Redmond Papers 15,176; Dillon refused to negotiate with Lloyd George on the grounds that he had been betrayed in the negotiations of autumn 1916. Wilson, ed., *The Political Diaries of C.P. Scott*, p. 282.

[106] Redmond and Dillon agreed that they should not even try to oppose the Parliament bill. Dillon to Redmond, 12 Apr. 1917, Redmond Papers 15,182.

[107] The temporary exclusion scheme was suggested by the Garden Suburb. Adams to Lloyd George, 16 Apr. 1917, L.G.P. F/63/1/4.

[108] Dillon to Redmond, 30 Apr. 1917, Redmond Papers 15,182.

[109] O'Connor to Redmond, 3 May 1917, Redmond Papers 15,215; *The Political Diaries of C.P. Scott*, pp. 282–283.

bill's passage.[110] O'Connor pursued Lloyd George to Paris and enlisted the support of Arthur Henderson and George Wardle in pressing for an early settlement, but even he was losing hope, and was especially afraid that the passions expressed in the Longford by-election would kill the chances of county option.[111]

The outcome of these haphazard negotiations depended heavily on Lloyd George's perception of the balance of power in England, Ireland and the United States. He chose to ignore warnings that American sentiment would regard 'nothing but a united Ireland' as a satisfactory settlement.[112] Balfour, who had just gone to the United States to arrange for full co-operation with Britain's new ally, reported that the Irish question was 'apparently the only difficulty we have to face here and its settlement would no doubt greatly facilitate vigorous and lasting co-operation of United States Government in the war' but a Most Secret annexe to his telegram reported that the majority of American Irish groups would in fact accept partition, although they would not welcome it in public.[113] In the early days of May the prime minister seemed convinced that he could not afford to offend Carson. Nonetheless he took up a suggestion from C.P. Scott that the Irish Council, which was being proposed by the drafting committee as a body which would decide whether Dublin legislation should be extended to the excluded northern counties, should be given the right to make legislative initiatives.[114] The decisions of the drafting committee, containing no concession to the Nationalist position save that the county plebiscites should be held shortly after the end of the war rather than after a three-year delay, were set out in a draft letter to Redmond. This was delayed by Lloyd George's absence in Paris, and his private advisers took advantage of the respite to urge more concessions; but at the same time the electors of South Longford undermined the Nationalist position by returning a Sinn Feiner, and Lloyd George began to think of further delay.[115]

By now, though, English Unionists were in a ferment over Ireland. On the one hand, there was a movement to block any settlement during the war; on the other hand, Walter Long pressed for action on the grounds that

---

[110] *Ibid.* p. 285.

[111] O'Connor to Redmond, 10 May 1917, Redmond Papers 15,215.

[112] Adams to Lloyd George, 30 Apr. 1917, conveying telegram Plunkett (in New York) to Adams, 29 Apr. 1917, Lloyd George Papers F/63/1/5.

[113] Balfour to Lloyd George (telegram) 5 May 1917, L.G.P. F/60/2/15.

[114] Scott to Lloyd George, 6 May 1917, L.G.P. F/45/2/9; Lloyd George to Duke, 9 May 1917, *ibid.* F/37/4/3.

[115] Adams to Lloyd George, 6 May 1917, containing draft letter to Redmond, Lloyd George Papers F/63/1/6; Plunkett Diary, 12 May 1917; Adams to Lloyd George, 13 May 1917, L.G.P. F/63/1/7.

'you are on the edge of a precipice as regards Ireland'.[116] On 15 May Philip Kerr, of the Garden Suburb, produced a new draft letter to Redmond which emphasised the provisional nature of the government's scheme.[117] That evening Lord Crewe learned by chance from Redmond that the Nationalist Party would support a proposal to submit the constitutional question to a convention of representative Irishmen. Crewe went to 10 Downing Street in the early hours of the morning to get this news to Lloyd George.[118] Coincidentally Professor Adams, Lloyd George's chief adviser on Irish affairs, submitted on the 15th and 16th a set of proposals emanating from T.P. Gill, a former Nationalist M.P., for an Irish Convention chosen to represent the principal religious and economic, as well as political interests in Ireland.[119] The War Cabinet went ahead with its discussions of Ireland in two meetings on 16 May. In the first Carson reiterated his insistence on exclusion by a 'clean cut' of the six counties; the second meeting approved Kerr's draft letter to Redmond, adding, as an afterthought, the suggestion of a representative convention.[120]

The afterthought saved the day for the government. Redmond's reply, made the next day after consultation with his parliamentary colleagues, rejected the draft bill but accepted the convention. Sir John Lonsdale,[121] for the Ulster Unionists, accepted either the bill, provided that the excluded area was not changed by amendments, or the convention. Midleton accepted the convention on behalf of the Southern Unionists, who feared above all things being deserted by their Ulster allies who could retreat into an excluded area. Even William O'Brien accepted, on behalf of the 'Independent Nationalists'.[122] This was a remarkable unanimity among the Irish parties, but they were agreeing only to change the venue of the argument, not to settle their differences. Fortunately this was all the government wanted, to enable it to get on with its other business. Meanwhile the Nationalist party won a valuable respite from its recent history of ignominious failure. This was none too soon, for the party had major financial problems: Dillon wrote to Redmond on 22 May that 'the plain

---

[116] Astor to Lloyd George, 14 May 1917, L.G.P. F/83/1/7; Long to Lloyd George, 15 May 1917, L.G.P. F/32/4/75.

[117] Turner, *Lloyd George's Secretariat*, pp. 94–95; Scott Diary, 15 May 1917, B.L. Add. MSS 50904.

[118] Crewe to Asquith, 16 May 1917, Asquith Papers 46.

[119] Turner, *Lloyd George's Secretariat*.

[120] War Cabinet Minutes, W.C. 140, 16 May 1917, CAB 23/1.

[121] Lonsdale, who sat for mid-Armagh, was the Irish Unionist whip.

[122] Redmond to Lloyd George, 17 May 1917, Redmond Papers 15,189; Lonsdale to Lloyd George, 17 May 1917, L.G.P. F/2/4/1; Patrick Buckland, *Irish Unionism* (Dublin, 1972), I, 90–95; O'Brien to Lloyd George, 17 May 1917, L.G.P. F/41/9/2. O'Brien's group was a splinter, based on Cork, which had left the official Nationalist Party when the main movement had repudiated the policy of land reform contained in Wyndham's 1903 Land Act. O'Brien himself, an author and journalist, had sat for a number of Southern Irish seats since 1883, and currently sat for Cork City.

truth is that unless you lodge security for £10,000 overdraft next week the Freeman goes — and with it the Party and the Movement.'[123]

In this atmosphere it was relatively simple for Adams and Duke to bring the different parties to agree on the composition of the convention, which opened on 25 July at Trinity College Dublin, with 101 members.[124] Despite vigorous efforts by Adams, Sinn Fein was not represented; and the Ulster Unionists who took part were bound by an agreement not to commit themselves to anything without reference to their party outside. Thus the extreme parties, who held the key to Ireland's stability, remained untrammelled by the convention. Frightened moderates of all colours gathered to discuss impossible futures in minute detail. Duke addressed the members in an opening speech full of laboured classicism and concluded, to the general horror, 'never despair of the republic'.[125] A fortnight earlier, Eamonn De Valera, for Sinn Fein, had defeated a Nationalist candidate by over 3,000 votes in East Clare, the seat left vacant by the death in action of John Redmond's brother William. This was the beginning of the end for an agreed settlement of the Irish question. In London the War Cabinet, greatly relieved, turned to the more pressing problems of the war: German submarines, the forthcoming offensive in Flanders, and the parliamentary row over Winston Churchill's return to the ministry.

The Growth of Opposition

During the final negotiations which led to agreement on the Irish Convention, Lloyd George asked Asquith whether he and his supporters would help the government put pressure on the Irish parties, and found him 'perfectly sterile'.[126] Asquith was now recognised as the leader of an opposition, though not a very energetic one. In the short term his fall in December 1916 improved the morale of Lloyd George's opponents in the parliamentary Liberal party. His administration's fall had been anticipated since the summer, and its principal detractors identified. Liberal backbenchers, indignant about conscription and the bungled Irish settlement, knew that however bad Asquith was as a trimmer of Liberal principles, Lloyd George was even worse. Accordingly, the *putsch* of 5–6 December wonderfully mended relations between Asquith and the back bench. Even

---

[123] Dillon to Redmond, 22 May 1917, Redmond Papers 15,182. The *Irish Freeman* was the principal Nationalist organ.

[124] Turner, *Lloyd George's Secretariat*, pp. 95–99.

[125] R.B. McDowell, *The Irish Convention, 1917–1918* (London: Routledge & Kegan Paul, 1970).

[126] *Scott Diary*, 15 May 1917, p. 292.

John Burns, who refused to join the 'mutual admiration society gathering' at the Reform Club on 8 December at which Asquith delivered his vale-dictory message to loyal Liberals, had changed his tone towards Asquith from the 'personal repugnance' he had felt towards an author of the war in July to benevolence towards a man 'whose troubles mainly spring from his too indulgent treatment of a jealous rival'.[127] By January William Pringle, a savage critic of the old Coalition, had accorded Asquith the title, which its subject had done much to cultivate, of 'fallen statesman'.[128]

The honeymoon between Asquith and the anti-government Liberals was short-lived. This was largely due to a fundamental difference of aims, which prevented either Asquith or his immediate circle — Crewe, Runciman, McKenna and Buckmaster — from picking up the leadership of opposition to the new Coalition, which their natural followers wished them to do. All that Asquith and his circle of ex-Cabinet ministers had in common with the disgruntled Liberal back bench was a distrust of Lloyd George. It soon became evident that this was not enough to make either a policy or a position. In the first six weeks after their deposition the ex-Cabinet showed no inclination to oppose at all. Runciman and Grey fell ill, Birrell had already retired and was in any case gravely ill, Asquith first moped,[129] then after recovering his health took to reading Lucian. Sir John Simon 'did not seem ... to have very clear ideas about Parliamentary action'.[130] If they had spoken out, the ex-Cabinet would have had to say the things for which they had been reviled by their back-benchers during the previous twelve months. Runciman's criticism of the Lloyd George administration was trenchant:

> What with 'cold feet' in one office and shallow minds in another, and courage alone in the highest we may well feel uneasy. In normal Cabinets these qualities correct or supplement each other, but in a directorate of the French revolution type the whole business becomes a gamble which may turn out well or may lead from one embarrassing confusion to another, until the mess is insoluble. ... It is George and no-one else who counts, and if he is a genius and truly great, if attention to detail and the practice of truth and the mind that can efface its ambition in the larger cause are all negligible in time of war then it was better that he should be alone in power. If he fails, then — the prospect is hideous. Germany cannot win, but there is yet time for us to lose, & a continuance of Salonika expeditions — 100,000 more men taken from France & sent there recently — a contempt for the shortage of tonnage, & the exhaustion of British credit in America and disaster will pursue us as surely as it now pursues Germany and Austria.[131]

---

[127] Burns Diary, 8 Dec., 15 Aug., 7 Dec. 1916, B.L. Add. MSS 46338.
[128] Pringle to Runciman, 18 Jan. 1917, Runciman Papers WR 161 (1).
[129] McKenna to Runciman, 15 Jan. 1917, *ibid*.
[130] Pringle to Runciman, *ibid*.
[131] Runciman to Emmott, 3 Jan. 1917, Nuffield College Oxford, Emmott Papers 6.

But this was a practical rather than a moral point, an objection to Lloyd George's inefficiency in fighting the war, not a contribution to the discussion which some anxious Liberals had been pursuing for more than a year about whether War and Liberal principles were compatible. Aware that this was the ex-Cabinet's position, the custodians of the Liberal conscience would not put themselves out for Asquith. On 7 January John Morley told Ramsay MacDonald that he had not written in condolence to Asquith 'because he thought he was reaping where he had sowed'.[132] Arthur Ponsonby, an outspoken opponent of the war, asked fiercely 'what the Liberal Party is, and who are its leaders',[133] refusing to commit himself either to Lloyd George or to Asquith. *Per contra*, those Liberals who wanted the war to be won efficiently were much less likely to support Asquith against Lloyd George, though they might regret the manner in which Lloyd George had assumed the premiership.

The problem of leadership was to bridge this gap and, failing a lead from Asquith, Runciman set out an agenda for opposition, writing to his leader on 29 January:

> As we have — all of us — alas, — to make speeches before Parliament meets, it would be helpful to know what line you approve of... In our demeanour difficulties arise more from our own anxiety on a number of topics and the extent to which public attention can usefully drawn to them, than by reason of any compunction one has for stepping behind the Shop Window. For instance, can anything be said or can any enquiry be made about the extension of our commitment at Salonica? Can we make any detailed (or brief) reference to the conservation of tonnage? Are we to omit all mention of the uninterrupted withdrawal of labour from the farms, which is leading in all the arable counties to less rather than more land being ploughed? Are the potato muddles and the maximum (or are they minimum) prices to pass without comment? Is Mr Hodge to be mentioned, or shall we postpone any enquiry into his authority for his decisions on steel &c.? He is a buffoon. If we ask all these questions, we run the risk of appearing to be captious, and yet we can hardly allow the larger topics to pass unnoticed. I am much impressed with the anxiety of the country to have some responsible men acting as their watchdogs.... We must not fail in this duty and we should be failing if we ceased to be vigilant, and equally failing if we do not give the country the impression they can rely on us. How to achieve that without appearing to be prompted by party feeling or lacking in concentration on the patriotic aim, is an art of which you alone are the master![134]

Even this exercise in walking on eggshells was too taxing for Crewe and Grey, who concurred with one another that 'the present Govt. must have the best chance the country can give it & we should leave it alone and not

---

[132] MacDonald Diary, 7 Jan. 1917, PRO 30/69/1753.

[133] Ponsonby to ? Robertson (chairman of the Liberal Association in Stirling Burghs, who was trying to sack Ponsonby as a candidate on account of his 'pacifism'), 10 Jan. 1917, Bodleian Library, Ponsonby Papers, MSS Eng. Hist c. 666.

[134] Runciman to Asquith, 29 Jan. 1917, Runciman Papers WR 161 (1).

embarrass it.'[135] Asquith preferred Grey's approach, and to the exaspera-
tion of Runciman and McKenna February was another quiet month on
the Liberal front benches. At the beginning of March Runciman noted
that '[McKenna] says that we *must* go on propping up our distinguished
jelly – the late P.M. to wit!....We must do our best to screw him up
to an emphatic speech on Ireland, & I want him to pronounce against
agricultural counties...'.[136]

March produced, in quick succession, two issues which demonstrated
the weakness of the opposition Liberals' predicament. Soon after the Irish
resolution discussed above, the government ran into difficulties with its
own supporters over the proposal to impose duties against the import of
cotton goods into India: a directly protectionist measure which injured
Lancashire. Asquith and his lieutenants were, in the event, unable to
make anything of either of these opportunities. The government's tactics over the Irish resolution were determined by negotiations with the
Irish party and Ulster Unionist members, not with opposition Liberals.
In the Commons Asquith intervened only to propose a commission of
inquiry. Despite Runciman's enthusiasm it would have been difficult for
him to do otherwise, since the constraints under which Lloyd George was
working had been allowed to determine Asquith's own policy in 1916,
to the annoyance of many of those Liberals who were now opposing the
government.

The Indian Cotton Duties debate was more difficult for the government
because it aroused intense feelings among Lancashire Liberal members,
prominent among whom was Sir Frederick Cawley, a leading figure in
the Liberal War Committee. The debate was set for 14 March and up to
the 10th there seemed to be some danger that this storm in a hotpot would
threaten the government's stability. William Buckler, the American diplomat who monitored Liberal feeling for Colonel House, reported that the
proposal 'will be attacked by McKenna and other leading Liberals', but he
also reported Runciman's view that the debate was 'likely to produce so
serious a breach that he and his colleagues on the front opposition bench
are rather embarrassed as they have no wish to upset the present government. I gather that they would much rather let it "hang itself" by getting
into difficulties over the conduct of the war.'[137] Runciman's diffidence
goes some way to explain the government's easy ride in the debate. The
serious, emotionally charged opposition to the proposals came almost entirely from the government's supporters, notably Sir Henry Norman and

[135] Grey to Crewe, 2 Feb. 1917, Crewe Papers C/17.

[136] Runciman to Mrs Runciman, 3 Mar. 1917, Runciman Papers WR 303 (2). 'Agricultural
counties' refers to Conservative proposals to consider area as well as population in determining the
number of parliamentary seats allotted to counties in the Representation of the People bill.

[137] Buckler to House, 10 Mar. 1917, Buckler Papers 654/I/1/4.

Sir William Barton; and among both Liberal and Unionist back-benchers on the government side, the Lancashire patriots were in a small minority. At the best estimate (Cawley's) Lancashire Liberals would cast 11 votes, out of more than 50 Liberals who were counted as supporters of the government.[138] Lancashire Unionists were no more significant numerically, though Derby, ever a weathercock, having decided on 10 March that they would cause no trouble, reversed himself two days before the debate.[139]

On the anti-Lloyd George Liberal side feelings were very mixed. The two Asquithian leaders with most Indian experience, Crewe and Montagu, agreed that to reverse a policy which had been announced in India would be a mistake: Montagu declared that 'I am not going to be a party to a resolution asking the Government to reverse its policy, or to a resolution which will be regarded by the Government as a Vote of Censure, nor can I sit quiet if either of these two courses is taken.'[140] Bryce, admittedly now an elder statesman, was glad that the *Manchester Guardian* was 'sending the Fiery Cross round Lancashire' but felt 'sincerely sorry for Lloyd George....One man in a Cabinet is helpless, even though he be Prime Minister — for he has no power of control except by the threat of resignation — & I suspect if he used that threat they would take him at his word & dissolve....If they did dissolve — it would be a wicked but a tempting course — they would come back with a Tory majority...'.[141] Recognising the tide of feeling, Ilbert predicted from the clerk's box on 12 March that 'Lancashire will be beaten on Wednesday by a big majority',[142] and the next day 'it became known that Asquith would not seriously attack [the duties]. Had he done so successfully, the Government would at once have dissolved Parliament, & the general impression is that Lloyd George's ministry would have won its way back to power with increased prestige. Asquith does not therefore wish to turn them out just at present...'.[143] Asquith's speech struck Bonar Law as an attempt to weaken the government's position,[144] but it had no such effect in the division lobby: the government, 'never in real danger',[145] had a large majority in which few Liberals participated on either side.

It is a delicate task to use the Indian Cotton Duties debate as a measure of the government's strength in March 1917 or of the coherence of the

[138] Cawley to Bonar Law, 9 Mar. 1917, B.L.P. 81/4/8.

[139] Derby to Bonar Law, 10 & 12 Mar. 1917, B.L.P. 81/4/13,15.

[140] Montagu to Crewe, 10 Mar. 1917, Crewe Papers C/34; cf. Crewe to Runciman (on the subject of Free Trade in general), 5 Mar. 1917, Runciman Papers WR 161 (1).

[141] Bryce to Scott, 11 Mar. 1917, Scott Papers B.L. Add. MSS 50909.

[142] Ilbert Diary, 12 Mar. 1917.

[143] Buckler to House, 16 Mar.1917, Buckler Papers 654/I/1/5. This observation of the feeling around Asquith is corroborated by Astor to Lloyd George, 13 Mar. 1917, Astor Papers 40/756.

[144] Bonar Law to the King, 14 Mar. 1917, B.L.P. 77/1.

[145] Ilbert Diary, 14 Mar. 1917.

Asquithian opposition. It is hard to believe Hardinge's report that '[I]t is perfectly clear to anybody who has any knowledge of the House of Commons that Asquith's popularity in that Assembly is undiminished while that of Lloyd George does not exist. Asquith has the House of Commons in the palm of his hand . . . ', not least because Hardinge himself had no direct experience and only indirect knowledge of the House of Commons, and was a man who detested Lloyd George.[146] Opinions about the relative strength of the government in the House differed sharply, and no witness was disinterested. Ilbert thought that Lloyd George was losing his hold on the Commons because he had got out of touch with it, and criticised his speeches on Ireland and Cotton.[147] Astor reported before the Irish debate that the Commons was 'on the whole, friendly to the Govt . . . '.[148] Neil Primrose[149] estimated in the middle of March that between 50 and 100 Liberals supported the government, against 50 or 60 Liberal and Labour M.P.s who were outright opponents.[150] Even allowing for vast optimism on the Lloyd Georgian side, 60 Liberal and Labour opponents could have little effect on a majority made up of the Unionist Party and the Lloyd George Liberals, even when, as was not often the case, help was forthcoming from the Irish Party.

Any advantage Asquith enjoyed, despite these figures, in his command of the House was neutralised by a paralysing reluctance to use it. The Cotton Duties debate, which brought 46 Liberals into the anti-government lobby of whom none were regularly supporters of the government, is of some use in delineating 'a clear split between the supporters and critics of the government',[151] but most of the Noes were Labour or Nationalist members, with a couple of Lancashire Unionists. It is therefore hard to believe that Lloyd George's place 'was secure for the moment only because Asquith appeared reluctant to assume it',[152] but much of the strength of the government lay in its power to intimidate the House of Commons by the threat of dissolution rather than in any command of the House's affections. In a real sense the government's strength from now on was to lie in its command of public opinion. In a show of bravado Runciman claimed to welcome the prospect of an election, but he does not seem to

---

[146] Hardinge, the former Viceroy of India who was now Permanent Under-Secretary at the Foreign Office, was writing to Valentine Chirol, the journalist. Hardinge to Chirol, 3 Apr. 1917, Cambridge University Library, Hardinge Papers 31. Cf. Bentley, *Liberal Mind*, pp. 54–55, which relies rather heavily on Hardinge's judgement.

[147] Ilbert Diary, 14 Mar. 1917

[148] Astor to Lloyd George, 5 Mar. 1917, L.G.P. F/83/1/2.

[149] Primrose was Rosebery's younger son. He had been a Liberal M.P. (for Wisbech) since 1910, and held junior office at the Foreign Office and the Ministry of Munitions. He was briefly Lloyd George's chief Liberal whip.

[150] Reported in Lloyd George to Derby, 15 Mar. 1917, L.G.P. F/14/4/27.

[151] Cf. E. David, 'The Liberal Party Divided 1916-1918', *Historical Journal*, xiii (1970), 515.

[152] Bentley, *Liberal Mind*, p. 55.

have expected to win it if it happened,[153] and the most plausible conclusion is that the Asquithian group therefore had no real leverage over the government in the spring of 1917.

The Reappraisal

Though it was difficult to appreciate at the time, May 1917 marked not only the end of the Coalition's honeymoon period but also a profound change in the political context of the war. A combination of military, diplomatic and industrial developments forced Britain's leaders to come to terms with the possibility of revolutionary change, and to set their minds to containing it at the same time as merely winning the struggle with the Central Powers. Perhaps the greatest event on the world stage in the spring of 1917 was the overthrow of the Tsarist regime in Russia, but this would have meant little in Britain had it not coincided with the upsurge of industrial unrest in Liverpool, Sheffield, Barrow-in-Furness and Coventry.

The May strikes were the first and best proof that Lloyd George was right to be fearful of the political consequences of unrestricted land warfare on the Western Front. They were occasioned by the withdrawal of the Trade Card scheme, described above.[154] Meetings were organised by the Joint Engineering Shop Stewards' Committee — a Rank-and-File organisation consisting largely of shop stewards belonging to the Amalgamated Society of Engineers — from the middle of April, when the War Cabinet's intentions were clear. The first stoppages took place on 30 April, led by local shop stewards' committees. The government's response was to reopen negotiations with the A.S.E. Executive, who discussed the new schedules with Addison and Henderson in the first week of May. This produced the intended result: the government made concessions on the details of implementation, while the union leaders appealed for support in stamping out Rank-and-File activities. On 11 May Addison and Henderson evolved a strategy for prosecuting the strike's ringleaders, and this was approved by Lloyd George and the War Cabinet on 17 May. Addison agreed to meet delegates from a national conference of strike committees which began to meet in London on the 15th, while preparations were made to arrest seven of the strike's leaders. Between 19 May, when the men were arrested, and 21 May when the strike was called off Addison negotiated with A.S.E. leaders and representatives of the strikers together, consistently refusing to meet the strikers alone, but hinting at conciliation so long as no further attempt was made to bypass the local and national of-

---

[153] Runciman to Mrs Runciman, 3 Mar. 1917, Runciman Papers WR 303 (2).
[154] See pp. 128–129.

ficials of the trade unions.[155] The prosecution was dropped, and a general return to work began on 21 May.

Both sides were shaken by this episode. The strikes had not engulfed the nation: many engineering centres worked normally, including the Clyde and Tyneside, and there was considerable disagreement among the strike leaders and extensive criticism of the tactics adopted by the shop stewards. Addison and the government achieved a measurable success by alternating concession with the deliberate use of prosecution to intimidate Rank-and-File leaders. On the other hand, the government's strategy of conciliating trade union leadership was clearly not adequate to the problem.[156] Widespread discontent gave the Left an opportunity to challenge both the government and the union hierarchies, and the War Cabinet was anxious to defuse tension by identifying the major causes of trouble.

The appointment of Commissions on Industrial Unrest at the end of the month, with six weeks to report, was evidence of some desperation, and although their final recommendations were blurred, the commissions helped to shape policy for the rest of the war. The reports were written by the chairmen of the regional commissions and reflected their different backgrounds and styles, but the range of information presented was enough to concern any government. One of the most cogent was Vernon Hartshorn's report on South Wales which, coming from a right-wing pro-war trade unionist, carried considerable weight. Hartshorn was sceptical of the importance of pacifist sentiment, but he urged that bad industrial relations practices and bad social conditions would inevitably lead to dangerous discontent. He concluded that it was essential to prepare openly for major reforms after the war, and the document was in essence a blueprint for a post-war political programme. The Barrow-in-Furness report was more explicit about the social upheaval of wartime, pointing to extreme overcrowding caused by the influx of labour into munitions towns.

Perhaps the most disturbing report was from the Yorkshire and East Midlands Commission, which observed bluntly that

> The result of this apparently universal distrust alike of the Trade Union Executive and of Government Departments who act with, and through them, has led to the formation of a vigorous defensive organisation for the protection of the workmen inside their own separate workshops, known as the 'Shop Committee' or 'Rank and file' movement, with Shop Stewards elected from the workers in every shop.

The commission described this as 'a most serious menace to the author-

---

[155] Wrigley, *David Lloyd George*, pp. 191–197.

[156] Too great an emphasis on negotiating with the 'leaders' of corporate bodies was characteristic of Lloyd George's style. For a more extended discussion of this point see John Turner, 'Experts and Interests: David Lloyd George and the dilemmas of the expanding state', in Roy Macleod, ed., *Government and Expertise* (Cambridge: Cambridge University Press, 1988).

ity and the entire work of the A.S.E. and other skilled workers' unions' and other unions were reported as feeling 'distrust in, and total indifference to, any promise the Government may make, while some referred [in evidence] to '"Russia" and openly declared the one course open to Labour was a general "down tools" revolutionary policy to secure reform that constitutional action was failing to effect.' The Yorkshire Commission took it upon themselves to recommend that the government 'should immediately take steps to dispel certain allegations now current that the aims of the Allies are Imperialistic and illiberal, by a declaration of these aims in the spirit of the various pronouncements of the past and present prime Minister, and of the formula that the object of the Allies is "to make the world safe for democracy" '. The main thrust of the report was to warn the government about the impact of war controls on political and industrial authority, but its analysis was ominously comprehensive. The force of these reports was lost in the summary prepared by George Barnes, which took the highest common factor in them and concluded that food prices and resentment of profiteering were the main causes of the strikes; but the War Cabinet and the House of Commons could not now ignore the impact of war on the country's political stability.[157]

In this way the commissions anticipated the rather more dramatic impact of the Stockholm episode, which followed Arthur Henderson's realisation, on the road to Petrograd, that in Russia the war had completely undermined the basis of civil society. To add to military defeat on the Western Front, bankruptcy at the hands of the Americans, collapse of the Entente Allies in East or West, and starvation under the submarine blockade, British politicians now had to worry about the very willingness of the working classes to accept their leadership. Permanent political reconstruction, at every level from the War Cabinet to the electorate, became a necessity.

---

[157] The reports, including the summary, are in *Reports of the Enquiry into Industrial Unrest*, P.P., 1917–18, Cd 8662–69, 8696, xv.

5

UNCERTAINTY
May to August 1917

The period of consolidation for Lloyd George's ministry came to an undignified end with the failure of the Nivelle offensive, the challenge of the engineers' strike, and the clumsy sidestepping of Irish difficulties in the middle of May. It had always been clear that the regime could not be all things to all men: now it could be seen how dissatisfaction with the government could lead to changes, some temporary, some permanent, in party structure and the wider political system.

Inevitably, the short-term consequences were easier to see than clear signs of long-term change. Discontent among dissident Liberals began to crystallise around the ex-Cabinet ministers, and Labour's anti-conscription minority became more vocally hostile to the government's policy. This much had been predictable even before the change of government. Yet subterranean movements in the Conservative Party, and shifts of opinion in the majority Labour group, also began to point to a political future in which the Conservative Party would reassert its identity against the suffocating embrace of Coalition, while Labour would emerge more openly as an exponent of class politics. On the government's side, setbacks in the conduct of the war sharpened hostility towards critics. The example of the disturbances in Russia after the formation of the Provisional Government introduced another concern. A coalition which had been set up merely to improve the execution of war policy now became a barrier against the corrosive effects of socialism. In the eyes of supporters, especially the Conservative back bench, the Coalition's future thus came to depend on its capacity to control change in the long run, as much as on its potential for winning the war. Politicians in both the main parties had worried about social upheaval since the 1890s, so this was not entirely new: nor were the frictions between Liberal and Conservative about how upheaval should best be contained, and who should pay the price. But until the beginning of 1917 the war had at least given them something else to think about, and when they began to think once more about the post-war world they were doubly alarmed. Slowly and unselfconsciously the Lloyd George Coalition began to make itself a counter-revolutionary government.

The course of political events was all the more difficult for contemporaries to predict, and for historians to follow, because of the different information and different perspectives which politicians brought to their work. Under the Asquith Coalition a great gulf had appeared between the front benches and the back, while the sense of distance between Liberal and Conservative ministers had been reduced though not extinguished. Under Lloyd George's government the political world was further stratified by access to information. In the centre, Lloyd George and his War Cabinet colleagues saw all the telegrams, heard all the briefings from senior military and naval officers, and enjoyed the benefit of private administrative intelligence from the War Cabinet Secretariat and Lloyd George's own Garden Suburb. Departmental ministers outside the War Cabinet attended the War Cabinet for their own departmental affairs, and evidently sometimes stayed on to listen to other departments' business. They were also invited to Lloyd George's working breakfasts, to which their junior ministers came as well. These affairs acquired a regular pattern during 1917, reflecting the need to give political rather than merely administrative direction, with Liberal and Conservative members of the government meeting on alternate Wednesdays to hear the prime minister's account of political events. Not all the eligible ministers attended every occasion, and it was clearly an inadequate substitute for regular communication and consultation in Cabinet. This created an important second tier of ministers, whose detached relationship with the inner circle gave plenty of opportunity to nurture grievances, whether against Lloyd George or against the Conservative leadership, or both. Walter Long and Lord Derby were especially active in this middle world, with Crawford a keen observer. Together with the third tier of politics — the parliamentary secretaries and whips who made up most of the large payroll vote in the House of Commons — these ministers held the key to the survival of the Coalition.

They did so because the back bench, which constituted the fourth tier, was weakened by partisan divisions and sheer lack of talent, and hamstrung by its lack of access to information. Apart from the dissident Liberal and Labour members, most M.P.s with a hint of capacity and a few without it had been included in the ministry in December 1916. Although there was plenty of room for right-wing discontent in 1917, there was no one to lead it. The greatest challenge to the Coalition came from the National Party, whose most prominent member, Brigadier-General Henry Page-Croft, had fallen out with his army superiors. Despite thirty years in a safe seat at Bournemouth, and political attitudes which returned to fashion in the

1920s, Page Croft was only able to reach junior ministerial office in 1940, at the age of 59: he was a natural rebel, but not a plausible alternative to the existing front bench. Not until Carson resigned from the War Cabinet at the end of the year did a real opposition leader emerge on the Conservative side, and Carson was by then obsessed with Ireland. The main body of Unionist M.P.s got most of its information and opinions from the *Morning Post*, the *Globe*, the *National Review* or the Harmsworth newspapers, while waiting for some sign of leadership from senior Conservatives among the second tier of ministers. They never got it: but most of the interesting political crises of 1917 centred on the question of whether one or other of those ministers would break away and exploit the latent hostility of Conservatives to the Coalition.

Among Liberals the lines of division were different but hardly clearer. At the highest levels of the party only Edwin Montagu ever managed to cross the slender bridge between Asquithian and Lloyd Georgian wings, becoming Secretary of State for India in June 1917. Winston Churchill, never a natural Asquithian, returned with obvious pleasure to the ministry at the same time, causing great turmoil on the Conservative benches. Apart from those two, Liberal ex-Cabinet ministers and other former office-holders fell naturally into two camps, with only Christopher Addison representing substantial political or administrative experience on Lloyd George's side. In addition Lloyd George had his whips: Neil Primrose until May 1917, then Frederick Guest, with a number of junior whips and parliamentary secretaries to be the nucleus of a Lloyd George Liberal Party within the Commons. This group was very small, with A.C. Beck, Frederick Kellaway and Thomas Macnamara being its most prominent members. The Liberal War Committee of 1916 appears to have remained in being, though its *raison d'être* had largely been made obsolete by the fall of Asquith's Cabinet.

Asquith had the rest of the former Liberal front bench and a body of whips, who controlled the dwindling resources of the 'official' party: John Gulland and Geoffrey Howard. Gulland and Howard were almost the only means of communication between the ex-Cabinet ministers and the main body of Liberal M.P.s. Asquith and the former ministers, though loquacious enough to the press, had been cut off from Lloyd George's opponents outside the ministry and found it hard to resume a dialogue with the back bench. Consequently a majority of Liberal back-benchers shared with their Conservative opponents a sense of isolation from both the government and the opposition front benches. Their information and opinions, too, came from newspapers, in their case the *Westminster Gazette* and the weekly *Nation* if they distrusted Lloyd George, the *Manchester Guardian* if they did not. Most Liberal M.P.s continued to support the government throughout 1917, while those who did not do so were slow to settle on the former ministers as their natural leaders.

Although Liberal and Conservative M.P.s considered themselves an essential part of the 'political nation', their isolation from the centre of power in mid-1917 was matched by their isolation from the population outside Westminster, an isolation which was at its most extreme in the last two years of the war. The suspension of conventional constituency activities, the conscription of party agents into the forces, and the very substantial movements of population during the war, especially in the major cities, left many M.P.s without the means to 'represent' their constituents or reflect their views confidently. Divining public opinion in wartime was more than usually a matter of intuition, reading the newspapers, or sheer guesswork. Anybody could guess: Lloyd George's Liberal entourage, whose roots in the constituencies were weaker than anyone else's, often guessed that the electorate was more sympathetic than the House of Commons towards the Coalition, and threatened M.P.s with a dissolution which would sweep many of them away. The wave of industrial unrest in the spring of 1917 shook Westminster's confidence in the level of popular support for the war and thus for the Coalition. Political calculations about the effect of a general election became more convoluted, and were further complicated by the general agreement that no election could take place until a new register could be drawn up under the Representation of the People Act.

No party was immune from doubt about its level of popular support, but the Labour Party found it particularly difficult to assess its own strength. Labour's local activities, especially the work of Trades Councils in dealing with welfare questions as well as industrial relations, gave the party useful access to popular opinion. But no one could be certain that in a confrontation with the Coalition this could be translated into political support: indeed no one could be certain that the Labour Party would be in confrontation with the Coalition at all if an election were called. During the consolidation of the Coalition Labour could be seen in simple terms as the sum of two tendencies. Like any other European socialist movement, it seemed to contain a 'moderate' (i.e. patriotic and pro-war) majority and an 'extreme' (anti-war) minority. In Britain the connection between the trade unions and the political wing of the Labour movement was more exclusive than elsewhere in Europe, and the trade unions were all to be counted on the patriotic side. In the eyes of Coalition leaders the ideal type of a right-thinking Labour politician was 'rampaging' John Hodge, who was both an M.P. and a leader of the steelworkers' union. The enemy was Ramsay MacDonald. This comforting dichotomy of patriotic and minority Labour politics began to break down in the spring of 1917, further confusing the political map. Labour M.P.s remained divided between pro-war and anti-war groups, but trade unionists in the country became increasingly sympathetic towards peace by negotiation and looked, through the fog, towards Russia as an example. When Arthur Henderson was forced out of the ministry in August 1917, Labour's centre of gravity moved away from the Coalition. Even though this did not lead to the consolidation of a high level of popular support for Labour, it was of momentous significance for the future of politics.

The interplay of Labour politics and the needs of the Coalition lent a unity to the period between the May strikes and the climax of the 'Stockholm affair' in August. Increasingly the working-class Left, whether in politics, on the shop floor, or in Russia, was identified as the enemy. The problem for politicians in the centre and on the Right was to settle their own differences and thereby increase their chances of defeating the threat. Unfortunately the war, which had caused the problem, gravely impeded its solution.

Analysis of the period, as before, must begin with the strategic dilemmas which the government faced, and the ill-fated decision to support Haig in his eagerness to attack through Flanders in 1917. This led ministers and their political opponents to reconsider the pressure towards a negotiated peace, which now became an important element in domestic politics. The climax of this reappraisal was the Stockholm incident of August 1917, in which Arthur Henderson as secretary of the Labour Party urged his party to send delegates to an International Socialist Conference at which German socialists were to be represented. This caused his colleagues in the War Cabinet to force his resignation, affecting the course of relations between Labour and the Coalition for the rest of the war. 'Peace' also added an extra flavour to the stew of factional issues within and between the major parties, helping to give some shape to a new alignment in opposition. To deal with these problems, the government was reshuffled in July and August, and serious discussions began within the Coalition about the best tactics for an eventual appeal to the electorate. The 'crisis' of December 1916 had overturned Asquith's leadership of the Liberal Party, but of itself it had not destroyed the old political order. The steady emergence of a Coalition political strategy, which involved an election to consolidate the reconstruction of the party system, cannot be attributed only to the overthrow of the Asquith Coalition. Discontent in the workshops and growing fear about the likely outcome of the war persuaded Lloyd George and his new colleagues that they should not return to the old party system, and that a political world safe for the new Coalition would have to be constructed afresh.

The Dilemmas of Strategy

After the débâcle of the Nivelle offensive the Coalition was under intense pressure to get its strategy right for the summer fighting on the Western Front. The Nivelle episode confirmed back-bench Unionist suspicions of the prime minister's character and motives. On the other hand, the government saw greater dangers than ever in the policy of giving the soldiers what they asked for: neither men nor munitions were available in quantities to be squandered. In the end the soldiers were given almost everything they wanted, and used their opportunity to fight the battle of Passchendaele, more accurately known as the third battle of Ypres.

In his memoirs Lloyd George was more defensive about his role in this decision than about any other episode in the war. 'And it is one of the bitter ironies of the war that I, who have been ruthlessly assailed in books, in the Press and in speeches for "interfering with the soldiers" should carry with me as my most painful regret the memory that on this issue I did *not* justify that charge.'[1] His explanation in 1934 was that he had no countervailing military advice to the optimism of Haig and Robertson, and that in the circumstances he could not have overruled the soldiers, who were, as he later discovered, concealing vital facts about the prospects of the campaign. It is now well established that the soldiers were indeed manipulating the War Cabinet's information,[2] but that is not a complete explanation of what went wrong.

The important changes to explain are the shifts in Lloyd George's views and the apparent balance of opinion in the War Cabinet in May and June of 1917. The Nivelle failure destroyed the morale of the French army and provoked widespread mutinies; but the future of French policy had been determined before the offensive was launched, by the change of government on 19 March which brought Painlevé to the Ministry of War and thus brought Pétain to the leadership of the French army in the last days of April. Respectively for political and for military reasons, neither man wanted to continue the attacks on the Western Front. The British government's main concern in May 1917 was therefore to maintain some sort of western offensive, and Lloyd George led the attempt. On 1 May in a War Cabinet discussion Lloyd George argued against a strenuous attack, but the majority of members, guided by Robertson and to a great extent by

---

[1] *War Memoirs*, p. 1304.

[2] Brian Bond, 'Soldiers and Statesmen: British civil-military relations in 1917', *Military Affairs*, October 1968, 62–75 is now superseded by Woodward, *Lloyd George and the Generals*, pp. 162–186; for a particularly blatant example, in which Haig concealed the implications of the French mutinies, see Robertson to Haig, 28 April 1917, Robertson Papers I/23/23 and John Terraine, *Haig: the educated soldier*, pp. 296–305.

an appreciation prepared by Smuts,[3] wanted to go on with the offensive. Lloyd George was therefore instructed to take this line in an inter-Allied conference in Paris on 4 May. This he did with considerable effect. Pétain, Haig and Robertson produced an agreed statement concluding that the Nivelle policy had failed and should be followed by a policy of attacks with limited objectives. Lloyd George resisted attempts by French politicians to suggest that offensives should be abandoned altogether. At the end of the conference both Lloyd George and his military advisers believed that the French would play their part in an offensive policy. Haig continued his preparations for a Flanders attack, even though Pétain and Robertson had grave doubts about the feasibility of launching an attack across low-lying ground which was subject to flooding.

The collapse of French military morale during May and early June was never fully revealed to the British G.H.Q., and little even of their information was passed on to the War Cabinet, but there was no shortage of hints, which Lloyd George had picked up at the Paris conference, that a major military effort might break the French army. The first stage in the Flanders campaign, the attack on Messines Ridge on 9 June, brought this weakness into the open because Pétain was unable to commit troops to the supporting attack. Haig did not pass this news on, despite promptings from Robertson, and responded obstinately to all doubts raised by Robertson about the level of support he could expect from the French army. He also seemed indifferent to warnings that the terrain was unsuitable for further attacks.

But it is unfair to Haig to suggest that his planning at this time was being carried on in defiance of civilian wishes. The 'civilian' position was far from clear. The British were faced by global strategic and economic problems which changed every week. The collapse of Russian military effort put all Eastern European activity in jeopardy, the entrance of the United States into the war, on which the French were relying, offered disappointingly little extra manpower, and decisions had to be made on the Salonika expedition, which was in a mess, and the campaign in Egypt and Palestine, which was offering unexpected opportunities. The engineering strikes and the manpower demands for food production restricted the flow of recruits. The War Cabinet system was facing a crisis of overwork in May, and was simply not taking enough decisions on these points. War Cabinet members did not know what they wanted, and this was the major reason for setting up a War Policy Committee on 9 June. Although its main work in the event was to adjudicate between Haig's Flanders plan and the alternative of a diversion of resources to Italy, its object was to

---

[3] General Smuts, the South African representative at the Imperial War Conference, had been co-opted to the War Cabinet.

review the whole strategic and economic position of the war. Moreover, the last coherent strategic appreciation which had appeared on the 'civilian' side — a report by Hankey prepared on 18 April, as Nivelle's attacks were failing — moved from an analysis of the risk of defeatism at home and the delicate economic and political position to the following conclusion:

> If the military operations now in progress on the western front do not promise big results — and at present the tendency is that they do not — we should conserve our strength in the main theatre until next year, when with America's co-operation, and with Russia reorganised, we may hope for better results. This does not mean that we must sit still. We must do the enemy all the damage we can. This can best be done by fighting a great battle with the object of recovering the Flanders coast, which would be the most effective way of reducing our shipping losses.[4]

Hankey, in short, was recommending support for Haig's Flanders offensive, as he had been doing since November 1916.

While no civilian member of the War Cabinet was fully committed to this analysis, no member had anything better to offer before the War Policy Committee met. It was agreed that some action had to be taken on the western front because any prospect of action anywhere else depended on keeping the Germans engaged there. Milner, who was later to be extremely sceptical of the Flanders offensive, had conceded to Robertson that the Palestine campaign was a 'secondary theatre'.[5] Moreover the Flanders offensive had been formally approved in March as part of the final settlement of the Nivelle question. Haig's attack on the Messines Ridge, which was in practice the beginning of the Flanders campaign, began on the day the War Policy Committee was set up, and had the *de facto* approval of the War Cabinet.

The War Policy Committee had been sitting for some days before it began to consider the question of the Flanders offensive. Milner, who was its progenitor, intended to begin with the Balkans and extend the discussion to shipping and labour supply questions. After the first meeting he complained that the prime minister 'had talked tosh at interminable length' and that he hoped that Lloyd George would soon tire of the committee and leave the other members to carry it on. By 15 June he had concluded that Lloyd George was 'as mad as a March hare'. But on 17 June, after the committee had been discussing casualties and the manpower situation with Macdonagh and Derby, he had come to the stark conclusion that 'we were not justified in throwing away so many men on the Western Front'.[6]

---

[4] Memorandum by M.P.A. Hankey, 18 Apr. 1917, P.R.O. CAB 63/20

[5] Robertson to Milner, 8 May 1917, Milner Papers 45.

[6] Thornton Diary, 11, 15 and 17 June 1917, Milner Papers 23/1. General Macdonagh was Director of Military Intelligence at the War Office.

Milner, of all people, seems to have been rather slow to come to this pessimistic conclusion about manpower. The shortage of men had been of manifest concern since January. Milner himself had been working on the reform of the National Service scheme for the whole of that time, frequently remarking that the war 'would end in a draw' or 'was gradually petering out', and that 'the position of Labour in the country was none too pleasant . . . war-weariness was fairly general.'[7] During May Lloyd George had put the position starkly to the military authorities, warning Robertson that

> the time had now arrived when we must face the fact that we could not expect to get any large number of men in the future but only scraps. He said this was because of the large demands for ship building, food production and labour unrest, and I [Robertson] am afraid that there is no getting away from the fact that there is great unrest in this country now as a result partly of the Russian revolution.[8]

Haig responded to this news, typically, by arguing that 'victory on the Western Front means victory everywhere and a lasting peace. And I have further no doubt that the British Army in France is capable of doing it, given adequate *drafts and guns*.'[9] Unlike Haig, both Derby and Robertson seem to have been affected by pessimism about the supply of drafts, Robertson believing that the supply would run out in the winter and Derby that it would run out very much sooner.[10] Robertson even opened his mind briefly, in early June, to the plan to reinforce Italy with guns, as an alternative to heavy fighting in the West. Haig closed it firmly for him.[11]

By the middle of June, therefore, the central question which the committee would tackle had been closely circumscribed. Any plan to shift large resources to the alternative theatres had been given up in advance, for although the civilians disliked the casualty rates on the Western Front none of them shared Lloyd George's belief in the East. Robertson was Haig's mouthpiece, and had stifled major doubts about Haig's Flanders plan because on balance he was more afraid of the results of sending reinforcements to Italy. The committee had nothing else to do but decide whether the Flanders offensive should be continued. Nevertheless, the positions to be taken by the various participants even on this single issue were still uncertain, except for Lloyd George on the one side and Haig on the other. It was a tentative and rather bewildered committee which finally adjudicated on Haig's plan.

[7] Thornton Diary 2 Apr., 4 May, 29 Apr. 1917, Milner Papers 23/1.
[8] Robertson to Haig, 26 May 1917, Haig Papers 113.
[9] Haig to Robertson, 28 May 1917, quoted in Blake, *Private Papers*, p. 233.
[10] Rawlinson Diary, 30 May 1917; Derby to Lloyd George, 26 May 1917, L.G.P. F/14/4/46.
[11] Haig Diary, 9 June 1917, Haig Papers 114.

Bewilderment made for indecision, and it took six weeks for a clear opinion to emerge. When on 20 July the War Cabinet finally agreed to Haig's plans for an attack, it was clear that the decisive factor had been Lloyd George's unwillingness to overrule the soldiers. Haig presented his strategic plan on 19 June. Lloyd George responded by raising the manpower question, harking back to the arguments pressed so strongly by McKenna in 1916 which he had then opposed: 'He wanted the country to be able to last. He did not want to have to face a Peace Conference some day with our country weakened while America was still overwhelmingly strong, and Russia had perhaps revived her strength. He wanted to reserve our strength till next year.'[12] On June 21 further argument between Lloyd George and Haig led to no result. Haig's diary note reveals as much about his own attitudes as it does about the committee:

L.G. made a long oration, minimising the success gained, and exaggerating the strength of the enemy. His object was to induce Robertson and myself to agree to an expedition being sent to support the Italians. It was a regular lawyer's effort to make black appear white! He referred with a sneer to my optimistic views. I told him that war could not be won by arithmetic and that the British Army being in touch with the enemy was able to realise how much the latter's *moral* had decreased. L.G. stated also that he had grave misgivings as to the correctness of the advice given by the Military Advisers of the Government. 'Robertson,' he said, 'had changed his opinions!' The P.M. so insisted on sending an expedition to Italy that I thought he had already promised support to the Italians.... [13]

It is clear that the intellectual quality of this debate was never going to be high. Haig's scepticism of the 'arithmetic' of war was matched by Robertson, who 'pointed out to the Committee that an officer of 40 year's soldiering was bound to base his views partly on military experience and instinct and knowledge of the service, and similar considerations which it was difficult to formulate briefly in writing'. Lloyd George had already observed that 'Similar reasons to those given now had always been adduced as to why we should do better than last time, and he had always been told that by applying the lessons of the past we should succeed. The experience had not unnaturally made him feel sceptical...'.[14] It was a conflict of authority, not of reason, and the outcome depended on political will.

By simply refusing to admit that alternative plans could work, Haig and Robertson eventually won the day. The decision to support Haig's plans was unpalatable to the War Policy Committee, but after 21 June the only ground for delay was a legitimate doubt about French intentions. Robertson had said in Paris in early May that the Flanders attack could

[12] 7th Meeting of the Cabinet Committee on War Policy, 19 June 1917, CAB 27/6.

[13] Haig Diary, 21 June 1917, Haig Papers 114.

[14] 10th Meeting of the Cabinet Committee on War Policy, 21 June 1917, CAB 27/6.

not succeed without active support from the French. Although Robertson found Pétain at the end of June 'like a man without a jot of confidence in the future . . .', and Henry Wilson had by then decided that the French could not mount a major attack, the military argument in favour of a Flanders offensive was quickly inverted, so that a Flanders offensive was held to be necessary precisely because the French would not fight on without it. As late as 16 July the Committee was still trying to make up its mind between strengthening the Italians and supporting Haig, but it discovered 'No new arguments & no new conclusions', and agreed two days later to allow Haig to continue.[15] Formal approval by the War Cabinet duly came on 20 July.[16] According to Henry Wilson ' . . . except Smuts all the War Cabinet believe that we cannot beat the Bosh'.[17]

The Dilemmas of Peace

The idea that victory might be unattainable had by now become one of the most important facts of political life, affecting the conduct of domestic politics as well as the private calculations of the War Cabinet. In the first months of the new Coalition the peace movement had been merely a minor political irritant. Nevertheless, with the departure of most of the leading Liberals from the government it was potentially a nucleus around which opposition might coalesce. Ministers therefore continued to treat any sign of 'pacifism' as an unpatriotic act, hoping to frighten M.P.s away from outright support.

The change of government in itself hardly encouraged any action by the parliamentary supporters of a negotiated peace. But the appearance of President Wilson's Peace Note in December encouraged the U.D.C. and some of its parliamentary sympathisers at least to talk. Richard Lambert, H.B. Lees-Smith, F.W. Hirst and Ramsay MacDonald prepared a memorandum for Lloyd George's benefit in January, urging 'an active diplomacy'.[18] The reception of Wilson's note, including the German reply which was felt to be 'fatal', had a depressing effect on the movement, suggesting as it did that the United States might now enter the war. This would inevitably deny the anti-war progressives their chief ally and comfort. Norman Hapgood and William Buckler from the U.S. embassy had been careful to preserve their contacts with Liberal groups in Britain as an adjunct to their diplomatic work with the government, and although

---

[15] Milner Diary, 16 July 1917.
[16] W.C. 191A, 20 July 1917, CAB 23/13.
[17] Rawlinson Diary, 23 July 1917, Rawlinson Papers 1/7.
[18] MacDonald Diary, 30/31 Jan. 1917, MacDonald Papers P.R.O., PRO 30/69/1753.

contact was to be continued their use, in the radicals' eyes, was that they were neutral.[19] Both Hapgood and Buckler were still definitely suspicious of Balfour and Cecil, now in charge at the Foreign Office, because they were 'hopeless' and 'somewhat indifferent, not to say frigid, about our possible participation in the war, because they do not know where we get off' on such subjects as the Pact of London, and the partition of the Balkans.[20] During the winter and early spring of 1917 the difficulty of pressing the government towards a negotiated peace was more than usually apparent. For once the government was known to be opening up conversations, albeit indirectly, with the German government, and the bellicose answers received from Berlin were discouraging to supporters of negotiation.

The Russian revolution in March and American intervention in the war on the Entente side in April made both the government and the peace movement think again about peace terms. Meanwhile the Dominion prime ministers, who arrived in London in late March for the Imperial War Conference, made it clear through Smuts of South Africa and Borden of Canada that they wanted a clearer statement of war aims, and preferably one which would not jeopardise possession of conquered imperial territories.[21] United States entry into the war did not, in the event, weaken the informal efforts made by American diplomats to bring the British government around to the idea of 'conversations': Buckler was still interested in mid-April in the Cabinet discussions of the previous November about the Lansdowne memorandum, which he explored with Runciman.[22] As Hardinge noted to Chirol, 'There is a great deal of nibbling for peace going on, and it is very distracting as there is no definite policy over here.'[23] The greatest stimulus to open political discussion of peace came from European and Russian socialists. Huysman, the secretary of the International Socialist Bureau (the Second International) proposed on 22 April that an international conference of socialists should be convened at Stockholm to resolve differences within the international socialist movement. This was taken up by the Petrograd Soviet on 15 May, and a joint committee issued an appeal to socialists on 11 July.[24]

[19] On relations between Radicals and the American government, see L.W. Martin, *Peace without Victory: Woodrow Wilson and the British Liberals* (New Haven, Ct: Yale University Press, 1958).

[20] MacDonald Diary, 30/31 Jan. 1917, reporting conversation with Hapgood; Buckler to House, 7 Feb. 1917, Buckler Papers 654/I/1/4, based on information from Noel Buxton.

[21] Records of the meetings are in CAB 32/1 and papers in CAB 17; see also C.E. Carrington, 'The Empire at War, 1914–1918', in *The Cambridge History of the British Empire* (Cambridge: Cambridge University Press, 1959), III, 605–644; N.G. Garson, 'South Africa and World War I', *Journal of Imperial and Commonwealth History*, viii (1979), 68–85; John S. Galbraith, 'British War Aims in World War I: a commentary on "statesmanship" ', *ibid.*, xiii (1984), 25–45.

[22] Buckler to Runciman, 13 Apr. 1917, Runciman Papers WR 161 (1).

[23] Hardinge to Chirol, 18 Apr. 1917, Hardinge Papers 31, f. 318.

[24] David Stevenson, *The First World War and International Politics* (Oxford: Oxford University Press,

This initiative created as much tension within the Labour Party as in the government. The Executive refused by nine votes to four to recognise the Stockholm conference because it was pro-German, but decided to send a delegation to Russia and to hold a conference of Allied socialists in June. MacDonald fumed. 'Here are great chances for this child of my heart & I am doomed to sit & listen to & witness the most appalling proofs of its imbecility.'[25] Others shared his view that there were great opportunities, at least for something. Trevelyan tried to work up support for an amendment to the third reading of the Consolidated Fund bill, 'declaring that the Allies' terms should be revised in view of Russia's attitude to Constantinople & no dismemberment'. MacDonald refused to support him, apparently on the ground that Trevelyan was doing everything 'off his own bat'. In the Secret Session of parliament on 10 May, according to MacDonald, 'Churchill made a good even if vulnerable speech pretty much on our lines strangely enough — no immediate prospects of a complete military victory, revival of diplomacy, Russia is out.'[26]

Although Lloyd George's attitude in the Secret Session was typically belligerent, he was already worried about the threat of military collapse in Russia. He had suggested to the War Cabinet on 9 May[27] that it might be worthwhile to consider the attempt to make a separate peace with Austria, and on 22 May, prodded by Buckler from the American embassy, he met Noel Buxton to discuss methods of detaching Bulgaria.[28] Simultaneously Lloyd George and the War Cabinet were assessing the significance of a letter from the Austrian Emperor to Prince Sixte of Bourbon,[29] which appeared to suggest that Austria was ready for negotiations. Arthur Henderson was sent as the War Cabinet's representative to meet the Russian government, and both he and Lloyd George were anxious that the Labour Party should also send a deputation to Russia.[30] Despite resistance from the Italians (who expected gains at Austria's expense from the Treaty of London) Lloyd George pressed his colleagues on 8 June to persist with moves towards Austria.[31] On the same day Lord Derby wrote to the prime minister 'I send you over Ramsay MacDonald's views as to terms of peace and I am bound to say if he would stick to them I do not think his visit [to Russia as a Labour party delegate] could do the slightest harm'.[32]

1988), p. 157. See also H. Meynell, 'The Stockholm Conference of 1917', *International Review of Social History*, v (1960), 1–25, 202–225.

[25] MacDonald Diary, 9 May 1917, MacDonald Papers, PRO 30/69/1753.

[26] MacDonald Diary, 10 May 1917.

[27] W.C. 135a, 9 May 1917, CAB 23/13.

[28] Buckler to House, 22 May 1917, Buckler Papers 654/I/1/6.

[29] The Emperor's brother-in-law, who was an officer in the Belgian army.

[30] Barnes to Lloyd George, 1 June 1917, L.G.P. F/4/2/6.

[31] W.C. 159a, 8 June 1917, CAB 23/13.

[32] Derby to Lloyd George, 8 June 1917, L.G.P. F/14/4/51.

Buckler noticed 'the growth of pro-Austrian sentiment is ... making for greater advances than you would gather from the Press .... Milner is now said to be pro-Austrian ... '.[33] Correspondingly, the War Cabinet became very anxious that MacDonald should be allowed to go to Russia, and put pressure on the Seamen's and Firemen's Union to lift its ban on his travelling there.[34] MacDonald even dined with Lloyd George at Walton Heath on 8 June to discuss war aims.

By July the government was giving clear signs of its willingness to hear, and perhaps adopt, the views of the anti-war radicals about a settlement with Germany's allies, if not about negotiations with Germany. Speaking in Glasgow Lloyd George left the future of both Mesopotamia and the German colonies 'for settlement by the Peace Conference'. According to Buckler this greatly heartened the 'liberal advocates of "no annexation"' because it represented a retreat from the right of conquest.[35]

Henderson's meetings with Russian politicians convinced him that a move towards peace was necessary to prevent the early collapse of the Provisional Government, and he believed that civilian unrest could force Britain down the same road.[36] He telegraphed this view to the Foreign Office while still in Russia. Hardinge and Balfour were alarmed that

> a voice has been raised in a responsible quarter advocating an early peace on the ground that it is doubtful whether some of our Allies can be relied upon to prolong the war, and that if peace is in consequence to be unsatisfactory we had better choose the most propitious moment for making it .... Once the idea that we shall have to accept an early and inconclusive peace takes root it may rapidly develop into a strong and dangerous growth, and I am anxious that it should be destroyed if possible ... [37]

As the more conservative members of the government woke up to what was happening, the *affaire Henderson* took on a political colour which effectively destroyed even covert co-operation between Lloyd George and the peace movement. Henderson on his return from Russia outspokenly proposed that a conference should take place in Stockholm. On 25 July

---

[33] Buckler to House, 14 June 1917, Buckler Papers 654/I/1/6.

[34] W.C. 165, 19 June 1917, CAB 23/3. The union, under the leadership of Havelock Wilson and 'Captain' Tupper, had instructed its members to 'black' any ship in which MacDonald attempted to travel. Barnes found Wilson 'considerably piqued at what he regarded as discourtesy on the part of the Workmen's and Soldiers' Council, which had never acknowledged his congratulatory telegram on the success of the Russian Revolution'. The ship in which MacDonald attempted to leave Aberdeen on 13 June was unable to sail. The episode is discussed in detail in Marquand, *Ramsay MacDonald*, pp. 213–215.

[35] Buckler to House, 5 July 1917, Buckler Papers 654/I/1/6.

[36] See J.M. Winter, 'Arthur Henderson, the Russian Revolution, and the Reconstruction of the Labour Party', *Historical Journal*, xv (1972), 753–773 for the best discussion of Henderson's experience in Russia.

[37] Hardinge to Sir Francis Bertie (Paris) and Sir Rennell Rodd (Rome), 31 July 1917, Hardinge Papers 31, ff. 368–370, 393–395.

the National Executive Committee of the Labour Party, on his advice, decided to call a special conference of the party to decide whether to send delegates, and Henderson, MacDonald and Wardle were selected to go to Paris to consult French socialists on the form it should take.[38] Meanwhile MacDonald moved a resolution during the supply debate, urging on 26 July that the British government should restate its own peace terms in view of the Reichstag's recent resolution against annexations. This suggestion was very badly received by the House. Not only did it find only nineteen supporters, it raised directly the issue of peace with Germany, which had not been contemplated even by the most flexible of Cabinet members or government supporters. Outhwaite, warning of 'virtually a revolutionary feeling' in the working classes, won no sympathy for his cause.[39] The ferocity of the House's response, which was matched by Unionists in the Cabinet, appears to have shifted the prime minister's perceptions. On 1 August Buckler predicted that Henderson's trip to Paris with MacDonald and his evident conversion to the view that war aims needed restatement 'alarms the "knockout" advocates, and we are perhaps approaching the moment when a struggle between them and the pro-negotiation forces will break out within the Cabinet'.[40]

This was prescient. Sensing the danger, Lloyd George told his Liberal ministerial colleagues at breakfast on 1 August that both America and France were opposed to a Stockholm conference with German delegates. The meeting decided unanimously that Henderson should not be allowed to go to such a conference as a member of the War Cabinet.[41] For all that, ministers were anxious that Henderson should not be forced to break with the War Cabinet, and both Bonar Law and Lloyd George tried to make it easy for him to stay in and avoid humiliation.[42] Lloyd George therefore supported him in the House of Commons in the evening, even though he had attacked him fiercely in Cabinet in the afternoon.[43] The Commons calmed down a little, but the Unionist attack was maintained in government. Carson on 4 August urged that the government should decide explicitly not to allow any delegates to go to Stockholm, remarking that 'it takes a good deal of argument to persuade [the Unionist back bench] that the Govt. was not behind Henderson in his visit [to Paris]', and pressed his opinion home on the 7th and 8th.[44] On 8 August the War Cabinet decided to refuse passports to Stockholm delegates, but at

---

[38] Labour Party Archives, N.E.C. minutes, 25 July 1917.

[39] H.C. Debs., xcvi, 26 July 1917, 1479–1590.

[40] Buckler to House, 1 Aug. 1917, Buckler Papers 654/I/1/6.

[41] Addison Diary, 1 Aug. 1917, Addison Papers 98.

[42] Bonar Law to Croal (editor of The Scotsman), 3 Aug. 1917, B.L.P. 84/6/99.

[43] Hankey Diary, 4 or 5 Aug 1917. Sanders noted that Henderson was badly received by the House but 'Lloyd George got him out of it in a very adroit speech'. Real Old Tory Politics, p. 89.

[44] Carson to Lloyd George, 4 Aug., 7 Aug., 8 Aug. 1917, L.G.P. F/6/2/42,43,44.

Henderson's insistence agreed not to announce this until he had had a chance to influence the Labour Conference, scheduled for 10th, to make up its mind against the conference — or so the decision appeared to Derby, though Lloyd George explained to Carson that it was the anti–Stockholm Labour members who wanted the delay.[45]

The events of 10 August seem to have been marked by dissimulation on both sides. During a Cabinet meeting in the morning, Lloyd George produced a telegram sent by Nabokoff, the Russian *chargé* in London, suggesting that the Russian government wanted to dissociate itself from the Stockholm conference. The accuracy of this telegram as an indication of Russian official opinion is in doubt, since it might have been solicited by the British ambassador, Buchanan. It was passed to Henderson at the Labour Conference. At lunchtime on the 10th, Henderson wrote to Lloyd George that

> Mr Sutherland forwarded me the telegram signed by Nabokoff on your instruction. I had already seen it and in the course of my speech, I took the opportunity of intimating that there had been a modification in the attitude of the new Government as compared with the old to the proposed conference.
>
> The conference has adjourned till two o'clock with no debate, in order that the different sections can take counsel as to the course they are prepared to support when we resume this afternoon.
>
> I think I ought to inform you that after the most careful consideration I came to the conclusion that I could take no other course than to stand by the advice I had given the day after my return from Russia. I endeavoured to make a statement of the position as I found it in Russia and since my return, both pro and con. It is absolutely impossible to estimate what decision the conference will reach. If you would like to see me at its conclusion, I shall leave myself at your disposal, for an appointment.[46]

At 6 p.m. the War Cabinet met and, in view of the fact that Henderson appeared to have gone back on his promise to oppose the conference, decided to force him to resign. Lloyd George saw Henderson and told him that his 'retention of the position of secretary to the Labour Party was no longer compatible with [his] membership of the government'.[47] Henderson's resignation was made public the following day, and his place in the War Cabinet was taken by G.N. Barnes, supposed by his new colleagues to be docile and predictable.

[45] Derby to Philip Sassoon, 14 Aug. 1917, Derby Papers, DER (17) W.O. Correspondence; Lloyd George to Carson, 9 Aug. 1917, L.G.P. F/6/2/45.

[46] Henderson to Lloyd George, 10 Aug. 1917, L.G.P. F/27/3/14.

[47] W.C. 210, 10 Aug. 1917, CAB 23/3.

The Dilemmas of Faction and Interest

Besides its significance for war policy, the Stockholm incident was the climax of an important reconstruction of attitudes in domestic politics. The Unionist Party during the spring and early summer of 1917 was manifestly sullen about the Coalition. A steady undercurrent of sectional grievances, from the Irish question to the food production campaign, rasped on Tory nerves and Bonar Law's leadership was once again under threat. Henderson's visit to Paris with Ramsay MacDonald at the end of July had evoked enormous hostility in the Commons, scarcely smoothed over by Lloyd George's conciliatory speech in the adjournment debate since a good many Tory back-benchers seem to have concluded from it that Lloyd George was behind the whole thing. Carson's renewed pressure in the War Cabinet represented a more fundamental resistance to the direction which the Coalition was taking, and Lloyd George's decision to force the breach with Henderson reflected the danger of trifling with Unionist sentiment. To that extent the prime minister and War Cabinet were being disingenuous when they attributed their grievance against Henderson to the fear of international complications and the effect on the morale of the British population. To the right wing of the Coalition, this was an important opportunity for a showdown with Labour and radical Liberalism: an opportunity to begin the redefinition of the party system. Meanwhile the hopelessness of Liberal reunion was borne in on the Liberals in the Coalition.

Until August, Lloyd George behaved towards his erstwhile colleagues as though he hoped to maintain the Coalition in being without splitting the Liberal Party, and as though in the long term he looked for reconstruction on different lines. The introduction of the Corn Production bill at the end of April came at a difficult moment in relations between the Government and the opposition Liberals. Lloyd George and his immediate colleagues — notably Addison and Frederick Guest — were embarrassed by the government's weakness in the House of Commons and anxious to retrieve some support from Asquith. McKenna and Runciman, especially the latter, were looking for an opportunity to score the parliamentary triumph which had slipped through their fingers during the Indian Cotton Duties debate, and found it in the debates on the Corn Production bill. Their efforts began with Runciman's speech on the first reading:

> ... I stated the case in forcible style, to the delight of many of our party and all the ex-Cabinet *barring the two Jews*. They liked my vigour — our party — and so far as I can see I made the Tories angry ....
>
> At all events we have made a start with the effective assertion of our views at last. There are still many of our week-kneed fellows who think that an election on

the topic will be forced by Bonar as the result of our attitude — poor creatures. I
am unrepentant. Asquith &c praised me loudly, but he will never vote against the
Government...[48]

It was not only the Tories who were annoyed: Addison 'was suddenly
seized with the desire...to speak in the House on the Food Production
Bill which Runciman opposed in a shocking speech yesterday...if anything can it is this kind of opposition to the Government which makes
one furious. Our difficulties both in shipping and food supplies up to the
present time are more due to Runciman than to any other man.'[49]

The process of testing Asquith's intentions and those of his immediate
associates began early in May. In short order Lloyd George offered the
Washington embassy to Grey (though with reluctance and at Balfour's
suggestion),[50] with the promise of wider powers than a career diplomat
would expect; offered Asquith a seat in the Cabinet; and offered a Ministry
of Reconstruction (as yet only notional) to Montagu. Only the last of these
offers was accepted, but then it was withdrawn. Asquith himself, so he
told the King's secretary Stamfordham, had advised Grey that he 'might
find himself seeing more eye to eye with President Wilson as regards the
conduct of the War and the aims of Peace than with the "Knockout" views
of Mr Lloyd George' and might therefore have to resign, to widespread
and damaging embarrassment. To the suggestion that he should himself
join the government, which was conveyed by the Master of Elibank on 9
May, Asquith's response, as described to Stamfordham, was

distinct, unmistakeable and decided. That 'under no circumstances would he ever
join a Government of which Mr Lloyd George was the Head as neither in character
nor capacity was he fit for his position. A man of great gifts, marked energy and force
of character he needs someone over & to control him and he knows this himself
— And, Mr A added, his Colleagues appreciate these feelings and also the almost
complete impossibility of things continuing as they are. Mr A does not believe that
the present system of government *will* last.[51]

It is not clear whether Lloyd George was, as Asquith believed, the
inspiration of this approach or whether he was entirely responsible for
its tone. Elibank appears to have set himself up as a broker between
the two leading Liberals, warning Asquith that Lloyd George might 'do
something desperate' like call an election, which would have the effect of
sweeping away every Liberal seat in Scotland.[52] Although Lloyd George
himself spoke to Asquith on 14 May, the conversation was confined to

[48] Runciman to Mrs Runciman, 24 Apr. 1917, Runciman Papers WR 303 (2).
[49] Addison Diary, 25 Apr. 1917, Box 98.
[50] Hankey Diary, 16 May 1917, Hankey Papers.
[51] 'Secret' Memorandum by Stamfordham, 18 May 1917, RA GV K 1185/2.
[52] *Ibid*.

Ireland, and it was left to Elibank to interpret one man to the other on the subject of Cabinet changes. He does not seem to have accepted Asquith's 'distinct, unmistakeable and decided' answer as final, for he advised Guest to 'Reconstruct, by including Asquith', and returned to Lloyd George to report progress.[53] On 17 May he saw Asquith again, confiding his fears of confusion and chaos if Lloyd George were left to govern without the ballast of Asquith in the Cabinet, but with no further success. The next day Montagu wrote to Asquith explaining that he had accepted a post in a Ministry of Reconstruction; Asquith replied in pained tones.[54]

The attempt to win Asquith was not abandoned. At Whitsuntide — 27–28 May — the house-party at Asquith's country home, The Wharf, included Lord Reading, the Lord Chief Justice. He suggested to Asquith that McKenna's acceptance of a directorship of the Midland Bank and his presumed consequent abandonment of politics 'wd remove a great obstacle in the way of possible reconstruction of the government'. Asquith ridiculed the suggestion that McKenna would bow out of politics, insisted that both he and Runciman were essential to a sound war administration, and proceeded (according to his own account) to abuse the present government and its personnel in the roundest terms. His contempt for the War Cabinet system, 'a hopeless & unworkable experiment', was only exceeded by his detestation of Lloyd George:

> I had learned by long and close association to distrust him profoundly. I knew him to be incapable of loyalty or lasting gratitude. I had always acknowledged & did still to the full, his many brilliant and useful faculties, but he always needed to have someone over him. In my judgement he had incurable defects, both of intellect and character, wh. totally unfitted him to be at the head...I could not associate myself with what [Reading] called 'the counsels' of any Govt. unless I had supreme and ultimate authority.

Except for that outburst, Asquith's note, which he appears to have sent only to Crewe among his supporters, grounded his decision to stay out of the government firmly on the alleged inefficiency of the War Cabinet system. This was consistent with his position before 4 December 1916, and was to an extent justified by the difficulties which were at that very moment troubling the War Cabinet and its staff.[55] His attitude contrasted with that of Crewe, who applauded his rebuff of Reading's offers, but observed that 'Badly as I think of the system, I doubt whether its defects have much real bearing on the course of the war, any more than

---

[53] Murray of Elibank to Asquith, 17 May 1917, Asquith Papers 18.

[54] Montagu to Asquith, 18 May 1917, and reply, *ibid*. 18. In the event Montagu entered the ministry as Secretary of State for India, after Chamberlain's resignation.

[55] Asquith to Crewe, 28 May 1917, Cambridge University Library, Crewe Papers C/40; on the War Cabinet's troubles see Turner 'The Higher Direction of War', *passim*.

the defects of the Coalition had, whatever they may have been.'[56]   On the other hand Asquith's other ex-Cabinet colleagues took offence at the government's policies, principally protection, the Corn Production Act,[57] compulsion, control of the press and (in some quarters) the 'knock-out blow'; while lowly Liberal agents simply saw that 'opinion moves strongly against the present P.M. especially among working men . . .' and that 'L.G. has offended the Irish nationalists by his attitude on the Ulster Problem.'[58] There were, in short, plenty of reasons for staying out of the close embrace of the Lloyd George Coalition; and Liberals of many persuasions and levels could agree to do so, so long as they did not enquire too deeply into each other's motives.

Gradually the combativeness of the Liberal front bench increased. On 22 May the regular meeting of ex-Cabinet ministers was urged by Samuel to appoint its own reconstruction committees to monitor the government's efforts. As McKenna explained to Runciman, he 'was opposed by cousin Edwin who told us that with the exception of the Trades sub-committee all the topics were being handled by Liberals and in a Liberal sense by the Government committee'.[59] The ex-Cabinet accepted Montagu's defence of the government and appointed only a Trade Committee: but within a month Montagu had forged an alliance with the ministry. 'You will not be surprised to hear that E.S.M. is going into the War Cabinet . . .', remarked Gulland to Runciman, 'As we say in Scotland, "Better a finger off an aye waggin!"'[60] The rumour was not strictly true — Lloyd George was still unwilling to create the new ministry of which he had spoken, and Montagu's incorporation into the government had to wait for the resignation of Austen Chamberlain and a consequent vacancy at the India Office — but it cut Montagu off from the ex-Cabinet.

Without Montagu's moderating influence the acerbity of front-bench Liberal attacks on the government increased, beginning with an intervention by Asquith in an attack on the War Office for its handling of the medical re-examination of wounded soldiers discharged from the forces. Asquith was urged to act by Pringle, and the news that he would speak put the government into a 'blue funk',[61] not least because it coincided

---

[56] Crewe to Asquith, 31 May 1917, Asquith Papers 18.

[57] 'The Runciman-McKenna gang are out to wreck the Bill.' Selborne to Milner, 23 May 1917, Bodleian Library, Milner dep. 45.

[58] See the views pressed respectively by Runciman and the agent for Kilmarnock Burghs upon Alexander Shaw, who was invited by Guest to become Scottish Whip for the Coalition Liberals. Correspondence, May 1917, in the Craigmyle Papers (in the possession of Lord Craigmyle). Shaw declined the offer after receiving Runciman's note, but before reading his agent's advice.

[59] McKenna to Runciman, 23 May 1917, Runciman Papers WR 161 (1).

[60] Gulland to Runciman, n.d., Runciman Papers WR 161 (1).

[61] McKinnon Wood to Runciman, 26 June 1917, Runciman Papers WR 161 (2); an analysis thoroughly confirmed by Derby to Lloyd George, 16 June 1917, L.G.P. F/14/4/52.

with the belief that the War Office 'as usual, has been making a beastly mess of things' and that Gulland was making special efforts to be awkward. Addison feared a cunning ploy in which the War Office Under-Secretary, Ian Macpherson, would be goaded into an aggressive stance before Bonar Law wound up for the government, 'and before you have had an opportunity of saying what the government will do etc. for Asquith to wind up his speech by saving the situation *for* the government again. This being afterwards suitably noted.' The parliamentary attack coincided with an electoral challenge from the Federation of Discharged Soldiers and Sailors, who put up a candidate in a Lancashire by-election against Derby's son Edward Stanley, an absentee candidate, and attracted the support of the Liberal M.P.s Pringle and Hogge.[62] Gulland was ill, and both government and opposition were distracted by the Mesopotamia report — which redounded little to Asquith's credit — but the sense of an impending clash was growing.

The passage of the Corn Production bill through the committee stages in early July provided yet another opportunity for Liberals to vote against a government measure on grounds of economic principle, and Tory organisers believed that 'It looks rather as if [Gulland's] party was now out for blood. A good many things are making the Government unpopular, and Asquith and Co may think they see their chance.'[63] The opportunity lay in combining anti-government Liberal back-benchers with Labour and Irish members who had specific sectional grievances against the bill, and the governmment had to face hostile votes of up to 100 members with a risk of being in a minority on the wages clauses. Only by pressure on pro-government Labour members was the difficulty averted. In fact the politics of food and the agricultural interest dominated parliamentary calculations in the middle of 1917, and the fate of parties and the ministry suddenly came to depend on a pre-war issue, revived in a new form.

The passage of the Act through its parliamentary stages did nothing to alleviate the stress on the food supply, and the reports of the Commissioners on Industrial Unrest emphasised that if food became short the impact in industrial areas would be severe. Pressure from the War Office to recruit men from agriculture did not let up, and the Board maintained its tillage programme. Late in May Milner was appointed by the War Cabinet to co-ordinate the tillage campaign, because other departments were refusing to help the Board of Agriculture by supplying petrol, or releasing men. Milner was faced with a stubborn rearguard action by Walter Long, who rarely missed an opportunity to complain to Prothero or anyone else who

[62] Addison Diary, 13 June 1917, Addison Papers 98; Addison to Bonar Law, 21 June 1917, Addison Papers 45; on the F.D.S.S. see Salvidge to Derby, 20 June 1917, Derby to Salvidge, 21 June 1917, Derby Papers 920 DER (17).

[63] Sanders Diary, 12 July 1917, *Real Old Tory Politics*, pp. 87–88.

would listen that 'Between us we are making the Country pacifist and Socialist' and that the ploughing policy was a policy of 'wanton destruction'.[64] He was encouraged in his view of the damaging political effects by Talbot, whom he quoted with evident pleasure as remarking that 'our agriculturists are gravely upset by the Corn Production Bill'.[65] Prothero continued to urge that the War Office should stop recruiting from agriculture, and Milner had to give Derby an instruction (which was however ignored) to that effect.[66]

Resistance to the tillage campaign and to the rest of the government's agricultural policy continued throughout the summer and autumn. The farmers' lobby was weakened by inconsistency. Philip Lytellton Gell, writing to Milner in July, protested that the government's failure to get on with the Corn Production bill was eroding the farmers' confidence: '...No class has been treated so inconsiderately, whilst they see the government — as usual — petting the trades unionists and factory labour. Farmers have less reason than any class to feel confidence in the Government's fair play. & now they are realising that Agriculture is to be worse represented in the H of C than ever, whilst the Nationalists and Rebels are still over-represented.'[67] On the other hand Long, pledging to support Prothero in the Commons over the clause which gave the Board powers to compel the tillage of derelict land because 'it is quite clear we are up against a party fight',[68] simultaneously made it clear that he believed the bill to be unpopular among farmers. He also kept up his attack on the tillage campaign, advising his own tenants that he supported Prothero in every way but that they should only plough land which would be more productive under the plough than it would be for dairying. With Derby taking the same position (and colluding with Long) it is hardly surprising that Prothero and Milner should feel exasperated.[69]

Another important feature of the politics of agriculture was its interaction with partisan dispute over the Representation of the People bill. Robert Sanders, who was brought back from Egypt in early May to be an assistant Conservative Whip, found himself almost immediately at the head of a rural Conservative counter-attack on the second reading of the bill. The report of the Boundary Commissioners, which proposed to take two seats from his county of Somerset, spurred him on; and at the committee stage, which began on 6 June, he began moves to persuade the

---

[64] Long to Prothero, 2 June and 27 May 1917, Long Papers 947/585.

[65] Long to Prothero, 12 June 1917, *ibid.*

[66] Prothero to Milner, 7 June 1917, Milner dep. 45; Milner to Derby, 12 June 1917, *ibid.*

[67] P. Lytellton Gell to Milner, 10 July 1917, Milner dep. 5.

[68] Long to Prothero, 24 July 1917, Long Papers 947/585.

[69] Long to Derby, 28 Oct. and 31 Oct. 1917, Long Papers 947/547; Long's circular to his tenants, Long Papers 947/660.

government to ensure that area as well as population was taken into account in redistributing parliamentary seats.[70] 'Agricultural counties' thus became the spearhead of a back-bench Conservative attack on the bill, whose contents had been shaped by compromises within the Speakers Conference and which was officially an agreed measure, being carried through the House by two Conservatives, Walter Long and Hayes Fisher, the President of the Local Government Board.[71]

Faced with the Corn Production bill and the Franchise bill, the Conservative back bench quickly succumbed to an acute sense of grievance and resentment against the party's leadership, against the Coalition, and against the Asquithian Liberals. Meanwhile the Liberal opposition began to sharpen its teeth for discussion of the details of the Franchise bill which were of particular concern to urban Liberals and urban Conservatives.[72] In this they were anticipated by the Conservative National Union, which had collected 150 amendments to the bill by 22 May, many of which were originated by the Lancashire association.[73] Political frustration and fear for the future made back-benchers on both sides of the House revert to outright partisan debate, with the added spice that the leaders on both sides were more inclined to stand pat on the bill as it had emerged from the Speaker's Conference. The result was a disturbed and uncooperative House of Commons, which ministers contemplated with growing despair.

The Dilemmas of Governing

A review of the Coalition's political standing in August, at the point of its first major resignation, reveals most of the important weaknesses which were to determine its behaviour in the coming months. June, July and August were full of pitfalls. In July the report of the Mesopotamia Commission was published. Although the commission had been set up under the Asquith Coalition, and criticised mainly the Government of India, the War Office, and a number of named military and naval officers, it reflected no particular credit on the new government. Austen Chamberlain, who resigned from the India Office in a characteristic gesture of slightly misdirected principle, was the only ministerial casualty. The government suffered, though, from the attack on Lord Hardinge, who had been Viceroy at the time of the campaign and was now Permanent Under-Secretary at the Foreign Office. He emerged with little credit from the

---

[70] Sanders Diary, 27 May, 10 June, 15 June, 6 July 1917, *Real Old Tory Politics*, pp. 84–87.
[71] See Pugh, *Electoral Reform in War and Peace*, pp. 104–106.
[72] Harcourt to Gulland, 29 May 1917, Bodleian Library, MS Harcourt dep. 448.
[73] Pugh, *Electoral Reform*, p. 106.

majority report, and a minority report from Josiah Wedgwood accused him of showing 'little desire to help and some desire actually to obstruct the energetic prosecution of the war'.[74] Hardinge, who disliked the Lloyd George regime, offered to resign but was persuaded to stay by Balfour. This led to attacks on Balfour for shielding a guilty man, generated by his old adversaries from the extreme Tariff Reform wing of the Conservative Party.

The furore over Mesopotamia coincided with the reconstruction of the ministry, a complex manoeuvre intended to remedy the political weaknesses which had become obvious in the first six months of the year. An important objective was to attract the few remaining waverers on the opposition front bench, of whom Edwin Montagu was the most attainable. As noted above, Montagu was wooed with promises of a new Ministry of Reconstruction, in which he could continue the work he was already doing as chairman of the Reconstruction Committee. Ministerial reorganisation had other purposes too. Obvious mismanagement at the Admiralty, and reputed mismanagement at the Ministry of Munitions, made Carson and Addison vulnerable. Addison was an easy target for the Conservative Right, but he was needed as the most credible Liberal in the ministry; Carson's administrative failings were obvious to his colleagues but his back-bench support made it impossible to remove him. Devonport fell ill, and a new Food Controller had to be found. Lord Cowdray's tenure of the Air Board was at risk 'because he cannot keep a place in the Government whilst negotiations are going on with respect to [his] Mexican oil interests'.[75] Churchill's re-emergence as a potential parliamentary critic made it important to shackle him to the administration, and grumbling among Labour and Conservative M.P.s suggested that a few more junior spaces could usefully be found on the government benches. Amid the distractions of running a war, it took Lloyd George and Bonar Law more than six weeks to bring about a reshuffle, while discontent mounted steadily.

The most troublesome part of the reshuffle was Churchill's return. His ambition had rebounded from the humiliation of being excluded in December 1916. His stock in parliament had risen rapidly since March, when he made a passionate and successful speech in defence of his Dardanelles policy in the debate on the commissioners' report. After this he had taken up the cause of soldiers who were recalled to the colours after being discharged with wounds, anticipating by two months the damag-

---

[74] *Report of the Committee Appointed by Act of Parliament to Enquire into the Operations of War in Mesopotamia*, P.P. 1917, xvi, 773, Cd 8610, p. 123.

[75] Addison Diary, 29 May 1917, Addison Papers 98. Cowdray's Mexican Eagle company was engaged in contract negotiations with the government. See Geoffrey Jones, *The State and the Emergence of the British Oil Industry* (London: Macmillan, 1981).

ing use which Asquith would make of the issue, and on 17 April he had been a leading critic of the suppression of the *Nation* by the War Office. Lloyd George recognised his grievance, and a *rapprochement* was organised through Guest. Churchill spoke in the Secret Session on 10 May, urging a postponement of the offensive. Immediately, according to his own account, he was approached by Lloyd George with a promise that he would be given a ministerial job as soon as possible.[76] In fact Montagu told Hankey before the debate that the prime minister had said before 5 May that both he and Churchill were to be offered jobs, and indirect approaches had been made to Churchill through Addison.[77]

The rumour that Churchill was to be offered the Air Board surfaced in the press and around parliament in the last days of May, and enraged Conservatives. A typical back-bench response came from Charles Beresford, who wrote to Bonar Law 'as head of the Unionist Party, to say that if Winston Churchill is appointed, I have a small Committee of well known and influential men, and we intend to hold meetings all over the country calling attention to Winston Churchill's career'. Typically of the objectors, Beresford went on to say that 'Personally I have no animus against him at all, in fact when we meet we speak and laugh, but I have the most violent feeling with regard to his ever being in office again...'.[78] The same feeling was forcibly expressed by leading Conservative ministers, including Curzon, Derby and Long; Sir George Younger warned, on behalf of the Conservative whips and Central Office, that 'his inclusion in the Government would prove disastrous to its fortunes'.[79] Cowdray warned that Churchill would merely use the achievements of the Air Board to advance his own career.[80] Younger's personal view was reinforced at a meeting of the National Union, where a resolution that Churchill's appointment would be 'an insult to the Navy and Army' was 'carried amidst cheers and with only two hands held up in dissent' in an audience of 300.[81] Lloyd George gave up this plan on 18 June, offering Churchill the Duchy of Lancaster instead, which he refused.[82] The only way left for Lloyd George to show his confidence in Churchill was to make a speech in his constituency, which he did at the end of the month, 'a sop

[76] Martin Gilbert, *Winston S. Churchill, Volume IV: 1916–1922* (London: William Heinemann, 1975), p. 17.

[77] Hankey Diary, 10 May 1917, Hankey Papers.

[78] Beresford to Bonar Law, 2 June 1917, B.L.P. 82/1/3.

[79] Curzon to Bonar Law, 4 June 1917, B.L.P. 82/1/4; Curzon to Lloyd George, 8 June 1917, L.G.P. F/11/8/12; Derby to Haig, 8 June 1917, Haig Papers 114; Derby to Lloyd George, 8 June 1917 (reprinted in Beaverbrook, *Men and Power*, pp. 359–360); Long to Balfour, 11 June 1917, Balfour Papers Add. MSS 49777, ff. 191–192; Younger to Lloyd George, 8 June 1917, with copies of other correspondence in B.L.P. 82/1/11.

[80] Cowdray to Lloyd George, 9 June 1917, L.G.P. F/11/2/3.

[81] Younger to Lloyd George, 9 June 1917, B.L.P. 82/1/11.

[82] Guest to Lloyd George, 18 June 1917, L.G.P. F/21/2/5.

to Winston for some scurvey treatment over the Air Board' as Geoffrey Robinson put it.[83]

Although the editor's seat at *The Times* was no guarantee of objectivity, Robinson's assessment of the state of politics at this point deserves respect.

> On the whole I think that the Government remains fairly strong in the country, and that it deserves to be strong on its record in the war and in foreign affairs. No doubt Lloyd George has proved himself a great diplomatist and stands very high in France and Italy. It is in domestic questions that he is likely to come to grief, and I put this down very largely to Bonar Law's incurable nervousness of the House of Commons.[84]

The most serious trouble in Robinson's eyes was the discharged soldiers question. The time had come for politicians to gossip, in their different styles, about the risk of subversion and dark 'influences' on popular feeling. Conservative Central Office had a long screed from the chairman of the Bradford and Shipley association complaining, almost in a single breath, about the Franchise bill, 'a gross violation and practically an absolute breaking of the Political Truce', the proposed limitation of liquor supplies, on the grounds that 'I have reason to believe that the revolution in Russia if not altogether due to, was considerably fostered, owing to prohibition of liquor', and increases in the price of tobacco and food. As a result, he protested, 'The present temper of the people is a fruitful source for propaganda on the part of the Union of Democratic Control and we see around us sedition openly preached without any action being taken.' This was passed to Carson, who passed it on to Lloyd George.[85] Guest assured Lloyd George that the Conservative Party in parliament 'mean[t] to support your leadership even at the expense of their personal feelings',[86] but forbearance could not be assumed indefinitely. The Unionist Business Committee (U.B.C.) expressed the back benches' disgruntlement at Bonar Law's failure to uphold Conservative interests. Hewins wrote to his leader on 5 July demanding 'a more vigorous application in public policy of principles upon which the Conservative Party, which is the majority in the House of Commons, could give far greater assistance than seems possible under present conditions', by which he meant both Tariff Reform and strong action against trade unions.[87]

In mid-July Conservative disgruntlement turned to rage as the reconstruction of the ministry was disclosed. Edwin Montagu replaced Cham-

---

[83] Robinson to Northcliffe, 28 June 1917, British Library, Northcliffe Papers 4890/93.

[84] *Ibid*.

[85] J.E. Fawcett to Sir John Boraston, n.d., enclosed in Carson to Lloyd George, 22 June 1917, L.G.P. F/6/2/34.

[86] Guest to Lloyd George, 18 June 1917, L.G.P. F/21/6/5.

[87] Hewins to Bonar Law, 5 July 1917, Hewins Papers 65.

berlain at the India Office, after Curzon had made a token protest; Carson was removed from the Admiralty and 'elevated' to the War Cabinet; Christopher Addison was removed from the Ministry of Munitions and given the new Reconstruction portfolio. Carson had been approached on 6 July, but had resisted.[88] The changes were made precipitately on 17 July, in an attempt to defuse trouble. Addison recorded that

> After the War Cabinet in the morning...L.G. took me aside with Bonar and said he felt he must make his Cabinet changes straightaway and that he wanted to put Montagu to India and bring Carson into the War Cabinet, making Geddes First Lord. He wanted me to take up Reconstruction straightaway....In the afternoon....Carson told me that L.G. had insisted on making the announcements to-night and that he did not intend to consult his colleagues, except Milner and Bonar, himself and myself. L.G. seemed to feel that if he delayed over it, he would raise a storm and not get them carried through at all...and that he intended to bring Winston to Munitions, if I went to Reconstruction.

Addison, who saw this as 'needless abruptness' had a further interview with his leader in which 'both of us got pretty angry'. Lloyd George's analysis of the position was that Long would lead a campaign against Churchill, that Balfour's threatened resignation, over the possibility of dismissing Hardinge over the Mesopotamia report, 'certainly cannot be afforded'. Addison concluded that 'altogether L.G. was in very deep waters and he knew it.'[89]

Perhaps because Carson's move was ostensibly a promotion, it aroused less heat than the other changes. On 27 July disaffected Conservatives took their chance to attack the bill creating the Ministry of Reconstruction, 'really just a job to pension off Addison who has been a hopeless failure at Munitions', and on the same day the Executive Committee of the National Union of Conservative and Unionist Associations (N.U.C.U.A.) repeated the attack on Churchill, demanding a full party conference.[90] Younger had already let it be known that he 'funk[ed] a conference' and that Bonar Law had 'the strongest objection to anything of the kind just now'.[91] Long, Cave and Talbot, the Conservative Chief Whip, claimed to have learned of Churchill's appointment only through the newspapers.[92] Hewins, on behalf of the U.B.C., complained to Bonar Law that

[88] Lloyd George to Carson, 6 July 1917, L.G.P. F/6/2/35, and further correspondence in F/6/2/36 & 37.

[89] Addison Diary, 17 July 1917, Addison Papers 98.

[90] Sanders Diary, 29 July 1917, *Real Old Tory Politics*, p. 88.

[91] Pencilled notes exchanged between Younger and Steel-Maitland at an N.U.C.U.A. meeting, 10 July 1917, Steel-Maitland Papers GD 193/390.

[92] Sanders Diary 20 July 1917, *Real Old Tory Politics*, p. 88.

We do not wish to conceal from you that most of the appointments... have shaken our confidence and impaired our hope of vigorous Government action... These appointments affect directly or indirectly all the problems to which we have referred, and the records of the Ministers concerned cannot be said to encourage the expectation that the efforts of the Government, either in their character or direction, will realise the aims we have defined.

The U.B.C.'s executive, after working itself into fury, convened a full meeting on 19 July and sent a deputation to Bonar Law, arranging with him to send a version of their letter to the newspapers. This was doctored to remove references to the appointments and thus appeared to concentrate on policy, but the thrust of their meeting with Bonar Law was towards personalities. Hewins

... explained our objections to Winston Churchill upon the ground of labour policy, to Montagu on the ground of his speech on Indian Government in the Mesopotamia debate, and to Addison on the ground of his record and predilections he is not a suitable person to put in charge of the Reconstruction Committee. [sic]

Bonar Law, after making clear that the Paris Resolutions were not the final word on post-war economic policy,

... turned to the Ministerial appointments on which he said he did not expect to be able to satisfy us. He explained his view of a Coalition Government. No doubt, he said, that if he had gone to Lloyd George and said that the appointments would not receive the support of the Unionist Party and that therefore he could not support them, these appointments would not have been made. It was quite competent for him to make these objections but he did not think such action would have been consistent with what a Coalition Government requires for its working.... during the last six months of Asquith's administration he had been aware that in supporting Asquith he had not had the sympathy of the Unionist Party. He thought that situation was intolerable and he was quite determined that he would not put up with it again. If we could not support Lloyd George's Government then he should resign and put an end to an impossible situation.

The deputation caved in sullenly, confirming Bonar Law's view that the best way to deal with dissidents was to threaten them. Hewins took his protest to Long, who characteristically damned his leader with faint praise:

B.L. is always very frank and straightforward & I am glad he told you about his position as regards the P.M. I do not agree with him and could not say anything — but now I can just as frankly say that I think the Party who keep this Gov. in office must be considered.[93]

The party who kept the government in office were far from pleased. H.A.L. Fisher heard from Cave that 'several members of his party had

[93] Hewins to Long, 24 July 1917, Hewins Papers 65; Long to Hewins, 25 July 1917, *ibid*.

said that they no longer wanted to get the whip' and concluded that Churchill's appointment was 'a fairly big error of judgement'. Fisher had already concluded that the appointment was 'the beginning of the end'.[94] Esher, in Paris, heard 'that the appointments of Winston and Montagu are really most unpopular, and that L.G. is supposed by his best friends to be off his head'.[95] Reading, on '*quite reliable* authority', warned Lloyd George that Bonar Law was upset by Churchill's appointment.[96] Churchill was certainly the most unpopular choice, but the other appointments had their detractors. The trouble with Montagu was that he knew too much about his new job, having served as Parliamentary Under-Secretary of State for India from 1910 until he was promoted to be Financial Secretary at the Treasury in February 1914. He had made a speech in the Mesopotamia debate on 12 July which criticised the Government of India not only for its administration of the war effort but also for its resistance to constitutional reform in India. He was immediately discussed as a successor to Chamberlain.[97] Curzon, protesting his personal admiration for Montagu, objected that his programme of Federal Home Rule for India 'will excite prodigious expectations while it must utterly fail of realisation'. Chamberlain wanted his Under-Secretary, Islington, to succeed. Balfour, initially doubtful, was persuaded by Lloyd George, who also reported the support of the King.[98] After an attempt to get Chamberlain to stay, Lloyd George arranged an exchange of letters between himself and Montagu in which the new Secretary of State averred that 'I should not dream of touching the great fabric of the Government of India without careful investigation.'[99]

Montagu's unbuttoned views had been rather different earlier in the month, when it was proposed to send Chamberlain on a grand tour to investigate Indian government. The India Office (with its 'indefensible and ludicrous' organisation) was partly to blame for the muddle in Indian administration, but Chamberlain was especially guilty:

He has covered himself with unimpeachable despatches and telegrams, but the real charge against him, Crewe, and the whole of the Indian conduct of the war, is that they never set themselves at the outset to do more than obtain for India itself a position of benevolent neutrality. They never attempted to fit Indian organisation to a part of the world war. It may well be that they were wise in this. They showed — and India knows that they showed — fear of Indian loyalty . . . . I do not believe

[94] Fisher Diary, 28 July 1917, Bodleian Libraray, Fisher Papers; *idem*, 18 July.

[95] Esher to Murray of Elibank, 22 July 1917, Elibank Papers 8804.

[96] Reading to Lloyd George, 22 July 1917, L.G.P. F/43/1/6.

[97] Addison Diary 13 July 1917, Addison Papers 98.

[98] Curzon to Lloyd George, n.d., L.G.P. F/11/8/13; Chamberlain to Lloyd George, 13 July 1917, L.G.P. F/7/2/7; Lloyd George to Balfour, and reply, 16 July 1917, L.G.P. F/3/2/25,26.

[99] Chamberlain to Lloyd George, 16 July 1917, L.G.P. F/7/2/6; Montagu to Lloyd George, 17 July 1917, L.G.P. F/39/3/23.

the public would tolerate for one moment Chamberlain's being allowed to consider the reform of the system of which he has been a conspicuous exponent. But be that as it may it cannot be right to send a man who has shown that he is intent on mending *the lavatory tap when the house is on fire*.[100]

As if the effort of being moderate for the benefit of Conservatives was not enough, Montagu by accepting office had to justify himself to his Liberal ex-colleagues, including Samuel, to whom he wrote on 27 July:

My conduct after our conversation must have surprised you.
    I find that the chance of getting my policy ratified or accepted by the Govt was too good to refuse — indeed that my Indian friends would never — and rightly — understand it if I refused.
    So believe me not unmindful of the disastrous formal consequences and the personal misunderstanding although I refused all other office and indeed this one under all other circumstances. I accepted and find myself isolated from my friends. So be it? But I owed you an explanation.[101]

His appointment was attacked in the Conservative press, and in the Asquith household his defection was worse received than that of Churchill, who was agreed to be 'only adopting a course which he had openly vowed he wanted to adopt'. Asquith himself would only comment that 'a Jew was not a fit person to attempt to govern India'.[102]

Even the lesser appointments caused trouble. Before he accepted office Montagu, as vice-chairman of the Reconstruction Committee, set up a number of sub-committees, whose membership offended the Conservative backwoods. Haldane, as chairman of the Machinery of Government Committee, was particularly unpopular,[103] and this unpopularity boiled over in late July in protests to Bonar Law, who asked for his removal. Montagu fiercely objected that 'if you wish to take action I shall understand and appreciate why it has been done, but I shall regard it, from the point of view of the decencies of public life, as deplorable', and nothing was done.[104] Farming Tories muttered without effect about Rhondda's succession to the Food Ministry. The ministerial reconstruction had succeeded only in that the appointments went through: the Conservative Party was not appeased, and only the appointment of Hayes Fisher, a dully reactionary London member, to the Local Government Board in succession to Rhondda went any way to please them.

---

[100] Montagu to Lloyd George, 5 July 1917, L.G.P. F/39/3/21.
[101] Montagu to Samuel, 27 July 1917, Samuel Papers A/155/V/3.
[102] Gainford's recollections of 19 July 1917 (written 24 July?), Nuffield College, Gainford Papers 43. Montagu had, of course, damaged his personal relations with Asquith by marrying Venetia Stanley.
[103] W.C. Bridgeman to F.S. Oliver, 16 Feb. 1917, Shropshire Record Office, Bridgeman Papers. Bridgeman was Parliamentary Secretary at the Ministry of Labour.
[104] Montagu to Bonar Law, 8 Aug. 1917, B.L.P. 82/3/11.

The Coalition's only hope of survival was now to rally its forces on a cry of unity against a common political enemy. The Corn Production Act, paradoxically, provided an opportunity because of the venom of Runciman's attack on it. The Radicals — always so called by Conservatives in this context, as though to emphasise continuity with pre-war politics — had for the moment consolidated the agricultural interest, which was the backbone of pre-war Conservatism, on the government's side.

Planning for Party Reconstruction

Although the fuss about ministerial reconstruction was extremely damaging to the Lloyd George Coalition, and must therefore be a large part of the explanation for Conservative reactions to the Stockholm incident, the Coalition's managers had seen trouble coming months before. At the time of the engineering strikes Lloyd George had occasion to change the Liberal Coalition Whip — Neil Primrose, the incumbent, was a rather reluctant Lloyd Georgian who wished to return to his regiment — and after toying with the idea of appointing Cecil Harmsworth, Lord Northcliffe's younger brother, finally appointed Frederick Guest.[105] Guest, sprung from a family of Unionist Free Traders, cousin to Winston Churchill and brother to the Irish Viceroy, Wimborne, was a robust politician. A Boer War veteran, he had been Churchill's assistant private secretary from 1907 to 1910, and won his first parliamentary contest in the family seat of East Dorset in January 1910. He was unseated on petition alleging malpractices, but returned in the December election, and soon became a junior Whip. Very much a War Liberal, he was French's A.D.C. from 1914 to 1916, and a known sympathiser with the Liberal War Committee.

Guest began work in the first weeks of May with a committee of Lloyd George's sympathisers including A.C. Beck and Christopher Addison, which planned the radical reconstruction of the Liberal Party while Murray of Elibank was busy planning to bring Asquith back into the fold. Even within Guest's committee there was disagreement about the extent of Liberal division and the best course for the future. Cecil Beck predicted that 'out of this disturbance of political thought and so far inarticulate desire for a more modern programme, there would evolve a new party suited by its instincts to deal with all the post-war problems in a democratic spirit and that its leadership naturally would descend on Mr Lloyd George.' Another member, probably Guest himself, urged that 'advanced radicalism and thoughtful labourism will eventually march triumphantly

---

[105] See Turner, *Lloyd George's Secretariat*, pp. 20–21.

side by side', and that a 'post-war coalition should include a section of Tory democrats'.

But the immediate problem was to combat the activity of John Gulland and Geoffrey Howard at the Liberal headquarters at Abingdon Street, and in this matter the discussion was not so pompous. All that mattered was to decide whether Asquith himself and his immediate supporters intended to make a fight of it. If not, it was thought that an aggressive campaign by the prime minister's side would be counter-productive, even though the Liberal Central Association was known to be working hard to prevent Lloyd George's sympathisers from being selected for by-elections. Asquith's speech to the Eighty Club on 3 May, in which he insisted that 'he would never countenance [Liberal dissensions], and he believed that was the universal sentiment of the party', though a travesty of what was going on in the party machinery, was reckoned a good guide to his own wishes; and the committee contented itself with the collection of a list of candidates, the establishment of an intelligence department to 'feel the pulse of Liberal opinion', and the cultivation of the press.[106]

Nevertheless the government's unpopularity in Scotland was recognised and an unsuccessful attempt made to recruit Alexander Shaw as a Scottish Liberal Whip with presumed Lloyd Georgian sympathies. After consulting Runciman and his election agent, Shaw declined, while making the point that 'post-war policy apart, the Coalition isn't so much worse than the last one'. Walter Roch, on the other hand, accepted appointment as Welsh Whip.[107] In addition Guest set up a 'literature' department and undertook to make contact with friendly editors. This was far from the active defence of Lloyd Georgian interests favoured by Beck, and Guest seems to have been influenced by his correspondence with Murray, whose advice was to '1. Avoid an election 2. Reconstruct, by including Asquith...'.[108] Murray had also told Lloyd George that if there was a general election 'You would lose every seat in Scotland.'[109]

As a result Lloyd George's whips had done very little in the spring and summer of 1917 to organise against Asquith's supporters. The Coalition Liberal M.P.s were adequately whipped, but Whips' notices were in fact sent to the whole party by both Guest and Gulland for their respective factions. Outside the House the Liberal organisations were allowed to get on with candidate selection for by-elections, even though the outcome

[106] 'Memoranda circulated by Capt. F.E. Guest', May 1917, Addison Papers 45.

[107] Guest to Shaw, 23 May 1917, Craigmyle Papers; Runciman to Shaw, 24 May, Shaw to Guest 24 May, David Moss (?) to Shaw, 27 May, ibid. Shaw, who had been elected for Kilmarnock Burghs in 1915 while serving at the front, sat as a Liberal until he retired in 1923. He was later managing director of P. & O., and a director of the Bank of England. Roch sat for Pembrokeshire from 1908 to 1918.

[108] Guest to Elibank, 11 May 1917, Elibank Papers 8804.

[109] Memo. by Stamfordham of a conversation with Asquith, 18 May 1917, RA GV K1185/2.

tended to follow Abingdon Street's wishes. The general election weapon, though discussed, was not for use; the Coalition's parliamentary majority was safe so long as the Conservatives maintained their consent, and public opinion was not a certain bulwark to Lloyd George's position. The erosion of this comforting state of affairs, through the debates on the franchise and on agricultural policy as well as the occasional shocks from the reports of the Mesopotamia and Dardanelles commissions, changed the basis for Guest's calculations, so that by August it had come to seem much more attractive to attempt the reconstruction of parties. Quite apart from its effect on the consolidation of the Labour Party, the Stockholm incident at last brought the older parties to the point of taking party reconstruction seriously.

6

FROM 'STOCKHOLM' TO 'LANSDOWNE'
August to December 1917

The late summer and autumn of 1917, introduced by the *affaire Henderson* and rounded off by the *affaire Lansdowne*, were turbulent months for the Coalition and its political opponents. The House of Commons was generally under-populated, and regular attenders were those more likely to be hostile to the government than the absentees.[1] The discontent of various sections of the House was expressed in opposition to different parts of the legislative programme. The Stockholm affair offended many Labour M.P.s and drove Henderson into opposition; the Corn Production bill irritated Liberals who disliked the grant of protection to farmers and Conservatives who disliked the wages clauses; the Petroleum bill, which was an attempt to encourage the extraction of oil by granting generous and exclusive licences to exploring companies, ran afoul of Liberals, including a number of solid government supporters such as Guest and Richard Denman. The Franchise bill had something for everyone: the sections dealing with Irish redistribution grated on the nerves of Irish members, Unionist and Nationalist alike, the retention of plural voting inflamed most of the Liberals, and the compromise over redistribution in rural areas annoyed Liberals who thought the Tories were getting too many M.P.s in agricultural counties and Tories who thought they were getting too few. The Alternative Vote proposals, which had enormous potential for reconstructing the party system if Liberal and Labour voters could use their second preferences to defeat Unionist candidates, so angered the Unionists that the government whips had to allow a free vote to deflect rebellion.[2]

Worst of all for the government, there was clear evidence that Asquith was now prepared to lead an oppositional move; but for the moment this was on the most unlikely issue. During September and October Lloyd

---

[1] Ormsby-Gore to Milner, 1 Nov. 1917, Milner Papers 372.
[2] See Pugh, *Electoral Reform in War and Peace*, pp. 119–135.

George was engaged in a complex attempt to outflank Robertson and Haig by finding an alternative strategy to the attack on the Western Front. His first line of attack was to commission reports from Henry Wilson and Lord French on the recent (Passchendaele) offensive. Robertson's response, co-ordinated with Haig, was to encourage press attacks on the prime minister in the *Globe* which was owned by a discontented Unionist businessman and edited by Leo Maxse, whose brother was a general on the Western Front. At its height the *Globe* campaign, echoed in the *Morning Post*, suggested that Lloyd George should be replaced by Asquith, who would not interfere with the generals.

Lloyd George's next effort, which reached fruition in November, was to propose the establishment of a Supreme War Council at Versailles, to co-ordinate Allied strategy. Covert opposition from Haig and the General Staff continued. On this occasion it was accompanied by serious mutterings in the House of Commons, in which Asquith himself was believed to share. Lloyd George put his proposals in a speech in Paris on 12 November: Asquith's commentary upon it in the Commons on 19 November constituted his first explicit criticism of the government's policy since his departure from Downing Street. To the despair of his followers, it was a low-key restatement of the *Morning Post*'s theme of 'Hands off the generals' rather than a questioning of the rationale of fighting a war *à l'outrance*, which was what his Liberal colleagues now wished to press. It was dangerous because it coincided with a tide of sentiment on the Unionist benches, which had already seen a small revolt by the National Party, and because it followed hard on the heels of parliamentary rows over the Petroleum bill and the fiasco of Lord Northcliffe's 'refusal' of the offer of the Air Board. It certainly marked no new departure in the ideology of opposition: as Haldane noted, 'the Liberals are not fertile at present. The feeling is that their work is now over for the present...'[3]

The publication of Lord Lansdowne's notorious letter in the *Daily Telegraph* on 29 November lent a focus to parliamentary discontents, and marked the end of a period of some confusion. Those Liberals who inclined to a negotiated peace saw it as a golden opportunity. 'How can we make him Prime Minister?' chirruped Arthur Ponsonby.[4] In fact the threat to the government lay in the possibility that Lansdowne's cautious and deeply conservative statement of war aims would win support from sufficient Unionists to embarrass the administration, weaken public support for the war if it were badly handled in public, and perhaps disrupt relations with the Entente. There was little thought at first on the government side either that Asquith had anything to do with it, or that it

[3] Haldane to his mother, 2 Dec. 1917, Haldane Papers 5998/145.
[4] Ponsonby to Lady Courtney, 29 Nov. 1917, Courtney Papers 12.

could make a significant difference to the balance of forces in the House of Commons. But the Lansdowne affair polarised politics in a way which had not previously been thought possible, and prepared the ground at last for a general election which might reflect the balance of political power during the war. The tribulations of the late summer and autumn, especially over the Representation of the People bill, had crystallised a pattern of voting among Liberal M.P.s in which the Coalitionists and anti-Coalitionists could easily be recognised. It had also helped to concentrate Unionist minds on the costs and benefits of the Coalition. The Lansdowne affair and its aftermath shaped these attitudes into a political campaign which could only culminate in an election.

The stratification of politics between ministers, back-benchers, and committed party sympathisers outside parliament gained in importance in this period. The War Cabinet saw the political process almost exclusively as a means to carry on the war and, to that end, to limit social damage during and after it. The House of Commons mattered mostly because it could obstruct this process, and much more attention was paid in the War Cabinet to the politics of 'Hands off the generals' than to any of the domestic issues which preoccupied the Coalition's business managers and in due course determined party allegiance in the post-war election.

After Stockholm

In the light of the political origins of the Coalition in December 1916, the War Cabinet's action in opening a breach between the government and the effective leader of the Labour Party was a momentous step. G.N. Barnes, the trade union M.P. from the A.S.E. who inherited Henderson's place in the War Cabinet, immediately warned Lloyd George that :

> ...the more I think of it the more I can see difficulties ahead in the event of severance with Mr Henderson.
>
> The vote yesterday is behind him: his going out now would weaken us very considerably. It would also raise the question of myself and other colleagues in the Government following him, and even if we did not, our usefulness to the nation would be immensely impaired by the appearance of only representing a minority, and he, representing the majority, having gone.
>
> I can see all the other, but with due deference, it seems to me that the other is mostly personal.
>
> Cannot an effort be made even now to retain him, and go on.[5]

The remaining members of the War Cabinet hesitated to widen the

---

[5] Barnes to Lloyd George, 11 Aug. 1917, L.G.P. F/4/2/9.

breach with Henderson too far, and on 11 August toned down Lloyd George's letter to the Labour leader. There was general agreement 'that the action of the Labour Party was likely to damage this country in the eyes of foreign Powers, who would say that British democracy had by its vote shown itself tired of the war, and that it would also be a serious blow to the Government' — reason enough to want the vote to have gone the other way, but not perhaps to justify the dismissal of Henderson after the event. More significant, perhaps, was the observation (probably by Hankey) 'that the present moment ... was one of really critical importance, when proposals of a plausible nature for peace had actually been made by the Pope, and other proposals of a plausible nature but tending towards an unsatisfactory peace were in the air.'[6] The dismissal of Henderson, accompanied by a letter which stressed first that Henderson by speaking as a member of the War Cabinet gave the delegates the impression that his views were shared by his War Cabinet colleagues, and second (a very strained objection) that he had mentioned the Nabokoff telegram in a 'very casual reference ... an indifferent summary', was more probably intended to clarify British relations with the Entente Powers. This was not entirely achieved: Buckler was convinced that Nabokoff had misinterpreted the Russian position,[7] and indeed the War Cabinet's attempt to explain and defend their attitude both to Henderson and the conference soon became entangled in inconsistency.

The War Cabinet meeting of 13 August spent some time discussing the presentation of its case and the limitation of political damage. Henderson had had to ask permission to read out official documents, and this enabled them to examine his case before it was put in the House. He proposed to read out a telegram of 2 August from Sir George Buchanan, which described the attitude of the Russian government and revealed certain divisions of opinion within it, which he evidently thought would justify support for the conference, and would also show that the War Cabinet had not at first opposed the conference even when they knew the Russian government's views. The War Cabinet decided to meet this point by insisting that the 2 August telegram expressed Buchanan's view, and that Nabokoff's telegram changed matters by expressing the considered and formal view of the Russian government. On the more substantial point that the War Cabinet had changed its mind since May 21, when Lloyd George telegraphed to Albert Thomas that he supported the Stockholm proposal, the summary in the minutes is revealing:

> The reasons for this change in attitude were, that in May the Russian Government was in the hands of the Workmen's and Soldiers' Committee, and, under its in-

---

[6] W.C. 212, 11 Aug. 1917, CAB 23/3.
[7] Buckler to House, 27 Aug. 1917, Buckler Papers 654/I/1/7.

fluence, were then inclined strongly in favour of the Stockholm Conference, and that the British Government were in this matter, to a great extent, influenced by their desire to support the authority of a newly formed body which had not yet firmly established itself. The consequence of the influence exerted by the Soviet, however, had been to shatter the discipline of the Russian army and the organisation of the nation, and the Russian government was at the moment taking measures to re-establish discipline in their forces by means which were absolutely contrary to the principles of the Soviet, and showed that the policy of the extreme revolutionaries had been discredited.

To permit the attendance of British representatives at the Stockholm Conference, which was tantamount to countenancing fraternisation between one section of the Allied British public and one section of the enemy public, would be very prejudicial to the policy which the Russian government was engaged on and was pressing forward, the very first item of which was the prohibition of fraternisation between Russian troops and those of the enemy.

It was recognised that no difficulty would be found in proving, on the above lines, that conditions had completely changed since May 1917, but that there would be considerable difficulty in doing so without embarrassing M. Kerensky.[8]

Despite this, and despite the fact that the Russian government had indeed been reconstructed, to the disadvantage of the Soviets, in the early days of August, it is unlikely that concern for internal Russian policy was in fact uppermost in the War Cabinet's collective mind. Lloyd George's speech in the House, and his published exchange of letters with Henderson gave rise to a 'complication' in Petrograd because Kerensky was annoyed to see it implied that he had wanted to stop the Stockholm conference. An urgent telegram was sent to Buchanan to prevent the Russian government from requesting the British government to allow delegates to go to Stockholm, a request which would have exploded the War Cabinet's case.[9] American diplomats understood very well that French and Italian vetoes were the real reason for Lloyd George's turning against the conference idea.[10] Since the War Cabinet were receiving steady reports of peace initiatives which, far from presaging an 'unsatisfactory' end to the war, actually offered the hope of dividing Germany from Austria, it is equally likely that their concern was not to stifle peace initiatives, but merely to keep those which came from Britain more firmly under their own control.[11] But this came at a heavy political cost: and the risk of losing the support of the Labour Party could not have been justified if there had not been corresponding domestic political pressures from the Coalition's Conservative supporters.

[8] W.C. 213, 13 Aug. 1917, CAB 23/3. This is quoted verbatim but without attribution by Lloyd George in *War Memoirs* II, 1138–1139. Henderson's account of the same transactions, given to Stamfordham and the King on 2 Nov., and quoted in RA GV Q 1157/12, simply cannot be reconciled with the other evidence.
[9] W.C. 217, 17 Aug. 1917, CAB 23/3.
[10] Buckler to House, 27 Aug. 1917, Buckler Papers 654/I/1/7.
[11] See Hankey's view, cited in Roskill, *Hankey: man of secrets*, pp. 420–421.

The Military Balance

Peace negotiations were also important because the decision to allow Haig his Flanders offensive had left the War Cabinet plunged in gloom. Lloyd George, in particular, continued to believe that a peripheral strategy — crippling one or other of Germany's allies — offered a better chance of success. The collapse of the Russian armies in mid-July, in the aftermath of their last successful offensive, forced the Western Allies to reconsider their strategy once more. On 25 and 26 July, at an inter-Allied conference in Paris, and again in conference with the French in London on 6 and 7 August Lloyd George urged that guns be sent from France to strengthen the Italian forces against Austria. Although Cadorna had asked for these guns a week before, and Foch had agreed in principle to send them, Robertson was able to turn both of them against the idea with the argument that it was unsafe to alter plans once they had been made. Robertson then summarised the General Staff's unvarying objection to peripheral attacks in a paper to the War Cabinet. He protested that the collapse of the Russian armies was an argument in favour of further concentration on the Western Front, to force the Germans to keep most of their troops there instead of sending them eastwards.[12]

The opposing argument was always implicit in the rows between civilians and generals which had now become commonplace. Before the second Anglo-French conference Lloyd George, with Milner, Balfour and Curzon, met Ribot, Painlevé and Albert Thomas with no soldiers present, to discuss 'the possibility of a separate peace with Austria'. This had been the ultimate purpose of Lloyd George's plan for reinforcing the Italian front, and the possibility was revived by news of further peace proposals emanating from the Vatican.[13] On 14 August Lloyd George told Stamfordham that he had 'secret information' that Austria might be about to throw over the German connection.

> The Prime Minister then began to expound his well-known theory that we had made an egregious mistake in not throwing our weight on to the side of Italy in order to smash Austria, take Trieste and then shake hands and make peace with Austria.... But the Prime Minister said it was hopeless to make any impression upon the Military Experts.... With regard to Men, we have *not* the superior proportion necessary for the attack.... In Guns we are only their equal, as to Ammunition we have far more than the Germans, but the latter have sufficient for the Defence.[14]

[12] Paper G.T. 1549, 29 July 1917, CAB 24/21.

[13] Rothwell, *British War Aims and Peace Diplomacy*, pp. 102–105; Stevenson, *The First World War and International Relations*, pp. 162–169.

[14] Memorandum by Stamfordham of an interview with Lloyd George, 14 Aug. 1917, RA GV K1185/4.

In mid-August, as the House of Commons absorbed the Stockholm crisis and the late summer rains reduced the country below the Passchendaele ridge to a quagmire, the case for sending guns to Italy became very strong. It also became associated with a scheme to set up an Allied General Staff to supervise strategy from the Channel to the Adriatic, which was first proposed by Foch in the Paris meetings and repeated in London in early August. Foch, who gave Robertson the impression that he had 'made up his mind that it is hopeless looking for good results on the West Front' was for the time being seen as Lloyd George's ally. Robertson complained to Haig that

> ...Lloyd George being keen on the Italian project for the time being and knowing that I am against it and that the French are for it, and as the French keep rubbing in that it is necessary to have a Central Staff at Paris, I can see Lloyd George in the future wanting to agree to some such organisation so as to put the matter in French hands and to take it out of mine. However, we shall see all about this.[15]

The inter-Allied staff had another proponent in Henry Wilson, formerly the British representative at French headquarters, who was very active during the last two weeks of August in lobbying members of the War Cabinet, with Lloyd George's support.[16] On 26 August the Italian government reported that the Isonzo campaign was going well and Lloyd George immediately proposed that guns and troops be sent, adding in his letter to Robertson that 'If the Allied Armies from the North Sea to the Adriatic were under one command I have no doubt as to the course which would be pursued. Surely our strategy ought to be based on the assumption that it is all one front.'[17]

Once more, civilian control of strategy became the issue of the moment. Foch arrived in London on 3 September to persuade the British to agree to allow 100 heavy guns to be sent from the French First Army to Italy. Robertson immediately summoned Haig to scotch the proposal. With the renewal of disagreement with the soldiers, the unity of the Cabinet now hung in the balance. After the War Cabinet meeting on 3 September Milner's private secretary

> ...found him in the depths of depression. The responsibility of having to reach a decision on this question was weighing on him very heavily.... He thought the P.M. meant 'to stick his toes into the ground over this question'. If he got his way he thought there would be a real crisis. The C.I.G.S. and Haig would of course be dead against it. It would be sure to leak out and there would be an outcry against the politicians for over-riding military opinion. Chief [Milner] thought it was a very nasty business.... I gathered that the Chief's own position was that he

[15] Robertson to Haig, 9 Aug. 1917, reprinted in Blake, *Private Papers*, p. 251.
[16] Wilson Diary, 20–27 Aug. 1917, Imperial War Museum, Henry Wilson Papers.
[17] Lloyd George to Robertson, 26 Aug. 1917, L.G.P. F/30/2/24.

was *very* sceptical of success on the Western Front this year, but he did not believe much in the P.M.'s particular plan, i.e., concentration on the Eastern front. The Military people would, of course, lay all the blame on the weather, and would claim that as being responsible for the failure to achieve anything on the Western front. He thought Haig did not quite realise sufficiently that our man-power was not inexhaustible . . . [18]

Haig met the War Cabinet on 4 September and predictably objected to the proposal. He was supported by Carson and Smuts, with Robert Cecil, representing the Foreign Office on the sidelines, noisily 'dissociating himself' from what was being suggested. The outcome was slightly unexpected. Haig, after offering 50 guns, went back to France and arranged for Pétain to send 100 on condition that they would be replaced in time for the next planned Flanders attack. 'This', as he observed 'ended the discussion on the question of guns in the most friendly way.'[19] Back in England, however, there was more permanent damage. Robert Cecil, a representative figure if not a major one, wrote to his cousin Balfour

> I have talked things over with Carson who agreed with me but acted more moderately. He urges me not to resign but I am very doubtful. You know I have long felt unhappy and uncomfortable. I dislike serving a Prime Minister whom I distrust. A divided ministry is never strong. Then who knows what may happen next. L.G. may over-ride the soldiers again in some far more vital matter. I have no confidence in his strategic intuition as B.L. has . . . . Still less do I like the way he treats Robertson and Jellicoe. And I greatly doubt the wisdom of some of his recent appointments.
>
> Finally I look forward with dismay to the chance of his conducting peace negotiations. So that the balance of my reason is for resignation sometime . . . [20]

Balfour, as was his wont, advised against resignation on the entirely typical grounds that 'You can see Lloyd George's faults, and they are not difficult to see. But do you think he can be improved upon out of our existing material?'[21] But Carson, 'all opposed to the meddling now practised by the Prime Minister and other politicians', advised Haig to confide in Asquith 'because the latter, though in opposition, has very great power' and assured Haig 'that the War Cabinet would not be allowed to interfere with [him or his] arrangements'.[22] The Conservative press, led by the *Morning Post*, became excited at the prospect of another dispute over strategy,[23] and the

---

[18] Thornton Diary, 3 Sept. 1917, Milner Papers 45.

[19] Haig Diary, 7 Sept. 1917, Haig Papers 117.

[20] Cecil to Balfour, 4 Sept. 1917, Balfour Papers, B.L. Add. MSS 49738, ff. 150–151. See also his draft letter of resignation in P.R.O. FO 800/196, ff. 240–245.

[21] Balfour to Cecil, 12 Sept. 1917, Balfour Papers B.L. Add. MSS 49738, f.160.

[22] Haig Diary, 14, 15, 16 Sept. 1917, Blake, *Private Papers*, pp. 254–255. F.E.Smith, after drinking heavily at lunchtime, took rather the same position, *ibid*. 14 Sept. 1917.

[23] See particularly the *Morning Post* for 5 Sept. 1917.

Coalition ministry was pushed into another period of public controversy with the General Staff.

Lloyd George himself was by now quite willing to be pushed. Robertson's response to the latest Italian proposal had been to make a fierce attack on civilian interference in the course of War Cabinet discussion on 28 August, and to gloss his remarks further as an addition to the minutes. His account was so inaccurate, particularly in its claims that the General Staff had not been consulted about the Italian campaign and that the War Cabinet's review of the Flanders offensive was unexpected and implicitly disloyal to the army, that Lloyd George ordered a contrary brief from Hankey. This was ready on 1 September, and Lloyd George took the problem away with him to Criccieth on his holiday, which began on 5 September. By this time, though, his Cabinet colleagues were fully aware of the potentialities of the dispute, and Milner was trying to restrain the prime minister's temper.[24] At Criccieth Milner recorded that 'we are none of us very hopeful of decisive results being achieved on present lines',[25] and at the same time in London Bonar Law told Robertson that he had 'lost absolutely all hope of anything coming of Haig's offensive'.[26] Lloyd George, soothed by Hankey and Milner,[27] held back from an onslaught on Robertson, and after returning to London was diverted by the news of another peace initiative from Germany, this time through Madrid, followed quickly by an approach to France through Switzerland.[28]

The September peace initiatives did not include detailed statements of the German terms, though it was assumed that a satisfactory settlement in the West would be achieved by large concessions to Germany in Russia — a prospect which Lloyd George was quite happy to contemplate. War Cabinet opinion tended against a compromise peace, with Milner and Bonar Law throwing their weight on the side of continuing the war. Before rejecting the overtures, Lloyd George demanded an assurance from the General Staff that Britain could defeat Germany even if Russia was forced to make peace. Unfortunately for him this was precisely what he got: visiting France to assess official French reactions, he was treated by Haig to a demonstration of the progress attainable in the Western offensive and a lecture on the impropriety of deserting Russia.[29] During his absence Asquith spoke at Leeds against any peace settlement which did not include German withdrawal from Russia, and his views were taken

---

[24] Milner to Bonar Law, 5 Sept. 1917, Milner Papers 144.

[25] Milner Diary, 17–20 Sept. 1917, Milner Papers 88.

[26] Bonar Law to Lloyd George, 18 Sept. 1917, L.G.P. F/30/2/25.

[27] Hankey Diary, 18 Sept. 1917, Hankey Papers 1/3.

[28] Rothwell, *British War Aims*, pp. 105–110.

[29] Hankey's notes of a meeting between Lloyd George and Haig, 26 Sept. 1917, CAB 1/25/16, quoted Woodward, *Lloyd George and the Generals*, pp. 202–203; Hankey Diary, reprinted in *Supreme Command*, II, 699–700.

up by the *Morning Post*. Politically, a compromise peace was at this point impossible to achieve.

Casting about for a way out of the impasse, Lloyd George returned to the plan of attacking Turkey in Palestine, but found himself frustrated again by Robertson, who put up Allenby to give a misleading account of the manpower and shipping necessary to mount a successful campaign.[30] The War Cabinet was more sympathetic to Lloyd George over this effort than over peace negotiations, and Haig's refusal to take over more of the French line, conveyed on 8 October, finally convinced them that they could no longer rely on Robertson and Haig for unbiased military advice. The War Cabinet was therefore open to Lloyd George's suggestion, made on 10 October, that Henry Wilson and Lord French should be invited to join a 'War Council' to discuss future strategy. The genesis of this suggestion is explained in Hankey's diary:

> ...the whole thing is a clever plot on L.G.'s part. Earlier in the year at Lindfield he sounded them out and ascertained this was their view, no doubt playing on their ambition and known jealousy & dislike of Robertson, by letting them see that he agreed, accompanying this no doubt with a good deal of suggestion. Then he lets Haig go on and even encourages him to do so, knowing that the weather was preventing a big success, in order to strengthen the argument. Then he guilelessly proposes the War Council, knowing perfectly well that the jury is a packed one, which will only report in one direction. By this means he fortifies himself with apparently unbiased military opinion on the great struggle with Robertson and Haig, which he knows he cannot face without it. The which intreague [*sic*], if unsavoury, is very skilfull [*sic*]. I am glad I had no hand in it...[31]

This assault on the 'Kitchener–Robertson agreement' predictably made Robertson think of resigning: Haig persuaded him to stay until his advice was actually rejected. It also forced Cabinet ministers to review their commitment to the Coalition: Curzon threatened to resign, promising that Balfour, Cecil, Carson and Derby would follow him.[32] Lloyd George consoled his colleagues and persuaded them to wait for the reports, but meanwhile raised the question of an inter-Allied war council with Foch, and tried to clarify his own strategic ideas in a long discussion with Hankey.[33] French and Wilson both submitted papers which discouraged the idea of an attack in Palestine, but both were scathing about the Western Front policy. Their documents were circulating among War Cabinet members when the Italians succumbed to a formidable attack by German and Austrian forces at Caporetto, and collapsed in a rout. It was immediately decided to send two divisions to Italy, preceded by Robertson, who

---

[30] Woodward, *Lloyd George and the Generals*, pp. 206–207.
[31] Hankey Diary 20 Oct., Hankey Papers 1/3.
[32] Hankey Diary 10 Oct. 1917, *ibid*.
[33] Hankey Diary, 15 Oct. 1917, *ibid*.

was in consequence not present when Lloyd George addressed the War Cabinet on 29 October.

This meeting can be taken as the beginning of the political crisis over the question of unity of command. The most exposed target was Derby, who recorded his bruises:

> Lloyd George was in a towering rage. He was most sarcastic and abusive and tried to attribute the whole of the Italian trouble to our General Staff. It was no good arguing with him and I left the room telling George Curzon and Arthur Balfour...that I proposed to send in my resignation at once. They begged me not to do so because they said that by doing so I should not achieve what I wanted which is namely support of you, and it would put them — they entirely agreed with me in my views — in a very awkward position.[34]

Over the next two days Lloyd George extracted from General Maurice, the Director of Military Operations who was acting for Robertson in the latter's absence, a draft constitution for an inter-Allied War Council, which was approved by the War Cabinet, over Derby's blundering objections, on 2 November. Henry Wilson was chosen to be the British representative if the arrangement was acceptable to the French, and the War Cabinet made it explicit that the new body would have the power to review and if necessary revise the strategic plans put forward by the general staffs of each of the Allies.[35] Lloyd George then took the plan to France and on to Italy, where he confronted Robertson. The first formal meeting of the Supreme War Council took place in Rapallo on 7 November, and despite Robertson's unconcealed rage began a process which was eventually to bring more than 200,000 British and French troops to bolster the Italian defences. It was an eventful day elsewhere, too: Allenby broke the Turkish line in Palestine, the Bolsheviks took the Winter Palace, and Haig mounted the final attack of his Ypres campaign.

Lloyd George returned to Paris and delivered a speech on 12 November in support of the new system which inflamed both the soldiers and their Conservative supporters. His condemnation of patchwork planning — 'stitching is not strategy' — was widened into an explicit attack on wasteful tactical methods and by implication the generals who used them. Despite careful preparation in the London press, this caused a storm not only in the extreme right-wing press but also among the Asquithian papers, especially the *Westminster Gazette* and the weekly *Nation*. The General Staff had for some time been working the press, through Gwynne of the *Morning Post*, St Loe Strachey of the *Spectator* and Maxse of the *National*

---

[34] Derby to Robertson (unsent) 29 Oct. 1917, Derby Papers DER 17 W.O. Correspondence.
[35] W.C. 259A, 30 Oct. 1917, CAB 23/13; W.C. 262 & 263, 2 Nov. 1917, CAB 23/3.

Review, and also in the United States.[36]   The paroxysm of resentment which overwhelmed the newspapers on 13 and 14 November was not therefore entirely surprising, nor was it unexpected that Asquith should now intervene to take the side of the generals. Austen Chamberlain, who spent that week at the front, was particularly active in working up Conservative opposition and told Curzon on Sunday 18 November, the day before the parliamentary debate that

> ...he found a good deal of feeling and agitation going on among the soldiers in general: and he tells me that he has found the same in the ranks of [Lloyd George's] Unionist supporters here.
> Indeed he shares it himself so much so that unless reassuring explanations are delivered in your speech he could not support the Govt and might be forced to vote against us.[37]

Against this Robert Sanders, one of the most experienced parliamentary organisers on the Conservative side, noted on 17 November that 'The prevalent idea now is that it will fizzle out.'[38] It did. Although Guest warned that 'Mr Asquith has not taken on this debate lightly',[39] Asquith's attack, based on a restatement of positions taken by the *Morning Post*, was not especially inspiring even for his own supporters, and Lloyd George had an easy personal victory.

Nevertheless the episode of the Paris speech was an ominous portent for the future. It was Asquith's first serious attempt to oppose; outright opposition from the Liberal front bench coincided with fundamental suspicion on the Unionist side. A few months later, in the Maurice debate in May 1918, the same recipe spelt disaster for the historic Liberal Party. For the moment it was merely a cause for disquiet. Robert Sanders, from the viewpoint of a rural Tory, was predictably pleased with Lloyd George's 'big personal success';[40] Cecil Harmsworth, writing across the intra-party divide to his old friend and colleague Walter Runciman, lamented that

> For the first time since the Boer War we have had open warfare between leaders of Liberalism, with their respective Liberal followers exulting in the swingeing blows dealt by the champions on the one side and on the other, and the Tories laughing in their sleeves at our egregious folly.[41]

[36] Brade to Beaverbrook, 11 Nov. 1917, House of Lords Record Office, Beaverbrook Papers C/60.
[37] Curzon to Lloyd George, 18 Nov. 1917, L.G.P. F/11/8/18.
[38] Sanders Diary, 17 Nov. 1917, *Real Old Tory Politics*, p. 91.
[39] Guest to Lloyd George, 17 Nov. 1917, L.G.P. F/21/2/7.
[40] Sanders Diary, 22 Nov. 1917, *Real Old Tory Politics*, p. 91.
[41] Harmsworth to Runciman, n.d., Nov. 1917, Runciman Papers WR 161 (2).

Here was an unmistakable sign that the pre-war party system might after all suffer permanent damage from the war.

Parliament and Opposition

The affair of the Paris speech forced the Coalition government to confront a House of Commons which for some months it had been trying to ignore. The balance of power in the House had begun to shift since Henderson's dismissal from the War Cabinet in August. The Labour Party's loyalty to the Coalition was strained, though this had no immediate effect in the division lobbies. In September the Conservative Right began to splinter, and a number of M.P.s led by Henry Page Croft set themselves up as the National Party. Their principles and programme were limited to an undifferentiated super-patriotism: they wanted harsh measures against aliens, extreme war aims, and an economic war-after-the-war against Germany. They also muttered against civilian control of strategy and the prospect of an Irish settlement which would concede very much to the Nationalists. It is clear that they enjoyed considerable sympathy from right-wing Conservatives in the country, and from a number of M.P.s who remained within the parliamentary party. Their appearance can therefore be interpreted as a renewal of the challenge to Bonar Law's leadership, which had done so much to bring about the Asquith Coalition in 1915. Meanwhile the generals' habitual supporters recognised Lloyd George's strategic initiatives as underhand attempts to establish civilian control over strategy, and duly objected. In private Asquith was known to be encouraging his principal supporters to take the same line. As a result the Coalition even by the beginning of October was far less secure than it had been in its early months, and the prospect of a successful hostile coalition was considerable: though it is hard to see how an alternative government could have emerged from a defeat engineered in this way. It was not clear how, with the existing House of Commons and the existing party structure it would be possible to create a firm basis for a different coalition government to carry on the war. Nevertheless, the partisan divisions in the Commons were hardening. Fifty or so Liberals voted consistently with the government on issues which challenged pre-war Liberal positions: the disfranchisement of conscientious objectors, the plural vote, the redistribution of Irish constituencies, and the strengthening of the Nationalist Party in Ireland by proportional representation. Nearly ninety were consistent opponents on the Irish clauses of the Franchise bill, and with the twelve Labour members who took the same position, these men made up the real parliamentary opposition, which persisted until the Maurice debate of May 1918, and afterwards.[42] But although the regular Liberal opposition outnumbered the regular Coalition Liberal contingent almost by two to one, it cannot be assumed that the rest of the Liberal parliamentary party — some eighty members — divided in the same way. In the circumstances of late 1917, with an overwhelming majority of the Unionist Party committed to the maintenance of the Coalition for the time being, inaction on the part of Liberals meant *de facto* support of the government. Moreover the balance of power in the Commons was still affected by the Irish party whose lack of interest in Westminster politics helped to keep the Coalition safe in late 1917.

The response of Lloyd George's immediate supporters was at two levels. The first was an attempt to restore the favourable balance of public opinion which had been assumed to exist in early 1917. On 3 October Hankey found Lloyd George 'very keen on getting out a great document giving an exposition of what the Government has done',[43] and returned to this theme on 8 October with Addison and Guest.[44] The result was the 1917 *War Cabinet Report*, which in the guise of an official account of stewardship presented a picture of the Lloyd George Coalition deliberately designed to emphasise the shortcomings of the Asquith regime. Addison discussed it with Lloyd George, Milner and Philip Kerr on 15 October:

> We . . . turned and discussed that it is pretty evident that Asquith, on the lines of the Ultra-Tories who are still disgruntled about Winston's appointment, is inclined to try to bring up some Parliamentary coup. I have been urging vehemently for some time that we should get together a record of the Government's achievements which, in some directions, are really splendid. I am quite sure that if they were set out properly they would make a great impression and effectively prevent any petty-fogging intrigues, in view of what has been done in the last ten months in comparison with the previous two years in food supplies, use of shipping, development of resources, home resources, especially ores etc. etc. . . . .[45]

It is clear, though, that at any rate the guests at that dinner party did not believe that the situation could be resolved without a reconstruction of parties. The discussion ranged over the progress of the 'Patriotic Labour' efforts being made by Victor Fisher, with Milner's encouragement. Addison recorded that

> Henderson, however, is being very active and Victor Fisher and his friends are apprehensive that he will be getting hold of their men in advance if they cannot come

---

[42] Pugh, *Electoral Reform in War and Peace*, pp. 130–133. See also Edward David, 'The Liberal Party during the First World War', Cambridge University M.Litt. thesis, 1968 and 'The Liberal Party Divided 1916–1918', *Historical Journal*, xiii (1970), 509–533.

[43] Hankey Diary, 3 Oct. 1917, Hankey Papers.

[44] Addison Diary, 8 Oct. 1917, Addison Papers 98. Addison here claims credit for the idea.

[45] Addison Diary, 15 Oct. 1917, *ibid*.

to some arrangement about seats. In the end, however, it comes down to a question of programme ... [and after the discussion cited above] It was finally arranged that this statement should be prepared and issued and that we should take our stand on it, in the meantime aiming to prepare and announce our Reconstruction programme at the end of the year. We then had a long discussion on the Programme and it was quite evident that, except on the Tariff issue, there would probably be no great difficulty in arriving at an agreement. Both L.G. and myself were very emphatic that any question of interference, especially with food, was to be absolutely ruled out. I promised to get something definite put together as soon as possible.[46]

The second level of action was therefore to take deliberate steps to bring about a more coherent grouping among the Coalition parties. During the next month nothing more was done about a programme, but the rumblings of discontent in the Conservative Party continued, and the building of bridges between the Coalition and 'Patriotic Labour' was put in hand. The Executive of the National Union of Conservative and Unionist Associations wished a national meeting of the association on a reluctant party hierarchy: Sir George Younger noted that '[i]f they had been able to force us into convening a Conference when it was first demanded in June or July, we should have been properly in the soup and the results might have been very serious, but I was glad to note a change of temper at the last meeting', and hoped that his ministerial colleagues would meanwhile 'arrange' any differences among themselves.[47] On the back benches, 'Patriotic Labour' sympathisers convened small meetings to agree to the proposition that '[It is] desirable to come to an understanding with the patriotic section of the Labour Party'.[48] Already, though, there were signs of local resistance by Conservative associations to the selection of any labour candidate, however patriotic, instead of traditional Unionists.[49]

Meanwhile the urgency of some sort of action to reconstruct the party system was underlined by the parliamentary turmoil over the Supreme War Council — with Addison complaining that 'there is no doubt that the General Staff and the Asquithites have made a very strong effort to discredit' Lloyd George[50] — and over the plural voting clauses of the Franchise bill. The maintenance of plural voting had been an agreed rec-ommendation of the Speaker's Conference, and therefore incorporated in the bill: opposition Liberals duly objected in a protracted session on 20 November, immediately following the debate on the Paris speech. At the weekly breakfast of Liberal and Labour ministers on 21 November, Lloyd George accepted Addison's advice to 'broach the general question of es-

[46] *Ibid.*

[47] Younger to Long, 19 Oct. 1917, Long Papers 947/599.

[48] Note, 15 Nov. 1917, Scottish Record Office, Steel-Maitland Papers GD193/99/2.

[49] See e.g. Neville Chamberlain to Steel-Maitland, 4 Nov. 1917, *ibid.*, on difficulties in North Worcestershire.

[50] Addison Diary, 19 Nov. 1917, Addison Papers 98.

tablishing the position with the Gullandites and bring matters, if necessary, to a head in determining who were and who were not our friends in the House'.[51] This was more than a reaction to a temporary parliamentary difficulty. Herbert Fisher recorded:

> Lloyd George spoke on necessity of a national party in the House and the country. I said a national party required a national programme. Opinion taken round the table. Some of the Labour men rather nervous... [52]

Quite clearly a national party also required a national 'cry'. This ingredient, essential to the Edwardian politics in which all the participants had reached their prime, was shortly to be provided by Lord Lansdowne.

The Irish Dimension

The final element in parliamentary calculation in November 1917 was Ireland. In the late summer it became obvious to Westminster politicians that Ireland was not a separate political stage with its own cast of characters playing to a different audience. While government and opposition absorbed the lessons of the Stockholm incident, they had also to recognise that the preservation of the Union was extremely important to the Conservative right wing. Anything which disturbed the future prospects of the Union also threatened the government's majority. The Coalition, naturally, tried to suppress Irish controversy altogether, but this was a policy foredoomed to disaster.

As the Convention was being launched it was clear that the government was buying time at a high price. Duke's policy of releasing Easter Rising prisoners, undertaken deliberately to smooth the way for Sinn Fein to enter the Convention or at least co-operate with it, enraged the Unionists. Minor riots in Dublin and Cork inflamed them further. Midleton complained that 'the action of the Government in deciding to release Sinn Fein prisoners, some of whom were convicted of grave crimes, gives us serious concern as to the coming Convention.... Apart from the disorders which will not improbably result, we apprehend that the effect on the Convention itself will be to stimulate the Extreme party to demands quite incompatible with any arrangement which we could enter...'.[53] Midleton was caught between a desire to co-operate with the government, in

---

[51] Addison Diary, 21 Nov. 1917, *ibid*.

[52] Fisher Diary, 21 Nov. 1917, Fisher Papers.

[53] Midleton to Lloyd George, 21 June 1917, L.G.P. F/38/1/2. Midleton, as St John Brodrick, was Secretary of State for War in Balfour's Cabinet, and was now the senior Southern Unionist in the Lords.

the national interest, and the deep suspicions of the Southern Unionist rank and file, which he largely shared. Though eventually persuaded to nominate Southern Unionists for the Convention, he continued to broadcast his complaints. To Bonar Law he remarked that 'You have always thought Ulster was the only key to the situation. We are now heartily, and very much against the grain, trying to help you out of the difficulties which we think would have been avoided by stronger policy in the past, which would also have facilitated a settlement.'[54] His views were made known to the Unionist peers and also to the War Cabinet, and on 4 July an extended meeting, attended by Duke, the Lord Lieutenant Wimborne, and Christopher Addison as well as War Cabinet members, heard him out.

The evident result was to confirm the War Cabinet in its policy and Duke, who was largely responsible for the prisoners question, in his authority in Ireland. Addison described Midleton's case as 'a long cock-and-bull story' from which no practical recommendations emerged, and concluded that Wimborne, who had travelled from Ireland to give evidence to the War Cabinet, was an 'unmitigated ass'. Duke, who complained on another occasion that if the Lord Lieutenant tried to debate the contents of the memoranda he submitted to the War Cabinet it would make his job impossible,[55] persuaded his colleagues that 'the whole thing evidently was an attack engineered by Midleton and others upon him'. Addison concluded that 'the effect of the whole afternoon was immensely to strengthen Duke's position and to provide a fine testimonial of his soberness and statesmanship.'[56] The government's policy at this point was to ignore Unionist protest about disorder and to be circumspect about taking action against Sinn Fein. Its rationale was neatly explained in early August by Hankey to his friend J. St Loe Strachey, editor of the *Spectator*:

> There is nothing that the enemies of this country would like better than to upset the Convention and the atmosphere in which it is working. Whether in the long run it will achieve the aims which all sober-minded men have at heart is, I fear, questionable, but there is no doubt that, at the moment, it is a very solid asset to us. By many people abroad it is understood, as it is intended to be understood, [& as it is,] a [very] real earnest of the intention of the British Government to seek a solution to the Irish difficulty, and so long as it can keep steadily at work this happy state of affairs should continue. It is a real asset to us in the United States, in the Dominions, in Russia, and among our Allies generally. Even if it fails of its ultimate purpose there is the possibility that it may create a Central party of moderate opinion in Ireland which will be able to hold its own against the Extremists on either side ... Hence,

---

[54] Midleton to Bonar Law, 19 June 1917, B.L.P. 82/1/17.
[55] Duke to Lloyd George, 16 July 1917, L.G.P. F/37/4/30.
[56] Addison Diary, 4 July 1917, Addison Papers 98.

it is very important not to upset, in its early stages, the Convention, and jeopardise whatever chances there are of good results . . . [57]

As a policy it was cynical but consistent.

It was soon evident that neither the freeing of prisoners nor the successful launch of the Convention had made it any easier to suppress Sinn Fein. Dublin Castle had seriously misjudged both the popular mood in Ireland and the nature of the Sinn Fein organisation, which was not the firmly led seditious conspiracy that prominent Unionists imagined. The authorities restrained themselves from arresting Sinn Feiners for seditious language as such, but continued to break up demonstrations which threatened to become violent, and to prevent drilling. One of the first victims of the new policy towards Sinn Fein was De Valera himself, who was arrested on 14 August for incitement. The immediate effect on the Convention was that Thomas Monteagle, a Sinn Fein sympathiser who was on the point of co-operating with the Convention secretariat, cried off,[58] and the Lord Mayor of Dublin, a Nationalist, threatened noisily to withdraw unless arrests of Sinn Feiners ceased. Sir Horace Plunkett, the Convention's chairman, protested.

> I got them to call off the arrest of de Valera [sic] and last night Hopwood wired me that no further action would be taken until Duke came over here. But here is the trouble.
> The policy of the government seems to be to let anybody say what they darn please, talking all the treason and sedition they like in the abstract, but if, when the military police (thinking it necessary for the public safety and for the defence of the Realm) prohibit meetings of drilled and armed men, speakers call upon mobs to disregard the prohibition and actually take part in the offence, arrests must follow. This the Authorities say de Valera has done more than once, making speeches of utmost violence. These speeches are censored, and de Valera is telling his friends, apparently, that he is doing nothing of the kind, but holding his hand and doing all he can to keep the country quiet, so as to give the Convention a chance.[59]

It was ironical that although considerable efforts had been made to get Sinn Feiners into the Convention, ministers and officials had little idea what Sinn Fein sympathisers in Ireland thought about the Convention and its chances. The most optimistic view came from experienced observers such as William Ormsby-Gore, who visited Ireland in September and reported that:

> I was told that the Sinn Fein movement is largely due to the stoppage of emigration combined with a fear that Redmond would agree to conscription in Ireland. There

[57] Hankey to Strachey, 2 Aug. 1917, House of Lords Record Office, Strachey Papers S/8/6/6. The words in parenthesis were added by hand to the TS letter.
[58] Monteagle to Adams, 15 Aug. 1917, L.G.P. F/66/1/47.
[59] Plunkett to Adams, 20 Aug. 1917, L.G.P. F/63/1/38.

is still an almost passionate fear of conscription, and a feeling that Redmond is too much 'in with' the British Government, then Sinn Fein became the fashion amongst the farmers, and is now developing itself in local politics. Hitherto the local government bodies have been largely composed of Redmondite townsmen, gombeen men, publicans, shopkeepers etc. Sinn Fein means to capture the local councils. County Leitrim Sinn Feiners are quiet people, they don't want another rebellion. If the Convention produces an Irish Parliament they will be quite satisfied, and the extremists will soon be discounted. Unionists and Nationalists expect and hope that the Convention will produce something in the end, and even Sinn Feiners would be glad if it did. There is no desire to hurry its deliberation.[60]

Advice of this sort could be conveyed to Lloyd George through Adams, his private secretary with responsibility for Irish affairs, if Lloyd George could be persuaded to listen. It was more difficult to affect the behaviour of Dublin Castle, which annoyed even moderate Nationalists by seizing arms from the National Volunteers but not from the Ulster Volunteers, and thus persuading many Nationalists that the Government of Ireland wanted the Convention to fail. The Lord Mayor of Dublin made his protest in public, adding to a torrent of anti-government speeches. Duke was forced on to the defensive, seeking out prominent Nationalists to persuade them that the military had acted with 'much care and moderation' and that the seizures and arrests had been successful in keeping 'the treasonable proceedings of certain Sinn Fein leaders within the bounds of safety'.[61] His real concern had been that the moderate (Redmondite) Nationalist Volunteers were on the point of joining forces with the separatist (anti-Redmondite) Irish Volunteers, taking their arms with them, but the over-riding need to keep the Convention afloat inhibited him from saying so too prominently in public.[62]

The task of convincing even the most moderate Nationalists that the government's policy was not both brutal and ineffective was made virtually impossible by the death in Mountjoy prison on 28 September of Thomas Ashe, a Sinn Feiner held without trial since the Easter Rising. Ashe had gone on hunger strike, and was force-fed. Shortly afterwards he died, either of starvation or because of the trauma of force-feeding. 'Isn't it like Ireland's luck', wrote Plunkett, whose efforts to bring the Convention towards agreement on specifics seemed about to bear fruit.[63] Dillon used Arthur Henderson as an intermediary with the Cabinet, wiring that 'Deaths of any more prisoners would arouse desperate feeling. All prisoners for political offences should be immediately put under special rules.'[64] Sinn

---

[60] 'Observations made on recent Visit to Ireland', Ormsby Gore to Adams, 11 Sept. 1917, L.G.P. F/70/20/7.

[61] Duke to Adams (telegram) 20 Sept. 1917, L.G.P. F/65/5/19; *The Nation*, 5 Sept. 1917.

[62] Redmond to Lloyd George, 31 Aug. 1917, L.G.P. F/37/4/31.

[63] Plunkett to Adams, 28 Sept. 1917, L.G.P. F/64/3/2.

[64] W.C. 242, 1 Oct. 1917, CAB 23/4.

Fein called for vengeance for the 'murder' of Ashe. Duke warned the War Cabinet that more of the forty prisoners still detained under D.o.R.A. would probably go on hunger strike, and it was decided to remove 'ring-leaders' to English prisons: but neither the British government nor the Irish administration was prepared for the demonstrations of popular feeling at Ashe's funeral on 4 October. A mile-long procession, in defiance of the Defence of the Realm regulations, followed the cortège, and pistols smuggled in the hearse were used to fire a military salute. Sympathetic observers thought that the occasion compared in importance to the funeral of Parnell, giving to Sinn Fein prisoners, and thus Sinn Fein itself, 'political' status.[65] Duke in fact did confer a special status on the Sinn Fein prisoners, at which an unsympathetic Unionist observed that 'in the twinkling of an eye De Valera has become the . . . outstanding man in Ireland'.[66]

The blow to British policy convinced Lloyd George that Duke and much of the Dublin Castle administration would have to be replaced; he canvassed Plunkett for suggestions and sent his secretary, William Sutherland, to make enquiries in Ireland. Sutherland discovered that the officials 'were very frank about each others' faults'[67] but could not find a better team, while Plunkett could only suggest obscure candidates for Duke's job.[68] The uncomfortable truth, for the War Cabinet, was that the intensity of feeling aroused by Ashe's death could not be contained by the exercise of powers under D.o.R.A.: nothing that Duke or the Castle could do would persuade Irish public opinion that Ashe was a criminal, and the remaining prisoners, 'fanatic and ready to face death', could easily twist the knife.[69]

Moreover, the Convention was reaching a critical stage. Nationalists and Unionists were on the point of a major disagreement over 'fiscal autonomy': the powers of an Irish parliament to raise funds by customs and excise duties, which could imply a commercial policy at odds with Great Britain and might cut Ulster industries off from British markets. The Nationalists insisted on 'autonomy', and to get it were prepared to offer large concessions in the new Irish constitution which would give Ulster a veto over legislation. Efforts by Plunkett and the Convention's secretariat to bring the two sides together by elaborate procedural ploys were frustrated by the anger roused by Ashe's death. Nationalists were determined not to let the Convention stifle the expression of their anger in order, as Duke wryly observed, 'to do something to re-establish their

---

[65] *The Nation*, 6 Oct. 1917.
[66] Crawford Diary, 5 Oct. 1917.
[67] C.P. Scott to Dillon, 19 Oct. 1917, B.L. Add. MSS 50904, f. 75.
[68] Plunkett Diary, 5 & 9 Oct. 1917.
[69] War Cabinet Minutes 249, 15 Oct. 1917, CAB 23/4.

still waning popularity in Ireland',[70] while leading Unionists attacked the weakness of the Irish government. Dr Bernard, the Protestant Archbishop of Dublin, warned that there was 'no hope' for the Convention.[71]

The very gravity of the situation determined Redmond's next move. In the House of Commons he launched a fierce attack on Dublin Castle, but contrived to forgive Duke and the British government. This was as well, since Unionist intransigence was threatening to cause a breakdown in the Convention, which would have been fatal to the Nationalist Party. In the House of Commons, Unionist pressure was mounting for a redistribution of Irish seats under the Franchise bill, now in the committee stage, and the whole future of Irish Nationalism was looking bleak unless the government would somehow step in to save the party. Consequently, in early November, Redmond appealed to Lloyd George to bring pressure on the Ulster members through Carson. On 13 November he warned that:

> Unless some power outside now intervenes, the Convention will prove abortive, and no-one knows better than yourself what that will mean. It will mean governing Ireland at the point of a bayonet. Do not imagine that anything else will be possible. Sinn Fein will be omnipotent, and you will be forced to appoint a Military Governor. The Nationalist Party will be helpless, and will inevitably disappear, and you will have a scandal in Ireland which will echo right round the world, and the effect of which will most undoubtedly be very serious, in America especially.[72]

Lloyd George's reply was hardly encouraging: Carson 'cannot get his people to go the lengths of the proposals put forward by the Nationalists'.[73] In the Convention Lord Londonderry tried to put forward a scheme of federal devolution, but his Unionist colleagues would not allow it to proceed.[74] On 22 November Duke told the War Cabinet that the Convention was on the point of collapse, and leaders of the various parties were asked to meet Lloyd George.[75]

Crisis in the Convention forced the Irish question upon ministers as they began to think about the reconstruction of politics on the mainland. It was an unwelcome subject, and the Coalition's main aim was to prevent its reaching Westminster at all if possible. The War Cabinet hardly had time to deal with it, yet it was important that the Irish party should not be given any reason to act concertedly against the government. As ever, their compliance had to be won without offending the Ulster Union-

---

[70] *Ibid.*

[71] In a letter to Curzon, reported in W.C. 251a, 17 Oct. 1917, CAB 23/13.

[72] Redmond to Lloyd George, 13 Nov. 1917, Redmond Papers 15,189.

[73] Lloyd George to Redmond, 15 Nov. 1917, *ibid.*

[74] Plunkett to Adams, 16 Nov. 1917, L.G.P. F/64/4/12; cf. D.G. Boyce and J.O. Stubbs, 'F.S. Oliver, Lord Selborne, and Federalism', *Journal of Imperial and Commonwealth History*, v (1976), 68–70.

[75] W.C. 280, 22 Nov. 1917, CAB 23/4.

ists and their sympathisers, who constituted the most disaffected of the Conservative minorities.

Lansdowne

Lord Lansdowne's unique contribution to the Coalition's difficulties came in the form of a letter printed in the *Daily Telegraph* (because *The Times* had refused it) on 29 November 1917, calling for a reconsideration of Britain's stated war aims to take account of the costs of continuing a war which was threatening the fabric of European civilisation. Lansdowne, who had succeeded Salisbury as Foreign Secretary in 1900 and had done most of the work in the making the original *entente cordiale*, was an unlikely pacifist. His conception of European civilisation was far removed from that of the radical critics of pre-war foreign policy who eagerly took up his cause in 1917. His propositions amounted to a high-minded defeatism which, in view of the government's chronic anxiety about manpower shortages and the post-war international relations, might have been thought quite agreeable to reflective statesmen inside and outside the Coalition government. The currents of politics, both at home and abroad, made sure that there was no such meeting of minds, and in any case the leaders of the Coalition could not forget his support for the Asquithian side in December 1916. Nonetheless, the issues he raised could not be brushed aside.

The emotional departure of Henderson had blurred the continuity of relations between the British government and its 'pacifist' critics. Just as MacDonald's views on the proper end of the war had been found acceptable in May 1917, the war aims of the Labour Party as defined in their discussions about Stockholm, were acceptable not only to Herbert Samuel on the opposition front bench but also to belligerent pro-Coalitionists such as Geoffrey Dawson of *The Times*[76] While no public statements were made about peace by negotiation, the reality of peace negotiations continued during the autumn. In late September the German government made the limited offer of a settlement mentioned above,[77] which would ostensibly concede most of the Western Allies' wishes but take advantage of Russia's weakened state to extend German influence in the East. In the end this was rejected by the French government.[78] In Britain the discussion of war aims between the parties and within parliament was confined in range by the establishment of the three-party War Aims Committee.[79]

---

[76] Dawson to Northcliffe, 27 Aug. 1917, Northcliffe Papers 153.
[77] Above, pp. 235–236.
[78] Rothwell, *British War Aims*, pp. 105–110.
[79] Sanders Diary, 31 Aug., 3 Oct., 5 Nov. 1918, *Real Old Tory Politics*, pp. 89, 91.

As a result, domestic political discussion of peace was in a flat spot while the Passchendaele campaign slithered to a halt and the collapse of the Italian army further weakened the hope of an Eastern solution to Britain's strategic problems. The futility of warmaking re-emerged as a political issue with the publication of Lansdowne's letter. Lansdowne wanted a restatement of British war aims which would remove the impression that Britain wanted to crush Germany militarily and economically and exclude her from the intercourse of civilised nations after the war. The most contentious part of his proposal was a suggestion that the British interpretation of the 'freedom of the seas' should be negotiable, so that it should not bear too heavily on German interests. At the time Lansdowne's motives seemed impenetrable, and in the absence of any evidence from his own papers they seem likely to remain so. Crawford thought that 'the explanation must to some extent be sought in the vexation and annoyance he feels at being out of office'.[80] There is no evidence to support Dr Bentley's hint that it was specifically intended to create movement in domestic politics.[81] To his sorrowing Unionist friends Lansdowne maintained that his postbag revealed a great deal of support for his views in the country 'from people whom no one would include in the category of cranks';[82] and the most likely explanation of his intentions is the most obvious one: that he wished to express a direction in which foreign policy could move. It is probable that Balfour knew about the letter beforehand — a draft of it, dated 6 November 1917, is in his papers[83] — but far from certain that he approved of it, since his attitude at the time to Austrian peace initiatives was seen by Hankey as frosty.[84] Still less can it be ascertained whether Balfour or Cecil actually inspired the note, which the *Morning Post* and other Unionist newspapers suggested. In these allegations we are probably seeing a last blow struck by disgruntled Tariff Reformers against the Hotel Cecil.[85] Official comment, led in the event by Robert Cecil, was firmly opposed to Lansdowne's suggestions, at least as taken literally.

But the reception of Lansdowne's initiative did not, indeed could not, stop at a refutation of his proposals for war aims. Conservative and Liberal leaders had to defend themselves in their own parties. Philip Kerr, the prime minister's secretary, noted that 'Talbot tells me that some Tories thought it all right until Bonar Law at the Tory meeting turned it down, *Note* the confirmation of Bonar Law's leadership at that meeting was, no doubt, largely assisted by the letter and it formed a text of which he made

---

[80] Crawford Diary, 1 Dec. 1917.
[81] Bentley, *Liberal Mind*, p. 60.
[82] Lansdowne to Austen Chamberlain, 2 Dec. 1917, Austen Chamberlain Papers AC 13/3/7.
[83] Memo., 6 Nov. 1917, Balfour Papers, B.L. Add. MSS 49730, ff. 291–299.
[84] Hankey Diary, 28 Nov. 1917, Hankey Papers 1/3.
[85] See the Duke of Northumberland to Gwynne, 29 Nov. 1917, Gwynne Papers 21.

full use.'[86] Waldorf Astor, another of Lloyd George's entourage, noticed Tory approval for the document even after Bonar Law's intervention,[87] and Strachey from the *Spectator* clearly expected to find agreement from Austen Chamberlain to the proposition that Lansdowne had said the right things in the wrong tone.[88] Lloyd George himself expressed a rather similar view to H.A.L. Fisher on 5 December, though he complained to Lord Islington that the letter had nearly wrecked the Paris conference on inter-Allied unity of command.[89]

Another factor serving to make Lansdowne a political issue was the response of the official Liberal Party. McKenna led the ex-Cabinet in urging Asquith to come out in favour of the letter, and back-bench pressure led by Noel Buxton and Josiah Wedgwood contended that negotiated peace was an issue which would re-unite Liberalism.[90] Another view of the same point was taken by Philip Kerr: 'If this Pacifist attitude crystallises and the Government decides to challenge it, there could be no better issue upon which to split the Liberal Party. War Liberals will not mind voting, if necessary, against their fellows on such an issue.'[91] Potential cracks in the Liberal Party were mirrored on the other side. Robert Cecil, complaining of the newspaper attacks on Lansdowne, observed that 'Lansdowne is not a traitor, nor is he senile, still less is he corrupt, and to suggest these things about him merely tends to throw doubt on the strength of the case of his opponents.' He went on to regret the tone, but very little of the content, of Lansdowne's letter and returned to the question of attacks:

> I may be a very bad judge of the opinion of the generality of my fellow-countrymen, but I think I do know something about the mental attitude of the landowners, and their friends, and I am quite satisfied that sooner or later they will very much resent the violence of the attacks on Lansdowne, and if they weaken in support of the war, I personally believe that one of our most important forces will have disappeared.'[92]

Correspondingly, Austen Chamberlain complained to Strachey that Lansdowne had come out against the idea of fighting an economic war after the war; Strachey was at pains to insist that his own failure to mention this in the *Spectator* did not spring from closet Free Trade opinions.[93]

---

[86] Kerr to Lloyd George, 4 Dec. 1917, L.G.P. F/89/1/9.

[87] Astor to Lloyd George, 5 Dec. 1917, Waldorf Astor Papers WA 40/756.

[88] Strachey to Chamberlain, 5 Dec. 1917, Strachey Papers S/4/5/7. He was wrong.

[89] Fisher Diary 5 Dec. 1917, Fisher Papers; Crawford Diary, 6 Dec. 1917: Islington was Under-Secretary for India.

[90] 'It seems to many Liberals important that this country should express itself on the ultimate peace settlement. Too much influence is exerted by Conservatives with prussian traditions.' Circular by Wedgwood and Buxton, 1 Dec. 1917, Pringle Papers II/56.

[91] Kerr to Lloyd George, 4 Dec. 1917, L.G.P. F/89/1/9.

[92] Cecil to Lloyd George, 5 Dec. 1917, L.G.P. F/6/5/10.

[93] Strachey to Chamberlain, 10 Dec. 1917, Austen Chamberlain Papers AC 13/3/99.

Because of the strident condemnation of Lansdowne in the *Daily Mail*, *Morning Post*, and elsewhere in the Conservative press, it was assumed that negotiated peace would now become an issue between the government and its parliamentary opponents. To some extent this was true, since the exponents of negotiation were still active; but at first neither Lloyd George or Asquith made it an opportunity to split the Liberal Party. On Asquith's side torpor and timidity might have played their part; more probably, his public statements were calculated to be as consistent as possible with his earlier statements on war aims, and the result was a position close to that of the government. On the government side, Lloyd George's well documented irritation with the effect of Lansdowne's letter on negotiations with the Allies had apparently worn off by the time he made a major war aims speech on 14 December.[94] By then Asquith had made his own speech (in Birmingham on 11 December),[95] and the two were not far apart in insisting on a secure peace based on the restitution of territory by Germany without a major assault on Germany's post-war position. Like Lansdowne, Asquith stated that he would not insist on changes in the German government; whereas Lloyd George, pursuing a rhetorical line which he had used since the Russian revolution and which was by now rather threadbare, pressed for a 'democratic' peace which, he argued, would not be practicable unless Germany became a democracy.

This left plenty of room for confusion. Sanders was convinced on 20 December that 'Asquith was strongly pressed by his colleagues to take the Lansdowne line in his Birmingham speech. But he stood firm.'[96] A week earlier, though, Buckler had reported to House that 'Asquith like Lansdowne disclaims all intention of insisting on changes in the German government, in short he has carried out the demands which Crewe, Samuel, Runciman, McKenna and the other Liberal leaders put forward.'[97] In fact Asquith had not capitulated to the wishes of the more radical advocates of a negotiated peace, and he had explicitly rejected Lansdowne's desire to curtail sea warfare. Nor had Lloyd George committed himself to the economic war after the war which his more extreme Unionist followers wanted.

On the government side this fudging was no mere accident. While public debate over war aims unsettled both the House of Commons and some of the Entente allies, an intense private activity was going on, because of authentic but secret peace initiatives emerging from Austria. The

---

[94] *The Times*, 15 Dec. 1917.

[95] *The Times*, 13 Dec. 1917. Asquith shared a platform with Austen Chamberlain, who not only praised his patriotism since his retirement but also remarked on the consistency of his views, a point taken up also by *The Times* on 14 December.

[96] Sanders Diary, 20 Dec. 1917, *Real Old Tory Politics*, p. 94.

[97] Buckler to House, 13 Dec. 1917, Buckler Papers 654/II/5/8.

Supreme War Council meetings which Lloyd George had been attending when Lansdowne's letter was published had been used to concert the Entente response to these initiatives: hence Lloyd George's embarrassment when Britain's firmness had been called into question by allies who could not believe that Lansdowne had acted without official encouragement.[98] Moreover Woodrow Wilson had addressed Congress on 4 December, calling for a peace based on justice and a reparation of wrongs, liberation of subject peoples in Austria-Hungary and Turkey, and a new set of leaders in Germany: a much more demanding war aim than Lansdowne's.[99] Lloyd George's rhetoric during December and January was tuned not only to the needs of domestic politics, but also to the needs of covert and overt diplomacy.

With the approval of the Allies, but against the resistance of Balfour and the Foreign Office, the War Cabinet sent General Smuts to Switzerland in December. He met Albrecht Mensdorff, formerly Austria's ambassador in London, in a Geneva suburb on 18 December. The discussion was amicable but inconclusive. Smuts put forward the proposition which had been popular in government for some months, that Austria would be left intact as a counterweight to Germany in Central Europe, not dismembered in the interests of the subordinate nationalities within the Empire. He refused to discuss a general peace, and Mensdorff refused to contemplate a separate peace between Austria and the Entente, so these negotiations could proceed no further: but Smuts came away with the useful point that Mensdorff did not believe that the Central Powers could even contemplate a shift in their position over negotiations until they had an up-to-date statement of Allied war aims.[100] In that sense Lansdowne was swimming with the tide of policy: but it was in everybody's interest to pretend that he was not.

Lansdowne's letter and the surrounding clamour had little impact on British foreign policy. Its lasting consequence was to ensure that for the rest of the war the division between the Coalition and its opponents would be expressed primarily as a matter of war to the end or a negotiated peace, whether or not the real divisions arose from domestic or foreign affairs. Lansdowne's public statement, whatever its intentions, must be seen as the first substantial step towards the Coupon Election of 1918, and a grave though not mortal blow to the political system of Victorian and Edwardian Britain.

[98] Crawford Diary, 6 Dec. 1917.
[99] *The Times*, 5 Dec. 1917.
[100] These encounters are described in Turner, *Lloyd George's Secretariat*, p. 162.

7

THE OPENING OF THE CAMPAIGN
December 1917 to February 1918

Calculation and Compromise

For the next three months the Coalition was to find itself unpopular in the House of Commons and simultaneously unloved by public opinion, which had hitherto been regarded as its mainstay. Lansdowne's letter cast confusion on the Lloyd Georgian plans for a more coherent Coalition. Addison, with Fisher and apparently Lloyd George as well, was prepared to contemplate an open breach with the Asquithian Liberals. Freddie Guest, with a more regular contact both with the Commons and the constituencies, feared that such a breach would play into the hands of the Conservatives. At the beginning of December the position of the Conservative leadership was assured by Bonar Law's competent handling of the N.U.C.U.A. meeting which had been forced on him, and Guest calculated that in any event Bonar Law would carry three-quarters of the Conservative back bench with him. Guest interpreted tentative discussions between younger Tory M.P.s and the Victor Fisher group not as evidence of the likelihood of a national party, but as a warning that the Conservatives could come to an agreement with Labour and perhaps, on certain terms, with the Irish, thus 'leaving both the Official Liberal Party and the Lloyd George Liberal section out in the cold'. and therefore 'many Tories would regard with equanimity an open rupture between the Prime Minister and Mr. Asquith'.[1] Guest further suggested that whatever Unionist M.P.s and their leaders might be prepared to do in co-operation with Lloyd George, the Unionist organisation in the country would 'exert great pressure to

---

[1] Guest to Lloyd George, 3 Dec. 1917, L.G.P. F/168/2/3.

prevent them becoming his political followers'. Guest was also impressed with the strength of the official Liberal machine and the degree of Liberal suspicion in the country of Lloyd George's connection with Milner and Carson. He believed that Liberals were in general anxious for a reunion of the party after the war. As to Labour, he reckoned that the parliamentary party, except for MacDonald and a few others, was solidly behind the government on war measures, but insisted that 'I do not think . . . that at the present time there is any hope of getting the Labour Party to join up with any other party or section for a general political programme.'

Concluding that both Liberals and Labour would resent an early general election, and that the only party to gain from an election on the old register would be the Tories, Guest urged that he should be allowed to continue what he called a 'Defensive' policy, avoiding a *casus belli* with the Official Liberals. But even this defensive scheme envisaged an election on the new register in July 1918, which Guest suggested should be

> . . . an appeal to the country on the 'Prosecution of the War', in other words, a khaki election, in which case only the Pacifists and declared anti-Government members will have to be fought. The Liberal Party which is unlikely to declare for Pacifism, would be forced to support the Government. This would result in the return of a similar Coalition Government, but would give greatly increased power and authority to the Prime Minister.

The next steps should therefore be to prepare 'the terms of an arrangement between the three sections of the Coalition' and a 'reconstruction programme' to appeal to Labour, Liberal and Conservative sympathisers.

Guest's analysis was accepted in Lloyd George's immediate circle. A meeting on 21 December between Lloyd George, Milner, Victor Fisher, Addison and Astor discussed future policy. The gathering was alarmed at Henderson's moves to reconstruct the Labour Party:

> . . . not so much from the fact that he is organising the party with a great many candidates — but from the fact that his personal vanity and weakness might precipitate him at any time into bringing about a condition at home with organised labour which might make only for a patched up peace, with all the possibilities of progress and reconstruction and insecurity afterwards which that would mean. There is probably inevitably a split coming in the Labour world, for the fact is the very small tail of the Labour Parliamentary and other organisations of the I.L.P. and others really seem to have captured the machinery of the organisation, the mass of the Trades Unionists leaders would probably find themselves left in the lurch on being committed to a programme with which neither they nor the bulk of their members have much sympathy. Fisher is getting, so he says, a comprehensive organisation through the country backed by solid Trades Unionists and the only point really is when the split is to come. There can, however, be no getting away from the fact that at present the tail is wagging the dog — from one's pretty extensive knowledge of the parties concerned, the metaphor really becomes more mixed than ever, owing to the fact that the brains are in the tail.

It is important to note that political planning at this stage was concerned with long-term developments in the Labour movement. These were not very successful prophecies — an editor preparing Addison's diaries for publication in 1934 noted 'In the light of later events, this [paragraph] beats a Greek tragedy for irony! Omit or Emend?' (it was omitted) — but they amounted to more than a simple concern for wartime politics. Nevertheless, on Guest's analysis, it was vital to fight a wartime election, and the meeting agreed to prepare a programme to answer the expected Labour challenge: a programme 'at all events sufficiently definite, although, of course, not elaborated with such details as would be necessary, if it were frankly a post-war election'. Addison could not, however, persuade the meeting that the party organisations of the three sections of the Coalition should immediately fuse.[2]

Addison persisted with his efforts to bring the sections of the Coalition into a more permanent relationship. On 4 January he suggested to Lloyd George that ministers of all parties should be convened in groups to discuss reconstruction problems; this was an alternative to an earlier plan, by which only the Liberal ministers would meet.[3] Nevertheless, he was keen to attend a meeting of the London Liberal Association, addressed by Asquith. 'I went deliberately in order to emphasise the fact that we were all Liberals together — Asquith was very friendly to me afterwards';[4] and it is clear that the attempt to consolidate the Coalition did not at this stage imply the general exclusion of opposition Liberals. The potential enemy was the Labour opposition. Indeed, plans for joint discussions of reconstruction among senior Coalition ministers languished until after the Nottingham conference of the Labour Party, at the end of January, had emphasised the degree to which anti-government feeling pervaded the rank and file. Significantly, the party did not call upon Labour ministers to withdraw from the government, as some of them had been expecting.[5] More anxiety was caused by the vociferous support for a 'democratic peace', not because this was a direct attack on the government's policy — the conference welcomed Lloyd George's recent war aims speech 'so far as they are in harmony with the war aims of the British labour movement' — but because it indicated the lines on which a Labour challenge to the Coalition could succeed. Asquith, in some ways a more nervous observer than ministerial Liberals, detected a 'tumultuous pacifism' which he associated with dangerous unrest.[6] Even so, Henderson was known in

---

[2] Addison Diary, 21 Dec. 1917, Addison Papers 98.

[3] Addison to Lloyd George, 4 Jan. 1918 and Lloyd George to ministers, undated. Addison Papers 13.

[4] Addison Diary, 5 Jan. 1918, Addison Papers 96.

[5] Milner to Lloyd George, 15 Jan. 1918, L.G.P. F/33/3/3, reporting the views of Hodge.

[6] Stamfordham to the King, 31 Jan. 1918, RA GV Q1284/2.

February to take the view that if the war had to continue it would be better if Lloyd George stayed in office to carry it through.[7]

The government's perception that the pro-Lansdowne movement was unlikely to take wing at the end of 1917 without help was shared by the Radical Liberals who had consistently been in touch with the American embassy. Josiah Wedgwood and Noel Buxton circulated for signature a letter to Asquith which placed 'Lansdowne' firmly in the context of the fissile Liberal Party:

> They note that even among Conservatives there is a strong body of feeling hostile to extravagant aims such as the destruction of Austria, and they are deeply puzzled when they understand from your own utterances that while the Government has tended to follow the more moderate section in this matter, the Liberal leader takes the extreme view. We know for a fact that a considerable section of the most active Liberals, feeling the want of material for the exercise of party loyalty and enthusiasm are tending to sever their party ties. Can the defection be arrested? It is becoming clear that the war is continued because a settlement based on restoration would not be a 'Victory', but the keener Liberals hold that Liberalism has something deeper to say than this. They see that the issue is at bottom the old issue between Liberal and Tory . . . We believe in the Party truce, but the party truce applies to the conduct of the war, not to the statesmanship which deals with the settlement.[8]

The government's response to the Lansdowne letter was at first panicky, but the panic was more fully expressed in the jingo newspapers than by ministerial statements, and by the time Lloyd George made his first pronouncement on the subject, on 14 December, he was prepared to dismiss Lansdowne with no more than heavy irony. He also propounded a set of new aims, in particular discounting any desire to destroy the Austrian Empire, which was in content if not in tone compatible with a great deal of 'progressive' opinion.[9]

The letter and the debate which it engendered had a considerable impact in the press — which with only the committed Liberal and Labour journals as exceptions took an abrasive line against Lansdowne's suggestions — among officers in the army, where Lansdowne won extensive support, in the senior ranks of the Conservative Party, especially on Balfour and Robert Cecil, and on Milner and Smuts, who represented 'imperial

---

[7] Memo. by Sir Francis Bertie and others 18 Feb. 1918, FO 800/175/116–117; also in L.G.P. F/52/1/15.

[8] Draft circular letter, signed by Wedgwood and Noel Buxton, 1 Dec. 1917, Pringle Papers II/56. The letter was signed by 23 M.P.s: Richard Acland, Wedgwood, Buxton, Alexander Shaw, Leif Jones, Athelstan Rendall, Sir William Collins, Richard Holt, Joseph Bliss, Gerald France, J.F.L. Brunner, Sir Godfrey Baring, Harry Nuttall, Ellis Davies, Percy Harris, Albion Richardson, J.G. Hancock, Sir Walter Runciman, Timothy Davies, Arthur Richardson, Sir J. Barlow, W. Pringle and E.J. Kelly. Buckler described them as 'a new group of "moderates", untarred by the brush of "pacifism"'.

[9] Turner, *Lloyd George's Secretariat*, pp. 158–161.

thinking' in the War Cabinet.[10] It brought into sharp focus the problem of maintaining the Labour movement's support for the war, which had been on ministerial minds since Henderson's awkwardness over Stockholm. But, although Lloyd George's immediate followers blamed senior opposition Liberals, notably Loreburn, for the tone of the letter, it made remarkably little difference to the relations between the two sides of the Liberal Party. If anything, it served to compound the embarrassment of Asquith's relations with his 'supporters' on the Liberal back benches. Besides the pressure of Radicals like Wedgwood, Asquith had to face urgings from his wife and threats from his front-bench colleagues, who warned that they would 'feel compelled to make a fuller and stronger statement' if he whittled down his endorsement of Lansdowne, as he appeared to be doing in his speech in Birmingham on 9 December.[11] As a result by mid-December, following his speech on war aims, he and his followers felt themselves committed to 'restitution and security' as in August 1914, not to the desiderata in Balfour's January 1917 note;[12] but no clarion call had emerged for a new political alignment.

Although anti-government Liberals began to organise for opposition, the attitude of the Asquithian leaders remained ambiguous. Leif Jones, by the end of December, was 'hopeful that before long we shall have...a regular, critical & active opposition, wh. will soon lead to a better government'.[13] In contrast Samuel, hearing that he might be offered the Home Office in place of Cave, thought that 'It might be made, perhaps, the occasion for a reconciliation all round' and did not predict Asquith's attitude.[14] In fact the developing discussion over war aims served if anything to bring Asquith, who with Grey met Lloyd George to discuss the prime minister's war aims speech on 3 January, closer to the government and rather further from his nominal supporters. The national and international debate on war aims was promoted by President Wilson, who promulgated his Fourteen Points on 8 January. As Asquith cogitated and McKenna put on record his strong preference for staying out of office,[15] minor figures such as Beauchamp in the Lords and Richard Holt in the Commons began to press their leaders that 'something might be done in support of Lord

[10] On the officers see Buckler to House, 13 Dec. 1917, Buckler Papers 654/II/5/8; corroborated by Victor Cazalet (from the Household Bn, B.E.F.) to Austen Chamberlain, 31 Dec. 1917, Austen Chamberlain Papers AC 13/3/8, see below p. 266.

[11] See e.g. Margot Asquith to Pringle, 3 Dec. 1917, Pringle Papers V/3 and Margot Asquith to Lord Courtney, 9 Dec. 1917, British Library of Political and Economic Science, Courtney Papers 12; Buckler to House, 10 Dec. 1917, Buckler Papers 654/II/5/8.

[12] Buckler to House, 13 Dec. 1917, Buckler Papers 654/II/5/8; see above, p. 251.

[13] Leif Jones to Courtney, 22 Dec. 1917, Courtney Papers 12.

[14] Samuel to Mrs Samuel, 9 Jan. 1918, Samuel Papers A/157/904.

[15] McKenna to G.H. Holden (London, City and Midland Bank), 1 Feb. 1918, Churchill College, McKenna Papers MCKN 7/2/1.

Lansdowne'[16], and Pringle was encouraged (by H.Wilson Harris of the *Daily News*) to co-ordinate his efforts with Arthur Henderson.[17] Holt, however, was 'sorry that Asquith had no warmer words for Wilson's last address',[18] and indeed Asquith once more made it clear in his behaviour that he had little in common with the 'Asquithians'.

The government was somewhat unsteady in February but this was because of the rumour and counter-rumour preceding the removal of Sir William Robertson as C.I.G.S., not because of any enthusiasm for a peace-by-negotiation coalition. Asquith and Lansdowne might have met in the second week of February for some sort of discussion, though in the end it was understood on the government side that they both decided that Lloyd George would have to stay in office:[19] the source for the conspiracy is Esher, an imaginative witness. When sacked, Robertson was careful to put his position before Asquith for use against the government, at first through Gwynne of the *Morning Post* (who had won the support of Hogge and Pringle over a ban on his paper occasioned by an article by Repington), and then face to face.[20] Margot Asquith, 'up to her elbows in intrigue',[21] lobbied everyone from Gwynne to Pringle in an attempt to create a coalition to replace the government.[22] But, as Stamfordham observed, 'The idea of a Lansdowne Ministry is absurd. L would never undertake such a job',[23] and it is hard to see how Asquith could have united the opposition Liberals, on the cry of 'hands off the generals', which he had tried with so little success the previous autumn. Buckler's generally percipient reports emphasised in mid-February that 'The failure of the Prime Minister to carry the House with him in yesterday's debate was due not to any pacifist movement, but to general dissatisfaction as to the handling of the Army Command.'[24] There were still many reasons for disliking the Lloyd George Coalition; it was still impossible for the different dissident elements to grow to dislike one another less than they disliked the prime minister. Asquith finally conveyed to Margot — who does not always seem to have listened to what she was told — that 'If any one is ass enough to force

---

[16] Beauchamp to Runciman, 4 Feb. 1918, Runciman Papers WR 169 (2).

[17] Harris to Pringle, 8 Feb. 1918, Pringle Papers II/61.

[18] Beauchamp to Runciman, 13 Feb. 1918, Runciman Papers WR 169 (2).

[19] Esher to Hankey, 13 Feb. 1918, L.G.P. F/23/2/14 (Esher's handwriting is nearly illegible: the true reading might be 'M.A.' for Margot Asquith); Hankey to Lloyd George, 15 Feb. 1918, L.G.P. F/23/2/15.

[20] Gwynne to Asquith, 11 Feb. 1918, Gwynne Papers 14; Gwynne to Hogge and others, Gwynne Papers 6; Robertson to Asquith, 16 Feb. 1918, Asquith Papers 32.

[21] Haldane to sister, 18 Feb. 1918, Haldane Papers 6013/13.

[22] Margot Asquith to Pringle, 14 Feb. 1918, Pringle Papers II/65; Gwynne to Margot Asquith, 18 Feb. 1918, Gwynne Papers 14; Haldane to sister, *supra*.

[23] Stamfordham to Bertie, 21 Feb. 1918, FO 800/191/324.

[24] Buckler to House, 11 Feb. 1918, Buckler MSS 654/II/5/8.

a division [on the dismissal of Robertson] it will give the Gov. an easy victory if not a triumph', and the intriguing died away.[25]

The disintegration of the 'Lansdowne–Asquith combination' marked the end of the impact of the Lansdowne letter on the Asquithian opposition. The flatness of parliamentary opposition in February and early March, despite a difficult international position, food shortages, and considerable labour unrest, indicates how little had been built upon the effusions of partisan sentiment in December over petroleum, Lansdowne, and the franchise bill. (Gulland, the Liberal Chief Whip, was also ill). The continuity in the anti-government roll-call in the various divisions was significant, but the numbers of anti-government Liberals remained small. There was no sense in which the 'Asquithian opposition' was either very Asquithian, or opposed on a specific ground on which a body of members could be united. It is particularly significant that Asquith himself showed little interest in the subject dearest to the Liberal heart — peace. His criticisms were consistent with the behaviour of an ex-war minister, and his efforts to mobilise opposition, such as they were, were easily portrayed as mischievous. For the most part, his interventions were mild, and his rising stature among opposition Liberals in the spring of 1918 was based not on anything he did, but on what Lloyd George seemed always to be doing to the Liberal conscience. This disjuncture between Asquith and the Asquithians was to take on a more ironical form during the crisis brought about by the German spring offensive in March.

The Robertson Problem

As so often happened under the Lloyd George Coalition, more immediately pressing reasons for action arose from the attitudes of the Tory right wing, provoked by the generals. The final confrontation between the War Cabinet and Sir William Robertson as C.I.G.S. took place in February, and Robertson's resignation was engineered on the 16th of that month. Almost simultaneously, an attack was launched on the ministry by Austen Chamberlain, who complained at the number of newspaper proprietors who held office, and at the use made of the press by Lloyd George through his private secretary, William Sutherland.[26] The immediate outcome was a meeting of the Unionist War Committee, which included backbench M.P.s and peers, 'to see if they could decide on a policy with respect to L.G., particularly with regard to selecting one whom they could support

---

[25] Margot Asquith to Pringle, 18 Feb. 1918, Pringle Papers II/67.
[26] *H.C. Debs* cii, 19 Feb. 1918, 656–657.

as his successor'.[27] Although the party had been restive in the Coalition during 1917, this was the first open attack on Lloyd George rather than Bonar Law. The novelty was often repeated in the years to come, though without success until the Carlton Club meeting of October 1922.

If nothing else, Robertson's last stand brought the enemy nearer to collapse than ever before in the annals of the Great War: but like the obstinate Germans, Lloyd George doggedly picked himself up and continued the fight. Military historians have now dug deeply into the story of civil–military relations between the establishment of the Supreme War Council and the resignation of Robertson, and others have explored the rapid evolution of war aims which went on at the same time.[28] Bureaucratic politics, geopolitical accidents and personal infighting explain a great deal of what went on, though the motives of the main actors do not emerge clearly except in the context of British political developments over the winter of 1917–18.

The immediate consequence of the establishment of the Supreme War Council in November 1917 was to give Robertson a focus for his grudges. Where before he could merely complain of being ignored or being made to repeat himself, he now had a specific institutional target against which opposition could be rallied; and the press campaign which he inspired on returning from Rapallo was unusually specific and for that reason effective.[29] He also had a personal target in Henry Wilson, whom he disliked. The intensity of Unionist resistance in the Commons[30] forced the government to modify its public presentation of the Supreme War Council, so that Lord Hardinge, no friend to the administration, could write that

> ...so far as I can judge there is no intention to upset Lloyd George but I think there are a good many people who wish to read him a lesson. In any case it is quite clear that he has changed the aspect of the inter-Allied Conference from what he intended it originally to be in order to meet the criticisms of those who were ready to attack him. If the Chiefs of the General Staff are allowed to be present at the Conference then the inter-Allied Conference merely becomes a sort of committee of liaison and no harm be done. But this will have to be very clearly defined in order to satisfy Robertson and the Army Council.[31]

---

[27] Addison Diary, 20 Feb. 1918, Addison Papers 96.

[28] The fullest recent account of civil–military relations is in David Woodward, *Lloyd George and the Generals*, pp. 221–281; war aims are covered in V.H. Rothwell, *British War Aims and Peace Diplomacy* and K.J. Calder, *Britain and the Origins of the New Europe* (Cambridge: Cambridge University Press, 1976).

[29] *The Globe*, 15 Nov. 1917; Repington, *First World War*, II, 131.

[30] See e.g. the machinations reported in Austen Chamberlain to Hilda Chamberlain, 20 Nov. 1917, Austen Chamberlain Papers AC 5/1/47.

[31] Hardinge (Permanent Under-Secretary at the Foreign Office) to Sir Rennell Rodd (ambassador in Rome), 19 Nov. 1917, Hardinge Papers 35, ff. 205–206.

Robertson's acquiescence was dearly bought. He tried to hamstring Wilson by defining his role as Permanent Military Representative to the Supreme War Council in such a way that he was subordinate to the Army Council.[32] In early December the Army Council ordered Wilson to submit to them any plans he intended to put forward at Versailles.[33] This battle of attrition, though tiresome, annoyed the War Cabinet less than two events on the battlefronts. On 20 November Haig launched a surprise attack at Cambrai, using nearly 400 tanks to penetrate the German line. Robertson tried to delay the transfer of troops to Italy, and St Loe Strachey from the *Spectator*, a doggedly faithful organ of the High Command, advised Haig that 'Nothing could have been more timely, both from the military and the political point of view'.[34] On 30 November the Germans counter-attacked successfully, wiping out most of the British gains and pushing further back into the British lines. Both the reverse and the High Command's delay in reporting it to the government disquieted the War Cabinet.[35] On 11 December Allenby, who was discovered to have a five-to-one numerical advantage over the Turks in the Palestine theatre, entered Jerusalem, making nonsense of his request for 13 divisions to mount the attack when the War Cabinet had wanted him to do so. That day Lloyd George moved against Haig and Robertson by suggesting to Derby that they be moved sideways to make way for others. Derby refused, but agreed to purge Haig's staff of Charteris, the intelligence officer whose consistently wrong forecasts had helped to shape the case for the Flanders offensive, and Kiggell, Haig's Chief of Staff.[36] The episode illustrated the political difficulties of getting rid of the senior soldiers, but it also seems to have confirmed Lloyd George in an intention to get rid of Derby as well.

Cambrai brought the fighting season to an end, and December was consumed in arguing about the manpower necessary to fight in 1918. The 'manpower crisis', which elbowed most other political and administrative business out of the way, marked the complete collapse of trust between the War Cabinet and the General Staff over the allocation of manpower between the military and the civilian war effort. Lloyd George, Curzon, Barnes, Carson and Smuts made up a Manpower Committee, which met first on 10 December. Its opening brief, from Hankey, pointed out that

---

[32] Robertson to Derby, 15 Nov. 1917, Robertson Papers I/20/11; Derby to Lloyd George, 18 Nov. 1917, L.G.P. F/14/4/77.

[33] Correspondence in L.G.P. F/23/1/31.

[34] Strachey to Haig, 29 Nov. 1917, Strachey Papers S/8/1/4.

[35] W.C. 292, 5 Dec. 1917, CAB 23/4.

[36] Derby to Lloyd George, 11 Dec. 1917, L.G.P. F/14/4/83 and subsequent correspondence in the same file. There were over 100,000 Allied fighting troops in Egypt and Palestine, against 21,000 Turkish combatants.

...the whole of the present difficulties were anticipated by the responsible Government Departments, although the more acute economic trouble has been much slower in developing than they anticipated. From the earliest days of the War until the present Government came into office the Government of the day, rightly or wrongly, always decided in favour of increased military effort and not much was done until the present year to strengthen our economic side. The result is that the economic position has become a threatening one .... [37]

The manpower problem was not entirely about military manpower, though that issue created most of the heat. While the War Cabinet's attempts to control Haig's use of manpower had been spectacularly unsuccessful, its efforts in the civilian economy were scarcely more distinguished. The thrust of policy since 1915 had been to increase the size of the civilian labour force by introducing women and unskilled men either to replace skilled workmen who also happened to be fit for military service, or merely to allow the redeployment of skilled men for more efficient production. Resistance from the trade unions and the shop stewards' movement had slowed this process down, but the labour force had expanded considerably.[38] From the spring of 1916 onwards, governments had to deal with two problems in parallel: the allocation of men between civilian and military needs, and the allocation of men within the civilian economy. Montagu's scheme of 'industrial compulsion' in December 1916 had been devised to meet the second problem, but this had been blocked by the terms on which the Labour party entered the Coalition. Between January and August 1917 responsibility for civilian manpower lay to some extent with Neville Chamberlain, the Director of National Service. His scheme, the War Munitions Volunteers, was an attempt to achieve Montagu's ends by voluntary means, a 'Derby scheme' for industrial compulsion. Like the original Derby scheme, this simply did not work, though Lloyd George's famous denunciation of it does not grapple with the real difficulties which Chamberlain faced, and which prevented him from reallocating more than 19,951 male volunteers and 14,256 women.[39] The most important of these, after the intransigence of the War Office, was the vested interest of the Ministry of Munitions and the Admiralty in controlling their own supplies of skilled labour. The allocation of other economic resources, such as raw materials, energy and transport, was steadily brought under control in 1917 by the Ministry of Munitions, the Coal Controller, the Shipping Controller, and finally the

[37] 'Note by the Secretary', Manpower Committee Papers, M.P.C. 2, CAB 27/14; also in L.G.P. F/191/4.

[38] See the discussion in P.E. Dewey, 'Military Recruiting and the British Labour Force during the First World War', *Historical Journal*, xxvii (1984), 199–223.

[39] These figures were revealed by the Select Committee on National Expenditure as the numbers dealt with between the establishment of the department and 1 August 1917. Chamberlain resigned a week later. Lloyd George, *War Memoirs*, I, 801–816.

War Priorities Committee, established in September 1917, which adjudicated between the Admiralty and the Ministry of Munitions over such scarce resources as steel and rubber. Yet no government department or War Cabinet committee grasped the nettle of allocating labour. Auckland Geddes, who succeeded Chamberlain in August 1917 and reconstructed his department as a Ministry of National Service, fought off until May 1918 all attempts to bring labour under the committee's aegis.[40] Since he himself had to work 'in consultation with the Departments concerned' when establishing the relative priority of different forms of civil work, this left a vacuum. Thus although Geddes's department had strong views about the use of men, and could identify major shortages in the manpower available for agriculture, forestry and building merchant ships, it had no power to get men out of one sector of the civilian economy and into another. As a result some of the shortages in the civilian economy, like some of the shortages in the army, could be attributed to bad distribution within it, rather than the crude imbalance between civilian and military effort.[41]

The Manpower Committee had to meet these problems as well as dealing with the usual obfuscation of the military authorities. Hankey, who had been working on the same issues since the autumn of 1915, considered the War Office's figures 'utterly unreliable'[42] because they were twisted to support the argument of the moment. The War Office's demands extended to 600,000 fit men to be taken from the civilian economy by November 1918. This was supported by a virtual admission that the army in France had fought itself to a standstill in 1917. Haig argued that his army was exhausted by the campaigns of 1917, and that he would remain on the defensive in 1918.[43] The Director of Military Operations, General Maurice, declared that 'we must spare no effort in placing every available man and gun in France as early as possible in the New Year', because 'it is only to be expected that the enemy will do his utmost to gain victory before America develops her military strength'.[44] The committee urged a removal of able-bodied men from Ireland and from the home forces, the redeployment of fit men from administrative and transport jobs in France into the fighting divisions, and an alteration in the balance of divisions so that each would have 9 rather than 12 infantry battalions, with the same number of artillery, machine-gun and engineer troops.[45]

[40] See the papers of the War Priorities Committee in CAB 40/2 and CAB 40/3, especially Minutes of the 10th Meeting, 14 Jan. 1918.

[41] See Grieves, *Politics of Manpower*, pp. 90–148.

[42] Hankey Diary, 6 Dec. 1917, Hankey Papers.

[43] 'Memorandum on the Question of an Extension of the British Front', 15 Dec. 1917, CAB 27/14; Robertson in W.C. 302, 19 Dec. 1917, CAB 23/4.

[44] Maurice to Lloyd George, 18 Dec. 1918, L.G.P. F/44/3/40. This paper, a report on operations in 1917, was prepared for a parliamentary statement on war aims, delivered on 19 Dec.

[45] The fullest statement of the committee's conclusions is in its report on 1 Mar. 1918, though

Military historians have argued at length about whether Lloyd George and the War Cabinet were at this point intending to keep the army short of recruits. Woodward, who defends Lloyd George from the charge of starving Haig of men and thus causing the disaster of March 1918, makes the point that 'the government was taking a calculated risk (which was both political and military) by not providing more recruits for the army', and asserts that the maintenance of Britain's staying power for a long war was 'not his only, or even his primary, motive in refusing to meet the demands of the army.... Lloyd George was once more using manpower to force Haig to change his methods'.[46] Though perceptive about Lloyd George's attitude to Haig, this interpretation rather stands the problem on its head. The army, which suffered 'permanent casualties' at the rate of 51,000 a month, was demanding drafts on a scale which could not be met from the civilian economy without political as well as economic disruption. The political problems were real ones, not invented by Lloyd George to control Haig.

On 18 and 19 December the prime minister prepared his ground for a major parliamentary statement which would review the campaigns of 1917 and rally the House against Lansdowne. His meetings with junior ministers — Conservatives at breakfast on 18 December and Liberals and Labour the following morning — were dominated by the acceptability of any further proposals for a 'comb-out'. The Liberals reassured him that the trade unions should be consulted according to the previous agreement with Henderson, though the Labour members suggested that the shop stewards were not so powerful as before.[47] The whole group, except for Ian Macpherson, told him not to conscript Ireland. With the Conservatives he was more open (and had a better amanuensis).

> ...cigars were handed out and the prime minister mused aloud about manpower; how Russia had failed, how Italy had weakened, how tardy has been American intervention and how slow its fruition. How difficult and obstructive Labour has been, notably the highest grades of skilled labour such as the engineers — 'The House of Lords of Labour' as he slyly called them, but how insolent is the aristocrat of the labour market! Lloyd George still smarts under the cool and offhand manner with which they have threatened national necessities — and their attitude on the new bill will probably determine its success. And Ireland? What is to be done about conscription? Lloyd George seemed to make no concealment of his own belief that Ireland ought to be conscripted, but he fears the immediate result. It would inevitably smash up the Convention which still gives a ray of hope. Probably

many of its decisions had been implemented before then. Haig had been opposing the reconstruction of divisions since early in 1917. He also wanted to preserve his cavalry forces.

[46] Woodward, *Lloyd George and the Generals*, p. 236, and see Woodward, 'Did Lloyd George starve the British Army of Men prior to the German Offensive of 21 March 1918?', *Historical Journal*, xxvii (1984), 241–252.

[47] Fisher Diary, 19 Dec. 1917, Fisher Papers.

Conscription would be followed by a defeat of the government in the H of C — in any case the normal conduct of business would become impossible. There would be scenes of violence — Dillon would be carried screaming out of the Chamber.... [48]

And so on. Lloyd George hinted that he would try to get the trade union movement to demand Irish conscription, but made it clear that without the support of organised labour he would not touch Ireland. It was explicitly assumed within the government that the supply of manpower for any purpose was approaching its limit.

In this way politicians as well as generals were brought face to face with the question posed by Lansdowne. Was it worth continuing the war? While the manpower discussion continued some minor efforts were going on to lure the Turks into a separate peace,[49] and, as noted in the previous chapter, Smuts had travelled to Switzerland to meet Mensdorff, the former Austrian ambassador to Great Britain. The Smuts–Mensdorff conversations were an opportunity to tell the Austrians that Britain might not after all wish to dismember the Austrian Empire. They would have had no sequel if Czernin, the Austrian Foreign Minister, had not on 25 December made public comments on the peace terms then being negotiated between the Russians and the Central Powers at Brest-Litovsk. Czernin's point, expressed in carefully guarded language, was that a peace based somehow on 'no annexations and no indemnities' was at least a point of departure for negotiation. On 28 December the War Cabinet decided to make an appropriate public statement of British war aims. It was assumed, rightly as it turned out, that Germany was not at that moment interested in negotiations. The point of making a statement about war aims was to defuse domestic opposition to the war and to make it possible for negotiations to be opened later.[50]

During the discussions in this and subsequent meetings it became clear that part of the War Cabinet was now genuinely afraid of the breakdown of civil order, and that estimates of the prospects of victory, in 1918 or later, varied considerably. On 27 December Lloyd George received Milner, just returned from a meeting of the Supreme War Council and

...plunged in medias res on the subject of possible peace and whether it was of any use trying to continue the war. [So Milner told Thornton, his private secretary] Chief was obviously knocked very flat, although, as he said to me, he had been thinking of little else during the past year.[51]

[48] Crawford Diary, 18 Dec. 1917.

[49] Turner, *Lloyd George's Secretariat*, pp. 78–80.

[50] W.C. 307A, 28 Dec. 1917, CAB 23/13; Balfour to Cecil, 28 Dec. 1917, Balfour Papers, Add. MSS 49738.

[51] Thornton Diary, 27 Dec. 1917, Milner Papers 23.

Robertson, for his part, repeated to the War Cabinet the blunt statement of confidence in eventual victory very much like his response to Lansdowne's previous memorandum in November 1916. On that occasion, it will be remembered, Lloyd George was on his side.[52]

But Robertson's was not the only voice among the soldiers during the winter of 1917–18. An officer in the Guards Brigade wrote at the end of the year:

> It was the fact of the Northcliffe Press's violent & unseemly abuse of Lord L's letter that made it such a big thing out here. If only they had ignored it, no one would have taken such extreme views on it, but as it was officers out here (3 generals I know included) took it up as a kind of gospel-truth & its author as the champion of their cause — i.e. peace on moderate terms. In fact the other night at the Officers Club I overheard 3 officers drink to Ld. L. Of course either extreme is absurd but what people don't realise, & what G.H.Q. cannot realise, is that the ordinary Tommy & junior officer has no idea at all why we are fighting & no ultimate aim or achievement is put before him — He has absolutely nothing to look forward to except Death, if lucky a wound. He knows that if he survives one battle he is due for the next.... All we want is — A definite statement of our peace terms (not vague terms — i.e. freedom of the seas but facts) — and those *if* they are refused — of course we go on until we get them — until then we must naturally not loosen our hold. Forgive this... but people don't seem to realise the extraordinary extent of feeling both among men and officers here, & if they don't soon do something — they must expect them to welcome letters like Lord L's.... Of course we shall win the war — no one doubts that — but whether we shall win by 'fighting' — no one quite believes that now — & the talk of 'knock out blows' etc simply infuriates the soldier here...[53]

The significance of this letter lies partly in its recipient — Austen Chamberlain — and partly in its author, an officer in an élite regiment who was obviously critical of some aspects of Lansdowne's position. At the same time there was perceptible unrest among civilians of the same class. Violet Markham wrote to Strachey of 'the extent of the evil among our own class. Opinion always filters down from the top, and if the well-to-do classes and the intellectuals throw in their hand most certainly the workers will do the same.'[54]

It was more predictable that Sir John Simon, now an R.F.C. officer, should write to Herbert Samuel that 'The soldiers are not nearly such fire-eaters as some of those who speak in their name and I find a good deal of uneasiness at the notion that France was aiming at new territory.... That is not what our men thought they were fighting for.'[55] The main flaw

---

[52] CAB 24/37, G.T. 3145, 29 Dec. 1917.

[53] 'Victor' [Cazalet] (Household Bn, B.E.F.) to Austen Chamberlain, 31 Dec. 1917, Austen Chamberlain Papers AC 13/3/38. Chamberlain was not then in office, and seems to have made no attempt to communicate this view to those of his Conservative colleagues who were.

[54] Violet Markham to Strachey, 2 Jan. 1917, Strachey Papers S/18/5/1.

[55] Simon to Samuel, 28 Dec. 1917, Samuel Papers A/155/V/6/9–10.

in all this evidence of élite unrest, ironically, is its estimate of opinion in G.H.Q. Smuts visited Haig and his staff in January, and found Haig 'strongly in favour of an early peace' in which Britain would keep the German colonies, allow Germany to annex Courland and expand towards Russia. Haig argued that the French and Italians might collapse at any time and 'doubted whether America would be a really serious military factor even in 1919 at her present rate of progress'.[56] At the same time Hankey warned that 'The army is tired of war, and there is a general feeling that peace is not very distant, or at least that the diplomatists ought to be feeling the ground in that direction.'[57]

Although the shifting opinions of Haig and his staff were not known to the War Cabinet as they made their decisions about war aims, they had had warnings about opinion among the troops. The Ministry of National Service, through its intelligence branch, knew that 'a great many of the discharged soldiers were in a very disgruntled state, on account of the way in which they had been messed about .... the men were thoroughly war-weary .... they spoke most bitterly of the waste of life during the continued hammerings against the Ypres Ridge this Autumn.'[58] Lloyd George on hearing this 'wished the Military Authorities to realise how profoundly he was dissatisfied with this expenditure of life, and of the very serious results it was having on the national outlook'; he later told the War Cabinet that 'it was absolutely necessary, before making further demands upon the nation's manpower, that the Government which handed over these men to the Army should see that everything possible was done to conserve their lives.'[59]

The War Cabinet had failed throughout 1917 to get Haig to change his tactics. A further attempt to force 'French' tactics upon him, by commending the more effective use of artillery, fell foul of the generals' trade union and Anglo-French politics: the French officer summoned to advise the Manpower Committee on casualties was briefed to explain that although French casualties had latterly been lower, there could be no comparison between casualty levels in small-scale attacks and the huge battles in which Haig was, and would be involved.[60] Since the French wanted to increase the rate at which British drafts were sent across the Channel, no French staff officer could be expected to say anything else. Failing any real control of casualty levels, and fearful of the impact on the economy as well as the army of widespread discontent, the War Cabinet

[56] Smuts to Lloyd George, 21 Jan. 1918, L.G.P. F/45/9/9.

[57] Hankey to Lloyd George, 22 Jan. 1918, L.G.P. F/23/2/11.

[58] Geddes in Second Meeting of the Manpower Committee, 11 Dec. 1917, CAB 27/14.

[59] Lloyd George in Third Meeting of the Manpower Committee, 11 Dec. 1917, CAB 27/14; W.C. 300, 17 Dec. 1917, CAB 23/4.

[60] Colonel Duffieux in Anglo-French Conference, 18 Dec. 1917, CAB 27/14.

had to attempt either to shorten the war or to bolster public support for
the idea of further sacrifice.

The Caxton Hall Speech

The outcome was a war aims statement made on 5 January. This was a
carefully prepared document, first drafted by Hankey, Philip Kerr and the
prime minister, then reconstructed by Smuts and Cecil. Balfour kept his
distance. He was alarmed at the proposal, made by Cecil and Smuts, to
bear Turkey's war debt, and more alarmed still at Smuts's proposal to approve the war aims of the Bolshevist Russians. 'It, the Bolshevist formula,
applies well enough to Europe, in a general way, though even in Europe it
is not without its difficulties. But it cannot reasonably be made to apply, in
my opinion, to German colonies.' He also made the uncomfortable point
that it was inconsistent to promise the Austrians that Britain did not wish
to dismember their Empire, while assuring the Bolsheviks that 'Bohemia,
Moravia, Croatia etc. are to determine, each for itself, what their future
status is to be.' Balfour's reaction was to be impatient with any discussion
of war aims, 'a problem in which I take no very great interest because, as
it seems to me, there is not the slightest difficulty in defining what ends
we want to achieve by the War. The real difficulty is to find out how
far we shall be able to attain them, and how far our Allies are prepared to
fight till they are attained: — and no amount of defining will help us to
solve either of these problems...'.[61] It was attitudes such as this which
confirmed Lloyd George, Milner and others in the view that Balfour was
unfit for his job. Between them, Cecil and Balfour had correctly defined
two facets of the problem facing the War Cabinet: to manage the attitudes of their enemies, who must be induced to negotiate on reasonable
terms, and to manipulate their allies, who must be induced not to give up
too soon. Cecil boldly assumed that the British people would not give
up, but made no serious effort to address the third question, of how their
resilience could be maintained.[62]

Another consideration was that the Labour Party was evolving its own
set of war aims. A draft, prepared by the Executive, was published shortly
before Christmas and discussed by the parliamentary party on 19 December, in preparation for a special conference held on 28 December.[63] The
Morning Post and the *Globe* detested the proposals, and they certainly re-

[61] Balfour to Cecil, 29 Dec. 1917, B.L. Add. MSS. 49738. See Turner, *Lloyd George's Secretariat*,
pp. 161–165 for the Downing Street contribution.
[62] Cecil's memorandum is in G.T. 3181, CAB 24/37.
[63] Barnes to Lloyd George, 20 Dec. 1917, L.G.P. F/4/2/1.

flected the powerful influence of the Lansdowne letter on radical thinking about peace; but the only difference of substance between Labour's assumptions and the War Cabinet's assumptions was that the Labour Party, like Lansdowne, conceded in advance that it would be undesirable to mount economic sanctions against Germany after the war. This was a Free Trade position, deliberately contrasted to the prevailing sentiment of the Coalition. In that sense, but in that sense alone, the Labour initiative had to be outflanked. Otherwise there was a broad consensus at the end of 1917, inside and outside government, that a fresh declaration of British war aims, leaving open the possibility of a negotiated peace, was both desirable and necessary. Milner, whose reputation as a diehard was ineradicable in Liberal and Labour circles, confirmed this in conversation with Buckler, whom he told that he

> personally does not doubt that some agreement will be reached within a few months, unless interfered with by the cross-currents of Labour 'diplomacy' both here and in Russia. He deplored Henderson's repudiation of all intention to penalise German industry, because this is the very sword which must be held over Germany's head. When she has climbed down, & not till then, it can and will of course be dropped.
> He regards military victory as impossible because too slow and universally destructive, but thinks that in control of 'world supplies' the Entente *have* the victory already, & Germany knows it.[64]

The war aims speech which emerged from these discussions was therefore the product of consensus, not of conflict. On 5 January, addressing an audience of trade unionists conveniently present at the Caxton Hall, Lloyd George delivered a paper 'composed as to two-fifths by Smuts, one fifth by the Prime Minister and two fifths by [Robert Cecil]'.[65] The text had been discussed in advance with Asquith and Grey, as part of an endeavour initiated by C.P. Scott and carried on with some reluctance on Lloyd George's part (but even more on Asquith's and more still on Grey's) to 'bring about an understanding as to war aims between the two wings of the Liberal party'; Ramsay MacDonald had also contributed his view in conversation and in a long letter.[66] Its content, calling for a peace on the basis of national self-determination in Europe, the retention of the German colonies, and preferably, but not necessarily for a change of regime in Germany, was less interesting than the reaction it evoked in observers outside the governing circle, who imposed upon it their own interpretations both of its diplomatic and its domestic political significance. Lord Newton, a professional diplomat, 'saw Lansdowne & asked him what he

---

[64] Buckler to House, 3 Jan. 1918, Buckler Papers 654/II/5/10.
[65] Cecil to Balfour, 8 Jan. 1918, Balfour Papers, B.L. Add. MSS 49738.
[66] *Scott Diary*, p. 324; Macdonald to Lloyd George, 1 Jan. 1918, Macdonald Papers, PRO 30/69/1162.

considered the difference to be between Ll. George's speech and his letter. Said everyone had been asking him that . . . '.[67] Maxse of the *Globe* hoped that 'the National Party will not remain silent and idle while Lloyd George makes himself the mouthpiece of "Defeatism" in our country'.[68] Buckler concluded that 'everybody is feeling the working class volcano under their feet (that is I think the chief determining factor in L.G.'s case)';[69] Newton thought that Lloyd George had explained to Woodrow Wilson that 'his speech was practically dictated to him by Labour people here. Fact is that they will refuse to go on with war much longer, by all appearances.'[70] The *Nation* chose to regard the speech as the 'early sequel of the Lansdowne Letter'.[71] C.P. Scott was struck most by the evidence it contained that the government was prepared to offer Germany a free hand in Russia in return for a settlement in the West which was satisfactory to France and Italy.[72] The speech, indeed, was all these things, except perhaps for defeatism. Its significance was emphasised by Woodrow Wilson's speech of 8 January, in which he spelled out the Fourteen Points which were to cause so much trouble at the Paris Peace Conference. At the time no dissonance was noted between Wilson's position and that of Lloyd George.

The content and provenance of Lloyd George's Caxton Hall speech both support the argument that after the initial flurry of irritation the issue of a negotiated peace, as raised by Lansdowne, was not allowed to become a threat to the domestic political structure at the end of 1917. It was extremely easy for Lloyd George and the War Cabinet to construct a definition of war aims and a stance on the issue of negotiated peace which satisfied the Labour Party, Asquith, the Unionist members of the War Cabinet, and, in substance, Lord Lansdowne. The objections of the National Party and the *Globe* were marginal. Even the radical Liberals who had pressed Asquith, against his own views and better judgement, to support the Lansdowne letter were unable to find a foothold in Lloyd George's speech, except on one point, which had not even appeared until long after Lansdowne. Discussing the Bolsheviks' peace policy, Lloyd George observed that

> The present rulers of Russia are now engaged without any reference to the countries whom Russia brought into the War, in separate negotiations, with their common enemy. I am indulging in no reproaches; I am merely stating facts with a view to making it clear why Britain cannot be held accountable for decisions taken in her ab-

[67] Newton Diary, 8 Jan. 1918.

[68] Maxse to Page Croft, 8 Jan. 1918, Churchill College, Page Croft Papers CRFT 1/10/37.

[69] Buckler to Arthur Hugh Frazier, quoted in Frazier to House, 16 Jan. 1918, House Papers 466/I/58/F282.

[70] Newton Diary, 9 Jan. 1918.

[71] *The Nation*, 12 Jan. 1918.

[72] *Scott Diary*, 7–8 Jan. 1918, p. 329.

sence, and concerning which she has not been consulted or her aid invoked.... *The democracy of this country means to stand to the last by the democracies of France and Italy and all our other Allies.* We shall be proud to fight to the end side by side with the new democracy of Russia, so will America and so will France and Italy. But if the present rulers of Russia take action which is independent of their Allies we have no means of intervening to arrest the catastrophe which is assuredly befalling their country.

This was smartly criticised by the *Manchester Guardian* in a passage which so stung Lloyd George that he rebuked Scott in a letter;[73] Massingham of the *Nation* observed to Buckler that the prime minister had spoken of Russia 'like a narrow little Welsh attorney'.[74] But at this point there was no great enthusiasm for Russia's cause within the Labour Party, and the issue was not pursued. Though partly upstaged by Wilson's 'Fourteen Points' speech, the Caxton Hall performance successfully dominated the discussion of war aims inside and outside the British government.

The Dismissal of Robertson

Whatever they wished to do, Lloyd George and his colleagues were obliged after January 1918 to go on fighting the war, trying to do so without risking immediate defeat and without incurring so many casualties that Britain would be fatally weakened during peace negotiations. Their major fear, ever present since 1916 and aggravated by Russia's collapse, was that France or Italy would be forced out of the war; and their policy had to be modified to suit their Allies' importunities. In early 1918 this course led them through a political minefield, as they tried to get Haig to agree to an extension of his line to relieve the French, and tried to get Haig and Robertson together to agree to the creation of a mobile inter-Allied reserve which could be used in the new campaigning season to reinforce the Western Front wherever the Germans chose to attack. These two issues in turn provoked Robertson's resignation and, as a result of the German attack on 21 March, also threw Lloyd George into conflict with the opposition in the Commons in the Maurice debate.

Both the creation of the Reserve and the extension of the line tested the machinery of the Supreme War Council. The extension of the British line was first agreed at a conference at Boulogne in September, but the plan was frustrated by the demands of the Ypres campaign and the despatch of troops to Italy. In December the French demanded an extension of the British line to Berry-au-Bac, 37 miles further than had been agreed

[73] Lloyd George to Scott, 15 Jan. 1918, L.G.P. 45/2/10.
[74] Buckler to House, 26 Jan. 1918, House Papers 654/I/1/7.

in September. Even Lloyd George resisted this, and the question was remitted to the Versailles staffs, who decided on 10 January to split the difference, by assigning a further 14 miles to Haig. At the same time Clemenceau was lobbying for a strategic reserve, with some initial support from Robertson, who wanted such a reserve put under a Generalissimo rather than under the Permanent Military Representatives at Versailles. This idea was deflected by Wilson, who advised that to put the reserve under Versailles would 'gain most of the advantages of a Generalissimo and suffer few of the disadvantages'.[75] The question of a reserve and its ultimate command were discussed at the Supreme War Council on 30 January – 2 February, in the presence of the premiers. This meeting was 'at times heated & quite unfit for the general public'.[76] Foch accused the British of refusing to supply enough men to the Western Front; Clemenceau demanded the immediate abandonment of 'sideshows' such as Turkey; Haig and Pétain warned that they did not have enough men to resist a German attack, though Haig had recently told the War Cabinet that he did not expect one; Robertson and Haig told the assembled company that the general reserve should be controlled by the Allied Chiefs of Staff, not by Versailles. The outcome was that Lloyd George got support for the Turkish campaign by undertaking that no troops would need to be moved from France, and an Executive War Board was created out of the Permanent Military Representatives, with Foch as chairman, to manage the general reserve. The question of extending the line towards Berry-au-Bac was referred to Haig and Pétain. So far, Lloyd George had won most of his points.[77]

It would have been very surprising if the decision of the Supreme War Council had settled anything finally. The ministerial party returned to a political storm not unlike the reception Lloyd George had received after his Paris speech in November. The tone of the press on this occasion was set by Col. Repington, recently dismissed from *The Times* by Milner's acolyte Geoffrey Dawson.[78] Repington went immediately to the *Morning Post*, whose editor, Gwynne, was being warned that 'there is a conspiracy of which L.G. and some other members of the W.C. are the instigators to get rid of Haig & Robertson. They are furious however at the way Northcliffe has managed the attack which is considered to have failed owing to its stupidity of method.'[79] The 'attack' in question was an

[75] Wilson to Milner, 14 Jan. 1918; Milner to Lloyd George, 18 Jan. 1918, L.G.P. F/38/3/2.

[76] Milner Diary, 31 Jan. 1918. Milner Papers 89.

[77] This and the preceding paragraph are based on Woodward, *Lloyd George and the Generals*, pp. 253–260; see also the minutes of the Supreme War Council in CAB 28/3/I.C. 39–42.

[78] Milner to Lloyd George, 18 Jan. 1918, L.G.P. F/38/3/4.

[79] Northumberland to Gwynne, 22 Jan. 1918, Gwynne Papers 21. Northumberland, a notable Diehard, held a junior position at the War Office. He helped to rescue the *Morning Post* in 1924.

article by Lovat Fraser in the *Daily Mail*, criticising the General Staff which had appeared with no help from Lloyd George on 21 January. Repington's first *Morning Post* article appeared on 24 January, an attack on the manpower decisions. He spent the period of the Supreme War Council in Paris, where he was fed information by the French.[80] From there he placed a telegram in the *Morning Post* of 8 February, which was taken up by the *Globe*. Amery, who warned Lloyd George of the likelihood of a 'raging, tearing press attack' took the view that the only way to deal with the consequences was to move quickly to control the War Office. To political tacticians, the danger of press attacks so closely supported by the War Office made drastic action essential. The reaction to Lovat Fraser's article, which provoked the Unionist War Committee to pass a resolution of support for Haig and Robertson in the Commons on 24 January, made it clear that the Coalition's Conservative supporters might well resist an attempt to purge the whole High Command. It was certain that Asquith, who was being fed information by the General Staff,[81] would ask awkward questions and perhaps turn out the supporters who had backed his attack on Lloyd George's Paris speech in November. This was the classic parliamentary trap which the Coalition could not risk.

Lloyd George's first expedient had been to divide Derby from Haig and Robertson. On 11 January he offered Derby the Paris embassy, which after consulting Balfour Derby turned down.[82] Lloyd George did not give up, and told Hankey on 3 February that he wanted to put Balfour into the War Cabinet, Milner at the War Office, and Cecil at the Foreign Office, with Derby going to Paris.[83] Although Robertson's intention was that Haig, Derby and himself should stand or fall together, Haig had already undermined this position by musing to Derby that 'Without wishing to judge [Sir Francis Bertie] as an ambassador, I can honestly say that he has been of very little help to us, and I feel sure you might be a real help to the army in France if you were at the head of our Embassy in Paris.'[84] Although Derby was perhaps naive enough to believe that Robertson and Haig 'being soldiers are debarred from speaking and stating their cases and I am the only mouthpiece through which their defence can come'[85] he

---

[80] Probably not directly by the British General Staff: Amery, who was a secretary at Versailles, heard only on 2 February that Repington was in France, so he was unlikely to have been in contact with officers at Versailles. Amery to Lloyd George, 3 Feb. 1918, L.G.P. F/2/1/15.

[81] Reading to Lloyd George, 1 Feb. 1918, L.G.P. F/43/1/13 reports a conversation with Asquith on 30 January who told him 'of discontent he had heard of because of [the proposal to attack in Palestine]...He also spoke with great concern about the relative numbers of German and Allies on the Western Front, and said that according to his information Germans would be in distinct superiority of numbers'. Either Asquith believed the *Morning Post*, or he had these figures from the General Staff.

[82] Derby to Lloyd George, 18 Jan. 1918, L.G.P. F/14/5/2.

[83] Hankey Diary, 3 Feb. 1918, Hankey Papers.

[84] Haig to Derby, 26 Jan. 1918, Haig Papers 123.

[85] Derby to Balfour, 24 Jan. 1918, L.G.P. F/3/3/2.

was well aware of what Lloyd George was trying to do: unfortunately for his comrades he was chronically indecisive, and this obliquity on Haig's part did not help his resolve. Robertson warned him on 2 February that 'The Army, the Army Council, the C.I.G.S., the Cs in Chief, will look to you, their Minister, to see that they are not placed in an impossible, unfair, and impractical position.'[86] Derby duly wrote a petulant note to Lloyd George to the effect that he 'might as well have been a dummy for all the advice I have been asked for',[87] but this cut no ice with the prime minister.

Derby then breakfasted with Lloyd George, to be told that Haig had agreed with the main principle of the Versailles decisions. This led Derby to another crisis:

> He then went on to talk about Robertson, and between you and me, whatever happens I think he is quite determined to get rid of him, and herein comes the difficulty of my position. If it is really so that you agree with the principles, provided the question of conveyance of orders is settled, then I should be justified in remaining in office, because it would be only a question of Robertson opposing a scheme to which you had given your assent. If, on the other hand, you are in agreement with Robertson, and Robertson is got rid of because he won't agree to it, then, naturally, I should have to go too.[88]

Robertson, who had heard Lloyd George make the same statements about Haig's view, let him know that 'It would help me if you could *incidentally* drop a line to Derby and say what you think about the Reserve question...'.[89] In the light of these two letters, Haig's response, that 'I consider general reservoir desirable but do not concur in system set up for commanding it', was a great deal less than a wholehearted endorsement of Robertson's position.[90] Esher reported to Milner that Haig 'is perfectly placid, having accepted the Versailles decision without further ado' and even suggested that Haig had avoided Repington during the recent conference.[91] From that point, Robertson's fate was sealed.

On 8 February, after seeing the *Globe* article, Milner guessed that Haig was 'too loyal to lend himself' to Robertson's purposes, but might resist the full development of the General Reserve. 'It is no use having a great rumpus & getting rid of Robertson, if the policy is to be side-tracked for quite different reasons by Haig.'[92] This was prescient on both counts:

[86] Robertson to Derby, 2 Feb. 1918, Derby Papers 920 DER (17), War Office Correspondence.
[87] Draft Memo, 4 Feb. 1918, Derby Papers 920 DER (17), War Office Correspondence.
[88] Derby to Haig, 7 Feb. 1918, Haig Papers 123.
[89] Robertson to Haig, 7 Feb. 1918, *ibid.*
[90] Haig to Derby (telegram), 8 Feb. 1918, Derby Papers 920 DER (17), War Office Correspondence. Cf. Woodward, p. 262, who considers that Haig was indicating that he would support Robertson.
[91] Esher to Milner, 9 Feb. 1918, Milner Papers 351.
[92] Milner to Lloyd George, 8 Feb. 1918, L.G.P. F/38/3/10.

but Lloyd George took the view that if Haig could be separated from Robertson he could be rid of Robertson with the minimum of political difficulty. Derby, Milner and the prime minister discussed the way forward at breakfast on 9 February, deciding that Robertson should be superseded. Lloyd George then prepared a draft statement on the relations between the War Office, the War Cabinet and Versailles in which Henry Wilson would be appointed Deputy Chief of the Imperial General Staff and retain his seat at Versailles, and the Secretary of State would regain the powers of giving military advice to the War Cabinet which Kitchener had been forced (by Lloyd George among others) to give up to Robertson in 1915. When Milner expressed doubt at this, Lloyd George produced an alternative in which Wilson would become C.I.G.S and Robertson would be sent to Versailles.[93] This dramatic illustration of Lloyd George's talent for thinking in terms of men rather than administrative structures left Milner unconvinced, but it had the right effect on Haig.

Haig arrived in London at 3.30 p.m. on 9 February, and Derby immediately told him that Robertson was going to be sacked and that Haig's opinion on that question would not be asked. In his interview Haig 'warned the P.M. and Derby of the distrust in which Henry Wilson is held by the Army' and noted that the plan to make Wilson and Robertson exchange posts came as a 'pleasant surprise' to Derby, 'who evidently was much exercised in his mind as to how to get out of his present difficulty with Robertson. The latter had lately become most difficult to deal with and lost his temper quickly...'.[94] Otherwise, in Lloyd George's words, Haig's 'attitude was perfectly correct'. Derby was also 'delighted', and Macpherson, the Under-Secretary at the War Office, was sent to tell Robertson the news.[95] The most important axis in military–civilian politics, between Robertson and Haig, was broken.

Robertson and his allies had not given up, however, and the battle moved to new terrain. The *Morning Post* published Repington's attack on the General Reserve scheme on 11 February (Monday). This provoked the War Cabinet to consider suppressing the paper, but in the end a prosecution under the Defence of the Realm Act was as far as they were prepared to go. Gwynne consolidated the attack by passing Robertson's views and a history of the weekend's transactions, including the observation that the Army Council was ready to resign *en bloc*, to Asquith for use in the Commons.[96] Derby wavered, and suggested to the War Cabinet on

---

[93] The story can be reconstructed from Milner's diary for 9–16 February and correspondence in L.G.P. 38/3/13.

[94] Haig Diary, 9 Feb. 1918, Haig Papers 123.

[95] Lloyd George to Milner, 9 Feb. 1918, L.G.P. F/38/3/11.

[96] Gwynne to Asquith, 11 Feb. 1918, Gwynne Papers 14; Asquith to Gwynne, promising to give it 'my best consideration', same date, *ibid*.

12 February that Robertson should be kept on after all, winning support from Balfour and Cecil. In the afternoon, Asquith launched Gwynne's attack in the Commons, after the King's Speech. It was noted that Lloyd George's speech on the Address was

> ...a deplorable fiasco. He had a bad cold and looked and spoke like a beaten man....Rumour says that Repington & McKenna have been seen together! Certainly LG spoke as if Asquith & Repington were playing the same game.[97]

Walter Long, who was temperamentally inclined to side with the generals, warned Balfour that 'The feeling in the House was *bad*; while John Burns, who described Lloyd George as 'the shimmering pantaloon', noted that 'HHA has been to a great extent restored or resurrected to his old position of authority and leadership.'[98]

The following day, apparently reinforced by the mood of the House, Derby attempted to reopen the discussion, but Lloyd George refused, and the question was again remitted to the War Cabinet, which met on 14 February. Robertson was allowed to state his case, and it was at this meeting that the outcome of the crisis appears to have been determined. Robertson refused to compromise; the War Cabinet agreed to offer him either Versailles, as deputy C.I.G.S., or the job of C.I.G.S. under the new arrangements; and Balfour was delegated to get an agreement from him in the afternoon. The afternoon meeting had no effect on Robertson, but the day's events markedly affected the political balance. Derby was ordered by the prime minister to offer the post of C.I.G.S. to Plumer. Robertson had not yet resigned, and the War Cabinet had not yet found a successor, but the result of Robertson's determination to stick to his guns was that both Curzon and Balfour 'had changed their opinions and no longer supported Sir W.R.'[99] During the next day, 15 February, Lloyd George and Milner, the War Cabinet members chiefly concerned, still did not know whether Robertson had decided to resign,[100] though Robertson himself seemed, in a letter to Haig, to think that he had not.[101] The uncertainty alarmed Guest, who reported 'incalculable harm' in the Commons, and Long, who after seeing Robertson was 'horrified at the idea of a change now of all moments'.[102] On this uncertainty, and on Plumer's predictable refusal to serve which reached the War Cabinet by telegram late in the

[97] Sanders Diary, 13 Feb. 1918, *Real Old Tory Politics*, p. 101.

[98] Long to Balfour, 14 Feb. 1918, Balfour Papers B.L. Add. MSS 49777; Burns Diary, 12 Feb. 1918, B.L. Add MSS 46340.

[99] Stamfordham's memorandum, 18 Feb. 1918, Royal Archives, RA GV F 1259/32. Robertson was careful to keep the monarch fully informed.

[100] Milner Diary, 15 Feb. 1918, Milner dep. 89.

[101] Robertson to Haig, 15 Feb. 1918, Haig Diary, Haig Papers 25.

[102] Guest to Lloyd George, 15 Feb. 1918, L.G.P. F/21/2/12; Long to Bonar Law, 15 Feb. 1918, B.L.P. 82/9/2.

afternoon, depended Robertson's survival. On 16 February, Lloyd George and Milner took the War Cabinet through the question again, agreeing over Derby's objections to give Robertson another opportunity to choose between Versailles and his present post with restricted powers.[103] This was put directly to Robertson, who declined either appointment and was thereupon replaced as C.I.G.S. by Henry Wilson.

The War Cabinet had acted at last. The only question was whether they could survive the political consequences. Robertson had talked to Asquith on 15 February, and on the 16th he sent him a full statement of his position for Asquith to use in the Commons.[104] Derby's intentions were still unknown, to the intense irritation of Milner, who complained that nothing

> will induce [Lloyd George] to part with his Derby. He is possessed by the idea of not losing any member of his team if he can possibly help it...What happens now is that, while good men like Chamberlain and Carson occasionally leave him, all the corkers remain. Derby has been the curse of this thing from the beginning. He has clung to us like a shirt of Nessus, and will continue to cling until he has poisoned the whole body. I have said this as often and as offensively as I can to everyone of my colleagues, but they...are of opinion that Derby is in some mysterious way popular, or influential, or a source of strength, or what not.[105]

On the other hand Robert Cecil's intentions were plainly to resign.[106] Enormous efforts were now put into keeping the ministry together for the forthcoming parliamentary discussion, expected on Tuesday 19 February. Bonar Law persuaded Derby not to resign, 'though not until Derby had resigned and then withdrawn his resignation once or twice'.[107] Lloyd George himself, though suffering from a cold, persuaded Cecil into a very tentative reconciliation with the Coalition,[108] while the job of bringing Walter Long round from 'the point of resignation' fell to Bonar Law, with help from Hankey and Derby. Milner had to deal with Unionists outside the government, seeing Austen Chamberlain and Salisbury separately on 18 February.[109]

The effort was not in vain. Lloyd George's parliamentary performance on 19 February was convincing, and Asquith's objections 'not damaging'.[110] Even Haig conceded that Lloyd George made out 'an excellent

---

[103] Milner Diary, 16 Feb. 1916; W.C. 347a, 16 Feb. 1917, CAB 23/13.

[104] Robertson to Asquith, 16 Feb. 1918, Asquith Papers 32.

[105] Milner to F.S. Oliver, 16 Feb. 1918, Milner Papers 354.

[106] Cecil to Bonar Law, 17 Feb. 1918, B.L.P. 82/9/6.

[107] Hankey Diary, 17 Feb. 1918, Hankey Papers. Hankey shared Milner's view of Derby as 'a danger to the state at the War Office'.

[108] Cecil to Lloyd George, 18 Feb. 1918, L.G.P. F/6/5/19.

[109] Milner Diary, 18 Feb. 1918, Milner Papers 89.

[110] H.A.L. Fisher Diary, 19 Feb. 1918, Fisher Papers.

case for himself which the bulk of the House (not understanding military matters) thoroughly endorses. Indeed Sir William comes out of the controversy as a "mulish irreconcilable" individual',[111] and Sanders noted that 'Asquith did as badly as L.G. did the week before'.[112]

Unhappily for the Coalition, the War Cabinet's good case on the Robertson issue did not teach the Unionist back bench to love Lloyd George, and suspicion was quickly displaced into the attack, mounted by Austen Chamberlain almost immediately after Lloyd George's statement, on the prominence of newspaper proprietors in the government. Beaverbrook, recently appointed Minister of Information, was widely disliked because of his dubious activities within the Conservative Party. Northcliffe, who had been appointed Director of Propaganda in Enemy Countries at the same time, was widely detested, most recently because of the Lovat Fraser attack on the generals in the *Daily Mail*. But Chamberlain's move was also based on a guess at the mood of the Conservative party, which his correspondents were telling him would like to see a change in the leadership of the party and a reconstruction of the government.[113]

Ireland

The re-emergence of an Irish problem in the midst of the government's troubles seemed to justify Westminster politicians in their preference for burying the Irish Question as deeply as possible. The Irish storm which was ready to break in March 1918 had in fact presented itself to Lloyd George when he returned from Paris at the beginning of December into the thick of the row over Lansdowne's letter. The Convention's leaders, facing the breakdown of their discussions, demanded an audience with the prime minister. Lloyd George was briefed by his secretary Adams, who travelled to Ireland to interview the contending parties and recommended that the government should take up a scheme put forward by Midleton, leader of the Southern Unionists in the Convention, which would allow limited fiscal powers to an Irish parliament. But Lloyd George's meetings on 5 December did no material good, and the Convention delegates reverted to attitudes of sullen mutual mistrust. For another two months relations between the War Cabinet and the Convention's leaders were left in the hands of Adams, who painstakingly created the elements of an agreement between Midleton, the Ulster Unionists, and the more moder-

[111] Haig Diary, 20 Feb. 1918, Haig Papers 123.
[112] Sanders Diary, 3 Mar. 1918, *Real Old Tory Politics*, p. 101.
[113] F.S. Oliver to Chamberlain, 19 Feb. 1918 (referring to 'our talk last night') Austen Chamberlain Papers AC 14/6/74.

ate Nationalists influenced by Redmond and Stephen Gwynn, while Lloyd George pleaded the Cabinet's preoccupation with manpower difficulties to postpone a direct discussion with his colleagues.[114]

In Lloyd George's correspondence with Redmond the seeds of a fatal ambiguity were already present. Redmond sought a 'definite assurance' that 'if we could come to an arrangement with the Southern Unionists...you would be prepared to propose that arrangement in the House of Commons, and to fight the Ulster Unionists on this point'; Lloyd George replied that there would have to be provisions 'to meet in the most reasonable way the difficulties of Ulster'.[115]

A resolution of Irish difficulties depended on the resolution of parallel difficulties within the government: while Southborough, the secretary of the Convention, could write to Redmond that 'My outlook on the position is that "our Ulster friends" will sit tight, that they won't go away, & that they will rely on a quarrel between you and the S. Unionists',[116] Lloyd George had to deal with Carson, whose following on the Unionist back bench, for reasons unconnected with Ireland, was still considerable. Redmond had to deal, as well, with the intransigence of the Bishop of Raphoe, Dr O'Donnell, who insisted that the Southern Unionists had not given ground on the essential point of Irish customs.[117] Redmond had a worse time than the prime minister. He could temporise by exploiting O'Donnell's energy in a tactical manoeuvre within the Convention: the bishop's plan, reserving customs and excise to an Irish parliament, was to be kept in reserve until Ulster had been forced, by Nationalist support for Midleton's plan, into open hostility to a settlement. After that he was in further difficulties, for Lloyd George refused to confirm his oral promise to fight Ulster if Ulster refused to co-operate, and Redmond could not offer his own more aggressive supporters any guarantees that a deal with the Southern Unionists alone would give them what they wanted. O'Donnell was therefore in a stronger position when pressing to reject Midleton's motion embodying his compromise with Redmond and Gwynn, on the ground that it did not give Ireland the fiscal settlement that the Nationalists wanted, and would not even guarantee that a settlement would come to pass. Against him, Stephen Gwynn defended the optimistic

[114] Turner, *Lloyd George's Secretariat*, pp. 103–109; Lloyd George to Redmond, 11 Dec. 1917, Redmond Papers 15,189. Stephen Lucius Gwynn, an author and journalist, was elected Nationalist M.P. for Galway in 1906. A Protestant (his father was Professor of Divinity at Trinity College Dublin) and an Oxford graduate, he was one of the few Nationalist M.P.s whose political career and memories did not stretch back to Parnell.

[115] Redmond to Lloyd George, 11 Dec. 1917, and reply, Redmond Papers 15,189.

[116] Southborough to Redmond, 14 Dec. 1917, Redmond Papers 15,228. Southborough, formerly Sir Francis Hopwood, had been moved sideways from the Admiralty to take up the secretaryship of the Convention.

[117] O'Donnell to Redmond, 23 Dec. 1917, Redmond Papers 15,217.

view in meetings of the Nationalist group, in an increasingly suspicious atmosphere generated by O'Donnell among the county councillors who made up most of the Nationalist delegation.[118]

The full convention reconvened on 4 January, and Redmond prepared an amendment welcoming Midleton's proposal provided it formed part of an agreed Irish settlement — a form of words advised by Southborough to avoid an explicit challenge to Ulster.[119] Redmond once more pressed Lloyd George for an assurance 'not merely of your own goodwill in this matter, but of the intention of the Cabinet to carry out a settlement on the Southern Unionist lines, should we be able to arrive at it',[120] but no promise came. The amendment, when finally put on the agenda, was welcomed by Southborough and Plunkett but spurned by O'Donnell;[121] and Lloyd George's assurance, when it finally arrived, was unhelpful. He wrote to Redmond, for announcement to the Convention, that he had discussed it in Cabinet 'and I find that there is a very large measure of agreement with the view which I have taken that the best hope of settlement lies along the lines of the Southern Unionists' proposals — every effort being made at the same time to provide reasonable safeguards for Ulster Unionist interests within the Irish Parliament...'.[122] This arrived too late to help Redmond influence the Nationalist group, which was swayed by the bishops led by O'Donnell, and in any case did not in any sense promise the Cabinet's support against Ulster. Redmond therefore declined to move his amendment, and warned Lloyd George on 15 January that there was 'no probability whatever' of agreement between Nationalists and Southern Unionists and that it was 'up to you to propose a settlement of your own'.[123] Lord Macdonnell, a sympathetic independent member of the Convention, feared that the episode would cost Redmond the Nationalist leadership, and the spectacle of the bishops 'running amok' emphasised the deep divisions within the Nationalist group.[124] His own contribution, an amendment to Midleton's motion which would give Irish customs to the United Kingdom parliament for the duration of the war and there-

---

[118] Redmond to O'Donnell, 26 Dec. 1917, Redmond Papers *ibid.*; O'Donnell to Redmond, 27 Dec. 1917, *ibid.*; Gwynn to Redmond, 29 Dec. 1917, Redmond Papers 15,192.

[119] Southborough to Redmond, 1 Jan. 1918, Redmond Papers 15,228.

[120] Redmond to Lloyd George, 4 Jan. 1918, Redmond Papers 15,189.

[121] Southborough to Redmond, 11 Jan. 1918, Redmond Papers 15,228; Plunkett to Redmond, 12 Jan. 1918, Redmond Papers 15,221; O'Donnell to Redmond, 14 Jan. 1918, Redmond Papers 15,127.

[122] Lloyd George to Redmond, 14 Jan. 1918, Redmond Papers 15,189.

[123] Redmond to Lloyd George, 15 Jan. 1918, *ibid.*

[124] Macdonnell to Lady Macdonnell, 17 Jan. 1918, Bodleian Library, Macdonnell Papers Eng. hist. 218. Macdonnell was an Irish Catholic landowner and a former member of the Indian Civil Service. He had also been a senior civil servant in the Irish Office.

after until the question could be considered by a Royal Commission, was rejected by Midleton.[125]

Procrastination in Downing Street had by now fatally damaged the prospects for a settlement in the Convention. Lloyd George's reluctance to think about Irish problems was eased a little by Carson's resignation from the War Cabinet on 21 January, supposedly in protest at the treatment meted out to his protégé Admiral Jellicoe by his successor as First Lord, Sir Eric Geddes. Although the prime minister was not inclined to move very much further, he responded to an appeal from Plunkett to invite leading members of the Convention once more to meet him in London. His open letter to the Convention spoke of the importance of a settlement agreed among all parties, and thus avoided any suggestion that the Cabinet would intervene to cut the Gordian knot.[126] It was left to Plunkett to decide when to read the letter. Midleton wanted it postponed until after a vote had been taken on his amendment, which was timetabled for 24 January, while Redmond urged that it should be read, if at all, before any division was taken. After some heated correspondence Redmond's wishes were met, Midleton's motion was not voted upon, and thus an 'open deadlock' avoided. The Convention adjourned forthwith to enable its leaders to meet the prime minister.[127]

Lloyd George himself was engaged at the Supreme War Council at Versailles, and the interval before his return was occupied by breathless efforts on the part of Adams, Plunkett and the Convention secretariat to contrive a position for him to take. After a number of meetings with Ulster delegates and Carson, besides continuous contact with the Southern Unionists, Adams and Plunkett put forward a four-part proposal, which they hoped would advance the Midleton proposal without committing the government to it. Their suggestions included a joint commission on customs, drawn from the Irish and United Kingdom parliaments, to be set up a year after the end of the war, during which interval the Irish parliament was to have no power over customs or excise; an Ulster Committee in the Irish parliament; alternate parliamentary sessions in Dublin and Belfast; and the location of the industrial departments of the new Irish administration in Belfast.[128]

This became policy, in so far as it was a policy, simply by being suggested by Adams to a War Cabinet meeting on 13 February, when ministers

[125] Midleton to Adams, 17 Jan. 1918, L.G.P. F/66/2/3.

[126] Redmond to Lloyd George, 18 Jan. 1918, Redmond Papers 15,189; telegram Lloyd George to Redmond, 19 Jan. 1918, *ibid.*; Redmond to Lloyd George, 21 Jan. 1918, and Lloyd George to Plunkett, same date, *ibid*.

[127] Plunkett to Redmond, 23 Jan. 1918, Redmond Papers 15,221; Redmond to Plunkett, 23 Jan. 1918, Redmond Papers 15,189; Macdonnell to Lady Macdonnell, 24 Jan. 1918, Macdonnell Papers Eng. hist. 218.

[128] Cf. Turner, *Lloyd George's Secretariat*, pp. 106–109.

were preoccupied with the attempt to dismiss Robertson. Walter Long protested that 'he felt convinced that the majority of those who thought with him in Parliament would never agree to the handing over of Customs to an Irish Parliament': but this was not the proposal, and Lloyd George's final negotiating position, as agreed by the War Cabinet, offered little positive support to any party in the Convention. He was instructed to make clear that the government would only accept a settlement during the war which included a single Irish Parliament, sitting in Dublin, and preserved Westminster control over customs and police for the duration of the war.[129]

Clad in this rather skimpy garment, the prime minister entered the conference chamber with a group of slightly sullen Convention delegates. Asked by Midleton, at the end of a querulous discussion, whether the government would support the Convention in proceeding without Ulster's consent, he was unwilling to give an answer; nor did he give any clear answers in separate conversations with the different groups of delegates the next day.[130] The government was now, in effect, faced with the choice of coercing Ulster or coercing Nationalist Ireland. Carson laid claim, on Ulster's behalf, to the promises made at the beginning of the war, when the Home Rule Act was placed, suspended, on the Statute Book: 'I can assure you, that the Ulster people who have suffered severely in the loss of their men at the Front, will regard it as an act of treachery if the promises are broken and Ulster is put under a Home Rule Parliament.' Suggesting that neither Sinn Fein nor the extreme Nationalists could accept any settlement 'consistent with the interests of Great Britain', he brought into argument a suggestion which had been canvassed in England during 1917, especially by F.S. Oliver and Lord Selborne, but had not been considered at all in the Convention: the possibility of resolving the differences between Ulster and the South by setting up a federal system for the whole United Kingdom, or at least a partial system for Ireland, pending the establishment of a fully federal system.[131] Discussion in London during the next few days revealed that the government in Westminster, though now increasingly responsible for the nature of any settlement, could no more agree about it than could the Convention. Balfour and Long in the War Cabinet carped at any alternative to partition.[132]

Plunkett, Shaw and Adams embodied their four-point plan in a draft letter for Lloyd George to send to Plunkett; Lloyd George, Milner and Philip Kerr tried to amend it, apparently to meet Carson's views, but

[129] W.C. 345, 13 Feb. 1918, CAB 23/5.

[130] *Procès-verbal* in L.G.P. F/66/6/1.

[131] Carson to Lloyd George, 14 Feb. 1918, enclosed in Carson to Selborne, 18 Feb. 1918, Selborne Papers 84.

[132] W.C. 351, 22 Feb. 1918, CAB 23/5.

were dissuaded by argument from Adams and Plunkett.[133] The letter was sent, and read by Plunkett to the Convention on 26 February. It did not have the intended effect. Provost Mahaffy of Trinity College, an 'old fool' in Plunkett's eyes, who sat as an independent in the Convention but whose sympathy for the Southern Unionists was quite open, forced a debate on law and order and the Convention was adjourned in some acrimony. When it resumed the next day, although Mahaffy was denied his law and order discussion by a strict party vote, tempers were frayed and the discussion was continued much in the same spirit as it had been before Lloyd George's intervention.[134] Dunraven, another independent member chosen for his sympathy for moderate Nationalism, supported the Lloyd George scheme, and at Midleton's suggestion Macdonnell prepared a set of resolutions which would bring it into practice; Stephen Gwynn finally proposed an amendment which would accept Lloyd George's fiscal proposals and declare a Free Trade agreement between Ireland and Great Britain for ten years after the establishment of the Irish Parliament, but explicitly declare that parliament to be the Irish taxation authority.[135]

The Gwynn amendment, probably the last chance of reaching agreement within the Convention, failed to take off. Midleton declined to support it, and the prime minister, though exhorted personally by Gwynn, refused to commit the government to accepting it if it were passed.[136] The Convention met on 5 March to discuss Macdonnell's scheme, which was presented in the form of six resolutions but embodied almost exactly the four-point plan worked out in the prime minister's secretariat in the middle of February.[137] A day of confusion and intransigence from the Bishop of Raphoe was followed by private discussions in which Plunkett was convinced that the majority of the Nationalist delegates was coming round to accepting the Macdonnell scheme.[138] On 6 March the Convention gathered, and heard that John Redmond had died. The members immediately adjourned for a week. When they reconvened on 12 March Macdonnell's resolutions (except for one) were carried by small majorities.[139] As soon as the fiscal problem was disposed of in this way, the remaining details of an Irish constitution were settled in a rush, on the basis of rec-

[133] Plunkett Diary, 25 Feb. 1918.

[134] Plunkett to Redmond, 26 Feb. 1918, Redmond Papers 15,221; Plunkett to Adams, 27 Feb. 1918, L.G.P. F/64/7/1.

[135] Macdonnell to Lady Macdonnell, 27 Feb. 1918, Macdonnell Papers, Eng. hist. 218. McDowell, Irish Convention, pp. 168–170; Plunkett Diary, 2 Mar., 5 Mar. 1918; Plunkett to Adams, 2. Mar, 5 Mar. 1918, Plunkett Papers; Midleton to Adams, 1 Mar. 1918, L.G.P. F/65/2/2.

[136] Gwynn to Adams, 31 Mar. 1918, L.G.P. F/66/2/29.

[137] Macdonnell to Lady Macdonnell, 5 Mar. 1918, Macdonnell Papers Eng. hist. e. 220; Same to same, 6 Mar. 1918, ibid. Eng. hist. c. 218

[138] Plunkett to Adams, 5 Mar. 1918, Plunkett Papers.

[139] Macdonnell to Lady Macdonnell, 12 & 13 Mar. 1918, Macdonnell Papers Eng. hist. c. 218

ommendations made in the Grand Committee (the Convention's working sub-committee) in the previous autumn. The Ulster Unionists, as a matter of policy, divided 'against everything that could have been alleged to have been agreed on' and supported an exclusion proposal. Finally, after some further controversy between Plunkett and members of the Convention, and even more between the members themselves, a chairman's report was drafted and approved on 9 April by 44 votes to 29 — the minority consisting of 18 Ulster Unionists and 11 Nationalists sympathetic to the Bishop of Raphoe. The Convention was then adjourned *sine die*.[140] On the same day Lloyd George told the House of Commons that because of the successful German attack on the Western Front, which had begun on 21 March, a Military Service bill would be introduced which would extend conscription to Ireland for the first time. Nationalist M.P.s protested; in Ireland what remained of the organised Nationalist Party allied itself with Sinn Fein to mount an anti-conscription campaign.[141]

The final six weeks of the Convention is so much a chapter of dismal accidents, from Mahaffy's inflammatory speechmaking through Redmond's death to the ghastly co-incidence of British collapse on the Western Front, that it is tempting to ascribe the ultimate failure of constitution-making to the Irish bad luck which Plunkett was so happy to cite. A sounder explanation looks further back, to the reconstruction of popular Irish politics in the wake of the Easter Rising. The Convention had largely succeeded in the government's intention of taking the Irish constitutional question out of Westminster politics. It had also succeeded almost completely in removing it from Irish politics as the Southern political system, at any rate, developed in 1917 and 1918. The erosion of support for the Redmondite Nationalist Party, which had proceeded apace after Easter 1916, was helped rather than hindered by the disappearance of active Nationalist local politicians (notably the thirty-three county-council chairmen who constituted the core of the Nationalist bloc in the Convention) into purdah in Trinity College between July 1917 and April 1918. When they emerged, blinking in the light of the anti-conscription campaign, it was to discover in such Nationalist strongholds as East Clare that the carefully organised, interdependent socio-political community of Nationalist Ireland, where farmer, priest and politician supported one another's aspirations in all directions, had simply become the Sinn Fein organisation. The link between the Redmondite party and the community had not so much been broken as dissolved. Sinn Fein had not superseded Nationalism; Nationalism had become Sinn Fein. But it was not only on the Nationalist side that the complex evolutions of Convention politics, which had nearly

[140] McDowell, *Irish Convention*, pp. 174–176.
[141] A.J. Ward, 'Lloyd George and the 1918 Irish Conscription Crisis', *Historical Journal*, xvii (1974), 107–129.

produced a 'settlement' between Nationalists and Southern Unionists, had lost touch with the realities of Southern Irish politics. By March 1918 the Southern Unionist party was on the point of splitting, with a substantial rank-and-file group supporting a 'Call to Unionists' which was printed in the United Kingdom press on 4 March. The 'Call' was an unequivocal demand for the maintenance of the Union, conceived explicitly as a repudiation of Midleton and his policy of negotiation with the Redmondites as exemplified in the Convention. The 'Call' led shortly afterwards to an outright split in the Southern Unionist party, and eventually, after the general election, to the secession of the Midletonites to form the Unionist Anti-Partition League. The only party to have maintained living links with its extra-convention organisation during the Convention months was the Ulster Unionist group, which had consequently maintained the stern intransigence which other parties would have maintained if they could have brought influence to bear on their representatives in the Convention. The Irish Convention was an example of élitist politics at its most ineffectual; Irish popular politics, confronted by an attempt to circumvent old problems in meetings behind closed doors, merely reasserted itself by choosing new institutional forms. In the case of Nationalist Ireland it was largely Sinn Fein; in the case of Southern Unionism, the Southern Unionist Committee. In April 1918, after a Convention, a clutch of by-elections in which Sinn Fein had consistently embarrassed the Nationalists, a massive Sinn Fein drilling movement, a conscription crisis and a number of minor parliamentary confrontations, the Irish Question had distinguished itself, not by changing, but by remaining ineffably the same.

Its unchanging nature also reasserted itself in Westminster politics. Old Irish quarrels inspired politicians on all sides of the House, but especially on the Unionist back benches, to keep party conflict alive during the greatest political crisis of the war, in which the Coalition was nearly swept away with the unfortunate Fifth Army in the aftermath of Germany's last offensive. Without Ireland, without the miserable and confused legacy of the Convention, the crisis of March to May 1918 would have taken a markedly different form.

8

POLITICS AND THE CRISIS
March to October 1918

The Impact of Ludendorff

The German attack on the Western Front in March 1918 rolled the British Armies back 40 miles to the line of the Somme and completed the process, begun in December 1916, which destroyed the British party system as it had existed in 1914. The sudden military reverse led within eight weeks to the parliamentary crisis known as the 'Maurice debate'. Challenged directly by the Asquithian opposition for the first time since December 1916, and also by a section of Unionist back-benchers led by Carson, Lloyd George won a striking personal victory in the Commons. His more hawkish supporters promptly set up a Lloyd George Liberal organisation and prepared to attack Asquithians in the next general election. The schism in the historic Liberal Party was never healed. In the same few weeks, a fatal blow was struck to the Union between Great Britain and Ireland. The introduction and subsequent withdrawal of conscription in Ireland destroyed the Nationalist movement and with it the fragile hope of compromise; in the short term it also threatened the government's political base in the Unionist Party. After the Coalition's fortunes were restored by the Maurice debate, the Irish Question remained, the bitter legacy of an English political crisis. Thus Ludendorff's last great offensive was a turning point in modern British history, in a way that the Maurice debate and even the Easter Rising, on their own, were not.

The German attack against the British Fifth and Third Armies began on 21 March. On 22 March Lloyd George intervened at the War Office to increase the flow of recruits and troops returning from leave to France, and the next day the War Cabinet agreed to send 18-year-old recruits to the trenches.[1] On 24 March Milner crossed to France to meet Clemenceau and some of his ministers at Doullens, where in a conference with the British and French generals on 26 March it was decided to give Marshal Foch a 'co-ordinating authority' over the armies on the Western Front. Foch was soon given 'strategic direction' of all Allied armies (on 3 April) and finally made 'commander-in-chief' (on 14 April).[2] The point of these efforts was to make better use of existing reserves in France by putting them under a single commander, and to bring as many soldiers as possible from England; but the intensity of the German attack argued for a further effort to increase the total number of soldiers at the expense of the civilian economy. On 25 March the War Cabinet decided to extend the age limits for military service, which would henceforth run from 17 to 51, and to include Ireland in the legislation for the first time.[3]

Both decisions were controversial and both were ambiguous in their origins. Men recruited under the extended Military Service Act would not arrive in time to affect the battle in France, and it was not certain that Ireland would yield as many men as would be needed to enforce conscription. In the early days of the German advance War Cabinet ministers, though conscious of acute military danger, saw political opportunities in the situation. Milner wrote to Lloyd George on 28 March:

> If there is a great disaster, we are, as a Govt., 'down & out' whatever we do, & we may as well fall gloriously over a big effort to retrieve the situation.
>
> If, on the other hand, 'the plague is stayed', we are in for a long and dragging fight.... [The Germans] are certain to keep on pushing, &, if they do not break us now, they will break us later, unless we can keep on sending substantial reinforcements.... Unless we can hold out another year, & that depends on what we do now — when people are thoroughly frightened & prepared for anything, a bad peace is a certainty.
>
> I should prefer to let someone else make it.
>
> If we survive this crisis & people settle down for a little bit, we shall never have another chance of getting the necessary men, & a fresh push a few months hence will catch us, without reinforcements, & with less room behind us to fall back on.[4]

The same argument was applied to Ireland. Robert Cecil, by conviction an opponent of Home Rule, observed that 'its only chance of success would be to carry it with conscription by a rush as a war measure. And that can only be done on the wave of intense feeling that now prevails.'[5]

---

[1] W.C. 371, 23 Mar. 1918, CAB 23/5.

[2] Woodward, *Lloyd George and the Generals*, p. 287.

[3] W.C. 372, 25 Mar. 1918, CAB 23/5. The original proposal had been to set the upper limit at 55.

[4] Milner to Lloyd George, 28 Mar. 1918, L.G.P. F/38/3/2.

[5] Cecil to Lloyd George, n.d., L.G.P. F/6/5/24.

From outside the governing circle F.S. Oliver made a similar point to Selborne:

> From our own point of view....there is obviously something to be drawn out of the turmoil. When men's minds are violently perturbed is the time to snatch decisions on matters which they regard as of secondary importance.[6]

Accordingly the crisis atmosphere was nourished, but the new Military Service Act was carefully planned. Impatient ministers outside the War Cabinet wanted parliament summoned 'forthwith' and Cecil tried to start a 'movement' which Walter Long refused to join.[7] Lloyd George and Bonar Law insisted on postponement.[8] The major source of delay, besides drafting difficulties, was the Irish problem, and in particular American responses to it. Ireland had been exempted from all previous Military Service Acts. It was included now firstly to appease Unionists inside and outside the government, and secondly to anticipate working-class resentment of the extended age limits in Great Britain. To persuade Ireland to accept conscription, and to persuade official and unofficial opinion in the United States that conscription did not mean the abandonment of Home Rule, the War Cabinet adopted a 'dual policy': Home Rule and conscription were to proceed side by side. This could only work if all Irish parties, the United States government and the Irish American community, and trade unionists and Unionist back-benchers in Britain could be persuaded, simultaneously, that they were getting what they wanted. This proved impossible, but while the chance of success remained the War Cabinet tried boldly to be all things to all sections.

The political risks of the 'big and comprehensive' scheme of extended conscription were underlined by Barnes, who complained to Lloyd George about the proposed age limits for English recruits on 26 March.[9] But the Irish question came swiftly to the front. The decision to conscript Ireland was taken on 25 March, but at subsequent meetings the War Cabinet wrung its withers about whether to introduce Home Rule before, after or at the same time as conscription. Warnings from all quarters in Ireland, official and unofficial, Unionist and Nationalist, did not shift them from the decision to conscript, but the decision to introduce Home Rule simultaneously was clinched by the United States government.[10] On 2 April Balfour put the government's case for Irish conscription before Colonel

---

[6] Oliver to Selborne, 27 Mar. 1918, Selborne Papers 84/86–7.

[7] Cecil to Lloyd George, 29 Mar. 1918, L.G.P. F/6/5/23; Long to Bull, 29 Mar. 1918, Bull Papers 4/17, declining to link himself with 'Hotel Cecil "of the later creation"'.

[8] Lloyd George to Cecil, 29 Mar. 1918, L.G.P. F/6/5/24; Bonar Law to Derby, 1 Apr. 1918, B.L.P. 84/7/18.

[9] Barnes to Lloyd George, 26 Mar. 1918, L.G.P. F/4/2/26.

[10] W.C. 373, 374, 375, 376, on 26, 27 (twice), & 28 Mar. 1918, CAB 23/5.

House, who at the direct inspiration of Woodrow Wilson prophesied that it 'would accentuate the whole Irish and Catholic intrigue which has gone hand in hand in some quarters in this country with the German intrigue'.[11] On 5 April the War Cabinet decided to take the measures together: on 6 April the rest of the government was told, and on 7 April the terms of the new Military Service bill were made public.[12] Response was passionate but varied. The A.S.E., representing the most important and volatile section of the industrial workforce in Britain, balloted its members and found them in favour of the new measures by a small majority.[13] The Irish Convention, which had been on the point of reaching a minimal compromise, fell apart and the more militant Nationalists threw in their lot with Sinn Fein. The Irish M.P.s walked out of the House of Commons — an action which in itself probably improved the government's chance of keeping control of the House — while in Ireland Sinn Fein, with the overt support of many Catholic clergymen, prepared to use violence to resist conscription.[14] By the time the bill was introduced in parliament on 9 April, it was clear that the government's policy could go badly wrong in a number of ways.

From the beginning, the government's public handling of the crisis was inept. Lloyd George's Commons speech introducing the new measures was ineffective: read from notes and lacking in enthusiasm.[15] Irish opposition was noisy, and the prime minister's explanation of the military position caused 'disgust' among officers on the Western Front. Both Liberal and Labour opponents decided that the government was tottering at the edge of a precipice. George Lansbury urged the ever-sympathetic Pringle to 'make a real effort to kick George out' and continued:

> It is an appalling business to take over, but a few brave men are needed, especially men who won't care about the Press but rely on the people. The Press is not the people, and there is a tremendous volume of opinion against George and his conduct, not only of the War, but of the aims and objects of the War. A rallying point is needed, and it should be found in the House of Commons.[16]

Buckmaster expressed the same excitement to Loulou Harcourt:

[11] Balfour to House, 2 Apr. 1918, House Papers 466/I/13/B69; House to Balfour, 3 Apr. 1918, Wiseman Papers 90/69.

[12] W.C. 383, 5 Apr. 1918; W.C. 385, 6 Apr. 1918, CAB 23/6.

[13] Barnes to Lloyd George, 10 Apr. 1918, L.G.P. F/4/2/28.

[14] R.B. McDowell, *The Irish Convention 1917–1918* (London: Routledge & Kegan Paul, 1970); A.J.Ward, 'Lloyd George and the Irish Conscription Crisis in 1918'; W.C. Minutes, 10 Apr. 1918, CAB 23/6; Turner, *Lloyd George's Secretariat*, pp. 113–116.

[15] H.A.L. Fisher Diary, 9 Apr. 1918; Sanders Diary, 14 Apr. 1918; Memo. by Stamfordham to the King, 9 Apr. 1918, RA GV K1290/1.

[16] Lansbury to Pringle, 11 Apr. 1918, Pringle Papers II/74.

The introduction of the Man Power Bill has caused more acute discontent than any measure since the commencement of the War.... Many people are anxious beyond all things that Asquith should take the lead and end a situation which they believe to be full of menace and disaster to the country. And, though Asquith will not move — and on the whole I think he may be wise — his reluctance will be misinterpreted and may shake the confidence of some of his followers. The crisis is so serious that it is impossible to foresee what might happen if the Government were thrown down; but, on the other hand, it must be remembered that people are saying openly that it is this government that has brought us to the edge of ruin and they believe that its continuance will precipitate the final catastrophe.[17]

It would be almost a month before the English dimension of the crisis began to threaten the government's position. Even the Labour Party seemed more concerned about Ireland: Barnes declined to vote in the division on the Irish clauses of the new bill, and other Labour ministers were rumoured to be considering withdrawal from the government unless Home Rule were brought in.[18] Lloyd George anticipated a challenge from the Asquithians over Irish conscription, and proposed to Bonar Law that:

If they succeed in defeating that part of the Bill, we ought to consider very carefully our next step. It should be resignation or dissolution. They are relying a good deal on the unpopularity of the 40–50 call-up, the men between these ages probably representing 30% of the electorate of this country. Our immediate duty is however quite clear. We must press these proposals through the House with all the support at our command on the ground that the military need is overwhelming.[19]

But the greatest threat came from the Unionist Party. As early as 5 April Guest reported that 'I believe the Tory Party will break the Government rather than split their Party over Home Rule.' He therefore began to negotiate with Tory M.P.s who were sympathetic to a federal solution, in which Ulster and the South would be separate provinces within the United Kingdom. Although his contacts, who probably included Leo Amery, promised a hundred Tory votes if a Home Rule bill were introduced on federal lines he remained pessimistic: 'they must not be too much relied on. The movement is still academic and many of their members will succumb to caucus control.'[20] Carson warned Bonar Law that Home Rule must not be mixed up with Irish conscription and demanded that Bonar Law call a meeting of the Unionist Party before proceeding further.[21] About 120 Unionists, peers and M.P.s, attended a meeting of

---

[17] Buckmaster to Harcourt, 12 Apr. 1918, Bodleian Library, Harcourt Papers dep. 448.
[18] Samuel to Mrs Samuel, 14 Apr. 1918, Samuel Papers A/157/911.
[19] Lloyd George to Bonar Law, 10 Apr. 1918, L.G.P. F/30/2/31.
[20] Guest to Lloyd George, 5 Apr. 1918, L.G.P. F/21/2/16.
[21] Carson to Bonar Law, 8 Apr. 1918, B.L.P. 83/2/9.

the Unionist War Committee on 16 April, addressed by Carson, in which the tone was 'distinctly adverse' to Home Rule.[22]

Nevertheless the War Cabinet, for want of a better idea, pressed ahead with the dual policy. A War Cabinet committee was set up on 15 April, including Long as chairman, Smuts, Addison, Hewart, Cave, Fisher, Curzon, Barnes, Duke and Austen Chamberlain. Chamberlain was about to rejoin the administration as a member of the War Cabinet: he made it a condition of his entry that any Irish settlement should be compatible with a federal scheme.[23] The committee's remit was to produce a Home Rule bill as quickly as possible. At the beginning Addison accused Cave of partisan bias and foot-dragging, but Long was anxious for progress.[24] On 17 April Lloyd George made a 'very able' appeal in the House of Commons for Unionist support for Home Rule. Samuel doubted whether it would have much effect on them: 'Everything now depends on the character of the Irish Bill which is soon to be produced.'[25]

To conciliate the Unionists, the Home Rule bill committee was persuaded by Long and Chamberlain to adopt a federal scheme.[26] From the Liberal side Addison objected, observing that the major proponents of federalism, such as Cave on the committee and Selborne and Salisbury outside, would not be sorry to see Home Rule postponed.[27] On 23 April, at Chamberlain's prompting, Lloyd George plumped 'impetuously' for federalism in the War Cabinet, but the matter was referred back to the drafting committee without clear instructions, and Addison and Barnes continued to press for a settlement on the lines of the Convention's report.[28] During the next weeks Addison complained that Long was 'using Fisher a good lot' because he was more compliant than Addison or Barnes: this was partly true, but Fisher had also been strongly influenced by Professor Adams of Lloyd George's Garden Suburb, who was sympathetic to federalism. Moreover Fisher, like Addison, soon began to voice objections to the proposal to impose conscription immediately.[29] Liberal sympathies for Irish Nationalism were still active in April 1918.

---

[22] Sanders Diary, 17 Apr. 1918.

[23] J.E. Kendle, 'Federalism and the Irish Problem in 1918', History, lvi (1971), 207–230.

[24] Addison Diary, 15 and 16 Apr. 1918, Addison Papers 96; cf. Christopher Addison, Four and a Half Years (London: Hutchinson, 1934), p. 511; cf. minutes of the Committee on the Home Rule Bill, 15 Apr. 1918, CAB 27/46.

[25] Samuel to Mrs Samuel, 17 Apr. 1918, Samuel Papers A/157/913.

[26] Minutes of the Committee on the Home Rule Bill, 16 Apr. 1918, CAB 27/46.

[27] Addison Diary, 19 Apr. 1918, Addison Papers 96; cf. Addison, Four and a Half Years, p. 514.

[28] W.C. 397, 23 Apr. 1918, CAB 23/6; H.A.L.Fisher Diary, 23 Apr. 1918, Fisher Papers; Addison Diary, 23 Apr. 1918, Addison Papers 96.

[29] Addison Diary, 26 Apr. 1918; cf. Fisher Diary, 26 Apr. reporting conversation with Adams, and Fisher to Lloyd George, 27 Apr. 1918, L.G.P., F/16/7/24; Turner, Lloyd George's Secretariat, pp. 113–119.

This was not emphasised when Lloyd George met Unionist ministers on 25 April. Bridgeman pointed out that 'many Unionists regarded themselves as bound by a pledge not to leave Ulster to be forced into a Home Rule scheme which she regards as unfair, and that unless Carson can exonerate them from the pledge they will be unable to vote for Home Rule. The federal idea is the only hope.' Lloyd George 'seemed favourable to it'.[30] Carson was in no mood to lift any pledges. On 27 April he wrote menacingly to Bonar Law predicting 'nothing but disaster' if Home Rule was forced on Ulster.[31] Even ministers, such as the ever-conscientious Robert Cecil, began to discover that their past pledges were strictly expressed.[32] In the last days of April the feeling among Unionist M.P.s began to alarm Lloyd George and Walter Long. While Leo Amery, a Federalist partisan, urged that 'probably 150' Unionists would vote for a Federal bill, with most of the rest abstaining, Long warned his committee that Unionist opinion had 'hardened'.[33] Long had already urged Bonar Law to make it clear to his bewildered Unionist colleagues that Home Rule was not being raised in order to placate the Nationalists, which it clearly was not doing, but as a result of a Cabinet bargain with Barnes.[34] By 30 April Lloyd George was talking to a shocked Fisher of the need to allow Ulster to contract out of any Home Rule measure.[35] What was worse for the government, it soon became apparent that the promise of Federalism was not enough for the Unionist Party outside Westminster. A questionnaire sent to local agents by Central Office on 26 April revealed a strong feeling in favour of maintaining safeguards for Ulster and a marked lack of enthusiasm for Federalism.[36]

Disorder in Ireland was a further source of irritation to the Unionist Party, and was made an issue by Carson's pointed accusation that in pursuit of its dual policy the government was overlooking seditious disorder in the South of Ireland.[37] There was little confidence in the Irish government. Duke's tenure of the Chief Secretaryship had been insecure since February, and he was ready to resign when the German attack overtook the government.[38] During April his job was offered to Clyde, the Lord Advocate, to Fisher, and to Addison. Other names suggested included

---

[30] Bridgeman Notes, 25 Apr. 1918, *Modernisation of Conservative Politics*, p. 132.

[31] Carson to Bonar Law, 28 Apr. 1918, B.L.P. 83/2/33.

[32] Cecil to Lloyd George, 29 Apr. 1918, L.G.P. F/6/5/26.

[33] Amery to Lloyd George, 29 Apr. 1918, L.G.P. F/2/1/22; Fisher Diary, 29 Apr. 1918, Fisher Papers.

[34] Long to Bonar Law, 26 Apr. 1918, B.L.P., 83/2/29.

[35] Fisher Diary, 30 Apr. 1918, Fisher Papers.

[36] Papers and correspondence in B.L.P. 83/3/11.

[37] Carson to Bonar Law, 27 Apr. 1918, B.L.P. 83/2/33.

[38] Cf. Adams to Lloyd George, 22 Feb. 1918, L.G.P. F/63/2/13; Long to Lloyd George, 4 Mar. 1918, L.G.P. F/32/5/10; Duke to Lloyd George, 22 Mar. 1918, L.G.P., 37/4/47.

Kellaway and Sanders.[39] The choice finally lit on Edward Shortt, described by Sanders as a 'dark horse' who 'started life in Boraston's office as a L[iberal] U[nionist]'.[40] In 1918 he was a Liberal, believed to have Asquithian sympathies, who had voted against the Irish clauses in the Military Service Act. He took the precaution of assuring himself of Long's support before accepting the job,[41] but his name alone could not reassure the Unionist back bench. At first Lloyd George and Bonar Law proposed to set up the Lord Lieutenancy in commission, with three Lords Justices chosen to inspire confidence in Britain and Ireland. The first name proposed was Lord French, the Commander-in-Chief, Home Forces, who was at that time in Ireland supervising military preparations for the enforcement of conscription. It was proposed that French should be joined by Lord Midleton and by James Campbell, the Irish Lord Chief Justice, a Protestant and a Unionist. On 28 April Wimborne was told brusquely to resign so that the Lords Justices could be appointed.[42] However Midleton, who did not believe that Home Rule could be enforced immediately and wanted large powers to go ahead with enforcing conscription, stated his objections in such terms that the government could not accept them.[43] This left French, who shared Midleton's view of the condition of Ireland, to accept the Lord-Lieutenancy in guarded language. Accepting that Home Rule and the enforcement of conscription were still the policy of the government, he went on to observe that:

> The condition of Ireland is such that neither policy can, in my opinion, be carried out till the authority of the country has been re-established and, in particular, an end has been put to the relations which I know exist between the Germans and the rebels in Ireland.
>
> I understand that it is in order to deal with such a situation that it is proposed to set up a quasi-military Government in Ireland with a Soldier as Lord Lieutenant.[44]

The way was now clear for a policy of 'thorough' in Ireland. French in Dublin, supported in London by Long, whom Lloyd George appointed as the War Cabinet's vice-gerent for Irish matters, pursued a policy which appealed to the majority at Westminster and in Great Britain. The consequences in Ireland, bad though they were, took second place.

---

[39] Fisher Diary, 16 Apr. 1918; Addison Diary, 17 Apr. 1918, Addison Papers 96; Addison to Lloyd George, 17 Apr. 1918, *ibid.*

[40] Sanders Diary, 29 Apr. 1918.

[41] Long to Lloyd George, 25 Apr. 1918, Lloyd George Papers F/32/5/26.

[42] Wimborne to Lloyd George, 28 Apr. 1918, L.G.P. F/48/1/8.

[43] Midleton to Lloyd George, 30 Apr. 1918, L.G.P. F/38/1/12.

[44] French to Lloyd George, 5 May 1918, L.G.P. F/48/6/10.

The Parliamentary Threat

In the early days of May the government's parliamentary position was critical. The immediate shock of the German attack and the Military Service Act had been overcome, but two issues threatened the future. The first was a series of ministerial changes in the service departments. In late April the War Cabinet had appointed Milner to co-ordinate French and British military efforts, in concert with the French government. The weaknesses of War Office administration which he reported to the War Cabinet persuaded Lloyd George that the time had come to remove Derby from the War Office. He was sent instead to the Paris embassy. Milner took over the War Office, leaving a vacancy in the War Cabinet which was in due course filled by Austen Chamberlain. Derby's removal from the War Office had been expected since the dismissal of Robertson in February; the Paris embassy was decidedly the loser in the transaction since Derby spoke no French. Chamberlain's appointment consolidated the support of a significant number of Unionists who had approved of his recent attack on the government for containing too many press lords.[45] This was all the more useful since his arrival coincided with a fresh wave of parliamentary excitement over the resignation of Lord Rothermere as Secretary of State for Air.

The Rothermere–Trenchard affair was yet another example of the ambiguity of the government's relations with its Unionist supporters. It was compounded of two elements: the perennial Commons hostility towards newspaper proprietors in government, which had been stirred up by Chamberlain, and the deep suspicion in the Unionist Party of civilian attempts to control military affairs. Rothermere, a newspaper proprietor himself and also brother of Lord Northcliffe, had been appointed Secretary of State for Air in November 1917, with instructions to unite the Royal Naval Air Service and the Royal Flying Corps in a single Air Force. He had somewhat negligently asked for Sir Hugh Trenchard, a staunch opponent of the fusion of the two services, as Chief of the Air Staff; and from the moment the Air Council was established on 3 January 1918, there was friction over policy and methods between Rothermere and his chief military adviser. This was readily made public by officers serving in the Air Ministry, including Sir John Simon and Lord Hugh Cecil, who alternated at will between staff jobs in the Air Force and attendance at Westminster.[46] An 'atmosphere of intrigue and falsehood'[47]

---

[45] See above, p. 278.

[46] A simple factual account of the Rothermere–Trenchard affair is in Sir Maurice Dean, *The Royal Air Force and Two World Wars* (London: Cassell, 1979), pp. 24–31; see also Malcolm Cooper, *The Birth of Independent Air Power* (London: Allen & Unwin, 1986).

[47] Sir David Henderson to Bonar Law, 26 Apr. 1918, B.L.P. 83/2/30.

predictably interested the parliamentary opposition as well as the hostile press.

On 12 April Rothermere won the War Cabinet's approval for a reconstruction of the Air Force, including the creation of an Independent Air Force to operate strategically in France, and some consequential changes in the staff at the Air Ministry.[48] Four days later Trenchard asked to be relieved of his duties and 'removed himself in civilian clothes to a seat in Green Park'.[49] He was replaced by Major-General Frederick Sykes. Lt.-Gen. Sir David Henderson, the Vice-President of the Air Council, promptly followed Trenchard in resignation. The affair was taken up by the *Morning Post*, and Rothermere contrived to publish his own version of the dispute. Even the government's natural supporters were alarmed. Bridgeman observed:

> It is a bad thing that Trenchard & Henderson have resigned from the Air Ministry. It is said to be because Trenchard wished to be free to meet the military demands★ of the Admiralty & War Office before using any of his force for bombing German inland towns & that Rothermere refused. If so Rothermere ought to be sacked. A letter from Rothermere to Walter Faber, giving a sort of explanation of his differences with Trenchard — & a very feeble one — appeared in the Times — but Walter Faber whom I saw the day it appeared, never received it, and had not written to him. Such are the ways of our journalist statesmen.
> ★I heard afterwards that this was not the cause of difference, but that Rothermere would give orders, without telling Trenchard, to the men under him — and also that R. was perpetually changing.[50]

Simon and Cecil immediately took the issue up in the Commons. 'Hands off the generals' was a popular cry, and the government's position was further weakened by John Baird, Rothermere's Parliamentary Under-Secretary, who after some hesitation warned on 22 April that he would not defend Rothermere's scheme of organisation in the Commons.[51] The next day Rothermere resigned, complaining of the indiscipline of Simon and Cecil, and pleading ill-health and the effective completion of his task to justify the timing of his decision.[52] Upon Bonar Law's urgent plea that 'There would be a much better chance of avoiding an Air debate on Monday if Lord R's resignation was announced and his letter appeared on the tape before the House meets', and after the exchange of letters had been doctored by Lloyd George and Beaverbrook to remove the plaintiveness about Simon and Cecil, the resignation was publicly accepted on

[48] W.C. 390, 12 Apr. 1918, CAB 23/6.

[49] Andrew Boyle, *Trenchard* (London: Collins, 1962), p. 278.

[50] Bridgeman Notes, 18 Apr. 1918, *Modernisation of Conservative Politics*, p. 131.

[51] Baird to Bonar Law, 18 Apr. 1918, B.L.P. 83/2/19; Baird to Lloyd George, 22 Apr., L.G.P. F/44/5/5.

[52] Rothermere to Lloyd George, 23 Apr. 1918, Lloyd George Papers, F/44/5/6.

25 April.[53] Robert Donald of the *Daily Chronicle* wrote to Runciman that 'The government is getting unpopular and most people think it is breaking up, if it is not actually riding for a fall.'[54]

At first it was believed that Rothermere's resignation had saved the day for the government. Buckmaster, reporting 'seismic disturbances' to Harcourt, nevertheless thought that 'Rothermere's retreat in accordance with plans to occupy arranged new positions has probably defeated the debate'. He also observed that Rothermere 'told Trenchard five lies in one day, which is more than a plain blunt soldier man can bear'.[55] Amery, never a good judge of the House, wondered to Lloyd George 'why the Cocoa and Old Port Coalition cannot realise that you have never held a stronger hand than at the moment'.[56] But Cocoa and Old Port, encouraged by Sir Edward Carson, forced a debate in the evening of 29 April. Lloyd George's 'vague and ill-constructed' defence was enough to save a defeat only because Hugh Cecil offended the House by his 'intemperate and ill-judged attack' on the prime minister.[57] 'But although L.G. got off easily he had no sort of a personal triumph,' wrote Duncannon to Derby. 'The House does not appear to have been sympathetic to him as a whole. A certain section appears to be becoming more and more bitter against him & to rejoice at any opportunity of showing hostility to him which they no longer attempt to disguise.'[58]

The Coalition by now needed all the parliamentary support it could get. With the Irish Nationalist Party once more in active opposition after eight months' moratorium while the Convention sat, and Labour restless about the conscription provisions, the government faced possible defeat if too many of its own supporters abstained on any issue. For once the possibility of a concerted opposition attack, led by Asquith, was significant. Asquith himself was slightly roused. Buckmaster reported to Harcourt on 22 April:

> He is more full of spirited and genuine irritation against the Government than I have seen him since the day when our Government fell.
>
> Two things seem specially to have contributed to his anger... The one was the appointment of Lord Derby as ambassador to France, and the other the muddle of the Government over Ireland.
>
> He did not take the view that Lloyd George did it in order to tumble down. He regarded it as a piece of muddling incompetence, and I think it shocks the orderly nature of his mind....

[53] Bonar Law to Lloyd George, 25 Apr. 1918, L.G.P. F/30/2/33; Rothermere to Lloyd George, 25 Apr. 1918, L.G.P. F/44/5/7; Lloyd George to Rothermere, 25 Apr. 1918, L.G.P. F/44/5/8; Beaverbrook, *Men and Power*, pp. 228–236.

[54] Donald to Runciman, 26 Apr. 1918, Runciman Papers WR 169.

[55] Buckmaster to Harcourt, 28 Apr. 1918, Harcourt Papers dep. 448.

[56] Amery to Lloyd George, 29 Apr. 1918, L.G.P. F/2/1/22.

[57] Crawford Diary, 30 Apr. 1918.

[58] Duncannon to Derby, 30 Apr. 1918, Derby Papers 920(17) British Ambassador Correspondence.

In truth, I can see but little hope in the near future. The darkness deepens. The military position was regarded by him with no less alarm than it is by myself; and he said repeatedly that this army of manoeuvre about which so many statements were being made was a mere phantom with no substance and reality at all.

The only contribution I made was to urge that circumstances too strong for our control might at any moment dissolve the government and that we ought to be ready with a plan whenever this occurred. I suggested that one good thing might be to restore Robertson, Jellicoe, and Trenchard without delay, and he discussed personnel of the Government much as before. That is, he made no mention of inclusion but he dwelt emphatically on exclusion and said that nothing would induce him to serve in any capacity whatever in a Government of which the present Prime Minister was a member.[59]

As Asquith brooded, a second threat to the ministry lurked in the wings. After Haig's 'back to the wall' order of 12 April a rumour had surfaced at Westminster that Lloyd George was personally responsible for the shortage of troops in France and thus for the reverses during the early days of the German offensive.[60] On 22 April Lloyd George protested to Milner about the previous week's official summary of the military situation. This purported to show that in four weeks of fighting a slight Allied advantage in troop numbers on the Western Front had been converted into a German superiority of 333,000 rifles. Lloyd George went straight to the political heart of the argument:

Unless . . . the figures supplied to me by the Staff a fortnight ago were deplorably misleading, this paper ought instantly to be revised and the Ministers amongst whom it is circulated warned of the serious error for which it is responsible. If on the other hand I was misled a fortnight ago and the House of Commons and the country through me, then it is time that the Department responsible for information should be thoroughly overhauled.[61]

Unknown to Lloyd George, G.H.Q. in France was politically active at this time, and probably responsible for the rumours. Lord Gorell, a young staff officer, recalled later that his superiors

were so incensed by Lloyd George who in their view refused the divisions urgently asked for & then lied about the figures . . . & regarded him so much as a national danger that they would have welcomed *anyone* as Prime Minister in his stead: & I came over unofficially armed with certain facts and figures to gauge public opinion. A couple of days convinced me that Lloyd George was the only possible prime Minister & that in any case a swap over then would be disastrous.[62]

By now Lloyd George and his government urgently needed a 'personal

---

[59] Buckmaster to Harcourt, 22 Apr. 1918, Harcourt Papers dep. 448.

[60] Samuel to Mrs Samuel, 17 Apr. 1918, Samuel Papers A/157/913.

[61] Lloyd George to Milner, 22 Apr. 1918, L.G.P. F/38/3/25.

[62] Bodleian Library, Gorell MSS Diary 1915–1919, p. 18.

triumph' in the House: the combination of Asquithian and Carsonite critics was tiresome and dangerous. Asquith's enemies outside the government showed signs of alarm. 'Over Trenchard the ship rocked heavily' remarked Esher, reflecting though that 'There is nothing to fear so long as Asquith shrinks from office.'[63] From the opposite viewpoint, Asquithians saw new opportunities. Runciman told his wife:

> The House of Commons is lifeless, & much turns on Asquith's attitude toward the Government. I want him to tell them that he must withdraw his support from the Prime Ministership of L–G who has not produced results, that he does not propose to take his place (to do so would give a discrediting personal flavour to a Government so formed). This act of renunciation should be accompanied by a promise of general support to an administration with a Conservative at its head while it waged war effectively.[64]

From the other end of the Asquithian spectrum, T.E. Harvey asked if it were 'possible that our front bench may make a definite move before long with a view to getting a change of Government, a government which may prepare the way politically & diplomatically for peace'.[65]

Divided in purpose before the final struggle had even begun, the government's Liberal opponents were caught unawares by the publication in various newspapers on 7 May of General Sir Frederick Maurice's remarkable letter, which accused Lloyd George and Bonar Law of misleading parliament and the public on a number of military issues, including the Allied rifle strength in France at the beginning of 1918, the Allied strength in the Middle East, and the War Cabinet's responsibility for forcing Haig to extend his line in January 1918. These allegations, made with the authority of the Director of Military Operations, seemed to confirm Westminster and press rumours of the War Cabinet's responsibility for the March débâcle. Asquith, who had no part in the preparation of the letter,[66] was warned of its impending publication by Maurice on 6 May and raised the question in the House on the 7th. 'In replying to Asquith I would not in the least adopt an apologetic tone. Quite the reverse,' Lloyd George wrote to Bonar Law, 'I am glad this opportunity has arisen to dispel the miasma of lies which is oppressing the air.'[67] Despite this advice, Bonar Law stumbled in his reply, and offered to submit the question of his own and the ministry's veracity to a committee of judges. Fortunately for the government, Asquith insisted that the question should be discussed by the

[63] Esher to Wilson (copy), 1 May 1918, L.G.P. F/47/7/24.

[64] Runciman to Mrs Runciman, 1 May 1918, Runciman Papers WR 303 (2).

[65] Harvey to Runciman, 6 May 1918, Runciman Papers WR 169.

[66] It was apparently written by Maurice after consultation with Repington.

[67] Lloyd George to Bonar Law, 7 May 1918, B.L.P. 80/2/20.

House and 9 May was set for the debate.[68] The debate gave Lloyd George the opportunity he had wanted. He told George Younger cheerfully after a breakfast meeting with Conservative ministers on 9 May that '[t]his time I have been caught out telling the truth'.[69]

Lloyd George's more excitable enemies scented victory. Carson, now thoroughly disaffected because of the government's Irish policy, cross-questioned Bonar Law during the exchanges on 7 May. Gwynne of the *Morning Post* expected the government to disappear after the debate, and Margot Asquith entered the Gallery remarking 'God Almighty can't save the Government. They are out this afternoon.'[70] Soberer minds recognised that the statements made by Lloyd George and Bonar Law were ambiguous,[71] and Runciman explained to Buckler that 'he did not expect any startling results as there were so many ways in which inaccurate statements could plausibly be explained and he intimated that Mr Asquith is not anxious to assume the reins at the moment.'[72] In the event, Runciman's tactical management ruined the opposition's case. Asquith's attack on the government bogged down in his 'act of renunciation'. He announced that his motion was neither a vote of censure nor a suggestion that he should replace Lloyd George as prime minister. These observations, as Bonar Law remarked with understandable smugness to the King, neither convinced the majority in the House nor pleased his followers.[73] Lloyd George's refutation of Maurice's specific charges, based on information worked up from Cabinet and Supreme War Council papers by the tireless Hankey, satisfied a House which was evidently impatient with Asquith; and the division, taken before dinner, went to the government by 293 votes to 106.

The Political Consequences of General Maurice

The size of the government's victory in the Maurice debate was evidently a surprise to many observers. In part it was the personal triumph which Lloyd George had needed since the dog days of mid-April. As much as Asquith had ever been an alternative prime minister, his credibility was now destroyed. 'I have never seen such a complete collapse as Asquith's yesterday,' wrote Waldorf Astor, 'You couldn't find him with a magnify-

[68] Beaverbrook, *Men and Power*, pp. 253–254.

[69] Crawford Diary, 9 May 1918.

[70] Gwynne to Asquith, 8 May 1918, Gwynne Papers 14; Crawford Diary, 6 Dec. 1918, reporting the recollection of Mrs Lowther, the Speaker's wife.

[71] Haldane to mother, 8 May 1918, Haldane Papers 5999/174.

[72] Buckler to House, 9 May 1918, Buckler Papers 654/II/5/12.

[73] Bonar Law to the King, 9 May 1918, B.L.P. 78/1.

ing glass, although Gulland was seen supporting and pushing him into the Division lobby.'[74] Even Godfrey Collins, the assistant Asquithian Whip, was forced to conclude that 'Asquith is unacceptable as a War prime minister to even the Liberal Party.'[75] But the personal factor was less significant than the range of party attitudes revealed by the vote. Buckler observed that the division list revealed the membership of the 'New Opposition', with only one Unionist ('a freak') and only half the Liberal Party voting with Asquith.[76] In fact this was only half true. Only six Labour M.P.s voted against the government, the rest abstaining, and the Irish members were absent. However, the debate settled the question of Unionist loyalty to the Coalition. At a meeting of the Unionist War Committee on 8 May Carson had tried to persuade back-benchers to take an independent line, supporting neither Lloyd George nor Asquith. After Amery had intervened to urge that the important thing was to keep Asquith out of office, the committee adjourned with 'a general sense that, whatever happened, we were not prepared to let Asquith come back'.[77]

All this did not amount to an overwhelming vote of confidence in Lloyd George. As one of Derby's innumerable correspondents observed:

> There is no doubt that this House of Commons are determined to veto any possibility of Asquith's return to power and this gives an idea of enthusiasm for Ll.G. which is also very far from the case. Of course the real difficulty is that while all recognise the force of L.G.'s qualities, everyone has a doubt of his veracity. Otherwise all this contretemps would never occur. The head of a government must above all things be honest. Personally I should far prefer what for want of a better term I will call a Tory administrator.... There are several names suggested but none seems to impress at all.[78]

But the prospect of an Asquith government sobered Lloyd George's Tory critics. Harcourt observed that 'the fear of H.A. as an alternative will prevent any govt. defeat.... I know most of my Tory acquaintances agree that a pure Tory Govt could not carry on war with Liberalism & Labour etc on its flanks.'[79]

The debate's message for the Liberals was no less ambiguous. It was true that Liberal M.P.s had not united in support of Asquith as prime minister, though since he had not asked them to do so, it was difficult to draw precise conclusions from the vote. His intimates decided that he was

---

[74] Astor to Garvin, 11 May 1918, University of Texas Harry Ranson Humanities Research Centre, Austin, Texas, Garvin Papers, Recip Astor I.

[75] Runciman to Mrs Runciman, 12 May 1918, Runciman Papers WR 303 (2).

[76] Buckler to House, 10 May 1918, Buckler Papers 654/II/5/12. The Unionist freak was Aubrey Herbert.

[77] *The Leo Amery Diaries*, I, 220–221, 8 May 1918.

[78] Londonderry to Derby, 12 May 1918, Derby Papers 920 DER (17), British Embassy Corr.

[79] Harcourt to Runciman, 21 May 1918, Runciman Papers WR 169.

unacceptable as a war leader, and without dismissing him entirely from calculation began to think of promoting Grey as an alternative to Lloyd George.[80] They also decided to strengthen anti-government whipping in the Commons.[81] On Lloyd George's side, the debate gave ammunition to the more hawkish members of his entourage who had been urging him since the spring of 1917 to set up a Lloyd George Liberal organisation. Addison and Guest immediately canvassed Liberal M.P.s, and sought newspaper support from Beaverbrook and Hulton.[82]

For all this, the omens for an infant Lloyd George organisation were not good. Between the autumn of 1917 and March 1918, Lloyd George's closest advisers had been trying to bring about a working alliance with the government's Unionist supporters. When it became necessary to draw up a common programme for a general election, the prospective marriage ran into difficulties: Curzon and Cecil spoke out against common action with Lloyd George 'on the ground that he is such a dirty little rogue'[83] and they cannot have been alone in the party. On 16 March Guest proposed optimistically to Younger that 'The traditional difficulty of getting either L.G. Liberals to support a Conservative against all comers and [sic] vice versa, can only be overcome by setting up, temporarily, a completely new organisation, both in name and premises. I suggest "Government Coalition", "National", or "National Reform" '.[84] This did not appeal to Unionist organisers. On 24 March Sanders noted:

> I have been engaged in various confabs lately as to a working agreement with ... the Lloyd George Liberals. I had a long talk with Bonar Law about it at Downing Street yesterday. He is all for alliance ... The point of difference with Guest is whether they should follow the L.U. precedent and start a separate organisation, or as he prefers have a new joint party. The latter will never do. Guest reckons on about 10% of Liberals following LG.[85]

The Maurice debate had a double impact on Guest's plan. On the one hand, it suggested that at least for war purposes, Lloyd George could count on far more than 10 per cent of Liberal M.P.s. On the other hand, the discussions within the Unionist Party between 7 and 9 May had confirmed that Unionist support for Lloyd George was a product of war, which could not be counted on in any other circumstances than an Asquithian challenge for the war premiership. As a result, despite their early belligerence, Lloyd

[80] Ibid.
[81] Runciman to Mrs Runciman, 12 May 1918, Runciman Papers WR 303 (2).
[82] Addison Diary, 16 May 1918, Addison Papers 96.
[83] Sanders Diary, 3 Mar. 1918.
[84] Guest to Younger, 16 Mar. 1918, B.L.P. 83/1/9.
[85] Sanders Diary, 24 Mar. 1918.

George's Liberal intimates moved carefully in the days after the debate. A tactical conference on 17 May yielded the cautious conclusion that:

> in our opinion, it is not, at this moment, expedient, even if it were practicable, as it does not appear to us to be, to set up separate organisations in the constituencies; but, in our opinion, the present activities of the Whips' Department should be developed and continued.[86]

A more extreme caution was expressed by Cecil Harmsworth, Lloyd George's private secretary, who had served as a parliamentary private secretary with Runciman and McKenna under the Asquith Coalition and felt himself bound by affection to the leading Asquithians as well as to Lloyd George. He wrote to Runciman the day after the debate:

> what is Genl. Maurice to us or are we to Genl. Maurice? & why should it be considered that on a point of principle the Liberals in the Govt. must necessarily take a different, and antagonistic, stand from that of a Liberal outside the Govt? I am equally familiar with both sides & I observe no such rigid divergences.
>   Is it too late to stop the rot?
>   .... Of course it may be said that it really does not matter what act of suicidal folly the Liberal Party now commits — that Arthur Henderson's liberally scattered candidatures will result in the defeat of Asquithites and Ll-Georgeites all over the country. Nobody can safely predict what will happen at the next General Election &, whatever ensues, a united Liberal Party must always be an important desideratum.— I write to you because I am unwilling to see the Liberal Party shipwrecked without uttering a word of protest. I am not a Liberal by birth or training, religion or convention, but simply because I have believed in Liberalism & still believe in it as a political force. Why should I be squeezed out by the unaccountable folly of Genl. Maurice's letter in the Press? I am only one of a very large number who decline to be squeezed out.[87]

In the last days of May the less cautious of Lloyd George's supporters had the better of the argument. The prime minister visited Scotland and addressed the Scottish Liberal Federation who, according to Addison, 'dropped their Asquith-Gullandite attitude altogether and cried enthusiastically in his support. It is quite evident that the feeling in Scotland has strengthened in favour of L.G. — whatever the machine might say.'[88] The election campaign was on: and for the moment the Asquithians were the enemy, at least in the eyes of Lloyd George's Liberal supporters. Their problem was to impose their priorities on their Conservative allies, some of whom still distrusted the prime minister and feared Labour as much as Asquith.

---

[86] Guest to Lloyd George, 17 May 1918, L.G.P. F/21/2/22.
[87] Harmsworth to Runciman, 10 May 1918, Runciman Papers WR 169.
[88] Addison Diary, 30 May 1918, Addison Papers 96.

A Strategy for Electoral Victory

Contemplation of a general election was resumed at a rather lower pitch than before, with both Conservatives and Lloyd George Liberals somewhat chastened by recent political events. Guest took the chair on the 17 May at the meeting of Lloyd George Liberals mentioned above. His colleagues included Addison, Churchill, Hewart, Montagu, Illingworth, Sir Edwin Cornwall, Dudley Ward and the Rev. Shakespeare. Besides concluding that it was neither expedient nor practicable to set up a separate Lloyd George Liberal organisation in the constituencies, they decided that the process of preparing a 'Liberal' policy for presentation to the country should begin.[89] This was a substantial retreat from February's aspirations to write a joint programme. The same sense of distance is conveyed in Conservative discussions. Desultory negotiations with the British Workers' League continued, with growing evidence that constituency parties did not like the proposed arrangements; these talks were not linked, as they had been earlier in the year, with close co-operation with the Lloyd George Liberals in a patriotic Coalition.[90] Nevertheless Guest and his assistant, Dudley Ward, were able to make a number of arrangements over seats with Sanders at Conservative Central Office. Sanders tried, without success, to get his leaders to work on a joint programme with Lloyd George.[91]

As a result, Guest was by July becoming anxious for the future of the Lloyd George Liberal group. A difficulty appeared when Sir Eustace Fiennes, the Liberal member for Banbury and a supposed Lloyd Georgian, accepted the Governorship of the Seychelles. Guest expected an Asquithian to be put forward for the seat, who would expect and get an unopposed return because of the political truce. He explained to Lloyd George:

> I must here mention that the Conservative Party have no fault to find whatsoever with the carrying out by Gulland of the Truce obligations with them; and although they see regretfully that its operation is detrimental to your own Liberal supporters, there is no doubt that there is a tendency on their part to leave things alone, until such time as a definite Coalition alliance for the purpose of a General Election is publicly announced.
>
> I am inclined to avoid an open rupture if it is quite certain that a programme and an alliance can be agreed upon and announced before the House rises in August.
>
> By that time I shall be in a position to inform your Liberal supporters that they are immune from contest, which will place us in a position strong enough to make what terms we like with the official Liberal Party. I have good reason for saying that the official Liberal Party are stating that the next Election will be a Truce Election!

[89] Guest to Lloyd George, 17 May 1918, L.G.P. F/21/2/22.
[90] See Sanders Diary, May and June 1918, *passim*.
[91] Sanders Diary, 14 July 1918.

This is a trick to evade contests and obtain a similar immunity — an immunity *to which we shall not necessarily agree.*

In the meanwhile I have asked the Conservatives to extort the following pledge:–
'To support Mr Lloyd George, the Prime Minister, and the Government, in all Divisions which are declared by them to be Votes of Confidence or necessary to the vigorous prosecution of the War.'

If you approve of my recommendation, it becomes vital that the Alliance should be completed without delay, failing which there is a danger that we shall fall between two stools and be forced to fight on our own.[92]

There seems little doubt that throughout this period Lloyd George, whenever he had the time to attend to domestic politics, was pushing the idea of an early general election. The proposal came to the ears of Derby at the Paris embassy, who thought it 'madness', though apparently more for diplomatic reasons than because of its likely domestic impact; and Derby complained to Long.[93] The tone of Long's reply suggests a shift in senior Tory thinking, and the beginnings of an explanation for it:

There is a very great change taking place in the country: the Socialists are increasing considerably in certain districts and are becoming very pugnacious and this has thoroughly frightened the middle class and led a great many of those who were our most bitter political opponents to reconsider their position, to approach leaders of our Party, and to express the hope that all moderate men who believe in the Empire and in fair play will unite to resist the attacks of the Socialists. I am convinced that this is the only policy that can lead to success. I entirely share your views about L.G. but I think we must face the fact that, unless some catastrophe happens, in all human probability we shall go to the country as a Government with him as our leader. I can see nobody else who is likely to command the support of the country.

If I discuss one or two men quite openly you will I am sure understand it is not because I have any personal feeling in the matter. I do not care who is Leader so long as we get a strong man who will lead us along the right path. George Curzon has been taking some active steps towards offering some guidance to the Party, but he won't go down with our people. This is very unfortunate. He is brilliant and I think a very delightful person, but our men won't have him.

Bonar Law has certainly fallen away though he has done his work most admirably in the House of Commons and I do not know why he does not command greater support among our people in Parliament and in the country. But he certainly does not occupy the position that he did and unless there is a change he would not receive anything like widespread support and therefore, having regard to these facts and to the further one that L.G. though he is Leader has no Party of his own and must therefore look to us to give him a Party I think that we ought, without very much more delay, to make up our minds definitely on certain subjects and tell him that if he is prepared to put them in his programme we are prepared to support him. Personally, I feel very confident that he would be more than ready to meet us.[94]

[92] Guest to Lloyd George, 13 July 1918, L.G.P. F/21/2/27.
[93] Derby to Long, 5 July 1918, Long Papers 947/547.
[94] Long to Derby, 10 July 1918, *ibid*.

The rapid development of Coalition election plans in July emerged, therefore, from the coincidence of Guest's growing impatience with the predicament of the Lloyd George Liberals, Conservative fears of the impact of labour organisation, and the perennial reflection that Lloyd George was a better leader for the Conservative Party than either Bonar Law or Curzon. As Long was urging the preparation of Conservative proposals to put before Lloyd George, Guest was pressing the Lloyd George Liberal committee to draw up an agreed programme with the Conservatives, sign an agreement over seats, and get Lloyd George to make a general policy statement as soon as possible, to be elaborated in the election campaign. Guest urged on Lloyd George that:

> I am fortified in my view that your chief considerations should now be:—
> (1) How to safeguard your supporters in the House of Commons; and
> (2) To enable us to get candidates into the field.
> As far as the *electors* are concerned you may rest assured that a *big majority* will vote for your continued leadership during the War.
> I therefore trust that you will, at any rate, take some preliminary steps to force the pace.
> With reference to the *'khaki'* voters, especially abroad, could not something be done to ensure their vote being cast for the Government? [95]

The 'crisis' which had followed the German spring offensive had transformed British politics, though not in the way that most contemporaries and many historians thought it had. Although Asquith had been the reluctant and fumbling leader of the protest during the Maurice debate, the conflict, and thus the Coupon Election which confirmed the disappearance of the pre-war party system, had its roots in Conservative revulsion against the necessary compromises of Coalition, the cooling of Labour's enthusiasm for the war, and the historic hatred of Irishman for Irishman. There was no 'new opposition' of Labour and radical Liberal; antagonisms within the Liberal Party were by now personal, not doctrinal; and the confrontation between Asquith and Lloyd George was based on bile and bungled opportunism, not on policy or principle. All that remained was for the Coalition's organisers to dress up the election as a vote of confidence in the government's conduct of the war. Fortunately the war began to go well, at least to public appearance, although the Coalition's leaders remained pessimistic for months to come. Though Haig's tactics might have done little to win the war for Britain and her allies without the determination of Ludendorff to match error for error, his summer's fighting did much to win the election for Lloyd George.

[95] Guest to Lloyd George, 13 July 1918, L.G.P. F/21/2/27.

A Victory for Strategy?

While party organisers busied themselves with the electoral struggle to come, their principals were preoccupied with the very present struggle in France. The German attack on 21 March was followed by two further successful offensives. On 9 April an attack through Flanders drove British forces back in the region of Armentières and the La Bassée Canal, prompting Haig's notorious 'Backs to the Wall' Army Order of 11 April. The apparent tardiness of Foch in moving reserves northwards for battle alarmed the War Cabinet, but they persisted in their support for unity of command. An emergency agreement with the American commander, General Pershing, provided for fresh American divisions to be attached to the British army; this antagonised Clemenceau and put further pressure on the Doullens agreement. A further German attack on the French forces around the Chemin des Dames followed in late May, and brought the Germans once again within 50 miles of Paris by early June. The Chemin des Dames offensive was a last desperate throw, but this was not obvious at the time. Only with the limited success of a British counter-attack at Hamel in early July, and the more spectacular achievements of the Battle of Amiens — the 'black day' for the German army noted by Ludendorff on 8 August — was it possible for the generals to look forward to defeating Germany in the West. Even then they did not expect victory in 1918 and their civilian masters did not confidently expect it at all. The dilemmas of strategy remained, and the political problem of civil–military relations survived into the post-Maurice era. Only the total collapse of Germany and its allies could entirely remove it from domestic political calculations.

The long-overdue eviction of Derby from the War Office enabled Lloyd George to take a closer interest in military policy. Protesting with some justice that War Cabinet business was too congested, he instituted the 'X' committee, consisting only of himself, Milner and Sir Henry Wilson, which after 14 May met before War Cabinet meetings to review the military situation. Lloyd George's success in the Maurice debate had gone some way to removing controversy about strategy from Westminster politics; the X committee removed it from the day-to-day scrutiny of the War Cabinet. This did not change the nature of the problem. Milner, once ensconced in the War Office, proved reluctant to attack the generals with the vigour which Lloyd George expected.

The knife-edge military balance in France set the tone for the politics of expectation which occupied Lloyd George and his colleagues. The arrival of the Dominion prime ministers for the 1918 Imperial War Cabinet brought open debate on the prospects for victory. Haig continued to argue for a decision on the Western Front. Wilson, as C.I.G.S., presented in late July a memorandum on military policy for 1918 and 1919 which suggested that Britain's position outside Europe was now secure, so that all efforts had to be concentrated on a Western Front victory in 1919.[96] Milner and Smuts even argued that there would not be enough men to support an active campaign in 1919. They therefore pushed back their estimate of the end of the war to 1920, and suggested that unless the British Empire was to be fatally weakened the level of activity in France should be reduced to 35 divisions, the balance to be deployed overseas.[97] As the discussion progressed in successive meetings it became clear that Wilson was willing to persist. In mid-August Lloyd George presented the case for delaying the offensive until 1920, but was inhibited from pressing it by the Dominion prime ministers — especially Hughes of Australia — by acrid moral pressure from Clemenceau and by the scepticism of Curzon, who was still attached to the idea of a vigorous prosecution of the war.[98] Nevertheless he continued to urge that Haig conduct his operations so as to limit casualties, and began to carp at Wilson for being 'Wully redivivus'.

The Amiens victory did not persuade the War Cabinet that Haig was right. Indeed, it was the middle of September before Lloyd George and his civilian colleagues showed confidence in an eventual military victory in the West. Even then they did not expect it in 1918. Haig's forces moved towards the Hindenburg line in early September, and in the middle of the month the Bulgarian army was defeated in an attack mounted from Salonika. Allenby broke through towards Damascus, which he reached on 1 October. A major victory by the American First Army, at St Mihiel on 13 September, resulted in huge German losses in guns and prisoners. On 29 September British troops broke through the Hindenburg line. Even yet, Lloyd George and Milner demanded that Haig reduce British commitments to the offensive and husband his manpower for 1919.

It was Haig's misfortune that though his preferred strategy of attacks on the Western Front had at last seemed to succeed, he could never get the civilian government to agree with him about either the present or the future course of policy. In early October Lloyd George at last decided that Haig had been right about the collapse of German morale and powers of resistance, and that Germany could, consequently, be defeated in 1918. Haig had by then begun to change his mind, and warned the X committee on 19 October that Germany would be able to hold its new lines well into 1919.[99] Three weeks later the Armistice was signed.

---

[96] 'British Military Policy 1918–1919', 25 July 1918, Imperial War Cabinet Papers, CAB 25/85.
[97] Committee of Prime Ministers, 31 July 1918, CAB 23/44.
[98] Committee of Prime Ministers, 16 Aug. 1918, *ibid.*
[99] X Committee minutes, 19 Oct. 1918, CAB 23/17.

9

'A SORT OF MIDLOTHIAN CAMPAIGN'
July to December 1918

The electoral battle joined

While Lloyd George and his ministerial colleagues were still preoccupied
by the fighting, political organisers found time in July to prepare for a general election. All now assumed that it was to be fought during the war.
Lloyd George and Bonar Law interviewed a deputation from the National
Unionist Association (including Selborne and Younger, the chairman of
the party) and conveyed so strongly the impression that an election was
imminent that Bonar Law had to amend Sanders's draft minute of the
meeting 'so as not to suggest that we are definitely contemplating an election'.[1] On 19 July the committee of Lloyd George Liberals under Addison
dusted off the heads of policy which had been prepared in March.[2] The
next day Guest submitted to the prime minister his proposals for a deal
about seats with the Conservatives, which would give Lloyd George 114
Liberal supporters, 15 Labour supporters and 17 from the British Workers' League.[3] On the 21st Sanders noted that Lloyd George's mind 'is
going strong for an election. He seems to me to be on the look-out for
some sensational cry. He says it is "the sauce" that makes a programme
digestible ... '.[4] Lloyd George passed the draft 'Heads of Policy' on 24
July, and the Unionist leaders met the same day to discuss their own doc-

---

[1] Bonar Law to Sanders, 22 July 1918, annotated on Sanders to Bonar Law, 19 July 1918, B.L.P.
83/5/18.
[2] 'Opinions expressed at, and Notes of, a Conference held at 12 Downing Street on Friday, July
19th', Addison Papers 72.
[3] Guest to Lloyd George, 20 July 1918, L.G.P. F/21/2/28.
[4] Sanders Diary, 21 July 1918, *Real Old Tory Politics*, p. 107.

ument. Cecil maintained his opposition to a link with Lloyd George, but Curzon was converted and the others 'favour[ed]' it. Guest, with perhaps unwitting condescension, informed Sanders that 'his people trust & like Bonar, Austen & Cave but not Balfour & Walter Long...'.[5] Meanwhile the official Liberal Party set to work on their programme, whose drafting had begun in February.[6]

Guest soon got cold feet. On 3 August he appealed to Lloyd George to be cautious about an alliance with the Unionists on the basis of an agreed programme which went beyond the war. His reason was essentially that a public statement in favour of colonial preference by Walter Long on 24 July, and the subsequent public discussion of colonial preference as a possible subject of agreement between the parties, 'has shown that the one desire of your opponents is to get hold of some issue which they can exaggerate and use to your detriment'. He also wanted Lloyd George to take all of his Liberal colleagues into his confidence. Developing this theme, he made it clear that he feared the odium of breaking up the Liberal Party by putting forward a joint programme: he even suggested that 'the return of the bulk of the Liberal Party, becoming accustomed to your leadership, may not, in the end, prove to be a disadvantage in dealing with the Unionist party'. He finally suggested a war election only, with the adoption of President Wilson's League of Nations policy as 'a means of separating the sheep from the goats', on the grounds that Wilson had vowed not to admit Germany to the league until it had eschewed militarism, while 'The Asquithians (except Mr. Asquith) Lansdownites and Pacifists are prepared to enter into negotiations at any time with the German Government in its present vicious form'. His strategy was therefore that

> If the Government were to adopt the former interpretation as its Programme I believe that the long looked for cleavage between ourselves and our opponents would be brought to light and that the majority of the Electors would range themselves under your banner and that the popular Election cry would be:-
> *'NO PEACE WITH GERMAN MILITARISM'*[7]

Sanders gained the impression that Guest 'funk'ed Tariff reform, and attributed his nervousness to this alone. Lloyd George seems not to have been so concerned, 'let[ting] it be seen quite plainly... that he was all for an early election'.[8] To his Liberal associates he let it be known that he was 'perfectly willing to make his statement such that might lead to the drop-

[5] Sanders Diary, 28 July 1918, *ibid.*
[6] Samuel to mother, 24 Feb. 1918, Samuel Papers A/156/553; Samuel to wife, 28 July 1918, *ibid.* A/157/932.
[7] Guest to Lloyd George, 3 Aug. 1918, L.G.P. F/21/2/30.
[8] Sanders Diary, 9 Aug. 1918, *Real Old Tory Politics*, p. 107.

ping of some of the others, [i.e. not Bonar Law] particularly Walter Long and Hayes Fisher, who are not only useless but thoroughly mischievous'.[9] The Lloyd George draft manifesto, as prepared by Addison's committee, was given to the Unionist hierarchy in the first week of August.

Guest's conviction that a 'war only' appeal was the right one did not affect his enthusiasm for the creation of a Lloyd George party; indeed it seemed to give him the excuse he had long wanted to organise the breach for Lloyd George's benefit. In preparation for a final conference on election plans, which took place at Lloyd George's Criccieth house from 17 to 20 August, Guest put forward a draft proclamation, appealing personally and directly to the electors to support Lloyd George as a war minister.

> I do not think, if the tone is sufficiently spiritual, that it will be regarded, except by those who do not matter, as a personal bid for power in the ordinary sense. You will, I am sure attract the support of those who wish to see this country led safely through the period of reconstruction which all fear may become chaotic, Bolshevik, piratical or anarchistic, unless sanely steered.

The practical implications of this strategy were not entirely clear, though Guest suggested that 'a definite party' would have to be formed, and it is clear that he still envisaged co-operation with the Unionist organisation rather than an attempt to split the Unionists as well as the Liberals.[10]

What does seem clear is that Guest still hoped to get over the obstacle of the programme, on which agreement with the Unionists remained a difficulty. Long still insisted that imperial preference must be part of the appeal to the electorate,[11] and from his convalescence in Wiltshire broadcast his doubts about 'the wisdom of a General Election in the winter or early days of the new year' because of anticipated shortages of food and coal.[12] Addison found this particularly irritating, recording on 22 August that:

> The Morning Post and the high Tories are, of course, anxious to precipitate L.G. into a Tariff Policy which would hopelessly disintegrate his own Liberal following. We must take adequate measures in some industries in some form or another, but beyond that I object as vehemently as ever to Tariff quackery, but this issue is the most difficult one we have to negotiate with the Tories. Bonar, Balfour and Carson, however, will present no difficulties, nor will Milner, and it would be an unmixed blessing if some others, as the result, be dropped, particularly the Walter Long, Hayes Fisher group, who are a serious handicap to the Government.[13]

[9] Addison Diary, 7 Aug. 1918, Addison Papers 99.

[10] Guest to Lloyd George, 16 Aug. 1918, L.G.P. F/21/2/31; Guest to Addison, 17 Aug. 1918, Addison Papers 72.

[11] Long to E. Talbot, 17 Aug. 1918, Long Papers 947/593.

[12] Long to Derby, 17 Aug. 1917, Long Papers 947/548; Long to Bonar Law, 19 Aug. 1918, B.L.P. 83/6/30.

[13] Addison Diary, 22 Aug. 1918, Addison Papers 99.

From the other side Edmund Talbot was concerned that 'we must have some kind of a programme on social and reconstruction matters. If we don't look out L.G. may stampede us into something at the last minute on some cry or other which may split us',[14] while Crawford feared 'ill-considered schemes and promises'.[15]

As a result of this doubt and mutual suspicion, the various participants were in fact quite ready to close on a minimum programme which would protect all the Coalition partners against the excesses of the others. Lloyd George's chief supporters at Criccieth, including Addison, Hankey, Philip Kerr and the assistant whip Dudley Ward, prepared an outline programme which emphasised welfare provision, notably the Health Ministry which was Addison's main reconstruction aim. Long offered Bonar Law the outline of a limited 'war only' programme, which amounted to a vigorous prosecution of the war, 'determined and unsparing' control of aliens, imperial preference, post-war control of raw materials (i.e. the Paris Resolutions), guaranteed employment for the returning troops and the relaxation or abandonment of government control of industry. If this seemed slightly unhelpful, it should be read in the context of Long's change of heart in acceding to the proposal to hold an election at all while the war continued. But with Long still convalescent, the initiative in Unionist planning still lay with Bonar Law, who personally favoured Lloyd George's plan to press on with an election. The Addison/Guest/Dudley Ward/Henry Norman programme was sent to the Unionist programme committee under Younger: it went to Clyde for comment, but Sanders concluded that 'there should be no great difficulty about agreement'.[16] The outstanding difficulty — Ireland — was as yet not discussed. Bonar Law's acquiescence in the prime minister's plans made for considerable resentment among his senior colleagues. Younger, the party chairman, was 'dead against' an election in November because he feared the effect of continued hardship, though he did not omit to plan the outline of a Coalition arrangement which would recognise the loyalty of 90–95 Lloyd George Liberals and, by drawing a line at the Maurice debate, outflank any attempt at 'death-bed repentances in the House'.[17]

Bonar Law continued to vacillate.[18] But during September the sheer logic of organisation compelled the Unionists to make plans for the election, and Younger grew impatient with Long's continual sniping at the

---

[14] Talbot to Long, 22 Aug. 1918, Long Papers 947/594.

[15] Crawford to Derby, 27 Aug. 1918, Derby Papers 920 DER (17) British Embassy Corr.

[16] Sanders Diary, 30 Aug. 1918, *Real Old Tory Politics*, p. 108.

[17] Younger to Long, 31 Aug. 1918, Long Papers 947/682.

[18] 'I have no very clear idea in my own mind yet what we ought to do', Bonar Law to Long, 31 Aug. 1918, B.L.P. 84/7/75, Long Papers 947/682; Bonar Law to Carson 2 Sept. 1918, B.L.P. 84/7/77.

development of the election proposal: 'I can't make out what he is driving at,' Younger wrote to Bonar Law on 16 September 'In one sentence he talks about a Coalition election and in the next demands absolute freedom to the constituencies in putting up candidates. That would be a pretty way to play the game, and if he thinks LG would lead on such terms he is very greatly mistaken. He listens to the tittle-tattle of every irresponsible person & changes & chops about like a weathercock . . . . Our lot is difficult enough without our pitch constantly queered by a prominent member of the party.'[19] Long was, however, right that the initiative lay with Lloyd George rather than the Unionist Party.

The election campaign began, in fact if not in theory, with a major speech at Manchester on 12 September, drafted by the Addison/Guest committee. It was intended to prepare the ground for a Coalition appeal, and it was written to provide a Coalition Liberal gloss on the points already agreed with the Unionists: for instance that imperial preference did not mean food taxes. The speech promised rapid decontrol of industry, safeguarding of industries, though not by a general tariff, and a broad measure of social reconstruction primarily aimed at the returning troops and their dependants. In this way it came very close to the preferences of the Unionist hierarchy in focusing its domestic policy on returning troops and on decontrol, while avoiding altogether the glaring problem of Ireland. Part of the Lloyd George Liberal strategy was that the election plan should be confirmed in public as late as possible, largely because the prime minister's organisation was in a very weak state. Sanders later remarked that it was meant to be the beginning of 'a sort of Midlothian campaign', but Lloyd George caught the 'flu and the triumphal sequel was frustrated.[20]

The effort to postpone general knowledge of Lloyd George's intentions was all the more successful: on 13 September Arthur Murray could write to an American correspondent that 'I am not sure that he has yet made up his mind', and the Canadian minister Sir George Perley was in doubt as late as 20 September.[21] Guest was exultant at the impact of the Manchester speech:

> . . . I gather that the visit has been an astounding success and a tremendous personal triumph. I feel sure that it is another vindication of the policy you have adopted

[19] Younger to Bonar Law, 16 Sept. 1918, B.L.P. 84/1/13. This was a response to Long to Younger, 12 Sept. 1918, Long Papers 947/599, sent after an interview between Long and Bonar Law.

[20] Sanders Diary, 29 Sept. 1918, *Real Old Tory Politics*, p. 109. Text in *The Times*, 13 Sept. 1918.

[21] Murray to Willert, 13 Sept. 1918, Elibank Papers 8807; Perley to Borden, 20 Sept. 1918, Borden Papers 51806.

of declaring political war on no-one and of hoisting a banner round which all and sundry may rally.[22]

But decisions had yet to be made about the nature of Lloyd George's open appeal to the electorate. Sir Henry Norman urged that although a personal appeal by the prime minister might succeed, it would be safer to make a Coalition appeal; and also pointed out that the necessary organisation could not be set up until Lloyd George had made it clear whether or not he proposed to fight on a Coalition ticket. Norman also advised on an early election on a 'non-party' reconstruction programme, arguing that the 'war only' appeal was too narrow.[23] But the difficulties posed by delay were now more obvious in organisational matters than in the programme. On 25 September Guest submitted two alternative plans for a Coalition agreement: a 'Truce' plan, based on the proposition that in the new parliament Unionists and Liberals would each have the same percentage as in the old parliament, thus leaving the Liberals to sort out their own differences so that Lloyd George Liberals received Conservative support and the Conservatives had a free run against those not certified as Lloyd George supporters; and an alternative scheme by which Guest would obtain immunity for 107 ministers and supporters, the right to fill vacancies left by supporters, and the right to contest 105 other seats carved out of the old Liberal seats and other good Liberal chances. Guest calculated that the second form of agreement would give Lloyd George 114 certain seats and a good chance in 105 others, whereas the percentage basis was to be preferred because 'it is a deeper test of the good faith of the Unionists'. Guest was sanguine about the prospect of splitting the Liberal Party by the percentage method, because he argued that 'when it comes to the test the official Liberal Party will cave in, and the doubtfuls will come over to us'.[24]

The possible impact on the official Liberal Party was obvious to all observers, and in an attempt to mitigate the damage the Master of Elibank acted as an intermediary on the same day between Lloyd George and Asquith to try to include Asquith in the government. According to Arthur Murray, Lloyd George offered Asquith the nomination of three Secretaryships of State and six Under-Secretaryships, but made the condition that both Irish conscription and the general election should go ahead. Asquith demurred to both these conditions and declined to serve under Lloyd George, which Arthur Murray thought 'petty-minded'; Elibank remarked that 'the inwardness of Mr A.s attitude is that he does not really trust either Lloyd George or Balfour, and could not therefore serve in government with them. He spoke strongly on these lines also.... Unless I am very

[22] Guest to Lloyd George, 14 Sept. 1918, L.G.P. 22/2/37.
[23] Memo. by Norman in Guest to Lloyd George, 19 Sept. 1918, L.G.P. 21/2/39.
[24] Guest to Lloyd George, 25 Sept. 1918, L.G.P. F 21/2/40.

much mistaken, in these two conversations I have been present at the obsequies of the Liberal Party as I know it.'[25] The conference of the National Liberal Federation at Manchester heard Asquith with enthusiasm on 27 September, and followed him in deploring an early general election.[26]

The opposition of the Asquithian Liberals and the breakdown of negotiations with Asquith seems to have hardened Lloyd George in his determination to go ahead with an election. At Danny Park on 27 September Bonar Law, Balfour and Lloyd George discussed the prospects for an election. Bonar Law, in a long reflective letter to Balfour about the outcome of these discussions, argued for an early election mainly on the grounds that without a Coalition government under Lloyd George the Conservative Party in the immediate future would suffer by being forced to the right in opposition to 'a combined Liberal and Labour party.... The only chance I think of a rational solution to these questions [he had mentioned land reform, the liquor trade and industrial conditions] is that they should be dealt with by a government which has so secure a support, not of one section but of both, that there would at least be a chance that the reforms which undoubtedly will be necessary should be made in a way which was as little revolutionary as possible.'[27] It was necessary, though, to settle outstanding problems of Tariff Reform and the Welsh Church, left over from the outbreak of war. Bonar Law dealt crisply with the latter problem in a brief interview with the Bishop of St Asaph, which he reported to Lloyd George: 'He is very moderate. All he wishes is the Glebes = £10,000 a year and a lump sum of two million.'[28]

Tariff Reform was more difficult, since the National Party was agitating, on its own account and through the Tariff Reform League, so as to embarrass the official Unionist leadership. Walter Long grumbled 'have you ... reason either to wonder or complain if those who are organising the Prime Minister's Party for him view without any great dislike a movement which tends to strengthen the Nationalist Party against the legitimate Unionist Party, and therefore create a body of support which I have no doubt would be easily transferred to the Prime Minister as a personal asset.'[29] As so often before, Younger and the party's officials had to press Bonar Law for clear instructions.[30]

Law's hesitation was not entirely his own fault. The Diehard group which had opposed a link with Lloyd George in the spring were still

[25] Arthur Murray's diary, 25 Sept. 1918, Elibank Papers 8815; Elibank to Lloyd George, 26 Sept. 1918, L.G.P. F/41/5/10 and Elibank Papers 8804; memo. by Murray of Elibank, *ibid.*

[26] Samuel to wife, 26 Sept. and 27 Sept. 1918, Samuel Papers A/157/939 & 941.

[27] Bonar Law to Balfour, 5 Oct. 1918, Balfour Papers B.L. Add. MSS 49693 ff. 272–281.

[28] Bonar Law to Lloyd George, 10 Oct. 1918, L.G.P. F/30/2/51.

[29] Long to Bonar Law, 4 Oct. 1918, B.L.P. 84/2/5.

[30] Sanders Diary, 13 Oct. 1918, *Real Old Tory Politics*, p. 109.

a force to be reckoned with,[31] and the question of Tariff Reform was still outstanding. Lloyd George in mid-October declined to accept Tariff Reform and refused to amend the Welsh Church Act, but otherwise offered to the Tories that he would advise his Liberal supporters to form a Coalition with them, in Guest's words 'for the attainment of a victorious peace and for the carrying out of a Democratic Programme of Reconstruction'.[32] Despite this gentle truculence, he was under pressure from his own supporters to close a deal with the Conservatives because, as Henry Norman said, 'many experienced Parliamentarians and influential outside politicians, strongly urge the necessity of an immediate Election before the Bolshevists can take further advantage of peace prospects.'[33] Lloyd George therefore began to force the pace. Sanders noted at a breakfast meeting of Tory ministers

> On the question of an election L.G. said if we put it off till some time after peace the inevitable discontent that would arise during the period of settling down might lead to a regular Bolshevic government. Younger has not been able to get anything definite out of Bonar as to agreement on policy. L.G. told him that Bonar put up a real ultra-Tory programme, said he could not have that and hinted that he was being approached by the Asquith people. Now L.G. will draw a programme of his own and see if we cannot agree on it.[34]

The gulf was bridged with the help of Carson, who as chairman of the Cabinet's two committees on post-war economic policy had worked closely with Addison about tariff matters and knew the field and its noisiest inhabitants intimately. On 21 October he addressed a paper, co-authored with F.S. Oliver, to Lloyd George:

> If we are to face the real facts which confront the country after the war in framing our economic policy it is essential that we should get rid of all predilections which arose out of our old controversies with reference to Free Trade and Tariff Reform. Indeed nothing could be more disastrous than that the question of reconstruction should be in any way mixed up with party controversies and not be discussed on a purely national basis.... We cannot for a moment anticipate that these people [soldiers and munitions workers and their families] will be content to return to the old conditions and indeed our policy ought to be to take care that their standards should be further improved [rather] than diminished. In other words we must aim at demonstrating to them that out of the sacrifices they have been called upon to make there would arise a fuller share of the profits accruing from their labour.[35]

---

[31] Derby Diary, 16 Oct., extract in Balfour Papers B.L. Add. MSS 49744 ff. 79–80, reporting a conversation with John Baird.

[32] Guest to Lloyd George, 21 Oct. 1918, L.G.P. 21/2/43.

[33] Norman to Lloyd George, 17 Oct. 1918, L.G.P. 21/2/42.

[34] Sanders Diary, 20 Oct. 1918, *Real Old Tory Politics*, p. 110.

[35] Carson to Lloyd George, 21 Oct. 1918, L.G.P. 6/3/18.

This was to be achieved by the increase of domestic industrial production, but the precise means were not to be specified. This draft, criticised by Lloyd George as 'too long', formed the basis of a statement agreed between Lloyd George and Bonar Law (and submitted to Carson) on 25 October,[36] as a result of which Sanders could comment that 'negotiations for a party agreement are getting a little forrarder'.[37] Meanwhile Bonar Law was engaged in dealing with his own right flank by 'squaring the National Party'.[38] This was not entirely successful: Page Croft appeared willing to support the Coalition, but Bennett Dampier, the National Party's principal organiser, was dead against it and was intriguing to remove Croft from the leadership of his splinter party.[39]

Pressure of time was now acute, as the collapse of the German army on the Western Front made an armistice seem imminent. On 29 October Guest reported to Lloyd George that he had reached agreement with Bonar Law about the number of Liberal candidates to be supported by Conservatives: 100 of the 'old Guard' and 50 others, in addition to any Labour supporters of the Coalition. A letter was drafted in late October, which Lloyd George was to send to Bonar Law, setting out the terms of the Coalition's agreement to fight the election.[40] Even at this late stage the supporting cast on either side was uncertain about what the principals were up to. Sir George Riddell, Lloyd George's closest confidant among newspaper proprietors, complained that the advertising material suggested by Guest 'created the impression that the capitalists had put up a big fund to jockey the working classes, and that they are using you as an instrument',[41] while Salisbury, who had chaired a Unionist War Committee meeting on 30 October, wrote to Bonar Law that 'it is your duty to have a party meeting without delay'.[42] Unionist sensitivities were further aroused as Lloyd George summarily dismissed Hayes Fisher, the President of the Local Government Board, for incompetence in preparing the electoral register so that soldiers could vote, and Bonar Law reacted angrily to this further threat to the unanimity of the Conservative Party.[43] On the other side, Walter Long was quoted, without his permission, as insisting on Tariff Reform as part of the Coali-

---

[36] Bonar Law to Carson, 25 Oct. 1918, B.L.P. 84/7/96.

[37] Sanders Diary, 27 Oct. 1918, *Real Old Tory Politics*, p. 110.

[38] *Ibid.* and Edward Goulding to Bonar Law, with enclosures, 24 Oct. 1918, B.L.P. 84/2/8,9.

[39] Sanders Diary, 27 Oct. 1918, *Real Old Tory Politics*, p. 111.

[40] Guest to Lloyd George, 29 Oct. 1918, L.G.P. F/21/2/43; Sanders Diary, 3 Nov. 1918, *Real Old Tory Politics*, p. 111.

[41] Riddell to Lloyd George, 31 Oct. 1918, L.G.P. F/43/7/7.

[42] Salisbury to Bonar Law, 2 Nov. 1918, B.L.P. 84/3/5.

[43] This oft-told tale can be followed in B.L.P. 84/3/1–2; L.G.P. F/15/4/16–17; Sanders Diary, 3 Nov. 1918, *Real Old Tory Politics*, p. 111; and Frank Owen, *Tempestuous Journey* (London: Hutchinson, 1954), pp. 503–504.

tion platform, and was obliged to protest for fear of damaging Coalition unity.[44]

Lloyd George pressed on. On 5 November he saw the King to request a dissolution, arguing that 'For every reason it seems to be the unique moment to appeal to the electorate, now that a great load is, as it were, removed from the mind of the people by the early prospect of a termination of the War, and it is important that the Election should take place now, rather than at a later period when demobilization may be in progress and thousands of both the military and civil population thrown out of employment, thereby causing considerable unrest in the country.' He also suggested that 'the women' were more likely to vote 'sanely' now than later on when there might be discontent. The King objected that the government had parliamentary support both to wage war and make peace, and that Asquith had promised continuing support, but his objections were brushed aside. Lloyd George promised an election 'before any unrest is likely to occur', and the dissolution was granted.[45]

Going to the Country

In December 1918 Westminster politicians 'went to the country' for the first time in eight years. The country to which they went was by now strange territory to most of them. The electorate had increased by 2.5 times and most constituency boundaries had been redrawn. The political truce had put an end to routine political work during the war, and there was little time for good canvassing between the dissolution and the poll. After four years of obsession with the war as they heard about it in the House of Commons and read about it in the newspapers, M.P.s were suddenly forced to confront their constituents directly. This was not always a happy moment, and for some days the concerns of Westminster, especially the details of the Coalition election appeal and the distribution of the Coupon, seemed to affect M.P.s more than the likely behaviour of the voters. When they began to campaign in earnest, even the experienced candidates found it hard to know what was going on. Their reports, and those of the party agents, were uncertain about popular feeling, and only a few themes emerged from a mass of contradiction.

One of these themes, though, helped to change the style of the Coalition's campaign: after the first week, instead of emphasising the reconstruction issues which had featured in the published manifesto, the Coali-

---

[44] The culprit was George Terrell, M.P., president of the National Union of Manufacturers, a strongly pro-tariff body.

[45] Stamfordham Memo., 5 Nov. 1918, RA GV K 1348/11.

tion's leaders played up reparations and indemnities. This was thought to be successful, but even on the eve of the poll the national organisers of all parties could only predict a Coalition victory, without being able to explain it. Nobody really knew how the women had voted, nor the absentee voters in the armed services, nor the new male voters who would have been disenfranchised by the old system. The idea of national unity, which the Coalition had made its own, was popular in the national press, but the provincial press was deeply divided on the old partisan lines. There was plenty of evidence to suggest that the Coupon arrangements were offending voters, but plenty of evidence on the other side. Until the very end Labour was considered to be a threat, and special efforts were made to frighten the electors away from 'Bolshevism'. In the end the Coalition's victory was greater than anyone had predicted, and Labour's performance was worse. The best prophets were those who had said that the old politics would be swept away, but none of them had said clearly what would take its place.

The campaign was launched openly on 12 November, the day after the Armistice. Lloyd George met Liberal M.P.s at 10 Downing Street and Bonar Law held a meeting of Conservatives at the Connaught Rooms. Each leader defended the decision to fight as a Coalition, but in rather different terms. Lloyd George's promise of bold social and economic reconstruction on Liberal lines was leaked to *The Times* (probably by Sutherland or Philip Kerr). It caused turmoil among the Conservatives, who had been persuaded by Bonar Law that a Liberal-led Coalition was the only means to contain Bolshevist-inspired demands for radical change.[46] This reflected the uncertainties which still remained about the long-term future of the Coalition and of the Liberal Party. Plenty of Tories disliked Lloyd George for all the old reasons: Robert Cecil rarely missed a chance to reserve his position on subjects like Welsh Church disestablishment, over which he resigned during the campaign, while Walter Long managed to support the principle of coalition while rejecting most of the details.[47] Liberals were also uneasy about the Coalition. Even the loyal H.A.L. Fisher had declined when Guest asked him before the meeting to move a vote of thanks, choosing to decide after he had heard the prime minister's speech.[48]

For once, Lloyd George was probably not being disingenuous when he told Sanders, the Unionist deputy whip, that at the Liberal meeting he had spoken impromptu and under pressure and was 'anxious to make things

[46] Sanders Diary, 16 Nov. 1918, *Real Old Tory Politics*, pp. 113–114. The report, dated 12 November and apparently ready for leaking, is in Kerr's papers, Scottish Record Office, Lothian Papers, GD40/17/1025.
[47] Cecil to Bonar Law, 11 Nov. 1918, B.L.P. 84/3/12.
[48] H.A.L. Fisher Diary, 12 Nov. 1918, Fisher Papers.

easy for his Liberal followers'. He had done it so well that Asquith wrote to him on seeing reports of the meetings, to arrange an interview.[49] On Wednesday 13th Asquith made a speech to a Liberal dinner in which, as Smuts wrote, he 'subscribe[d] with both hands to [Lloyd George's] whole programme and nothing but your programme. He fears the extinction of his rump and the dissolution of the Liberal Party.'[50] Although Lloyd George's critics jumped to the conclusion that newspaper talk of Liberal *rapprochement* was an attempt by Lloyd George to 'get the most useful of the old gang in as ballast to himself',[51] the supplicant on this occasion was certainly Asquith, not the prime minister. After meeting the Coalition ministers at breakfast on Thursday 14 November and deciding to go to the polls on 14 December, Lloyd George saw Asquith. Nothing came of the meeting. Asquith reported to Runciman that 'there would be *no* proposal for any reconstruction of the Govt, at any rate until after the Election': the difficulty on Lloyd George's side was apparently that the arrangements between Guest and Younger over seats could not be disentangled.[52] The Liberal Lazarus had got up and laid hands on the sick-bed from which the Master of Elibank had tiptoed sadly away some two months before, only to succumb to the smothering logic of electoral organisation.

Even so the series of public meetings which followed did not immediately make the battle lines clear to everyone. The Labour Party met on 14 November and decided to withdraw from the Coalition. This was greeted by the remaining Labour ministers with open distress. Stephen Walsh, who had an impregnable seat in the Ince division of Lancashire, simply ignored the decision and over the course of a week persuaded the Lancashire and Cheshire Miners' Federation to endorse his candidature and let him go on supporting the Coalition and abusing the 'camarilla' at the head of the Labour Party.[53] Even those who accepted the authority of the delegate conference, like Clynes and Brace, were profusely regretful in their explanations to Lloyd George.[54] Labour was therefore not immediately recognised as an open opponent of the Coalition. The position of the Liberals was even more ambiguous. Because of the newspaper discussion of 13 and 14 November, the tone of Asquith's speech on the 14th, and the conduct of a large Liberal meeting addressed by Asquith at the Caxton Hall on the 18th, many assumed that Asquith and his supporters were supporting the Coalition from outside. The Coalition manifesto, published

[49] Asquith to Lloyd George, 13 Nov. 1918, L.G.P. F/42/5/4.

[50] Smuts to Lloyd George, 14 Nov. 1918, L.G.P. 45/4/22.

[51] Lady Gainford to Gainford, 14 Dec. 1918, Gainford Papers 97.

[52] Asquith to Runciman, 15 Nov. 1918, Runciman Papers WR 302; H.A.L. Fisher Diary, reporting a conversation with Gordon Hewart, 14 Nov. 1918, Fisher Papers.

[53] Walsh to Bonar Law, 24 Nov. 1918, B.L.P. 84/3/21.

[54] Clynes to Lloyd George, 21 Nov. 1918, L.G.P. F/10/5/6; Brace to Lloyd George, 23 Nov. 1918, L.G.P. F/5/6/6.

on 21 November, invited 'every section of the electorate, without distinction of party, to support the Coalition Government in the execution of a policy devised in the interest of no particular class or section . . . '.[55] Yet certain Liberal candidates were to be proscribed. Some did not see the point of this, especially when Lloyd George admitted that many of the Asquithians now 'pressing him to admit them to the fold' had supported the previous Coalition government in the House.[56]

Within Lloyd George's circle, both Fisher and Montagu took the matter up.[57] Montagu made his case at a meeting of Liberal ministers on 20 November:

> I felt very apprehensive that the arrangements made as regards candidatures for the new Parliament may in the long run on the one hand vitiate the authority of the new Parliament as representative of the nation, and on the other hand exclude from the new House of Commons Liberals who, while not necessarily voting for you on every occasion, would give you, in the policy which I know you have at heart and upon the success of which the future of our country depends, more support than some of the Conservatives who will be returned as Coalitionists will find it possible to give you.[58]

Historians have accepted this implied claim that the Coalition candidates were less progressive than the Asquithians, and that the 1919 House of Commons was therefore more reactionary than it need have been.[59] The conclusion might be right, but the premises are suspect, for the political opinions of uncouponed Liberals were as varied as those of their couponed brethren. The 'Asquithian' Liberals included most of the 'Liberal millionaires', such as Richard Holt and Percy Molteno, who had opposed Lloyd George's social and fiscal reforms before the war, as well as established radicals such as Josiah Wedgwood, C.T. Needham and R.L. Outhwaite. On the other hand, although some very reactionary Conservatives got the coupon they might well have won without it: some uncouponed Conservatives won handsomely against couponed Liberals. But many Liberal candidates shared Montagu's optimistic vision of a truly progressive Liberal Party wrapped in the Coalition banner, and they begged for 'the letter'. Haldane had a visit from Percy Allen, of the Central Liberal Association, who told him that 'he does not think that Asquith will have more than 50 followers in the new H of C and is much concerned. Even the Daily News is now saying that there is no leadership.'[60]

[55] 'The Coalition Manifesto', TS, 21 Nov. 1918, L.G.P. F/168/2/7.

[56] Crawford Diary, 14 Nov. 1918.

[57] Fisher to Mrs Fisher, 18 Nov. 1918, Fisher Papers.

[58] Montagu to Lloyd George, 21 Nov. 1918, L.G.P. F/40/2/22.

[59] Roy Douglas, 'A Classification of Members of Parliament elected in 1918', *Bulletin of the Institute of Historical Research*, xlvii (1974), 74–94.

[60] Haldane to Elizabeth Haldane, 22 Nov. 1918, Haldane Papers 6013/48449.

It would have been very surprising if some Liberals had not decided at this point to leave the sinking ship. Sir Charles Hobhouse, who had been Postmaster-General in the last Liberal Cabinet, was unusual only in his plain speaking. He approached Guest on 15 November:

> ...and wished me to convey to you that, in view of the two speeches delivered by yourself and Mr. Asquith on Tuesday and Wednesday last respectively, he found his position in politics so difficult that, if he could find employment out of the House, he would not stand again. He wished me to ask you whether you would care to give him the vacancy on the Board of Directors of the Suez Canal Company, in return for which he would undertake to hand you over East Bristol.

This was a brave shot, but the price was too high for Guest, who wanted Hobhouse left 'to flounder harmlessly in disgruntled and leaderless opposition'.[61] Guest was right: Hobhouse took only 7.6 per cent of the poll in East Bristol, standing against a couponed Liberal.

Conservative organisers had their difficulties too, now that the Guest–Younger discussions were revealed. On 23 November Bonar Law had 'ten abusive telegrams' from Liverpool alone, where Sir Albert Salvidge, the local Tory boss, saw the chance to make a clean sweep for his party, and resented the protection given to Liberal candidates by the Coupon.[62] As Salvidge explained to Derby, 'I am sorry to say that things in Liverpool are not very satisfactory... It is impossible for the people in London to settle a matter of this sort without consultation with us here and if they attempt it they must take the consequences. If they had left us alone we should have won ten seats!'[63] In Liverpool the Conservative machine largely controlled the Coupon: in Manchester, where Liberalism was stronger, Liberals and Conservatives both decided to have a free fight without the Coupon. In Scotland Liberals warned that the Coupon might do more harm than good, but elsewhere it was in strong demand.[64] Guest believed that the Tory whips were responding by dragging their feet: he complained to Lloyd George that 'we have not yet obtained the "real goods" up to the number (150) for which you, rightly, stipulated.'[65] Bonar Law and Churchill were set up as a court of arbitration, but even this did not satisfy local Conservatives who believed that their hour had come. Dissident

---

[61] Guest to Lloyd George, 15 Nov. 1918, L.G.P. F/21/2/97.

[62] Fisher Diary, Fisher Papers.

[63] Salvidge to Derby, 23 Nov. 1918, Derby Papers 920 DER (17) Salvidge Correspondence. The Conservatives did win ten of the eleven Liverpool seats, including the Fairfield division where a Liberal, Captain Joseph, held the coupon; the Scotland division, as expected, was held by T.P. O'Connor for the Irish Nationalist Party. In Fairfield the Unionists put up Major J.B. Cohen, who had fought with the Liverpool regiment and lost both legs. Cohen supported the Coalition programme, and was supported by De F. Pennefather, a Couponed Unionist candidate. Unionist tactics were *ad hominem* and effective; *The Times* on 10 December described them as 'unreasonable and ungracious'.

[64] Sanders Diary, 27 Nov. 1918, *Real Old Tory Politics*, p. 117.

[65] Guest to Lloyd George, 15 Nov. 1918, L.G.P. F/21/2/97.

Conservatives opposed 18 Coalition Liberal candidates, and defeated four of them.

It would be wrong, though, to assume that the Coupon caused offence only to those who had not been chosen to receive it. Consider the response of Alfred Pease, a former M.P. for Cleveland and a Liberal traditionalist in an area where his family had dominated Liberal politics for generations. Writing about the Cleveland contest to his brother, the former Liberal Whip Jack Pease, now Lord Gainford, he observed:

> The candidates are Samuel a London *Jew* out for *himself* — 'Liberal' (caucus — John Fred Wilson & O'Connell Jones). A stranger Sir Somebody Something 'Coalitionist' comes from somewhere — Knows nobody & nothing here (caucus — Ld Guisborough's selection) & Dack — a decent Cleveland miner, probably the best of the lot — (caucus — I.L.P. or Bolchevists) —
> Representation of & Voice of people &c — all sludge — Most people in Cleveland do not want a Jew but a Christian & want a Cleveland man but not a Bolchevist but there it is — I should not think Samuel will get in but it is difficult to tell as Dack is by no means certain to get the whole Labour vote — which here is not Bolchie — I expect many will vote for the Coalition.[66]

The strongest theme in this witches' brew of resentments is suspicion of Westminster manipulation, a feeling common to Conservatives and Liberals. It illustrates the fragile basis on which national party organisation had grown up since the great nineteenth century Reform Acts. Party leaders, abetted by the professional political class which was beginning to dominate the House of Commons and of which Herbert Samuel was a successful example, tried to impose central offices, candidate lists, and national decision-making on local parties which had been run by the likes of Arthur Pease. Local activists had given only grudging consent before 1914. Party discipline was resented when it conflicted with local needs, especially the desire for a local man. The coupon arrangement was another step towards centralisation, which in itself hastened the decline of Liberal morale. The Conservatives, better placed to resist Westminster's threats even in 1918, were more resilient and by 1921 were ready to rise up against the Coalition, but even they were never again to enjoy

[66] Alfred Pease to Gainford, 24 Nov. 1918, Gainford Papers 97. The Conservative Coalitionist was Sir Park Goff, who won the seat with 8,701 votes, a majority of 91 over the Labour candidate. Samuel polled 7,089. 'Jack' Pease (Joseph Arthur Pease, Lord Gainford) sat for Tyneside from 1892 to 1900 but moved out — to Saffron Walden and later to Rotherham — after his defeat in the 1900 'Khaki' election; he was the only career politician among the Peases, being Chief Whip 1908–10 and holding various ministerial offices until December 1916. Alfred Pease sat for York from 1885 to 1892, and for Cleveland from 1897 to 1902. Their father, Sir Joseph, had been M.P. for South Durham from 1865 to 1885 and then for Barnard Castle until his death in 1903; their grandfather, Joseph Pease, held South Durham from 1832 to 1841. Henry Fell Pease, another member of Pease and Partners, sat as a Liberal for Cleveland from 1885 until his death in 1896, being succeeded by Arthur Pease (brother of Jack and Alfred). Henry's father, another Henry Pease, held South Durham from 1857 to 1865.

their pre-war autonomy. By reducing local political activity without correspondingly putting Westminster to sleep, the war had brought about a lasting shift in relationships between the centre and the localities. To many local politicians in 1918 the distribution of the coupon symbolised this unwelcome change.

It would have been easier for them to understand it if the Coalition organisers had been able to reveal a transparent logic behind their decisions. The first principle of selection had been to reward service and to find places for all the faithful. Since so many sitting members retired in 1918, this did not fill all the places available, but where sitting members were given the Coupon it was important that they should be given some assurance of victory. In these cases the Coupon should have prevented the appearance of Conservative candidacies in Liberal seats and vice versa. This would have been acceptable during the war, but was clearly unsatisfactory in peacetime, especially in marginal seats where Conservatives were hoping for victory. This difficulty was all the greater where the Coalition candidate was not a sitting member. In allocating the Coupons to such constituencies, Guest and Younger were trying to balance numbers between Conservatives and Lloyd George Liberals while matching parties as far as possible to the seats which they were likely to win. But they could hardly say this in public, since the agreement on a fixed number of Coalition Liberal seats was not acknowledged. Instead they pretended that they were choosing, from those available in the constituency, the best man to support the Coalition in the future. Both Conservatives and uncouponed Liberals could quickly make a nonsense of this claim by declaring that they were potentially more loyal to the Coalition than the couponed candidate. A typical move of this sort was made by W.H. Gritten, three times a Unionist candidate in The Hartlepools and three times defeated, who complained that the Liberal selected for the Coupon in his seat had a poor record in the war. His local association supported him and he won an easy victory.[67] On the other side Evan Cotton appealed unsuccessfully through Montagu as 'a sitting member of the House of Commons in a Liberal seat who intends to support the Prime Minister's policy', but who was being passed over in favour of a Conservative.[68] No scheme of allocation could have eliminated such cases entirely, but the methods adopted produced them in dozens. Faced with the difficulty H.A.L. Fisher

---

[67] For more on Gritten see John Turner, 'The British Commonwealth Union and the General Election of 1918', *English Historical Review*, xciii (1978), 555 and the *Northern Daily Mail* for 6 Dec. 1918.

[68] Cotton to Montagu, 16 Nov. 1918, enclosed with Montagu to Guest, 18 Nov. 1918, L.G.P. 40/2/21. Harry Evan Cotton was a barrister with Indian experience who had subsequently been a Progressive member of the L.C.C. He took the East Finsbury seat at a by-election in July 1918. His competitor was Lt.-Col Martin Archer-Shee, who had held the Finsbury Central seat for the Conservatives since 1910. Archer-Shee abandoned the Coalition because of its Irish policy in 1921.

proposed to 'let Liberals & Tories fight it out freely without official candidatures', but this was dismissed by Bonar Law on the grounds that 'it
would have meant collision between him and Lloyd George.'[69] This was
at the heart of it: whatever the reality, Lloyd George and Guest believed
that they had got the best available bargain in the coupon arrangement,
and were unwilling to jeopardise it. To protect it, they had to steamroller
the constituencies.

On 26 November the list of candidates was published; 'all or nearly all
quite meaningless & obscure' as Fisher noted.[70] The press on both sides
now picked up the revulsion of feeling which had been widespread among
aggrieved politicians, and Lloyd George became nervous. He urged Guest
to get on with 'the Committee of Managers that Addison suggested and
which we approved last week' and demanded the formation of 'Area L.G.
committees'.[71] He asked Sanders 'if anyone could get at Northcliffe' and
received a discouraging answer: not unjustified, since Northcliffe, whom
Lloyd George had rebuffed when he asked to be sent to Paris as part of the
peace mission, was writing friendly letters to Page Croft of the National
Party and giving free publicity to the Labour Party.[72] The Asquithian
press, predictably, objected to the Coupon altogether, while even the
Express under Beaverbrook's guidance criticised the exaction of pledges.[73]
The possible consequence was not lost on Lloyd George's opponents.
McKinnon Wood made the point to Runciman:

> The publication of the list of certified candidates which would turn a Tory minority
> of only 15 in Scotland into a Tory majority and have a similar effect in Glasgow (only
> three Liberals having been blessed) has caused a remarkable revulsion of feeling here.
> When I was in Glasgow early in November the Coalition idea was preponderating
> in every Liberal Club, now both Scottish and Liberal sentiment are thoroughly
> offended. The rascals have over-reached themselves. It has become a clear straight
> fight now and I am quite happy. My plain speaking Election Address which would
> have scandalised many of my friends a week ago is now quite right...[74]

Guest's committee of managers met for the first time on 29 November
and its first report was on the state of the press: 'It is to be noted that
there is very little criticism of the Coalition programme — except in
Labour journals... — but there is all but universal condemnation of what

[69] Fisher Diary, 23 Nov. 1918, Fisher Papers.

[70] Fisher to Mrs Fisher, 26 Nov. 1918, Fisher Papers. Amendments to the list were still being
published until 12 December, to mounting hilarity and contempt in the press.

[71] Lloyd George to Guest, 27 Nov. 1918, L.G.P. 21/2/48.

[72] Sanders Diary, 27 Nov. 1918, *Real Old Tory Politics*, p. 117; Northcliffe to Page Croft, 28 Nov.
1918, Page Croft Papers CRFT 1/17/4.

[73] See e.g the *Westminster Gazette* for 26 Nov. 1918 and telegram of 26 Nov. 1918 addressed
to Arthur Murray in Elibank Papers 8807; Beaverbrook to Churchill, 26 Nov. 1918, Beaverbrook
Papers C/85.

[74] McKinnon Wood to Runciman, 28 Nov. 1918, Runciman Papers WR 169 (2).

is variously called "traffic in seats", "ticket-of-leave candidates", etc. This condemnation has grown daily, and is as common in openly friendly and moderate journals as in those notoriously hostile.'[75]

Serious campaigning began in the last days of November, with most candidates issuing their addresses and making set-piece speeches to public meetings. This was the style of pre-war politics, and both candidates and the parties' headquarters expected to judge the progress of the campaign from public response on these occasions. But the evidence of public response is difficult to interpret. Not much can be gleaned from election addresses about the tone of the campaign. Most Conservative addresses were devoted to general support of the Coalition and an appeal to the electors to return the government which had won the war and could therefore be relied upon to govern well in peace. The Coalition programme was supported in general and anodyne terms. Coalition Liberal addresses were little different, though more detailed emphasis was laid on the proposals for reconstruction in the Coalition manifesto. Neither party made very much at this stage of the reparations question, although most Coalition candidates took up the assertion that the Labour Party was fundamentally Bolshevist. This reflected a press campaign justifying British intervention in Russia, which had been organised covertly by the Foreign Office at the War Cabinet's request.[76]

On the other side, Labour addresses concentrated on social reform while independent Liberals, at least in England, were most likely to emphasise the distasteful characteristics of the election while usually offering support to Lloyd George. So anxious were the uncouponed Liberals that the *Times* correspondent in the north of England noted on 10 December that 'I have yet to discover an Asquithian Liberal who does not vie with his official Coalition opponent, whether Liberal or Unionist, in proclaiming his acceptance of Mr Lloyd George's programme.' A case in point is Samuel in Cleveland, whose contest was a microcosm of the Liberal dilemma in 1918, with a Conservative Coalitionist and an independent and popular Labour candidate also standing against him. His election address came in two forms, one addressed separately 'To the WOMEN VOTERS of the CLEVELAND DIVISION' to illustrate the point that this new element of the electorate was to be treated cautiously. His hopes and fears were helpfully indicated in bold type:

> There is to be a Labour candidate at this election. Some working people may think that a Labour candidate ought always to be supported merely because he **is** a Labour candidate. **But is it a good thing that our politics should be divided simply**

[75] Guest to Lloyd George (memorandum), 29 Nov. 1918, with enclosure, L.G.P. F/20/2/99.
[76] R. Cecil to Lloyd George, 20 Nov. 1918, L.G.P. F/6/5/47.

on lines of class? ... That is a question that the new women voters should ask themselves.

Parties are useful in politics. They help us to organise opinion and instruct the voters. **But there may be too much party spirit** ... Mr Lloyd George ... wishes to continue, for the settlement following the war, the union of parties which happily prevailed during the war. He wishes to use that union in order to pass, by common agreement, a number of Bills for the benefit of the people ... **In this I think he is right. If I am returned to Parliament I shall support him in that policy.**[77]

The voters cannot have learned much from addresses such as these, in which at least two candidates in a single constituency seemed to be standing for the same thing. Early responses were mixed, and varied a great deal from constituency to constituency. Coalition Liberal candidates reported a lot of trouble from 'the furious campaign of the "Cocoa Press" against the Coalition' (Cecil Harmsworth, Luton), mentioning particularly the effect of the *Daily News*. Albert Illingworth's agent found his local association (Lancs., Heywood and Radcliffe) in 'a state of ungovernable fury over the action of the Whips in officially sanctioning the candidature of Tories against Liberals. The effect has been to put the vast majority of Liberals in Lancashire against the Prime Minister and to have undone the great impression he made at Manchester in September.' Sir Henry Norman said much the same for Blackburn, as did Sir Joseph Davies in Crewe, and a number of Welsh candidates. The consensus was that this would drive advanced Liberals into Labour's arms. Except for those who were opposed by renegade Conservatives, Coalition Liberal candidates were preoccupied with the challenge from Labour, and looked anxiously for signs of a split in the working-class electorate. Sir George Toulmin in Bury, who discerned 'a pronounced movement from Liberal to Labour', also detected an interest in 'the exaction of full reparation from Germany and punishment from Kaiser downward'. But this report, which was echoed by others, followed Lloyd George's Newcastle speech which promised that the authors of the war would be brought to justice. The earliest reports discussed a much wider set of interests, including a dread of conscription and fears about the restitution of trade union rights (Athelstan Rendall, Gloucestershire Thornbury); pensions (Sir William Stephens, Salford West); and security of tenure for allotment holders (L. Haslam, Newport).[78] A particularly touching report came from J.D. Hope, contesting Berwick and Haddington, who found 'Minimum wage of 25/- in Corn Production Bill causing trouble. Please let me know how I voted.'

By the beginning of December both Coalition party organisations were registering concern about the electors' apathy, while the Lloyd George

[77] Samuel Papers, A/63/3.
[78] 'Synopsis of Confidential Reports from Lloyd George Liberal Candidates: first batch of reports', n.d. L.G.P. F/167/1/1.

Liberals were further concerned about the confusion and hostility stirred up in potential Liberal voters by the Coupon arrangement itself. The sharpening of the campaign in its last two weeks reflected these fears. Conservative reports in the first week of December were dominated by the electorate's interest in getting an indemnity from Germany, repatriating Germans, punishing the Kaiser, and keeping German goods out after the war.[79] On the other side Addison put to Lloyd George that:

> ... it was clear to me from my experiences of last week, so far as they had gone, that the necessity for some machinery for seeing that justice was meted out to highly-placed German criminals — or at least those thought to be responsible for inhuman conduct in the war; that they should be tried beginning with the Kaiser; for making Germany pay, as much as possible, and for the return to Germany of interned enemy aliens, seemed to be as prominently in the public mind as any other issues.[80]

At the same time Lloyd George, whose election plan was to make major speeches in major towns for reporting by the national press, was being pulled in other directions by local Liberal interests which reflected local fears. In Leeds, before his great speech on 7 December, he was urged to 'appeal for united support on the lines outlined in his letter to Mr Bonar Law and either leave out any direct reference to Mr Asquith and his followers, or in the alternative deal with them in a most conciliatory way, as otherwise the Liberal Party which we have kept united in Leeds will be rent from top to bottom and a considerable part will vote Anti-Coalition.'[81] T.J. Macnamara, priming him for his last major speech in London shortly before polling day, issued a list of seven subjects all of which, apart from a reference to the Coalition's 'vigorous prosecution of the war', emphasised the new Coalition as a vehicle of social reconstruction in the interests of the working classes. Neither the Kaiser nor Germany was mentioned. Macnamara underlined his advice that 'You should flatly deny that you or your colleagues mean to perpetuate conscription' and concluded that the Coalition should promise 'to meet the aspirations of the people by dealing with all social problems with a largeness of grasp and a spirit of determination the like of which we have not seen before'.[82] Guest also emphasised at this stage in the campaign that a statement on conscription was necessary because 'it is being used against Govt candidates

---

[79] 'Extracts from Confidential Reports by Unionist Central Office Agents on Subjects in which the Electors are most interested', 3 Dec. 1918, L.G.P. F/167/1/1.

[80] Addison Diary, 2 Dec. 1918, Addison Papers 99.

[81] William Farr (Hon. Sec. Leeds Liberal Federation) to Guest, 4 Dec. 1918, L.G.P. F/21/2/50. The speech — reported in *The Times* on 9 Dec. 1918 — contained no direct reference to Asquith, but defended the Coalition against charges of reaction and contrasted the performance of his Coalition against Asquith's. Asquith replied on 9 Dec., *The Times* 10 Dec. 1916.

[82] Macnamara to Lloyd George, 10 Dec. 1918, L.G.P. F/36/1/19.

by Asquithians & Labour'.[83]

Lloyd George in fact dealt with conscription in a speech at Bristol on 11 December; but it was in this speech also that he turned his earlier cautious statements about German reparations into an impromptu promise that 'we shall search their pockets for it.' Even so, there was a marked and deliberate caution in the text of his speech, which was full of warnings that Germany's capacity to pay was limited, and that it might therefore be impossible to claim the full cost of the war.[84] He was following a line first taken by Sir Eric Geddes, who had promised a Cambridge audience that 'we will get everything out of [Germany] that you can squeeze out of a lemon and a bit more', a phrase later to be improved to 'squeezing Germany like a lemon until the pips squeak'. Geddes's speech was hardly reported at the time, and like Lloyd George he was insistent that there was a limit to Germany's capacity to pay.[85] Certainly by the end of the campaign there was a marked convergence between Lloyd George and the more robust elements in the Conservative Party. Leo Amery had observed in November that 'His speeches and manifestoes are good reading and full of zeal — and there is no one who really holds a candle to him in that line.' By the end of the campaign Lloyd George had adopted Amery's own prescription; 'I have gradually cut down my social reform programme to a few generalities, plus a little about dumping and British industries and tell them about the Peace Conference and what it means to the country, and go wholeheartedly for a strong policy including the Kaiser punishing as well...'.[86] However, this election tactic must be put in perspective. Lloyd George's own instincts were of course pugnacious: Henry Wilson recorded on Armistice night that 'LG wants to shoot the Kaiser. Winston does not.'[87] Until the late stages of the campaign, though, he had emphasised the reforming aspects of the agreed Coalition programme, and kept his cries for reparations in bounds, in particular by referring repeatedly to Germany's ability to pay. His belated interest in the uttermost farthing, which was never unqualified, appeared in response to a fear among his circle of the likely consequences of electoral apathy and the loss of Coalition Liberal seats because of local difficulties and confusion. After the polls had closed H.A.L. Fisher noted that 'LG committed a great tactical error in not coming out against conscription earlier',[88] and it was while repairing that error that he created a distraction by raising the electoral temperature

[83] Guest to Lloyd George, 10 Dec. 1918, L.G.P. F/21/2/51.

[84] *The Times*, 12 Dec. 1918.

[85] Keith Grieves, *Sir Eric Geddes* (Manchester: Manchester University Press, 1989), pp. 72–73.

[86] Amery to Mrs Amery, 26 Nov. 1918, *Leo Amery Diaries*, p. 246.

[87] Wilson Diary, quoted by Martin Gilbert, *Winston S. Churchill. Vol IV. 1916–1922* (London: William Heinemann, 1975), p. 166.

[88] Fisher Diary, 15 Dec. 1918, Fisher Papers.

over reparations. He was prepared for a Liberal backlash against it by an analysis of Asquith's speeches which showed that he too had steadily become more precise and emphatic about getting Germany to pay the cost of the war.[89] The 'Khaki' campaign was not edifying, but its cynicism reflects Lloyd George's fears of being outflanked by the Conservatives as well as his determination to confine the rise of Labour.

The Poll

A rather strained optimism was typical of the Coalition Liberal organisation in the last days before polling day. In Scotland and Wales most candidates were reported as 'confident' or 'very hopeful', but in England the picture was less clear. London had a particularly high proportion of 'Doubtfuls' and 'Hopefuls', but reports from the East Midlands and Yorkshire were also mixed: the candidate for Hull N.W. was described as 'Hopeful (probably lose).'[90] The Conservative machine, with more agents on the ground, ventured a prediction of the outcome on 11 December. On the basis of 'guesswork', and complaining that 'it is extremely difficult to give an opinion that is worth anything at the present time', the agents predicted 399 Coalition victories in England, leaving 129 for the non-Coalition parties.[91] This exaggeration of the strength of the opposition was typical of Coalition thinking in the last days of the campaign. Labour, rather than the Asquithian Liberals, was most feared, and the agents worried about issues such as the Lancashire cotton strike and the conscription rumour. Only after Lloyd George's Bristol speech did the organisers breathe easily.

The country, with the exception of the service voters, went to the polls on 14 December 'in a drizzle of rain and in a complete absence of interest and excitement' according to Crawford, whose view was widely shared.[92] The final turnout was 57.2 per cent, rather more than the Whips expected but very low compared with turnouts greater than 80 per cent in the 1906 and 1910 elections.[93] The new enlarged electorate was quite as difficult to reach as the politicians had said, but it is not clear whether apathy or confusion was most to blame. Female voters seem to have turned out in good numbers, and most of the politicians who bothered to comment on them shared the view that their political intelligence was limited and their

[89] Untitled paper, n.d., L.G.P. F/168/2/2.

[90] Guest to Lloyd George, 10 Dec. 1918, L.G.P. F/21/2/51.

[91] 'Forecast of Result Based on Reports Received from Unionist Central Office Agents', 11 Dec. 1918, L.G.P. F/48/9/1. No prediction was made for Scotland or Wales.

[92] Crawford Diary, 15 Dec. 1918.

[93] Guest's prediction reported in H.A.L.Fisher to Mrs Fisher, 15 Dec. 1918, Fisher Papers 5/2. The 1886 turnout of 74.2 per cent had been the lowest experienced under the 1885 franchise.

sympathies mostly with the Coalition. Richard Holt and Arthur Haworth wrote separately to Runciman on 17 December to blame the defeat which they both expected on the female vote 'which came up freely & I feel sure was hostile' when the male working-class vote was low. Haworth thought that 'the working class vote, and especially the women among them, have been all out for the Kaiser's head,'[94] a feeling which was clearly shared in Asquith's constituency.[95] Liberal dissatisfaction was mirrored in the reports of Sir Albert Salvidge, based on Liverpool's experience but including gossip about the rest of Lancashire. In his constituencies 'the women polled exceedingly well and there is also no doubt an overwhelming majority of them voted for our men.'[96] In a more measured review Guest noted:

> They polled proportionately more heavily than the men, but whether from a sense of novelty or of duty does not appear certain. As was to be expected they displayed interest in social questions such as housing, health, and so on, but all impressions and reports agree that women showed more determination even than the men in demanding full war indemnity from Germany and punishment of the Kaiser and his fellow criminals.
>
> In the great majority of cases wives and husbands seem to have voted on the same side. On the whole it does not seem that their enfranchisement led to their taking a more active part than hitherto in actual election work, such as canvassing and so on. A large number of meetings, however, for women alone was held.[97]

Until the results were declared, and even afterwards, the full impact of this 'incalculable factor' newly introduced by the Representation of the People Act could only be guessed.

The other source of great uncertainty was the service vote. Almost every soldier was entitled to be an elector, because the Act had given the vote to all men over 19 who had seen active service. An elaborate and rather unwieldy system of postal and proxy votes was devised to ensure that this section of the electorate could record its opinions. Voters on active service in the United Kingdom or on the Western Front were entitled to postal votes, while other service voters were allowed to nominate proxies. It was administratively impossible for these men to exercise their vote on the day of the poll, since the interval between nominations and polling was only eight days; so the count was extended over the Christmas holiday to allow the forces' postal votes to be returned. Coalition ministers were very anxious about this exercise. In some, mainly Con-

---

[94] R.D. Holt to Runciman, 17 Dec. 1918, Arthur Haworth to Runciman, 17 Dec. 1918, both in Runciman Papers WR 169. Cf. Crawford's remark that 'They allowed themselves to be swayed by flattery and personal considerations, often saying quite openly and without a trace of cynicism that they were going to support the best-looking man!' Crawford Diary, 17 Dec. 1918.

[95] Stuart R. Ball, 'Asquith's Decline and the General Election of 1918', *Scottish Historical Review*, lxi (1982), 44–61.

[96] Salvidge to Derby, 31 Dec. 1918, Derby Papers, 920 DER Salvidge Correspondence.

[97] Guest to Lloyd George, n.d. (before 30 Dec. 1918), L.G.P. F/21/2/59.

servative, circles the soldiers were thought to be an important element in
the Coalition's potential support. In early 1918 this had caused concern
when the arrangements for putting soldiers on the register had been disrupted by the German offensive in March. In due course just over 3.9
million service voters were registered for the United Kingdom; some of
these were duplicate registrations and many soldiers were omitted from
the register. For the election 2.7 million postal ballot forms were issued.
The problem was to make sure that they reached their destination and,
quite as important, to make sure that they were used.[98]

This problem had been raised as early as July by Guest, who wondered
'with respect to the *"khaki voters"*, especially abroad, could not something
be done to ensure their vote being cast for the government?'.[99] As Hayes
Fisher at the Local Government Board struggled deeper into the mire
over the register, the question of how the soldiers would use their votes
paled beside the risk that they would be unable to vote at all because of
the Coalition's bungling. By 29 October 'The Prime Minister doesn't
mind if he [Hayes Fisher] is drowned in Malmsey wine, but he must be a
dead chicken by tonight.'[100] Hayes Fisher's swift removal to the Duchy
of Lancaster probably did not affect the number of ballot papers issued,
and the parliamentary row did not entirely die away. By early December
Milner, who as Secretary of State for War had at first been blamed for
lateness in getting ballots to the troops, was content that 'the vast majority
of them' would be able to vote if they wished. But now he feared that
they did not wish to, and wrote anxiously to Haig that

> It is no business of mine, as Secretary of State for War, *how* the men vote, and the
> last thing I want to do is to try to exercise the slightest influence upon them as to
> the direction, in which they should use the political power which we put into their
> hands. But I should regard it as unfortunate, both for the country and the Army, if
> they did, in large numbers, abstain from voting at all...It is the duty of every man
> to try to the best of his lights to help his country to a right decision by voting for
> the man or party which he believes will most conduce to a good result.

Endearingly, he suggested that the men's understandable confusion at
getting a ballot paper merely containing two or three unknown names
could be helped by having 'someone at hand — an officer or "padre" —
who could enlighten them'. Haig, in character, replied that everything
possible had been done but pointed out the lack of information available
in France.[101] This was a problem the Coalition organisers already had

[98] 'Absent Voters', *P.P.* 1918, Cd. 9156, ; cf. the discussion in Pugh, *Electoral Reform*, pp. 172–173.
[99] Guest to Lloyd George, 13 July 1918, L.G.P. F/21/2/27.
[100] Owen, *Tempestuous Journey*, p. 504; but see also the extensive correspondence in B.L.P. 84/7/97–98 and 84/2/10–11, and in L.G.P. F/30/2/53.
[101] Milner to Haig, 5 Dec. 1918, Haig Papers 134.

partly in hand: press advertising was directed to the newspapers which circulated among the troops, and extra quantities were sent abroad in the days immediately after 14 December, carrying advertisements urging soldiers not to waste their chance to vote.[102]

These efforts had very little effect. The count was closed on 28 December. By that time, according to the Post Office, 641,632 soldiers had voted; 3,200 soldiers' ballots arrived too late. Understandably, Lloyd George refused to allow these figures to be published.[103] The very low poll undoubtedly reflected apathy, and irritation against politicians who thought that an election was more important than getting the troops home. The preferences of the soldiers who did vote need not have reflected the political preferences of the army as a whole, since officers were far more likely to have voted than the men; but it is likely that the absentee vote, when cast, favoured the Coalition. Salvidge's opinion was that 'although the soldiers' vote was not overwhelmingly in our favour there is little doubt we had a considerable majority of these votes'.[104]

The Results

In the short term, at least, the simple calculations of Tory advocates of the soldier franchise and Coalition exponents of an early post-war election seem to have been justified. As a 'Khaki' election, it succeeded beyond all expectation. On 17 December, with all except the soldiers' votes cast, Conservative Central Office made its final prediction. With agents still complaining about the bad canvass, the guess was that the Coalition would have a majority of 265 over all other candidates. The Tory machine looked forward to 356 Conservative victories (including 14 without the Coupon), 5 National Party, 5 British Workers' League, 134 Coalition Liberals, 44 Asquithian Liberals, 73 Labour, and 7 independents. This was a remarkably good prediction of Coalition Liberal performance. The rest of the figures seriously underestimated the strength of the uncouponed Conservatives, and overestimated the strength of Labour and the opposition Liberals. When passing the figures on to the prime minister, Younger insisted that there was 'steadily accumulating evidence that the Labour Organisation was used effectively', and suggested that the estimates should be discounted by '*at least* 25%. Even then the results would be extraordinarily good'.[105]

[102] Guest to Lloyd George, 18 & 19 Dec. 1918, L.G.P. F/167/1/2.
[103] A.H. Illingworth to Lloyd George, 7 Jan. 1919, with annotations by J.T. Davies, L.G.P. F/28/4/9.
[104] Salvidge to Derby, 31 Dec. 1918, Derby Papers, Salvidge Correspondence 920 DER.
[105] Younger to Lloyd George, 17 Dec. 1918, L.G.P. F/48/5/1.

When the result was declared on 28 December it was discovered that the victory compared well with the 'landslide' which had brought about the Liberal–Labour–Irish majority in 1906. In the 1919 parliament of 707 M.P.s the Coalition could muster 332 Conservative, 132 Liberal, and 22 Labour and other members elected with the coupon, with a further 52 sympathetic uncouponed Conservative and National Party members and up to 16 uncouponed Liberals to boot: a possible total of 554. In 1906 the Liberals and their likely supporters had held 513 seats in a House of 670.[106] The distribution of votes was somewhat less favourable in 1918: only 53 per cent of votes cast for the Coalition and its friends against 56 per cent for the pro-Liberal parties in 1906. Nonetheless, it was a famous victory. Robert Sanders claimed it as 'partly for L.G. and quite as much for the Conservative party',[107] while Walter Long insisted that 'there had been for years a steady movement in what we call Conservative directions....and it is only natural that it should find its results in the Election...'.[108] Couponed Conservatives had prospered; and eight uncouponed Conservatives had been returned against couponed Liberals, with a further twelve who had defeated Liberals in constituencies where no coupon had been issued.[109] To all appearances the long run of defeats since 1906 was over, and the Conservatives' time had come. But 1918 cannot be explained simply as 1906 in reverse. The election registered changes in party geography and in the politics of class; it also showed the early effects of the 1918 Representation of the People Act. Its results, further analysed in Chapter 11, are a testament to the good luck and perhaps the good judgement of the Coalition organisers.

[106] Made up in 1906 of 400 Liberals, 30 Labour and 83 Irish Nationalist. In practice the Westminster parliament of 1919–22 had 634 members, since the 73 Sinn Fein M.P.s did not take their seats. 1918 estimates of Liberal support for the government are taken from Guest to Lloyd George, 30 Dec. 1918, L.G.P. F/21/2/55.

[107] Sanders Diary, 5 Jan. 1918. *Real Old Tory Politics*, p. 122.

[108] Long to Derby, 31 Dec. 1918, Long Papers 947/548.

[109] Roy Douglas, 'A Classification of the Members of Parliament elected in 1918'.

10

A NEW POLITICAL LANDSCAPE
I – Capital and Labour

The Coalition government fought the election campaign, from its beginnings in 1917, to control change by creating a safe party system. Outside party politics, competition among other powerful institutions also threatened the political stability whose preservation had become the Coalition's domestic war aim. The war extended the role of the state and brought government into closer contact with capital and labour. This engagement need not have lasted into the peace: R.H. Tawney famously made the point that the extension of state control in wartime withered soon afterwards because it had neither ideological purpose nor long-term plan.[1] But the war did create new expectations for the use of the state's power, and corresponding disappointment when it was not used. Although most critics of post-war change, like Tawney, regretted the failure to press on with the 'progressive agenda' of the Edwardian years, by no means all the expectations were 'progressive' in that sense.[2] With some important exceptions, the attitudes of Liberal Coalitionists towards post-war social reconstruction were markedly more enthusiastic than that of their Conservative colleagues, while Conservatives retained a commitment to Tariff Reform which the Liberals rejected. The Labour opposition had its own demands, while the opposition Liberals disliked much of what they heard but feared the electoral consequences if they stood out against it. Reconstruction therefore helped to keep party identities alive within the Coalition. At the same time, many of the pre-war social issues discussed in Chapter 1 were revived, but usually in an altered form. The war did

---

[1] R.H. Tawney, 'The Abolition of Economic Controls, 1918–1921', originally written in 1941, reprinted in J.M. Winter, ed., *History and Society: Essays by R.H. Tawney* (London: Routledge & Kegan Paul, 1978), pp. 129–186.
[2] See Scott Newton and Dilwyn Porter, *Modernisation Frustrated: the politics of industrial decline in Britain since 1900* (London: Unwin Hyman, 1988), pp. 31–64, for a rare modern attempt to deal with the aspirations of social-imperialist reformers.

not stop politicians' arguing about Tariff Reform, health insurance and denominational education, but it did change the language used and shift their natural alliances inside and outside parliament.

The war also brought organised interests to the forefront of political change. The best-known example is the shop stewards' movement. Although its influence was temporary and perhaps overstated, the existence of a semi-formal network of labour activists radically altered the terms on which wages and conditions were negotiated in the later part of the war, and put pressure on the government to develop a conciliatory labour policy which would deflect insurrectionary movements in peacetime. It also compelled the established trade union hierarchy to shift to the left. The shop stewards had their counterpart among the employers, in the proliferating trade and business interest groups which combined commercial activities — conventional price-fixing and wage-bargaining functions — with the desire to speak directly to government. The new business groups had a more permanent effect on the structure of business politics than the shop stewards had on the trade union movement, mostly because the *ancien régime* in business politics was not so deeply rooted. But they, too, were partly responsible for shifting business's traditional spokesmen — business M.P.s — further towards the extreme in their demands. Given the need to mobilise the war economy, the government had to meet both these movements part way; the result was a consistent attempt to incorporate organised interests in order to control them. Businessmen and trade unionists were given jobs within government, and new consultative bodies were created to bring their wishes directly to the attention of ministers and departments. The interest groups themselves were recognised as authoritative spokesmen of their 'constituencies'. Some writers have seen this as the beginning of a process which during the twentieth century has reduced the significance of parliament and elevated the institutions of the 'extended state':[3] this depends on whether the interests or the politicians controlled the agenda, and during the war it seems to have been the politicians.

So large a range of political functions was carried out at this boundary between government and other organised elements in society that it would be impossible to approach it all in detail. The discussion which follows is therefore limited to a few themes which illustrate either the structure or the content of 'non-party politics' as it interacted with party politics during the war. The effacement of Free Trade, as a party issue as well as a policy problem, is important because of the intensity of pre-war feeling about Tariff Reform; but the question of state intervention in

[3] Especially R.K. Middlemas, whose *Politics in Industrial Society* (London: André Deutsch, 1979) has been influential.

overseas trade went beyond tariffs, and the discussion below touches the incorporation of business interest groups into government to implement a variety of policies. On the other hand, the troubled history of industrial relations at the end of the war reflects a general dissatisfaction with state intervention on the shop floor, shared by politicians, employers and trade unionists alike. It also illustrates starkly the continuity between wartime and pre-war and post-war concerns. The same continuity is illustrated in a vignette of social reform, the 1918 Education Act. This, the 'Fisher Act', shows particularly well how the war's amplification of the national efficiency issue was unable to drown out other, more traditional political and administrative attitudes.

A theme common to all of these issues is that policy could neither be made nor implemented by the state (and the party system) alone. This was perceived in all the belligerent powers to some degree: in Germany the lesson was learned superficially, in France rather more thoroughly.[4] But this emphatically did not mean that outside interests, particularly business interests, captured the apparatus of the state. Much less did direct bargaining between capital and labour supplant the political process. In contrast to the received wisdom, the experience of war suggests that the state had very little need to give ground to the institutions of what Middlemas has intriguingly called the 'extended state'. Pluralism, not corporatism, was the fruit of wartime change. On the other hand, there is not much here to suggest that 'the apparent change in the attitudes of businessmen, and their new willingness to accept centralised restrictions upon business and industry' were a very prominent part of business politics, let alone amounting to 'a hymn of praise to the new partnership between the state and private industry'.[5] The initiative lay with ministers and officials, and business and labour attitudes to the state were always fractious and often hostile.

The Strange Death of Laissez-Faire

One of Lloyd George's best debating points, when defending his credentials as a Simon-pure Liberal, was to remark that it was Reginald McKenna who abandoned Free Trade.[6] The McKenna Duties were imposed in the 1915 September Budget principally to limit imports and thereby to free shipping for essential war services. The 33 per cent duties on certain lux-

---

[4] Gerald Feldman, *Iron and Steel in the German Inflation, 1916–1922* (Princeton: Princeton University Press, 1977); John Godfrey, *Capitalism at War: industrial policy and bureaucracy in France, 1914–1918* (Leamington Spa: Berg, 1987).

[5] K.O. Morgan, *Consensus and Disunity* (Oxford: Clarendon Press, 1979), p. 18.

[6] *Scott Diary*, 26 Jan. 1917, p. 257; but he also seemed to Scott to regard Free Trade as 'part of the played-out programme of a hidebound Liberalism ...'.

ury items remained in force until 1931 (with a brief lapse from 1924 to 1926 caused by the Labour chancellorship of Philip Snowden) and were one of the few protective measures imposed by British governments before the resort to a tariff system in 1931. As noted above,[7] the employment of tariffs for any purpose in war or peace was controversial, and the opportunity to score points was immediately taken up by Conservatives who helped to persuade a not unwilling government to participate in the Paris Economic Conference and set up the machinery to work out how to implement Britain's commitments under the Paris Resolutions.

Thereafter, the Paris Resolutions were a touchstone of virtue for an important section of the Conservative back bench and for front-benchers such as Carson and Milner. Since they were an apparent concession to the economic logic of Tariff Reform, this was to be expected. Rather more surprising was their enthusiastic adoption by leading Liberals. During the war, and for a few months afterwards, Free Trade as it had been understood before the war was thrust to the margins of politics. Grumpy back-benchers such as John Burns recited Free Trade shibboleths in parliament and in their diaries: 'Just as coquetting with National Service led to compulsion so the desire to be "practical" "reasonable" and "patriotic" spell new Imperialist will lead Liberals into Protection and Reaction'.[8] This made very little impact on their leaders, and in the election campaign even Asquith was to be heard supporting the general principles of the Paris Resolutions.

The return to more familiar party battle lines in 1919, which culminated in a joint Liberal/Coalition Liberal manifesto in September of that year, appears at first to confirm that the wartime Liberal softening on Free Trade was an aberration. The Finance bill for 1919 contained an imperial preference clause, which enraged opposition Liberals and discomfited Coalitionists. The resurrection of some forgotten but glorious platitudes, such as Runciman's rediscovery that 'It was the Free Trade system of taxation alone which had enabled the Treasuries of the world to raise funds wherewith to conduct the war',[9] helped to restore a sense of Liberal identity. Protection was an obstacle to fusion between Coalition Liberals and Coalition Conservatives, and the issue therefore shaped the post-war party system at a critical moment. Nevertheless the ideological content of Free Trade, like that of Tariff Reform, had withered. The debate between Free Trade and protection was no longer the major focus of discussion about redistribution of wealth, social policy, or state intervention in the economy; each of these issues had developed its own momentum and its own discourse during the war. Instead, it had become a technical matter

---

[7] Chapter 3, pp. 115–116.

[8] Burns Diary, 27 Feb. 1917, B.L. Add. MSS 46339.

[9] Speaking at Edinburgh, 24 Oct. 1919, reported in the *Liberal Magazine*, xxvii (1919), 550.

of official support for industry and commerce, in which government departments, pressure groups and trade associations contributed as much to the policy outcome as did the politicians.

The crumbling of Free Trade politics began early in the war. Although the contradiction was readily forgotten later, it was embarrassing to exponents of an open world economy that the free trade which had brought Britain huge commercial revenues and the financial strength to sit out a long war had also allowed certain economic functions to lapse in Britain. The discovery of 'strategic industries' led the Board of Trade to set up a committee in July 1915 under Sir Algernon Firth, chairman of the Association of British Chambers of Commerce (A.B.C.C.). The committee eventually reported in February 1916 in favour of protective measures for a number of small trades, though of these only magnetos, electrical apparatus and laboratory glassware were genuinely of strategic importance.[10] Before its report, though, the climate in Britain had been changed by revelations of German proposals for an economic *Mitteleuropa*, and by the parliamentary discussion of the Budget in September. McKenna's duties — on motor cars, cinema films, clocks and musical instruments — were specifically designed to restrict imports and their yield was expected to be no more than £1.01 million in a full year, in a Budget which promised to raise £106 million. McKenna defended them as a war-only measure, and was supported by Bonar Law's declaration that Tariff Reformers in the Cabinet had not tried to influence the Budget.[11]

Not all M.P.s, especially Liberal M.P.s, were convinced; and whatever Cabinet members were doing, there is much evidence of increased activity by lobby groups. The Unionist Business Committee and the Tariff Commission were especially active, in contact with Walter Long in Cabinet and also with leading protectionist businessmen. W.A.S. Hewins, the U.B.C. secretary, worked closely with Sir Vincent Caillard, of Vickers Ltd, to prepare a case for the September Finance bill debates, and Vickers gave the Tariff Commission £2,000 for its work in December 1915.[12] In January 1916, while parliament was thoroughly excited about the Military Service bill, Hewins brought forward a debate about the success of the blockade and the need for co-operative Dominion effort to suppress German trade competition after the war. This was met by Runciman with his somewhat premature declaration that 'commercially Germany is a beaten nation', and a promise that ' . . . we must see to it that having ended this

---

[10] The trades in question were paper-making, printing, stationery, jewellery and silversmithing, cutlery, fancy leather goods, glassware, china and earthenware, toys, brushes, electrical apparatus and magnetos.

[11] *H.C. Debs*, 5s, 1915–1916, lxxiv, 1302–1436, 13 Oct. 1915.

[12] Caillard to Hewins, 26 Sept. 1915, Hewins Papers 58/133; Caillard to Hewins, 1 Dec. 1915, Hewins Papers 58/166.

war victoriously we do not give Germany a chance of reconstructing her commercial position'.[13] This, and the acceptance of Hewins's motion by the House, was recognised as a success for Tariff Reformers.

In the leading chambers of commerce the need for an aggressive post-war economic policy was canvassed enthusiastically. The London chamber set up an essay prize on the subject. 'The men who are starting it are all good Tariff Reformers,' remarked a sympathiser to Hewins, 'and they are only affecting to be moderate in order to rope in a lot of men who were formerly free-traders, and who don't want their "conversion" to be too much advertised at the moment.'[14] Minds were also changing in the Manchester chamber, where protectionists who had long been a sullen minority succeeded in referring back a motion from the directors (the chamber's executive committee) which proclaimed the virtue of Free Trade. The Birmingham and Leeds chambers both passed resolutions against post-war trade with Germany.[15] The A.B.C.C., which like most of the provincial chambers had been neutral about fiscal policy before the war because of divisions among its members, was also induced in March 1916 to pass a string of resolutions including demands for 'Reciprocal Trading Relations and Tariffs' to establish an order of preference between British Empire, allied, neutral and former enemy concerns, and 'Navigation Laws'.[16] A leading protagonist of this change of stance was Arthur Samuel, a Norwich shoe-manufacturer and later a Conservative M.P., who was simultaneously to be found recommending a policy of post-war discrimination against Germany to the Institute of Shipbuilders, even though it would cost £30 million a year.[17]

The idea that the war was an opportunity to capture trade was understandably attractive to British merchants, though it had some paradoxical effects not anticipated by protectionist politicians. The widespread notion that Britain's wealth and consequent war-making potential was based on a high volume of international trade made it difficult for some traders to appreciate the need for restrictions on trading with the enemy, if the effect of this trade was to make profits for Britain. Official policy was also ambivalent, so that it was not until the end of 1916 that clear limits

[13] H.C. Debs, 5s, 1915–1916, lxxvii, 1357–1358, 10 Jan. 1916.

[14] Sir Joseph Lawrence to Hewins, 11 Jan. 1916, Hewins Papers 59/28. Lawrence, a keen Tariff Reformer, had been a Conservative M.P. from 1902 to 1906. He was chairman of the Linotype company and a colleague of Dudley Docker as a director of British Westinghouse. He was later concerned with the establishment of the British Commonwealth Union.

[15] Thirty of the Manchester directors resigned in protest. [Manchester Chamber of Commerce] Journal, xxxv (1916), 89, and commentary in Liberal Magazine, xxiv (1916), 101; The Times, 1 Feb. 1916.

[16] A.B.C.C. Executive Committee Minutes, Special Meeting, 14 Mar. 1916, Guildhall Library A.B.C.C. Papers 14476/8.

[17] Notes of a speech delivered 24 Feb. 1916, Churchill College, Cambridge, Mancroft Papers MANCR 2/1.

were laid down to prevent merchants who were eager to capture neutral trade from engaging in activities which might transfer valuable industrial goods to Germany.[18] Businessmen found it difficult to reconcile these limits with official encouragement to export more, and the frustrations they met were an important source of the demand for improved financial facilities in the post-war period. The Association of British Chambers of Commerce and the London chamber were particularly vociferous.

The restive spirit among chambers of commerce, largely representing merchants, also afflicted manufacturers. Here the leading spirits were more openly protectionist in their antecedents. They included Dudley Docker, whose pre-war activities have been noted in Chapter 1, Hugo Hirst of the General Electric Company, and a number of other bankers and heavy industrialists. Docker was responsible for launching the Federation of British Industries in April 1916. In due course the F.B.I. was to subsume the 'Central Association of Employers' Associations', set up by disaffected Lancashire and Birmingham manufacturers in December 1915, and the Employers' Parliamentary Association, which dated back to the 1911 National Insurance Act. It also tried to absorb the British Manufacturers' Association (B.M.A.), another Docker product, based in Birmingham, which had been set up in 1914 as a protectionist lobby organisation.[19] Other active manufacturers' groups included the British Engineers' Association, an organisation for promoting exports formed in 1912, and the British Electrical and Allied Manufacturers' Association, founded in 1911 by Hirst and others.[20] The manufacturers' groups were hostile to the chambers of commerce, whom they suspected of being soft on tariffs because of their high merchant membership, and they quickly began to manoeuvre for direct access to government, using parliamentary and political connections to help them.

Though fearful that Tariff Reformers were using businessmen to forward their case, Liberal ministers were anxious to please the business groups. They tended to respond more directly to the chambers of commerce, which were longer established. In early 1916 McKenna promised state aid to traders after the war; Runciman, sharing a platform with Bonar Law at the Associated British Chambers of Commerce, agreed with his

[18] John McDermott, ' "A Needless Sacrifice": British businessmen and business as usual in the First World War', *Albion*, xxi (1989), 263–282; ' "Total" War and the Merchant State: aspects of British economic warfare against Germany, 1914–1916', *Canadian Journal of History*, xxi (1986), 61–76. See also Jonathan S. Boswell and Bruce R. Johns, 'Patriots or Profiteers? British businessmen and the First World War', *Journal of European Economic History*, xi (1982), 423–445.

[19] A fuller account of these organisations is in John Turner, 'The Politics of Organised Business in the First World War', in John Turner, ed., *Businessmen and Politics* (London: Heinemann Educational, 1984), pp. 33–49.

[20] R.P.T. Davenport-Hines, 'Trade Associations and the Modernisation Crisis of British Industry, 1910–1935', in H. Yamazaki and M. Miyamoto, eds, *Trade Associations in Business History* (Tokyo: University of Tokyo Press, 1988), pp. 205–226.

colleague that 'security must be regarded as even greater than opulence'; Montagu told a Cambridge audience that 'We in the past treated all nations as nearly as we could equally. But look back at the history of this war, and see the use Germany made of her trade, and just ask ourselves the question whether we can ever afford or dare to let that happen again?'[21] Although none of this amounted to a commitment to tariffs, it was a clear message that Liberal ministers were not prepared to rebuff the business pressure groups, even though there was no shortage of ideological ammunition on the Free Trade side from such fresh publications as J.A. Hobson's *The New Protectionism*, which appeared in July. The principal occasion for making concessions was the Paris Economic Conference, where the British negotiators were an ideologically balanced team of Crewe and Bonar Law. The Paris Resolutions fell short of a *Zollverein* for the Allies after the war, but by setting out a staged plan for applying sanctions against Germany after the war they did represent an Allied commitment to preventing Germany's economic recovery. Britain's acceptance of the resolutions, qualified by an agreement that the purposes should be obtained using whatever fiscal policy each country saw fit to adopt, became the government's commercial policy; and so it rested for more than twelve months after the conference in July 1916.

Asquith responded to the Paris Resolutions by setting up the Balfour of Burleigh Committee on Industry and Trade after the War, which became the focus of parliamentary and lobby pressure over tariffs. The committee itself was balanced politically, including Hewins and Lord Faringdon[22] as Conservatives, Alfred Mond, Lord Rhondda and J.A. Pease as Liberals, George Wardle for the Labour Party and Richard Hazleton for the Irish Nationalists. The chairman, who pointed out that he had been a member of nine Royal Commissions since 1874, was a Unionist Free Trader who had been ejected from the Conservative Cabinet in 1903. He warned at the beginning that 'some people might attribute to me an undue adherence to special fiscal doctrines'.[23] The committee co-opted the chairmen of a number of Board of Trade industry committees which had been set up by Runciman earlier in the year, and set to work.

In the long run, the Balfour of Burleigh Committee was of limited significance for economic policy. Its final recommendations for restrictions on post-war trade were overtaken by events: the United States government flatly refused to co-operate in international post-war arrangements

[21] McKenna at the A.B.C.C., 28 Feb. 1916, *Liberal Magazine*, xxiv, 72; Bonar Law and Runciman to the same audience, 19 Apr. 1916, *ibid.*, 166; Montagu at Cambridge, 19 Feb. 1916, *ibid.*, 68.

[22] Faringdon was a banker, stockbroker and railway director. He had close links with Dudley Docker.

[23] First Meeting of the Committee on Industry and Trade after the War, 25 July 1916, P.R.O., Board of Trade Papers, BT 55/8.

based on the Paris Resolutions, and at the end of the war the German economic threat seemed so small that it was not allowed to stand in the way of restarting international trade.[24] It also spent much time and paper on well-known lost causes such as decimal coinage and standardisation of measures. But as a catalyst for political developments, it was of high importance. It was the first policy committee to listen systematically to organised interest groups; it was an important practical link between Tariff Reform activists and business pressure groups; and it crystallised a view of economic policy which its Liberal members shared with the Conservatives.

The committee began its work under the cooling shadow of the Asquith Coalition's 'Reconstruction Committee' a committee of ministers which the prime minister had set up in March 1916 to co-ordinate investigations about post-war reconstruction. The Reconstruction Committee established non-ministerial sub-committees which occupied themselves with examining a range of social and economic problems including health and education provisions. It quite deliberately worked through existing government departments, and its sub-committees and working groups tended to contain strong representation from civil servants and tame experts.[25] Characteristically, the Reconstruction Committee's contribution to Balfour of Burleigh's terms of reference was to soften them by removing any mention of a policy for Britain which would 'render it independent of foreign supplies'.[26] Moreover the committee was given a secretary from the Board of Trade, Percy Ashley, who took extensive 'guidance' from the Permanent Secretary, Sir Hubert Llewellyn Smith. At first the permanent officials tried to control the committee by rationing its information. Ashley and Llewellyn Smith denied any knowledge of memoranda on the Paris conference which would contain 'the considered opinion of the Board' on its outcome.[27] But it was too much to expect that such an emotive subject could be cooled by these tactics; moreover Percy Ashley was the brother of the protectionist economist W.J. Ashley, and his undoubted professional objectivity and discretion was tempered by his great familiarity with the arguments and interests of the protectionists. The second meeting of the Balfour of Burleigh Committee duly produced heated argument about post-war policy towards Germany and the concept of an 'essential industry'.[28]

[24] See the discussion in Peter Cline, 'Winding Down the War Economy: British plans for peacetime recovery, 1916–19', in Kathleen Burk, ed., *War and the State*, pp. 157–181.

[25] See the discussion of the education group, 'essentially a small, select official group', in Sherington, *English Education*, pp. 59–61.

[26] Vaughan Nash (secretary to the Reconstruction Committee) to Balfour of Burleigh, 4 July 1916, BT 55/8.

[27] Percy Ashley to Llewellyn Smith, 22 July 1916, 26 July 1916, *ibid*.

[28] Minutes of Second Meeting, 17 Aug. 1916, *ibid*.

Both businessmen and Tariff Reform politicians on the committee saw the danger that official and Liberal instincts would smother an aggressive trade policy. Hewins had recently explained to the National Women's Unionist Association that '... the military wrecking of Germany would not be enough. You have to do it economically.';[29] and the business committees which had been examining individual industries had for the most part mandated their chairmen to press for post-war restrictions on German economic revival. Hewins, with some help from Faringdon, resisted Balfour's chairmanlike instinct to defer consideration of the trades' committees reports until the relevant ministries had been consulted, threatening that '... the Committee might lay itself open to criticism if more rapid progress ... was not made on arriving at some definite conclusion'.[30] Even so, there were important differences between Faringdon and Hewins. The former was prepared to press for post-war import prohibitions but not to endorse a general tariff as a permanent policy. The trades committee chairmen were also more circumspect about a general tariff than they were about specific and temporary protection: they were particularly annoyed at a report from the War Trade Intelligence Department suggesting (rightly, as it turned out) that the German economy would be unable to compete in the immediate post-war period.[31] Tariff Reformers outside the committee were alarmed. John Gretton warned Hewins about Faringdon:

> You must remember that he is by training and experience a financier with large interests abroad under his care. A tariff is essentially a manufacturer's proposition, and it therefore seems time to call the producers to your support. Would Dudley Docker's thousand pounds be any use to you?[32]

Parliamentary discord in the autumn of 1916 inflamed the discussion of post-war policy. Apart from the Nigeria debate, raised largely by Bonar Law's Conservative opponents,[33] Tariff Reformers put forward an awkward motion on 14 November about the domestic food supply, which was an opportunity to snipe at various failings in the government's control of shipping and raw materials, and also to raise questions about imperial preference. The proposers were Hewins and De F. Pennefather, an active member of the U.B.C. and of the Associated Chambers of Commerce,

---

[29] Address, 13 July 1916, Hewins Papers, 24/163.

[30] Fourth Meeting, 15 Sept. 1916, BT 55/8.

[31] Memo. by H.W.C. Davies, discussed in Fifth Meeting, 12 Oct. 1916, *ibid*.

[32] Gretton to Hewins, 13 Oct. 1916, Hewins Papers 60/146. The Docker reference is presumably to the £1,000 subscription put up by each founding member of the Federation of British Industries; see Turner, 'Politics of Organised Business', p. 37.

[33] Discussed in Chapter 3, pp. 114–115, 128.

with a record of Tariff Reform publications.[34] While the B.E.A. and the
B.E.A.M.A., now joined by the British Empire Producers' Association,
kept up their propaganda about post-war trade, and Conservative politicians encouraged the diversion of businessmen's profits into quasi-political
bodies such as the London Imperialists, there was steady pressure on the
Balfour of Burleigh Committee to incorporate the pressure groups directly
into policy-making, so that the government could work closely with business interests. At this point the cross-currents of opinion and interest became so complex that the trade warriors were temporarily thwarted by
official (and Liberal) inertia.

The rapid and well-funded advance of the Federation of British Industries (F.B.I.) seemed at first to promise greater business influence in
policy-making. The organisation's director, Roland Nugent, was a former Foreign Office official with experience in commercial matters. With
Docker and Caillard, who were the leading spirits on the federation's
council, he was determined to create a single-minded business organisation with authority to speak for business to government. To this end he
arranged a merger between the F.B.I. and the Employers' Parliamentary
Association (E.P.A.), which took effect in January 1917, and set about 'to
manoeuvre the Associated Chambers [of Commerce] into the position of
being regarded as a representative body of Merchants, and us into the position of being a representative body of Manufacturers . . . '.[35] He advised
former colleagues in government that ' . . . it would be a great mistake
to ignore the [Trade] Associations which, as a general rule, are far more
active and powerful bodies than Chambers, at any rate as far as industrial interests are concerned'.[36] He wrote directly to Lloyd George with
a list of manufacturers' concerns, and promised the F.B.I.'s co-operation
in resolving them.[37] He won a degree of recognition from the Balfour
of Burleigh Committee, which heard him, with Caillard, expound the
F.B.I.'s post-war recommendations on 15 February.[38] This activity staked
out a large claim by an important interest group.

As an exercise in manipulation it was frustrated by deep divisions in the
'business interest'. The F.B.I.'s merger with the E.P.A. had frightened off
a number of Lancashire members of the E.P.A., who believed it would
create a pro-tariff body; Sir Charles Macara, a founder of the E.P.A.,
noisily resigned. To placate those Free Traders who remained in the
merged organisation, F.B.I. officials launched a questionnaire survey of

---

[34] *H.C. Debs*, 5s, 1916, lxxxvii, 14 Nov. 1916.

[35] Nugent to Docker, 15 Jan. 1917, University of Warwick Modern Archives Centre, FBI Papers
FBI/D/Nugent/2.

[36] Nugent to W. Spens (Foreign Trade Dept), 13 Jan. 1917, *ibid*.

[37] Nugent to Lloyd George, 15 Jan. 1917, *ibid*.

[38] Eighteenth Meeting, 15 Feb. 1917, BT 55/8.

their members, hoping to develop a policy which would be acceptable because it would at least appear to have risen spontaneously from the grass roots. At the same time they bickered with the British Manufacturers' Association, whose effective leader was now George Terrell M.P., in the hope that some common action could be taken even though 'they are virtually a Tariff body and we are not.'[39] A meeting of manufacturers' organisations on 20 March made little difference. Nugent briefed Caillard, who was to represent the F.B.I., that the B.M.A. had been 'trying to steal our thunder for some time, and this *must* be put an end to, or they may develop into a serious nuisance'.[40]

As a result, what Professor Cline has described as the producers' 'most direct and extensive opportunities for participating in post-war planning for production and its circumstances'[41] were squandered. In early 1917 there was no single manufacturers' view, let alone a 'business view' which would subsume the desires of manufacturers, merchants and bankers alike. The most vociferous political friends of business were associated with Tariff Reform, and occupied a pivotal position in the Balfour of Burleigh Committee. There they forced the pace, encouraging a reluctant chairman to write to Lloyd George in January recommending imperial preference, albeit in rather weak terms.[42] But the fragmentation of business interests gave their opponents plenty of leverage, even on the committee. The Caillard–Nugent evidence was particularly revealing. Hewins coached his witnesses through an explanation of their recommendation for a central selling agency or export combine which would mimic German methods of overseas trade, then continued:

Q. Would you think it possible to form that sort of combination if you leave the other branches of your policy unaffected?
A. No, certainly not. I think it would be absolutely impossible.
Q. It must be part of a great national economic policy?
A. Certainly.
Q. Otherwise it would have no chance —
A. None whatever.

And so the F.B.I. witnesses marched into a rather obvious trap set by Wardle, whose Labour instincts were all for Free Trade.

Q. I presume you would regulate prices?
A. There must be a regulation of prices if you come to a general selling agency . . . .
Q. I presume therefore that if you had foreign selling in a collective way, it would develop into home selling in a collective way?

---

[39] Nugent to Docker, 1 Mar. 1917, FBI/D/Nugent/1.
[40] Nugent to Caillard, 20 Mar. 1917, FBI/D/Nugent/2.
[41] Cline, 'Winding Down the War Economy', p. 167.
[42] Fifteenth and Sixteenth Meetings, 1 Feb. 1917 and 2 Feb. 1917, BT 55/8.

A. I should think it very probably might.

Q. In that case you would also have power to fix prices at home —

A. Yes.

Q. Do you think that this is a power that can be safely left in the hands of a federation of manufacturers?

A. I think quite.

Q. You do think so?

A. I do not think it has ever acted in restraint of trade so far ...

This answer, which was probably unrivalled in the annals of official inquiries until the benefits of coal-dust to miners' lungs were expounded to the Sankey Commission, did not convince. The confidence of Liberal and Labour members of the committee was further eroded when Caillard and Nugent called for legislation to make 'the ordinary objects of associations such as the regulation of prices and output become legal objects, [so that associations should consequently be] able, as in Germany, to enforce their rules in this respect upon their members.'[43]

Noises off from squabbling manufacturers' associations, and the leaked knowledge of the Balfour of Burleigh Committee proceedings, warned the opposition front bench that the defence of Free Trade might acquire political salience once more. In January Sir Charles Henry, a Liberal M.P. who (with Churchill, Handel Booth, Sir Alfred Mond, Sir J.H. Dalziel and six other Liberals associated with the Liberal War Committee) had voted against the government during the Nigeria debate, set out with Sir Edward Goulding, an old Tariff Reform hand, to rally Liberal support for the Paris Resolutions and imperial preference.[44] Lloyd George airily assured C.P. Scott that a deviation on Free Trade would not break up the Liberal Party.[45] McKenna was still trying to curb the activities of the Free Trade Union, which threatened to embarrass the party leadership. By mid-February Henry had collected 14 names, which, though hardly enough to rock the Liberal Party, was quite enough to cause a damaging row if the planned deputation to Lloyd George were undertaken.[46] The confidence of the Liberal ex-ministers was shaken by the Indian Cotton Duties debates, not least because of the evidence that the bulk of the parliamentary Liberal party seemed indifferent to the underlying principle. Montagu began to distance himself from his colleagues on the issue. In

---

[43] Evidence 18, Questions 558–581, in BT 55/10. For a discussion of price-fixing arrangements before 1914 and of the anomalous legal status of trade associations, see John Turner, 'Servants of Two Masters: British trade associations in the first half of the twentieth century', in Yamazaki and Miyamoto, *Trade Associations in Business History*, pp. 176–178.

[44] Henry to Goulding, 22 Jan. 1917, Hewins Papers 64.

[45] *Scott Diary*, 26 Jan. 1917, p. 257.

[46] Goulding to Bonar Law, 16 Feb. 1917, B.L.P. 81/3/10. The members concerned were Sir John Bettell, Sir Edward Beauchamp, J.A. Bryce, W.H. Cowan, Sir Eustace Fiennes, Ellis Griffith, Sir Hamar Greenwood, Sir Charles Henry, Sir George Croydon Marks, Sir William Pearce, Sir Herbert Raphael, Sir Joseph Walton, Ivor Wason, and Sir Ivor Herbert.

May Asquith's colleagues set up a committee to shadow the Balfour of Burleigh Committee, recognising at last that although the tendency of every other reconstruction sub-committee was acceptable to Liberals, the trade warriors were in the ascendant there.[47]

Within the government, Free Trade was embattled. The arrival of the Dominion prime ministers in London in March was the occasion for setting up a committee on the 'Non-territorial Desiderata of Peace', consisting of Milner, Henderson and the Dominion representatives. Milner wanted Hewins to attend as an adviser, but Henderson temporised and only consented on condition that J.M. Robertson, a Liberal M.P. who had written on Free Trade, was brought in as a counterweight.[48] Since the committee had many other things to do, such as deal with an embryonic League of Nations proposal, Henderson's touchiness on the issue is notable. Soon afterwards Long was to be found pressing Balfour to set up a department of economic policy in the Foreign Office by taking over the staff of the Tariff Commission; and although this did not happen immediately, the eventual establishment of the Department of Overseas Trade, a joint venture between the Foreign Office and the Board of Trade, saw another known Tariff Reformer, Arthur Steel-Maitland, installed at its head.[49]

Although politicians' sensitivities were most easily aroused by discussion of tariffs, the businessmen involved in reconstruction committees had a wider repertoire of policy expedients. One of the most controversial was the British Trade Corporation (B.T.C.), invented by the Board of Trade committee on Financial Facilities for Trade after the War under the chairmanship of Lord Faringdon. The corporation was designed to answer one of the common demands of organised business groups, for a source of capital for export projects. The committee which devised it comprised a number of bankers and industrialists with pre-war links to Business Leagues as well as the Tariff Reform movement, of whom the most prominent were Dudley Docker, Rupert Beckett, a banker and a member of the family which owned the *Yorkshire Post*, and Huth Jackson, also a banker. The committee had large ambitions. They sought a Royal Charter for the new body, and an annual payment of £25,000 from public funds for commercial intelligence work. They collected a list of subscribers who together were expected to put up £1 million, and who included a large number of the bankers and armaments manufacturers subsequently involved in the British Commonwealth Union or the 'Cellulose Scandal'. They suggested that members of the board of directors (which was to include many of their own number) would participate as bankers, drawing bonuses for good performance and enjoying the opportunity to act as

[47] McKenna to Runciman, 23 May 1917, Runciman Papers WR 161/1.
[48] Milner to Hewins, 18 Apr. 1917, Hewins Papers 64.
[49] Long to Balfour, 16 May 1917, Balfour Papers B.L. Add. MSS 49777.

agents for the companies supported by the corporation. They drew upon the weight of polemical evidence, much of it supplied by themselves or their companies, which attributed Germany's export achievements to close co-operation between bankers and industry. Their scheme was disclosed to the world in May 1917.[50]

With such a provenance the content of the report was not surprising. Nor was the parliamentary opposition, which came from a mixed bag of Liberals and Unionists, mostly with banking connections, who feared the appearance of a privileged competitor.[51] After substantial amendment the charter was granted and the B.T.C. began operations in July. Its activity during and after the war was exotic in the extreme: most of its business was done on the periphery of revolutionary Russia, with anti-Bolshevik regimes, and it surrendered its charter in 1926, after passing its dividend in each of the previous five years.[52] As an example of the trade-warrior mentality it could hardly be bettered, and its rise and fall were determined by the unwillingness of the Foreign Office after the war to give it the official support which to Docker and his friends was the prerequisite of national economic success. Its gestation, however, gives a rather different insight into the making of policy in 1917. The charter was put forward with considerable force and enthusiasm by Sir Albert Stanley, the President of the Board of Trade, who was briefed on the merits of the proposal and the weaknesses of the opposition. Officials in the Board of Trade put up no significant opposition to the scheme, and provided a brief in its defence. Llewellyn Smith even collected details of Sir Frederick Banbury's own business ventures to confirm that the B.T.C. directors would not be taking unprecedented privileges.[53] The scheme failed at the first parliamentary attempt because Stanley was not in the House and the Whips could not guarantee a Government victory in a division; Austen Chamberlain was called in to defend the government's position but had not read the charter until he was sitting on the front bench at 4.30 in the afternoon. Bonar Law, whose sole contribution from the Treasury had been to challenge the proposal for a guaranteed government payment for commercial intelligence, was unrepentant, especially after

[50] Faringdon's exposition to the Balfour of Burleigh Committee, Thirty-first meeting, 10 May 1917, BT 55/8; Parliamentary discussion 17 May 1917, *H.C. Debs*,5s, 1917, xc, 17 May 1917, cols 1835 ff.; list of subscribers and other details in BT 13/83/1. On the cellulose affair, see D.C. Coleman, 'War Demand and Industrial Supply; the "dope scandal", 1915–1919'.

[51] Opponents included Clifford Cory (Lib.) and J.T. Walters (Lib.), but also George Faber (Con.), who was Rupert Beckett's brother-in-law and partner in Beckett & Sons of Leeds, as well as Sir Frederick Banbury, the member for the City of London, who was opposed to almost everything on principle.

[52] Its business is described in Davenport-Hines, *Dudley Docker*, pp. 142–148.

[53] H.A.P. to Llewellyn Smith, 23 May 1917, BT 13/83/1.

learning the proposed remuneration terms for directors.[54] Without trying to obstruct the proposal, senior ministers were not obviously willing to push forward such a scheme of government–business co-operation even when Commons objections were obviously self-interested. Part of the explanation was the Treasury disdain of which Docker and his allies were wont to complain; part of the explanation was simple muddle; but it is also apparent that the elaborate committee structure which seemed so porous to business interests did not in fact give them direct access to the influence which they so badly wanted.

Uncertainty of direction was the hallmark of policy on the Paris Resolutions. The War Cabinet at first gave little attention to Balfour of Burleigh's interim recommendations for imperial preference and import restriction. Mond, who had left the committee on appointment to the ministry, urged Lloyd George in February to have a discussion among ministers since he thought that Liberal members, who he believed had changed their minds about free trade in response to the evidence they had heard, would want a chance to inform and persuade their colleagues.[55] Despite the intermittent parliamentary discussion provoked by events such as the Indian Cotton Duties debate, imperial preference was left to the Imperial War Conference. There was no discussion at the heart of government and consequently no action. The U.B.C. became agitated and urged Bonar Law in July that 'the stability of our present relations with our Allies depends upon action on the lines of the resolutions passed at the Paris Economic Conference and the Imperial War Conference, and [the U.B.C. is] not satisfied that the work of inquiry and investigation now carried on by so many committees will lead to tangible results in the near future'.[56] Part of the trouble was that the Reconstruction Committee gave no strategic guidance to its sub-committees; nor had it laid down a timetable of work. The resolution of this problem was imminent, but hardly to the liking of Hewins and his colleagues.

The great ministerial reshuffle of July 1917 brought economic policy once more to the fore, but only by accident. As described above, the origins of the reshuffle were complex; its important outcomes were to get Carson out of the Admiralty, where he was ineffective, and to get Addison out of the Ministry of Munitions to make way for Churchill.[57] The corollary of these moves was that Carson was found a place in the War Cabinet, which helped reassure his back-bench supporters that he had lost no influence, and Addison went to a newly formed Ministry of

[54] Chamberlain to Bonar Law, 18 May 1917, B.L.P. 81/6/18; Bonar Law to Chamberlain, 20 May 1917, B.L.P. 84/6/85.
[55] Mond to Lloyd George, 27 Feb. 1917, L.G.P. F/36/6/12.
[56] Hewins to Bonar Law, 5 July 1917, Hewins Papers 65.
[57] See above, Chapter 5.

Reconstruction. Addison was extremely cross about this move — 'a day in which a bomb fell not only into my own career but into the Ministry of Munitions and the Government generally' — and tried without success to stipulate for membership of the War Cabinet. Instead he got the right to reorganise the Reconstruction Committee and a rather ambiguous mission to encourage departments to undertake reconstruction enquiries.[58] The U.B.C. was horrified at all the new appointments, and commented to Bonar Law that Addison was 'not a suitable person to put in charge of the Reconstruction committee', apparently on the grounds of his presumed Free Trade 'predilections'. The upshot was a heated deputation which Bonar Law skilfully cooled down by making a veiled threat of resignation and a restatement of the government's post-war economic policy. His exposition did not please Hewins, who simply disbelieved the assertion that the government was doing the best it could by resolving to denounce the Most Favoured Nation agreement with Germany. Hewins's view, so far as it can be inferred from his correspondence, had already moved on to a desire to see preparations being made for a peace conference in which tariffs or other trade barriers could be used as bargaining counters against Germany.[59] The same view was apparently held in the British Empire Producers' Association, who saw Addison's appointment as 'a means of delay, & whittling down of any Preference policy . . . '.[60]

It is possible to discern at least four strands in debate about post-war economic policy in mid-1917. One is straightforward protectionism, espoused by the U.B.C. and by many of the most vociferous businessmen engaged in the reconstruction dialogues. The second is a hope that the threat of a post-war trade war would encourage Germany to make terms sooner rather than later. This was often introduced as a supporting point to the first, but it was in fact a free-standing policy which was adopted for a while by the government's Economic Offensive Committee (E.O.C.), set up by the War Cabinet on 20 August.[61] A third strand to be found is the comprehensive government–industry co-operation favoured by Docker, the F.B.I. and by the sponsors of the British Trade Corporation. A fourth, which eventually triumphed by default, is a concern for the stability of international trade in conditions of shortage which would certainly occur at the end of the war even if Germany was thoroughly beaten. Many policies could serve more than one of these aims. Professor Cline has observed that the bodies set up by government — the Economic Offensive Committee and the Economic Defence and Development Committee (E.D.D.C.)

---

[58] Addison Diary, 17 July 1917, Addison Papers 98, and agreement between Addison and Lloyd George, *ibid*.

[59] Hewins to Long, 24 July 1917, Hewins Papers 65.

[60] Sandbach Parker (B.E.P.O.) to Hewins, 30 July 1917, *ibid*.

[61] W.C. 223, 29 Aug. 1917, CAB 23/3.

which superseded it in June 1918 — embodied the second strand and moved on to the fourth. He makes the important point that senior ministers had no great confidence in an economic offensive as a means to win the war, but were in due course persuaded that the maintenance of controls would be necessary to ensure British access to raw materials after the war (rather than to deny German access).[62] The ministers most concerned, Addison at Reconstruction and Carson, who became chairman of the E.O.C., were persuaded earlier than most that there would be no specifically German threat at the end of the war. They therefore found themselves at cross-purposes with the raw protectionists such as Hewins but also with the active businessmen such as Docker, Faringdon and the couple of dozen industry and banking representatives who populated the Board of Trade committees. The two latter groups very often wanted the same institutional changes as Carson and Addison wanted, but wanted them for different reasons and therefore lost their enthusiasm rather earlier as the climate of war began to change.

This diversity of purpose, only partly recognised by Tawney and Cline, goes some way to explaining why official policy towards tariffs, post-war economic policy and the role of business groups emerged fitfully and in a different form from anything originally wanted by any of the participants. The first casualty was the Board of Trade's Imports-Exports bill, which was introduced in November 1917. This would in effect have prolonged the existing restrictions on trading with the enemy into the post-war period, by giving the Board of Trade control over exports. It was resisted by a combination of businessmen who disliked control and Liberal M.P.s who were by then convinced that protectionists had a stranglehold over government which had to be broken; and it was withdrawn. The contrasting experience of the Petroleum bill, the Non-Ferrous Metal Industry bill, and the Trading with the Enemy (Amendment) bill, all presented at about the same time, is instructive. Each of these bills was passed comfortably. All of them offended *laissez-faire* doctrine, and the Petroleum bill in particular, which expropriated mineral rights for the state so that they could be granted under licence to oil companies, shook Coalition Liberals in their loyalty. Richard Denman, Prothero's Parliamentary Private Secretary, resigned because he was criticised for disloyalty in objecting to the scheme, observing as he went that 'If anything could make attractive to me the position of a lapdog trained to wag its tail at all ministers, to sit up and swallow whatever food any of them may offer, it would be the fact of its being associated with personal service to yourself...'.[63] There was even some Conservative opposition from those who thought the government

---

[62] Cline, 'Winding Down the War Economy', pp. 169–178.
[63] Denman to Prothero, 5 Nov. 1917, Bodleian Library, Denman Papers, 1.

should work the oil itself rather than 'encourage exploitation by the Oil Kings'.[64] But in the absence of a comprehensive business coalition against the bill, it passed even in the restive House of November 1917. Of the other two bills mentioned, both concerned specific trades,[65] whose members largely welcomed them, and proposed merely to exclude Germans from participation after the war. No general tariff protection or state intervention was envisaged, and both bills passed. The Imports-Exports bill was held up until the end of the war, when it was quietly abandoned.[66]

Although a business Coalition could come together spontaneously in the Commons to resist change, no such coherence seemed to be possible behind any positive move. In November the U.B.C. set up new sub-committees to discuss 'Industry and Trade' and 'Finance', but they were frustrated by the lack of official action on which to comment. The theme of official action, pushed ahead in some part by Addison's activity as Reconstruction Minister, was towards control of raw materials and to the reorganisation of the Board of Trade to resemble more closely the Ministry of Commerce for which business groups had long been pressing, but both these developments were bemired in committees, leaving the pressure groups with little foothold. Control of raw materials occupied the attention of the Economic Offensive Committee and led to discussions about an Imperial Mineral Resources Bureau, but even when the 1918 Imperial War Conference took the matter up in June 1918 the purpose and scope of this body was still undefined. The tariff question, above all, remained unresolved. Carson was one of many politicians who took the view that 'the more we keep off the old controversy & make a start from "the lesson of the war" the better.'[67] When the 'old controversy' did come up in 1918, with Long's intervention in the pre-election campaign in favour of imperial preference, it was hurriedly shooed back into its kennel by Addison and Lloyd George. Open discussion of tariffs as an essential part of peacetime economic development awaited the parliamentary discussion of safeguarding in late 1919.

Of the commonest non-Tariff demands of business pressure groups, questions of consular and Board of Trade reform were met by the establishment of the Department of Overseas Trade in October 1917. This organisation, subject to the dual control of the Foreign Office and the

[64] Ormsby-Gore to Milner, 1 Nov. 1917, Milner Papers 372. At least one prominent 'Oil King', Lord Cowdray, was a Liberal.

[65] The Trading with the Enemy (Amendment) bill was concerned with German banking business in Britain.

[66] On the parliamentary atmosphere in November, see above, pp. 238–242. Compare the interpretation in this paragraph, emphasising the importance of party coherence, parliamentary organisation and interest coalitions, with Cline's emphasis on the popularity of anti-Germanism in 'Winding Down the War Economy', pp. 170–171.

[67] Carson to Gwynne, n.d., (1918?), Gwynne Papers 17.

Board of Trade, was welcomed by some businessmen, notably Lord Faringdon, who had chaired the committee which investigated the question
in 1916. Others, including Docker and Pennefather, who had submitted
minority reports, outspokenly condemned it.[68] The issue of a new ministerial structure was discussed by Haldane's Machinery of Government
reconstruction sub-committee. Subject to considerable pressure from suspicious civil servants, and disposed for their own reasons to be distrustful of
business interests in government, the members of the committee compre-
hensively rejected the idea that organised business should play a decisive
role in economic policy through access to a Ministry of Commerce and
its committees. In its dismissal of any such notion, the committee's report raised many of the questions which historians have asked about the
wartime relationship between organised interests and the state:

> What is aimed at is that the control and regulation which becomes necessary should
> be exercised virtually, not by a Ministry which would be specialised, competent, and
> expert, and able to safeguard the interests of the community as a whole; but by the
> influence of dominant corporate bodies representing either employers or workmen,
> upon a ministry which, it is asserted, ought to represent 'Industry' and could be
> made to express the views of 'Industry' (or of the particular industry concerned),
> as against those of the rest of the community. If we maintain that the supreme
> function of Government, and of every Minister, is to assert the common interest of
> the community as a whole, it seems indispensable to . . . negative the proposal for a
> Ministry which would actually represent the interests of those engaged in industry,
> whether employers or employed . . . . [69]

Although the Board of Trade did make small changes after the war, such
as the appointment of an advisory committee of businessmen which was
to be consulted at the President's discretion,[70] the intrusion of organised
business groups into policy-making was successfully resisted.

LAISSEZ-FAIRE AND THE IRON AND STEEL INDUSTRY

There were, nevertheless, signs by the end of the war that the state had integrated business organisations into the implementation of policy. This was
done because the aims of the Ministry of Munitions, the Board of Trade
and the Ministry of Reconstruction, and later the Ministry of Health, were
clearly unattainable without the assistance of non-governmental organisations. Much of the partisan energy of business groups was channelled into
doing the government's work, and without making any commitment to

[68] Davenport-Hines, *Dudley Docker*, pp. 134–137.

[69] *Report of the Committee on the Machinery of Government P.P.* 1918 Cd. 9230, xii, I, pp. 46–47.

[70] This had been suggested by a Board of Trade committee of businessmen chaired by Sir Clarendon Hyde (a colleague of Lord Cowdray in the Pearson civil engineering/oil conglomerate) and
published as the *Report of a Committee appointed to consider the Question of the Reorganisation of the Board
of Trade*, P.P. 1917, Cd 8192.

the political objectives of the business groups themselves, ministers and officials controlled events in what they conceived to be 'the common interest of the community as a whole'.

The incorporation of organised business groups as agents of policy rather than makers of policy was particularly favoured by the Ministry of Munitions in its labour relations, and as such is addressed below. But in trade matters both the Board of Trade and Addison's Reconstruction Ministry took initiatives which harnessed business energies to a post-war policy which resembled in kind but not in degree the state-backed trade war recommended by the Docker group. The emergence of a clear view among permanent officials was an important catalyst for change. In March 1917 Percy Ashley contributed a passage on trade combinations to Stanley's speech to the Associated British Chambers of Commerce.

> Combination must be met by combination. This involves a departure from our traditional habits and possible modification of the general state attitude towards industrial combinations.[71]

Over the next few months most of the industry committees set up by the Board of Trade reported. Their specific recommendations reflected the prevailing opinions, and often divisions of opinion, in the industries from which their members were drawn. Thus the Coal Committee rejected all forms of control and tariffs and confined itself to demanding a relaxation of the requirement that mine-owners should pay compensation for subsidence, while at the other extreme the Electrical Trades Committee wanted a full-blown anti-alien policy: prohibition of imports of enemy goods for three years, high import duties, regulation of enemy investment in electrical enterprises within the Empire, prohibition of dumping, a requirement that government departments, public bodies and companies supplying electrical energy under statutory powers should accept only British tenders for the supply of equipment, and safeguards to prevent national assets passing into 'alien hands', besides the usual demands for export finance.[72] These were by now the commonplace demands of the business lobby.

The Scoby-Smith Committee, on the iron and steel trade, was predictably among the most interesting. It recommended an ore-buying syndicate with government and private capital, and an export sales organisation. A large majority of the members wanted tariff protection, backed up as usual with imperial preference and anti-dumping measures, and recommended that the industry's trade associations and trade unions

---

[71] Ashley to Llewellyn Smith, 17 Mar. 1917, BT 13/75.
[72] Report of the Coal Committee, 25 Apr. 1917, in BT 13/76/1; of the Electrical Trades Committee, 18 Apr. 1917, in BT 13/89/7.

should be given legal powers to impose collective agreements on their respective members. The rationalisation of plant into more economic units
was commended. The fate of this report was almost a parable of industry–
government relations in the last years of the war. The report itself was
accompanied by a trenchant catalogue of Sir Hugh Bell's dissenting opinions. Bell, a Middlesborough ironmaster of impeccable Liberal credentials,
was opposed to almost every one of his colleagues' prescriptions, including
rationalisation and even the extension of consular services. He questioned
the propriety of using the taxpayers' money for 'any purpose' connected
with the support of the steel industry, and laid about the protectionists.

> There have been fifteen Parliaments since 1852; of these four have given majorities
> to the Conservative Party — some of which have been substantial. We [he was
> supported on some questions by J.E. Davison] submit that it would be the height of
> impropriety to seek to reverse the considered policy of more than two generations
> except after the most careful consideration and investigation . . . . It is quite impossible
> to conduct such an investigation while we are still in the state of excitement and anger
> which the bloodiest and most destructive war ever fought has inevitably produced. It
> should certainly not be begun as the result of an enquiry of the character conducted
> by this Committee, from whose deliberations all broad aspects of the case have been
> almost necessarily excluded.[73]

The interim report lay in the Board of Trade's files until the Reconstruction Ministry was set up. In July, members of the committee were
informed that their report would not be published because of the 'international political position'; a shorthand for fears about American and French
reactions.[74] A divided report, which did not precisely match the moment,
was best shelved.

Addison's new ministry, after considerable delay, recognised the government's interest in negotiating with 'General Standing Committee of
Employers representative of the Iron and Steel Trades', a body set up
by trade associations in the industry under Scoby-Smith's chairmanship.
The circumstances were telling. After the Economic Offensive Committee had laid down very broad lines of policy for raw materials control,
the Reconstruction Ministry set up the Central Materials Supply (C.M.S.)
Committee, under the same Clarendon Hyde who had chaired the committee on Board of Trade reorganisation. The C.M.S. committee was
interested in supplies immediately after the war, and wanted to deal with
representative organisations of manufacturers and traders. Hyde disclaimed
any interest in high policy or in tariffs.[75] He favoured discussions with

[73] Interim report, 31 Jan. 1917, BT 13/76/1.

[74] Draft letter to members of the committee, 10 July 1917, *ibid.*

[75] He was almost certainly a Free Trader by inclination, or so it would appear from his contributions
to the Balfour of Burleigh Committee and the Iron and Steel Trades Committee's 1916 discussions;
see BT 55/24.

authoritative representative bodies such as the F.B.I. and was dismissive of smaller self-appointed bodies such as the British Empire Producers' Organisation.[76] As the War Office supplied names of representative organisations known to its Contracts branch, so the Hyde committee collected information on employers' associations more generally.[77] After this material had been digested Addison began to approach trade associations to urge them to combine and strengthen themselves to assist the government.

The idea of an ore-buying combine, for example, had been accepted by the Board of Trade in January 1917, before the interim Scoby-Smith report had been submitted.[78] But it was only after a laborious evolution that the proposal emerged in a form which the Reconstruction Ministry would acknowledge. In October 1917 Percy Ashley pressed in Stanley's name for sections of the trades committees' reports 'which do not deal with matters of Government policy' to be published, and included raw materials buying among such items, together with education, apprenticeship, and standardisation of measures. The ministry noted that everything on his list except combines should be published, with the proposals for buying and selling combines held back until the Hyde committee had considered them.[79] The practical possibility of setting up such bodies in the steel industry was at last addressed in May 1918 when Addison met a representative of the National Light Castings Association (N.L.C.A.) — representing manufacturers of guttering, drainpipes and manhole covers — and agreed that it would be possible to 'form one body to deal with industrial and commercial questions in this industry'.[80] On 23 May Addison and G.H. Roberts, the Minister of Labour, spoke to a large meeting of steelmakers and urged them to form a comprehensive and representative association in the industry, and when it was set up, in July, Addison invited it to send a representative to the C.M.S. Committee. He also asked Scoby-Smith explicitly 'what branches of the Industry were represented in the Central Committee [of the I.S.T.C.] and in connection with which I could look to them for guidance and assistance.'[81]

The final act was to bring representatives of all industries together and involve them in a Priority Committee. This took place on 2 August, with

[76] Memo. of a conversation on 21 Nov. 1917 by C. Sandbach Parker (Secretary of B.E.P.O.) with corrections by Hyde, P.R.O. RECO 1/362.

[77] Wintour to Addison, 12 Sept. 1917, RECO 1/360; 'Memorandum on Industrial Combinations (with special Reference to the United Kingdom) and Legislation relating thereto' n.s. printed for the Reconstruction Ministry, Nov. 1917, RECO 1/376. The latter paper was probably written by John Hilton, author of the Reconstruction Ministry's later *Report on Trusts and Trade Combinations*.

[78] Ashley to Llewellyn Smith, 12 Jan. 1917, BT 55/9.

[79] Ashley to Vaughan Nash, 10 Oct. 1917, RECO 1/255; Nash to Addison, 10 Oct. 1917, *ibid*.

[80] Memo. by P.W. Barter of conversation between Addison and Mr King of the N.L.C.A., 8 May 1918, RECO 1/418.

[81] W. Thorneycroft to Vaughan Nash, 17 July 1918; Barter to M.H. Deakin (secretary of the I.S.T.C.) 7 Aug. 1917; Addison to Scoby-Smith, 13 Sept. 1918, all RECO 1/729.

about 100 manufacturers present, including two representatives from the F.B.I. Addison's line at this meeting was to explain to the representatives that there was going to be raw materials control, and that it was up to them to put forward names to be part of a standing committee which would judge priorities. This came as a considerable surprise to the assembled businessmen, who fell to discussing how much control there should be. The F.B.I. representatives took the view that 'while there can be little doubt that a certain measure of control, and the adoption of a system of priorities in certain directions is inevitable, it is most important that control shall be discontinued at the earliest possible moment.' They therefore wanted to get involved with the machinery of control instead of arguing about its essential merits. Addison, however, was firm. The standing committee would contain five government representatives, four or five manufacturers and two merchants; it would be a quasi-judicial, not a representative body; and the state, not the industries, would decide on the necessary measure of control.[82] As negotiations continued, the official position became clearer. A War Cabinet committee under Walter Long authorised the Reconstruction Ministry to set up a Central Raw Materials Board, and the ministry proposed a titular board consisting of five ministers with a body of assessors comprising civil servants and trade association representatives. This arrangement, which further reduced the standing of the trade associations, was approved by the War Cabinet in October.[83]

The striking feature of the Hyde committee's discussions and of Addison's use of them in 1918 was that the Reconstruction Ministry had recognised that control and co-operation in product and raw materials markets had to be accompanied by the same measure of control in dealings with labour. Addison's conception of the iron and steel organisation included all the wage-bargaining functions of a pre-war employers' federation. This had the attractions of logic: labour costs were an important part of manufacturing costs, and if efficiency was to be achieved by mitigating competition for other resources such as raw materials, it made good sense to regulate inter-firm competition over wage rates. Employer organisation at the industry level would also make it possible to deal more effectively with trade unions organised at the industry level. The Reconstruction Ministry was backing the development of Whitley Councils for industrial relations (discussed below), and wanted to see effective and responsible bodies represented on them. But logic had an uphill struggle against the conventions of the industry, which told in favour of separating 'commer-

[82] Memorandum by Sir Herbert Rowell and P.W. Rylands, 2 Aug. 1918; Rylands to Addison, 2 Aug. 1917; Addison to Rylands, 7 Aug. 1917; Rylands to Addison, 8 Aug. 1917, all in F.B.I. Papers, S/WALKER/112/4.

[83] Minute by H.W. Garrod (Ministry of Reconstruction) 20 Sept. 1918, RECO 1/408.

cial' from 'industrial' functions. In this sense the ministry was clearly ahead
of most business opinion.

Moreover, the Reconstruction Ministry's view of industrial combination, which was enshrined in its own reports and in a the work of its
Standing Committee on Trusts set up principally to examine the impact
of price combinations on the public interest, was very far from subservient
to businessmen's views or interests.[84] Combination was to be an instrument of economic policy, and therefore subject to public controls. The
Ministry of Reconstruction believed that the post-war economy would be
unstable, and did not believe that businessmen would of their own volition
do what was necessary to defend it. Addison and his advisers implicitly
doubted the F.B.I.'s assumption that combinations would not act in restraint of trade. His desire to see strong representative bodies reflected the
administrative convenience of dealing with a single agent; it did not mean
handing policy over to the interests concerned. Although a strong business
lobby had emerged during the reconstruction discussions, the tables had
been turned on the representative associations which had led it.

LAISSEZ-FAIRE AND SHIPS

A contrasting example is the case of shipping. Shipping and shipbuilding
were two mainstays of the pre-war British staple economy. Like all the
other staples except textiles, they were essential to a war economy. Moreover, shipping became controversial because of allegations of profiteering,
and shipbuilding was one of the industries whose productivity and labour
troubles caused anxiety to both the wartime Coalition governments. The
two industries, inevitably interdependent, were capital-intensive and per-
ilously exposed to the world economy. Although most of the leading
figures in both industries were known Free Traders, their objection to
tariffs was not matched by squeamishness about other forms of protection,
or anti-competitive practices. The major shipping lines were all involved
in international price-fixing.[85] The major shipbuilding companies had
close relations with the shipowners which certainly interfered with free
competition, though these arrangements were not always harmonious;[86]
much of the shipbuilders' business before the war had been with the Admiralty, which provided a comfortable return on capital though it was not
until after the war that the Shipbuilding Conference managed to suppress
price competition in naval work. Neither industry could ever ignore the

---

[84] *Report of the Committee on Trusts*, *P.P.* 1918, Cd. 9236, xiii, 789; papers of the Standing Committee, set up under the Profiteering Act, in BT 55/55. The Standing Committee was quickly sidetracked
into minor investigations during 1919.

[85] *Report of the Select Committee on Shipping Rings*, *P.P.* 1909, Cd. 4668.

[86] See e.g. P.L. Robertson, 'Shipping and Shipbuilding: the case of William Denny and Brothers',
Business History, xvi (1974), 38–39.

state, nor the state these industries; and the maintenance of control after the war was highly contentious, involving some powerful personalities. The outcome was a rapid decontrol which did neither industry any good, even though both had demanded nothing else throughout the war.

Runciman's Board of Trade, which was often attacked for its tenderness to profiteering shipowners, had realised in 1916 that the position of shipping and shipbuilding after the war would be difficult. The precise nature of the difficulty could not be predicted: perhaps great merchant losses would lead to excess demand for ships, perhaps the renewal of German competition would put pressure on both shipowners and shipbuilders, perhaps the restriction of trade would create a glut in the market. A departmental committee under Alfred Booth of Cunard, and including both shipowners and shipbuilders, was set to work in early 1916, along with the other committees noted above. By November 1916 it had become quarrelsome, and the shipbuilders demanded their own committee; but by then a clear line had emerged in an interim report. A Board of Trade official summarised this disdainfully as 'strafe the Germans and leave us alone', and went on:

> Both of these things are excellent things in their way, but if it should not be practicable to hamper the Germans as much as is hoped, the mere policy of leaving British shipping absolutely free to develop on its own lines will not carry us very far, and will not be much protection against foreign competition. Unless some measure of co-operation amongst British shipowners can be brought about, no real advance can be made. Of course, any such advance will be exceedingly difficult to effect, and it is very doubtful whether this particular committee can help very much in this direction.[87]

For the remainder of the war the Board of Trade, the Ministry of Shipping, and the Ministry of Reconstruction laboured in vain to persuade the industries to co-operate among themselves and with one another. The most extreme form of persuasion was the proposal to nationalise shipping, contained in a paper put to the War Cabinet in June 1917.[88] This alerted the shipowners, who presented themselves as a deputation on 13 July to demand guarantees against nationalisation, and to protest that the policy of building standard ships, to economise on labour and materials in the shipyards, produced a merchant fleet which would be unsuitable for postwar use. Here at least was the basis of a discussion about post-war policy, but the two sides were still far apart. In November the War Cabinet recommended that shipbuilding should be controlled for three years after the war, to secure the supply of ships to replace neutral losses (which the

[87] C. Hipwood, 'Minute on the Interim Report of the Committee on Shipping and Shipbuilding after the War', 11 Nov. 1916, BT 13/86/3.
[88] 'Shipbuilding Policy', G.T. 1407, CAB 24/20.

government had promised) and ensure that the right sort of ships were
built for the 'public interest'. This was promulgated to a background of
'grave anxiety' from the Booth Committee about merchant shipbuilding.[89]
The shipbuilders were by now very anxious about post-war competition,
and lobbied Lloyd George to protest that government yards being laid
down to build standard ships would compete with private yards after the
war.[90]   The Ministry of Reconstruction tended to favour a policy of
prohibiting shipbuilding for neutral owners, but this was rejected by the
Booth committee when it reported in January 1918.[91] The general tenor
of the report was hostile to the government's stated policy, and by the
beginning of 1918 tension between government and the industries was
running high.

There was more to this than disagreement over the details of post-war
shipping control. The shipowners were a small and articulate group. Although they were somewhat cantankerous they knew each other well and
many of them had a longer experience in public life than most businessmen. A number of prominent politicians had shipping links, including,
for example, R.D. Holt, an Asquithian Liberal and a Liverpool shipowner,
Walter Runciman, and Alexander Shaw. One of their most prominent
spokesmen was Lord Inchcape of P. & O., whose objections to state control had been well known since he had signed a hostile reservation to the
Selborne report on food production; while negotiating with the government about shipping he was conducting a fierce polemical campaign in
the press against all forms of state intervention, during and after the war.[92]
His energy and money, along with Lord Cowdray's, would be laid after
the war at the disposal of Anti-Waste politics. The shipbuilders were more
numerous, and lacked a trade association which might have lent coherence to their activities, but there was considerable overlap between the
traditionally merchant yards and the armaments firms such as Vickers and
Armstrongs. It was through this overlap that the Shipbuilding Employers Federation was brought into contact with the British Commonwealth
Union to take up an explicitly anti-Labour and anti-state position in the
spring of 1918.[93] The result was a tenacious hostility to any form of state
control which was resistant to argument and blandishment because it did
not depend on the specific predicament of the industries, but on more
general ideological commitment.

---

[89] Memorandum by the Committee on Shipping and Shipbuilding, n.d., BT 13/79/2.

[90] Untitled brief to the Prime Minister, by Cecil Harmsworth, 11 Oct. 1917, L.G.P. F/233.

[91] Full report and supporting minutes in RECO 1/281. Correspondence between Sir Frank Fielding and Reconstruction Ministry officials over the building prohibition in RECO 1/313.

[92] Stephanie Jones, *Trade and Shipping* (Manchester: Manchester University Press, 1989), pp. 117–
118.

[93] See below, pp. 379–384 and Turner, 'British Commonwealth Union'.

After the Booth report had been made public Addison, Stanley and Maclay, the Minister of Shipping, met representatives of the shipowners and shipbuilders on 14 March 1918. Addison had already accepted the shipowners' arguments that it would be better to release ships from control as soon as possible after the war, though his officials were less impressed by the industries' case.[94] The conference concentrated on shipbuilding rather than shipping control. Both the industries represented urged that controls would be unnecessary. Maclay hedged, promising that the government would consider the matter and give a reply as soon as possible. In the same meeting the shipowners dismissed any argument in favour of maintaining control over tonnage and undertook not to raise existing freight rates if ships were released from controls.[95]

Subsequent developments revealed differences of view on the government side. H.W. Garrod of the Ministry of Reconstruction reflected that the Booth committee

> ...make no attempt to see the dangers of an immediate relaxation of state control. They desire, for example, to have all government-owned ships sold to British shipowners at auction. But it is not suggested that the Government might become the victim in either case of a 'ring'. The Committee, again, feel acutely the shortage of shipping, but it does not occur to them that, in the transition period, there will be a shortage of other things than shipping e.g. raw materials; and that just because of this shortage of raw materials it will be essential to maintain for some time a state-control of shipping...[96]

Garrod continued to press for prolonged control both of shipping and of shipbuilding, urging though that

> ...with regard to the nature of the control, the shipbuilders should be brought to understand that in many particulars this is a question upon which the decision rests with them. The more the shipbuilders are able to achieve what the Government wants by means of Trade Councils, and again the more they are able to establish satisfactory arrangements as to wages and conditions with the Unions, the sooner will the Government be able to efface itself and relax control.[97]

One of his colleagues had already pointed out that shipowners' complaints about shortage of capital after the war were weakened by the high profits known to have been made.[98] These voices were set against Addison's own instincts and the trend of thought in the Ministry of Shipping, some of whose officials were ready to promise an early relaxation of controls on both industries.

[94] Vaughan Nash to Upcott, 4 Feb. 1918, RECO 1/281.
[95] 'Notes of a Conference held at the Ministry of Shipping 14 March 1918', RECO 1/282.
[96] Garrod to Vaughan Nash, 15 Apr. 1918, RECO 1/281.
[97] Garrod to Nash, 2 May 1918, RECO 1/282.
[98] Upcott to Nash, 23 Jan. 1918, RECO 1/281.

An attempt was made to resolve interdepartmental difficulties in May. Stanley wanted to propose a bill which would extend his ministry's shipbuilding powers after the end of hostilities. Without it, they would lapse with the Defence of the Realm Act. Addison, who was being advised by his Permanent Secretary that the shipowners and shipbuilders would be justified in pressing for a promise of early relaxation of controls,[99] suggested that the very minimum of powers should be taken. At a meeting of ministers and officials Albert Illingworth, from a Whip's viewpoint, advised that it would be easier to apply for comprehensive powers than only a few, against which Addison urged that a deal should first be struck with the shipbuilders. The conference agreed to recommend the extension of all powers for a year after hostilities ended, but the interest of its proceedings lies more in two *obiter dicta*. At the meeting Maclay 'thought it desirable not to consult the shipbuilders beforehand but to tell them what had been determined afterwards';[100] and afterwards John Anderson of the Shipping Ministry explained his reasoning to Reconstruction Ministry officials:

> What the shipbuilders fear is that at any time within the next few years we may have a labour government. This government would very likely be pledged at the polls to schemes of nationalization and if they found a system of control of shipbuilding (or shipping) actually in working order they would convert this by easy adjustments into a permanent nationalizing scheme. This being a fixed idea in the minds of the shipbuilders it is probably not possible to make any pronouncement which is likely to reassure them.[101]

The future of shipping and shipbuilding control was still in contention at the end of the war, and became one of the major issues of post-war reconstruction politics. Like many such issues, its outcome depended on international economic conditions which were scarcely imagined during the war, as well as on internal British politics.[102] The significance of this vignette of government-industry relations during the war is more general. Neither government nor the trades were completely agreed on their respective aims. The ministries concerned had different reasons for extending and maintaining control, and were therefore prepared to back away at different points. Their policy was affected hardly at all by a doctrinaire belief in the superiority of state control over *laissez-faire*. While Addison believed in the positive virtues of involving businessmen in decision-making and implementation, Maclay, perhaps more cynical, saw the advantages of taking decisions on his own. The shipowners and shipbuilders, on the other hand, scarcely bothered to consider whether state intervention could

---

[99] Nash to Addison, 4 May 1918, RECO 1/282.
[100] Garrod's account of the meeting in RECO 1/282.
[101] Garrod to Nash, 14 May 1918, RECO 1/282.
[102] See Susan Armitage, *The Politics of Decontrol*, for a full discussion.

help them because they were preoccupied with the larger threat to capitalist society. They were much farther away from the idea of a partnership with government, even an anti-socialist partnership, than the manufacturers of the F.B.I. If they had party-political affiliations, they were Liberal rather than Unionist; their rejection of the government's favoured economic policy was backward-looking. But they, like the protectionists of the steel industry, took full advantage of the government's dependence on them to define the limits of policy at the end of the war.

Educational Reform: the dog that did not bark

Although it very soon fell victim to the parsimonious spirit of the post-war Coalition, the 1918 Education Act was one of the more significant pieces of social legislation to be passed during the war. It addressed a subject which had been of central importance in pre-war politics. It provided for the establishment of a 'national' system of education, by specifying many of the aims which county and county borough councils should have when drawing up education schemes, and it proposed a system of half-time continuation schools in which children aged between 14 and 18 would receive not less than 320 hours of education a year unless they were in full-time secondary education. It deliberately avoided denominational questions, and between its introduction in August 1917 and the Royal Assent in August 1918 significant concessions were made to sectional interests, which reduced both the cost and the social and economic impact of reform. It might therefore appear to have been one of the 'smaller mice' produced by the labouring mountains of reconstruction politics; but its gestation reveals a great deal about the workings of politics and administration during the war.

Geoffrey Sherington has shown that the substance of the 1918 Education Act was derived from proposals made in the Board of Education immediately before the war. The political origins of those proposals had been the Nonconformist grievances against the Conservatives' 1902 Education Act. The collapse of the 1906 Education bill in the Lords had set back Liberal hopes of a rapid resolution of Nonconformist grievances, and it was not until 1911, again under pressure from organised Nonconformity, that J.A. Pease at the Board of Education suggested the lines of a bill which would redeem the Liberals' election pledges. This led to a Cabinet committee under Lord Haldane, which included Lloyd George, then Chancellor of the Exchequer, Runciman, who had just exchanged the Board of Education for the Board of Agriculture, Pease, and Lord Crewe, the Lord President. Haldane immediately began to work with

Board of Education officials to produce a scheme which would increase the quantity and improve the quality of post-elementary education, largely by increasing government grants and rearranging the powers of education authorities; it also took account of 'national efficiency' pressures in proposing an improvement of technical education and a measure of university reform. The draft bill which emerged from the committee's deliberations did not deal with university education, but did encompass reform of the local education authorities and also confronted Nonconformist concerns by encouraging the establishment of more council schools and prohibiting religious tests for head teachers in areas where the only school was a denominational institution. The two latter reforms, taken together, addressed what had become known as the 'single school' grievance, one of the most emotive issues to emerge from the 1902 Act. Unfortunately they were not enough for organised Nonconformity, which enlisted Lloyd George's support. As a result, although the pre-war Liberal government had provided considerable financial help for elementary education and was preparing to spend money on universities, technical education and teacher training as well, it had not, by the outbreak of war, reached agreement about legislative reform of the educational system.[103]

In the early months of war Pease, supported by Christopher Addison who was newly appointed as his Parliamentary Under-Secretary, concentrated on schemes for improving technical education and scientific research as a foundation for industrial and military strength. This idea was as old as Prince Albert, and had resonances in the quality press and the quarterlies. Their proposals, submitted in May 1915, faded with the Liberal government, leaving only the Department of Scientific and Industrial Research as a legacy.[104] Under the new regime Addison moved to Munitions as Lloyd George's deputy and Pease was replaced by Arthur Henderson. Henderson had been appointed to deliver the Labour movement to the Coalition, not to further educational reform, and no initiatives came from the Board until the appointment of the Reconstruction Committee in March 1916. At this point the permanent officials of the Board replied to the committee's circulars by dusting off the 1913 proposals. The Reconstruction Committee accepted this position, but with Haldane's inspiration also set up a sub-committee drawn partly from outside the Board to consider plans for post-war educational developments. It was this sub-committee, under Haldane, which selected as the 'main lines of advance' the establishment of compulsory daytime continuation classes for children between 14 and 18, and substantial improvements in teacher training and teachers'

---

[103] This and the following paragraph are based on Sherington, *English Education*, chs. 1 and 2.

[104] Roy Macleod and Kay Andrews, 'The Origins of the DSIR: reflections on ideas and men', *Public Administration*, xlviii (1970), 23–48; Ian Varcoe, 'Scientists, Government and Organised Research in Great Britain, 1914–1916: the early history of the DSIR', *Minerva*, viii (1970), 192–216.

pay.[105] Public discussion of education now included contributions from the Workers' Educational Association (W.E.A.), which wanted universal free education to 16, and the National Union of Teachers, which wanted a package of measures not unlike the Haldane proposals accompanied by the principle of universal free education as well as large increases in pay. A nascent science lobby had emerged in the form of the Neglect of Science Committee, while the National Education Association was still banging the drum for non-denominational education.

An important characteristic of the Reconstruction Committee was that it was not supposed to do anything: practical work remained the responsibility of departments and their political heads. In December 1916 Crewe, who had in August succeeded Henderson at the Board of Education, was ejected with his fellow Asquithians. His placed was filled by H.A.L. Fisher, vice-chancellor of the University of Sheffield. Fisher's ostensible qualification was that he was a professional educationalist and a Liberal. He had, however, publicly opposed the fashionable cry for an emphasis on science, and in Liberal politics he was an Asquithian, in the sense that he felt a disdain for the methods and character for which Lloyd George was known at the end of 1916. He owed his appointment, though, to his connection with the monstrous regiment of Welshmen which had developed around Lloyd George in late 1916 and which was a sub-group of a coherent body of Lloyd George acolytes, not all of them Welsh, who had been regularly associated with his reform schemes since 1911. Its members included Addison, David Davies, Waldorf Astor and Thomas Jones, an academic who in 1916 was serving as secretary of the Welsh National Insurance Commission.[106] It was Jones who, acting on the advice of Sir Henry Jones (Professor of Philosophy at Glasgow), proposed Fisher's name to Addison. Fisher was soon revealed as a very conservative reformer, very acceptable to the permanent officials and from the first able to command the respect of educationalists in the Labour movement. His views so closely matched those of his officials that he readily brought forward their proposals, which were passed hurriedly by the War Cabinet in February 1917.[107] His first parliamentary speech, promising higher pay and status for teachers, continuation schools, and an expansion of university education, was received with enthusiasm inside and outside the Commons, though it markedly failed to offer any radical change in the existing pattern of education.[108] Fisher could apparently look forward to a smooth passage for his bill.

[105] RECO 1/14, 'Report of Lord Haldane's Sub-committee', n.d., cited Sherington, *English Education*, p. 61.

[106] For further discussion of the coherence of Lloyd George's circle, see Turner, 'Experts and Interests', pp. 217–218.

[107] W.C. 75, CAB 23/1, 20 Feb. 1917.

[108] *H.C. Debs.*, xcii, 19 Apr. 1917, cols 1888–1970.

Nevertheless there were obstacles on the way. More radical reform was espoused by the education sub-committee of the Reconstruction Committee; this was set up in March as part of a reorganisation of the committee, and included Beatrice Webb, Marion Phillips, Seebohm Rowntree and Arthur Greenwood — all Radical, socialist or Fabian — as well as two members of the monstrous regiment, Tom Jones and Professor W.G.S. Adams, head of Lloyd George's private secretariat.[109] The education sub-committee proposed a school-leaving age of 16 followed by half-time secondary schools to the age of 18.[110] At the same time the W.E.A. was proposing its own alternative, and in May held a large conference of trade unionists, W.E.A. members and local authority representatives whose discussion was particularly aimed towards increasing equality of educational opportunity, and against the tendency for the education of working-class children to be seen as a direct preparation for employment.[111] On the other side, the newly formed Federation of British Industries found the economic costs of education a good subject with which to interest its members; the denominational interests woke up; and the Lancashire interest, already embattled because of the Cotton Duties issue, returned to its old concern for the availability of juvenile labour in the textile mills, with support from trade unionists.

The bill itself was introduced in August, but could not pass through all its stages by the end of the session, and therefore had to wait to be reintroduced in a modified form in March 1918. Forces outside parliament worked on it at the end of 1917; parliamentary effort was concentrated on the Second Reading and the committee stages in the spring of 1918. With the known support of the Anglican bishops and the Free Church Council, the Board could afford to be sanguine about the opposition of the Catholic Education Council, which wanted to see Catholic continuation classes, with state support, and thought that any full-time education beyond the age of 14 would be too expensive for poor parents.[112] Industrial interests were less tractable, and Fisher resorted to a speaking tour to overcome Lancashire's objections.[113] Response to his speeches was so enthusiastic that he told the War Cabinet that the industrial lobby was so cowed that it would not openly object to the bill.[114] This proved unduly optimistic, but Fisher's strategy was now to conciliate the denominations by concessions of detail and the education authorities by more explicit commitments to

[109] Dr Marion Phillips was a member of the I.L.P.; Greenwood was then active in the W.E.A.

[110] G.T. 1304, July 1917, CAB 24/19.

[111] Sherington, *English Education*, pp. 101–103.

[112] Catholic Education Council to Selby-Bigge, 26 Apr. 1917, P.R.O. ED 24/705, cited in Sherington, *English Education*, p. 109.

[113] He also went to Bristol and South Wales, where he was enthusiastically received; Herbert Lewis to Lloyd George, 17 Oct. 1917, L.G.P. F/32/1/9.

[114] G.T. 2370, 20 Oct. 1917, CAB 24/29.

respecting the existing powers and duties of the authorities. In this form the bill was discussed in the 1918 session.

Fisher's parliamentary position was strong because he could count on support from the Conservative leadership, and a benign indifference from most of the Conservative back bench.[115] Some trouble was of course expected from Sir Frederick Banbury, and duly came.[116] But with consistent support from Coalition Liberals and from the majority of Conservative members, including some such as Lord Henry Cavendish-Bentinck who generally took the side of Liberal or progressive Labour amendments, Fisher could be sure of winning any division on a substantive part of the bill. On matters of detail he was more vulnerable. The County Councils Association, for example, had a powerful advocate in Henry Hibbert, Unionist M.P. for Lancashire Chorley, who attracted support from other Lancashire M.P.s, Conservative, Liberal and Labour, for curtailing the hours required to be spent in continuation schools. Fisher had to concede, explaining that the opposition of Lancashire's Labour members, in particular Snowden and Clynes, made it tactically unwise to hold out for his original scheme.[117] Hibbert was a particularly effective — and lucky — lobbyist. As chairman of the Education Committee of Lancashire County Council he was trying to extend the local authority's role in secondary (full-time) education, and had had to win local support from employers and trade unionists alike. His attitude to the bill was governed by a desire not to jeopardise the gains he had made, and he was able to use his established connections as the basis of a parliamentary coalition. His position was rather different from that of Basil Peto, a businessmen with civil engineering and mining interests, who overtly wanted to maintain a docile juvenile labour force; Peto was in turn somewhat at odds with the F.B.I., whose 'Parliamentary Committee' was active in debates on the bill and met frequently in March 1918 to co-ordinate its tactics. While Peto was almost completely reactionary, the F.B.I. committee was divided, as it was on labour questions generally, between those who welcomed ameliorative social reform because it would improve the quality of the labour force and those who were more worried about short-term costs.[118] The F.B.I. position, as set out in its January 1918 *Memorandum on Education* and in the parliamentary interventions of its supporters, was a half-acceptance of Fisher's ideas which characteristically asked that the F.B.I.'s local organisations should be recognised as competent to be represented on local

---

[115] See Kevin Jefferys, 'The Educational Policy of the Conservative Party, 1918–1944', University of London Ph. D. thesis, 1984, ch. 2.

[116] *H.C. Debs*, civ, 13 Mar. 1918, cols 430–435.

[117] Fisher to Gilbert Murray, 8 June 1918, Fisher Papers 7.

[118] Jefferys, ch. 3, *ibid.*; Minutes of the Parliamentary Committee, F.B.I. Papers C/19.

education authorities. This was not a text on which to go to the barricades, and it readily succumbed to Fisher's tactical compromise.

As an example of social legislation, touching many aspects of national life and affecting the interests of workers and employers, the history of the Fisher Act tells a revealing tale. Despite a wealth of public comment about education during the war, it was devised in an intellectual climate which owed its shape to pre-war discussion and pre-war positions. The appearance during the war of new institutions such as the Reconstruction Committee and its sub-committees did not, in the event, deflect the Board of Education from its determination to carry through a systematic but small reform of the system put in place by the 1902 Act. The war rhetoric which supported it was cast in very general terms by Fisher, and owed little to the 'national efficiency' school of thought; specifically, it rejected any close connection between education and military strength. Education's role in the economy was at least as much to restrain social passions as to enhance productivity: Fisher told the F.B.I. that he hoped the education system for working-class youth would ' ... fill their minds with something like humane letters, or elements of science' and thus 'get a humane outlook throughout all the country and ... industrial relations more intelligently discussed'.[119] Correspondingly, little support is offered for the view that economic interest groups, especially those of a 'social-imperialist' persuasion, had a strong purchase on policy-making. A plurality of interests, some new but many old and familiar, competed for the Board's attention; the outcome was shaped by all but determined by none of them. In so far as there was a modernisation crisis, the experience of educational reform illustrates part of the explanation for it: a richly complex pre-war polity easily digested the temporary passions of the war and produced a result which fell far short of reformist aspirations.

Employers and Labour

It is a commonplace, but no less true for that, that during the First World War 'the Government found that it *needed* to recognize the labour movement as a force in the land in virtually all areas of State activity.'[120] Many of the important consequences of this need are reviewed in earlier chap-

---

[119] Notes of a deputation from the Federation of British Industries, 6 Feb. 1918, ED 24/657.

[120] Chris Wrigley, 'Trade Unions and Politics in the First World War', in Ben Pimlott and Chris Cook, *Trade Unions in British Politics* (London: Longman, 1982), p. 79. Wrigley's studies, in *David Lloyd George and the British Labour Movement* (Hassocks: Harvester, 1976) and 'The First World War and State Intervention in Industrial Relations' in Chris Wrigley, ed., *A History of British Industrial Relations. Volume 2* (Hassocks: Harvester, 1987), form a benchmark for all subsequent work on wartime industrial relations and the state.

ters: the entry of Labour politicians into both Coalition governments, the wariness which all wartime governments felt about introducing conscription and changing working practices, the careful trimming of the Lloyd George Coalition's expressed war aims in January 1918 to suit the language favoured by organised labour. Trade union leaders were also consulted formally by government departments over the implementation of a wide range of industrial legislation, so that by the end of the war it could be said without irony that trade unionists were 'allowed to give — like the clergy in Convocation — not only their votes as citizens but also their concurrence as an order or estate.'[121] Their new status recognised the rapid increase in trade union membership, from just over 4 million in 1914 to more than 6.5 million at the end of the war. The trend was not irreversible, for trade union influence and membership both waned swiftly during the post-war slump after 1921. Nevertheless, the rise of trade unionism as an extra-parliamentary political force seems to parallel, even outshine, the rise of the Labour Party in parliamentary politics.

Of course it was not so simple. The incorporation of trade union hierarchies into government committees had its political costs, of which the greatest was a heightened tension between trade union leaders and their members on the shop floor. Moreover the steady advance of trade union committee-men was contested by government departments, politicians and employers' groups who were, together, able to put strict limits on the concessions made to labour during the war. Neither higher living standards, nor control of the labour process, nor control of the labour supply were willingly granted to organised labour. Employers and government were always aware that peace would bring a renewal of pre-war industrial conflicts, and therefore tried to make sure that nothing done during the war would fundamentally weaken their position. In the event the slump did more harm to trade unionism than anti-labour politics could ever do, but pessimistic employers could not foretell the future. Competition with the labour movement stimulated employers to improve employers' organisations for wage bargaining, strengthen collaboration with government departments, and put time and money into political fringe movements. Extending the boundaries of the state to include labour and employers, the 'tripartitism' which Keith Middlemas in particular has seen as the means by which politicians marginalised the extremes in British politics, led in practice to robust conflict as much as to consensus.

The need to incorporate trade unionists and employers together in negotiations about wages and the labour process was felt early in the war. In December 1914 and January 1915 talks between engineering employers

---

[121] Sidney and Beatrice Webb in the 1920 edition of *The History of Trade Unionism* (London: Longman, 1920), p. 635.

and the Amalgamated Society of Engineers failed to solve the problem of labour shortage created by the rapid increase of War Office orders. The employers' desire, shared by the Board of Trade, was for an immediate relaxation of the workshop rules which before the war had given skilled craftsmen some control over the labour process in the engineering industry.[122] When the unions refused to agree to this, or to any relaxation of current overtime limits and the prohibition on non-union labour, the secretary of the Engineering Employers Federation, Allan Smith, asked the War Office to ban strikes and restrictive practices. This was declined.[123] Soon afterwards, though, at the instance of the Board of Trade, the Cabinet set up the Committee on Production to investigate the obstacles to increased munitions product After reporting on the detailed problems of labour supply — which included competitive bidding for labour by firms contracted to different government departments — the Committee on Production was converted on 24 February 1915 into an arbitration body for disputes arising on government work.[124] Meanwhile the lines on which labour agreements would be negotiated in the future were being laid down. To the background of an engineering strike on the Clyde, the Committee on Production issued four reports which called for relaxation of restrictive practices, matched by promises by the employers to revert to normal practices after the war. A specific agreement was ratified by the A.S.E. which allowed semi-skilled workers to work on shell fuses. In March Lloyd George negotiated the more comprehensive Treasury Agreements with a number of unions, of whom the A.S.E. was the most important but also the most reluctant. The basis of the Treasury Agreements was that trade unions would abandon strikes and submit disputes about working practices to arbitration, while the employers would accept a limitation of profits; and the main sticking point in getting union agreement was that the restrictions on profit seemed extremely lax.[125] The government's main interest was in continuity and economy of production, and to get continuity it was important that the arbitration system was recognised by the workers.

To this end the National Advisory Council of Labour (N.A.C.), consisting of union representatives drawn from the pre-war Industrial Council, was established to advise the Committee on Production and to act as a buffer between the committee and discontented unions by 'advising'

[122] *History of the Ministry of Munitions* (London: H.M.S.O.) I, Part 2, 37–47.

[123] Correspondence in MUN 5/8/171.

[124] The committee consisted of Sir George Askwith, the Industrial Commissioner at the Board of Trade, and civil servants from the Admiralty and the War Office. See Wrigley, *David Lloyd George*, pp. 94–97 and the *History of the Ministry of Munitions* I, Part 2, 146–154.

[125] Firms were to lose 80% of their 'excess' profits, the standard of calculation to be the three pre-war years which had in fact been prosperous for the engineering industry. All overheads arising from war work, and all capital expenditures, were allowed against the extra profits.

unions before they submitted cases to the committee. Significantly the A.S.E., which had been sticky about the Treasury Agreements, preferred to deal independently with the ministry.[126] It very soon extended its role in two ways. On the one hand, the Committee itself was a ready source of advice for the Ministry of Munitions (when it was set up in June 1915) about any issue concerning labour relations. Its advice was not always heeded, but it could and often did indicate the best way to persuade the trade union movement to accept a policy on which the ministry was decided. On the other hand, it set up a local organisation of advisory councils which worked with local arbitration committees in much the same way as the N.A.C. worked with the Committee on Production. These local advisory councils were further drawn into the management of labour relations when the employers on the government's Armament Output Committee pressed for local joint committees of employers and workers.[127]

The collaboration of national and local trade union leaders in the relaxation of workshop restrictions was emphasised in August after the failure of the War Munitions Volunteer scheme. This had been an attempt to increase the mobility of skilled labour by enrolling volunteers who would get union rates and conditions and a subsistence allowance if they worked away from home; it had not worked because there was an absolute shortage of labour. Lloyd George and Addison, his Parliamentary Secretary, went to the N.A.C. and told them that the scheme had failed and that there was now no alternative to the 'dilution' of skilled labour by female and semi-skilled workers brought in to do repetition work. Then, as Dr Wrigley has eloquently put it, 'the N.A.C. took it upon themselves to organise dilution'.[128] Lloyd George had made it clear that compulsory direction of industrial labour was the only alternative. Members of the N.A.C. made up the union side of the Central Munitions Labour Supply Committee (C.M.L.S.C.), whose chairman was Arthur Henderson, and the N.A.C. urged its local committees to co-operate, much as it had urged them to support the War Munitions Volunteer scheme. Although the A.S.E. maintained its practice of negotiating separately with the minister, it subscribed to the detailed regulations for dilution when the C.M.L.S.C. produced them in September 1915. But the A.S.E. leaders had been more reluctant to endorse them because their members, the most skilled of the organised groups within the industry, had most to lose.

During the winter of 1915–16 the government enforced dilution in the munitions factories by a mixture of negotiation and outright coercion.

---

[126] The Industrial Council was a body of employers and workmen set up by the Board of Trade before the war which could offer arbitration if the two parties to a dispute wanted it.

[127] Allan Smith at the Armament Output Committee, 20 Apr. 1915, MUN 5/7/171.

[128] Wrigley, *David Lloyd George*, p. 139.

After making highly visible concessions to grievances over the cost of living in the Rent Restriction Act, and cosmetic changes to the Munitions Act after lengthy and well-publicised discussions with the A.S.E. and the other unions, Lloyd George set about enforcing dilution in the engineering shops of the Clyde, which had long been recognised by the Ministry of Munitions as the hardest nut to crack. As described above[129] this task was undertaken with some skill and considerable ruthlessness. The shop stewards on the Clyde Workers' Committee were isolated in a dispute which was called on very limited grounds — the suppression of a newspaper and the restriction of a shop steward's right to organise his fellows — rather than the more popular and generally contentious issue of the cost of living. A.S.E. members were the pillars of the strike, but their Executive Committee did not support it. The government's subsidiary purpose in confronting the C.W.C., in fact, had been to strengthen the official trade union movement against the shop floor, so that the leaders, with whom the Treasury Agreements and other national and local agreements had been negotiated, could continue to make bargains which their members would keep. This was in the government's interest; it was also in the employers' interest, and the interest of the trade union hierarchy. After the spring of 1916, with the dilution programme in full swing and before the manpower shortage of the following summer had intervened to put further pressure on the labour market, the labour policy of the Ministry of Munitions looked successful. With the leading trade unions accepting both military conscription and dilution Lloyd George, who had championed both these causes, could feel content; and the employers who were given considerable support in their efforts to improve productivity could look to the government for continued help.

But it was in the summer of 1916 that a convulsion within the Engineering Employers' Federation (E.E.F.) revealed the strength of discontent on the employers' side. A Glasgow employer, J.R. Richmond, threatened to resign from the Federation because of 'the supine and inactive policy of the Federation during the past two years... [and] its failure to educate Government and public opinion in order to counteract the activities of Trades Unions....'. The occasion was a press announcement that Henderson was to be appointed head of a Labour Advisory Department.[130] In view of the regular meetings between Lloyd George as Minister of Munitions and the representatives of the E.E.F. and the Shipbuilding Employers' Federation (S.E.F.), the existence of the Armaments Output Committee where the leading contractors met civil servants to overcome restrictions on the supply of labour and raw materials, and the number of business-

---

[129] In Chapter 2, pp. 107–108.

[130] Minutes of the Emergency Committee, Warwick University Library, Modern Archives Centre, E.E.F. Papers, Minute Book 12.

men working as temporary civil servants in the Ministry of Munitions —
who far outnumbered trade unionists — this might seem unconvincing,
but it was deeply felt. The Birmingham Association of Engineering Employers supported Richmond's call that Allan Smith should withdraw in
protest from all government committees, and pressed for the federation to
'endeavour to have a representative in the House of Commons'.[131] The
two factors most likely to have stirred up this discontent were the general
politicisation of business during 1916, discussed above, which was centred
in Birmingham, and the tightening grip of the Ministry of Munitions'
costing department, whose pricing investigations had substantially reduced
the profits being made on high-volume munitions work.[132] Although the
Ministry of Munitions had created a political storm over its efforts to control the cost of labour and the freedom of workers through the Munitions
Acts, and thereby set its face in public against the interests of the workers,
the unsung achievement of its cost accountants was to redress the balance
somewhat against the interests of the employers.

In the autumn of 1916 the government's labour policy was further tested
by the evidence of an absolute manpower shortage. Military recruitment,
aided by conscription, was stepped up and resulted in shortages of skilled
and unskilled labour. The importation of Irish and colonial labour, and
the use of enlisted soldiers in labour battalions, mitigated the shortage
of unskilled workers on the docks, in building work, and in agriculture.
The only solution to the shortage of skilled labour was to press dilution
further, in particular in the engineering shops. The inevitable resistance,
which was strongest among members of the A.S.E., led in late 1916 to the
institution of the Trade Card scheme which handed over to the unions
themselves the responsibility for determining which workers were entitled
to exemption on the grounds of craft identity.[133] Although the Ministry
of Munitions had little intention of letting matters rest there, and was ac-
tively considering industrial conscription as the Asquith Coalition fell,[134]
the concessions when first made appeared to be considerable, and further
eroded the employers' confidence in the government. Both the newly
established Federation of British Industries and the more experienced Engineering Employers' Federation set about lobbying government for fuller
and more systematic consultations between government departments and
organised employers. They did it in competition with one another, and
disagreed over tactics and even over long-term aims, with the result that
they achieved very little before the end of the war. But their activity at

[131] Minutes of the Emergency Committee, 29 Sept. 1916, *ibid*.

[132] Above, pp. 83–86. See *History of the Ministry of Munitions* Vol. 3, Part 2 for a full discussion of contracts costing.

[133] See above. pp. 128–129 for a description of the scheme and its introduction.

[134] Grieves, *Politics of Manpower*, pp. 63–89.

the beginning of 1917 was the early origin of the National Confederation of Employers' Organisations, set up in 1919, and therefore helped to shape the politics of capital and labour for the inter-war period.

Under the Lloyd George Coalition employers, unions and government raised their eyes from immediate wartime problems and began to prepare for industrial conflict in peacetime. Employers agreed with politicians that the ground was moving beneath their feet and that without positive action the employers' side would suffer at the hands of an insurgent labour movement. Nevertheless, a split between traditionalists in the major employers' federations and innovators associated with the Federation of British Industries proved impossible to avoid. From the first the Engineering Employers' Federation was hostile to the F.B.I., on the grounds that in commercial matters such as price-fixing and combinations the interests of different sections of employers were 'varying and in many cases opposing'.[135] Subsequent friction between the two bodies suggests more deep-rooted suspicions. Under Allan Smith's influence the E.E.F. threatened to boycott the F.B.I. unless it promised to abstain from labour questions, but had to be satisfied with the establishment of a body called the Employers' Advisory Council (E.A.C.) which was sponsored by the F.B.I. but opened its membership only to employers' organisations with no commercial functions.

The F.B.I. agreed in January to withdraw from labour questions, but during the early months of 1917 the E.A.C. was yet another vehicle for its attempts to get itself recognised as the sole channel of communication between government departments and manufacturing industry. Smith, on behalf of the E.E.F., sabotaged this effort. His methods are instructive. He first agreed to join the Employers' Consultative Committee of trade associations summoned by the ministry and led by the F.B.I., but threatened to withdraw from it in June on the grounds that it had too readily accepted the ministry's proposals for concessions to the unions which could be used 'as a springboard for further concessions' after the war. He then negotiated directly with the Shipbuilding Employers' Federation and the larger employers' associations in textiles and steel.[136] His work was rewarded when the Ministry of Munitions reconstituted its Employers' Advisory Committee to consist entirely of members of the engineering and shipbuilding federations and the National Employers' Federation, a Birmingham group which had been formed in 1913 as a common front to deal with the Workers' Union before the war and retained its identity

---

[135] E.E.F. Emergency Committee 28 July 1916, E.E.F. Minute Book 12.

[136] For the Shipbuilders' response, see National Maritime Museum, Shipbuilding Employers' Federation Papers, Executive Board Minutes, 31 July 1917.

during the war.[137] Having persuaded the Ministry of Munitions not to recognise the F.B.I.'s authority, he turned on the F.B.I. itself and with the help of the textile employers, the Steel Ingot Makers' Federation and the National Federation of Building Trades Employers extracted a promise from the F.B.I. officials that they would stand by their agreement of January 1917.[138]

None of this improved the employers' chances of influencing the Ministry of Munitions. The ministry had an elaborate network of consultative committees on every matter from labour relations to contract pricing and supervision. Addison, on entering the ministry in December 1916 had asked his officials to establish formal machinery for consulting employers just as already existed for the trade unions; this led to the first Employers' Advisory Committee.[139] He also maintained, among others, the rather larger Employers' Consultative Committee; a Financial Advisory Committee (chaired by Sir Clarendon Hyde) appointed in March 1917;[140] and the Advisory Committee to the Minister of Munitions under Sir Arthur Duckham, which gave advice *ad referendum* on every sort of point from the use of factories after the war to the reorganisation of the contracts branch. The latter committee was happy to spawn even more committees, such as the committee to advise the head of the Priorities department, which was to consist of 'three men of the highest class of commercial knowledge'.[141] But the minister's attitude to the employers he consulted was fairly cool. When Harris Spencer, the outspoken secretary of the Midlands Employers' Federation, objected to the changes proposed in the 1917 Munitions of War (Amendment) bill on the grounds that his federation did not intend to be bound by agreements on which it had not been consulted, Addison briskly observed that he could not consult every affected party and 'statutes cannot be null and void because of that'.[142] His successor, Winston Churchill, was confronted in his second meeting of the Consultative Committee by a disgruntled Allan Smith who observed that 'our desire is

---

[137] Records of the Employers' Consultative Committee and of the Employers' Advisory Committee are in MUN 5/53 and MUN 5/79. The N.E.F., formerly the Midlands Employers' Federation, was yet another Docker body, but Docker supported many organisations with different and often competing aims. For Smith's correspondence and negotiations see E.E.F. Management Committee Minutes 29 June and 27 July 1917, Minute Book 13 and E.L. Hill to R.T. Nugent, 31 Aug. 1917, F.B.I. Papers D/Nugent/2.

[138] F.B.I. Employers' Advisory Council Minutes, 26 July and 9 Aug. 1917, F.B.I. Papers C/19/48.

[139] Addison to Stephenson Kent, 18 Dec. 1916, MUN 5/53.

[140] John Mann (Assistant Financial Secretary, Min. of Munitions), to Addison, 3 Mar. 1917 and memo. of appointment, 19 Mar. 1917, MUN 4/5326.

[141] Advisory Committee Report, 23 Jan. 1917, MUN 4/437; records of the Advisory Committee are in MUN 4/437 and MUN 4/1250; of the Financial Advisory Committee in MUN 4/5326.

[142] Minutes of Proceedings at a Conference between the Minister of Munitions and the Employers' Consultative Committee, 17 July 1917, MUN 5/53. But 17 July had not been Addison's best day; see pp. 220–221 above.

to assist the Ministry, but our difficulty has been that we, so far, have not been too frequently asked to do so.'[143] Employers were restive in 1917 because they thought they were being ignored, despite the apparatus of committees and councils which was supposed to bring their influence to bear on government.

The existence of the Ministry of Labour, above all, was a focus for grievance. The ministry was notoriously set up as a bribe to the Labour Party, and was considered by almost everyone else, except its ministers and officials, as a hindrance to the establishment of a coherent manpower policy. The Ministry of Munitions, the Shipyard Labour Department of the Admiralty, the Ministry of National Service and the War Office Contracts Branch all tried in some way to make parts of labour policy, resenting the existence of a Labour ministry; meanwhile the ministry complained, with justice, that 'we hardly ever have to bat on any but a spoiled wicket'.[144] In order to do the political job to which he had been appointed, John Hodge, the 'rampaging' first Minister of Labour, openly conceded demands made by the T.U.C. for labour representation on the Committee on Production and on advisory committees to supervise the labour exchanges.[145] The ministry also prepared legislation to strengthen the pre-war trade boards and the Restoration of Pre-war Practices bill, which appeared to enshrine the undertakings made to the labour movement at the time of the Treasury Agreements. While historians are generally agreed that the practical outcome of the ministry's initiatives was very small, it is still important that these initiatives were well publicised in 1917, and were associated with a ministry whose day-to-day work caused a great deal of trouble to employers. By appearing to do a great deal for labour, the ministry appeared to be doing harm to employers' interests, and won itself many enemies.[146]

The alienation of both unions and employers from government grew as the Ministry of Munitions and the War Office put further pressure on industry in response to the manpower crisis and the Ministry of Reconstruction began to develop its own views on industrial relations after the war. The committees advising the Ministry of Munitions resented the confident enthusiasm with which Churchill and his officials took up schemes such as works committees: Smith suggested in November that 'this scheme should be put in a pigeon-hole or somewhere else equally

---

[143] Meeting of the Employers' Consultative Committee, 14 Aug. 1917, MUN 5/79.

[144] Bridgeman Diary, Feb. 1918, *Modernisation of Conservative Politics*, p. 125.

[145] Lowe, *Adjusting to Democracy*, pp. 14–15.

[146] See Rodney Lowe, 'The Ministry of Labour, 1916–1919: a "still, small voice"?' in Kathleen Burk, ed., *War and the State*, pp. 108–134; on the Restoration of Pre-War Practices bill, see Gerry R. Rubin, 'Law as a Bargaining Weapon: British labour and the Restoration of Pre-War Practices Act 1919', *Historical Journal*, xxxii (1989), 925–945.

suitable, and that we should forget all about it',[147] but to no avail. Still worse was the episode of the $12\frac{1}{2}$% bonus. The Commissioners on Industrial Unrest had commented on the grievances of skilled men on time rates who were earning less than the dilutees and semi-skilled men who worked on repetition tasks without the tool-setting skills of the time-served engineers. One of the clauses of the August 1917 Amendment Act, to which Harris Spencer had objected, allowed the Minister of Munitions to set wage rates; and in October the $12\frac{1}{2}$% advance on time-rates was proclaimed. The policy was doubly flawed from the beginning. On the one hand, the scheme disrupted the structure of differentials between pieceworkers and timeworkers, and arbitrarily reversed a policy of moving towards piece rates which had been introduced earlier in the year. The Ministry of Labour and the Admiralty duly opposed it on these grounds. On the other hand, the public face of the scheme was muddled: rather than a straightforward redress of grievances, it was presented as a palliative for the rising cost of living. As a result its extension was demanded as of right by many other groups and the government was forced by degrees to concede it. By 24 January, after a series of damaging strikes which on this occasion were not confined to one or two centres but spread from Scotland to London, the War Cabinet had forced to announce a $7\frac{1}{2}$% increase to workers in piecework or premium bonus schemes.[148]

The bonus strikes gravely damaged the prospects for a successful tripartite relationship between government, employers and labour. The trade unionists who were involved in the various advisory committees consulted by the ministry had been powerless to stop either the policy itself or the angry reaction of the rank and file. The employers were also enraged: they had had to pay the bonus and stand the consequences of the strikes, and they had been ignored when they protested against the policy. As the government's responsibility for wage bargaining had come into greater prominence, they felt themselves the helpless victims of political bargaining. This was most acute when Auckland Geddes, Neville Chamberlain's successor as Minister for National Service, proposed to soften the blow of his new Military Service bill by more rigorous levies on excess profits.[149] This black period of the war was easily remembered afterwards when businessmen of all colours denounced the effects of state control upon industry and industrial relations.

These were black days in other respects for employers' organisations. In the last months of 1917 the pressure on managers was acute: labour shortage and Ministry of Munitions cost control were two arms of a pincer which sometimes squeezed very hard indeed. In July Dudley Docker's

[147] Employers' Advisory Committee, 29 Nov. 1917, MUN 5/53.
[148] Wrigley, *David Lloyd George*, pp. 219–222.
[149] See e.g. W.C. 310, 1 Jan. 1918, CAB 23/5.

Metropolitan Carriage Wagon and Finance Company, the main supplier of tanks, interrupted its production during hard negotiations about the ministry's right to audit its accounts. Other employers also expressed their dislike of being hunted by accountants and held up to calumny for alleged profiteering.[150] In the autumn a number of local engineering employers' associations led by Manchester withdrew their co-operation from the Ministry of Munitions' dilution officers; national officials of the E.E.F. went down at the ministry's request to urge them to relent.[151] Abused for their profits and denied the labour they needed, employers were losing what confidence they had ever had in the government's willingness or even ability to support their position.

It was in this climate that employers' attitudes to the labour movement became sharper and more aggressive. There were a number of strands in anti-Labour politics in early 1918. One of the most novel was the promotion of organisations which denied the relevance of class conflict. Since 1916 the Industrial League and later the National Alliance of Employers and Employed (N.A.E.E.) had been promoting co-operation between capital and labour. The Industrial League first appeared in July 1916: its inaugural meeting, attended by trade union and business figures, was concerned with problems arising from dilution. The National Alliance held its inaugural meeting on 9 December 1916; it was interested in demobilisation problems, and turned its attention to current relations between employers and employed on the formation of the Ministry of Labour. The National Alliance had greater official patronage. Neville Chamberlain chose its Birmingham launch on 20 January 1917 to make the first public announcement of his National Service scheme. It is perhaps a measure of his audience that it greeted this deeply flawed scheme with enthusiasm.[152] Both organisations clearly had a great deal in common, including some common Labour members, with the 'Patriotic Labour' movement which had also appeared in the middle of 1916: the difference between them seems to have been that the Industrial League drew its business supporters more from the British Engineers' Association, while the National Alliance was more closely linked to the Docker group and the F.B.I.[153]

---

[150] Davenport-Hines, *Dudley Docker* pp. 100–101.

[151] 'Minutes of Proceedings of a Conference with the Engineering Employers' Federation on Dilution', 20 Oct. 1917, MUN 5/71.

[152] Grieves, *Politics of Manpower*, pp. 103–104.

[153] D.A. Bremner, the secretary of the B.E.A., served on Industrial League Committees, while Docker and Hiley made a point of being present at the Birmingham meeting of the Alliance and F. Huth Jackson, another Docker associate, was active in its work. Its subscription list later included Docker, the F.B.I., a number of Docker companies, Sir Algernon Firth, Tootal Broadhurst and Company, and Huth Jackson; indeed the overlap with 'Patriotic Labour' at one end was nearly matched by an overlap with the British Trade Corporation (q.v. above, pp. 347–349) at the other. The B.E.A. and the Docker group of businessmen associated with the F.B.I. were not mutually exclusive groupings. On the Industrial League and the N.A.E.E. there is much useful evidence in

The idea that employers and workers could co-operate without the mediation of the state was a powerful one, and found its fullest reflection in the F.B.I.'s 'Committee on Industrial and Commercial Efficiency', which reported in December 1917 and proposed a comprehensive social security system paid for and administered jointly by trade unions and employers. The committee observed that they 'are convinced that no state action can have satisfactory results. One effect of the War has been to cause an almost universal dislike and distrust of State interference, which is always cumbersome, expensive, and irritating.'[154] This report, which caused a good deal of offence to the E.E.F., was of course rich in allusion. The idea of employer-provided welfare as a means of binding the workforce more and more closely to its employers looked back to the 1890s.[155] It was commonly associated with extreme hostility to trade unionism, though trade unions had also resented state interference in their own welfare schemes. The incorporation of trade unions into the F.B.I. scheme undoubtedly owed much to the *de facto* co-operation of trade union leaders, but not shop stewards, in dilution and other measures which had assisted employers during the war. The shared hostility to the state also reflected the tensions of industrial relations during the manpower crisis of late 1917. Here was a reason, if only a negative one, to identify the interests of employers with those of workers.

A very different approach was taken by the E.E.F., which made a study of post-war problems in late 1916 by circulating enquiries to its constituent associations. This initiative owed something to J.R. Richmond's discontented outburst of the previous August, in which he had suggested seeking local associations' views 'as to the means which should be taken to counteract the influence of Trade Unionism in determining the policy of the Government in industrial matters'.[156] Questionnaires were sent out in September, but not all had been returned by the end of March.[157] In the excitement over competing with the F.B.I. for representation at the Ministry of Munitions, Smith and his colleagues seem to have forgotten about their members' views on post-war reconstruction until the autumn, when a summary of responses was presented to the management committee with a 'Memorandum on Post-War Industrial Problems'.[158] Although the E.E.F. had no agreed report of its own, the officials' response to the F.B.I. report was blistering. They objected to the scale of the benefits

---

E.E.F. microfilm papers, O/98–O/101.

[154] 'Report of the Committee on Industrial and Commercial Efficiency', F.B.I. circular (in E.E.F. microfilm papers, F137/148).

[155] See Fitzgerald, *British Labour Management and Industrial Welfare*.

[156] Richmond to Smith, 25 Aug. 1916, reported in E.E.F. Emergency Committee, 29 Sept. 1916, Minute Book 12.

[157] Smith's report to the Executive Board, 30 Mar. 1917, Minute Book 12.

[158] 'Memorandum on Post-War Industrial Problems', Sept. 1917, E.E.F. Papers, I(1)7.

proposed, insisted that the state rather than the employer should bear the burden of sickness, and contradicting the F.B.I. committee's strictures against profit-sharing (which had been used as a disciplinary device in a number of federated firms, especially in the west of Scotland), condemned 'anything which tends to pauperise the workforce at the hands of the employer'.[159] Another section of their reply noted that only very large firms could afford such generous welfare schemes. Instead, the E.E.F. proposed to enter negotiations with the unions on concessions within the accepted limits of industrial bargaining, such as reductions in hours and increases in wages.[160]

This was all arguably a fair reflection of opinions in the engineering and shipbuilding industries, and all relevant to the matter in hand. But the E.E.F. response omitted probably the most important element in the context, which was that since mid-1917 the employers' associations in the engineering and shipbuilding sectors had been trying to create a strong confederation to deal with the feared explosion of labour militancy after the war, and greatly resented the F.B.I.'s attempt to cut across it. This constitutes a second strand in employers' thinking about labour relations at the end of the war. Undermining the F.B.I.'s bid to advise the Ministry of Munitions was only the first step towards a strong labour relations body under the control of the leading employers' organisations. The foundation of co-operation with the Shipbuilding Employers' Federation had been laid in January 1917 by the Marine Engine Builders' Committee of the E.E.F, which decided to approach the shipbuilding employers to discuss 'questions of mutual interest'.[161] Co-operation with the National Employers' Federation was discussed, at the instance as usual of the Birmingham Association, in October 1917. Hostility between the two bodies had been obvious at the Ministry of Munitions Advisory Committee. The N.E.F. in its first incarnation as the Midlands Employers' Federation had in effect been a breakaway group from the Birmingham Engineering Employers' Association, and was formed in 1913 to deal flexibly with the Workers' Union, which was then strong in the Midlands. E.E.F. members noted that they suffered from the effects of sympathetic strikes caused by 'extremely bitter' feelings against N.E.F. firms which did not treat skilled unions with respect or honour the pay awards of the Committee on Production.[162] But the virtues of co-operation were obvious. The N.E.F. agreed in November not to poach members from the E.E.F. and by February 1918 the officers of the E.E.F., the N.E.F. and the S.E.F. had

---

[159] 'Observations', 21 Jan. 1918, E.E.F. microfilm F137/145.

[160] 'Post-War Industrial Problems', 21 Jan. 1918, E.E.F. Papers I(1)12.

[161] M.E.B.C. Minutes, 9 Jan. 1917, E.E.F. Minute Book 12.

[162] Secretary of the Birmingham Federation of Engineering Employers to the Secretary of the E.E.F., 29 Oct. 1917, E.E.F. microfilm papers S10.

agreed to work towards a national confederation of employers' organisations. Powerful personalities were engaged. Smith for the E.E.F. tried to restrict the confederation to labour matters alone, and thus offended Sir George Carter of the S.E.F., whose federation had occasionally acted as a trade association.[163] During the *froideur* Harris Spencer of the N.E.F., under some pressure from Docker, brought about with Smith a fusion between the N.E.F. and the E.E.F. which became official in August.

This merger postponed the establishment of a confederation, but chimed in well with Smith and Docker's other scheme, which was to co-operate in establishing a number of ancillary organisations to fight the labour movement. One of these was the British Commonwealth Union (B.C.U.), which had made little progress since its foundation in late 1916 as the London Imperialists,[164] and badly needed the funds which the three employers' organisations were now prepared to plough into it. The other was the National Stability League, a propaganda and intelligence organisation specialising in engineering labour which had been set up by the F.B.I. in December 1917. This hardening of anti-labour politics reflected the political climate of early 1918. Many of those who had worked for some time on the assumption that the natural community of interest between employer and worker could be the basis of a lasting partnership were bewildered and frustrated by the persistence of strike action. Sir Vincent Caillard, a leading figure in the F.B.I., wrote to the prime minister in January 1918 enclosing papers on industrial unrest which he warned 'are misleading in so far as they imply that the recent strikes have been caused by genuine grievances.... no strike of any importance has occurred for some time that was not organised and led by men connected with revolutionary and anti-patriotic bodies...'.[165]

The hunt for propagandists and subversives was pursued with enthusiasm. The B.C.U. used its new wealth to begin drawing up blacklists of opposition M.P.s to be fought at elections, and searched for 'Patriotic Labour' men who could be subsidised to influence their fellows in a right-thinking direction. The National Stability League, with a subscription list including Docker, the F.B.I., the E.E.F., Vickers Ltd and a number of aircraft firms, also employed agents who proselytised in the

[163] S.E.F. Papers, Executive Board, 26 Mar. 1918.

[164] See above, p. 115 and Turner, 'British Commonwealth Union'.

[165] Caillard to Lloyd George, 19 Jan. 1918, L.G.P. F/6/1/10. Caillard was a director of Vickers Ltd, whose agent Sir Basil Zaharoff was in late 1917 the intermediary for bribes offered to certain Turkish politicians by the British government; this was his occasion for writing to Lloyd George. Caillard had been a Commissioner of the Ottoman Public Debt, and was familiar with corrupt Turkish politicians. Vickers' insight into labour relations can be judged from its contribution to the discussion on drunkenness and output in May 1915, in which a Vickers manager averred that management error accounted for less than 1% of delays in production, and shortage of raw materials about 17%, leaving more than 80% to be explained by drunkenness as a residual category. See Turner, 'State Purchase of the Liquor Trade'.

workshops. These agents were full of reports of subversion during February and March, while the effects of the January 1918 Military Service (Amendment) Act were felt: the Minister of National Service had been empowered to extend the age limits and also, in a separate decision, to issue a new Schedule of Protected Occupations. The War Cabinet, like the employers, were expecting disruption from the A.S.E.[166] In the event there was little disruption because the A.S.E. had taken a position which antagonised the other unions — they wanted to comb out dilutees before skilled men — but also because of the German spring offensive, which radically changed the climate of opinion, if only temporarily. In April a Sheffield agent of the N.S.L. reported that

> Now . . . is the moment for the Employers to deal with Shop Stewards and to prevent their going from one shop to another ostensibly for the purpose of their work but in reality for propaganda purposes. They should be told that they must remain in the shop where their work is. Employers need not be afraid of the Shop Steward's power as hitherto. Now is the time for any firm to get rid of men who are agitators or undesirable in the shop.[167]

Since subscribers to the National Stability League were paying to hear this sort of information, they were no doubt pleased to get it.

Despite Smith's overt hostility to the F.B.I., caused in large part by the simple fear of being superseded as an employers' organisation, the F.B.I. and the leading employers' organisations were in practice co-operating in 1918 in a concerted political attack on the labour movement. This was on the face of it a far cry from the public protestations in favour of employer–worker co-operation which characterised the F.B.I. report of December 1917. But in fact the two were not inconsistent. Both the National Stability League and the B.C.U. on the one hand, and the N.A.E.E. and the comprehensive welfare schemes on the other, were devices to break labour's resistance to capitalism. All the employers concerned in these developments were convinced that the state had either not tried, or tried and failed, to contain the labour movement. A combination of stick and carrot, overt and covert methods, kindness and coercion might redress the balance in the employers' favour. The main weakness in the employers' position, on labour matters as well as on the tariff and trade questions discussed in the previous section, was a tendency to factionalism, well admixed with personal rivalries. Internal dissension within the main employers' organisations had been almost as damaging as competition between them during 1916 and 1917. The minor revolt against Smith in 1916 was matched in the Shipbuilding Federation in 1917 by a move to impose 'well-defined and rigid rules' on members who had been flouting the federation's pol-

---

[166] Wrigley, *David Lloyd George*, pp. 224–225.
[167] 'Report No 735', 10 Apr. 1918, E.E.F. microfilm papers O/092.

icy on negotiations with labour.[168] This remarkable propensity to quarrel lasted until the Armistice and beyond.

The summer and autumn of 1918 were not marked by serious confrontation between employers and workers. This was partly due to the atmosphere of crisis which politicians created deliberately to force through the Military Service Act of April 1918,[169] but also to rationalisation of manpower planning which the Ministry of National Service was at long last able to achieve. Guerrilla warfare between the labour-using departments was almost eliminated, and the demands of the War Office firmly rebuffed. After the first panic, as the battle settled down and British and American forces began to force the German army back, deliberate efforts were made to return skilled men from the army to essential jobs in industry.[170] The transition was not painless: in June and July the so-called 'Embargo Strikes' over the enlistment of skilled workers challenged the government's determination to control the allocation of labour. But these were overcome by a show of determination, accompanied by a direct and successful appeal to the trade union leadership. Lloyd George and Churchill refused to talk to shop stewards, and told the Trade Union Advisory Committee that shop stewards were 'subversive . . . to labour progress'. Barnes urged Labour comrades that 'It will be absolutely impossible for us to maintain trade unionism in this country if this sort of thing is allowed to go on.'[171] The committee urged the militants to return to work; the government threatened to conscript strikers if they stayed out after 29 July; and the strikes were defeated.[172] Although discontent over wages and living standards persisted, the evidence suggests that the shop stewards' movement was in retreat by the summer of 1918, and the employers' effort was accordingly directed to post-war problems.

One important initiative in this direction was the attempt to create an 'industrial party' in the House of Commons. This was the work of the British Commonwealth Union, which set out to canvass potential candidates of all parties about their political opinions, but finally settled on a rushed policy of selecting and subsidising a limited number of sympathisers. They were rather a job lot: most were friends or contacts of the Docker group, fighting seats in the Midlands; some were disgruntled Unionist candidates who found themselves facing couponed Liberals; and the B.C.U. also supported Christabel Pankhurst as a super-patriotic candidate in Smethwick and a Lower Deck candidate for Rochester, as well as a couple of 'Patriotic Labour' candidates.

---

[168] Committee Minutes, 7 May, 4 June, 2 July, 14 Aug. 1917, S.E.F. Papers.
[169] See Chapter 8 above.
[170] Grieves, *Politics of Manpower*, pp. 193–199.
[171] Trades Union Advisory Committee, 25 July 1918, MUN 5/79.
[172] Wrigley, *David Lloyd George*, pp. 228–230.

The B.C.U. candidates joined a parliament in 1919 which hardly needed persuading of the importance of business, and their efforts were subsumed in the general Conservative back-bench distrust of the compromising tendencies of the post-war Coalition. The desire for an independent industrial group was the product as much of impatience — felt particularly by Smith and Docker — as of a rational calculation of political prospects, and even when setting it up some members of the Shipbuilding Employers' Federation doubted 'whether Members of Parliament could ignore their Party Whip'.[173] But as the Parliamentary Industrial Group, the B.C.U. M.P.s were particularly active between 1919 and 1923. Their first leader was Edward Goulding, an old Tariff Reform hand, but in the autumn of 1919 Smith himself entered parliament and undertook the leadership. Smith refused to be associated with protectionism, and led the group as a lobby in favour of state action to relieve employment. In practice this meant subsidies for railway building and electrification, which would provide orders for the firms with which many members of the group were associated. Smith and the group were also involved in the Gairloch conference in 1921, in which the post-war Coalition's policy towards unemployment was partly evolved. So long as Lloyd George was prime minister Smith was tolerated as an adviser and channel of communication, but his relations with Bonar Law and especially Baldwin were poor, and the group correspondingly lost cohesion. For all that, its survivors were still to be seen under the second Baldwin government, when disrespectful young Tories such as Harold Macmillan identified them as the 'forty thieves'.[174]

Another initiative from the summer of 1918 was to engage in preparatory negotiations about post-war conditions with the the trade unions, preferably avoiding both the government and the Labour Party. The leading employers' organisations had taken a cautious view of the reports of the Whitley Committee, which recommended the establishment of a structure of joint councils from works committees to national bargaining councils. Allan Smith had been a member of Whitley's committee — a sub-committee of the Reconstruction Committee — and had supported its reports as far as they reflected existing practice in the engineering industry, but his members were unimpressed. The proposals of the F.B.I. sub-committee did not survive the onslaught of engineering and shipbuilding employers, and the field was therefore clear for joint action by the two traditionalist organisations.

Even this was an uphill struggle, as Smith and Carter tried to urge their members towards a harmony that they only just felt themselves. Smith's plan to negotiate over shortening the working week was accepted, but

---

[173] Executive Board Minutes, 26 July 1918, S.E.F. Papers.

[174] See Terence Rodgers 'Sir Allan Smith, the Industrial Group, and the Politics of Unemployment', *Business History*, xxvii (1986), 100–123.

Carter and Smith openly disagreed when they met the trade unions in November, and the talks broke down in embarrassment and disarray.[175] This delayed plans for a national confederation of employers' organisations, so no organisation existed on the employers' side to match the T.U.C. when Lloyd George summoned the National Industrial Conference in February 1919.

The breakdown of the N.I.C. has been discussed by Kenneth Morgan, Rodney Lowe, and Rodger Charles.[176] Each of these authors writes in terms of the evaporation of wartime consensus, which is understandable from the fraught perspective of 1919. But the mixed provenance of the N.I.C., and the diverse aims with which participants entered it, tell a different story. The proposition that workers were discontented because they had too little part to play in the running of industry was the foundation of the Whitley committee's thinking, and it had been supported by the War Cabinet in September 1917.[177] The idea then bifurcated. Whitley's reports proposed the organisation of hierarchies of joint committees, industry by industry, in which employers and workers would meet at district, regional and national level to discuss wages and conditions, and by implication to agree on national bargaining procedures. A separate report proposed works committees. The outcome of this line of thinking was a number of 'Whitley Councils' in various industries. The Whitley committee envisaged that the councils in industries with little previous organisation would strengthen both unions and employers' organisations in those industries, with help from the Ministry of Labour; and that in highly organised trades the councils would subsume, or be subsumed in, existing national representative meetings. In practice the councils did promote unionisation in some unorganised trades, at least until the beginning of the post-war slump, but got little help from the government because of Treasury resistance.[178] In the organised trades, such as textiles, shipbuilding and building, the establishment of 'Joint Industrial Councils' had little effect on wage bargaining because both employers and unions preferred to retain existing machinery intact and deflect the J.I.C.s to other subjects.[179] The other leg of the idea of formal collaboration between employers and workers arose naturally from the War Cabinet's interpretation of the Industrial

[175] Eric Wigham, *The Power to Manage* (London: Macmillan, 1973), p. 98.

[176] Rodger Charles, *The Development of Industrial Relations in Great Britain, 1911–1939* (London: Hutchinson, 1973), pp. 229–249; Rodney Lowe, 'The Failure of Consensus in Britain: the National Industrial Conference, 1919–21', *Historical Journal*, xxi (1978), 647–675; K.O. Morgan, *Consensus and Disunity* (Oxford: Clarendon Press, 1979), pp. 57–59.

[177] W.C. 208, CAB 23/3.

[178] Rodney Lowe, *Adjusting to Democracy*, pp. 92–96 and 'The Ministry of Labour, 1916–1924: a graveyard of social reform?', *Public Administration*, lii (1974), 415.

[179] The building J.I.C., though, undertook the novel role of negotiating a policy of cost-plus tenders and expansion of the skilled labour supply to assist the post-war housing programme.

Unrest reports, which like Whitley emphasised the need for communication and the value of organisation on both sides of industry to dampen conflict. The initiative was taken by G.H. Roberts, who took over the Ministry of Labour from Hodge in the August reshuffle. With his Under-Secretary, Bridgeman, he was assiduous in promoting the Whitley principles but also in encouraging union expectations of a national conference to discuss industrial policy after the war. This was in due course incorporated into Lloyd George's campaign rhetoric and launched by Sir Robert Horne, Minister of Labour in the post-war Coalition, in February 1919.

The Ministry of Labour's expectation of the N.I.C. is quite clear. Bridgeman thought that

> The chief hope of industrial peace & progress after the war rests in my opinion upon the reorganisation of trade in such a way as to give the employees more interest in & knowledge of their trades & a better way of settling differences. If the capitalists miss this opportunity they will meet the most violent opposition from labour, and if the employees do not join in this movement and agree to abstain from restricting output in return for a better share of the profits they will drive capital out of the Country. In either event the prosperity of our country will be doomed.[180]

This was the position taken in public by Roberts and clearly endorsed by the War Cabinet. Ministry of Labour officials also believed that industrial problems 'can only be successfully solved by a policy of decentralisation' rather than by state interference.[181] This added up to a coherent justification for a national representative conference which would accept responsibility for the peacetime relationship between capital and labour. Unfortunately neither unions nor employers' organisations took that view of the proposal. On the trade union side neither Roberts (an engaged Coalitionist who resigned from the Labour Party to contest the Coupon election) nor his civil servants were completely trusted. On the employers' side there was no preparation for such a conference because what were considered the important issues, such as hours of work and wages, were being addressed by the individual employers' organisations. The National Industrial Conference, when it opened in February 1919, was thrust upon a distracted and indifferent industrial world by the Coalition government.

The result was predictable. Employers and trade unionists went on doing what they had been doing in the war. Over the 48-hour week and the question of minimum wages, a working sub-committee was set up which produced reports in favour of both. When referred to the main protagonists the propositions were simply rejected by the employers,

---

[180] Bridgeman Diary, February 1918, *Modernisation of Conservative Politics*, p. 126.

[181] H.B. Butler, deputy secretary to the ministry, in January 1918, LAB 2/218/ML 1059/3, quoted in Lowe, 'The Ministry of Labour, 1916–19: a "still, small voice"?', in Burk, *War and the State*, p. 124.

who thereby demonstrated that they attached no special authority to the conference; and it is hardly likely that the trade union side would have behaved differently if the main recommendations had not been to their liking. They had not so much changed at the end of the war because of an erosion of consensus, but rather had signally failed to change a wartime pattern of behaviour despite the blandishments of the Coalition.

A Modernisation Crisis?

Contemporary political rhetoric, and a good deal of historical writing, has placed the First World War at the centre of a critical period for the development of the British state in its relationship to the economy and to industrial society. How far does the history recounted above confirm this interpretation? Certainly there was a cluster of political and economic issues, recognised at the time, which seemed to converge. If words can make crises, the passionate demands of Dudley Docker and the ringing challenges of the shop stewards' movement both suggest that British capitalism was in crisis, and that the struggle for power and for change was a real one. The perceived failure of British industry in competition with other industrial nations, and the apparent difficulty of improving industrial productivity by changing working practices, seemed to indicate the nature of the problem. The demand that the state should intervene, somehow, was widespread. Although many historians have placed the most intense crisis in the post-war years, largely because of the increased intensity of strike activity in 1919–21 and 1925–26, there is a general inclination to look to the war for the origins of change. From many ideological perspectives, historians have described a government which responded to the challenge either by becoming openly oppressive,[182] by adopting a strategy of killing discontent by kindness,[183] or by expanding the institutions of the state to accommodate organised interests.[184]

Elsewhere in this book it has been suggested that the Lloyd George Coalition, over the period of its wartime ministry, became a deliberately counter-revolutionary force. Much of the change in party politics during the period can be explained by the pressures which this new role imposed, and in that sense the reactionary quality of the ministry is historically important. But seen from the viewpoint of the employers and trade unionists who also had an interest in the outcome of the war, it was not a very consistent or successful reaction. The subsequent political behaviour

[182] E.g. Keith Burgess, *The Challenge of Labour*.
[183] E.g. Mark Swenarton, *Homes Fit for Heroes*.
[184] E.g. Keith Middlemas, *Politics in Industrial Society*.

of capital and labour, even their behaviour during the formative year of 1918, reflects a loss of faith in the state's power either to achieve or to prevent change. It is this loss of faith which gives substance to the idea of a modernisation crisis. Two recent authors have presented a reductionist view of the war and immediate post-war period in which modernisers, represented by, among others, Dudley Docker, Beatrice Webb, H.A.L. Fisher, Addison and Haldane, with the support of movements such as the F.B.I., were opposed by 'liberal institutions' and the traditions of sound finance.[185] Although this emphasis on the dead hand of sound finance is supported by the importance of banking orthodoxy in the early 1920s — especially the role of the Cunliffe Committee and the Financial Facilities Committee in preaching the necessity for budgetary restraint[186] — it hardly does justice to the complexity of wartime politics in which these political strategies and alliances were formed. Any categorisation which brackets Dudley Docker and Lord Haldane should be looked at askance; this is all the more true when the political context of their action is examined.

It is clear from the experience of the so-called 'trade warriors' that the move towards a post-war economic war with Germany was deeply entangled in other, older political traditions. It was not just liberal orthodoxy, or Liberals, who undermined the movement towards a protectionist economy but the sheer complexity of economic interests represented at the heart of decision-making. On the other hand, there were at one level of analysis two distinct approaches towards capital–labour relations: the corporatist and conciliatory approach represented by the N.A.E.E and the robust confrontation favoured by the E.E.F. The difference was highlighted by the row over the F.B.I.'s memorandum of December 1917. Yet the protagonists in that argument were quite ready to combine in expensive covert political attacks both on the Labour Party and the shop stewards, without apparently feeling any contradiction. The failure of business pressure to come up with a plausible political case, either in the 1918 election or the negotiations during the National Industrial Conference in 1919, was manifest. But it was not divisions between modernisers and traditionalists which caused this failure. Traditional Smith of the engineering employers fell out with equally traditional Carter of the shipbuilders, but co-operated with modernising Docker and Caillard in the British Commonwealth Union.

A similar point can be made about attitudes to representation, and the extended boundaries of the state, which have exercised Professor Middlemas. No larger gap can be envisaged than that between Haldane's view of the relations between government departments and the society which they served, quoted above, and the F.B.I.'s vision of a Ministry of Commerce

---

[185] Newton and Porter, *Modernization Frustrated*, pp. 31–63.

[186] See *First Interim Report of the Committee on Currency and Foreign Exchanges*, P.P. 1918, Cd. 9182; *Report of the Committee on Financial Facilities P.P.* 1918, Cd. 9227.

which embodied business views. Yet both are recruited as modernisers. The failure of 'corporatism' to take hold during and after the war goes deeper. Official attitudes to organised interests, whether in the Ministry of Munitions, the Ministry of Labour, the Ministry of Shipping or the Ministry of Reconstruction, were cool and manipulative. An early re-alisation that government policy could not be implemented without the help of trade unions, trade associations and employers' organisations forced ministers and civil servants to work harder, but the structure of authority remained remarkably the same. The opportunity to take initiatives lay largely with the apparatus of the state. The fact that ministers did have the upper hand, and tended to use it ineffectively, was the main source of frustration among trade unionists and employers alike.

There was, in short, no single, simple modernising thrust opposed by liberal orthodoxy. Nor was there a simple conflict between capital and labour. The effect of war, both in exaggerating the productivity prob-lems of British industry and raising wide hopes about reconstruction, was however to change the relationship between the organised interests and the re-formed party system; to change the political landscape in which Liberal, Labour and Conservative politicians toiled. Businessmen of all sorts, as well as trade unionists, were after 1918 deeply suspicious of the state's ability to bring about constructive change. The pell-mell rush to decontrol was one, passing consequence of this spirit; another was the de-coupling of the trade union movement from the Labour Party, which only began in earnest in 1924. While politicians came increasingly to recognise the economy, and conflicts of interest within it, as the main subject of political concern, the major actors were convinced by the experience of 1917 and 1918 that it would be better to be left alone, to fight the class war or negotiate its end.

11

A NEW POLITICAL LANDSCAPE
II – The Electoral Map Redrawn

When the results of the Coupon Election were known, Archibald Salvidge, the Conservative boss in Liverpool, commented that 'We have reached our maximum of strength now in the country and of course in the future we cannot hope to hold the present position.'[1] His party had won 359 seats in Great Britain by attracting 39.5 per cent of the poll on a low turnout. Most gains were at the expense of the Liberal Party, which was left with 163 seats from 28.6 per cent of the poll, but Labour had continued on the steady track of its pre-war expansion, winning 60 seats with 23.6 per cent of the poll.[2] Did the war, or long-term social and economic change, or, as some have claimed, the new franchise bring about such a striking political transformation? In particular, did it bring about the rapid rise of Labour at the Liberals' expense and the restoration of the Conservative Party to the dominant electoral position it had lost in 1906?

The case for expecting the war to have been influential is strong. The war disrupted party politics at every level. It split the Liberal leadership, the Liberal parliamentary party, and the Liberal press: three pillars of the great edifice which was Edwardian Liberalism. The Liberal intelligentsia was also disturbed, though its influence over the mass of voters can be doubted.[3] More significant, perhaps, was the disruption of local party organisation when agents and officials went off to fight or turned their hands to recruiting or 'war work', and the ambiguous role of the central organisation. The coupon itself, whose use was partly influenced by war politics, confused and demoralised those potential Liberal voters who

---

[1] Salvidge to Derby, 31 Dec. 1918, Derby Papers 920 DER (17) Salvidge Correspondence.

[2] These proportions relate to Great Britain only, including the University seats. Twenty Irish Unionists, including three 'Patriotic Labour' candidates from Belfast, swelled the Conservative total at Westminster, but the other British parties did not contest Irish seats.

[3] Clarke, *Liberals and Social Democrats*, Ch. 6.

found themselves without a Liberal candidate to support.[4] Since the prosecution of war had been the major political issue for the last four and
a half years, the Liberals would seem likely to suffer from being deeply
and publicly divided about it. Asquithians, even Asquith himself, suffered
grievously from a public opinion which could not understand the subtleties of his objection to the Lloyd George regime, and dismissed him
and his like as a traitor.[5] Just when an enlarged electorate came to the
poll for the first time, in emotional circumstances, the Liberal Party was
divided, directionless, and unconvincing.

Everything which told against the Liberals would seem to have helped
the Conservatives. Because of the party's firm support for the Coalition
almost any sitting Tory M.P. who wanted one was able to have a coupon.
There was little room for doubt that the Conservatives were the militarist
and patriotic party, and many Conservatives won without the Coupon or
even against it. Divisions at the top of the party, though real enough,
scarcely reached the electorate. Disputes between the back bench and
the parliamentary leadership were being resolved at the end of the war,
though they were soon to break out again over the question of continuing
the Coalition, and the position of party leader was as strong as it had been
since 1903.[6] Local party organisation was no worse hit than the Liberals',
and Central Office was intact. Only the ultra-patriotism of the National
Party could threaten the loyalty of traditional Conservative voters, while
the war's events and atmosphere would be more likely to attract waverers
than to repel them. The result was as predictable as it was satisfactory, and
Younger had so little to complain of in January 1919 that he was reduced
to observing that 'The result is somewhat embarrassing and the new lot
will need some steering...'.[7]

The 'war' argument is more difficult to make for the Labour Party. One
source of confusion has been the ambiguous nature of Labour's achievement in 1918. Some historians have reckoned it very good, because
Labour's percentage of the total vote was so much greater than in 1910;
others have reckoned it very bad because there were only 28 more seats.[8]
Neither interpretation makes much sense, for reasons which will be made
clearer below. Some historians in groping towards the light have man-

---

[4] A.H. Taylor, 'The Effect of Electoral Pacts on the Decline of the Liberal Party', *British Journal of Political Studies*, iii (1973), 247, notes that where a three-cornered fight took place in 1922, the average drop in the Liberal vote since 1910 was 22.7 per cent if the constituency had been contested by a Liberal in 1918, but 28.7 per cent if the Liberals had withdrawn in favour of a Conservative because of the Coupon.

[5] Stuart R. Ball, 'Asquith's Decline and the General Election of 1918' *Scottish Historical Review*, lxi (1982), 44–61.

[6] J.O. Stubbs, 'The Great War...'.

[7] Younger to Steel-Maitland, 1 Jan. 1919, Steel-Maitland Papers GD 193/274/Y.

[8] David Marquand, *Ramsay MacDonald*, pp. 238–239.

aged to hold two contradictory views at once, giving reasons for Labour's success while denying that it had a success at all.[9] The best 'war' explanations of success are those which can be generalised to elections after 1918, when 'success' was in any case less ambiguous. Although Labour, like the Liberals, suffered from the prominence of its anti-war minority, it is held to have gained in public esteem from trade union participation in the war effort. The war also increased union membership, and thus implicitly added to the organised Labour vote. Moreover the local activity of the party, co-ordinated by the War Emergency Workers' National Committee and finally consolidated by the 1918 revision of the party's constitution, could not be matched by the other parties. Because Labour was not much involved in the Asquith Coalition, it could avoid blame for failure in the war without having to offend working-class sceptics by coming too close to Lloyd George. Then, so soon as war fever had been replaced by revulsion, Labour could turn MacDonald's notorious anti-war stance to advantage, in a way denied to prominent Liberals who had been associated with wartime government. In this view, the war goes some way towards making Labour look like a genuine mass party as well as a party of government.[10]

Though persuasive, the 'war' argument seems too good to be true. Was the pre-war political system unchanging? Would the Liberal Party really have held the working-class vote for ever if there had been no war? The case against the 'war argument' is made persuasively by historians of the Labour Party.[11] Sceptics point to the steady movement of trade unions into the Labour Party before the war, particularly the miners' unions whose support, it turned out, was so important for Labour in 1918. The growth of Labour support in municipal elections before 1914 is to these historians further evidence for the latent strength of the Labour movement. They assume that the MacDonald–Gladstone pact of 1903,[12] giving Labour a free run in certain constituencies in the 1906 election and in some places in 1910 as well, worked to Labour's advantage at first but later worked against the party by keeping Labour candidates out of winnable seats. This is clearly not a perfect explanation. Despite its municipal successes Labour did not prosper when it opposed the Liberals in by-elections after 1910. The electors' willingness to vote Labour did not apparently extend to parliamentary elections. Labour's leaders tried with varying degrees of enthusiasm to let go of the Liberal coat-tails, but it is not certain that social currents were running strongly enough in their direction to have made

[9] Pugh, *Making of Modern British Politics*, pp. 199–201.

[10] Pugh *Ibid.*; Marquand, *Ramsay MacDonald*, p. 243.

[11] In particular Ross McKibbin in *The Evolution of the Labour Party*, pp. 236–241.

[12] On which see Frank Bealey, 'The Electoral Arrangement between the Labour Representation Committee and the Liberal Party', *Journal of Modern History*, xxviii (1956), 353–373.

this a successful strategy even if it had had time to work.[13] Nevertheless it is still attractive to explain Labour's rise in terms of long-term social change. The politicisation of the Victorian working class was a complex process, in which the activities of the parliamentary parties and their local organisations played some part,[14] but which also owed a great deal to the situations in which working men worked, and the interplay of relatively constant attitudes, such as that to religion, with shifting events.

Chapter 1 described a complex pattern of interactions between social, religious and workplace factors in the determination of working-class political allegiance, a pattern which was changing slowly before the war. Working practices changed under the influence of new technology and economic fluctuations. Migration steadily changed the ethnic and religious composition of communities, just as it changed the basic class composition of some constituencies. Transient political events made certain combinations of class, religion and ethnicity important at certain times but not at others.

It was in this context that by 1910 the interaction of local and national deals between Labour and Liberal had established the Labour Party as a full partner, albeit a junior partner, in the progressive alliance. The events of 1911–14 put both national and local deals under strain. At the national level Ramsay MacDonald and Arthur Henderson, who were the only two parliamentary leaders of obvious ability, were sceptical of Labour's chances of survival as a fully independent party. MacDonald expressed a positively Augustinian determination to be fully independent but not yet, and had to restrain his local party in Leicester from putting his long view into effect prematurely by fighting a Liberal in a by-election in 1913. Labour activists all over the country were impatient with this attitude, but where they kicked over the traces, or found themselves forced to fight independently by unsympathetic local Liberals, the voters confirmed MacDonald's view. Labour lost four seats in by-elections between December 1910 and the outbreak of war, two to Conservatives, one to a Liberal and one to a Lib-Lab candidate: Labour was at the bottom of the poll in each case, just as it was in the ten other bye-elections it contested in the period. Meanwhile Labour's organising zeal was diminishing and few new branches were being established.

To all appearances the appeal of the New Liberalism, based on radical policies supposed to attract working-class voters, was maintaining working-class loyalty to Liberalism. The National Insurance legislation annoyed some trade unions, but only because it cut across their friendly

[13] R.I. McKibbin, 'James Ramsay MacDonald and the Problem of the Independence of the Labour Party, 1910–1914', *Journal of Modern History* xlii (1970), 216–235.

[14] J.A. Garrard, 'Parties, Members and Voters after 1867: a local study', *Historical Journal*, xx (1977), 145–163.

society functions and competed for their members' approval: it did not give them an issue on which to rally their members against the government, and the concession which included union benefits in the fund merely restored the status quo. The Liberals' 1906 industrial relations legislation smothered Labour's appeal as an independent party to protect trade union interests, while their leisurely response to the Osborne judgment on political funds, handed down in 1909 and remedied in 1913, hindered trade union support for the political movement. The strike wave of 1911–13 did not apparently increase working-class voters' identification with the Labour Party. Labour organisers expected their party to grow slowly, and their modest target for the 1915 election was based on the view that trade union sponsored candidates were most likely to succeed.[15] The I.L.P. and the Fabian Society could offer organisational skills, and were often responsible for growth in the number of branches, but they had a weaker grip on the electorate. The Labour vote was still based on a sectional appeal, which perhaps guaranteed it a minimum level of support but certainly set an upper limit to its electoral appeal. Its growth was also heavily influenced by regional variation in style and organisational methods, caused at least in part by the fragmentation of the movement's leadership at Westminster.[16]

Like the other parties, Labour launched out on the unknown in August 1914. Matthew *et al.* are convinced that the next four years did nothing significant for Labour's electoral support, and that their post-war growth was based on the franchise changes of the 1918 Representation of the People Act. Their argument depends on two assumptions: that the pre-war franchise discriminated against Labour, a point which will be examined further below, and that nothing happened during the war to change the social basis of Labour's support. The second assumption has its own baggage of corollaries. It rests on the belief that political preferences are more like tribal loyalties than anything else; that W.S. Gilbert was more or less right to claim that every child born alive was 'either a little Liberal or a little Conservative'; and that political man was the sum of a set of social variables such as class, religious allegiance, ethnic origin, occupation, and position in the wage hierarchy, which though not invariant were very slow to change. His vote 'expressed' these differences. Self-evidently, even the war could not have changed these variables enough, for a large enough part of the population, to account for Labour's electoral growth between 1910 and 1922. Since it could not, Matthew *et al.* find an alternative explanation in the franchise changes, which in their view increased the number of potential Labour voters without needing any change in

[15] McKibbin, *Evolution of the Labour Party* pp. 72–87.

[16] On which see esp. Duncan Tanner, *Political Change and the Labour Party* (Cambridge: Cambridge University Press, 1990).

the social characteristics of the population. One flaw in this reasoning is that between 1900 and 1910 the Labour proportion of the vote grew at the same rate as it did between 1910 and 1922, showing almost a fivefold increase in each period.[17] If society could not have changed enough to change political preferences during the war, it could not have changed enough in the Edwardian decade either, and we must look for alternative or at least complementary explanations for Labour's growth.

For the Edwardian period, some of these explanations have already been mentioned. Large and rapid changes in workplace politics had local consequences. Transient political events made some social characteristics temporarily more important. Personalities on the national political stage counted for a lot, and the relative standing of the two major parties in a three-party contest affected Labour's prospects. Each of these themes can be projected forward into the politics of war, and to them can be added the impact of two wartime issues, negotiated peace and the conscription question, on the political preferences of the working class. Working-class political choices begin to make sense only when they are treated not as a passive translation of social characteristics, but as an active response to events.

It is easy to list the wartime developments which might have affected the Labour vote, but much more difficult to measure their effects. Some of the more obvious have been mentioned earlier in this book: the rise to prominence of leaders such as Henderson and Barnes, whose ministerial service gave some credibility to Labour as a governing party; the work of the War Emergency Workers' Committee; the resilience of Labour's local political organisation, based on Trades Councils. Undoubtedly Labour used the war to strengthen its role as a party of social integration. The War Emergency Workers' National Committee, an offshoot of the National Executive Committee, identified Labour with welfare questions, both in the civilian workforce and among soldiers' dependants. The local Trades Councils, committees on which were represented the local branches of trade unions, became involved with poor relief in the early part of the war, putting the consumer's case to the Ministry of Food after 1916, and took part in local negotiations with government departments about

---

[17] Labour share of the U.K. vote (per cent):

1900	1.3
1906	4.8
1910 (J)	7.0
1910 (D)	6.4
1918	20.8
1922	29.7

The annual rate of change is greater between 1900 and December 1910 than it is between December 1910 and 1922. Choice of January 1910 as the datum point would further increase the disparity.

the allocation of labour, especially under the Lloyd George Coalition.[18] These were services with which the political organisations of the other parties did not compete. Liberal and Tory agents helped in recruiting, sold war bonds, and made propaganda about war aims, but they did not undertake case-work about individual grievances, nor claim to represent a section of the community in its dealings with the government. Wherever there was a Labour candidate, the party's propaganda in 1918 emphasised this direct contribution to the common welfare.

The growth of trade union membership during the war, accompanied by greater activity especially during the strike movements of autumn 1915, spring 1916, spring 1917 and winter 1917–18, has also been claimed as a foundation for subsequent Labour growth. Union membership has been shown to be closely related to Labour voting in studies of more recent elections, and it has been argued that the psychological support offered by the trade union was vital in the early part of this century when the act of voting Labour was seen as deviant.[19] The war, by creating an industrial boom, increased the number of trade unionists from 4.145 million in 1914 to 6.533 million in 1918.[20] What is less certain is that these members all represented potential Labour votes, for although the leadership of the unions, and the T.U.C., were committed to the Labour Party by the end of the war, they could not command their members. Some of the more intense episodes of strike activity had thrown up difficult political issues for the trade union movement, especially in the last two years of the war. The 1917 engineering strikes, for example, had been led by shop stewards whose socialist commitment was undoubted, and who later emerged as Labour activists and M.P.s. But closer study has made it clear that the decision to follow the strike was based on more complex discontents. Some of these, like the rent issue in Glasgow, fed directly into Labour politics, though not in 1918. Discontent about food prices was general but transient. Conscription, 'badging' of essential workers, and the dilution of skilled labour, had an atavistic significance. Although the leaders spoke freely of 'Bolshevism', the substantial content of some British Bolshevism in 1917 and 1918 was discrimination against female labour and the preservation of wage differentials between skilled and unskilled workers.[21] The defence of traditional working practices and social arrangements

[18] See e.g. Turner, *Lloyd George's Secretariat*, p. 31, on the work of the Port Labour Committees.

[19] Chris Chamberlain, 'The Growth of Support for the Labour Party in Britain', *British Journal of Sociology*, xxiv (1973), 474–489.

[20] Some of these were women, many of whom would be under 30 and therefore without the vote. See Chris Wrigley, 'Trade Unions and Politics in the First World War', in Ben Pimlott and Chris Cook, *Trade Unions in British Politics* (London: Longman, 1982), pp. 79–97 for a general discussion. Note that the growth in membership was a function of economic growth, persisting until 1920, when it reached 8.348 million, and then declining.

[21] Waites, *Class Society at War*, esp. pp. 120–159; but see J. Smith, 'Labour Traditions in Glasgow

could appear revolutionary, but it was also compatible with xenophobic patriotism, as shown by C.B. Stanton's by-election success in Merthyr in November 1915, which followed the South Wales miners' strike. If the Labour Party became identified with internationalism it could forfeit the support of these men, and there is some evidence that in 1918 it did so. On the other hand, where candidates like Ben Tillett and Will Thorne had a consistent pro-war record they could usually rely in 1918 on tacit support from the Coalition, which saved them from attack and cleared the way for a higher Labour vote.

The war also transformed, quickly and permanently, the circumstances which had made Irish minorities inaccessible to the Labour Party and had kept part of the Jewish minority out of politics altogether. The most dramatic effects of the Easter Rising, the Convention, and the conscription crisis of March–May 1918 were in Ireland, where the Nationalists steadily lost their grip on a once loyal population. In England only one Irish Nationalist candidate — T.P. O'Connor in the Scotland Division of Liverpool — had established a position. First elected in 1885, and with 78 per cent of the vote in 1910, he was difficult to shift and there was no Sinn Fein candidate in 1918 to oppose him. Elsewhere the Roman Catholic Irish vote had traditionally provided much of the Liberal minority in Lancashire. The actions of Liberals in government, before and after December 1916, gave them little reason to hope for Home Rule from that quarter, and even in 1918 they appear to have drifted towards Labour. After the 1921 Treaty the irrelevance of the Liberal Party to sectional Irish interests was painfully obvious. This allowed the Roman Catholic Irish vote, which was almost without exception working-class, to drift behind the Labour Party. The 1921 census reports, for England and Wales, numbers of residents born in the area later to become the Irish Free State; and while this is not an exact count of those who would properly regard themselves or be regarded as 'Irish voters' it indicates the geographical distribution of the Irish population at the end of the war. With trifling exceptions (Derby and Merthyr Tydfil), the areas where more than 2 per cent of the population was Irish born were all in inner London or Lancashire, with the highest proportions recorded in Liverpool. Some areas with port towns approached this figure, as did the Lancashire mining districts.[22] In Scotland the Irish vote was mostly on Clydeside, where even before the war the Irish electorate had touched 13 per cent in some Glasgow con-

---

and Liverpool', *History Workshop*, xvii (1984), 32–46, who defends the socialist credentials of the Glasgow leaders.

[22] The figures cannot, unfortunately, be attributed to individual constituencies, where of course the proportions Irish-born would sometimes be far higher and the 'Irish electorate' higher still. In terms of 'constant units' (see Appendix I for details) there were 14 constant units, covering 39 constituencies, where the Irish-born population exceeded 2 per cent.

stituencies.[23] This was a formidable advantage to Labour, especially where the party's organisation could be built upon Irish community links.

The Jewish experience was different. Smaller than the Irish community, more heavily concentrated in one area (the East End of London), and even less likely to be enfranchised before the war, the Jewish immigrant community was highly politicised. It was also divided socially from the politically active Jewish community long established in England, and lacked the opportunity to exercise itself politically in an English context. Opposition to Tsarist Russia was the strongest issue uniting Jewish immigrants, and during the war this immediately brought a number of their most active members into conflict with the authorities over conscription. Jewish socialists who did not want to be pressed into service on the same side as Nicholas II were natural sympathisers with the internationalist wing of the Labour movement. Conscription tribunals in the East End, dominated by Liberal and Unionist politicians, were hostile to their appeals and the resulting demonstrations consolidated an alliance between Jews and socialists, and revived anti-semitic feeling in the rest of the electorate.[24] Although anti-alien feeling among prospective Labour voters remained high right through to the 1918 election, the Jewish vote had nowhere else to go. With increasing enfranchisement, it provided a solid core of Labour votes in the East End, combining in some areas with the Irish vote to create a dominant coalition.

Explanations of voting choice in the longer term are commonly associated either with 'expressive' theories, which maintain that voting choice is a function of the group with which the voter associates himself, or with 'instrumental' theories which maintain that voters self-interestedly pick governments which will do them good, judging by past performance or by the promises made in election campaigns, rewarding success and punishing failure. Most studies of early twentieth-century British voting patterns have taken an 'expressive' viewpoint. The question asked is not whether social grouping influences electoral choice, but whether class, as a superordinate social grouping, has superseded other allegiances in the twentieth century. This question lends itself to fairly rigorous statistical testing, but to show that one sort of social grouping has superseded another is not to prove that the 'expressive' viewpoint is the right one. 'Instrumental' theories about electoral choice are difficult to examine within a single election, because usually only the results of a series of elections will confirm or refute an hypothesis.

Two sorts of question are in mind in the study described here. The first is the conventional 'expressive' hypothesis. Kenneth Wald and W.L.

---

[23] Pelling, *Social Geography*, pp. 400–402.
[24] Alderman, *London Jewry and London Politics*, pp. 59–65.

Miller have both argued, in long-term studies of electoral behaviour before and after the First World War, that class and religion were the main
determinants of voting choice.[25] Although they differ about the timing of
the change, they agree that class has risen in importance while religion has
declined. Wald, in particular, argues that the 1918 election was a watershed in which class overtook religion; he demonstrates this by comparing
the elections of 1885 to 1929 according to the correlates of Conservative voting, and shows that while class differences between constituencies
appeared to account for little of the variation in the Conservative vote
in elections before 1918, they seemed to leap in importance in 1918 and
maintain this position in all subsequent elections until 1929. Wald's 'cleavage model', adapted from the work of Miller and Raab, seeks to predict
Conservative voting from a combination of variables measuring Anglican,
Nonconformist and Catholic presence in constituencies, the proportion
of the electorate involved in agriculture, and a class variable based on the
definitions used in the 1951 census.[26] Although he finds a sharp change
at the 1918 election, this conclusion must be treated with considerable
caution. His early class measures are necessarily very imprecise, derived
by converting information from the 1891 census into the categories used
in the 1951 census. This unavoidable error of measurement has an important corollary: it would reduce the apparent correlation between class and
Conservative voting, whatever the underlying relationship. Thus some of
the changes he notes are probably to be explained by greater measure-

[25] Kenneth D. Wald, *Crosses on the Ballot* (Princeton, N.J.: Princeton University Press, 1983);
William L. Miller, *Electoral Dynamics in Britain since 1918* (London: Macmillan, 1977).

[26] The table of standardised regression coefficients below indicates his results more fully. See
Appendix I for further explanation of regression models.

	Anglican	Non-conformist	Catholic	Per cent Agriculture	1951 Class	Multiple R^2
1885	0.31	−0.27	0.35	−0.16	0.23	0.25
1886	0.29	−0.33	0.21	−0.18	0.39	0.21
1892	0.24	−0.36	0.08	−0.09	0.10	0.12
1895	0.07	−0.37	0.22	0.07	0.15	0.14
1900	−0.03	−0.02	0.45	0.04	−0.04	0.21
1906	0.23	−0.38	0.10	0.20	0.09	0.20
1910, Jan.	0.26	−0.49	0.20	0.20	0.18	0.30
1910, Dec.	0.44	−0.39	0.22	−0.05	0.27	0.32
1918	0.47	−0.28	0.03	−0.56	0.65	0.43
1922	0.32	−0.40	0.07	−0.17	0.70	0.46
1923	0.49	−0.33	0.07	−0.14	0.67	0.53
1924	0.34	−0.30	0.10	−0.15	0.66	0.49
1929	0.52	−0.29	0.11	−0.37	0.68	0.58

Source: Wald, *Crosses on the Ballot*, p. 214

ment errors in the earlier data. This doubt is confirmed by the steady improvement in the explanatory power of his model from 1892 onwards. Although the relative explanatory power of class seems to increase, the apparent influence of Anglicanism is markedly higher in the later period than in the earlier, while the Nonconformist coefficients are much the same. The improvement in the whole model is driven by improvement in the explanatory power, and thus in part by the improvement in measurement, of the class variable. A second major doubt lies in the choice of 1918 as the moment of dramatic change. This seems arbitrary, since the ten years between 1900 and December 1910 also saw a very large apparent change in the coefficient for class, if not quite as big as that between 1910 and 1918. This earlier change would support the 'revisionist' view of Clarke, McKibbin and others who have seen a growth of class politics in the pre-war period. The evidence presented is not sufficiently clear-cut, nor is the data sufficiently reliable, to support Wald's swingeing declaration that there was 'a dramatic alteration of cleavage bases between 1910 and 1918, a movement of the vote from a confessional to a class alignment'. But his claim that the finding 'leads inescapably to the conclusion that the rise of Labour and the decline of the Liberals are bound up in the same packet with the substitution of class for religion as the major social force underlying the British party system',[27] is rather more plausible, if only because the rate of expansion of Labour voting between 1900 and 1910 was in fact almost as great as the rate of expansion between 1910 and 1918. All in all, there is not enough longitudinal evidence in his study to make the 1918 election into a watershed.

There are nevertheless some important questions to be asked about 'expressive' influences on voting in 1918, and their relationship both to the electoral tactics of the competing parties and to the final outcome of the election. Since Conservative voting, in particular, was affected by the selective withdrawal of Liberals under the Coupon arrangement, it is important to ask whether this masked the religious effect which had previously favoured Conservatives in Anglican areas, while allowing the class effect to hold firm. Another important question is whether 'expressive' effects vary from region to region. The greater questions, though, are raised by the franchise changes. Matthew, McKibbin and Kay have proposed a clear 'expressive' explanation of voting, but linked it to the appearance of a new class of voter, the previously unenfranchised male. If they are right, constituencies with a higher proportion of new voters should show a leaning towards Labour. Moreover the appearance of women, 40 per cent of the electorate completely neglected by Matthew *et al.*, poses the question of whether women voted 'expressively', and if so, how.

---

[27] Wald, *Crosses on the Ballot* pp. 214–215.

The other challenge is to explore the effect of wartime politics and political organisation, making the assumption that some of the variation in voting patterns between constituencies would be accounted for by 'expressive' social variations, leaving other variation to be explained by such things as the political background of the candidate, the intensity of local political organisation during the war, special characteristics of constituencies such as a history of strikes or the presence of controversial groups such as the Irish or Jewish immigrants. The fact that the 1918 election was the first under the new franchise and the new boundaries makes it impossible to study *change* between 1910 and 1918 as a dependent variable, to be 'explained' by the events of the period. The best that can be done is to compare one constituency with another at one moment, to assess how much of the difference between them can be accounted for by differing experiences.

It is possible to measure some of these and similar effects, and compare them with the putative effects of the change in the franchise, with a comprehensive study of election results in 1918 and some reference to 1922, in relation to what can be discovered about the social characteristics of each constituency. This has required some laborious statistical work, for the details of which the reader is referred to the appendix. The centrepiece of this study has been an analysis of the correlates of the Labour vote. This is largely because the Labour Party was the only political grouping which was, more or less, fighting alone with a clear attitude to the other parties. All the others were either entangled in coalition, and therefore drawing support from many who might be considered erstwhile or potential opponents, or feuding within their parties and therefore unable to present a clear identity to the electorate. Nevertheless the conclusions refer also to the relative success of Conservatives and Liberals, and to the long-term decline of the Liberals as an electoral force. The study is confined to Great Britain because the electoral fate of Ireland, North and South, was so profoundly affected by the collapse of the Union that it seemed impossible to make useful comparisons between the British and the Irish experience; moreover the focus of attention has been the lives and times of the mainland parties, which were scarcely affected by electoral developments in Ireland.

It is tempting to argue that the 1918 election was so exceptional that it carries no lessons for the long run. This would be more plausible if the Labour Party's share of the vote in 1918 did not fit so smoothly into the progression of increasing Labour shares from 1906 to 1929, and if the Liberal defeats had been comfortably reversed in the calmer atmosphere of 1922. The Coupon election was unique — all elections are — but it was also an important member of a series of elections which steadily transformed British electoral geography.

Table 1: The Results, 1918

	Total votes	Share of votes cast	Candidates	M.P.s elected	Unopposed returns
ENGLAND					
Coalition Conservative	3,097,350	36.9	318	295	40
Other Conservative	317,281	3.7	34	20	0
Total Conservative	*3,414,631*	*40.6*	*352*	*315*	*40*
Coalition Liberal	962,871	11.6	95	82	12
Coalition Labour	39,715	0.3	4	3	1
Coalition NDP	121,673	1.6	15	8	0
Coalition Independent	9,274	0.1	1	1	0
Total Coalition	*4,548,164*	*56.5*	*467*	*409*	*53*
Liberal	1,172,700	14.7	232	25	2
Labour	1,811,739	22.6	291	42	6
Co-operative	37,944	0.5	7	1	0
Irish Nationalist	8,225	0.1	2	1	1
National Party	94,389	1.2	26	2	0
NDP	20,200	0.2	7	0	0
Discharged Soldiers'	12,329	0.1	5	0	0
Others	345,188	4.4	114	5	1
Total	*8,050,878*	*100.0*	*1,151*	*485*	*63*
WALES					
Coalition Conservative	20,328	3.9	2	1	0
Other Conservative	39,264	7.4	6	3	0
Total Conservative	*59,592*	*11.3*	*8*	*4*	*0*
Coalition Liberal	207,377	39.2	19	17	4
Coalition NDP	22,824	4.3	1	1	0
Total Coalition	*289,793*	*54.8*	*28*	*22*	*4*
Liberal	51,382	9.7	10	3	2
Labour	163,055	30.8	25	9	5
Others	24,804	4.7	8	1	0
Total	*529,034*	*100.0*	*71*	*35*	*11*
SCOTLAND					
Coalition Conservative	336,530	30.8	34	28	1
Other Conservative	21,939	2.0	3	2	0
Total Conservative	*358,469*	*31.8*	*37*	*30*	*1*
Coalition Liberal	221,145	19.1	28	25	7
Coalition Labour	14,247	1.3	1	1	0
Coalition NDP	12,337	1.1	2	0	0
Total Coalition	*606,198*	*53.8*	*68*	*56*	*8*
Liberal	163,960	15.0	33	8	0
Labour	265,744	22.9	39	6	0
Co-operative	19,841	1.8	3	0	0
NDP	4,297	0.4	1	0	0
Others	66,671	5.6	21	1	0
Total	*1,126,711*	*100.0*	*165*	*71*	*8*

Table 1: The Results, 1918 *(continued)*

	Total votes	Per cent of votes cast	Candidates	M.P.s elected	Unopposed returns
IRELAND					
Unionist	289,213	28.4	36	23	0
Nationalist	228,902	22.0	56	6	0
Sinn Fein	495,345	47.0	100	72	25
Others	25,765	2.6	12	0	0
Total	*1,039,225*	*100.0*	*204*	*101*	*25*
UNIVERSITIES					
Coalition Conservative	18,530	45.2	8	8	0
Other Conservative	3,757	9.2	4	2	0
Total Conservative	*22,287*	*54.4*	*12*	*10*	*0*
Coalition Liberal	5,197	12.7	3	3	0
Total Coalition	*27,484*	*67.1*	*15*	*13*	*0*
Liberal	742	1.8	1	0	0
Labour	5,239	12.8	6	0	0
Nationalist	1,070	2.6	2	0	0
Sinn Fein	1,762	4.3	2	1	0
Others	4,673	11.4	6	1	0
Total	*40,970*	*100.0*	*32*	*15*	*0*
UNITED KINGDOM					
Coalition Conservative	3,472,738	32.5	362	332	41
Other Conservative	671,454	6.2	83	50	0
Total Conservative	*4,144,192*	*38.6*	*445*	*382*	*41*
Coalition Liberal	1,396,590	12.6	145	127	23
Coalition Labour	53,962	0.4	5	4	1
Coalition NDP	156,834	1.5	18	9	0
Coalition Independent	9,274	0.1	1	1	0
Total Coalition	*5,760,852*	*53.2*	*614*	*523*	*65*
Liberal	1,388,784	13.0	276	36	4
Labour	2,245,777	20.8	361	57	11
Co-operative	57,785	0.6	10	1	0
Irish Nationalist	238,197	2.2	60	7	1
National Party	94,389	0.9	26	2	0
NDP	24,497	0.2	5	0	0
Discharged Soldiers'	12,329	0.1	5	0	0
Sinn Fein	497,107	4.6	102	73	25
Others	467,101	4.4	161	8	1
TOTAL	*10,786,818*	*100.0*	*1,623*	*707*	*107*

Source: Calculated from election data, with corrections in voting share for two-member seats using methods defined in Craig, *British Electoral Facts* (2nd edn, London: Macmillan, 1971), p. xiii. The total for the Coalition includes uncouponed Conservatives because they were *de facto* supporters of the new government and opponents of Labour and the Asquithian Liberals. Fifteen of the 'Other' candidates were Labour supporters, three of whom (one each in England, Scotland and Wales) were returned.

The Results

The national figures of votes cast and seats won in the Coupon election, summarised in Table 1, point to the bare outline of political change since the Liberal hegemony of 1906–14, even though direct comparisons are difficult because of the 1918 redistribution. In England the 352 Conservative candidates, couponed and uncouponed, took 42.6 per cent of the vote and won 315 seats out of 485; in December 1910, fighting 436 constituencies out of 456, they had polled 48.8 per cent of votes cast but won only 234 seats.[28] Their gain was almost entirely at the expense of the Liberals, whose share of the vote dropped from 44.4 per cent to 26.3 per cent, giving them 82 seats with the coupon and 25 without it. Most of these gains were permanent: all but a handful of English seats won by Conservatives in 1918 remained in Conservative hands until the Second World War. Liberals were able to reclaim a number, mostly in 1923, but these soon reverted to the Conservatives. The Labour Party's performance in England was unimpressive, even though it polled 22.6 per cent of the total vote, against 6.4 per cent in December 1910. The extra votes came entirely from extra candidatures (291 in 1918 against 44 in 1910): 42 English seats went to Labour, 8 more than in 1910. Twenty seats corresponded to seats held in the old House, while 21 were new: but only in the Midlands did Labour win seats in distinctly new areas. Gains in seats were made equally from Conservatives and Liberals. Labour suffered temporary losses in London and the North-East, and some long-term losses mostly in Lancashire and Cheshire.

The English picture of Conservative advance, Liberal retreat, and slow forward movement by Labour contrasted sharply with the rest of the United Kingdom. Ireland was scarcely touched by redistribution in 1918, but the old political map was nearly erased. Sinn Fein took all the South outside Dublin, where the Unionists held only Rathmines, and Waterford which remained in Nationalist hands. The Nationalists were driven back on the Catholic communities of Ulster, where five members of the old parliamentary party held on to their seats. Ulster Unionism clung to the laager of the six counties. Wales, on the other hand, seemed almost untouched. Welsh Liberal M.P.s, with 26 of the 34 Welsh seats in the old House, had for the most part been loyal to Lloyd George and the Coalition. Twelve sitting members and 7 others received the coupon: all were elected, along with 2 other Liberal candidates. One of the two couponed Conservatives was defeated and 3 of the other 6 candidates won. Conservatives thus added only one seat in Wales. The Liberals' loss of 6 seats

[28] Note that in terms of the share of total votes cast won by each candidate, this was a worse performance than in 1918.

and Labour's corresponding gain owed something to a shift in the voters' allegiance but more to redistribution, which gave seats to mining areas in the South at the expense of rural counties in North and Central Wales. The Liberal collapse in Wales was to be postponed until 1922, when the party was reduced to 10 seats.

The Scottish experience in 1918 was different again. Of the 70 Scottish seats in 1910, the Liberals held 58, the Conservatives 9, and Labour 3. In 1918, after extensive redistribution, the Liberals kept only 33 seats out of 71: Labour doubled its total to 6 and the Conservatives jumped to 30. The Liberals thus suffered to about the same extent as in England, and the Scottish Labour candidates outstripped their English brothers, while the Conservatives, largely through the good offices of the Coalition, seemed to have become equal partners with the Liberals in Scottish politics. But Scottish Tories, unlike English Tories, were unable to keep the spoils in the 1920s. Their 1918 gains, mostly in the industrial districts of the West of Scotland, were picked off by Labour in 1922, and only once thereafter (in 1931) did Labour drop below 20 seats in Scotland. The Conservatives' later gains in Scotland were made at the expense of the Liberals in Eastern and Highland areas. The coupon and the muddle of Liberal organisation gave a number of industrial and mining seats to the Conservatives in 1918 which otherwise would have gone directly to Labour.

Seats won in British elections do not precisely reflect votes cast. The distribution of candidatures, shown in Table 2, and share of the vote for opposed candidates, shown in Table 3, indicate the regional variation in pro-Labour sentiment, and give some indication of the regional variation of support for the government parties. There were few areas in which Labour contested fewer than half the seats, but by far the most profitable English regions in terms of votes were Lancastria, the Midlands and the North of England. Wales was comparable to the most profitable English regions; the West of Scotland was comparable to the Bristol region; and in the East of Scotland Labour's performance was remarkable.

Tables 2 and 3 also raise interesting questions about the relative strength of the two main opposition parties at the polls. In Wessex, Devon and Cornwall, and East Anglia opposition Liberal candidates were more successful than Labour candidates; elsewhere the opposite was true.[29] The disparity in favour of Labour was particularly marked in Bristol, Lancastria and Scotland, where Labour was doing well, and in the South-East where both opposition parties were doing badly. It is significant that in English regions where Liberalism's vigour was witnessed by a comparatively large number of couponed Liberals — in Yorkshire and especially in the North

[29] Except for the unfortunate Highland Land League candidates who carried the Labour banner in the Highlands.

Table 2: Regional Distribution of Candidatures, 1918

	Conservative		Coalition Liberal		Liberal		Labour		Total seats
London	44	*6*	13	*1*	30	—	33	*1*	59
South East	69	*4*	8	—	33	—	54	—	79
East Anglia	10	*1*	3	*3*	9	—	7	—	17
Central	9	*4*	5	*1*	6	—	9	—	18
Wessex	15	*3*	2	*1*	11	—	9	—	19
Bristol	15	*1*	7	—	12	—	15	—	23
Devon & Cornwall	12	*1*	1	—	13	—	6	—	16
West Midlands	28	*6*	4	*2*	22	—	28	—	43
East Midlands	19	*3*	8	—	17	*2*	22	—	34
Lancastria	56	*4*	12	*2*	27	—	56	*3*	75
Yorkshire	27	*3*	21	*1*	27	—	43	*2*	55
Northern England	15	*3*	11	*1*	20	—	29	*1*	36
Wales	8	—	15	*4*	8	*2*	22	*5*	35
Highlands	1	—	5	*2*	4	—	3	—	8
East of Scotland	12	—	7	*4*	14	—	14	—	26
West of Scotland	23	*1*	11	*1*	16	—	33	—	36
Totals	363	*40*	133	*23*	269	*4*	383	*12*	579

Note: Unopposed candidatures shown in italic.

of England — even the opposition Liberals seem to have held their own against Labour; where Liberalism was under attack by a particularly rampant Unionism, as in Lancastria, Labour candidates carried the standard of opposition. In Wales there was very little Conservatism and five of the eight Conservative candidates stood without coupons; the Coalition was represented by the Liberal Party; opposition Liberalism was weak; and Labour was a determined and successful opposition, though part of its strength, as will be seen later, came from a decision by the Coalition whips not to issue coupons against Labour candidates in mining districts.

This picture of the distribution of Labour's voting strength contrasts with the distribution of Labour's gains, mentioned earlier. Of the regions where Labour's share of the vote in contested seats was above 30 per cent only the Midlands saw Labour make substantial gains. In Lancastria and the East and West of Scotland Labour was either checked or even pushed back. This testifies to the effectiveness of the Coupon allocation, which appears to have minimised the advantage to Labour of splits in the anti-Labour vote.

Another perspective is shown in Figure 1, in which plots of the distribution of each major party's votes are compared across six categories of constituency.[30] The comparison between Labour and Conservative

[30] For descriptions of the constituency types and the boxplot display, see Appendix I.

Table 3: Percentage Share of the Vote, 1918

	Conservative	Coalition Liberal	Liberal	Labour
London	57	49	21	24
South East	67	49	19	28
East Anglia	53	63	41	29
Central	53	56	22	39
Wessex	55	73	33	25
Bristol	59	56	25	34
Devon & Cornwall	59	59	36	25
West Midlands	58	37	21	34
East Midlands	51	63	31	35
Lancastria	57	42	26	36
Yorkshire	52	60	26	30
North of England	45	50	30	34
Wales	39	60	33	36
Highlands	53	63	45	20
East of Scotland	52	57	39	46
West of Scotland	55	62	20	33

Note: Each party's share shown as the percentage of votes cast in all seats contested by that party.

experience is powerful, if unsurprising. In urban constituencies, Labour did markedly better in working-class areas than in middle class areas, with mixed-class areas in between. The opposite was true for the Conservatives. There is more significance in the mining areas, where Labour's achievement surpassed its performance in urban working-class areas even though the large number of unopposed returns would tend to depress the apparent level of support. This relationship did not hold in Scotland, where urban working-class constituencies were more enthusiastic for Labour than their English counterparts and the mining constituencies, which were few in number, did not stand out very far. Labour also did somewhat better in rural and urban/rural areas than in urban working-class areas, though the difference was not very large.

The experience of the Liberals, in both their guises, was more problematic. Couponed Liberals were almost entirely excluded from urban middle-class seats. In all other areas they outperformed their Labour and Asquithian opponents, but their comparative advantage was less in mining areas. Their best performances were registered in mixed-class, urban/rural and rural areas, and in urban working-class seats they outperformed the Conservatives. Opposition Liberals trailed badly behind Labour except in urban/rural seats, where they kept up, and fully rural areas where they were conspicuously successful.

Figure 1: Shares of the Vote in the 1918 Election

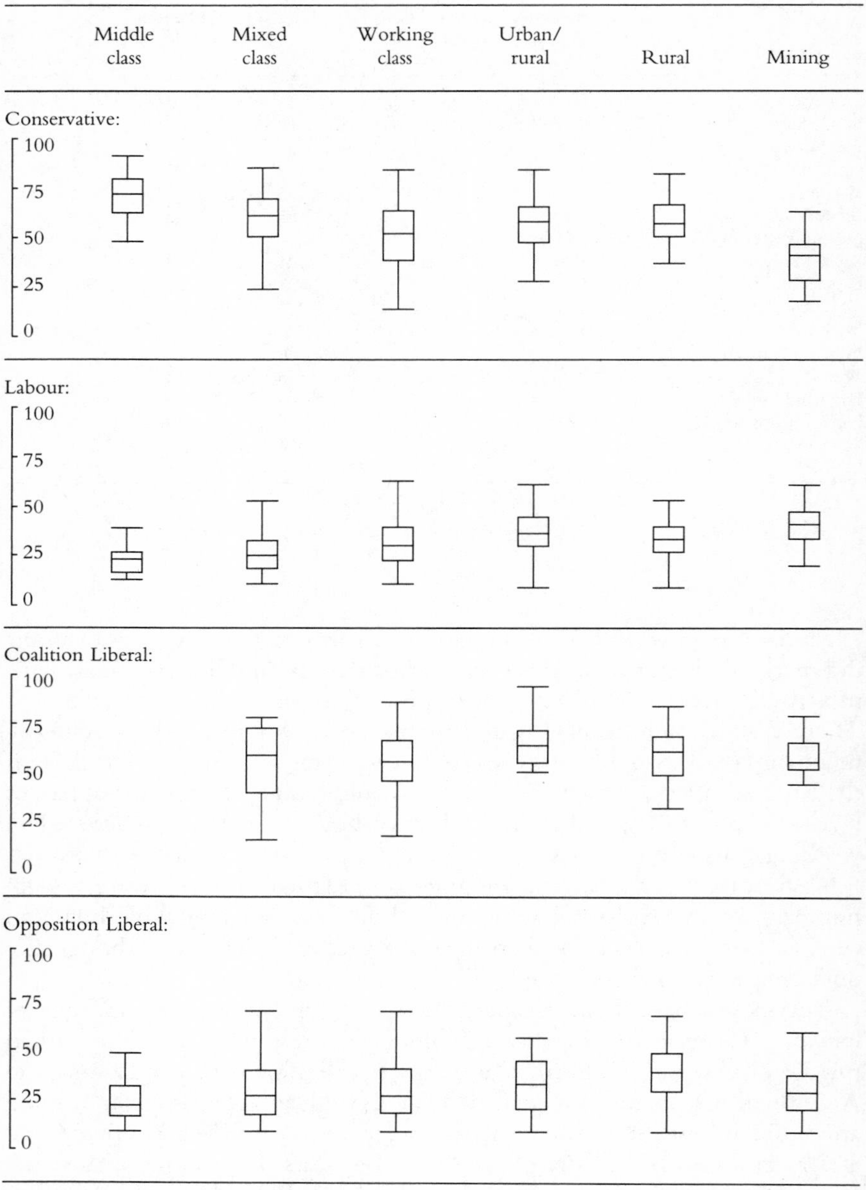
Middle class
Mixed class
Working class
Urban/ rural
Rural
Mining
Conservative:
Labour:
Coalition Liberal:
Opposition Liberal:
100
75
50
25
0

Source: Constituency data files.
Note: For further information on boxplots, see Appendix I. There were too few Coalition Liberals to plot in middle-class seats.

Another important inference to be drawn from these plots is the class-based appeal of the Couponed parties taken together. Although the Coalition Liberals made a better showing in urban working-class seats than their coalition partners, the Coalition as a whole was strongest in urban middle-class areas and progressively weaker as the middle class electorate was diluted; though in mining seats Coalition Liberals, often former Lib-Labs in Durham and Wales, outperformed even the Labour Party.

The Context

THE COUPON AND THE CANDIDATES

The distorting effect of the Coupon and the strategic decisions of the party organisations in what was in essence a three-party system can be illustrated by the regional spread of candidatures. As Table 3 showed, the efforts of the contending parties were not distributed evenly across the country. Two main themes emerge: the regional disparities in the allegiance of Liberals and correspondingly the balance between Liberals and Conservatives in the allocation of coupons, and the geographical and social spread of Labour candidatures. Among Liberals the extreme cases are Wales, whose Liberal M.P.s were predominantly loyal to Lloyd George and duly received their coupons, and Devon and Cornwall, where there were six times as many uncouponed as couponed Liberals. More generally, Liberal coupons were more generously distributed and acknowledged in the North than in the South. The process was complicated and it is hard to disentangle cause and effect in those constituencies where no sitting Liberal M.P. was involved, and there were some complaints that potentially loyal Liberals had been shunned in favour of Conservatives. Lancastria was an obvious exception to the general rule that Coalition Liberalism prospered in northern regions. In some cases, Lancashire candidates of both parties were reluctant to acknowledge the need for a coupon and there were proportionately more couponless contests than anywhere else except in Wales. Moreover, the strength of sentiment in the Conservative organisation was such that uncouponed Conservatives were more frequently run against couponed Liberals there than anywhere else. The combination of sentiment and the coupon thus ensured that Liberalism in either form was much more likely to survive in Yorkshire, the North of England, Wales and Scotland than elsewhere. Coalition Liberals were over-represented in working-class, rural and mining constituencies, and under-represented in middle-class constituencies.

The geographical concentration of Conservative M.P.s in the South East and Lancashire, already evident before the war, was strongly reinforced by the allocation of coupons. Couponed Conservatives were also quite likely to turn up in the West Midlands, and relatively unlikely to be put forward in the North of England, Wales, the East of Scotland, and Yorkshire. In Wales and the North of England, local parties were inclined to make up for this by putting forward unofficial candidates; and in Lancashire, as Salvidge's correspondence shows, the local parties thought that an average crop of coupons was not enough. Predictably, Conservative coupons were skewed towards middle-class and mixed-class constituencies and rural constituencies, and were much less frequent in working-class and mining constituencies; unofficial candidatures were much more likely to be found in working-class constituencies.

It is notable that rural seats were much less likely than urban seats to do without the coupon, for whatever reason, and much more likely to see unopposed returns of Coalition candidates; in that sense, deference was alive and well in the countryside. But the influence of large rural constituencies in Scotland and Wales is very large in this calculation; in England, Labour and uncouponed Liberals were in many areas able to capitalise on political ferment in farming areas, and did so to good effect.

Coupon allocation also influenced the Labour experience, as intended. Douglas and his successors are right to point out that the majority of sitting Labour members were given a free run by the Coalition organisers. This was to be expected. Until the Labour Party conference in November decided that it would not enter the election as part of the Coalition, these men were expected to be given coupons of their own: 16 seats were reserved for them in Guest's discussions with Younger, and no hostile coupons were issued against them when the election was called. But this did not leave the sitting members entirely unaffected. Of the 42 seats held by Labour in 1910, six had been lost in by-elections: two members had had the whip withdrawn and become *de facto* Liberals. One member retired in 1918, leaving 33 sitting Labour members to campaign in the 1918 election. Of these 33, four (George Barnes, George Wardle, G.H. Roberts and James Parker) held on to their Coalition offices, defied the party's decision to fight independently, and stayed in Parliament as Coalition Labour M.P.s (Parker moved from Halifax to Cannock; the others stayed put). Robert Tootill joined the British Workers' League, and retained his Bolton seat with Coalition support. Twenty-eight Labour M.P.s were left to stand as official Labour candidates, of whom ten were returned unopposed and a further eight won in contested elections of which only four were opposed by couponed candidates.

In exercising the choice not to oppose Labour M.P.s Younger and Guest seem to have been guided by a number of considerations. The very few 'pacifist' Labour M.P.s were opposed: Jowett in Bradford, Snowden in Blackburn, MacDonald in Leicester. Coupons were also issued against most of the Labour M.P.s who had voted against the government in the Maurice debate: Frank Goldstone (Sunderland) and Thomas Richardson (M.P. for Whitehaven, who fought in Leicestershire Bosworth in 1918) fell victim here, but not J.W. Taylor, who sat for Chester-le-Street. The remaining sitting Labour members, and a couple of trade unionists who sat in the 1910–18 Parliament as Liberals, were either protected by the Coupon or given a clear run, sometimes against disgruntled 'independent Labour' candidates. G.H. Roberts, who was disowned by his local Labour Party in Norwich when he joined the Coalition Ministry, was opposed by an official Labour candidate when he accepted the Coupon. In assuring themselves of the return of these members and others like them, Guest and Younger were getting not only a 'Patriotic Labour' caucus in parliament, but also a group with identifiable views on peacetime issues. The sitting trade union M.P.s returned in 1918 were almost entirely what contemporaries and some historians have called 'moderate'; that is to say they were solidly right-wing. Havelock Wilson, the seamen's leader who fought as a Coalition Liberal, is an extreme case: he ended his political career as a Companion of Honour and boasted in *Dod's Parliamentary Companion* that he had kept his union out of the General Strike. But there is a continuum between him and J.H. Thomas, whom Lloyd George later trusted not to support the miners in 1921 because he 'wanted to be Prime Minister', and who was returned for Derby with tacit Conservative support: and through to William Brace, returned unopposed in Abertillery, and Vernon Hartshorn, a new member returned unopposed in Glamorgan, Ogmore, both of whom exhibited extreme 'moderation' during coal disputes in the 1920s. In declaring explicitly that the Labour Party was to be unopposed in the South Wales coalfield, Guest and Younger were preparing their ground for peace as well as protecting the Coalition in war.

Consideration for the Labour Party certainly did not extend to those who were trying to extend its ground. The Labour Party stayed away from middle-class urban constituencies and rural constituencies, and, as expected, favoured working-class and mining seats. Very few new Labour candidates, whatever their ascertainable opinions on the war, were given a free run by the Coalition. Instead the forces of the National Democratic Party were concentrated in areas where Labour expansion was feared: especially Durham and the East and West Midlands. There were ironies here. While trying to defeat Thomas Wing, a worthy but tedious Asquithian who had voted against the government in the Maurice Debate, the Coalition gave the Coupon in Durham, Houghton-le-Spring to an N.D.P. candidate who came bottom of the poll, leaving Wing to be defeated by Robert Richardson, a local miners' candidate. In the West

Midlands N.D.P. and Coalition Labour candidates fared reasonably well, taking Cannock, Hanley and Duddeston: in the East Midlands Labour candidates defeated N.D.P. candidates in Notts, Broxtowe and Notts, Mansfield, and only Ramsay MacDonald succumbed to attack in Leicester West. Except in Lancashire, where the Coupon was often kept hidden, Labour expansion into new areas took place against organised Coalition opposition. Labour's distribution of effort was shaped partly by the leadership, but mostly by the initiative of local organisations. Consequently the party fought some unprofitable seats, especially in London and the South-East.

The result was that Labour had a clear run in only 12 seats, half of them in mining areas. Of the 381 opposed candidates who stood as official Labour candidates or who can otherwise be identified as Labour candidates[31] 36 were exempted from Couponed opposition; but 20 of these faced Conservative opponents who protested loyalty to the Coalition, and a further 12 had to fight opposition Liberals. Among those facing a contest from a major-party rival, the average Labour share of the vote was 30 per cent for those who faced a coupon and 40 per cent for those who did not. In this limited sense, therefore, the coupon could be regarded as worth 10 per cent of the vote.

THE NEW ELECTORATE

The basis of the 'franchise' explanation for Labour's success after the war is the appearance in the electorate of new social forces because of the 1918 Act. Two-thirds of the 'new' voters were women; the rest were men who for one of a number of reasons were not enfranchised under the old legislation. Neither category of new voter was evenly distributed across the country.

The distribution of the female electorate is shown in Table 4a. There were fewer female voters in industrial areas and mining areas, and many more in middle-class urban areas and coastal resorts. Poor employment opportunities explain the flight from industrial areas; the middle-class and resort areas had high proportions of domestic servants, mostly female, and wherever elderly people gathered women's greater longevity ensured that they were strongly represented. Moreover the terms of the Act, which gave the vote to women over 30 who would have qualified for the local government franchise or whose husbands would have qualified, tended to work against the enfranchisement of working-class women much as the pre-1918 franchise had discriminated against working-class men. Table 4b shows the social correlates of female enfranchisement based on the constant

Table 4a: Average Percentage of Women in Electorates

	Middle class	Mixed class	Working class	Urban rural	Rural	Mining	Regional average
London	42	42	40	n.a.	n.a.	n.a.	41
South East	43	40	40	41	42	n.a.	41
East Anglia	42	40	n.a.	41	40	n.a.	41
Central	42	43	41	40	41	n.a.	41
Wessex	46	41	n.a.	40	40	n.a.	41
Bristol	44	41	40	42	42	40	42
Devon & Cornwall	45	44	42	45	41	n.a.	43
West Midlands	43	40	39	40	40	39	39
East Midlands	n.a.	41	41	41	40	38	40
Lancastria	41	39	40	41	40	39	40
Yorkshire	39	40	41	40	40	38	40
North of England	n.a.	38	38	39	40	38	38
Wales	n.a.	39	38	39	41	36	38
Highlands	n.a.	n.a.	n.a.	37	35	n.a.	35
East of Scotland	39	41	39	39	41	36	40
West of Scotland	39	34	37	37	39	36	37
Type Average	42	40	40	40	40	37	

Source: Constituency data file.
Note: Arithmetical means of constituency proportions for all U.K. constituencies.

Table 4b: Predictors of the Proportion of Women in the Electorate

Predictor	Beta	S.E. Beta	T	Sig. T
Finance	.65	.069	9.48	.0000
Agricultural	.21	.066	3.15	.0020
Male Textile	.21	.056	3.74	.0003
Mining and Quarrying	−.26	.068	−3.85	.0002
Electrical	−.21	.064	−3.28	.0013
(Constant)			63.92	.0000

$R^2 = .61$
$S.E. = .014$
$F = 42.97$
$Sig.F = .0000$

$N = 137$ constant units in England and Wales.

Source: Census data file.

unit census figures for occupational characteristics of the population. It is fairly easy to predict the proportion of women in an electorate from a combination of variables measuring the occupational characteristics of the area: more than 60 per cent of the variance can be explained in this way, and a great deal of this is associated with the presence or absence of males occupied in the financial sector. It is evident therefore that the differing proportions of women in constituency electorates are to be explained partly by variations in the female proportion of the adult population and partly by differences in the rate of enfranchisement of women in communities with different occupational structures.

This leads to some rather surprising conclusions about the female vote at the 1918 and subsequent elections. In all studies of elections between 1918 and 1931 a strong correlation between the proportion of female voters and a constituency's propensity towards Conservative voting is clearly established. But this does not necessarily mean simply that women voted Conservative. The results reported above suggest that the female proportion of the electorate is in fact a fairly sensitive index of the class structure of a community, and that 'middle-class' constituencies consistently had a higher proportion of women in the electorate. The strong relationship between partisan allegiance and the female voter indicates a class-based, as well as a gender-based, politics; but at the same time it calls into question the working definitions of 'class'.

In the special circumstances of 1918 the differential enfranchisement of women had a further twist. A corollary of the results reported above is that the female electorate was more closely associated with the 'middle class' *within* as well as *between* communities.[32] Since the women were almost all at home and a significant proportion of the male electorate were on active service and therefore much less likely to cast their votes, the effective electorate in 1918 was substantially more 'middle-class' than it would have been if *either* there had been no war *or* there had been no female electorate of the sort set up by the 1918 Act. The interaction between a war and women electors was particularly potent. If any of the specifically female attitudes recorded in contemporary political anecdotes could be relied upon they would have tended to augment the effect of this interaction: both contented Coalitionists and aggrieved Labour men noted the enthusiasm of women as wives and mothers of the dead and wounded

[32] Although it is possible that working-class women in middle-class communities were more likely to be enfranchised than working-class women in working-class communities, the parsimonious interpretation of the figures is that in any community the middle-class women were more likely to be enfranchised, and that this is what explains the link between occupational structure and the proportion of women enfranchised. This would also be consistent with the legal conditions for enfranchisement of women, which favoured the wives of established householders and those who were householders in their own right. Moreover, any age-based franchise tends to discriminate in favour of longer-lived social groups.

for vengeance against the Germans, which led them to support the Coalition appeal. But the observation, noted below, that the female proportion of the electorate weighed more against Labour than against opposition Liberals suggests that class differences were of greater significance.

The other major new element in the electorate was the 'new male' voter; individuals who would probably not have been enfranchised under the 1883–5 legislation, but who got the vote now by being over 21 or by virtue of active service in the forces. This is a more elusive group than women, because by definition it cannot be separately enumerated. The two ways to approximate the numbers of new male electors are by county, taking the difference between the 1915 electorate and the male electorate in 1918 as a decent approximation of the numbers of extra voters, or by an estimation procedure using the county figures to derive a relationship between social and occupational characteristics and the growth in the electorate. The second method can be used to estimate the proportion of new voters in each unit of analysis.

There is a weak but discernible relationship between the occupational characteristics of the counties and the proportion of their 1918 electorates which appear to be 'new': high proportions of 'new' voters are associated with low proportions of miners, agricultural workers and professional workers, and the three variables together account for nearly 40 per cent of the variance in apparently 'new' voters. This makes it possible to estimate the proportion in each unit of analysis by using the same variables. This estimate can then be used as an independent variable in the analysis of voting; but it is no more than an estimate and must be treated with reserve.

An Empirical Study of Voting in 1918

Most of the investigations reported here take the form of fitting regression equations to data about voting outcome as a dependent variable and various social and political variables as predictors. The units of analysis are either constituencies or 'constant units' consisting of groups of constituencies about which census data can be collected.[33] To seek a partial explanation of the voters' choice in the 1918 election a number of social

[33] The multiple regression equation takes the form of a linear additive combination of the independent variables, and the analysis provides an estimate — the standardised regression coefficient — of the contribution made by each independent variable to 'explaining' variance in the dependent variable. The reliability of this coefficient can also be estimated. The proportion of variance explained by the whole model is given by multiple correlation coefficient R^2. A fuller account of the nature of regression and multivariate analysis-of-variance models, their limitations, and the definitions of the variables used, can be found in Appendix I.

Table 5a: Predictors of the Labour Vote, 1918

Predictor	Beta	S.E. Beta	T	Sig. T
No Major Party Opponent	.26	.04	6.15	.0000
Against a Coupon	−.19	.04	−4.49	.0000
Mining Seat	.22	.05	4.51	.0000
Women Electors	−.28	.05	−5.82	.0000
Roman Catholic Priests	−.13	.05	−2.95	.0034
Candidate Chosen by Nov. 1918	.10	.04	2.37	.0182
Agricultural	.20	.05	4.23	.0000
(Constant)			9.05	.0000

$R^2 = .35$
$S.E. = .10$
$F = 23.84$
$Sig.F = .000$

$N = 375$ United Kingdom Constituencies.

Source: Constituency data file.

and occupational measures were taken from the 1921 census to indicate the occupational structure (and as a working inference the class structure) of constituencies and groups of constituencies. As explained more fully in Appendix I, these measures could for the most part only be applied to groups of constituencies rather than to individual constituencies. Moreover the 1911 and 1921 censuses give information about occupations which is very difficult to interpret in terms of any accepted theory of class structure. A complementary but crude way of establishing the class structure of constituencies was to use the sixfold typology pioneered by Pelling, who divided London constituencies into middle-class, mixed-class and working-class types; to this the three categories of urban/rural, rural and mining were added by Neal Blewett to cover the whole of England.[34] In the present study this has been extended to Scotland and Wales. Other constituency characteristics explored were the proportion of women voters on the register and the proportion on the register who were likely to have been 'new' male voters. A further important set of figures concerned the religious complexion of constituencies.[35] In the discussion which follows the 'models' presented are not the only ones which were explored: the tables give examples of relationships discovered, but it is not suggested

[34] The first two categories are defined by the proportion of the constituency's area covered by urban districts, the last by an estimate of the proportion of miners in the electorate.

[35] This was inferred from the census data on the distribution of clergymen, following methods developed by W.L. Miller. Fuller descriptions of the measures, together with grave warnings about their reliability, appear in Appendix I.

that the 'predictors' of the voting behaviour of constituencies are the only determinants of the outcome.

Table 5b: Predictors of the Conservative Vote, 1918

Predictor	Beta	S.E. Beta	T	Sig. T
Sitting Liberal	−.14	.04	−3.60	.0004
Established Labour Candidate	−.12	.04	−2.87	.0044
Coupon in Favour	.30	.04	7.54	.0000
Professionals	.19	.05	3.49	.0006
Metal Workers	.09	.05	1.98	.0485
Electrical Workers	.17	.04	3.93	.0001
Women Electors	.16	.05	3.49	.0006
Catholic Priests	.11	.04	2.63	.0088
Middle Class Seat	.11	.05	2.34	.0197
Mining Seat	−.19	.04	−4.40	.0000
Working Class Seat	−.11	.05	−2.49	.0132
London Seat	−.10	.04	−2.26	.0245
(Constant)			−.36	.7182

$R^2 = .47$
$S.E. = .11$
$F = 27.71$
$Sig.F = .0000$

$N = 357$ United Kingdom Constituencies.

Source: Constituency data file.

SOCIAL, OCCUPATIONAL AND RELIGIOUS CORRELATES OF VOTING CHOICE

The analyses were concerned both with changes in the electorate brought about by the 1918 Representation of the People Act and with more stable characteristics of the population which could be measured in the census. Tables 5a–5d illustrate the sort of relationships identified. The proportions of both women and new male voters in the electorate varied considerably from constituency to constituency. As shown below, a high female proportion in the electorate was correlated with Conservative voting, and with Coalition voting, but not apparently with Liberal voting; and it told heavily against the Labour vote. The simplest explanation is that women tend to vote Conservative more than men; this is supported by survey studies of more recent elections, and also corresponds to the perceptions of the party organisers of all colours in 1918, who reported that women were particularly likely to vote for the Coalition and particularly likely to respond to patriotic appeals. But since women voters were not distributed randomly across the country, and since the effect was much stronger on the Conservative vote than on the Coalition vote, it is prudent to take account of the reservations noted above and conclude that the very strong 'female' propensity to vote against the Labour Party was also an indication of the well-established middle-class bias against Labour. A study of the effect of the enfranchisement of all women under the 1928 Representation of the People Act, the so-called flapper vote, tends to the same conclusion.[36] It is noteworthy that when the female proportion of the electorate was excluded from the analyses the 'London effect' increased markedly, though not enough to suggest that the significance of the female vote was entirely a matter of regional variation.

The role of new voters is also problematic. The analyses at constituency level suggest that their presence was positively but very weakly correlated with Labour voting. This is an awkward result. If valid, it calls into question Tanner's supposition that the new franchise was irrelevant to Labour's rise, but does not offer very strong support to the Matthew, McKibbin and Kay thesis that the franchise was the most important determinant of change.

The tables also show the effect of including religion and a measure of class. It is evident that the variation apparently accounted for by social variables is less substantial than the variation brought about by manipulations of the structure of the contest. The determinants of the Conservative vote in the model noted in Table 5a are particularly interesting. That the party should do better in middle class seats than in mining or working class seats is not surprising. That it should, taking other considerations into account, do less well in London than elsewhere is tantalising, as is the apparently favourable impact of workers in the electrical and metalworking trades. The odd distribution of electrical workers, associated with modernising industry where trade-union affiliations were weakest, is likely to be a partial explanation for this phenomenon; and within working-class constituencies metal-working was associated with the West Midlands, where Liberal Unionism was strong. But the dominant note is political organisation — the favourable effect of the Coupon and the resistant qualities of sitting Liberal members and established Labour organisations — and the association of Conservative voting with high proportions of professional workers and women voters. The association of Conservative voting with a strong representation of Catholic priests, which would normally be expected to imply the presence of a self-aware Irish community, is at first sight odd: a plausible explanation is that it reflects the density of Irish settlement in Lancashire and the West of Scotland, where it stimulated anti-Irish feeling and thus an Orange shade of Conservatism.

---

[36] Turner, 'Sex, Age and the Labour Vote in the 1920s' in Peter Denley and Deian Hopkin, eds, *History and Computing II* (Manchester: Manchester University Press, 1989), pp. 243–254; and see Jorgen Rasmussen, 'Women in Labour', *Electoral Studies* (1984), 47–63.

Table 5c: Predictors of the Uncouponed Liberal Vote, 1918

Predictor	Beta	S.E. Beta	T	Sig. T
Electrical Workers	−.26	.07	−4.02	.0001
Agricultural Workers	.17	.07	2.59	.0100
Middle Class Seat	−.14	.06	−2.48	.0139
Couponed Opponent	−.15	.06	−2.66	.0083

$R^2 = .19$
$S.E. = .13$
$F = 17.24$
$Sig.F = .0000$

$N = 267$ United Kingdom constituencies.

Source: Constituency data file.

More surprisingly, perhaps, the measurable differences between constituencies on religious variables appear to have had little overall effect. In Miller's constant-unit analyses the impact of sectarian variation was about half as strong as the impact of class. The presence of Catholic and Anglican clergy was associated with lower Labour votes, and the presence of Nonconformist clergy was, to a rather lesser extent, associated with higher Labour votes. Distinguishing as Miller does between sectarian effects (caused by differences in the denominational balance) and 'religiosity' effects (caused by the overall saturation of clergymen, not by the intensity of belief), one can say that religiosity effects were unusually low in 1918, less than half what they were still to be in 1974. The effect of sectarian variation was higher than in any subsequent year, but even so paled in significance before the arrangements made by the Coalition organisers. In the present analysis only the presence of Catholic priests seems to have had a marked impact, and that only on the Labour and Conservative votes. This is largely because sect in 1918 discriminated between Conservative and Liberal candidates, not between Conservative and Labour or between Conservative and all others; and the Coupon had ensured that even in three-way contests the conflict between Conservative and Liberal was not interpreted as a traditional party fight by all potential Liberal voters.

This perspective suggests that the distribution of the Labour vote in the 1918 election was influenced heavily by the Coupon, as intended and expected, and that, for whatever reason, the Coalition did disproportionately well in constituencies where women voters were strongly represented. The Coupon was intended to stifle the effects of opposition, and it worked.

Table 5d: Predictors of Aggregated Coalition Vote, 1918

Predictor	Beta	S.E. Beta	T	Sig. T
Professional Workers	.11	.052	2.17	.0308
Electrical Workers	.17	.044	3.88	.0001
Women Voters	.13	.050	2.56	.0107
Mining Seat	−.20	.046	−4.25	.0001
Middle Class Seat	.12	.050	2.39	.0173
(Constant)			1.21	.2250

$R^2 = .20$
$S.E. = .15$
$F = 23.38$
$Sig.F = .0000$

$N = 440$ United Kingdom constituencies.

Source: Constituency data file.

REGIONAL STRENGTHS AND WEAKNESSES

Even when the relationships in Tables 5a–5d are examined, a great deal of variation is left to be accounted for. A direct way to look at this is to tabulate the average residual — the difference between a party's actual share of the vote and the value predicted by the model — for each combination of region and constituency type.[37] This gives an immediate picture of the areas and constituency types in which any of the political groupings seems to have been over-performing or under-performing consistently. In terms of an expressive theory of voting, it shows the extent to which Labour seems to have capitalised on such strength as it drew from the social structure of the constituencies which it fought. Nothing more than a partial survey of spatial variation in voting behaviour in 1918 is possible here. But even the limited glimpse which it gives can indicate why the problem of explaining the overall decline of Liberal voting and its replacement by the habit of voting Labour has proved so intractable and controversial among historians who have concentrated upon generalisations at the national level.

The most important inference to be drawn from this exercise is that Labour's weakness in London was greater than could be accounted for by measurable social and religious indicators. This under-performance in fact continued throughout the inter-war period. This can be left to stand as an example of genuine regional differences in electoral behaviour,

[37] In the residual tabulation shown here the residuals are 'standardised' before tabulation, that is the raw residual is divided by the standard deviation of all residuals.

Table 6: Geographical Distribution of Labour Residuals from Table 5a

	Middle class	Mixed class	Working class	Urban rural	Rural	Mining	Regional average
London	−.14	−.23	−.28	n.a.	n.a.	n.a.	−.20
South East	−.06	−.38	.48	−.21	.60	n.a.	−.02
East Anglia	.14	−.88	n.a.	n.a.	.17	n.a.	−.28
Central	.17	.38	.81	.91	.83	n.a.	.91
Wessex	−.42	−.66	n.a.	.36	.36	n.a.	−.18
Bristol	.88	−.15	1.56	−.83	.46	2.94	.55
Devon & Cornwall	−.23	−.28	−.70	1.75	−1.31	n.a.	.16
West Midlands	n.a.	.60	−.17	.15	.43	n.a.	.15
East Midlands	n.a.	−.48	.21	.08	−.07	.12	−.03
Lancastria	.21	.06	.18	−.40	n.a.	1.42	.13
Yorkshire	−.99	−.49	.12	−1.09	−1.96	.22	−.24
North of England	n.a.	−.62	.08	.84	−.24	.04	−.10
Wales	n.a.	−.36	.59	.57	.41	−.25	−.01
Highlands	n.a.	n.a.	n.a.	.68	−1.09	n.a.	−.50
East of Scotland	−1.26	−1.26	.74	−.44	−.05	3.05	.06
West of Scotland	−.53	−1.30	.19	.20	−.08	−.25	−.02
Type Average	−.08	−.33	.15	.04	.13	.16	.00

Source: Constituency data file.
Note: The more extreme figures in the body of the table are for categories which include only one or two constituencies, such as the isolated mining constituency of Forest of Dean in the Bristol region. For that reason the marginal averages for type and region are of rather greater significance.

to be explained by the influence of communities upon their members; or it could be suggested that notwithstanding the occupational structure of working-class communities in London, the industrial structure, and thus the labour process, favoured smaller workshops, less unionisation and higher labour mobility, and thus discouraged the class solidarity which encouraged Labour voting elsewhere. Unfortunately the available data does not give a systematic insight into variations in the labour process.

The apparent under-performance of Labour candidates in Yorkshire and the West of Scotland mining and mixed-class urban seats is more surprising. Labour did well in Scotland, but the model would predict that it should have done better. This was an area of robust Liberalism, crippled but not destroyed by the Coupon, but the beneficiary in 1918 was the Conservative Party. The unusual proportion of three-way contests, which were concentrated in the burghs and the industrialised or miner-dominated seats in the central counties, does much to explain this. Liberalism had enough vigour to split the historic anti-Conservative vote, suppressing Labour's appeal. But it did not have the resilience to survive the post-war Coalition with its organisation intact, and in 1922 the advantage flowed to Labour, which won electoral victories that corresponded more closely to its roots in Scottish industrial society. In 1918 there were also some special reasons for Labour's local weaknesses in Scotland. The circumstances of Coalition inevitably gave a remarkable boost to Bonar Law in Glasgow Central, where the Labour candidate struggled to get a decent vote; and in Lanarkshire, which should have been a good area for Labour, the Conservatives gained from outstanding performance of Walter Elliott, later reckoned one of the most impressive of new Tory members, in Lanark, and Arthur Buchanan, a local landowner, in Coatbridge. In Yorkshire, except in the mining seats, Labour candidates found it difficult to push ahead. Here the greatest obstacles, apparently, were the Coalition Liberals.

Wales also had structural peculiarities in the 1918 election, in its case a dire shortage of Conservatives coupled with the Coalition organisers' decision to allow unopposed Labour victories in the strongest Labour seats. When opposed, therefore, Labour candidates were on average less favourably placed than they were to seem in 1922. Official Labour did its cause no good, either, by putting up a candidate in Aberdare against C.B. Stanton, who could have held the seat against John the Baptist himself and had little difficulty against the Rev. T.E. Nicholas, who took a mere 21 per cent of the vote for Labour. However if only the seats fought in both years are examined it appears that Labour in Wales was quite close to its 1922 strength by 1918, and that with few exceptions Labour victories after 1918 can be accounted for by the misfortunes of the other parties. One such exception was Neath, where Labour's share of the vote was nearly doubled between 1918 and 1922, and by moving into Aberavon Ramsay MacDonald raised his party's share from 35.7 per cent to 46.6 per cent. But in Pontypridd, for example, Labour first won the seat on a massive turnround in July 1922, when the Liberal T.A. Lewis was defeated on going to the polls on appointment as a Whip, and they held the seat in the general election of October 1922 with only 5 per cent more of the poll than they had lost with in 1918. Their victory was made by the successful intervention of a Conservative, who apparently took Liberal votes. Stanton's magic ceased to work in Aberdare and in 1922, fighting as a Liberal, he lost heavily to Labour.

Especially when compared with results for 1922 in the same constituencies, the regional variations in Labour's performance are thus powerful evidence of the success of the Coupon in defusing a latent but very real threat from the Labour Party in industrial areas of England and in Wales and Scotland. In London, and in most of the mainly agricultural counties, Labour was weak where it was represented at all, and its weakness was greater than predicted by socio-economic models. However there is a slight but undeniable hint that, taking other factors into account, Labour was slightly stronger than would be expected in the most rural areas of the English counties, where wages were lowest and conditions harshest. It would still never have been able to win an agricultural seat, but in some areas, notably East Anglia, the impact of wartime policies and politics on agriculture gave it a fillip.

Some of the examples are telling. In King's Lynn E.K. Hemmerde, an anti-Coalition Liberal, withdrew from the contest and recommended Liberals to support a local organiser of the Agricultural Labourers' Union, W.B. Walker. This was not a solitary case, and the tendency was remarked by Buckler in one of his reports to Colonel House.[38] Moreover, Walker polled 49.1 per cent of the vote. The 1922 result suggests that in this case Liberals had split almost evenly between Walker and the Coalition Conservative. After 1922, Labour dropped markedly, and only won the seat in 1945 (with 48.7 per cent of the vote). Edwin Montagu, facing another Agricultural Labourers' Union candidate in his Cambridgeshire seat, found that 'notwithstanding...that he only decided to fight the Sunday before Nomination Day, he made me fight as I have never fought before and in this Conservative Constituency, so Conservative as to be usually Liberal, he frightened Conservatives and Liberals almost out of their wits.' Montagu's explanation was that

when the farmer could terrorise the labourer, he voted — he had to vote — with him. Now that the farmer cannot sack the labourer, either because he is a Trade Unionist or because there is such a scarcity of labour, all the young labourers, all the boys who are growing up, and indeed, some of the old ones, are determined on revolutionary ideas and will swallow any talk such as my opponent Stubbs (why do Labour candidates always get the right names?) fed them on.

With the additional difficulties that local mineral deposits had been worked by the Ministry of Munitions, paying up to £4 a week when local wages

[38] Buckler to House, 3 Dec. 1918, Buckler Papers 654/II/5/12.

had only just been raised to 30/- by the wages boards, and that the voters did not believe that the Tories would 'back you up in a really democratic agricultural policy', poor Montagu evidently felt that his couponed seat had been unduly hard work.[39] He won comfortably, but Labour's 35 per cent of the vote was hardly dented throughout the inter-war period, and Stubbs finally took the seat in 1945.

Above all though, Labour's voting strength in 1918 rested upon the mining seats, even more than on working-class seats in industrial and other towns. Even in mining communities the Coupon was a potent weapon, but Coalition organisers were most concerned with damage limitation: to allow a miners' candidate a free run, especially when he was unlikely to be a vigorous opponent of the Coalition in the new parliament, was a cheap and fairly safe option. The comparison between 1918 performance, by-election performance, and the behaviour of mining electorates in 1922, discussed below, suggests that the mining vote for Labour, strong as it was in 1918, strengthened further, and on average showed more solid gains during the immediate post-war period than other Labour electorates. This was true in Scotland, where as noted above the Liberal vote had first to be destroyed by Conservative intervention aided by the Coupon, but the ex-perience of the West Riding of Yorkshire was particularly telling. Increases in the Labour share in mining constituencies from 1918 to 1922 varied between 25 per cent and more than 50 per cent, mostly at the expense of Liberals. In a poignant contrast the notorious Spen Valley division, an ur-ban working-class constituency with a relatively low proportion of miners whose rejection of a Coalition Liberal candidate in December 1919 — 'the beginning of a psephological earthquake' according to Cowling[40] — jolted Conservative confidence in the utility of the Coalition arrangement, returned its Labour member in the 1919 by-election with a *lower* share of the vote than he had had in 1918. In 1922 his share declined even further, and Sir John Simon was returned as an independent Liberal because the Coalition Liberal candidate of 1919 was replaced by a Conservative. The contrast between mining and non-mining seats could not be more clearly expressed.

The residuals from the better-fitting models of Labour voting can also be used to examine individual constituencies and small groups of con-stituencies, posing interesting questions. Surprisingly high Labour polls in Wednesbury and West Bromwich suggest some survival of the anti-government spirit of the engineering strikes, but this is hardly confirmed by the poor Labour performance in Greenock and the rather ordinary showing in the working-class constituencies of Glasgow, where only John

[39] Montagu to Lloyd George, 16 Dec. 1918, Lloyd George Papers F/40/2/24.
[40] Cowling, *Impact of Labour*, p. 26.

Wheatley in Shettleston managed to put up an unusual performance at 49.8 per cent. Some unexpectedly high Labour polls in the Bristol region — especially Bristol East, the Forest of Dean and the Frome division of Somerset — were related to the humiliating collapse of local Liberalism, though the direction of cause and effect is far from clear. In Bristol East and Frome, neither of which was wholly transformed by the boundary reform, the Conservative vote was little changed by comparison with the run of pre-1914 elections, while a solid Liberal vote was exchanged in 1918 for a solid Labour vote. The humiliation of Hobhouse[41] was encompassed at East Bristol. Part of the explanation was that Frome was influenced by miners. In the Forest of Dean, ineluctably a miners' constituency with social characteristics described by Pelling as 'frontier conditions',[42] the Conservatives withdrew in favour of a Coalition Liberal candidate who was nevertheless trounced.

Despite the generally weak performance of Labour in London, there were pockets of strength in East London and the heavily urbanised areas of Essex and Kentish London. In the 1918 election these pockets were associated with sitting members, such as Will Thorne and Arthur Henderson, or with notable figures such as Lansbury. Stepney and Whitechapel, where the turmoil of anti-conscriptionist and anti-immigrant politics was greatest, had low enfranchisements and low turnout. In those areas the advance of Labour by 1922 and 1923 was unusually rapid, reflecting the effective organisation of the Irish and Jewish labour movements, and their co-operation, in the years after the war. This co-operation had not been achieved in December 1918.

A survey of unexpectedly high Labour polls throughout the country suggests that prominent trade unionists were particularly well favoured; for example John Hodge in Manchester, Gorton had all the advantages of being a sitting member, a former minister, a local trade unionist and a large personality, with none of the disadvantages of a Coupon against him. Ben Tillett was also left alone in Salford North. Even against a Coupon, James Sexton in St Helens won Labour's third general election victory since 1906, in a constituency whose strong Labour traditions have been noted in Chapter 1.[43] The contrasting experience of Bonar Law's Labour opponent in Glasgow, or the unfortunate independent Labour candidate in Shoreditch who opposed Christopher Addison (and H.G. Chancellor, himself well known as a sitting and radical Liberal), suggests that famous names could cut both ways. This in turn leads to the conclusion that politics at national level had its own specific impact on voters who might choose Labour. Over and above any 'expressive' reasons for casting or

[41] See above, p. 321.
[42] Pelling, *Social Geography*, p. 156.
[43] See above, p. 29.

withholding a Labour vote, electors in 1918 were responding to personality and the flow of Westminster politics.

It is hardly even noteworthy that Conservative and Liberal candidates were able to attract support in some areas which was much greater than anything predicted by the measurable characteristics of the constituencies. The robustness of local idiosyncrasy has been documented for the British electorate up to the present day; R.J. Johnston has made a particularly effective study of geographical variation in the flow of the vote in the 1983 election, with the advantage of very convenient data.[44] The consequence of the Coupon arrangement was that the voters' choice was anticipated; Liberals were put where Liberals were expected to win, and their victories — commonly over Labour candidates — were therefore bigger than they probably would have been without a Coupon. Opposition Liberals, of course, were in a different predicament. The appearance of a Liberal without a Coupon suggested either that a sitting member or a candidate selected by a local party before the end of the war was a known Asquithian, or that national organisers thought that the Conservatives stood a better chance of winning. These two points were uncorrelated. Since uncouponed Liberals, in addition, often presented the electorate with an appeal which was nearly indistinguishable from that of a Coalition candidate, it is especially difficult in these circumstances to know what a vote cast for an uncouponed Liberal was supposed to mean.

The geographical distribution of Conservative and Liberal electoral victories, and also to an extent of their shares of the vote, therefore represents the intentions of the Coalition organisers just as much as it reflects the wishes of the voters. These intentions did not include any radical changes in the balance between Conservative and Liberal, and as noted above this was not always welcome to local party organisations, especially on the Conservative side. Correspondingly, efforts to correlate Liberal shares of the vote with the occupational characteristics of constituencies are not very fruitful. The overall effect was to maintain a Liberal presence in rural areas, such as Devon and Cornwall, where it had been strong before the war, but otherwise to confirm the Conservative hold on most agricultural seats and most middle-class urban areas. In Liverpool, most of London,

---

[44] R.J. Johnston, *The Geography of English Politics* (London: Croom Helm, 1985). Johnston has used the BBC/Gallup survey of voting intentions, which gives occupation and various measures of social class for each respondent. He used the whole panel to estimate the relationship between the independent variables and voting choice, then used census data — available for each constituency — to predict the vote for each constituency based on the make-up of that constituency in terms of the class indicators. He then mapped the differences between predicted and actual votes. The result was a series of cogent cartograms showing that Labour did better in the North and Midlands, and worse in London and the South-East, than any of the available social-class predictors would suggest; Conservative experience was almost a direct reflection of this.

and Birmingham 'popular' Conservatism was impervious to Liberal and Labour attack even in working-class seats.

Taking into account the predictors of Conservative success, there were still some unexpected results. Some Liberal sitting members managed to limit the damage caused by the Coupon: Sir Willoughby Dickinson in St Pancras North, for example, held his couponed Conservative opponent down to 41 per cent of the vote in a three-way contest, and in Islington South Thomas Wiles took 46 per cent against a Coalition Conservative. Although both men lost their seats, they held a significant share of the vote. Godfrey Collins in Greenock, J.A. Macdonald in Falkirk, and William Wedgwood Benn in Leith defended themselves well in respectable Scottish burgh constituencies. Although the prominent Asquithian ex-ministers felt very sorry for themselves, most put up rather better performances than their back-bench ex-colleagues: for example McKenna's defeat at Pontypool, where he came third after the Coalition Conservative, or Runciman's loss of Bootle, were not significantly worse than that of other Liberals in those areas.

In South East London the absence of coupons in Kennington and Southwark North seems to have told against the Conservative candidates, though in Lambeth North the sitting Conservative, Sir W.H. Gastrell, a Tariff Reformer and a senior figure in the Primrose League, managed to lose convincingly to the Liberal chairman of the Borough Council despite the advantage of a coupon. In general, with the notable exception of Hodge, mentioned already, and Arthur Henderson in East Ham, serious and unexpected Conservative defeats and near-misses were at the hands of Liberals rather than Labour candidates. At the other end of the scale the astounding victory of the Potato Controller, J.W. Dennis, who carried 86 per cent of a very low turnout against a Liberal in Birmingham Deritend, is only a trifle more difficult to explain than the victory of Col. Albert Buckley with 84 per cent of a much higher poll in Lancashire, Waterloo. Buckley was a Unionist with a Free Trade record and a good claim to be a war hero; his new constituency was carved out of Southport and the suburban areas of Ormskirk, with a strong middle class presence. Birmingham Deritend was part-successor to the old, solid working-class South constituency whose M.P. was Leo Amery. Amery had been unopposed at a 1911 by-election and moved on to an easy victory in Sparkbrook, the other seat carved out of Birmingham South; Dennis got the credit, and traditional West Midlands working-class Unionism held its own.

Among opposition Liberals, the most surprising results outside London and Scotland were at first sight those in the North East: the Seaham and Spennymoor divisions of Durham, and the two Middlesborough seats. But Evan Hayward in Seaham, and Penry Williams and Walter Thomson in Middlesborough might have gained some advantage from the Coupon, which all were offered and all refused; none had Conservative opposition. Nor did Sam Galbraith in Spennymoor, an old Lib–Lab member who was disappointed to be opposed by an official Labour candidate. George Lambert in Devon, South Molton, was a sitting member who once appeared on a Coalition list although he was opposed by a Coalition Conservative. The good fortune of these Liberals is probably a comment on the ambiguities of the Coupon, not on the political colour of their region; but the three very low Liberal polls in Frome, Yeovil and Swindon, including a humiliating 8 per cent for Sir John Barlow in the Frome seat which he had held since 1892, correspond to a marked shift to Labour by former Liberal voters in the Bristol region.

1918 and 1922 Compared

Figure 2 shows boxplots of the shares of the vote received by each of the major groups in the 1922 election, and can be compared with Figure 1 on page 408. The plots show starkly how the electoral performance of the parties varied between different types of constituency, and further analysis reveals a distinct regional pattern which was to prove permanently unfavourable to the survival of the Liberal Party.

With very few exceptions, Labour improved its performance between 1918 and 1922 in the seats which it fought at both elections. Nevertheless there are significant differences between regions and constituency types. Of the 14 urban middle class constituencies which Labour contested twice, 10 showed an increase and four a decrease. In mixed class constituencies the ratio was 59 to 17, and in working class areas 86 to 24; these comparisons reinforce the impression that in the towns some sort of latent class-based voting choice was somehow suppressed in 1918. In urban/rural areas the ratio of 28 to 14 was essentially the same as in middle-class urban constituencies, but the unusually strong Labour performance in rural areas was checked in 1922, with 20 constituencies showing a decline against 15 showing an increase. The only regions where increases were more numerous than decreases in rural seats were East Anglia, Wales, and the West of Scotland. Labour's strength in mining constituencies was very much reinforced in the post-war period. Although the average gain was about the same as in working-class urban seats, the benefits were more evenly spread, with 38 seats showing an increase and only 5 (3 of them in the East Midlands) showing falls. This is consistent with the mining seats' having already achieved a higher Labour vote in 1918: a 'ceiling effect' prevented the stronger constituencies from going very much higher, so the large advances of those who were catching up only brought the average

Figure 2: Shares of the Vote in the 1922 Election

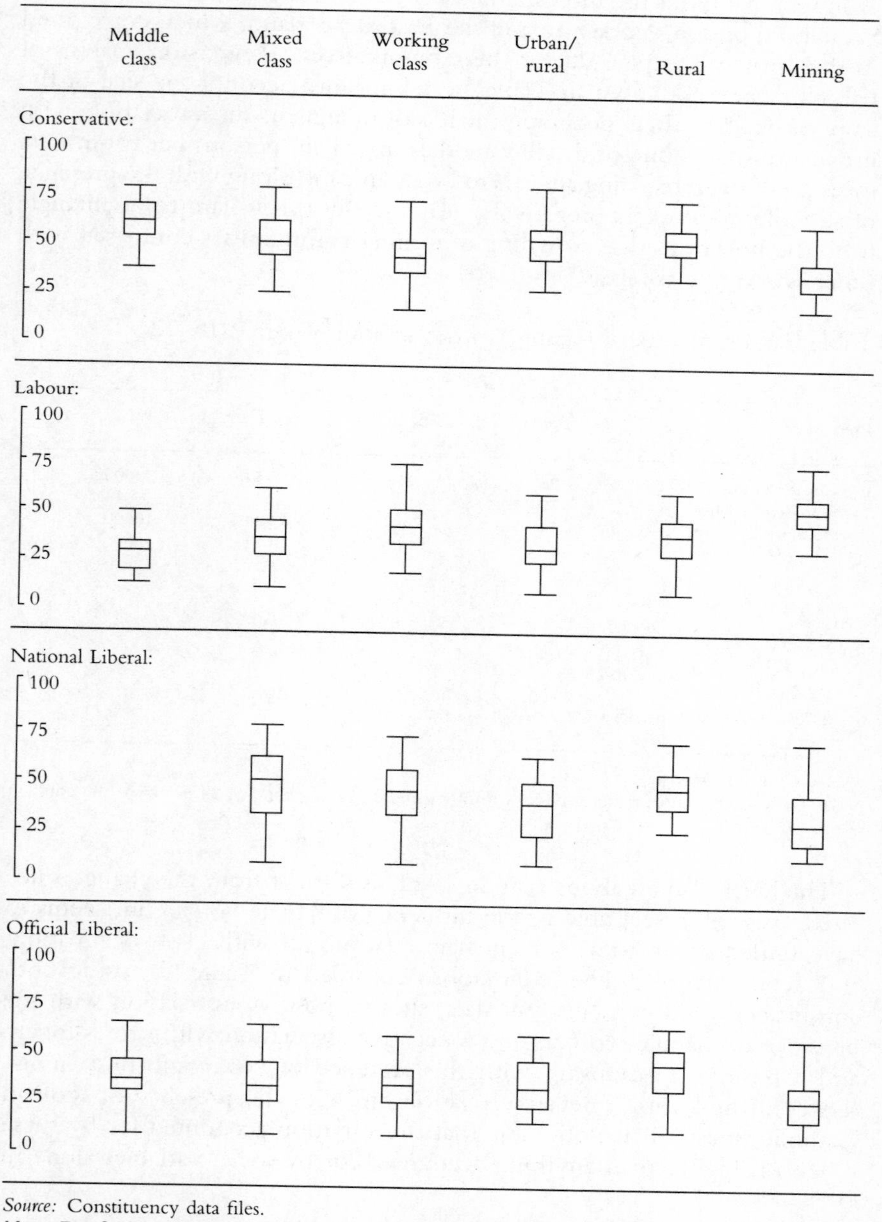

Source: Constituency data files.
Note: For further information on boxplots, see Appendix I. There were too few National (Lloyd George) Liberals to plot in middle-class seats.

gain to the same level as that of urban working-class seats.

In regional terms the most marked Labour increases were in the West of Scotland, London, Yorkshire and the East of Scotland, which correspond to the areas of sharpest fall for the Conservatives. Regression analysis of Labour's gains as shown in Table 7a, taking into account the size of the gains as well as their geographical location suggests an association with urban stress: it is one of the few models in which 'persons per room' as a measure of overcrowding appears to be significant, along with the presence of agricultural workers (negatively related). But this is hard to disentangle from the notorious overcrowding of mining communities compared with other working class areas.[45]

Table 7a: Predictors of Change in the Labour Vote, 1918–22

Predictor	Beta	S.E. Beta	T	Sig. T
Persons per room	−.26	.07	−3.51	.0005
Nonconformist Ministers	.19	.06	3.23	.0014
Agricultural Workers	−.24	.08	−3.11	.0020
(Constant)			5.01	.0000

$R^2 = .17$
$S.E. = .10$
$F = 21.0$
$Sig.F = .0000$
$N = 268$ U.K. constituencies contested at both elections.

Source: Constituency data file.
Note: These coefficients predict variations from a general upward trend of 24 per cent (the constant term).

The level of the Labour vote in 1922, as distinct from the change since 1918, was still susceptible to the influence of female voters, but seems to have settled down to a more prosaic relationship with class, occupation, and denomination. The explorations recorded in Table 7b, using both constituency and constant unit data, show a positive association with the presence of manual workers and a negative association with professionals, and a positive relationship with the presence of Nonconformist ministers compared with a negative relationship with the presence of Roman Catholic priests. It is noticeable that the variation accounted for by these models is higher than anything accounted for by social variables alone in 1918.

[45] The relationship is in any case not overpoweringly strong, the two variables together accounting for no more than 20 per cent of the variance.

Table 7b: Predictors of the Labour Vote, 1922

Predictor	Beta	S.E. Beta	T	Sig. T
Women Voters	−.35	.05	−7.33	.0000
Established Candidate in 1918	.22	.04	5.00	.0000
Persons per room	.25	.05	5.26	.0000
Nonconformist Ministers	.15	.04	3.42	.0007
Roman Catholic Priests	−.11	.04	−2.57	.0163
Textile Workers	.11	.04	2.41	.0163
(Constant)			12.77	.0000

$R^2 = .38$
$S.E. = .10$
$F = 37.23$
$Sig.F = .0000$

$N = 348$ United Kingdom constituencies.

Predictor	Beta	S.E. Beta	T	Sig. T
Non-manual Workers	−.73	.08	−8.23	.0000
Professional Workers	−.29	.07	−4.09	.0001
Nonconformist Ministers	.46	.08	5.84	.0000
Constant			11.37	.0000

$R^2 = .54$
$S.E. = 10.26$
$F = 48.54$
$Sig.F = .0000$

$N = 121$ United Kingdom Constant Units

Source: Constituency and Constant Unit data files.

At first sight the experience of the Conservative Party seems paradoxical. Its average loss in share of the vote between 1918 and 1922 was 8 per cent. In no sub-category of region and constituency type did the party show more gains than losses, and its average losses were worst in middle class urban seats and best (being about zero) in mining seats. Even in rural areas its share of the vote fell. Of middle class urban seats, 40 witnessed a decline in Conservative share while only 4 saw an improvement; of mining seats, by contrast, 7 showed an improvement against 10 which declined. The greatest losses were in the West of Scotland, which proved not to be natural Conservative territory after all. In Lanark, for example, Elliott and Buchanan were both faced by a 14 per cent swing to Labour; Elliott comfortably retained his seat but Buchanan was hit by the intervention of a Liberal who took 11 per cent of the vote, leaving Labour comfortably ahead.

Yet the Conservatives made a small net gain in seats in 1922. It appears that they did so by retaining many seats with reduced majorities, while gaining a number through the withdrawal of Coalition Liberals from seats where no Conservative had been put forward in 1918. The large increase in Conservative share of the United Kingdom vote, from 32.5 per cent in 1918 to 38.5 per cent in 1922, was achieved largely through the seats which had been left fallow in 1918. It is a safe inference that the Coalition had temporarily attracted a large number of Liberal voters through the Coupon, and that contemporary Conservative claims to have won the 1918 election by their own efforts were grossly exaggerated. Moreover the various models which account for Conservative voting in terms of social variables, an example of which is shown in Table 8, are rather less idiosyncratic for 1922 than for 1918. The most successful predictors are the proportion of professionals in the occupied workforce, the wealth of the constituency (marked in the example by the number of persons per room: the more comfortable the accommodation the greater the propensity to vote Conservative), the proportion of miners, and the extent to which Anglican clergy predominated over other clergymen in the district. Most models show that the areas with the highest proportion of agricultural workers were, other things being equal, less inclined to vote Conservative; this reflects the success of Liberals in rural areas in that election. The proportion of women in the electorate, which was so compelling in the 1918 election, slips behind the social composition of the male labour force and the denominational tendency of the population in its apparent political importance. Taken together these observations suggest that an underlying denominational factor in Conservative voting was suppressed or obscured by the circumstances of the 1918 election. It also suggests that some element of the 'female' propensity to support the Coalition in 1918 was more than just a reflection of class and religious allegiance: that there was something truly gender-linked in the women's vote which backed Lloyd George and the Tory party.

These impressions are partly confirmed by the fate of the Liberal candidates in seats contested at both elections. Almost all National Liberal candidates, fighting as successors to the Coalition Liberal tradition in 1922, saw their share of the vote decline when confronted by Conservative opponents. The few exceptions were in seats where a third party had withdrawn, and those where a candidate fighting in 1918 with National Democratic Party or British Workers' League support had been succeeded by, or redefined himself as, a more conventional Liberal. Seats fought by an uncouponed Liberal in 1918 and again by an 'official' Liberal in 1922 show a more varied and interesting pattern. In most respects their experience was very much like that of Labour, with more gains than losses in share of the vote in five out of the six categories of seat; where

Table 8: Predictors of the Conservative Vote, 1922

Predictor	Beta	S.E. Beta	T	Sig. T
Miners and Quarrymen	−.19	.06	−3.36	.0000
Working-Class Seat	−.26	.05	−5.43	.0000
Mining Seat	−.21	.05	−3.79	.0002
Textile Workers	−.16	.04	−3.46	.0006
Agricultural Workers	−.37	.06	−6.07	.0000
Persons per room	−.31	.06	−4.95	.0000
Anglican Predominance	.13	.05	2.50	.0130
(Constant)			4.11	.0000

$R^2 = .38$
$S.E. = .10$
$F = 34.71$
$Sig.F = .0000$

$N = 380$ United Kingdom constituencies.

Source: Constituency data file.

it differed, it reflected Labour experience as though in a mirror. In all urban categories and in the 'urban/rural' group there were more gains than losses in share of the vote, as though to mark a recovery from the calumnies of the 1918 campaign. In rural seats the official Liberals made a very strong recovery, with 26 seats showing an improvement against 9 showing a decline. The exception was in East Anglia, which suggests that Liberals were regaining agricultural territory lost to Labour except in the most heavily unionised areas. Correspondingly, 9 mining seats showed a reduction against 4 which showed an improvement, as though the consolidation of Labour at Liberal expense was advancing most rapidly in those seats; 2 of those 4 were in the East Midlands, where Labour's advantage in mining seats was least evident.

So bizarre were the political circumstances of 1918 and 1922 that it is worth asking whether the Liberal party taken as a whole in 1922, without regard to differences of label which were often obscure or controversial at the time, showed any regularity of experience. Some influence of social variables is detectable: the Liberal share of the vote is negatively associated with the presence of manual workers on the one hand and of professional workers on the other. There is variation between countries — a 'Welsh effect' and a 'Scottish effect' — which seems to subsume any relationship between denominational strength and the propensity of a constituency to incline towards a Liberal. Taken together, these observations suggest that any 'expressive' quality to the Liberal vote had become thoroughly unhinged by 1922. It has already been observed that withdrawals under the Coupon arrangement appear to have had a damaging effect on the

Liberals' capacity to recover in subsequent elections.

Comparison of 1922 results with those of 1918 illuminates some of the strange qualities of the Coupon election. It is clear that the withdrawal of Liberals under the Coupon had a heavier long-term cost than the concomitant withdrawals of Conservatives, since the Conservatives had no apparent difficulty in moving back into old territory to compensate for the absence of Coupon victories. Comparison of Labour performance in the two elections suggests that the powerful regional and occupational concentration of Labour voting, which has been characteristic of the party since the First World War, was visible but not fully established in 1918. The mining areas had not pulled away from all other categories of constituency, as they were to do in and after the 1922 election. The unsettling effect of the war on farmworkers had a temporary effect in 1918, but only in a few areas was it consolidated in subsequent elections. In other respects the 1922 result sharpened, rather than changed what was apparent in 1918: Labour's distinctive appeal in urban working-class constituencies was even more precisely mirrored by Conservative appeal to the middle class; beleaguered Liberals could match neither the Conservative appeal to the middle classes nor the Labour appeal to the miners, and their fine showing in the agricultural counties did them little good.

1918 and the new political geography

Both the election campaign described in Chapter 9 and the results analysed here make it clear that the 1918 general election was a deliberate and largely successful effort to hold back the advance of the Labour Party. The distortion of the Coupon makes it difficult to interpret the results for the Conservative Party; Conservatives did well, but they did so as part of a coalition, and it is impossible to tell for certain whether Conservatism or the Coalition was the appeal which lured potential Labour or Liberal voters away. But it is possible to draw conclusions about the rise of Labour and the decline of Liberalism. Firstly, the relationship between the new electorate and the rise of Labour is too contradictory to be reconciled with the 'franchise' theories first expounded by Matthew, McKibbin and Kay. The 1918 Act's major contribution to electoral change was to enfranchise women. Although it cannot be said for certain that they voted *as women* against the Labour Party, the sharp class-bias of the female franchise manifestly worked against Labour's interest in the short term. Labour's strength against the Coalition was apparently founded on trade union organisation and the habit of Labour voting built up *over long periods* in mining districts and urban working-class areas, with considerable impetus from the politics of personality. There was no sudden explosion of Labour strength, either in 1918 or later in 1922, and no 'Big Bang' theory is therefore necessary. Nor would it be compatible with what little can be observed about constituencies where new electors were particularly strongly represented. Secondly, important regional variations in Labour and Liberal performance in the difficult conditions of 1918 weaken any explanation cast purely in terms of class or sectarianism, or the transition between the two. Regional variation was more important than the national effects of class variation. Thirdly, the Coupon was an important discipline for the governing parties in a three-party system. Without it, Labour's share of the vote, constituency by constituency, would have produced many more Labour M.P.s, as it did in 1922.

The fragility of explanations based on class or sect is particularly striking, because it calls into question the very essence of 'class' as a political concept. Although it would be convenient to regard the 1918 and 1922 elections as part of a transitional stage in electoral history, between a largely sectarian political environment of the 1890s and a class-based politics more typical of the inter-war years, the messy reality of electoral allegiance rather suggests that the state of transition was almost permanent. The Liberal Party, after all, was still to have a good run for Lloyd George's money after 1922. In 1929 it even regained ground in middle-class constituencies where it had lost to the Conservatives in 1923 and 1924. In 1931 the vehemence of popular reaction to the financial crisis was such that Labour voters were in a minority among working-class electors. Throughout the inter-war years Labour's national share of the vote was grounded not just on trade unionists, but more specifically on special groups of trade unionists, particularly miners. What can be regarded as Labour's electoral bedrock is much more parsimoniously defined in geographical or even geological terms than in social terms; it included the coalfields, and wherever there were no coalfields the allegiance of the urban working class to Labour was fluctuating and conditional. Even after the 1945 election victory, which appeared to cement the relationship between the Labour Party and a fairly homogenous working class, steady changes in social structure associated with education and economic developments soon began to chip away at the 'traditional' working class. While the link between Labour and the working class still held, the working class itself began to shrink and diversify.[46]

It is therefore much more satisfactory, despite the rhetoric of class used so freely by politicians of all shades during the Coupon election, to look to a different and more fragmented model of electoral change. During the

[46] For a compact discussion see A. Heath, R. Jowell and J. Curtice, *How Britain Votes* (Oxford: Pergamon, 1985), pp. 25–43.

war changes in the labour process and the external threats to trade union expectations made large local impacts on working class electors, whether in munitions areas affected by strikes and overcrowding or rural areas suffering from the politics of envy. Ethnic loyalties, such as those of Jewish and Irish minorities, were aroused and transformed by wartime events. But this transformation did not take effect immediately, and long-term changes were still significant. Strike-hit areas, for example, were not prominent among the areas of high Labour polls; but trade union leaders, sometimes the very men whose accommodation with the government had been the despair of active trade unionists, were reliably returned with healthy shares of the vote. Labour, as a political rather than an industrial movement, was hardly revolutionary. It was, rather, a coalition of convenience in which the practice and language of socialism had a mediating, not a determining role. But it was potentially a formidable coalition, and well worth the effort which the Lloyd George Coalition put into restraining it.

12

A PERSPECTIVE

Political systems are about government, and in Britain during the First World War the challenges of government were at least as great as the competition for office which obsessed Edwardian politicians. The cry which united most British politicians was a demand for victory at almost any price. The call for 'more vigorous prosecution of the war' had the same almost liturgical quality as the appeal to 'national efficiency' had had in the first decade of the century. It was a substitute for thought, but instead of simplifying politics it made the pursuit and exercise of power more uncertain. War transformed the struggle for resources in British society. Acts and omissions of government changed the distribution of wealth and stirred up or kept alive conflicts between employers and workers. Traditional social, regional and religious differences were complicated by the trauma of war but rarely suppressed. Ideological fissures in educated society were reconsidered in the light of new problems but, again, were rarely made to vanish. Worse still, victory when it eventually came merely restated all the controversial questions about Britain's relations with Europe, with her overseas possessions, and with the United States. The loss of international economic hegemony, in particular, guaranteed that the distribution of wealth and industrial power would be a continuing element in political debate. Meanwhile the parliamentary struggle, especially the survival tactics of the Lloyd George Coalition, laid waste the Edwardian party system.

Historians have shown a natural desire to give straightforward answers to straightforward questions about the connection between the social and economic trauma of war and this transformation of party politics. The results are discussed in Chapter 1. Favoured perspectives have ranged from the grossly mechanistic among Marxist approaches, in which the movement of great social forces is seen as the cause of political change, to the extremes of contingent explanation represented by the high politics school.

Some writers locate the critical moment of change in the war, as the product of Liberal collapse; some look before it, to the inevitable consequence
of Labour's advance; some look afterwards to the fine calculations of the
supporters of the post-war Coalition. Although reductionism of some sort
is essential to historical writing, the main theme of this book is to challenge
these particular manifestations of it. Nobody should be forced to decide
whether the Labour Party had begun an inexorable rise before 1914, or
whether, by contrast, the Liberal Party still had life in it, or even whether
the Conservatives would have won an election in 1915. These questions
can only be answered with the preface 'if the war had not happened': but
it did happen, and the larger and more immediate job is to explain what
happened during the war and why, and then to relate this to the past and
the future.

This book began with the premise that the fundamental political issue
in early twentieth-century Britain was the power of the state. The scope
of state activity was as controversial as the question of who controlled the
state. The most important political innovation of the Edwardian decade
was to use, or promise to use state power to win the support of the electorate; the 'squalid argument' embodied as much in the haphazard social
innovations of the 1906–14 Liberal governments as in Chamberlain's Tariff
Reform campaign. Public policy, in the form of tariffs or Dreadnoughts
or old age pensions or elementary education, was used not only to appease
or stimulate known sections of the electorate, but to shape and manipulate
the electorate as it grew in size. Politicians recognised that some traditional
social formations such as Nonconformity were weakening, and some like
organised Labour were strengthening. Their aim was to control and profit
from these developments, rather than be overwhelmed by them. For this
it was essential to be in office and to use the apparatus of the state. A
political stance based on opposition at Westminster and tight control of
local politics, which had served both Liberals and Conservatives well in
the nineteenth century, was simply not good enough for the new era.

The state had by 1914 become anything but the 'neutral switchboard' of
pluralist theory or the passive instrument of bourgeois hegemony favoured
by Marxist interpretations. Political parties, once the means by which
court factions manipulated the Commons and an unreformed electorate,
then the tangible expressions of sectional interest in Victorian society, had
become political actors in their own right. The state which they controlled was increasingly potent and centralised. External threat — the
German menace — was sporadically used to partisan effect, but its major
consequence was a massive increase in central government expenditure,
which put further strain on the taxing power of the state, and a spasm of
authoritarianism exemplified in the Official Secrets Act. Internal threat to
the status quo was met sometimes with violence, as when strikers were

shot by the army 'in support of the civil power', more often by systematic conciliation and bargaining. Above all, both major parties used their legislative opportunities carefully, to create partisan advantage by centralising social functions. The Conservatives squashed radical opportunities in the school boards by subsuming the boards into county councils which were more often under Conservative control. The Liberals used the National Insurance legislation to substitute state welfare agencies for the motley of private and co-operative friendly societies, charities and trade unions which had won the allegiance and the affection of the workforce. The old cries of sentiment and sectionalism were still heard, but they were augmented by the measured use of state power.

Even before 1914 it was evident that the machinery of the state was scarcely powerful enough for the demands being made upon it. The outbreak of war, soon followed by efforts to mobilise the war economy for the production of munitions, confirmed what was already feared about Westminster's ability to influence the civilian population. The additional problem of controlling admirals and generals, and reconciling the demands of the army with the war economy's need for men, at last finished off the Edwardian hopes of the political parties. The rush to coalition in 1915, often interpreted as a conspiracy of the front benches against the back, was no less a rushing together of leading politicians in fear that their principal means of controlling the external world was about to break down.

This fear was probably better understood by the Liberals than by their erstwhile opponents. Senior Conservatives probably believed, and their back-bench followers certainly believed, that things would change dramatically for the better when Conservative ministers had charge of the offices of state. The most perspicacious were disillusioned almost immediately by the deliberations of the Dardanelles Committee, which concluded that although the operations at Gallipoli were not successful it would be too costly to abandon them. The failures of the immediate past were reinterpreted as evidence of the intractability of the problems facing any government, rather than the culpable errors of political opponents. This was necessary since the Conservatives now bore collective responsibility for the conduct of the war.

But still the partisans of a more vigorous prosecution of the war hoped that a more skilful and ruthless use of the state's power would create the opportunity for victory. It was easy for them to hope, but only so long as the complicated economic problem of manpower allocation was reduced to the simple ethical problem of the state's right to call on the lives of its citizens. During the unhappy life of the Asquith Coalition divisions among the political élite steadily diverged from the concerns of ordinary backbenchers, which were in turn less and less attuned to any form of public opinion. Lloyd George, Churchill and most of the Conservative ministers retained their confidence in the governing potential of the state; sceptical Liberals, led by McKenna at the Treasury, increasingly doubted that anything within the government's power could bring about the necessary conditions for victory against a determined enemy.

It was during this period, though, that the moral climate of warmaking came to exclude critics from any serious hearing. The moral tone of 'business as usual' was pervasive in the early months of the war. Although it has been shown by historians that the Liberal government was not dogmatically committed to *laissez-faire* methods in the control of the war economy, there is no doubt that many sections of the population, from businessmen to trade unionists and from Nonconformist clergymen to Unionist grandees such as Lord Lansdowne, simply did not believe that the outbreak of war meant a radical discontinuity with pre-war attitudes to public and private conduct. Businessmen made profits, sometimes by trading indirectly with the enemy; trade unionists pressed wage claims and disrupted munitions production; some ministers of religion preached war resistance; Lord Lansdowne wondered out loud whether Anglo–German rivalry was bad enough to fight a war about. During 1915 and 1916 such attitudes were marginalised. Even outright opponents of the war became more circumspect in their public and parliamentary statements. Ministers, led by Asquith, simply never referred to an alternative policy. Of all the dissident elements in the Cabinet only Lansdowne, who was too deeply established to care very much what people thought of him, maintained an open and dispassionate attitude to the war during 1916, which culminated in his provocative November memorandum.

From the viewpoint of Lloyd George and his sympathisers, who slowly came to include Bonar Law and one or two Conservative leaders who thought he was a lesser evil than Asquith, the failures of 1916 were largely caused by divisions at the top. At the time, and also in the retrospect of his memoirs, Lloyd George insisted that dozens of opportunities for the exercise of power were lost, from Crawford's earnest pleas for food control to the civilian Cabinet's reluctance to say boo either to Kitchener or to Sir William Robertson. Nervelessness in the hands which held the levers of power was, in this view, the besetting sin of the Asquith Coalition. The *putsch* of December 1916, with its rather misleading overtones of administrative reform, was designed bluntly to change the leadership so that the state's power could be directed properly.

Within six months of this political success, Lloyd George and his coadjutors had realised that something more profound was wrong. During 1916 the sense that political power was being misdirected was common to Liberals and Conservatives of all levels of seniority. Radical Liberals disliked the Conscription Acts as much as Unionist Conservatives disliked the apparent chicanery of the Irish settlement. The Asquith Coalition had too few friends for survival. Undoubtedly there were many Conservatives who saw the Lloyd George Coalition as a way of directing power as they would have it directed, and welcomed a practical political victory over war-shy Liberals. Having won this victory, they soon came to recognise its hollowness.

In short order the new government discovered that it was impossible to create a parliamentary majority without making restrictive promises to Labour, impossible to control strategy against the pro-military instincts of the Conservative back bench, impossible to satisfy military and civilian demands for manpower at the same time, impossible to coerce an industrial population into limitless improvements in productivity, and impossible to please the Irish Nationalists without upsetting Ulster Unionists. The dawning realisation, which unhappily coincided with the political and military collapse of Russia, reordered the priorities of those in power. For the first time since the outbreak of war, the prime minister and his immediate allies began to think of breaking up the existing parliamentary parties instead of simply yoking them together to maintain a coalition in office. Civil–military relations were an important spur: the ruthlessness with which the military authorities exploited the government's political weakness convinced the War Cabinet that change would eventually be necessary.

Between the early summer of 1917, when Lloyd George's minions first began to discuss their attitudes to the opposition Liberals, and the end of the year when Lansdowne's letter was used to flush out organised political resistance, each of the pre-war parties came under some pressure to split into loyalist and anti-government wings. The split in the Labour Party had been defined by the crisis in the party at the outbreak of war. The conscription crises of 1916 had shown how pro-war Labour men, especially trade unionists in the parliamentary party, could be drawn back towards opposition by specific issues. With Russia in disarray, the government made tentative approaches to Ramsay MacDonald which might have brought some of the anti-war faction over to the government on the peace issue. When this failed, partly because pro-war Labour in the shape of Havelock Wilson was too belligerent to co-operate, government organisers and the War Cabinet were forced to draw the line closer to the pro-war pole. Even this was fumbled during the Stockholm affair, because Conservative back-benchers, and some ministers, were unwilling to accept the necessary fudging from Arthur Henderson. The result, with Henderson's departure, was that the pro-war, pro-government wing of the Labour Party was smaller than it need have been and unable to expand to keep pace with the expansion of the 'official' Labour Party out of doors during the winter of 1917–18.

The muddle of Stockholm was largely caused by the determination of Conservative Party organisers and the more influential among its parliamentary leaders to prevent the split in the party which Lloyd George's plans would have implied. Even this simple aim was muddied by resentment of Bonar Law's apparent acquiescence in Lloyd George's more controversial policy inclinations. But Bonar Law, advised by Sir George Younger, was careful not to create conditions in which more than a handful of disgruntled back-benchers would follow rebels such as the National Party dissidents. To soothe the Unionist Business committee, and more senior malcontents such as Carson, the Conservative leader joined his War Cabinet colleagues in taking a hard line against Henderson. This gave him some political capital to spend, and his adroit handling of the Lansdowne controversy gave him more, but much of it was used up by the row over Robertson's dismissal in February 1918. Between then and the Maurice debate, the adherence of the Conservative Party to the Coalition was under more strain than ever before, and more than at any time until long after the war was over. Confidence in Bonar Law's leadership slumped, with Austen Chamberlain and Carson as two active House of Commons men excluded from office and Selborne and Salisbury leading the awkward squad in the House of Lords. Courageously, Bonar Law clung to the principle of coalition and urged the party organisers to prepare the machine for a coalition election. But the depth of co-operation between Conservatives and the Lloyd George Liberal organisation was strictly limited by Conservative reluctance to split the historic Unionist Party.

By contrast, the Liberal Party offered little resistance to the Coalition's attempts to split it. Indeed, the problem for Coalition organisers was that the party was too much inclined to split, and to do so on lines which were inconvenient for the government's purposes. This is witnessed by the repeated efforts to bring Asquith back into the administration. Had any of these attempts succeeded, it is highly unlikely that the whole contingent of semi-pacifist Liberals, sympathisers with the U.D.C., and disgruntled 'Liberal millionaires' would have come with him. Nor would Runciman and McKenna, loathed by Lloyd George and loathing him in return. Almost certainly Herbert Samuel would have done, though, and so would many solid Liberal back-benchers whose position in their constituencies would have qualified them for consideration for the Coupon in 1918 and significantly changed the balance of the post-war Coalition. Coalition Liberal organisers were repeatedly frustrated by Asquith's unpredictable and often petulant ventures into opposition in 1917 and early 1918. Although opposition Liberals saw the affair of the Lansdowne letter as an opportunity to bring about a Lansdowne–Asquith axis, Lloyd George played it as an effort to bring Asquith, a known opponent of a negotiated peace, closer to the government and to separate him from the anti-war Liberals. The terms of the Caxton Hall speech were just as much directed to Asquith as they were to war-weary trade unionists.

From this perspective, Asquith's failing was that he had come to detest and distrust Lloyd George, and that without doing much to encourage it he had become a natural focus for disgruntled members of the governing élite, whatever their party or allegiance. The government's critics came to him, and he therefore found himself at the head of — leading would imply too active a role — parliamentary excitements over the re-enlistment of medically discharged soldiers in the summer of 1917, over the Strategic War Council in November, over the sacking of Robertson in february and most disastrously over General Maurice's allegations against Lloyd George and Bonar Law in May. Since nothing he had done since his resignation had endeared him to the rank and file on the Tory back bench, none of these moves could have brought him back into office at the head of a robust alternative coalition. This point was made trenchantly by the Conservative back-benchers who rallied to the government against Maurice's charges, but it could have been inferred at any of the previous small crises. Asquith's determination to return as leader or not at all ensured that when the Liberal Party did split the dividing line would rest between him and Lloyd George, instead of cleanly between the pro-war and anti-war Liberals, and would leave both halves of the party weakened and incapable of recovering ground from Labour.

While the battle lines were being drawn, the shadow of a general election was never far away. The meaning of this spectre has not always been clear to historians, largely no doubt because it varied almost from month to month. At first, when the Coalition was in parliamentary difficulties in the early summer of 1917, the assumption among the Lloyd George Liberals who discussed it was that a quick war election under the existing franchise might return a more tractable House of Commons, which would give the War Cabinet a freer hand to control policy. At this point the unwanted M.P.s were both the opposition Liberals and the more discontented Tories, and the Coalition's appeal would have been over the heads of both parties. In those circumstances the advantages of going to the country were very finely balanced. Asquith's attitude to the war was opaque, and the success of any move against recalcitrant Tories depended on the Conservative Party machine's willingness to co-operate. Lloyd George's personal popularity, on which success would depend, was extremely uncertain. It was therefore easy to shelve the project. When it reappeared, after Stockholm and after the summer recess, it was different. Now the difficulty was not simply in the House of Commons but in public opinion — reported by the censors, in the newspapers, through the medium of trade union organisation and in other ways — which had begun to question the wisdom of fighting the war as the Coalition was fighting it.

The purpose now contemplated by Lloyd George's closest advisers, and also by senior Conservatives, was not so much to take advantage of the current of public opinion as to use political activity to change its direction. The target was Labour, especially its more pacifist elements and the rank-and-file movement which threatened industrial production. Consequently the stand-off between the two wings of Liberalism was deliberately minimised, at least by Christopher Addison, and discussions between Coalition Liberals and Coalition Conservatives went on as though a war-only election was all that was wanted.

Even if the party organisers had had time to draw breath between parliamentary crises, and even if the leading politicians in government had been able to commit time to electoral work as well as to manpower shortages and strategic conundrums, they now faced a new constraint. The imminence of electoral reform under the Representation of the People Act would have made it extremely difficult to justify an election before the new franchise had come into effect. Not only was the government forced to postpone an election, it was forced to reconsider the means by which an election under the new franchise might be fought and won.

Until the March crisis, negotiations within the Coalition about election plans and programmes moved fairly slowly. During the period of intense activity immediately following the German breakthrough they were interrupted completely, and the subsequent row about Irish policy and then the Maurice affair prevented a single-minded push. By the time conversations were resumed seriously the terms of alliance had changed once more. Many groups and individuals in the Coalition agreed that they wanted a Coalition election but not what they wanted it for. While there were some who still wanted to dish the Asquithians, many Liberal and Conservative Coalitionists wanted above all to make sure that the Labour Party was divided in the next parliament, whether in war or peace. For some the ideal election cry would still have been 'the more vigorous prosecution of the war'; others would have preferred an appeal on peace and reconstruction issues whose hidden purpose would have been to return a sounder war ministry; yet others wanted a 'war' cry to guarantee a safe government in peacetime; and as the weeks wore on it became more and more obvious that the election would be fought at or near the end of the war, so a peacetime programme would be almost obligatory. Until August there was no confidence at the top that the war would be over before 1919, and as late as September there was no open acknowledgement of an election plan. Programmes for an election were still in contention as late as October, not least because neither the purpose of keeping a coalition in being nor its likely duration were agreed between Liberal and Conservative Coalitionists.

With this level of uncertainty among contemporaries it is difficult to speak of the Coupon election being either a wartime election designed to secure a war ministry or a peacetime election designed to take advantage of wartime emotion to return a conservative administration; nor can it safely be said that it was first one of these things and then the other. Once the two leaders had decided to fight as coalition partners and persuaded their followers to agree, the immediate purpose was to win as large a majority as possible. The Coupon was the principal means to that end. The Coalition programme also helped, and the content of the election campaign, especially after the change of tone in the middle, was carefully tuned to what the electorate seemed to want. But as Chapter 11 shows, it is unwise to generalise too broadly about the response of the electorate to the campaign itself.

The Coupon election secured a Coalition victory, but it did not make the political world safe for the Coalition. This was in part because pre-election disagreements about the purpose and scope of coalition simply carried over into the post-war government. The minimum interpretation was that the Coalition existed to keep Labour down by electoral manipulation. This was especially vulnerable to the evidence of by-elections from 1919 onwards, which seemed to show Conservatives that there was nothing to be gained from an anti-socialist alliance with the Coalition Liberals. A more constructive interpretation of the purpose of the Coalition was that it existed to channel the uses of state power most effectively in order to maintain prosperity and social stability. This was the interpretation favoured by Addison, Eric Geddes and many others who had come to prominence during the war. It was accompanied by a good deal of rhetoric, much of it sincerely meant, about the common interest of employers and workers and their shared need for state intervention to regulate society in the general good. It was a logical extension of the progressive agenda which had inspired New Liberals and Fabians, and some ministers including Lloyd George and Churchill, before 1914. And it was the most prominent victim of the collapse of consensus in 1920–21.

Probably the most important political effect of the First World War was to create this aspiration as an ideological and political movement centred on the Coalition, and then to pack it with the seeds of its own destruction. The opportunity was created by successive Cabinet crises during the war, which marginalised many of those who would have opposed it in all parties. The growth of government during the war provided models which were applied, hastily, to post-war problems. The need to design an election programme which successfully discriminated between the Coalition and its opponents, rather than between the traditional parties in their pre-war ideological plumage, prompted ministers to launch a number of schemes whose value as social palliatives was if anything enhanced by the unrest which was to follow in 1919.

The irony was that the war had also discredited this particular marriage of ideology and political organisation. Organised Labour, inside and outside parliament, had always been suspicious of state intervention while tolerant of its benefits if those included redistribution of wealth. The experience of war heightened that suspicion among trade unionists and those whom they sponsored in parliament. Conscription, confusion in industrial labour policy, and clumsy intervention in the wage-bargaining process had enraged the skilled unions; widespread manipulation of the labour process had stimulated the general unions and broadened the appeal of the skilled unions to the semi-skilled. More than that, the intervention of the state in society outside the workplace had very often been seen as prejudiced against the working class. The continual profiteering scandals, and the specific grievances against bad housing and inadequate food supplies which had surfaced in the reports of the Commission on Industrial Unrest, exploded the myth of the neutral state. A yearning for genuinely free collective bargaining was a natural reaction to intrusive state activity in industrial relations; a principled resistance to state control, in such forms as Guild Socialism as much as rank-and-fileism, was also a common reaction. Outside the workplace the war gave little reason for confidence that if given power the state would use it in the interest of the working class. The evolution of the Labour Party Constitution of 1918, in a political atmosphere which cannot have allowed any of the participants to forget the flaws in state control, reflected the desire of Labour activists to tolerate state intervention only if the state's apparatus were in Labour hands.

Such a reaction chilled any hopes of state-organised collaboration between capital and labour, despite the lingering rhetoric of Whitleyism and the painful fiasco of the National Industrial Conference of 1919. The Coalition, especially those ministers not associated with wartime intervention such as Addison and Geddes, tried to keep the principle alive but their pitch had been queered by the war. Neither direct intervention, nor the arm's-length approach of tripartite intervention at the boundaries of the 'extended state' was of interest to trade unionists or the Labour Party.

The employers' experience of state intervention mirrored that of labour. Here again, the organised employers had reaped great rewards from collaboration with the state and enjoyed the fruits of their efforts, sometimes to the tune of millions. But the end of the war saw no celebration of the advantages of state intervention or of tripartite bargaining. Businessmen had floated the idea of new apparatus such as the Ministry of Industry, and trumpeted the virtues of cartels and selling combines. Faced with the government's suggestion that they should make do with new governmental institutions which they did not control, and should adapt their own organisations to the national interest as defined by government departments, they became depressed and cantankerous. Their annoyance soon spilled over into the Conservative back benches, and duly scuppered developments such as the Ministry of Transport bill which embodied Geddes's proposals for sweeping economic reform. Instead, organised employers preferred to deal directly with labour; and when the grandiose F.B.I. plans for a welfare system controlled by employers and unions fell by the wayside, capital and labour soon reverted to a familiar state of chronic hostility.

Thus the war not only destroyed the old Liberal Party by smashing its leadership into fragments, but also destroyed the only child of pre-war Liberalism which the war itself had seen into life. This lends perspective to the hoary question of the war's contribution to the death of Liberalism. In its heyday the Liberal Party had adapted to changing social and electoral conditions by evolving new policies and allowing the institutions of the party to grow to fit them. This had been easier in government than in opposition, and in the immediately pre-war governments it had been very successful. By preventing the party from taking advantage of change, the war fixed old patterns of Liberal doctrine. As Bentley has shown, Liberal doctrine almost seemed to regress in the post-war years. The political conditions of the post-war Coalition — determined by the priorities which the Conservative Party had developed during the last year of the war — prevented Coalition Liberals from doing enough with the state apparatus, and they duly withered.

By denying the power of unfettered government to the Liberals after 1918, the Coalition and the Coupon election virtually guaranteed that the party would not be able to manufacture an electoral appeal. But the results of the Coupon election strongly suggest that near-irreparable damage had already been done to its position by December 1918. The case for this conclusion is partly based on the strong evidence that middle-class voters preferred Conservatives to Liberals when they wanted to oppose the Labour Party; partly on the number of constituencies in the traditionally Liberal areas especially of the Celtic fringe which fell first to Conservatives and in subsequent elections to Labour; partly on the degree to which Liberal victories over Labour in areas of traditional Liberal strength were only won by Conservative withdrawal under the Coupon. To some extent Liberal losses against Conservative coupons can be discounted as artificial (but only to the extent that Liberal victories with the coupon must also be discounted). On the other hand, the long interval since the last election meant that only a small fraction of those voting in 1918 would ever have voted Liberal before. Meanwhile millions of new voters had been created by time and legislation. Even if the Liberal Party had lost no voters, it faced the challenge of encouraging those new voters to give their support. It failed.

Britain's political experience in the First World War had much in common with that of other belligerent countries. Parties on the left tended to split into pro-war and anti-war elements. Party government was unstable and the coalitions which succeeded party government were also unstable. The challenge of mobilising a war economy heightened conflict between the state and industrial workers; the challenge of devising a rational military strategy strained relations between the civil power and the armed forces. But by surviving long enough to be on the winning side, the British government ensured that the regime itself was secure at the end of 1918. Even the challenge from the military hierarchy, which was powerful and persistent and had in Germany effectively replaced civilian leadership, was contained in Britain, though there were some difficult moments when the opposition sought to exploit the government's difficulties. As a result, the social and political conflicts of war were contained within a party structure in a representative political system and were, with minor exceptions, kept off the streets. The state itself, though discredited, still existed and continued to be a political weapon available to the Lloyd George Coalition. The political consequences of the years of greatest stress — the crisis of war in which the Lloyd George Coalition was battling to understand and control events — were not revolutionary but counter-revolutionary. The alignment of the governing parties against Labour undercut historic Liberalism. The invention of a rhetoric of employer–worker collaboration lightly disguised a heightened conflict over the process of production. Not only Conservative politicians, but also the possessing classes whom they aspired to represent, had survived the crisis of war with their power largely intact and their opponents in disarray. It was a small and expensive victory, but it was enough.

APPENDIX I
The Election Study

This appendix provides a description of the methods used and the assumptions underlying them, so that their contribution to the main argument of the book can be assessed. It gives a basic introduction to the terminology used, but does not attempt a full exposition of statistical methods, for which alternative references are given. It also discusses the sources used and the choices made among alternative methods of analysing the data.

The quantitative analysis of voting behaviour

'THEORY' AS A NECESSARY EVIL

The point of making a quantitative study of the Coupon Election was to judge the success of the political strategies of the competing parties and to put the post-war election in the context of long-term electoral change. Historians of the early 20th century have generally assumed that the electors' choice is mainly determined by the associations between parties and particular social groups, and have asked how and why those associations have changed over time. This has been described as the 'expressive' theory of voting choice.[1] An alternative approach has been to argue that voters make rational calculations of the benefits to be expected from the different parties, and vote accordingly.[2] This is the 'instrumental' theory of voting. The two are not mutually exclusive. Voters may, for example, incline to

---

[1] It is the basis of David Butler and Donald Stokes, *Political Change in Britain* (2nd edn, London: Macmillan, 1974), which was in turn derived from the classic American study, A. Campbell, P.E. Converse, W.E. Miller and D.E. Stokes, *The American Voter* (New York: Wiley, 1964).

[2] H. Himmelweit, P. Humphreys, M. Jaegar, and M. Katz, *How Voters Decide* (London: Academic Press, 1981); this approach can be traced to Anthony Downs, *An Economic Theory of Democracy* (New York: Harper & Row, 1957).

one party or other because they identify it with their own social group, but make a choice 'on the day' because they expect some benefit from a party if it is returned to office or think they have suffered loss from a party in government. Informal expert commentaries on elections, and indeed the classic series of 'Nuffield' studies of British elections since 1945, have often pursued both approaches together. Such pragmatism is inevitable, since the evidence which might distinguish between the theories is difficult to obtain and intractable once gathered.

The central problem for 1918 is to explain the relative size of the vote for candidates of the main contending groups — Conservative, Coalition Liberal, Opposition Liberal, and Labour — and thus to account for the partisan structure of the new parliament in 1919. In an unequal electoral system such as that of the United Kingdom, the proportion of seats won in Parliament is not closely determined by the proportion of votes cast. The first-past-the-post system is notorious for discriminating against third and fourth parties; in 1918 it also provided complex tactical opportunities for the Coalition, which was trying to maximise the number of Coalition M.P.s returned. The issue of the Coupon and the enforced withdrawal of Conservative or Liberal candidates in many constituencies were tactics designed explicitly to limit the voters' choice even more than it was limited by the single-member system. Thus although the voters' choice is important, the fact that it was constrained makes it all the more difficult to study.

There is no thought here of confirming or denying a general theory about voters' behaviour from the evidence of the 1918 or 1922 elections. The aim is an acceptably accurate description of what happened at the end of the war, and the expressive and instrumental theories are no more than shorthand expressions to describe the range of possible explanations. If they are theories at all, they are very strictly confined to the elections in question.

MODELLING THE PAST

The notion of 'fitting' a statistical 'model' to quantitative data about the past is alien and repulsive to many historians. It need not be so. A statistical model does no more than offer a simplification of complex reality, just as all historical accounts are simplifications of the past. The aim is to produce a useful description which 'fits' the data. This might be no more than an arithmetical mean of the observations of a particular variable, such as unemployment rates in each parliamentary constituency. Once the mean is calculated it can be said that some constituencies have higher than mean rates and some lower; the 'fit' is the mean, with the difference between a constituency's rate and the mean for the whole country being known as the 'residual' for that constituency. The model can easily be made more interesting by dividing the country up into regions, each of which would have its own mean unemployment rate which would be different from the national mean. The fit is now made up of two components, the national mean and the difference between the national and each regional mean; the constituency residual is now the difference between the constituency's rate and the mean rate for the region to which it belongs. Once this is done the sum of the residuals is much smaller than it was when the fit was only the national mean, and it can be said that the model 'explains' more of the variation in the rates of unemployment than a model incorporating the national mean alone, and is therefore a better fit.[3] In general, a statistical model can be seen as an equation:

$$Data = Fit + Residual$$

There are many possibilities for the form of the fit. Sometimes it can be achieved simply by subdividing the units of observation into smaller groups, as described above. Sometimes it can be achieved by finding a relationship between one varying quantity and another, so that, for example, higher unemployment rates are associated with higher concentrations of young workers. The proportion of young workers is seen to 'predict' the unemployment rate and thus to provide a fit to the data, using the regression method described in more detail below.

However a fit is achieved, it presents challenges and opportunities to historians and social scientists whose concern is with cause. The statistical methods themselves offer no help here: they are arithmetical techniques which reveal the strength of relationships and the goodness of fit between a model and its data. They can demonstrate regional variation in unemployment rates, but say nothing about whether 'region' causes the differences; no more can they say that concentrations of young workers cause unemployment. Historians who have given up worrying about causes will have no anxieties on this score, but it is important that those who have not are careful to recognise what the statistical model can and cannot provide. Any general proposition that young workers cause unemployment or Methodists cause Labour voting can be supported by a statistical model, but only in the sense that if it proves impossible to fit a model of Labour voting which incorporates Methodists it is difficult to sustain the causal hypothesis. Even if the fit is good, some theoretical insight drawn from outside the data is necessary to make sense of it.

In order to make sense of a quantitative past, historians must usually have theories which they state formally as hypotheses and then test using statistical models such as the regression analyses under discussion here.

[3] This is, of course, a very informal description of the technique known as Analysis of Variance.

Such theories will take such forms as 'a high level of female enfranchisement will, other things being equal, be associated with high levels of
Conservative voting', 'high average incomes are associated with Conservative voting' or 'a high proportion of newly enfranchised male voters will
be associated with high levels of Labour voting'. Although the statistical
methods are indifferent to causality, most such theories will in practice
have been devised with some causal assumptions in mind. It is important
to recognise that even if investigation confirms the associations, it has not
ipso facto confirmed the causal analysis.

MODELS AND MEASUREMENT

The use of theory in this way, to produce a formal statement of quantitative relationships which can then be tested against the evidence, poses a
number of further problems. Theories relate two or more abstract quantities. Measuring these abstract quantities for real historical entities is fraught
with difficulty. It is simple to ask whether class is associated with the
propensity to vote Labour or Conservative; impossible to find a measure
of class for which a number can be associated with each geographical area
(let alone each constituency, but that is a separate problem). If historians
could agree on a definition of class which could be associated with the
categories used in the decennial census, enormous progress would have
been made, but class itself is a concept with a complicated theoretical history. A Weberian preoccupation with socio-economic status, identified
by consumption habits and wealth, is common in modern discussions of
electoral analysis.[4] Straightforward Marxist analysis of class is concerned
with the individuals' relationship to the ownership and control of industrial capital. Both concepts are partly subsumed in the notion of class as a
function of occupational prestige, which was very influential in Edwardian
thinking about class structure. The efforts described by Wald[5] indicate the
dimensions of the problem for the electoral historian: he first constructs
an entirely plausible model of a working class consisting of several overlapping groups 'defined by their role in the production process', and then
constructs measures of the geographical concentration of these groups from
the Registrar-General's categories I to VIII used in the 1911 Census. This
is done with care, but with the honest admission that the groups measured
do not, and cannot, exactly match their definitions. The census categories
themselves are arbitrary and ideologically charged even in their attribu-

---

[4] Compare M. Kahan, D.E. Butler and D.E. Stokes, 'On the Analytical Division of Social Class',
British Journal of Sociology xvii (1966), 123–30 with Patrick Dunleavy, 'The Urban Basis of Political
Alignment: social class, domestic property ownership, and state intervention in consumption process',
British Journal of Political Science ix (1979), 409–443.

[5] Kenneth D. Wald, *Crosses on the Ballot* (Princeton N.J.: Princeton University Press, 1983), pp.
98–108, 122–127.

tions of particular occupations to broader occupational groupings. By the time of the 1901 and 1911 Censuses the occupational classifications used had come to 'place more emphasis on levels of skill, and the distinctions between making and dealing and administration',[6] and it was from such a hierarchical scheme of occupational value and esteem that the categories I to VIII were devised. Unfortunately the scheme of classification does not define the workers' role in the production process, because it refers to the occupation rather than its industrial (or non-industrial) context. Wald therefore makes ingenious approximations, which give an estimate of the 'concentration of manual workers in factory or factory-like situations'.[7] Other historians have lamented the absence of any measure of class in the 1921 Census, but constructed indices of the presence of middle-class voters from a summation of workers in commerce, finance, public administration and the professions, leaving the working-classes to be defined by subtracting these middle-class occupations (perhaps with the addition of agricultural workers) from the total of occupied males.[8] This again links occupational status, rather than role in the production process, to voting outcomes. Since the labour process was so important in Edwardian politics, and so intimately bound up with popular reactions to governmental action during the war, this loss of focus is particularly regrettable for a study of the 1918 election.

The problem of measuring religious affiliation, an essential component in all studies of electoral behaviour, is even more acute. After the traumatic religious census of 1851, which revealed the fragility of the Anglican hegemony, no direct religious questions were asked in the decennial censuses. Studies of post-1918 elections have used counts of clergymen of the various denominations as an approximate index of the religious commitment and denominational colour of areas; Wald's study of the 1884–1910 electoral system tapped further sources such as enrollments in denominational and public elementary schools and the denominational affiliation of local education committees recorded in an unofficial survey at the turn of the century, while Kinnear explored church year-books for some constituencies. These are worthy and ingenious exercises, but they all measure external correlates of religious commitment and denominational affiliation (and do so in an unavoidably arbitrary fashion) when the underlying theory is about something else: the relationship between the structure of a voter's religious beliefs or the strength of his denominational affiliation on

[6] Edward Higgs, 'Structuring the Past: the occupational, social and household classification of census data', *Computing and History Today* 4 (August 1988), 26; see also Edward Higgs, *Making sense of the Census: the manuscript returns for England and Wales, 1801–1901* (London: HMSO, 1989).

[7] Wald, *Crosses on the Ballot*, p. 125–126.

[8] Michael Kinnear, *The British Voter: an atlas and survey since 1885* (London: Batsford, 1968) p. 122; Miller, *Electoral Dynamics*, p. 112.

the one hand, and his voting decisions on the other. Such ills are endemic in quantitative history, but they should not be overlooked simply because they cannot be cured.

Studies of contemporary electoral behaviour enjoy an incalculable advantage over historical studies in that the voters themselves are accessible: a sample of them can be asked how they voted and in what constituency, and then asked other questions about their social and economic background and their attitudes to identified political issues. From survey data of this kind, modern theories of voting behaviour have been built up and tested.[9] No such surveys were made of British voters before 1945, nor can historians of early twentieth-century voting use the poll-books upon which much good work has been done for the period before 1872. All work on national elections must therefore be carried out using constituencies, and often larger units, as the units of analysis. Votes are recorded by constituencies; the social and economic characteristics of constituencies can occasionally be discovered and otherwise the characteristics of larger units incorporating more than one constituency can be ascertained; the two can be related in a statistical model. This approach has a number of drawbacks but it is the only means of generalising from the unsatisfactory data available.

TECHNIQUES

In explaining the distribution of the vote in British parliamentary elections, usually expressed as the proportion of votes cast for each contending party in each constituency, any quantitative study must attempt to relate the votes cast to another set of countable or categorisable features of voters or constituencies. Most studies of electoral behaviour have used *linear regression models* to relate a *dependent variable*, in other words a characteristic of the constituency whose quantity needs to be explained, such as the Labour share of the vote, to one or more *independent variables*, or characteristics which might be thought to cause variation in the dependent variable, such as the proportion of trade unionists or ethnic minority voters in the electorate, the average level or distribution of income, or the mix of manufacturing and service employment. This can be understood schematically from Figure 1, in which values of a dependent variable are plotted against the corresponding values of an independent variable:

---

[9] For a good introduction see W.L. Miller, *The Social Survey Method in the Social and Political Sciences* (London: Frances Pinter, 1983).

Figure A1: Scatterplot of an Imaginary Relationship

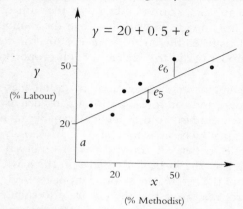

(% Methodist)

Note: Each circle represents a constituency, plotted with the appropriate values of *x* and *y*. The errors or *residuals* for the fifth and sixth constituencies are shown in this plot: the residual is the difference between the *observed value*, as plotted and the *predicted value* derived from the regression line. The intercept term, *a*, is the level at which the regression line crosses the *y* axis, and represents the predicted value of *y* if *x* were zero.

each point on the plot represents a constituency. The *regression line* is the straight line which 'best fits' the scatter of points. This can be expressed as an algebraic function of the form:

$$y = a + bx + e$$

Where for each constituency *y* is the value of the dependent variable, *a* the *intercept term*, or the value which *y* would apparently have if *x* were zero, *x* the value of an independent variable, *b* the coefficient by which *x* must be multiplied to get a corresponding value in *y*, and *e* the *error term*, or the difference between the value of *y* calculated from $y = a + bx$ and the actual value of *y* for the particular observation.

The regression line is calculated so that the errors are minimised; if the errors themselves were used directly in the calculation, negative errors would cancel out positive errors, so the calculation is based on the squares of the errors, and coefficients are calculated for *a* and *b* which will minimise the *sum of squares* of the errors. The technique is therefore commonly known as *least squares* regression.[10] In a set of observations

[10] Formulae for calculating the various statistics employed here are not given. There is an introductory discussion in Roderick Floud, *An Introduction to Quantitative Methods for Historians* (London: Methuen, 1979), pp. 151–153, which can be followed up in C.M. Dollar and R.J. Jensen, *Historian's Guide to Statistics: quantitative analysis and historical research* (New York: Holt, Rinehart and Winston,

like this the *variance* of the variable y is defined as the sum of the squared differences from the mean value of y, divided by one less than the number of observations; the *error variance*, correspondingly, is the sum of squared residuals from the fitted line, divided by one less than the number of observations. If when a line is fitted the error variance is small in relation to the total variance, the model is said to 'explain' a high proportion of the variance in y.

The historian is looking for an 'explanation' of differences between constituencies in the proportions of votes cast for a particular party. In a regression model, what is wanted is an independent variable such as average household income, for which the scatter of points is closely grouped around the regression line so that e is small for each observation. This *goodness of fit* is measured by the *correlation coefficient*, which is calculated from the sum of squares of the errors and is conventionally written as r. It takes values between zero, indicating that there is no discernible relationship, and 1, indicating perfect correspondence. In extreme cases, though, a very good fit could be obtained if all values of y were very much the same, whatever the value of x. One is therefore looking further, for a variable for which differences in x make appreciable differences in y so that b, the *regression coefficient* or *slope* of the regression line, is large. If two variables plotted together show a high correlation and an appreciable regression slope, they can be said to be closely related.

If the observations are part of a random sample taken from a larger population of possible observations, and if certain other conditions are satisfied, one can calculate the probability of getting the observed relationship in a sample drawn from a population in which no true relationship existed. If this probability is low, it is likely that the calculated relationship is genuine, though this does not help to decide whether it is important. These probability calculations are known as *significance tests*. When the data are not sample data, but are instead the whole population of possible observations (which is often the case in historical work) the problem of deciding whether an observed relationship means anything is more difficult.[11] Most researchers using non-sample data adopt rules of thumb, in which the statistics computed for the purpose of significance tests are used as a guide to whether the correlation or regression coefficient is worth considering further.

The linear regression model using one independent variable is a great simplification of a complex reality. It is highly unlikely that a single variable will make it possible to predict very much of the variation in another. One would expect that the average household income in a

1971). Some especially useful further techniques are given in J.W. Tukey, *Exploratory Data Analysis* (Reading, Mass.: Addison Wesley, 1977).

[11] See Floud, *An Introduction to Quantitative Methods*, p. 185.

constituency would influence the Labour vote and thus help to predict it; but so might the proportion of Methodists. The first resort in such a case is to the *multiple regression model*, taking the form:

$$y = a + b_1 x_1 + b_2 x_2 + e$$

Here x_1 may be income and x_2 may be Methodists; b_1 and b_2 are the corresponding regression coefficients. There could of course be more than two independent variables. The usual *caveat* that the relationships are being estimated 'other things being equal' is in practice met by including as many of the 'other things' as possible as additional terms in the regression, and leaving the rest for the error term. There is a single correlation coefficient for the whole equation, known as the *multiple correlation coefficient*, which is a measure of the goodness of fit of the whole model and is conventionally written as R. Derived from R is R^2, the squared multiple correlation coefficient. The usefulness of R^2 depends on the fact that it is equivalent to the proportion of the variance in y which is 'explained' by the whole model.

The analyses are greatly complicated by the fact that the British party system in 1918 contained three and more parties, often competing within the same constituency. The proportion of the votes cast for each party in such a system are significantly affected by the presence and attractiveness of *both* of the other parties competing. Forty per cent of the vote to Labour means one thing if 60 per cent went to Conservative, and quite another if Conservative and Liberal were split 35 per cent to 25 per cent. In describing a constituency's political behaviour it is therefore desirable to indicate not only the share of the vote going to one party, but a measure of its behaviour in a three-party system, if only in the form of one party's lead over another. Unfortunately this is made almost impossible by the Coupon.[12]

By systematic testing of different sets of independent variables with the appropriate analyses, the historian can find out which combinations are most closely related to the dependent variables or combinations of variables which seem interesting. Variables which do not improve the goodness of fit, or in other words do not add to the power of the model to predict the outcome, can be discarded. Those that do help prediction will be retained, until a combination is found which accounts for as much as possible of the variation. The result is a formal, quantitative statement of the relationship between certain measured characteristics of constituencies, and another, measured characteristic, the proportion of votes cast for a particular party or the index of partisanship. For each independent variable, the regression

---

[12] For a method appropriate to a more stable and 'normal' election, see Miller, *Electoral Dynamics* pp. 114–126.

coefficient indicates the effect that that variable has on the dependent variable when the simultaneous effects of all the other variables in the model are taken into account. By using the *standardised regression coefficient* it is possible to compare the impact of different variables on the dependent variable.[13] Models of voting behaviour constructed in this way can be very elaborate, and can sometimes seem to 'explain' a high proportion of the variation in the proportion of votes cast for a particular party. R^2 reaches .4 or 40% in some of the regression models reported in this study. It is a long way from this to a causal explanation of a particular pattern of voting.

Moreover, there are special problems associated with regression analysis when applied to aggregates such as constituencies. Many theories of voting behaviour are mainly concerned with the decisions of individuals. Translating them to constituency level, or higher, for the purpose of measurement brings its own problems. Supposing that it is hypothesised that miners are more likely to vote Labour than Conservative and women more likely to vote Conservative than Labour. To test these hypotheses the proportion of miners and women in the electorate will be incorporated in a multiple regression with the party vote as a dependent variable. If, for Conservative voting, it is found that the regression coefficient for miners is negative and for women is positive, one might imagine the hypothesised relationship confirmed. But in fact it is quite possible for the observed relationship at the aggregated (constituency) level to be precisely opposite to the true relationship at individual level. Take, as two famous examples, Irish voters in Liverpool and Jewish voters in New York. All contemporary evidence suggests that the Liverpool Irish voted for Irish Nationalist candidates when they could, otherwise for Liberal candidates before 1918 and often Labour candidates afterwards. Regression analysis, however, produces a positive correlation between the proportion of Irish adults in the population and the level of *Conservative* voting. Similarly, Jews in New York were until recently known from survey data to favour the Democrats, but Congressional districts with high proportions of Jewish inhabitants were inclined to return Republicans. In both of these cases this mismatch arises because the target group are an identifiable minority. In New York, Jews have tended to move from the immigrant

---

[13] This statistic takes into account the differing variance of each of the variables concerned: if the values of a variable range from 15 to 150 with a mean of 45, the significance of a difference of ten points between two constituencies is rather less than it would be if the variable took values which were mostly between 10 and 30, so before calculating the regression coefficient the values of each variable are *standardised* by subtracting the mean and dividing through by the *standard deviation*, which is the square root of the variance of the variable. The resulting standardised values have a mean of zero and a standard deviation of 1; whatever the units of measurement and whatever the underlying variance of the variable, a value of, say, greater than 2 or less than -2 is very unusual and 'means' the same for each variable. Consequently the values of the regression coefficients are comparable. Unstandardised regression coefficients are heavily influenced by the units of measurement and cannot be compared directly with one another.

districts of first settlement to affluent middle-class areas where their Gentile neighbours are disproportionately Republican. In Liverpool, the Irish population lived in working-class districts where the non-Irish population were prone to sectarian bigotry, carefully organised by local Conservative politicians. The more prominent the Irish minority, the more effective the bigotry. In the only seat where Irish voters were actually a majority (the Scotland division) an Irish Nationalist MP was regularly returned until 1929. The misleading consequence of such a regression analysis is known as the 'ecological fallacy'.

Another trap which causes trouble in any regression model but is particularly dangerous in historical models which use aggregate rather than individual-level data and also try to draw causal conclusions, is the problem of variables not stated in the model. If the dependent variable — voting preference — is largely determined by an independent variable which has not been measured, and the regression model includes a second independent variable which is correlated with the first and perhaps caused by it *but which does not itself have any causal significance with respect to the dependent variable* a regression analysis will duly show a high correlation between the dependent variable and the independent variable in the model; the unwary may well infer that there is a causal link between them. The geographical distribution of some characteristic (for example of female voters) may be determined by some unconsidered factor such as the economic structure of a region, which may be having a direct effect on voting behaviour. This would show up in a regression model as a positive relationship between female voters and, say, Conservative voting, and could easily appear in that form even if the female voters themselves were more disposed to vote *against* Conservatives. This difficulty is compounded by the problems of measurement described above. One might try to derive a set of measures to indicate economic structure and include it in the model to control for its effects; but if, because of inadequate sources, that set of measures were to be a fairly inexact representation of the actual economic structure of the constituency, it would not appear to be correlated either with voting behaviour or with female enfranchisement.[14]

The problem of variables not included in the analysis is related to the problem caused by 'multi-collinearity': the occurrence of two independent variables in the regression which are highly correlated with one another. One might find the number of farmworkers highly correlated with the numbers of Methodists. In this case, the estimates provided by a least-squares analysis of both the correlation coefficients and the regression coefficients of the two variables with respect to the dependent variable

[14] Upon this rock the study reported in Turner 'Sex, Age and the Labour Vote...' nearly foundered.

will be unsafe. The usual cure is to leave out one variable, or to combine the two into an index which represents the property to which they both apparently refer. This is rarely a very appealing solution for the historian, who may be very interested in the separate contribution each is making, and may find the relationship between the two a challenging problem in itself. But very often in the models reported in Chapter 11 the delicate choice of which variables to include has been a revealing problem in itself: in some of the models the close correlation between financial workers and high female electorates has made it possible to construct two equally powerful models showing very different groups of explanatory variables by allowing women voters to stand as surrogate for finance workers or *vice versa*, or by using regional dummy variables.

REPORTING RESULTS IN FIGURES AND TABLES

Apart from simple cross-tabulations, two types of report are particularly used in Chapter 11. For describing the level and spread of variables such as share of the vote, use is made of the *boxplot*, a graphical technique developed by John Tukey. The purpose of a boxplot is to indicate not only the central value of a variable, which could be done simply with the arithmetic mean or the median, but to show how values are grouped around that central value, and to make it possible to compare sets of data quickly by eye. In a set of data which has been ordered from the lowest value to the highest, the *median* is the 'middle value' which divides the set of data into two equal sized groups of which half are higher than the median and half lower. The dataset is also divided into *quartiles*: the first and third quartiles mark off one quarter and three quarters of the values (the second quartile, of course, is the median). The *inter-quartile range* is the difference between the values of the first and third quartiles. The interquartile range is used as a measure of the *spread* of the data set. The boxplot shows the range of values between the first and third quartiles literally as a box, with the median shown as a line across it. The observations outside the interquartile range are given special treatment: a 'step' is calculated as 1.5 times the interquartile range, and the values of two 'fences' are calculated as one step above the upper quartile and one step below the lower quartile. Anything beyond a fence is identified as an *outlier* and identified separately; the values nearest to the fences but still inside them are identified as the *adjacent values*, and a line, sometimes known as a 'whisker' is drawn from the box to the adjacent values. The result is shown in Figure A2.[15]

---

[15] An excellent introduction to the use of boxplots is in Catherine Marsh, *Exploring Data* (Oxford: Polity Press and Basil Blackwell, 1988); for a fuller treatment, see Tukey, *Exploratory Data Analysis*.

Figure A2:   A Simple Boxplot

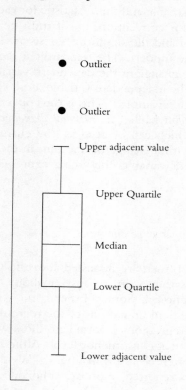

Note: The boxplots in Chapter 11 are simplified further by the omission of outliers. The presentation of boxplots can also include the fences and 'outer fences', defined as the distance two steps beyond the quartiles, and distinctions can be made between outliers and 'extreme outliers' which lie beyond the outer fences.

The other heavily-used report is the table of results from regression analysis. Reporting the results of regression analysis in historical studies is all too much a matter for the investigator's preference or prejudice. In Chapter 11 a conventional form is adopted in which the multiple regression coefficient, R^2 is reported, together with the *standardised* regression coefficients for each variable included in the equation. Two significance tests, the T statistic for each variable and the F statistic for each model, are also reported out of respect for convention; but it must be remembered that this is not a sample study and the significance tests are best seen as a guide to the robustness of the models. The standardised regression coefficients should be read as 'the change in the dependent variable associated with a change of one unit in the independent variable, both variables being expressed in terms of standard deviations.' This is the convention adopted by Wald in *Crosses on the Ballot*; Miller, in *Electoral Dynamics*, reports the *semi-standardised coefficients*, which can be read as 'the change in the dependent variable associated with a change of one unit in the independent variable, with the independent variable only being expressed in terms of standard deviations.'

Alternative analyses

The various regression models used are discussed above in Chapter 11 in the context of the questions they seem to answer about the social and economic basis of political choice. Some further comment is necessary about the technical properties and limitations of the regressions.

The most straightforward regressions reported are those which use only the data which can be gathered at constituency level. Although regressions using the whole set of contested elections in English, Welsh and Scottish constituencies are sometimes reported, most are subdivided so that only a certain part of the country is covered. Often the dependent variable used further limited the number of cases investigated (where, for example, no Labour or Liberal candidate stood). Dummy variables (e.g. 1 for constituencies where a coupon was issued, 0 for constituencies where it was not) were sometimes employed as an alternative to dividing the constituencies into two groups, especially where the number of constituencies in a regression was much reduced for other reasons.

Greater complexity arose when constant-unit data was used. One set of regressions used the constant unit itself as the unit of analysis; another used constituencies, but attributed to each constituency the socio-economic characteristics of the constant unit of which it was a part. Both approaches created major problems in interpretation.

Using the constant unit as a unit of analysis produces regressions which are comparable with those produced by Miller and Wald in their long-term studies of electoral change. The independent socio-economic variables are measured across the constant unit; the dependent variables, usually share of the vote, have to be calculated by an arbitrary method to allow for unopposed returns and different contest structures. The technique used is to sum the votes for each party across all the constituencies in the unit, and to attribute to unopposed candidates the votes they would have received if the voters in their constituencies had turned out at the rate typical of the constant unit, and all voted for them. This tends to inflate the apparent popularity of parties with unopposed returns.[16] This is unsatisfactory, but hardly more so than the alternative, which is to take the dependent variable as, for example, Labour votes as a proportion of all votes cast in constituencies in which Labour candidates stood. If this is attempted, the population for which the independent variables are measured is not the same population as that for which the dependent variable is measured. That might not matter, but it detracts from the point of using constant units. Furthermore, it is difficult to interpret comparisons between each party's share of the vote when it is thus defined. The procedure of multiplying up is therefore adopted here with tepid enthusiasm. Nonetheless, the full constant unit method is valuable precisely because it is comparable with other studies.

The alternative is to use constituency-level data for all variables available at that level, complemented by constant-unit data for socio-economic variables available only at the higher aggregation. This has the effect in a least-squares regression that any correlation existing between the constant-unit level variable and the constituency-level independent variable is likely to be underestimated, as is the coefficient of the slopes for the constant-unit variables; the multiple correlation coefficient R^2 will also be reduced. This is the price paid for more meaningful estimates of the relationship between the dependent variables of voting choice and structural variables such as new voters, female voters and the contest structure.

Throughout the study it was expected that measurable variables would not provide a complete explanation of the voting outcome. This was not simply because measurements were inherently inaccurate and the units of analysis inconveniently mismatched, but also because other factors such as the personality of the candidates, the experience of the campaign in individual constituencies, and aspects of a constituency's experience untapped by the measures used would all play a part in determining the number of voters willing to cast a ballot for a particular candidate. The quantitative model was intended to serve as a foundation on which other explanations could be built. For that reason the residuals were of especial importance.

---

[16] Miller defends the procedure thus:'It is probably true that if the unopposed candidate had been opposed his opponent would have gained some of the votes allocated to him, but it is equally true that if the two candidates in a straight fight had been opposed by a third candidate they would both have taken less [sic] votes than they actually received. In that sense the notional vote allocated to an unopposed candidate is consistent with our acceptance of votes recorded elsewhere.' *Electoral Dynamics* p. 108.

To compare a result with the result predicted in that constituency from what was known about its occupational structure, contest structure and electoral composition would indicate its individuality and pose questions about the performance of a candidate or the results of a speech which could not otherwise be posed at all.

Sources for the 1918 study

A major premise of the study was that no 'expressive' theory of voting behaviour would be sufficient to explain the outcome of the election or even the proportion of votes cast in individual constituencies, but rather that social and economic factors must be taken into account in explaining the response of the electorate to the unusual conditions in which the election was held. Data bearing on the social and economic characteristics of constituencies (more precisely, on the aggregations of constituencies which could be combined to produce areas for which census data was available) were therefore used. All census data were taken from the machine-readable dataset assembled by W.L. Miller for his *Electoral Dynamics*, and it is right to re-iterate here the great debt which all electoral historians owe to Professor Miller both for the elaboration of the method of 'constant-unit' analysis and for making the constant-unit data available in machine-readable form.[17] In addition to socio-economic data the study used data on votes cast for each candidate in each constituency derived from F.W.S. Craig, *British Parliamentary Election Results 1918–1949*.[18] The same source furnished details of the apparent party label of each candidate. Information on the prior existence of Labour party organisations and candidatures was taken from F.W.S. Craig, *British Parliamentary Election Results, 1885–1918*[19]

and from Ross McKibbin, *The Evolution of the Labour Party*, pp. 73–76., while data on the presence of miners was derived from Roy Gregory, *The Miners in British Politics*, pp. 96–7, 138–139, 174–175. Registration data on the number of male and female voters in each constituency in 1918 and the number of voters entitled to a postal vote because of military service, were taken from *Return of Parliamentary and Local Government Electors*, P.P. 1918, Cd 138, xix, 925. For the purpose of estimating the proportion of new voters in the electorate, figures for the old electorate were taken from the *Return relating to Parliamentary Constituencies* of 1915, aggregated as described below. Supplementary information on the political background

---

[17] It is available from the ESRC Data Archive.
[18] Third edn., Chichester: Parliamentary Research Services, 1983.
[19] London: Macmillan, 1984.

of candidates was taken from House of Commons division lists. Each of these sources, and the method of deriving variables from them, is described in turn below.

LEVELS OF ANALYSIS

Britain suffers from an official determination, unique among civilised countries, to make the social basis of electoral choice opaque to historians. Electoral analysis depends on the opportunity to link voting figures to census data. In Britain voting figures for parliamentary elections are only released for parliamentary constituencies, not for sub-units such as wards or precincts as is customary in other countries. These units are uncomfortably large in themselves, considering the socio-economic variations which can be expected within constituencies, but insult is added to injury by the fact that the boundaries of parliamentary constituencies in the early part of the twentieth century did not coincide with the administrative units for which census data was gathered or published. It is therefore impossible to determine the social composition of more than a few parliamentary constituencies from the published census. For all others it is necessary to aggregate constituencies until an area is defined whose boundaries correspond to an area defined by aggregating censal units such as boroughs, county boroughs or administrative counties. This method was pioneered by W.L. Miller, and has also been followed by Wald. For the 1918 to 1974 period it produces 161 'constant units' for which both voting data and census data can be derived.[20]

In an ideal world it would have been possible to carry out all the analyses at the level of constituencies. But, as noted, the major census data is only available in large aggregations of censal units. Basic political data is, of course, available for constituencies, but some measures which include estimates of three-party interaction can only be calculated in larger units. Any data which relates to the period before the 1918 boundary revision can only be related to post-1918 data by aggregating even further, to the level of administrative counties. Consequently three datasets were prepared for the study in which political and miscellaneous data was measured at the constituency level, at the level of 'constant units' and at the level of administrative counties. Census data was incorporated at the level of constant units and counties; and in the constituency-level dataset, census data measured for each constant unit was attributed to each of the constituencies within that unit.

[20] Miller, *Electoral Dynamics*, p. 98–100. Miller's concern is to produce units which are 'constant' across a number of elections, but no significant additions are possible if this condition is relaxed.

The social and economic data of particular interest in this study related to the occupational composition of the population, derived from the 1921 Census as being the nearest in date to the election. Undoubtedly there were shifts in occupational structure between 1918 and 1921 caused by the economic shocks of demobilisation, boom and slump, but these changes are irrecoverable. Other variables used included measures of the population density and housing stress, and measures of the numbers of Anglican, Roman Catholic and Nonconformist clergymen as an indicator of religious tendencies.[21] The variables used in the analysis are listed in Table A1.

POLITICAL DATA

The election results and registration data were available by constituency, and are listed in Table A2.

The history of the Coalition government and the nature of the campaign suggested other explanatory variables which might be important in explaining the response of the electorate to the choices put before them. Since the Labour party was so much the focus of Coalition attacks, and since it attempted to expand its range so dramatically in the last year of the war, it seemed that some measure of the deeprootedness of Labour politics in any constituency would be appropriate. A number of variables were therefore calculated to signify sitting Labour members or previous Labour candidatures within the area covered by the constituency, the proportion of votes won by a Labour candidate in the most recent general election contested, and a declared intention to contest seats known by 1914.[22] Except for the proportion of votes won, these were all 'dummy' variables ($0 = absent1 = present$). In all cases the constituencies to which the information referred did not match the constituencies as they existed in 1918; where pre-war constituencies had been divided the values were attributed to all successors, and because the variables were being used to test the effect of 'immunisation' by previous exposure to Labour politics it was held arbitrarily that if any part of a constituency had been affected by a Labour candidacy or organisation it acquired the tincture of that earlier political activity.

Another political variable, MAURICE, took the value of 1 when one of the opposition candidates had voted against the government in the Maurice Debate. This was included to test the proposition that the elec-

---

[21] For a discussion of the value of clergymen as an index of religious affiliation, see W.L. Miller and Gillian Raab, 'The Religious Alignment at English Elections between 1918 and 1970', *Political Studies* xxv (1977), 227–251.

[22] McKibbin, *Evolution of the Labour Party*, pp. 73–76.

Table A1: Census Variables from 1921 Census by Constant Unit

I *Aggregate numbers*

Agricultural labourers
Miners and quarrymen
Men employed in metal trades
Men employed in electrical trades
Male textile workers
Female textile workers
Transport workers
Workers in financial sector
Employees in local government and public administration
Professional workers
Clerks not included above
Male domestic servants
Female domestic servants

Rooms per person
Persons per acre
Persons born in Northern Ireland
Persons born in Southern Ireland
Persons born in Ireland (unspecified)
Males speaking Welsh only

Anglican clergymen
Roman Catholic Clergymen
Other (i.e. Nonconformist) clergymen

Males over 12
Males over 12, unoccupied and retired
Males over 12, neither retired nor gainfully employed
Total population, male and female

II *Calculated Variables*

Occupied Males
All occupational categories expressed as a proportion of occupied males
Middle class by occupation: clerks, professional workers, financial workers and local government workers
Working class by subtraction: occupied males minus agricultural workers and middle class by occupation
Anglican clergymen per head of population
Roman Catholic clergymen per head of population
Other clergymen per head of population
Anglican clergymen as a proportion of all clergymen

Note: It was not possible to obtain counts of all variables for all areas, and certain categories, such as Welsh speakers, were only counted in census districts where their presence mattered for administrative reasons. The problems of using these counts of occupations as an approximation for class structure are discussed in the text, as are the dangers (and advantages) of counting clergymen. The original dataset was prepared by W.L. Miller for *Electoral Dynamics in Britain*.

Table A2: Constituency Data

I *Results for 1918 and 1922 General Elections*

Conservative votes
Coalition Liberal votes
Opposition Liberal votes
Labour votes
Votes for 'Other' candidates:
> National Party, Coalition NDP, Uncouponed NDP, Co-operative (or second Labour, if two Labour candidates), Discharged Soldiers & Sailors, Independent, Independent but known to be Liberal, Independent but known to be Conservative, Irish Nationalist, Prohibitionist, Highland Land League, Independent Democrat, British Socialist Party, Christian Socialist

II *Electorate*

Total on register
Male voters
Female voters
Male voters entitled to service vote
Occupation (plural) voters

III *Calculated variables*

All party votes as proportion of the total votes cast and as proportion of the total electorate.
Females and service voters as proportion of registered electorate.
Estimates of 'new male' voters calculated from a regression model of changes in the male register between 1915 and 1918 against census variables, using administrative counties as constant units.

---

torate punished such behaviour when reminded of it (as it always was) by Couponed candidates. It was closely related to the dummy variable for a sitting Asquithian Liberal member, and as a result had a paradoxical effect: Conservatives facing 'Maurice' candidates generally had lower shares of the poll than their fellows in other constituencies.

The most tendentious additional variable was an estimate of the number of 'new' voters in each constituency, included in order to address the Matthew, McKibbin & Kay thesis that the voters newly enfranchised by the 1918 Act were less likely to vote for the old parties and more likely to vote Labour. Since almost every constituency boundary was changed by the 1918 Act, it was impossible except in a very few cases to estimate the numbers of new voters by subtracting the number of voters on the 1915 Register from the number of male voters on the 1918 Register.[23] The procedure adopted was similar to the 'constant unit' method used by

---

[23] Even this procedure would not, of course, have been a direct estimate of the number of voters who had not previously been able to cast a vote, because even without franchise changes the electorate 'turns over' continuously as some electors die and some reach the age or other status which qualifies them for inclusion. But Matthew et al. are really concerned with categories of voter, not individuals, and a direct subtraction would have indicated the approximate numbers in categories not previously enfranchised.

Wald and Miller. A number of 'cross-register' units were aggregated, each containing one or more complete constituencies under the 1885 distribution and one or more under the 1918 distribution. In England and Wales these units were, almost without exception, administrative counties. Since one important consequence of the redistribution had been to incorporate urbanising areas into borough seats, while redividing very large boroughs, the old borough constituencies very rarely provided the basis of constant units. In Scotland the redistribution was very much more radical, especially in the Lowlands, and many cross-register units included more than one county. Throughout the country the match between the perimeters of the old constituency groups and the new constituency groups was checked both by reference to the Boundary Commission maps and the acreages and population numbers for the 1911 census which are reported both in the 1915 register and the 1918 Register. Frequently the reported census populations, and less frequently the acreages, differ while the mapping and the constituency descriptions in the Boundary Commission reports appear to match. Since this is apparently due in part to corrections made to the Census after the 1915 register was prepared, the maps have been preferred to the sums; but these discrepancies should be noted as a source of concern. At the end of the process the proportion of 'new male' voters was not found to be very influential after all.

CLASSIFICATION OF CONSTITUENCIES

Two variables were used in the analyses to categorise constituencies. As an alternative to the constant-unit analysis favoured by Wald and Miller, Pelling in his *Social Geography of British Elections* and Blewett in his analysis of the 1910 elections used constituency classifications of socio-economic structure. These were somewhat *ad hoc*, but have the advantage that they attach information to the constituency rather than to a larger unit. They classified seats into Mining, Rural, Mixed Urban/Rural and three sorts of urban constituency, Working Class, Mixed Working/Middle Class and Middle Class. These distinctions worked reasonably well for London constituencies, where Pelling used Booth's survey to determine the number of female domestic servants per head of population, and thus to grade the social standing of a constituency. Outside London, inspection of maps makes it possible to determine to what extent a constituency is made up mostly of rural districts or partly of urban districts, and thus to assign it between the Rural and Urban/Rural categories. Blewett used Gregory's estimates of the mining electorates to identify a number of Mining seats. The allocation of urban seats outside London to one of the three urban categories is extremely uncertain. Census data on which it could be based is recoverable only for boroughs (and is thus no better than the constant-unit

census data), and for divided boroughs Blewett used anecdotal evidence
largely from newspaper election reports to assign constituencies between
the three categories. The value of this exercise, as he would be the first
to point out, depends on whether the analytical categories actually reveal
meaningful differences in the behaviour of constituencies. For the 1918
constituencies used in the present analysis, a similar grading procedure was
followed for English constituencies, relying heavily on value-judgements
made by Blewett and Pelling as well as on independent inspection of maps,
so that there was some chance of consistency between the studies. The
result is no less *ad hoc* than Blewett's, and indeed probably more so; the
classifications are advanced very hesitantly, and the large number of urban constituencies assigned to the Mixed Class category indicates, above
all, the investigator's own unease with the results. In view of the com-
plexities of boundary drawing in Scotland and Wales, and the absence of
very convincing anecdotal evidence for all but a few constituencies this *ad
hoccery* is even more uncertain in the Celtic fringe. In intermediate stages
of the analysis the cross-classification of constituency type and region was
frequently used to examine residuals from a regression as a guide to what
additional variables might be included to improve the model. In the final
analysis some categories, such as Middle Class and Mining, clearly stand
out more than the others.

The division of the country into larger regions was undertaken with
more confidence, partly because it permits comparison with the results
presented by Blewett and Pelling and partly because it does produce categories which seem to discriminate between different sorts of constituency
behaviour. The basis of the distinction is Fawcett's *Provinces of England*
adopted by Pelling and Blewett as the basis for assigning constituencies to
groups and lightly adapted in this study since some re-drawn boundaries
crossed Fawcett's lines. Appendix II shows all the constituencies classified
by region and type.

A final important consideration when attempting to analyse electoral
outcomes was the structure of each contest and the presence or absence
of the Coupon. Whether the dependent variable was the Conservative,
Coalition Liberal, Opposition Liberal or Labour vote it was expected that
the nature of the competition would significantly influence the proportion of the voters prepared to cast a vote for any party. Labour might be
expected to perform differently in the absence of a Coupon, or in the absence of any major party competition, than in a contest with a couponed
major-party candidate, and it was of central interest to discover whether
performance against couponed Liberals was better or worse than performance against Conservatives (couponed or uncouponed). The share of
the vote received by any party in a two-party contest would be expected
to be different from that in a three-party contest. A number of variables

were therefore employed as classification variables, sometimes as dummy variables and sometimes to split the constituencies into groups so that separate regressions could be tested. In the event there were comparatively few contests in which three major-party candidates competed, with or without the Coupon; and the distribution of Coupons between Liberals and Conservatives was such that differences in constituency type and region seemed to count for far more in Labour's performance than whether the opponent was Conservative or Liberal.

APPENDIX II
Classification of Constituencies

This Appendix is a list of all constituencies in Great Britain, classified by their region and attributed constituency type. For a discussion of these attributions, see Appendix I.

London

Middle Class
Camberwell, Dulwich
Chelsea
City of London
Hackney North
Hampstead
Holborn
Kensington South
Lambeth, Brixton
Lambeth, Norwood
Lewisham East
Lewisham West
Paddington South
St Marylebone
Wandsworth, Balham and Tooting
Wandsworth Central
Wandsworth, Clapham
Wandsworth, Putney
Wandsworth, Streatham
Westminster Abbey
Westminster St George's

Mixed Class
Battersea South
Deptford
Fulham East
Fulham West
Greenwich
Hammersmith North
Hammersmith South

Islington East
Islington North
Kensington North
Paddington North
St Pancras North
St Pancras South West

Working Class
Battersea North
Bermondsey, Rotherhithe
Bermondsey, West Bermondsey
Bethnal Green North East
Bethnal Green South West
Camberwell, Peckham
Finsbury
Hackney Central
Hackney South
Islington South
Islington West
Lambeth, Kennington
Lambeth North
Poplar, Bow and Bromley
Poplar, South Poplar
St Pancras South East
Shoreditch
Southwark Central
Southwark North
Southwark South East
Stepney, Limehouse
Stepney, Mile End
Stepney, Whitechapel and St George's

Stoke Newington
Woolwich East
Woolwich West

South East

Middle Class
Southend On Sea
Bromley
Hythe
Kent, Sevenoaks
Ealing
Hornsey
Willesden East
Willesden West
Middlesex, Acton
Middlesex, Spelthorne
Middlesex, Twickenham
Middlesex, Uxbridge
Middlesex, Wood Green
Kingston Upon Thames
Richmond Surrey
Wimbledon
Surrey, Chertsey
Brighton
Hastings
Sussex (East), Eastbourne

Mixed Class
Ilford
Essex, Romford
Hertfordshire, Watford
Rochester, Chatham
Rochester, Gillingham
Kent, Chislehurst
Kent, Dartford
Kent, Dover
Kent, Gravesend
Kent, Isle of Thanet
Edmonton
Middlesex, Brentford and Chiswick
Middlesex, Enfield
Middlesex, Finchley
Middlesex, Harrow
Middlesex, Hendon
Croydon North
Croydon South
Surrey, Mitcham

Working Class
East Ham North
East Ham South
Leyton East
Leyton West

Walthamstow East
Walthamstow West
West Ham, Plaistow
West Ham, Silvertown
West Ham, Stratford
West Ham, Upton
Camberwell North
Camberwell North West
Tottenham North
Tottenham South

Urban/Rural
Essex, Colchester
Essex, South Eastern
Hertfordshire, Hemel Hempstead
Hertfordshire, Hertford
Hertfordshire, St Albans
Kent, Canterbury
Kent, Faversham
Kent, Maidstone
Kent, Tonbridge
Surrey, Eastern
Surrey, Epsom
Surrey, Farnham
Surrey, Guildford
Surrey, Reigate
Sussex (East), Lewes

Rural
Essex, Chelmsford
Essex, Epping
Essex, Harwich
Essex, Maldon
Essex, Saffron Walden
Hertfordshire, Hitchin
Kent, Ashford
Sussex (East), East Grinstead
Sussex (East), Rye
Sussex (West), Chichester
Sussex (West), Horsham and Worthing

East Anglia

Middle Class
Cambridge

Mixed Class
Great Yarmouth
Norwich
Ipswich

Urban/Rural
Isle of Ely
Suffolk (East), Lowestoft
Suffolk (West), Bury St Edmunds

Rural

Cambridgeshire
Huntingdonshire
Norfolk, Eastern
Norfolk, King's Lynn
Norfolk, Northern
Norfolk, Southern
Norfolk, South Western
Suffolk (East), Eye
Suffolk (East), Woodbridge
Suffolk (West), Sudbury

Central

Middle Class
Bedfordshire, Bedford
Berkshire, Windsor
Oxford

Mixed Class
Reading

Working Class
Bedfordshire, Luton
Northampton
Wellingborough

Urban/Rural
Peterborough

Rural
Bedfordshire, Mid
Berkshire, Abingdon
Berkshire, Newbury
Buckinghamshire, Aylesbury
Buckinghamshire, Buckingham
Buckinghamshire, Wycombe
Daventry
Kettering
Oxfordshire, Banbury
Oxfordshire, Henley

Wessex

Middle Class
Bournemouth

Mixed Class
Dorset, Southern
Portsmouth Central
Portsmouth North
Portsmouth South
Southampton

Urban/Rural
Dorset, Eastern
Hampshire, Aldershot
Hampshire, Fareham
Hampshire, New Forest and Christchurch
Hampshire, Winchester

Isle of Wight
Wiltshire, Salisbury
Wiltshire, Swindon

Rural
Dorset, Northern
Dorset, Western
Hampshire, Basingstoke
Hampshire, Petersfield
Wiltshire, Devizes

Bristol

Middle Class
Bristol Central
Bristol West
Cheltenham
Bath

Mixed Class
Bristol North
Bristol South
Gloucester

Working Class
Bristol East

Urban/Rural
Wiltshire, Westbury

Rural
Gloucestershire, Cirencester and Tewkesbury
Gloucestershire, Stroud
Gloucestershire, Thornbury
Somerset, Bridgewater
Somerset, Frome
Somerset, Taunton
Somerset, Wells
Somerset, Weston Super Mare
Somerset, Yeovil
Wiltshire, Chippenham

Mining
Gloucestershire, Forest of Dean

Devon & Cornwall

Middle Class
Devonshire, Torquay

Mixed Class
Cornwall, Penryn and Falmouth
Exeter
Plymouth Drake
Plymouth Sutton

Working Class
Plymouth Devonport

Urban/Rural
Cornwall, Camborne

Cornwall, St Ives
Devonshire, Barnstaple
Rural
Cornwall, Bodmin
Cornwall, Northern
Devonshire, Honiton
Devonshire, South Molton
Devonshire, Tavistock
Devonshire, Tiverton
Devonshire, Totnes

West Midlands
Middle Class
Warwickshire, Warwick and Leamington
Mixed Class
Smethwick
West Bromwich
Wolverhampton West
Staffordshire, Burton
Staffordshire, Lichfield
Birmingham, King's Norton
Dudley
Worcester
Working Class
Walsall
Wednesbury
Wolverhampton, Bilston
Wolverhampton East
Birmingham, Aston
Birmingham, Deritend
Birmingham, Duddeston
Birmingham, Edgbaston
Birmingham, Erdington
Birmingham, Handsworth
Birmingham, Ladywood
Birmingham, Moseley
Birmingham, Sparkbrook
Birmingham, West Birmingham
Birmingham, Yardley
Coventry
Urban/Rural
Herefordshire, Hereford
Shropshire, Shrewsbury
Shropshire, The Wrekin
Staffordshire, Cannock
Staffordshire, Kingswinford
Warwickshire, Nuneaton
Warwickshire, Rugby
Warwickshire, Tamworth
Worcestershire, Kidderminster
Worcestershire, Stourbridge

Rural
Herefordshire, Leominster
Shropshire, Ludlow
Shropshire, Oswestry
Staffordshire, Leek
Worcestershire, Bewdley
Worcestershire, Evesham
Mining
Staffordshire, Stafford

East Midlands
Mixed Class
Leicester East
Leicester South
Grimsby
Lincoln
Nottingham Central
Nottingham South
Working Class
Derby
Leicester West
Nottingham East
Nottingham West
Urban/Rural
Derbyshire, High Peak
Leicestershire, Harborough
Leicestershire, Loughborough
Leicestershire, Melton
Holland with Boston
Grantham
Nottinghamshire, Bassetlaw
Nottinghamshire, Rushcliffe
Rural
Derbyshire, Southern
Derbyshire, Western
Rutland and Stamford
Brigg
Gainsborough
Horncastle
Louth
Nottinghamshire, Newark
Mining
Derbyshire, Belper
Derbyshire, Chesterfield
Derbyshire, Clay Cross
Derbyshire, Ilkeston
Derbyshire, North Eastern
Leicestershire, Bosworth
Nottinghamshire, Broxtowe
Nottinghamshire, Mansfield

Lancastria

Middle Class
Wallasey
Manchester Exchange
Southport

Mixed Class
Birkenhead West
Cheshire, Northwich
Cheshire, Wirral
Bootle
Liverpool, East Toxteth
Liverpool, Edge Hill
Liverpool, Everton
Liverpool, Exchange
Liverpool, Fairfield
Liverpool, Walton
Liverpool, Wavertree
Manchester, Rusholme
Manchester, Withington
Salford North
Salford West
Lancashire, Stretford
Lancashire, Waterloo
Lancashire, Widnes
Newcastle under Lyme

Working Class
Eccles
Preston
Rossendale
Stockport
Cheshire, Crewe
Cheshire, Macclesfield
Cheshire, Stalybridge and Hyde
Accrington
Ashton under Lyne
Barrow in Furness
Blackburn
Bolton
Burnley
Bury
Liverpool, Kirkdale
Liverpool, Scotland
Liverpool, West Derby
Liverpool, West Toxteth
Manchester, Ardwick
Manchester, Blackley
Manchester, Clayton
Manchester, Gorton
Manchester, Hulme
Manchester, Moss Side
Manchester, Platting
Nelson and Colne

Oldham
Rochdale
St Helens
Salford South
Warrington
Lancashire, Clitheroe
Lancashire, Darwen
Lancashire, Farnworth
Lancashire, Heywood and Radcliffe
Lancashire, Ince
Lancashire, Middleton and Prestwich
Lancashire, Mossley
Lancashire, Royton
Lancashire, Westhoughton
Stoke on Trent, Burslem
Stoke on Trent, Hanley
Stoke on Trent, Stoke

Urban/Rural
Cheshire, Altrincham
Cheshire, City of Chester
Blackpool
Lancashire, Chorley
Lancashire, Fylde
Lancashire, Lancaster
Lancashire, Lonsdale
Lancashire, Ormskirk

Rural
Cheshire, Eddisbury
Cheshire, Knutsford

Mining
Leigh
Wigan
Lancashire, Newton
Staffordshire, Stone

Yorkshire

Middle Class
Sheffield, Ecclesall
Sheffield, Hallam
Sheffield, Park

Mixed Class
York
Birkenhead East
Kingston upon Hull, Central
Kingston upon Hull, North West
Kingston upon Hull, South West
Bradford North
Leeds Central
Leeds North
Leeds North East
Sheffield Central

Sheffield, Hillsborough
Wakefield
Yorkshire (West Riding), Pudsey and Otley

Working Class
Huddersfield
Kingston upon Hull, East
Bradford Central
Bradford East
Bradford South
Dewsbury
Halifax
Leeds South
Leeds South East
Leeds West
Sheffield, Attercliffe
Sheffield, Brightside
Yorkshire (West Riding), Colne Valley
Yorkshire (West Riding), Elland
Yorkshire (West Riding), Keighley
Yorkshire (West Riding), Shipley
Yorkshire (West Riding), Sowerby
Yorkshire (West Riding), Spen Valley

Urban/Rural
Yorkshire (North Riding), Scarborough and Whitby
Yorkshire (West Riding), Penistone
Yorkshire (West Riding), Pontefract
Yorkshire (West Riding), Ripon
Yorkshire (West Riding), Skipton

Rural
Yorkshire (East Riding), Buckrose
Yorkshire (East Riding), Holderness
Yorkshire (East Riding), Howdenshire
Yorkshire (North Riding), Richmond
Yorkshire (North Riding), Thirsk and Malton
Yorkshire (West Riding), Barkston Ash

Mining
Barnsley
Batley and Morley
Rotherham
Yorkshire (West Riding), Doncaster
Yorkshire (West Riding), Don Valley
Yorkshire (West Riding), Hemsworth
Yorkshire (West Riding), Normanton
Yorkshire (West Riding), Rother Valley
Yorkshire (West Riding), Rothwell
Yorkshire (West Riding), Wentworth

North of England

Mixed Class

Darlington
The Hartlepools
South Shields
Stockton on Tees
Sunderland
Newcastle upon Tyne, Central
Newcastle upon Tyne, East
Newcastle upon Tyne, North
Newcastle upon Tyne, West
Tynemouth
Wallsend
Middlesbrough East
Middlesbrough West

Working Class
Carlisle
Gateshead
Durham, Jarrow

Urban/Rural
Cumberland, Whitehaven
Cumberland, Workington
Durham, Durham
Northumberland, Berwick upon Tweed
Yorkshire (North Riding), Cleveland

Rural
Cumberland, Northern
Cumberland, Penrith and Cockermouth
Northumberland, Hexham
Westmorland

Mining
Durham, Barnard Castle
Durham, Bishop Auckland
Durham, Blaydon
Durham, Chester Le Street
Durham, Consett
Durham, Houghton Le Spring
Durham, Seaham
Durham, Sedgefield
Durham, Spennymoor
Morpeth
Northumberland, Wansbeck

Wales

Middle Class
Cardiff Central
Cardiff East
Cardiff South
Swansea West
Newport

Working Class
Swansea East

Urban/Rural

Caernarvon District of Boroughs
Carmarthenshire, Llanelly
Flintshire
Glamorganshire, Gower
Glamorganshire, Llandaff and Barry
Merionethshire
Monmouthshire, Abertillery

Rural
Anglesey
Brecknockshire and Radnorshire
Caernarvonshire
Cardiganshire
Carmarthenshire, Carmarthen
Denbichshire, Denbigh
Monmouthshire, Monmouth
Montgomeryshire
Pembrokeshire

Mining
Denbighshire, Wrexham
Merthyr Tydfil, Aberdare
Merthyr Tydfil, Merthyr
Rhondda East
Rhondda West
Glamorganshire, Aberavon
Glamorganshire, Caerphilly
Glamorganshire, Neath
Glamorganshire, Ogmore
Glamorganshire, Pontypridd
Monmouthshire, Bedwellty
Monmouthshire, Ebbw Vale
Monmouthshire, Pontypool

Highlands

Urban/Rural
Inverness Shire and Ross and Cromarty, Inverness

Rural
Aberdeenshire and Kincardineshire, Central
Aberdeenshire and Kincardineshire, Eastern
Aberdeenshire and Kincardineshire, Kincardine and Western
Caithness and Sutherland
Inverness Shire and Ross and Cromarty, Ross and Cromarty
Inverness Shire and Ross and Cromarty, Western Isles
Orkney and Shetland

East of Scotland

Middle Class
Edinburgh West

Mixed Class

Aberdeen South
Edinburgh North
Edinburgh South
Leith
Stirling and Falkirk District of Burghs

Working Class
Aberdeen North
Dundee
Montrose District of Burghs
Dunfermline District of Burghs
Kirkcaldy District of Burghs
Edinburgh Central
Edinburgh East

Urban/Rural
Fife Eastern
Midlothian and Peeblesshire, Northern
Roxburghshire and Selkirkshire
Perthshire and Kinross Shire, Perth
Stirlingshire and Clackmannanshire, Clackmannan and Eastern
Stirlingshire and Clackmannanshire, Western

Rural
Forfarshire
Banffshire
Berwickshire and Haddingtonshire
Midlothian and Peeblesshire, Peebles and Southern
Moray and Nairnshire
Perthshire and Kinross Shire, Kinross and Western

Mining
Fife Western

West of Scotland

Middle Class
Ayr District of Burghs

Mixed Class
Glasgow Central

Working Class
Dumbarton District of Burghs
Glasgow, Bridgeton
Glasgow, Camlachie
Glasgow, Cathcart
Glasgow, Gorbals
Glasgow, Govan
Glasgow, Hillhead
Glasgow, Kelvingrove
Glasgow, Maryhill
Glasgow, Partick
Glasgow, Pollok

Glasgow, St Rollox
Glasgow, Shettleston
Glasgow, Springburn
Glasgow Tradeston
Greenock
Paisley

Urban/Rural
Dunbartonshire
Renfrewshire, Eastern
Linlithgowshire

Rural
Argyll
Dumfriesshire
Galloway
Lanarkshire, Lanark
Renfrewshire, Western

Mining
Ayrshire and Bute, Bute and Northern
Ayrshire and Bute, Kilmarnock
Ayrshire and Bute, South Ayrshire
Lanarkshire, Bothwell

APPENDIX III
List of Primary Sources

GOVERNMENT RECORDS

Cabinet	*CAB*
Board of Trade	*BT*
Foreign Office	*FO*
Ministry of Labour	*LAB*
Ministry of Munitions	*MUN*
Ministry of Reconstruction	*RECO*
War Office	*WO*

PRIVATE COLLECTIONS

Association of British Chambers of Commerce Papers	*Guildhall Library*
Addison Papers	*Bodleian Library*
Astor Papers	*Reading University Library*
Austen Chamberlain Papers	*Birmingham University Library*
Balfour Papers	*British Library*
Beaverbrook Papers	*House of Lords Record Office*
Bonar Law Papers	*House of Lords Record Office*
Borden Papers	*Public Archives of Canada*
Bridgeman Papers	*Shropshire Record Office*
Buckler Papers	*Yale University Library*
Bull Papers	*Churchill College Archive Centre*
Burns Diary	*British Library*
Courtney Papers	*British Library of Political and Economic Science*
Craigmyle Papers	*In the possession of Lord Craigmyle*
Crewe Papers	*Cambridge University Library*
Curzon Papers	*India Office Library*
Denman Papers	*Bodleian Library*
Derby Papers	*Liverpool City Library*

Engineering Employers' Federation Papers	*University of Warwick Modern Archives Centre*
Elibank Papers	*National Library of Scotland*
Emmott Papers	*Nuffield College Library*
Federation of British Industry Papers	*University of Warwick Modern Archives Centre*
H.A.L. Fisher Papers	*Bodleian Library*
H.A. Gwynne Papers	*Bodleian Library*
Haig Papers	*National Library of Scotland*
Haldane Papers	*National Library of Scotland*
Hankey Papers	*Churchill College Archive Centre*
Harcourt papers	*Bodleian Library*
Hardinge Papers	*Cambridge University Library*
Hewins Papers	*Sheffield University Library*
House Papers	*Yale University Library*
Ilbert Diary	*House of Lords Record Office*
Lothian Papers	*Scottish Record Office*
Kitchener Papers	*Public Record Office*
Lloyd George Papers	*House of Lords Record Office*
Long Papers	*Wiltshire Record Office*
Long Papers	*British Library*
MacDonald Papers	*Public Record Office*
Macdonell Papers	*Bodleian Library*
McKenna Papers	*Churchill College Archive Centre*
Mancroft Papers	*Churchill College Archive Centre*
Milner Papers	*Bodleian Library*
Northcliffe Papers	*British Library*
Page Croft Papers	*Churchill College Archive Centre*
Plunkett Papers	*Plunkett House, Oxford*
Pringle Papers	*House of Lords Record Office*
Rawlinson Papers	*Churchill College Archive Centre*
Redmond Papers	*Bodleian Library (microfilm)*
Robertson Papers	*King's College, London*
Rumbold Papers	*Bodleian Library*
Runciman Papers	*Newcastle University Library*
Samuel Papers	*House of Lords Record Office*
Scott Papers	*British Library*
Selborne Papers	*Bodleian Library*
Shipbuilding Employers' Federation Papers	*National Maritime Museum*
Steel-Maitland Papers	*Scottish Record Office*
Strachey Papers	*House of Lords Record Office*
Trevelyan Papers	*Newcastle University Library*
Willoughby de Broke Papers	*House of Lords Record Office*
Wilson Papers	*Imperial War Museum*
Wiseman Papers	*Yale University Library*

BIBLIOGRAPHY

Adams, R.J.Q., and Poirier, Philip, *The Conscription Controversy in Britain 1900–18* (London: Macmillan, 1987)

Addison, Christopher, *Four and a Half Years* (2 Vols, London: Hutchinson, 1934)

Alderman, Geoffrey, *London Jewry and London Politics, 1899–1988* (London: Routledge, 1989)

————, 'The Railway Companies and the Growth of Trades Unionism in the Late Nineteenth and Early Twentieth Century', *Historical Journal*, xiv (1971), 129–152

————, 'The National Free Labour Association: a case study of organised strike-breaking in the late 19th and the early 20th century', *International Review of Social History*, xxi (1976), 309–336

Anderson, Gregory, *Victorian Clerks* (Manchester: Manchester University Press, 1976)

Balderston, T., 'War Finance and Inflation in Britain and Germany, 1914–1918', *Economic History Review*, 2s, xlii (1989), 222–244

Balfour, A.J., *Economic Notes on Insular Free Trade* (London: Longman, 1903)

Barker, T.C., *The Glass-makers: the rise of an international company, 1826–1976* (London: Weidenfeld, 1977)

Barnes, John and Nicholson, David, eds, *The Leo Amery Diaries: Volume I, 1896–1929* (London: Hutchinson, 1980)

Barnett, L. Margaret, *British Food Policy during the First World War* (London: Allen & Unwin, 1985)

Bealey, Frank, 'The Electoral Arrangement between the Labour Representation Committee and the Liberal Party', *Journal of Modern History*, xxviii (1956), 353–373

Beaverbrook, Lord *Politicians and the War* (2 Vols, London: Butterworth, 1928 and 1930); (republished as one volume, London: Collins, 1960)

————, *Men and Power* (London: Hutchinson, 1956)

Bebbington, D.W., 'Nonconformity and Electoral Sociology, 1867–1918', *Historical Journal*, xxvii (1984), 633–656

Beckett, Ian, 'The British Army 1914–1918: the illusion of change', in John Turner, ed., *Britain and the First World War*, (London: Unwin Hyman, 1988)

Bentley, Michael, *The Liberal Mind* (Cambridge: Cambridge University Press, 1977)

————, 'Party, Doctrine and Thought', in Michael Bentley and John Stevenson, eds, *High and Low Politics in Modern Britain* (Oxford: Clarendon Press, 1983), pp. 123–153

————, *The Climax of Liberal Politics: British Liberalism in theory and practice 1868–1918* (London: Edward Arnold, 1987)

Bernstein, George L., *Liberalism and Liberal Politics in Edwardian England* (Boston: Allen & Unwin, 1986)

————, 'Yorkshire Liberalism during the First World War', *Historical Journal*, xxxii (1989), 107–129

Blewett, Neal, *The Peers, the Parties and the People: the general elections of 1910* (London: Macmillan, 1972)

————, 'The Franchise in the United Kingdom, 1885–1918', *Past and Present*, xxxii (Dec. 1965), 27–56

Bond, Brian, 'Soldiers and Statesmen: British civil-military relations in 1917', *Military Affairs*, October 1968, 62–75

Boswell, Jonathan S. and Johns, Bruce R., 'Patriots or Profiteers? British businessmen and the First World War', *Journal of European Economic History*, xi (1982), 423–445

Boyce, George, ed., *The Crisis of British Unionism* (London: Historians' Press, 1987)

————, *The Crisis of British Power* (London: Historians' Press, 1990)

————, 'Federalism and the Irish Question' in Andrea Bosco and John Pinder, eds., *The Federal Idea* (forthcoming)

Boyce, D.G. and Stubbs, J.O., 'F.S. Oliver, Lord Selborne, and Federalism', *Journal of Imperial and Commonwealth History*, v (1976), 68–70

Boyle, Andrew, *Trenchard* (London: Collins, 1962)

Boyle, T., 'The Liberal Imperialists', *Bulletin of the Institute of Historical Research*, lii (May 1979), 48–82

Brooks, David, *The Destruction of Lord Rosebery: from the diary of Sir Edward Hamilton, 1894–1895* (London: Historians' Press, 1987)

Brown, B.H., *The Tariff Reform Movement in Great Britain 1881–98* (New York: Columbia University Press, 1943)

Bunselmeyer, R.E., *The Cost of War: British economic warfare and the origins of reparations* (Hamden, Conn.: Archon, 1975)

Burgess, Keith, *The Challenge of Labour: shaping British society 1850–1930* (London: Croom Helm, 1980)

Burk, Kathleen, ed., *War and the State* (London: Allen & Unwin, 1982)

Burk, Kathleen, *Britain, America and the Sinews of War 1914–1918* (London: Allen & Unwin, 1985)

Cain, P.J., 'Political Economy in Edwardian England: the Tariff Reform controversy', in Alan O'Day, ed., *The Edwardian Age: conflict and stability 1900–1914* (London: Macmillan, 1979), pp. 35–59

Calder, K.J., *Britain and the Origins of the New Europe* (Cambridge: Cambridge University Press, 1976)

Carrington, C.E., 'The Empire at War, 1914–1918', in *The Cambridge History of the British Empire* (Cambridge: Cambridge University Press, 1959), III, 605–644

Ceadel, Martin, *Pacifism in Britain, 1914-1945: the defining of a faith* (Oxford: Clarendon Press, 1980)

Cecil, Lord Hugh, *Conservatism* (London: Williams & Norgate [Home University Library], 1912)

Charles, Rodger, *The Development of Industrial Relations in Great Britain, 1911–1939* (London: Hutchinson, 1973)

Clarke, P.F., 'British Politics and Blackburn Politics, 1900–1910', *Historical Journal*, xii (1969)

————, *Lancashire and the New Liberalism* (Cambridge: Cambridge University Press, 1971)

————, *Liberals and Social Democrats* (Cambridge: Cambridge University Press, 1978)

Cline, Peter, 'Winding Down the War Economy: British plans for peacetime recovery, 1916–19' in Kathleen Burk, ed., *War and the State* (London: Allen & Unwin, 1982), pp. 157–181

Coats, A.W., 'Political Economy and the Tariff Reform Campaign', *Journal of Law and Economics*, xi (1968), 181–229

Coetzee, Frantz, 'Pressure Groups, Tory Businessmen, and the Aura of Political Corruption before the First World War', *Historical Journal* xxix (1986), 833–852

————, *For Party or Country: nationalism and the dilemmas of popular Conservatism in Edwardian England* (New York: Oxford University Press, 1990)

Coleman, Donald, 'War Demand and Industrial Supply; the "dope scandal", 1915–1919' in J.M. Winter, ed., *War and Economic Development* (Cambridge: Cambridge University Press, 1975), pp. 205–227

Collini, Stefan, *Liberalism and Sociology* (Cambridge: Cambridge University Press, 1979)

Cooper, J. Milton, 'The British Response to the House-Grey Memorandum: new evidence and new questions', *Journal of American History*, lix (1973), 958–971

Cooper, Malcolm, *The Birth of Independent Air Power* (London: Allen & Unwin, 1986)

Cowling, Maurice, *1867: Disraeli, Gladstone and revolution* (Cambridge: Cambridge University Press, 1967)

————, *The Impact of Labour* (Cambridge: Cambridge University Press, 1971)

————, *The Impact of Hitler* (Cambridge: Cambridge University Press, 1975)

Cronin, James E., *Industrial Conflict in Modern Britain* (London: Croom Helm, 1979)

Currie, Robert, *Industrial Politics* (Oxford: Clarendon Press, 1979)

Dangerfield, George, *The Strange Death of Liberal England* (London: Constable, 1935)

Davenport-Hines, R.P.T., *Dudley Docker* (Cambridge: Cambridge University Press, 1984)

————, 'Trade Associations and the Modernization Crisis of British Industry, 1910–35' in Hiroaki Yamazaki and Matao Miyamoto, eds, *Trade Associations in Business History* (Tokyo: University of Tokyo Press, 1988), pp. 205–226

David, Edward, 'The Liberal Party during the First World War', Cambridge University M.Litt. thesis, 1968

————, 'The Liberal Party Divided 1916–1918', *Historical Journal*, xiii (1970), 509–533

————, ed., *Inside Asquith's Cabinet* (London: John Murray, 1977)

Davies, R., 'The Liverpool Labour Party and the Liverpool Working Class', *North West Labour History Bulletin*, vi (1979–80), 2–14

Dean, Sir Maurice, *The Royal Air Force and Two World Wars* (London: Cassell, 1979)

Dewey, Peter, 'Military Recruiting and the British Labour Force during the First World War', *Historical Journal*, xxvii (1984), 199–224

————, *British Agriculture in the First World War* (London: Croom Helm, 1988)

————, 'Nutrition and Living Standards in Wartime Britain', in D. Wall and J.M. Winter, eds, *The Upheaval of War* (Cambridge: Cambridge University Press, 1988), pp. 197–220

Dingle, A.E., *The Campaign for Prohibition in Victorian England* (London: Croom Helm, 1980)

D'Ombrain, Nicholas, *War Machinery and High Policy: defence administration in peacetime Britain 1902–1914* (Oxford: Clarendon Press, 1973)

Douglas, Roy, 'The Background to the "Coupon" Election Arrangements', *English Historical Review*, cccxlii (1971), 318–336

————, 'God Gave the Land to the People', in A.J.A. Morris, ed., *Edwardian Radicalism, 1900–1914* (London: Routledge & Kegan Paul, 1974)

————, 'A Classification of the Members of Parliament Elected in 1918', *Bulletin of the Institute of Historical Research*, xlvii (1974), 74–94

Dunbabin, J.P.D., 'British Elections in the Nineteenth and Twentieth Centuries: a regional approach', *English Historical Review*, ccclxxv (1980), 241–267

Egerton, George W., 'The Lloyd George War Memoirs: a study in the politics of memory', *Journal of Modern History*, lx (1988), 55–94

Emy, H.V., 'Lloyd George as Social Reformer: the Land Campaign', in A.J.P. Taylor, ed., *Lloyd George: twelve essays* (London: Hamish Hamilton, 1971)

———, *Liberals, Radicals and Social Politics 1892–1914* (Cambridge: Cambridge University Press, 1973)

Englander, David, *Landlord and Tenant* (Oxford: Oxford University Press, 1983)

Fair, John D., *British Interparty Conferences: a study of the procedure of conciliation in British Politics, 1867–1921* (Oxford: Clarendon Press, 1980)

Fanning, Ronan, 'The Irish Policy of Asquith's Government and the Cabinet Crisis of 1910' in A. Cosgrave and D. McCartney, eds, *Studies in Irish History Presented to R. Dudley Edwards* (Dublin: University College, 1979), pp. 279–303

Fawcett, C.B., *Provinces of England* (London: Williams & Norgate, 1919)

Feldman, Gerald, *Iron and Steel in the German Inflation, 1916–1922* (Princeton: Princeton University Press, 1977)

Fielding, Steve, 'Irish Politics in Manchester 1880–1914', *International Review of Social History*, xxxviii (1988), 261–284

Fitzgerald, Robert, *British Labour Management and Industrial Welfare, 1846–1939* (London: Croom Helm, 1988)

Fitzpatrick, D., *Politics and Irish Life* (Dublin: Gill Macmillan, 1979)

Foster, John, 'Strike Action and Working-class Politics on Clydeside, 1914–1919', *International Review of Social History*, xxxv (1990), 33–70

Fraser, Peter, 'Lord Beaverbrook's Fabrications in *Politicians and the War 1914–1916*', *Historical Journal*, xxv (1982), 147–166

Freeden, Michael, *The New Liberalism: an ideology of social reform* (Oxford: Clarendon Press, 1978)

French, David, 'Spy Fever in Britain, 1900–15', *Historical Journal*, xxi (1978), 355–370.

———, *British Economic and Strategic Planning 1905–1915* (London: Allen & Unwin, 1982)

———, 'The Rise and Fall of "Business as Usual"', in Kathleen Burk, ed., *War and the State* (London: Allen & Unwin, 1982), pp. 7–31

———, 'The Origins of the Dardanelles Campaign Reconsidered', *History*, lxvii (1983), 210–224.

———, *British Strategy and War Aims, 1914–1916* (London: Allen & Unwin, 1986)

Fry, Michael, 'Political Change in Britain, August 1914 to December 1916: Lloyd George replaces Asquith', *Historical Journal*, xxxi (1988), 609–627

Galbraith, John S. 'British War Aims in World War I: a commentary on "statesmanship"', *Journal of Imperial and Commonwealth History*, xiii (1984), 25–45

Gardiner, A.G., *The War Lords* (London: J.M. Dent, 1915)

Garrard, J.A., 'Parties, Members and Voters after 1867: a local study', *Historical Journal*, xx (1977), 145–163

Garson, N.G., 'South Africa and World War I', *Journal of Imperial and Commonwealth History*, viii (1979), 68–85

Gilbert, B.B., 'David Lloyd George, the Reform of British Landholding and the Budget of 1914', *Historical Journal* xxi (1978), 117–141

Gilbert, Martin, *Winston S. Churchill. Volume III, 1914–1916* (London: William Heinemann, 1971)

———, *Winston S. Churchill. Volume IV 1916–1922* (London: William Heinemann, 1975)

Godfrey, John, *Capitalism at War: industrial policy and bureaucracy in France, 1914–1918* (Leamington Spa: Berg, 1987)

Gooch, John *The Plans of War: the General Staff and British military strategy c. 1900–1916* (London: Routledge & Kegan Paul, 1974)

Gregory, Roy *The Miners and British Politics, 1906–1914* (Oxford: Oxford University Press, 1968)

Grieves, Keith, *The Politics of Manpower, 1914–1918* (Manchester: Manchester University Press, 1988)

——, *Sir Eric Geddes: business and government in war and peace* (Manchester: Manchester University Press, 1989)

Griffith Boscawen, Arthur, *Memories* (London: John Murray, 1925)

Grigg, John, *Lloyd George: from peace to war* (London: Methuen, 1985)

Hankey, Lord, *The Supreme Command* (2 Vols, London: Allen & Unwin, 1961)

Harmsworth, Cecil, *Pleasure and Problem in South Africa* (London: Harmsworth, 1908)

Harris, José, 'The Transition to High Politics in English Social Policy, 1880–1914' in Michael Bentley and John Stevenson, eds, *High and Low Politics in Modern Britain* (Oxford: Clarendon Press, 1983), pp. 58–79

Harrison, Brian, *Separate Spheres: the opposition to women's suffrage in Britain* (London: Croom Helm, 1978)

——, 'Women's Suffrage at Westminster 1866–1928', in Michael Bentley and John Stevenson, eds, *High and Low Politics in Modern Britain* (Oxford: Clarendon Press, 1983), pp. 80–122

Harrison, Royden, 'The War Emergency Workers' National Committee', in Asa Briggs and John Saville, eds, *Essays in Labour History 1886–1923* (London: Macmillan, 1971)

Hay, J.R., 'Employers and Social Policy in Britain: the evolution of welfare legislation, 1905–14', *Social History* (1977), 435–456

——, 'Employers' Attitudes to Social Policy and the Concept of Social Control, 1900–1920', in P.M. Thane, ed., *The Origins of British Social Policy* (London: Croom Helm, 1978)

Hazlehurst, Cameron, *Politicians at War* (London: Jonathan Cape, 1970)

Hewart, Gordon, *The New Despotism* (London: Ernest Benn, 1929)

Hinsley, F.H., (ed.), *British Foreign Policy under Sir Edward Grey* (Cambridge: Cambridge University Press, 1977)

Hinton, J.M., 'Rank and File Militancy in the British Engineering Industry, 1914-1918' London University Ph.D. thesis 1969

——, *The First Shop Stewards' Movement* (London: Allen & Unwin, 1973)

Hirst, Hugo 'Two Autobiographical Fragments', ed. R.P.T. Davenport-Hines, *Business History*, xxviii (1986), 124

Holbrook-Jones, Mike, *Supremacy and Subordination of Labour* (London: Heinemann Educational Books, 1982)

Hopkin, Deian, 'The Membership of the Independent Labour Party, 1904–10: a spatial and occupational analysis', *International Review of Social History*, xx (1975), 175–195

Howarth, Janet, 'The Liberal Revival in Northamptonshire, 1880–1895', *Historical Journal*, xii (1969), 78–118

Jalland, Patricia, 'United Kingdom Devolution, 1910–14: political panacea or tactical diversion?', *English Historical Review*, xciv (1979), 757–785

——, *The Liberals and Ireland: The Ulster question in British politics to 1914* (Brighton: Harvester Press, 1980)

Jefferys, J.B., *The Story of the Engineers* (London: Amalgamated Engineering Union, 1946)

Jefferys, Kevin, 'The Educational Policy of the Conservative Party, 1918–1944', University of London Ph. D. thesis, 1984

Jenkins, Roy, *Asquith* (London: Collins, 1964)

Johnston, R.J., *The Geography of English Politics* (London: Croom Helm, 1985)

Jones, Stephanie, *Trade and Shipping* (Manchester: Manchester University Press, 1989)

Joyce, Patrick, *Work, Society and Politics* (Brighton: Harvester Press, 1980)

Kendle, J.E. 'The Round Table Movement and "Home Rule All Round"', *Historical Journal*, xi (1968), 332–353

————, *The Colonial and Imperial Conferences 1887–1911* (London: Longman, 1970)

————, 'Federalism and the Irish Problem in 1918', *History*, lvi (1971), 207–230

————, *The Round Table Movement and Imperial Union* (Toronto: University of Toronto Press, 1975)

Koss, Stephen, *Nonconformity in Modern British Politics* (London: Batsford, 1975)

————, *The Rise and Fall of the Political Press in Britain. Volume II: the twentieth century* (London: Hamish Hamilton, 1984)

Laybourn, Keith, and Reynolds, Jack, *Liberalism and the Rise of Labour, 1890–1918* (London: Croom Helm, 1984)

Littler, Craig R., *The Development of the Labour Process in Capitalist Societies* (London: Heinemann Educational Books, 1982)

Lloyd George, David, *War Memoirs* (Popular edn., 2 Vols, London: Odhams, 1938)

Lowe, Rodney, 'The Ministry of Labour, 1916–1924: a graveyard of social reform?', *Public Administration*, lii (1974)

————, 'The Failure of Consensus in Britain: the National Industrial Conference, 1919–21', *Historical Journal*, xxi (1978), 647–675

————, 'The Ministry of Labour, 1916–19: a "still, small voice"?', in Kathleen Burk, ed., *War and the State* (London: Allen & Unwin, 1982), pp. 108–134

————, *Adjusting to Democracy* (Oxford: Clarendon Press, 1986)

Lunn, K., 'Political Anti-semitism before 1914: fascism's heritage' in K. Lunn and R.C. Thurlow, eds, *British Fascism* (London: Croom Helm, 1979), pp. 20–40

Macara, Charles, *Recollections* (London: 1922)

Machin, G.I.T., *Politics and the Churches in Britain 1869–1921* (Oxford: Clarendon Press, 1987)

MacCarthy, Desmond, ed., *H.H.A.: letters of the Earl of Oxford and Asquith to a friend: first series, 1915-1922* (London: Geoffrey Bles, 1933)

McDermott, John, ' "Total" War and the Merchant State: aspects of British economic warfare against Germany, 1914–1916', *Canadian Journal of History*, xxi (1986), 61–76

————, ' "A Needless Sacrifice": British businessmen and business as usual in the First World War', *Albion*, xxi (1989), 263–282

McDowell, R.B., *The Irish Convention, 1917-1918* (London: Routledge & Kegan Paul, 1970)

McEwen, J.M., 'The Coupon Election of 1918 and the Unionist Members of Parliament', *Journal of Modern History*, xxxiv (1962), 294–306

————, 'The Struggle for Mastery in Britain: Lloyd George versus Asquith, December 1916', *Journal of British Studies*, xviii (1978), 131–156

————, 'The Press and the Fall of Asquith', *Historical Journal*, xxi (1978), 863–883

————, 'Lloyd George's Liberal Supporters in December 1916: a note', *Bulletin of the Institute of Historical Research*, liii (1980), 265–272

McGill, Barry, 'Lloyd George's Timing of the 1918 Election', *Journal of British Studies*, xiv (1974)

McIver, Arthur J., 'Employers' Organisations and Strike-breaking in Britain, 1880–1914', *International Review of Social History* xxix (1984), 1–33

MacKenzie, S.P., 'Morale and the Cause: the campaign to shape the outlook of soldiers in the British Expeditionary Force, 1914–1918', *Canadian Journal of History*, xxv (1990), 215–232

McKibbin, Ross, *The Evolution of the Labour Party, 1910–1924* (Oxford: Clarendon Press, 1973)

McKinlay, Alan, and Zeitlin, Jonathan, 'The Meanings of Managerial Prerogative: industrial relations and the organisation of work in British engineering, 1880–1939', in Charles Harvey and John Turner, eds., *Labour and Business in Modern Britain* (London: Frank Cass, 1989), pp. 32–47

McLean, D., 'English Radicals, Russia and the Fate of Persia, 1907–1913', *English Historical Review*, xciii (1978), 338–352

McLean, Ian, *The Legend of Red Clydeside* (Edinburgh: John Macdonald, 1983)

Macleod, Roy and Andrews, Kay, 'The Origins of the DSIR: reflections on ideas and men', *Public Administration*, xlviii (1970), 23–48

Macready, H.W., 'Alfred Marshall and Tariff Reform, 1903', *Journal of Political Economy*, lxiii (1955), 259–267

Marder, A.J., *From the Dreadnought to Scapa Flow*, Vol. 5 (London: Oxford University Press, 1962)

Marlowe, John, *Apostle of Empire* (London: Hamish Hamilton, 1976)

Marrison, A.J., 'Businessmen, Industries and Tariff Reform in Great Britain 1903–1930', *Business History*, xxv (1983)

Martin, L.W., *Peace without Victory: Woodrow Wilson and the British Liberals* (New Haven, Ct: Yale University Press, 1958)

Marwick, Arthur, *The Deluge: British society and the First World War* (London: Macmillan, 1965)

Matthew, H.C.G., *The Liberal Imperialists: the ideas and politics of a post-Gladstonian élite* (Oxford: Clarendon Press, 1973)

Matthew, H.C.G., McKibbin, R.I., and Kay, J.A., 'The Franchise Factor in the Rise of the Labour Party', *English Historical Review*, xci (1976), 723–752

Meacham, Standish, ' "The Sense of an Impending Clash": English working-class unrest before the First World War', *American Historical Review*, lxxvii (1972), 1343–64

Melling, Joseph, 'British Employers and the Development of Industrial Welfare, c. 1880–1920', University of Glasgow Ph.D. thesis, 1980

——————, 'Employers, Industrial Harmony and the Evolution of Company Welfare Policies in Britain's Heavy Industry: West Scotland, 1870–1920', *International Review of Social History*, xxvi (1981), 255–301

——————, *Rent Strikes: the people's struggle for housing in West Scotland 1890–1916* (Edinburgh: Polygon Books, 1983)

——————, 'Whatever Happened to Red Clydeside?: industrial conflict and the politics of skill in the First World War', *International Review of Social History*, xxxv (1990), 3–32

Mews, Stuart, 'Urban Problems and Rural Solutions: Drink and Disestablishment in the First World War', in D. Baker, ed., *The Church in Town and Country* (Oxford: Blackwell, 1979)

Meynell, H., 'The Stockholm Conference of 1917', *International Review of Social History*, v (1960), 1–25, 202–225

Middlebrook, Martin, *The First Day on the Somme* (London: Allen Lane, 1971)

Middlemas, Keith, ed., *Thomas Jones: Whitehall Diary: Volume 1 1916–1925* (London: Oxford University Press, 1969)

——————, *Politics in Industrial Society* (London: André Deutsch, 1979)

Miller, William L., *Electoral Dynamics in Britain since 1918* (London: Macmillan, 1977)

Miller, William and Raab, Gillian, 'The Religious Alignment at English Elections between 1918 and 1970', *Political Studies*, xxv (1977), 227–251

Moore, Bill, 'Sheffield Shop Stewards in the First World War', in L. Munby, ed., *The Luddites and Other Essays* (London: Michael Katanka Books, 1971), pp. 245–261.

Morgan, K.O., *Wales in British Politics, 1868–1922* (Cardiff: University of Wales Press, 1970)

————, *Lloyd George: family letters 1885-1936* (London and Cardiff: Oxford University Press and University of Wales Press, 1973)

————, *Consensus and Disunity* (Oxford: Clarendon Press, 1979)

Morris, A.J.A., *Radicalism against War, 1906–1914* (London: Longman, 1972)

Murphy, R.P., 'Walter Long and the Conservative Party 1905–1921', University of Bristol Ph.D. thesis, 1984

————, 'Faction in the Conservative Party and the Home Rule Crisis, 1912–14', *History* lxxi (1986), 222–234

————, 'Walter Long, the Unionist Ministers, and the Formation of Lloyd George's Government in December 1916', *Historical Journal*, xxix (1986), 735–745

Murray, Bruce K., *The People's Budget* (Oxford: Clarendon Press, 1980)

Naylor, John, 'The Establishment of the Cabinet Secretariat', *Historical Journal*, xiv (1971), 783–803

Newton, Scott and Porter, Dilwyn, *Modernisation Frustrated: the politics of industrial decline in Britain since 1900* (London: Unwin Hyman, 1988)

Nimocks, Walter, *Milner's Young Men: the 'kindergarten' in Edwardian imperial affairs* (London: Hodder & Stoughton, 1970)

Nottingham, Christopher, 'Recasting Bourgeois Britain? The British state in the years which followed the First World War', *International Review of Social History*, xxxi (1986), 227–247

O'Brien, Anthony Mor, 'Keir Hardie, C.B. Stanton and the First World War', *Llafur*, iv (1986), 31–42

O'Day, Alan, *The English Face of Irish Nationalism* (Dublin: Gill Macmillan, 1977)

————, 'The Irish Influence on Parliamentary Elections', in Roger Swift and Sheridan Gilley, eds, *The Irish in the Victorian City* (London: Croom Helm, 1986)

Offer, Avner, *Property and Politics* (Cambridge: Cambridge University Press, 1983)

————, *The First World War: an agrarian interpretation* (Oxford: Clarendon Press, 1989)

O'Halpin, Eunan, 'H.E. Duke and the Irish Administration, 1916–1918', *Irish Historical Studies*, xxii (1981), 362–376

————, *The Decline of the Union: British government in Ireland, 1892– 1920* (Dublin: Gill Macmillan, 1987)

Oliver, F.S., *Ordeal by Battle* (London: Macmillan, 1915)

————, *The Anvil of War* (London: Macmillan, 1916)

Owen, Frank, *Tempestuous Journey* (London: Hutchinson, 1954)

Panayi, Panikos, 'Anti-German Riots in London during the First World War', *German History*, vii (1989), 184–203

Pelling, Henry, *Social Geography of British Elections 1885–1910* (London: Macmillan, 1967)

Phillips, G.A., 'The Triple Industrial Alliance in 1914', *Economic History Review*, 2s, xxiv (1971), 55–67

Pigou, A.C., *The Riddle of the Tariff* (London: Brimley & Johnson, 1903)

————, *The Great Inquest* (London: The Pilot, 1903)

————, *Protective and Preferential Duties*, (London: privately printed, 1906)

Pugh, Martin D., 'Asquith, Bonar Law and the First Coalition', *Historical Journal*, xvii (1974), 813–836

————, 'Yorkshire and the New Liberalism', *Journal of Modern History*, l (1978), 1139–1155.

————, *Electoral Reform in War and Peace* (London: Routledge & Kegan Paul, 1978)

————, *The Tories and the People, 1880–1935* (Oxford: Blackwell, 1985)

Purdue, A.W., 'The Liberal and Labour Parties in North-Eastern Politics 1900–14: the struggle for supremacy', *International Review of Social History*, xxvi (1981), 1–24

Rasmussen, Jorgen, 'The Political Integration of British Women: the response of a traditional system to a newly emergent group', *Social Science History*, vii (1983), 61–95

————, 'Women in Labour', *Electoral Studies*, iii (1984), 47–63

Reid, Alastair, 'Dilution, Trade Unionism and the State in Britain during the First World War', in S. Tolliday and J. Zeitlin, *Shop Floor Bargaining and the State* (Cambridge: Cambridge University Press, 1985), pp. 46–74

————, 'Glasgow Socialism', *Social History*, ii (1986), 89–97

Reynolds, J. and Laybourn, K., 'The Emergence of the Independent Labour Party in Bradford', *International Review of Social History*, xx (1975), 313–346

Rhodes James, Robert, *Rosebery* (London: Weidenfeld,1963)

Riddell, Lord, *War Diary* (London: Ivor Nicholson & Watson, 1933)

————, *The Riddell Diaries 1908–1923: a selection*, ed. J.M. McEwen (London: Athlone, 1986)

Ridley, Jane, 'The Unionist Social Reform Committee 1911–14: Wets before the Deluge', *Historical Journal*, xxx (1987), 391–413

Robbins, Keith, *The Abolition of War: the peace movement in Britain, 1914-1919* (Cardiff: University of Wales Press, 1976)

Roberts, Elizabeth, 'Working-Class Standards of Living in Barrow and Lancaster, 1890–1914', *Economic History Review*, 2s, xxx (1977), 306–319

————, 'Working-Class Standards of Living in Three Lancashire Towns, 1890–1914', *International Review of Social History* xxvii (1982), 43–65

Roberts, Richard, 'Businessmen, Politics, and Municipal Socialism', in John Turner, ed., *Businessmen and Politics: studies of business activity in British politics, 1900–1945* (London: Heinemann Educational Books, 1984), pp. 20–32

Robertson, P.L., 'Shipping and Shipbuilding: the case of William Denny and Brothers', *Business History*, xvi (1974), 38–39

Rodgers, Terence, 'Sir Allan Smith, the Industrial Group, and the Politics of Unemployment', *Business History*, xxvii (1986), 100–123

————, 'Employers' Organisations, Unemployment and Social Politics in Britain during the Inter-war Period', *Social History*, xiii (1988), 315–341

Roskill, Stephen, *Hankey: man of secrets* (London: Collins, 1970)

Rothwell, V.H., *British War Aims and Peace Diplomacy* (Oxford: Clarendon Press, 1971)

Royle, T., *The Kitchener Enigma* (London: Michael Joseph, 1985)

Rubin, Gerry R., 'Law as a Bargaining Weapon: British labour and the Restoration of Pre-War Practices Act 1919', *Historical Journal*, xxxii (1989), 925–945

Rubinstein, W.D., 'Wealth, Elites and the Class Structure of Modern Britain', *Past and Present*, lxxvi (1977)

Russell, A.K., *Liberal Landslide*, (Newton Abbot: David & Charles, 1973)

Sacks, Benjamin, *The Religious Issue in the State Schools of England and Wales, 1902–1914* (Albuquerque, N.M.: University of New Mexico Press, 1961)

Scally, R.J., *The Origins of the Lloyd George Coalition* (Princeton: Princeton University Press, 1976)

Searle, G.R., *The Quest for National Efficiency: a study in British politics and political thought, 1899–1914* (Oxford: Blackwell, 1971)

Semmel, Bernard, *Imperialism and Social Reform: English social-imperial thought 1895–1914* (New York: Anchor, 1968)

Shallice, A., 'Orange and Green and Militancy: sectarianism and working-class politics in Liverpool, 1900–1914', *North West Labour History Bulletin*, vi (1979–80), 15–32

Sherington, Geoffrey, *English Education, Social Change and War, 1911–20* (Manchester: Manchester University Press, 1981)

Sheffield, G.D., 'The Effect of the Great War on Class Relations in Britain: the career of Major Christopher Stone D.S.O., M.C.', *War and Society*, vii (1989), 87–105

Smith, Elaine, 'Jews and Politics in the East End of London', in David Cesarini, ed., *The Making of Modern Anglo-Jewry* (Oxford: Blackwell, 1990)

Smith, J., 'Labour Traditions in Glasgow and Liverpool', *History Workshop*, xvii (1984), 32–56

Snowden, Philip, *An Autobiography* (2 Vols, London: Ivor Nicolson & Watson, 1934)

Spears, E., *Prelude to Victory* (London: Jonathan Cape, 1939)

Spender, J.A., and Asquith, C., *The Life of H.H. Asquith* (London: Hutchinson, 1932)

Stevenson, David, *The First World War and International Politics* (Oxford: Clarendon, 1987)

Stevenson, John, 'More Light on World War One', *Historical Journal*, xxxiii (1990), 195–210

Stone, Norman, *The Eastern Front, 1914-1917* (London: Hodder & Stoughton, 1975)

Stubbs, J.O., 'The Impact of the Great War on the Conservative Party', in Gillian Peele and Chris Cook, eds, *The Politics of Reappraisal 1918-1939* (London: Macmillan, 1975)

————, 'Beaverbrook as Historian: *Politicians and the War, 1914–1916* reconsidered', *Albion*, xiv (1982), 235–253.

Swartz, Marvin, *The Union of Democratic Control in British Politics during the First World War* (Oxford: Clarendon Press, 1971)

Swenarton, Mark *Homes Fit for Heroes* (London: Heinemann Educational Books, 1981)

Swift, Roger, and Gilley, Sheridan, eds, *The Irish in the Victorian City* (London: Croom Helm, 1986)

————, *The Irish in Britain, 1815–1939* (London: Frances Pinter, 1989)

Sykes, Alan, *Tariff Reform in British Politics 1903–1913* (Oxford: Clarendon Press, 1979)

Tanner, Duncan, 'The Parliamentary Electoral System, the "Fourth Reform Act", and the Rise of Labour in England and Wales', *Bulletin of the Institute of Historical Research*, lvi, 134 (1983), 205–219

————, *Political Change and the Labour Party* (Cambridge: Cambridge University Press, 1990)

Tawney, R.H., 'The Abolition of Economic Controls, 1918–1921', originally written in 1941, reprinted in J.M. Winter, ed., *History and Society: Essays by R.H. Tawney* (London: Routledge & Kegan Paul, 1978), pp. 129–186

Taylor, A.H., 'The Effect of Electoral Pacts on the Decline of the Liberal Party', *British Journal of Political Studies*, iii (1973)

Taylor, A.J.P., *The Troublemakers: dissent over foreign policy, 1792–1939* (London: Hamish Hamilton, 1957)

————, ed., *Lloyd George: a diary by Frances Stevenson* (New York: Harper & Row, 1971)

Thompson, L.M., *The Unification of South Africa, 1902–1910* (Oxford: Clarendon Press, 1960)

Thompson, Paul, *Socialists, Liberals and Labour: the struggle for London 1885–1914* (London: Routledge & Kegan Paul, 1967)

Thorpe, Andrew, 'J.H. Thomas and the Rise of Labour in Derby, 1880–1945', *Midland History*, xv (1990), 111–128

Townshend, Charles, 'Military Force and Civil Authority in the United Kingdom, 1914–1921', *Journal of British Studies*, xxviii (1989), 262–292

Turner, John, 'The British Commonwealth Union and the General Election of 1918', *English Historical Review*, ccclxviii (1978), 528–559.

————, 'State Purchase of the Liquor Trade in the First World War', *Historical Journal* xxiii (1980), 589–615

————, *Lloyd George's Secretariat* (Cambridge: Cambridge University Press, 1980)

————, 'The Higher Direction of War', in Kathleen Burk, ed., *War and the State* (London: Allen Unwin, 1982), pp. 57–83.

————, 'The Politics of Organised Business in the First World War', in John Turner, ed., *Businessmen and Politics* (London: Heinemann Educational Books, 1984), pp. 33–49

————, 'Man and Braverman: British industrial relations', *History*, lxx (1985), 236–242

————, 'Sir Vincent Caillard', in David Jeremy, ed., *Dictionary of Business Biography: Volume I* (London: Butterworth, 1986), pp. 564–567

————, ' "Experts" and Interests: David Lloyd George and the dilemmas of the expanding state, 1906-1919', in Roy Macleod, ed., *Government and Expertise in Britain 1815-1919* (Cambridge: Cambridge University Press, 1988), pp. 203–223

————, 'Sex, Age and the Labour Vote in the 1920s', in Peter Denley and Deian Hopkin, eds, *History and Computing II* (Manchester: Manchester University Press, 1989), pp. 243–254

————, 'Industrial Relations and Business History', in Charles Harvey and John Turner, eds., *Labour and Business in Modern Britain* (London: Frank Cass, 1989), pp. 1–5

Varcoe, Ian, 'Scientists, Government and Organised Research in Great Britain, 1914–1916: the early history of the DSIR', *Minerva*, viii (1970), 192–216

Vincent, John, ed., *The Crawford Papers: the journals of David Lindsay, twenty-seventh Earl of Crawford and Balcarres 1871–1940 during the years 1892 to 1940* (Manchester: Manchester University Press, 1984)

Waites, Bernard, *A Class Society at War: England, 1914–1918* (Leamington Spa: Berg, 1987)

Wald, Kenneth D., *Crosses on the Ballot* (Princeton, N.J.: Princeton University Press, 1983)

Waller, Philip, *Democracy and Sectarianism: a political and social history of Liverpool 1868–1939* (Liverpool: Liverpool University Press, 1981)

Ward, A.J., 'Lloyd George and the 1918 Irish Conscription Crisis', *Historical Journal*, xvii (1974), 107–129

Webb, Sidney and Webb, Beatrice, *The History of Trade Unionism* (London: Longman, 1920)

Weinroth, Howard S., 'The British Radicals and the Balance of Power, 1902–1914', *Historical Journal*, xiii (1970), 653–682

————, 'Norman Angell and *The Great Illusion*: an episode in pre-1914 pacifism', *Historical Journal*, xvii (1974), 551–574

Whiteside, Noel, 'Industrial Welfare and Labour Regulation in Britain at the Time of the First World War', *International Review of Social History*, xxv (1980), 307–331

Wigham, Eric, *The Power to Manage* (London: Macmillan, 1973)

Williamson, Philip, ed., *The Modernisation of Conservative Politics: the diaries and letters of William Bridgeman, 1904–1935* (London: Historians' Press, 1988)

Wilson, Keith, *The Rasp of War: the letters of H.A. Gwynne to Lady Bathurst, 1914–1918* (London: Sidgwick & Jackson, 1989)

Wilson, Trevor, 'The Coupon and the British General Election of 1918', *Journal of Modern History*, xxxvi (1964), 28–42

————, *The Downfall of the Liberal Party* (London; Collins, 1966)

————, ed., *The Political Diaries of C.P. Scott* (London: Collins, 1970)

————, *The Myriad Faces of War* (Oxford: Polity Press, 1988)

Winch, Donald, *Economics and Policy* (London: Hodder & Stoughton, 1969)

Winter, J.M., 'Arthur Henderson, the Russian Revolution, and the Reconstruction of the Labour Party', *Historical Journal*, xv (1972), 753–773

————, *Socialism and the Challenge of War* (Cambridge: Cambridge University Press, 1974)

————, *The Great War and the British People* (London: Macmillan, 1985)

Wood, I.S., 'Irish Nationalism and Radical Politics in Scotland, 1880–1906', *Journal of the Scottish Labour History Society*, ix (1975), 21–38

Woodward, D.R., *Lloyd George and the Generals* (London: Associated University Presses, 1983)

————, 'Did Lloyd George Starve the British Army of Men prior to the German Offensive of 21 March 1918?', *Historical Journal*, xxvii (1984), 241–252

Wrigley, Chris, *David Lloyd George and the British Labour Movement* (Hassocks: Harvester, 1976)

————, 'The Ministry of Munitions: an innovatory department', in Kathleen Burk, *War and the State* (London: Allen & Unwin, 1982), pp. 32–56

————, 'Trade Unions and Politics in the First World War', in Ben Pimlott and Chris Cook, *Trade Unions in British Politics* (London: Longman, 1982), pp. 79–97; reprinted in 2nd edn (London: Longman, 1991), pp. 69–87.

————, 'The First World War and State Intervention in Industrial Relations 1914–1918', in C.J. Wrigley, ed., *A History of British Industrial Relations: Volume II* (Brighton: Harvester, 1987)

————, *Arthur Henderson* (Cardiff: Wales University Press, 1990)

Yearwood, Peter, ' "On the Safe and Right Lines": the Lloyd George government and the origins of the League of Nations, 1916–1918', *Historical Journal*, xxxii (1989), 131–155

Zeitlin, Jonathan, 'The Labour Strategies of British Engineering Employers, 1890–1922', in Howard F. Gospel and Craig R. Littler, *Managerial Strategies and Industrial Relations* (London: Heinemann Educational Books, 1983), pp. 25–54

————, 'From Labour History to the History of Industrial Relations', *Economic History Review*, 2s, xl (1987), 159–184

————, ' "Rank and Filism" in British Labour History: a critique', *International Review of Social History*, xxiv (1989), 42–102.

INDEX